The Oregon Companion

THE
Oregon
COMPANION

AN
Historical Gazetteer
OF
The Useful, The Curious,
AND
The Arcane

Richard H. Engeman

Timber Press
Portland • London

Front cover: (top) Harney County, 1941 postcard. J. H. Eastman photograph.
Steven Dotterer collection; (small images, clockwise) Oregon Historical Society,
OrHi 4785-a; Walter S. Bowman photograph. University of Washington Libraries, Special
Collections, UW27645z; Mason collection; Oregon Historical Society, CN 007874; *Oregon Journal*
photograph. Oregon Historical Society, OrHi 106089.

Back cover (from top): *Oregon Journal* photograph. Oregon Historical Society, OrHi 106089;
Mason collection; Schminck Memorial Museum; Everett Olmstead/Elite Studio photograph.
Historic Photo Archive, 9305-A4311-A; Steven Dotterer collection.

Spine: *Oregon Journal* photograph. Oregon Historical Society, OrHi 106089.

Frontispiece: Umatilla County exhibit, Lewis and Clark Exposition.
Image courtesy of Special Collections and University Archives, University of Oregon Libraries, PH037_0646

Opposite: The Skiway between Government Camp and Timberline Lodge.
Sawyer's photograph. Steven Dotterer collection.

Page 6: The Union Pacific Railroad streamliner *City of Portland* in 1935.
Everett Olmstead/Elite Studio photograph. Historic Photo Archive, 9305-A4311-A.

Page 14: Ezra Meeker poses with his wagon tent in 1913.
Albert H. Barnes photograph. University of Washington Libraries, Special Collections, Barnes 1889.

Map by Allan Cartography, Medford, Oregon.

Published in 2009 by Timber Press, Inc.

The Haseltine Building
133 S.W. Second Avenue, Suite 450
Portland, Oregon 97204-3527
www.timberpress.com

2 The Quadrant
135 Salusbury Road
London NW6 6RJ
www.timberpress.co.uk

Printed in the United States of America
Reprinted 2009

Library of Congress Cataloging-in-Publication Data
Engeman, Richard H.
    The Oregon companion : an historical gazetteer of the useful, the curious,
and the arcane / Richard H. Engeman.
        p. cm.
    Includes bibliographical references and index.
    ISBN 978-0-88192-899-0
    1. Oregon—History—Encyclopedias. 2. Oregon—History, Local—Encyclope-
dias. 3. Oregon—Description and travel—Encyclopedias. 4. Oregon—Geography—
Encyclopedias. 5. Oregon—Biography—Encyclopedias. 6. Oregon—Miscellanea—
Encyclopedias. I. Title.
    F876.E64 2009
    979.503—dc22
    2008032991
A catalog record for this book is also available from the British Library.

To my parents,
Bud and Jerre Engeman

Contents

Acknowledgments

In one sense, this work is based on the downloading, if you will, of more than three decades of mental accumulation of information about Oregon, acquired in the course of both school and work—and, of course, meticulously sifted, evaluated, arranged, and arrayed. It is also an outcome of many years of interaction between the author and an immense number of other people. My decades of professional work with archival and library materials—photographs, books, brochures, drawings, architectural plans, letters, diaries, business ledgers, maps, postcards, magazines, leaflets, sheet music, posters, menus, newspapers, timetables, recipes, scribbles, lithographs—almost always occurred in conjunction with questions from other people, or projects that other people were undertaking. Much of the information that I absorbed came before my eyes in the course of finding it for someone else.

So my first thanks go to the (literally) thousands of people I have worked with in the course of their research. Alas, I can not name them all, though many of them named me in their own acknowledgements. Their fascinating array of questions, problems, postulations, suppositions, and projects kept me occupied, personally and professionally, for many fruitful years.

Very special thanks go to Dale Johnson, former botanical editor at Timber Press, who first posited this book to me and whose unflagging support and encouragement (even after he left Timber Press to pursue studies in horological adjustment, becoming a watchmaker certified by the Watchmakers of Switzerland Training and Education Program) have a great deal to do with the fact that I finally did it. Eve S. Goodman, editorial director at Timber Press, also deserves thanks for seamlessly picking up the reins and calmly persuading me to continue and complete the book. James E. Eckenwalder of Toronto, distinguished taxonomist and author of the definitive reference on the conifer family (Timber Press, forthcoming), also deserves thanks. My college colleague, and a university colleague of Dale Johnson, Eckenwalder is himself a storehouse of arcane knowledge on many topics; he seems to have convinced Dale that I was similarly stuffed full of Oregon arcana and that I should be persuaded to lighten my burden through writing.

Glenn Mason and Steven Dotterer, dealer and collector, respectively, of and in regional historical photographs and paper ephemera, have my thanks for their excellent advice and suggestions, and for lending many images for use in this book. Heartfelt thanks are due to G. Thomas Edwards, Nicholas Starin, Kathy Tucker, and Steven Dotterer for their detailed reading of the manuscipt and for literally hundreds of helpful suggestions and questions. The staff, past and present, of the research library of the Oregon Historical Society, have been helpful to me over many years, especially Susan Seyl, Mikki Tint, Michelle Kribs, Geoff Wexler, Shawna Gandy, Elizabeth Winroth,

Arthur C. Spencer, Ken Lomax, and Steve Hallberg. Those historical society staff who worked on the Oregon History Project also deserve thanks: Marianne Keddington-Lang, the project instigator; and George Eigo, Kathy Tucker, Joshua Binus, Cain Allen, Melinda Jette, Dane Bevan, Trudy Flores, Sarah Griffith, Robert Donnelly, and Cara Ungar-Gutierrez. I hope I made good use of your good work. Thanks to David Milholland for many creative sparks. And I must reach back and extend tribute also to former colleagues at the University of Washington Libraries and the Southern Oregon Historical Society: you all helped me.

Finally, I am ever grateful for the support, love and encouragement of Terry E. Jess. I could not have done it without you.

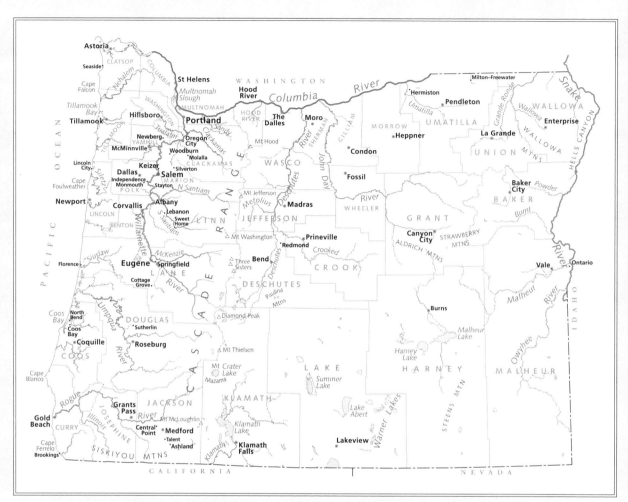

Oregon counties, county seats, and incorporated places with populations over 5,000 based on 2003 U.S. Census Bureau estimates. For reasons of space, many cities in the Portland metropolitan area have been omitted.

Introduction

What is a wigwam burner, and what did it burn and why did we burn it? Have bicycles always been such a big deal here? What is a Mazama? Why is Lincoln City such a long and dreary string of stores and parking lots? What is the story on the Donner und Blitzen, that Thunder-and-Lightning River that flows into the Lake of Bad Times? Why are Salem's busses called Cherriots?

If you had a handy encyclopedia of Oregon, a handbook with a historical perspective, you could answer some of those questions. Now you have it, in your hands. It is not only for newcomers, but for all of us who live here and still have questions about the state. There are 96,466 square miles in Oregon, and that is a lot of landscape. Over the small span of some two hundred years of recorded time, much has changed. Making sense of that much territory and that much change is not easy. This book might help.

What's here and what's not? And if it's not here, why not? The entries include physical places such as towns and cities, counties, rivers and lakes, mountains, and other features. All counties and all incorporated towns have entries. Natural features have been treated selectively, not exhaustively. People who have left a mark on Oregon—and who are no longer living—have entries, especially if their name is still before us as part of the name of a building or town or park. The book includes entries representing Oregon industries, products, crops, and natural resources. A selected number of entries deal with the state's indigenous wildlife, flora, and geology; such as iconic fauna (beavers and salmon), flora (huckleberries), and geology (Mount Mazama). Some entries are regionalisms, such as webfoot and wigwam burner, tree farms and hoedads.

This book is the work of one person, not of an academic committee overseen by a panel of wise and seasoned editors. As such, it has its own set of strengths and weaknesses; the author is more attuned to matters of transportation and less cognizant of the development of professional sports, for example. The bibliographies—which include recommended websites—can lead you to other sources of information about Oregon.

Oregon Yesterday and Today

Oregon a half-century ago was a different place. My mental reconstruction of that vanished time and place is embodied in recollections of an evening's drive along the northern Oregon Coast. After a family visit with my step-grandmother, the elegant and genial Eleanor (she was also officially a Lincoln County deputy sheriff, which added a note of intrigue to her status), my father, mother, sister, and I would drive west from Eleanor's house in the lumber mill town (and county seat—then) of Toledo, to Newport and the Coast. As a child fascinated by noise and motion, I was reluctant to leave behind the sights and smells of the Toledo mill, which ran day and night with screeching whistles, clouds of smoke and steam, a mill that was fed an endless supply of logs by a railroad with real steam-powered locomotives.

For the first darkening hour or so, we drove through small beach resort towns—Agate Beach, Taft, Oceanlake—and then snaked over Cascade Head to Neskowin. As the sun sank and darkness set in, the trip was punctuated by a succession of fiery landmarks: lumber mills in small towns where the byproducts of milling—bark, shavings, and saw-dust—were ruthlessly thrust into huge cone-shaped metal furnaces. These were wigwam burners, and in an era that did not make other uses of these wood scraps, the wigwam burners, sparks flying upward, were the markers of a prosperous community. Bay City, Garibaldi, Wheeler, Nehalem, even resort towns such as Cannon Beach and Seaside, and our hometown of Warrenton, were all anointed with the smoke of the wigwam burn-ers. The drive home would be punctuated time and again by an orange glow and a sweet smell of wood smoke. It had been like that for decades; we thought it would always be that way: we had a law requiring replanting logged-over lands, didn't we? Weren't the timber companies planting tree farms?

You will find a few wigwam burners still out there in former timber country. Today they are cold and rust-bound, stilled by pollution controls as well as by the realization that what was "waste" now has economic uses, and that the forest resources themselves are rapidly dwindling. Those surviving wigwam burners are Oregon artifacts that raise questions, from the newcomer and the longtime resident alike. Knowing something about them goes a long way to establishing context, and to understanding why and how things are different today—and how they look different, too.

Place names also raise questions and give context, names like that of the town of Union and the county of Malheur. So can paying attention to Oregon's landscape and its agriculture and industries. What is the history and significance of agricultural products such as nursery stock and vineyards? Are these new enterprises, or have they been around for a while? I hope this book will help you find at least the start of answers to these kinds of questions, and perhaps increase your understanding of how Oregon and its history fits into the much larger world around it.

I am solely responsible for what is written here. Your comments, questions, and reac-tions are gratefully solicited.

Notes on Using this Book

- Entries are alphabetical, letter-by-letter.
- Within each entry, words in **boldface** refer to other individual entries that may pro-vide additional information on the topic.
- All Oregon counties and all incorporated cities and towns have entries. The term "incorporated" refers to the establishment of local city or town government.
- There are entries for communities, rivers, mountains, and other geographical features,

and for plants, animals, crops, and notable terms and phrases. The selection of entries is extensive but it is not comprehensive.

• For persons, there are individual entries only for those who are deceased. Living persons are mentioned where appropriate, but do not have a separate entry or cross-reference.

• Quotations are cited within the entry; see the bibliography for more information on the source. Any unreferenced quotations are from Lewis A. and Lewis L. McArthur's *Oregon Geographic Names*, or the 1915 *Oregon Almanac*, both listed in the bibliography.

▶ Indicates photograph or illustration.

Oregon
A TO Z

Abernethy, George (1807–1877) George Abernethy was the first and only governor of Oregon's **provisional government**, which preceded its status as a United States territory. Abernethy was born in New York City in 1807, where he went into business as a young man. He married Anne Pope in 1830, and in 1839 the family, including two children, left for Oregon by ship with the Methodist missionary contingent headed by **Jason Lee**. He handled the mission's financial affairs for some twenty years, managing its store at **Oregon City**. His business acumen and Methodist connections put him in the position to become a political force among a group that favored connecting with the United States, rather than aligning with Great Britain, a position particularly favored by those associated with the still-powerful **Hudson's Bay Company**. Among the enterprises in which he engaged was the publication of Oregon's first newspaper, the *Oregon Spectator* (he tried to keep its voice from becoming too political, an attitude that frustrated its editors), and involvement with the Oregon Exchange Company, which issued the controversial **beaver money** as a local currency. During the 1840s, recently arrived emigrants to Oregon often paused and restocked at a field owned by Abernethy in Oregon City; it was known as Abernethy Green, and became the site of the End of the Oregon Trail Interpretive Center in 1993.

Abernethy was elected governor of the provisional government in 1845, and was re-elected in 1847. His wish for American control of the Oregon Country had come to pass by that point, and President James K. Polk signed the bill creating the Oregon Territory on August 14, 1848. Word reached Oregon City in 1849, shortly before the arrival of **Joseph Lane**, the newly appointed territorial governor. Abernethy had already prepared for the transition; he went back to his mercantile interests.

The devastating Willamette Valley **floods** of 1861 destroyed much of Abernethy's business and crippled him financially. He subsequently moved to Portland, where he continued in business and even operated the Methodist Book Concern there; his roots were firmly planted.

Many features borrow the Abernethy name: they include a road and a creek in Oregon City, a street and a school in Portland, a railroad station name and a lake in Lane County, and the I-205 bridge across the Willamette River at Oregon City.

▶ **Abert Rim** Abert Rim, a stunning wall of rock, overlooks Lake Abert in northern Lake County. The highly mineralized lake has no outlet; the rim looms up to 2,500 feet along its eastern border, one of the nation's highest fault block escarpments. Capt. **John C. Frémont** named both the lake and the rimrock for his commander, Col. John James Abert (1788–1863), who was the longtime Chief of the Topographical Bureau in Washington, DC.

Adair, Bethenia Angelina *see* **Owens-Adair, Bethenia Angelina**

Adair Village Adair Village in Benton County emerged from the remains of a World War II training encampment, **Camp Adair**, which once hosted some 33,000 troops. After the war, portions of the former camp were used by the Air Force until 1969. The Adair Village post office operated from 1947 to 1951, and the camp headquarters area has gradually evolved into a residential suburb of nearby Corvallis. After the Air Force ceased operations, that property, including individual houses, was sold. Adair Village was incorporated as a city in 1976, with the city hall located in one of the original wartime buildings. In 2007, Adair Village had a population of about 930.

Adams This Umatilla County community in wheat-ranching country was granted a post office in 1883, became connected by railroad with Pendleton the next year, and was incorporated as a municipality in 1893. It was named for settler John F. Adams. The 1900 census recorded 263 residents; by 1915, the town boasted a broom factory with brooms made "from home-grown broom corn," but apparently any prosperity it brought was short-lived. The town's population sank below 200 during the next century, rising to about 335 in 2007. The surrounding country-side is agricultural, while in recent years the town has become more a residential suburb of Pendleton than a retail center.

Adler, Leo (1895–1993) Born in Baker City, Leo Adler was one of three children of a Jewish merchant family; his father ran a music and jewelry store. Leo was involved in business from his youth, when he peddled magazines on the street and through the mails. That became the basis of his lifelong career, for his news distribution company grew to a staff of thirty and served seven western states. He retired at age seventy-seven, a millionaire bachelor who had already started a second career in public philanthropy benefiting the residents of his hometown, **Baker City**. In 1939, he bought a new pumper truck for the fire department; he was noted for frequently sending steak dinners to the fire crews by taxi. Over the years he contributed funds to the local hospital, to support local baseball teams and programs (he was an avid fan of baseball), to a wide variety of religious denominations, in support of other community sports and recreation programs, and for historic preservation. The Leo Adler Foundation carries on his work in Baker City and eastern Oregon; the family residence, his home for his entire

Abert Lake and Abert Rim as they appeared in 1946. J. H. Eastman photograph. Steven Dotterrer collection.

life, is open to the public through the Baker Heritage Museum.

> Law, Adair. *The Spark and the Light: The Leo Adler Story*. Boise, Idaho: Leo Adler Trust, 2004.

Adrian This small Malheur County farming town is situated on the west bank of the Snake River south of Nyssa. It came into being in 1913 as a station on a branch of the Oregon Short Line railroad. It was named for the Illinois birthplace of Reuben McCreary, who had tried to establish the town of Riverview on the east side of the Snake River. Riverview post office opened in 1911, and moved to the west side of the river after the arrival of the railroad; the name was changed to Adrian in 1919. The community was incorporated in 1972; its estimated population in 2007 was 185.

African-Americans in Oregon *see* **blacks in Oregon**

Agate, Alfred Thomas *see* **Wilkes Exploring Expedition**

agriculture The lure of good (and free or inexpensive) land for agricultural purposes through the **Donation Land Act** was the major impetus of the emigration of American settlers to Oregon in the 1840s and 1850s via the **Oregon Trail**. Agriculture has remained a mainstay of the Oregon economy. The Willamette Valley and the open lands of **French Prairie** and the **Tualatin Plains** were initial attractions: fertile land that was already cleared, primarily as the result of the Indian practice of annual burning to maintain the grasslands as forage for game animals. Early settlers planted a great deal of wheat, which was ground into flour at local mills. Wheat is still grown in the Willamette Valley.

Major agricultural areas also developed in the nineteenth century in the valleys of the **Umpqua River**, **Bear Creek**, **Rogue River**, and **Grande Ronde River**; dry land wheat farming took hold on the Columbia Plateau south of the Columbia River. In the twentieth century, irrigation projects brought agricultural development to the **Umatilla River** valley, **Treasure Valley** in Malheur County, **Deschutes County**, and the **Klamath Lake** region, where high-water-use crops such as potatoes, sugar beets, melons, onions, and alfalfa came into production.

The establishment of nurseries was important to the initial propagation of Oregon's apple, pear, and nut crops; since World War II, wholesale nurseries themselves have emerged as the most important component of Oregon's agricultural industry, providing ornamental plants and trees to retail nurseries across the nation. The **Willamette River** Valley has long been a leading producer of cane berry crops such as blackberries and loganberries, as well as strawberries, hops, mint, filberts (also known as hazelnuts), and seed crops such as ryegrass, fescue, red clover, and orchard grass. Since the 1960s, Christmas trees and lawn turf have emerged as new crops in western Oregon. Dairying was another pioneer-era enterprise that was once widespread in the state; it is still common, but is concentrated in a half-dozen areas. Poultry such as chickens and turkeys were once on every farm; today they are typically raised in huge batteries. The area around **Sutherlin** once was famous for its turkeys. Coastal areas once raised crops of bulbs such as daffodils and lilies; Curry County still does. And cranberries, grown extensively in Coos County, were once found in Clatsop County as well. Oregon had about 40,000 farms in 2007, a number that is slowly growing after many years of decline. The growth of **farmers' markets** in the 1990s and 2000s has given a new lease on life to small-scale farmers. About 90 percent of Oregon's 2007 crops were sent out of state. *See also* **cattle industry**; **irrigation**; **nurseries**; **seed industry**; **sheep raising**; entries for particular crops such as **wheat**; and entries for individual counties.

Ainsworth, John Commingers (1822–1893) John C. Ainsworth was one of the legendarily stalwart founders of Portland and one of Oregon's first captains of industry. He was born in Iowa and raised in Ohio, and received little education as a child. Orphaned as a teenager, Ainsworth went to live with a storekeeper uncle in Iowa. After working in retail and wholesale trades along the Mississippi, he jumped onto the river, becoming captain of a small riverboat. Struck with gold fever, young Ainsworth headed for California in 1850. However, in Sacramento he chanced to meet Oregon businessman Lot Whitcomb, who persuaded him to command one of the territory's first river vessels, the side-wheel steamboat *Lot Whitcomb*, launched on Christmas Day of 1850 on the Willamette River in Milwaukie.

Ainsworth proceeded to wrangle his way to a prominent place in Oregon's transportation and financial circles. His second marriage, in 1850, was to Nancy Jane White of Oregon City, daughter of a well-to-do farmer and investor, Judge S. S. White. The impressive temple-fronted Ainsworth house, built of wood in the Greek revival style, is on the National Register of Historic Places, located at Mount Pleasant in Oregon City on Lot Whitcomb Drive. After 1859, the family moved to Portland, where Ainsworth soon became one of the kingpins of the **Oregon Steam Navigation Company (OSN)**, which in the 1860s became the monopoly operator of transportation on the Columbia River. Fueled by the demands of gold rushes in the interior areas of Idaho, western Montana, and eastern Oregon, OSN made a fortune for its chief owners—Ainsworth, **Simeon G. Reed**, and **Robert R. Thompson**—carrying supplies from Portland to The Dalles, Umatilla Landing, and Wallula.

Foreseeing the changes that railroads were bringing to the transportation business, Ainsworth sold his shipping interests in 1880 and invested in banking, organizing the Ainsworth National Bank in 1883; this became the United States National Bank in 1891. Ainsworth and his family moved to California, where he died in 1893. Portland has an Ainsworth school and an Ainsworth street, and a rail-

road station in the Columbia River Gorge was named Ainsworth; also in the Gorge is a state park, the property donated by John C. Ainsworth's son and daughter-in-law.

▶ **Air Oregon** The deregulation of the airline industry in 1978 brought about the creation of Air Oregon, a local enterprise that was spearheaded by utility executive and power broker **Glenn Jackson**. The intent was to assure commercial air passenger service would continue to numerous smaller airports in the state such as Coos Bay and Pendleton, service previously provided by **West Coast Airlines**. Air Oregon was merged with Horizon Air in 1983.

Albany Like many communities dating from the early American migrations of the 1840s, the name Albany came west with the settlers, in this case with the Monteith brothers from New York State. Albany, the seat of Linn County, was well situated on the

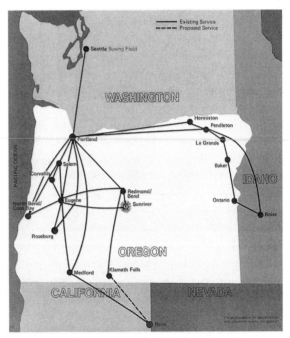

A map of Air Oregon routes in 1979 shows how the company tried to link small Oregon cities to gateways such as Boise, Seattle, Portland, and Reno. Author's collection.

Willamette River adjacent to rich valley farmlands, and soon became a river shipping point for grain and the site of a flour mill. A post office was established in 1850, and the city was incorporated in 1864; its population reached 3,079 by 1900. A Presbyterian school, Albany Collegiate Institute, was founded in 1867 and developed into the small Albany College; it moved to a new campus near Portland in 1942 and was renamed **Lewis and Clark College**.

Albany was connected with Portland by rail in 1870, and in the 1880s developed as a minor railroad and industrial center along the route between Oregon and California. A woolen mill opened in 1889. By the early twentieth century, Albany was a center for sheep raising, prune and hops culture, and walnut growing.

Although Albany was a relatively minor timber town in the Oregon scheme of things, in 1941 it became the host of the Albany Timber Carnival, which featured contests in logrolling, bucking and sawing, tree-climbing, and similar events. World War II pushed the next carnival to 1946, and it was held annually until it finally died of natural causes (the decline of the timber industry in the area) in 2005; a revival has been discussed.

Albany has been a leader in the historic preservation movement in Oregon. It boasts a number of excellent examples of small-town commercial and residential architecture from the 1880s into the 1910s; historic districts include the Thomas and Walter Monteith house, built in 1849. Agriculture and timber-related industry have been supplemented by such enterprises as rare metals production: zirconium, hafnium, and titanium. Some of this production takes place in the adjacent community of **Millersburg**. Albany's population reached 18,181 by 1970, and an estimated 47,470 in 2007.

Albina neighborhood, Portland Platted by real estate developer William Paige in 1872, Albina saw major growth after the arrival of the **Union Pacific Railroad** in 1884. The Union Pacific's principal freight terminals, yard, and maintenance facilities were built nearby, and the town's population was largely of immigrants from northern Europe. A historical remnant is the White Eagle Tavern, once a locus of social life for Polish workingmen. Albina was incorporated in 1887; in 1891 residents voted to merge with Portland. After World War II, when jobs brought many African-Americans to the Portland area, Albina became the center of the city's black residential and business district. A de facto ghetto was the result of pressures from real estate and banking interests; an abortive **urban renewal** project in the 1960s culminated in the so-called Albina riots of 1969. Much of the physical core of the 1890s Albina was gutted in the project; however, residential areas have subsequently undergone revival and gentrification, also a controversial process.

alder Four species of alder, a deciduous softwood tree or shrub, are native in Oregon. The red alder, *Alnus rubra*, is the most common, found especially along streams in the Coast Range. Alder wood long had little commercial value, and as fuel was not favored because it burns all too quickly, but in recent decades it has been increasingly harvested to make furniture and to produce pulp for papermaking.

alfalfa *see* **hay**

Alis Volat Propiis *see* **"She flies with her own wings"**

Aloha This unincorporated Washington County community is located between Beaverton and Hillsboro. The **Tualatin Plains** was densely settled by farm families beginning in the 1840s. The Aloha post office opened in 1912 (the origin of the name is mired in obscurity; it may be derived from Aloah Beach, Wisconsin, misspelled), and the neighboring populace was described as "suburban" as early as 1915, when "general farming, dairying, fruit growing and poultry raising" were the primary occupations. The Southern Pacific rail line through Aloha was electrified in 1914, giving commuters a ride to downtown Portland in forty-four minutes. Post–World War II population growth boomed after Intel built the first of several facilities in Aloha in the 1970s. With a population estimated in 2000 at more than 41,000, Aloha is a featureless sprawl of houses and industry atop the deep, rich soil of the Tualatin Plains.

Alphabet Historic District, Portland
see **Nob Hill neighborhood, Portland**

▶ **Alpine** An unincorporated community in rural Benton County, Alpine is located in the foothills of the Coast Range. While the location is only vaguely mountainous, the name alludes to the Alps. The Corvallis & Alsea Railroad reached the area about 1908, intent on reaching the lumber resources of the area. A post office opened in 1912, and by 1915, some 300 people were reported to live nearby, engaged in farming, dairying, livestock and poultry raising, lumbering, and operating shingle mills. The railroad was abandoned in 1950, but the crossroads community has endured; photographer James Cloutier documented its daily doings in the 1970s. The post office closed in 1976, the school in 2003 and the market in 2004. Two vineyards prominent in Oregon's recent success with pinot noir grapes, Alpine and Woodhall, were established nearby in 1976.

James Cloutier. *The Alpine Tavern: Photographs of a Social Gathering Place.* Eugene, Oregon: Image West, 1977.

Alsean Indians The Alsean Indians include the Yaquina and Alsea tribes, who spoke dialects of an isolated language group and lived along the Oregon Coast in the vicinity of Yaquina and Alsea Bays, respectively. They maintained close ties with the neighboring **Tillamook Indians** to the north and the **Siuslaw Indians** to the south. Their diet, shel-

Children playing outside the defunct Alpine Market in Alpine, 1968. Lee Mintoyne stands at the doorway of his appliance repair shop. James Cloutier photograph, courtesy of James Cloutier. Special Collections and University Archives, University of Oregon Libraries, PH263_55-20.

ter, clothing, and lifestyles were similar to those of other coastal peoples. Family groups lived in cedar-plank houses in villages near the ocean. Their homeland was geographically isolated from white settlements of the 1840s and 1850s, but their numbers were greatly reduced by introduced diseases. Significant white contact did not come until the establishment of the **Coast Reservation** in 1855, which placed hundreds of Indians from other southwestern Oregon tribes on their lands. The Alsean people remained; the remnant Alsea Reservation closed in 1875 and most residents were removed to the **Siletz Reservation**.

► **Alsea River** The Alsea River is best known for an elegant concrete span that once bridged the river's estuary at **Waldport**, designed by state bridge engineer **Condé B. McCullough** and opened in 1936. Structural deterioration required the replacement of the bridge, and public sentiment forged a new design that echoes that of McCullough and is equally handsome; it opened in 1991. The 49-mile river drains the Coast Range, rising in western Benton County and flowing west through Lincoln County. It is named for the **Alsean Indians** who lived along the river and its bay. The Alsea area became part of the **Coast Reservation** in 1855; this was reduced to a local Alsea Reservation in 1865. The reservation was terminated in 1875 and the remaining residents were removed to the **Siletz Reservation**. A guidebook in 1915 noted that "there is little open country in the Alsea Valley as the Alsea River and its tributaries wind tortuously in between steep timbered hills and mountains. What open country there is, is well developed agriculturally, several of the finest dairy farms in the state being located there." While dairying has diminished since then, in the 1990s goats were raised in the Alsea River valley to make **cheese**.

aluminum industry Bauxite, the mineral from which aluminum is made, is found nowhere in Ore-

Four seagulls sit atop four pilings on Alsea Bay, where the Alsea River meets the Pacific Ocean. The Alsea Bay Bridge was completed in 1936; corrosion required its replacement. Wesley Andrews photograph. Steven Dotterer collection.

gon in any commercial quantity or quality. However, the convergence of the World War II need for aluminum with the availability of cheap and plentiful hydroelectric power to process it, made the aluminum industry for several decades a major economic presence in Oregon and the Pacific Northwest. Aluminum was in demand by 1940 for aircraft production (Seattle-based Boeing was not far away), and soon was needed for other military purposes, particularly **shipbuilding** in the Portland area. An aluminum reduction plant was erected near the Columbia River in Troutdale in 1941, operated by Alcoa for the U.S. War Department; Reynolds Aluminum took it over in 1946 and it operated until 2001. Harvey Aluminum began construction of a plant in The Dalles in 1955, lured by the electricity of **The Dalles Dam**; the facility operated only intermittently after the 1980s. The changing economics of both aluminum manufacture and electric power production and distribution ended the industry in Oregon by 2005.

Amity A place of ostensible harmony, Amity was named in recognition of the successful resolution of a school siting dispute in 1849. A post office opened in 1852, and a railroad from Portland and Forest Grove came to town in 1879. It was incorporated as a city the next year, with a population of 215. Amity was born as and has remained an agricultural community, its nearby products reported in 1915 as fruit, especially prunes, hops, dairy products, wool, and livestock, with "English walnut orchards planted on hills to the east." By 2000, those Amity Hills were covered by the numerous vineyards of a burgeoning wine industry. Amity holds an annual daffodil festival in March, though it is not clear why it does so except that it brings visitors to town. Other tourist attractions include local wine-tasting rooms and the nearby Monastery of Our Lady of Consolation, where Brigittine monks make chocolate confectionaries that are much favored in the region. Amity's population in 2007 was about 1,480.

antelope *see* **pronghorn antelope**

Antelope This Wasco County trading community took its name from the Antelope Valley, named about 1862 for the once-common pronghorn—which is not an antelope, but is called one nevertheless. A post office was established in 1871, and the town was incorporated in 1901. When the Columbia Southern Railway in 1900 reached its terminus at **Shaniko**, several miles north of Antelope, it dealt an economic blow to the town. The 1900 census gave Antelope precinct a population of 249, more than it has had at any time since. Cattle- and sheep-raising have long been the economic mainstays in the area. From 1917 to 1921, the editor of the town newspaper, the *Herald*, was **H. L. Davis**, who made use of the experience in his Pulitzer prize-winning novel of early Oregon, *Honey in the Horn*.

Antelope's sleepy existence was shaken in the 1980s by the influx of religious communards who took over the nearby Big Muddy Ranch to build the town of **Rajneeshpuram**, under the direction of the charismatic **Bhagwan Shree Rajneesh**. As the nearest established governmental entity, Antelope became not only the site of a popular Zorba the Buddha Rajneesh restaurant, but also the target of a 1984 takeover that changed its name to Rajneesh (the vote: fifty-seven to twenty-two; many Rajneeshi had moved within the city limits). Local residents were incensed; relations were acrimonious, fueled by incidents such as the legalizing of nudity in the small Antelope public park. The cult soon, and spectacularly, imploded, and by a vote of thirty-four to zero the name reverted to Antelope in 1985. The post office name has remained serenely unchanged since its inception. Antelope's population was estimated at sixty in 2007.

Applegate, Jesse A. (1811–1888) Born in Kentucky, Jesse Applegate taught school and worked as a surveyor in Missouri. He was married in 1832 to Cynthia Ann Parker; the Applegates eventually had thirteen children. His brothers **Lindsay Applegate** and Charles Applegate and their families joined Jesse in 1843, as all came west on the **Oregon Trail**. In Oregon, Jesse Applegate became a major figure in the development of the **provisional government**. He began a farm in Polk County, built a sawmill, and again worked as a surveyor.

Both the Jesse and Lindsay Applegate families experienced tragedy on the last leg of their journey to Oregon: each lost a son to drowning in the Columbia River. That experience induced Jesse and Lindsay to join with **Levi Scott** in an effort in 1846 to open a new trail that avoided the dangerous river trek. (Another approach led to the creation of the **Barlow Road**.) This new route, entering Oregon from the south, was known as the **Southern Emigrant Road**; since 1950, the name Applegate Trail has often been used for this route.

In 1849, Jesse Applegate and his family moved south and settled near what became the town of **Yoncalla**, where he raised cattle and farmed. Jesse also continued to influence Oregon public life and politics—he was a Lincoln Republican—through letter writing and by meeting with public figures, to the extent that he became known as the "Sage of Yoncalla."

> Applegate, Shannon. *Skookum: An Oregon Pioneer Family's History and Lore.* New York: Beech Tree Books, 1988.

Applegate, Lindsay (1808–1892) The older brother of **Jesse Applegate**, Lindsay was from Kentucky, married Elizabeth Miller in 1831, and was the father of six sons; one son drowned in the Columbia River when the family emigrated to Oregon in 1843. Lindsay claimed land in Polk County, and with Jesse and **Levi Scott** worked to develop the **Southern Emigrant Road** in 1846. He served with **Joel Palmer** as a special Indian agent in 1855, helping to settle the **Rogue River Wars**. In 1860, Lindsay purchased the toll road over the Siskiyou Mountain summit south of Ashland on the **California-Oregon**

Trail. He also served briefly in the state legislature, and as special agent with the **Klamath** and **Modoc Indians** in the 1860s. The **Applegate River** is named for Lindsay; Applegate Peak commemorates his son Oliver Cromwell Applegate (1845–1938), who also served as Indian agent on the Klamath Indian Reservation. The small community of Applegate is named for the Applegate River.

Applegate Indians *see* Athapaskan Indians

Applegate River The Applegate River and its tributary, the Little Applegate, extend about forty miles in Jackson and Josephine Counties from headwaters in the Siskiyou Mountains to a confluence with the Rogue River west of Grants Pass. The valleys were the scene of major placer gold discoveries in the 1860s, leaving behind a tracery of rock tailings and abandoned ditches on the landscape. Applegate Dam, completed in 1980, impounds the upper reaches of the Applegate River.

Applegate Trail *see* Southern Emigrant Road

apples Oregon has native crabapples, but the first cultivated apples are credited to **John McLoughlin**, who planted them at **Fort Vancouver** in 1826; one of the five first trees still survives there. Apples were prominent in the nursery stock that came west with **Henderson Luelling** in 1847, and by the early 1850s there were sufficient apples growing in the Willamette Valley that they were exported to California, where gold miners paid fancy prices for fresh fruit. Commercial orchards came after 1900 with the development of refrigerated railroad cars and packing and storage facilities; in the 1910s, the **Bear Creek Valley** and the valley above **Hood River** became centers of apple culture, as did the Willamette Valley. The premium gift apple business grew in the 1930s with orchardists such as **Harry**

and **David**. Many orchardists switched to **pears**, a higher-value crop more suited to local conditions, in the 1940s and after.

Arch Cape A coastal resort community in Clatsop County, Arch Cape is named for a natural feature on Cape Falcon. A post office was established in 1912. The remote hamlet was at the end of a wagon road from Seaside; the completion of Arch Cape tunnel in 1940 placed it on the **Oregon Coast Highway**. It remains a small community of vacation and retirement homes.

English, David, and Alma English. *Arch Cape Chronicles: A Bit of Oregon Coast's Past.* Arch Cape, Oregon: D. and A. English; Seaside, Oregon: Frontier Publishing, 1993.

architecture Oregon's architectural heritage has its beginnings in the structures built by Native peoples of the region, such as the cedar-plank longhouses of the **Chinook** and **Kalapuyan Indians** on the Oregon Coast and in the Willamette Valley. Early Euro-Americans brought architectural ideas with them, making use of Native materials but rarely of Native techniques. The first structures were related to trade and defense, such as **Fort Astoria** and **Fort Vancouver**. American emigrant farmers of the 1840s and 1850s brought with them common building techniques and styles, such as the Greek revival style often found in early churches, houses, schools, and courthouses—executed in wood; rarely was brick or stone used extensively in early Oregon. In the late nineteenth century, trained architects such as **William Whidden** brought new styles and materials to the area. Architectural education came through teacher/practitioners such as **Ellis F. Lawrence** and the mentor system that brought **Albert Ernest Doyle** to prominence and helped to launch his protégé, **Pietro Belluschi**. By the end of World War II, Portland and Oregon were operating in the same architectural milieu as the rest of the nation—except that Oregon still favored wood and made

innovative use of it in residential work such as that of **John Yeon**. *See also* **Fort Dalles**; **Lewis, Ion**; **Unthank, DeNorval**.

Clark, Rosalind. *Oregon Style, Architecture from 1840 to the 1950s.* Portland, Oregon: Professional Book Center, 1983.

Vaughan, Thomas, and Virginia Guest Ferriday, eds. *Space, Style and Structure: Building in Northwest America.* Portland, Oregon: Oregon Historical Society, 1974.

Arlington Today a minor wheat-shipping port on the Columbia River, Arlington began its existence as a community named Alkali, located, as it is, at the mouth of Alkali Canyon in Wasco County. A post office with that name opened in 1881, just after the Oregon Railway and Navigation Company built a rail line along the riverbank. By 1883, Alkali was on a transcontinental railroad line and the name seemed to be too rustic and parochial. In 1885, the town was incorporated as Arlington (the post office name changed then, too), taking the middle name of early resident Nathaniel A. Cornish (whose daughter Nellie was to found in 1914 what is today Cornish College of the Arts in Seattle). In 1968, the construction of **John Day Dam** flooded the townsite, long picturesquely strewn along China Creek in Alkali Canyon. In the 1980s, a canyon south of Arlington was developed into a regional waste disposal site that receives garbage from as far as Seattle. The dam-related relocation and reconstruction has resulted in a town that is basically a freeway rest area. Its population in 2007 was estimated at 610.

Weatherford, Marion T. *Arlington, Child of the Columbia.* Portland, Oregon: Oregon Historical Society, 1977.

art We have no names to attach to the artists who were in Oregon before the arrival of Euro-Americans in the late eighteenth century, but surviving examples of stone artifacts, pictographs, and tools let us know there were many. Euro-American explorations such as those of Capt. **George Vancouver** and the **Wilkes Exploring Expedition** often carried artists in their crews, and sometimes artists came of their own accord, as did **Paul Kane** in the 1840s, and photographer **Carleton E. Watkins** in the 1860s and 1880s. The state's first entrepreneurial artist was **Eliza Barchus**, whose images of Mount Hood flooded the country in the early 1900s. The establishment of the **Portland Art Museum** helped make art more publicly visible in the early twentieth century, particularly after the opening of its Modernist building by **Pietro Belluschi** in 1932. **Julia Hoffman** helped bring the arts and crafts movement to Oregon, and to advance art education; her daughter, **Margery Hoffman Smith**, helped put art in public places such as **Timberline Lodge**. "Modern" art came to the fore when **Louis Bunce** and his wife opened the first art gallery in Portland that featured such works; and modern art was spoofed by the likes of "Mr. Otis," the alter ego of journalist **Stewart Holbrook**. Art patronage dates back to the days of the **Skidmore Fountain** and **C. E. S. Wood** in the late nineteenth century, and forward into the 1960s with **Jean Vollum**, close friend of artist **Hilda Morris**. *See also* **Morris, Carl**.

Allen, Ginny, and Jody Klevit. *Oregon Painters: The First Hundred Years (1859–1959)* Portland, Oregon: Oregon Historical Society Press, 1999.

▶ **Ashland** Located along the route of the venerable **California-Oregon Trail** at the base of the Siskiyou Mountains in Jackson County, Ashland was first called Ashland Mills. The site along dashing Ashland Creek provided power for a sawmill and a flour mill in the 1850s, both supplying necessities for the gold miners who had recently made a boomtown of nearby Jacksonville. The post office of Ashland Mills opened in 1855 (the "Mills" was dropped in 1871), and the town was incorporated in 1874; the census of 1880 gave Ashland a population of 842.

Ashland became an important division point on the **Oregon & California Railroad**; the golden spike connecting the two states by rail was driven there on December 17, 1887. The railroad became a major employer, and many of Ashland's historic residences and the brick commercial buildings on its plaza date from the railroad prosperity of the 1880s. Lithia Park was established in 1892, extending from the downtown plaza up Ashland Creek. The Ashland **chautauqua** began in the park in 1893, and it of-

This photograph was taken from the veranda of the Hotel Oregon in Ashland about 1915. The view looks to the west across the plaza. The hotel planted palm trees to emphasize Ashland's close connection with California.
Steven Dotterer collection.

fered summer lectures, physical training, and music into the 1920s. A huge beehive-shaped hall was built for the chautauqua.

During a burst of civic improvements in 1914, the city included the park in its efforts to promote Ashland as a resort city, bolstered by the appeal of the many mineral springs found in the vicinity. Noted San Francisco landscape architect John McLaren prepared plans for the park, which included trails, lawns, and fountains, including a drinking fountain for lithium-infused spring water. In 1925, the community-financed Lithia Springs Hotel opened, the tallest building in the city (it has remained so); the spring water was piped to it, too.

In 1926, Ashland became the site of a state teachers college, Southern Oregon Normal School, which has since morphed into **Southern Oregon University**. The city had earlier hosted a succession of church- and quasi-state-supported teachers' colleges between 1869 and 1909. Also in 1926, the **Southern Pacific Company** opened a new main railroad line between Oregon and California via Klamath Falls. This caused a major decrease in railroad employment in Ashland. Ashland's population in 1910 was 5,020; in 1940, it stood at 4,744.

The **Oregon Shakespeare Festival** began in 1935 through the efforts of **Angus L. Bowmer**. The foundation of the old chautauqua building became the foundation of a theater to showcase Shakespearean plays, and by the 1980s the festival had become the city's major economic engine. In the 1960s, some businesspeople seized upon the Shakespearean theme as a rationale for slathering the city's commercial facades with faux Elizabethan English false fronts—some of which are incongruously still in place amid the many restored Victorian-era historic structures.

Bolstered by timber production, a growing college, and the Shakespearean festival, Ashland's population increased rapidly in the late twentieth century, reaching 12,342 in 1970, 16,252 in 1990, and an estimated 21,630 in 2007. The city's attri-butes as a place for retirees was noted as early as 1915, and by the 1990s, they formed a major population segment, including many former Californians.

Atwood, Kay. *Mill Creek Journal: Ashland, Oregon, 1850–1860*. Ashland, Oregon: K. Atwood, 1987.

O'Harra, Marjorie. *Ashland: The First 130 Years.* Rev. ed. Ashland, Oregon: Northwest Passages Publishing, 1986.

Astor, John Jacob (1763–1848) This German-born New York businessman made his fortune in the fur trade. He came to the United States in 1784, and by 1810 was in a position to finance and equip two contingents of his **Pacific Fur Company** to the mouth of the Columbia. The first group arrived from New York City in 1811 aboard the *Tonquin* and established Fort Astoria in time to meet those who had traveled overland from Montreal, departing there in July 1810. The perilous trek of the overland group, which included **John Day**, formed the basis for one of the signal literary promotions of the **Oregon Country**, Washington Irving's *Astoria* (1836).

Irving, Washington. *Astoria; or, Anecdotes of an Enterprise Beyond the Rocky Mountains*. Philadelphia: Carey, Lea & Blanchard, 1836.

Astoria Astoria long claimed some kind of banner as the "oldest continuously American-occupied settlement in the West," based on the arrival of representatives of **John Jacob Astor's Pacific Fur Company** in 1811 and the establishment of **Fort Astoria**. It is a wobbly claim (for one thing, the British took over the fort in 1813 and held it until 1825), but not terribly important: its steep slopes are steeped in history in any case. Astoria is situated on a rugged point of land near the mouth of the Columbia River, capped by Coxcomb Hill (elevation 595 feet), which is in turn topped by the **Astoria Column**. The settlement was the site of the first American post office in the Far West (1847) and its first customs house (1849). In the 1870s and 1880s, the tremendous runs of **salmon** up the Columbia River fueled the development of commercial fishing and canning operations based in Astoria, while the success of the upriver port of Portland made Astoria the center of operations for ship pilots (such as **George Flavel**) licensed to navigate the river and its treacherous bar. Railroad fever boosted dreams of an economic boom in the 1880s; these went bust by 1893, and the eventual arrival of a railroad in 1898 brought modest prosperity. The railroad boosted timber operations, such as the large mill erected by A. B. Hammond, the railroad's owner.

It was a busy place. Astoria was incorporated as a city in 1876; the 1880 census reported a population of 2,803, making it the fourth largest city in the state after Portland, East Portland, and Salem. Timber and commercial **fishing** brought to Astoria a range of immigrants: **Chinese** came in the 1870s and 1880s and worked in canneries; **Finns**, Swedes, and other Scandinavians worked as fishers and loggers; Hammond's mill employed Sikhs from India. Many Scandinavian immigrants were socialists, and advocated cooperative businesses; the Union Fishermen's Cooperative Packing Company, founded in 1896 by Scandinavian gillnet fishermen, operated a major cannery until 1975. The Finns were numerous enough that there was a Finnish neighborhood, Uniontown (placed on the National Register of Historic Places in 1988), and several Finnish-language newspapers. One, *Toveri*, founded in 1907, became a daily paper in 1912; in 1930, its editor and several staff were arrested and deported for advocating communism.

Astoria celebrated its centennial as an American city in 1911, proud of the new brick Weinhard Astoria Hotel and its electric streetcar service. By 1915, Astoria boasted ten fish canneries and cold-storage plants, four sawmills, two shipbuilding operations, a can factory, four machine shops, a flour mill, and two creameries. Until that year, it also boasted many saloons (**prohibition** came early to Oregon). During World War I, the **shipbuilding** yards turned out wooden military and supply ships; the yards usually

built fishing vessels and small freight and passenger boats for the **mosquito fleet** that operated out of Astoria.

Astoria in 1920 had a population of 14,027; only Portland and Salem were larger. On the night of December 7, 1922, a fire started that consumed the entire business district of Astoria, including its brick hotel and its streetcars—virtually all of downtown Astoria was constructed on wooden pilings over once or present tidelands. It was a devastating blow. The city rebuilt: streets and buildings on concrete foundations, the new Liberty Theatre on the site of the old Weinhard Astoria Hotel, buses replacing the streetcars, and a new, eight-story Hotel Astoria. The crowning glory was the **Astoria Column**. But the 1930 census showed a population of but 10,349.

Astoria still had fish canneries, but fishing declined precipitously after the construction of dams on the Columbia River, beginning in the 1930s. The city marked its sesquicentennial in 1961; five years later, a highway bridge across the Columbia River opened, eliminating the last ferry crossing on the **Oregon Coast Highway**. In 1974, the last major seafood processor, **Bumble Bee Seafoods**, moved its headquarters from Astoria, and shuttered its operations in 1980. The last major timber related operation, worker-owned Astoria Plywood, closed in 1989; the population in 1990: 10,069. The city has since concentrated on tourism related to its historic resources: a concentration of Victorian houses (spared in the 1922 fire), the post-fire downtown architecture of the 1920s (including a renovated Liberty Theatre), and its Scandinavian heritage. The city has also become a significant retirement center and a center for art. Its estimated population in 2007 was 10,045.

Astoria Column This concrete structure, patterned after Trajan's Column in Rome, was designed by architect Electus D. Litchfield at the instigation of Ralph G. Budd, head of the **Great Northern**

Railroad, and with funds from Vincent Astor, great grandson of the fur trade magnate **John Jacob Astor**. The column is graphically entwined with images from regional history etched into the surface in a technique called sgraffito; the artist was Attilio Pusterla of Italy. The column was dedicated in 1926 as the culmination of the second of two "historical expeditions" that were conducted in 1925 and 1926 by the Great Northern Railroad, in the course of which several other historical monuments were erected along the railroad's lines west of Saint Paul.

Atfalati Indians *see* **Kalapuyan Indians**

Athapaskan Indians By the early 1800s, this native language grouping included a number of tribes located in present-day Curry, Josephine, Jackson, Coos, and Douglas Counties in Southwestern Oregon. Among these were the Upper Umpqua, in the watershed of the Umpqua River; the Upper Coquille in the Coquille River watershed; the Galice and Applegate along the Illinois and Applegate Rivers; the Chetco at the mouth of the Chetco River; and the Chasta Costa and Tututni along the coast and the lower reaches of the Rogue River. Athapaskan peoples are also found in Western Canada, Alaska, and the American Southwest, isolated from those groups in Oregon.

Bands and families typically moved seasonally to take advantage of food resources, such as berries, camas, trout, lamprey, and elk in the summer; in autumn, groups moved to fish camps to catch salmon—Chinook and coho—and to gather acorns, hazelnuts, and huckleberries; the winter villages were centers of rituals and socializing.

Most of these Indians, as well as the **Takelma Indians** to the east, were often referred to by white explorers and settlers as Rogue or Rogue River Indians, a term that came into vogue in the 1850s with several violent skirmishes between whites and Indians at the time of an influx of gold miners into Southwest Oregon, as well as some settlers. Efforts to make some kind of settlement with the tribes, such as the **Table Rock** treaty and reservation, were often thwarted by vigilante miners bent on Indian extermination; such encounters characterized the **Rogue River Wars**. The dismal outcome was the forced removal of surviving Indians from most of the region and their resettlement on the **Coast Reservation** (which shrank and then disappeared) and the **Siletz** and **Grand Ronde Reservations**. *See also* **Confederated Tribes of Grand Ronde**; **Confederated Tribes of Siletz**.

Miller, Jay, and William R. Seaburg. Athapaskans of Southwestern Oregon. In *Handbook of North American Indians*, vol. 7, Northwest Coast, 580–588. Washington, DC: Smithsonian Institution, 1990.

Athena The farm community of Centerville, Umatilla County, was located roughly midway between Pendleton and Walla Walla. A post office opened at Centerville in 1878, and the railroad arrived in 1884. In 1889, the local school principal successfully proposed that the town become Athena—Centerville was much too prosaic a name. Athena was incorporated in 1904, and the 1910 census reported a population of 586; wheat, peas, and corn are widely grown nearby. Scots immigrants were prominent in the area, and annual gatherings were held at Athena beginning in 1899. These ceased at the onset of World War I, but became the inspiration for the town's Caledonian Games, which have been carried on since 1976. A cannery was established in 1935 for the canning of **peas**, which have become a major crop in the area. In 2007, the population was estimated at 1,270.

Aumsville Aumsville today is a burgeoning small suburb of Salem, located in Marion County at the base of the rolling Waldo Hills. Its beginnings as a community date to the 1840s, when emigrant Americans claimed the land for farming. A community—

apparently first known as Hoggum for the plentitude of hogs in the vicinity—began to coalesce after Henry Turner (who is also the namesake of the nearby town of **Turner**) and his family built a gristmill in 1863. The town's name derives from that of Amos or Aumus M. Davis, son-in-law of Henry and Judith Turner, who died in 1863. The town was platted in 1864, and had a post office by 1868. A narrow-gauge railroad came through in 1880; by 1890, this line was part of a growing network of Southern Pacific Company branch lines in the Willamette Valley. Aumsville was incorporated in 1911, and it remained a rural service center with a population of between 150 and 300 for many decades. Since 1980, its population has expanded tremendously, and was estimated in 2007 at 3,300. It is the "Home of the Corn Festival," established in 1969; the area is a heavy producer of sweet corn for freezing and canning.

Some accounts of Aumsville's history refer to Aumsville as being located on, or at least close to, the wagon road connecting Salem with eastern Oregon over **Santiam Pass**; coincidentally, postcards of Aumsville can also be found emblazoned with the slogan, "On the road of a thousand wonders." It should not be assumed that Aumsville was one of the "thousand wonders," nor that the road to Santiam Pass was the road in question. The **"Road of a thousand wonders"** was a Southern Pacific Company advertising slogan, and the road was a railroad.

➤ **Aurora** The town of Aurora lies south of Portland near the Willamette River and its confluence with the Pudding River in Marion County. Named for the daughter of its charismatic founder, Dr. **William Keil**, Aurora began as a settlement of German Christian communitarian farmers in 1857. Keil brought a group of followers west from Missouri, where they had founded the community of Bethel in

The community band of Aurora lasted well after the formal termination of the cooperative colony. This photograph shows the band and a crowd that has come down to the Southern Pacific Company depot to see the exhibits aboard the company's farm demonstration train in 1910. The company partnered with Oregon Agricultural College (now Oregon State University) in this project. Oregon Historical Society, CN 007874.

1845. Among the immigrants was Dr. Keil's son Wilhelm, who died shortly before the move; his body traveled overland in a casket, preserved in alcohol. The Aurora Mills post office was opened in 1857 (it changed to simply Aurora in 1894). Aurora flourished into the 1870s, renowned for its brass band and for its food; travelers on the new **Oregon & California Railroad** stopped there for meals. Communal activity ended after Keil's death in 1877, and the properties went to individual farmers. The town was incorporated in 1893, and the 1900 census reported a population of 122; it was 229 in 1920. By 1915, Aurora was a small agricultural town, where "hops is one of the principal crops and dairying one of the most profitable industries"; **filberts** have also long been a notable product. Based on the remaining evidence of the Keil colony, part of the town was incorporated in the Aurora Historic District, which was placed on the National Register of Historic Places in 1974. Since the 1980s, Aurora has become a center for antique shops, and it has grown as a suburban residential area; its census count in 1970 was 306, and escalated to an estimated 955 in 2007.

Dole, Philip. Aurora Colony Architecture: Building in a Nineteenth-Century Cooperative Society. *Oregon Historical Quarterly* 92 (Winter 1991–1992): 377–416.

Snyder, Eugene E. *Aurora, Their Last Utopia: Oregon's Christian Commune, 1856–1883*. Portland, Oregon: Binfords & Mort, 1993.

► **aviation** In aviation's early years, daredevil pilot Silas Christofferson made headlines with stunts such as his 1912 flight off the roof of Portland's Multnomah Hotel. Commercial passenger air service along the Pacific Coast had its beginnings with Pacific Air Transport in 1926, which had an airmail contract between Seattle and Los Angeles. Planes made stops in Portland and Medford. Portland developed its first major airport on Swan Island in 1927, dedicated by none other than Charles Lindbergh. *See also* **Air Oregon**; **West Coast Airlines**.

West Coast Air Transport was another pioneer in the field of commercial aviation in Oregon. This brochure was published in 1929 to publicize the company's daily-except-Sunday flight between San Francisco and Seattle with stops in Oakland, Montague (a town near Yreka, California), and Portland; there was an additional flight between Seattle and Portland. A company limousine met each flight to take passengers to and from downtown ticket offices. Author's collection.

B

Bachelor Butte *see* **Mount Bachelor**

Bailey, Margaret Jewett "Smith"
see **literature**

► *Bailey Gatzert* The *Bailey Gatzert* was a sternwheel steamboat, built in Ballard (Seattle), Washington, in 1890 for service on Puget Sound. She was transferred to Portland in 1892 for use on the Willamette and Columbia Rivers, where she became a mainstay of The Dalles, Portland & Astoria Navigation Company, a fast and favorite boat on the run between Portland and The Dalles, and on excursions between Portland and Cascade Locks. Randall V. Mills relates that one day in 1914, with a load of passengers hoping to reach Portland in time to see the fabulous **Portland Rose Festival** evening electrical parade, the *Gatzert* left The Dalles at 3:10 p.m., stopped at four landings and wended through the locks at the Cascades, and docked at 9:03 p.m.— she averaged about twenty-three miles an hour on the water.

The *Gatzert* went back to Puget Sound in 1917, and was retired in 1926. She inspired music—the *Bailey Gatzert March*—and a postage stamp picturing her was issued in 1996. The real Bailey Gatzert (1829–1893) was a prominent Seattle businessman and mayor who is also the namesake of an elementary school there.

Baker, Edward Dickinson (1811–1861) Edward Dickinson Baker's residence in Oregon was

The sternwheel steamboat *Bailey Gatzert* is pictured somewhere on the lower Columbia River in a photograph by J. F. Ford probably taken about 1905. Oregon Historical Society, OrHi 37857.

exceedingly short, but his national stature has left the state with many reminders of him. He was born in England and came to the United States as a child, with his parents settling in Philadelphia. They moved to Illinois in 1825, and young Baker studied law and got into politics; he became a state representative in 1837, then a state senator and a U.S. Congressman. He resigned to serve in the Mexican-American War (1846–48), returned to Congress in 1849–51, and then set out for California, where he practiced law in San Francisco. Friends and political advisors persuaded Baker to come to Oregon in 1860, where the new state legislature elected him as a Republican to the U.S. Senate, along with the Independent **James W. Nesmith**. Baker raised volunteer troops for the Union at the beginning of the Civil War; he was a colonel when he was killed at the Battle of Balls Bluff, Virginia, on October 21, 1861. He was buried in San Francisco. In Oregon, **Baker County** and **Baker City** commemorate his service to Oregon, and Oregon's place in the history of America's **Civil War**.

Baker, George Luis (1868–1941) Riding on a wave of civic reform, George L. Baker was swept into Portland's mayoral office in 1917 for a 16-year ride, during which he oversaw the transformation of the city's waterfront and the construction of four bridges across the Willamette. Born in The Dalles, Baker came to Portland in 1889, where he worked his way up from stagehand to manager to **theater** owner of the Baker Stock Company. Being a theatrical impresario was vastly suited to Baker's outgoing nature; his talents at oratory and politicking complemented his business skills. First elected to the Portland city council in 1898, Baker was a supporter of the 1913 initiative that recast the framework of city government to a nonpartisan council, headed by a mayor whose powers were largely ceremonial. "Our George" led the city with the brio and dash of a theater magnate, while city affairs were conducted with careful attention to the needs of the business

elite. Baker's public face was tarnished in the 1920s by association with fiscal chicanery and an ill-advised attempt to curry favor with the Ku Klux Klan in his unsuccessful 1923 bid for the U.S. Senate. Baker is remembered in Portland as a rousing civic booster.

Baker City Baker City was named for the county of which it is the seat of government. Sited along the historic travel route that had become the Oregon Trail in 1840s and a road to the gold mines of the **Powder River** in the 1860s, Baker City was a post office point beginning in 1866, was named the county seat two years later, incorporated as a city in 1874, and in 1880 boasted a population of 1,258. The arrival of the railroad in 1884 doubled the population by 1890. The Eccles family of Utah and other investors began developing timber interests and other industries, including the **Sumpter Valley Railway**, which penetrated timberlands to the west of the city. By 1915, Baker City had "six saw mills, sash, door and box factories, cigar factories, brewery and ice plant, fire clay plant, granite cutting plant, foundries, machine shops and bottling works."

The city shortened—modernized—its name to Baker in 1911. The local availability of good building stone gave the city an imposing array of structures, including the Geiser Grand (1889) and Antlers Hotels, Saint Francis DeSales Catholic cathedral (1907) and Saint Elizabeth Hospital, and numerous business blocks and residences. On the verge of the Depression, the citizenry financed the fashionable Baker Hotel, a 10-story Art Deco skyscraper that has been the tallest building in the city since 1929—and the tallest in Oregon east of the Cascades for most of that time. Baker City's population in 1940 was 9,342.

The timber industry began a slow decline in the area in the 1960s, and the city's population remained stable; the 1970 census showed 9,354 residents, and it declined in the next decade. Since then, Baker City has increasingly capitalized on its history as an economic engine. The downtown business district was placed on the National Register of Historic Places in 1978, and the imposing Geiser Grand Hotel reopened in 1998 after a major renovation. In 1989, the citizens voted to change the name of the city from Baker back to Baker City. Baker City's population in 2007 was estimated at 10,105.

Baker County Baker County was created from Wasco County in 1862, named for Col. **Edward Dickinson Baker** of the Union forces, killed at the Battle of Balls Bluff in 1861. The Wallowa Mountains on the northeast and the Blue Mountains to the west frame the valleys of the Burnt River and Powder River, which both flow into the Snake River along the county's eastern border. Union County was sliced off from the northern portion of Baker County in 1864, and in 1887 Malheur County was created from the southern section. In 1901, a final adjustment was made to the boundaries when an area known as the panhandle, between the Powder River and the Wallowa Mountains, was restored to Baker County. The current land area is 3,089 square miles.

Historically, the Burnt River and Powder River valleys were at the northern edge of territory inhabited by the **Northern Paiute Indians**. Euro-American explorers and trappers passed through the area beginning in the 1810s, and the **Oregon Trail** of the 1840s traversed it, but extensive incursions first occurred with the discovery of **gold** on tributaries of the Powder River in 1861. Auburn, one of the ephemeral mining camps, was the first county seat; government moved to **Baker City** in 1868. In the 1870 census, the county's population was 2,804.

After the blush of the gold rush, Baker County's development was slow until the arrival of a transcontinental railroad line, which opened in 1884 between Portland and Omaha and points east. The county's population jumped to 6,764 in 1890, and to 15,597 in 1900—and that population plateau remained in place for more than a century; the esti-

mate for 2007 was 16,435. More than half of the county's inhabitants reside in Baker City.

The construction of the narrow-gauge **Sumpter Valley Railway** into national forest land in the Blue Mountains fostered a logging and lumbering industry that lasted until the 1980s. Livestock raising and mining have been other mainstays of the county's economy. The county's golden heritage is evident in ghost towns such as **Sumpter** and **Granite**. It is also marked by a stranded relic of industrial gold mining that remains in Sumpter: a dredge that participated in the decades-long roiling of the gravels of the Powder River, a process that created a valley of denuded heaps of river rock that extends for many miles.

Balch, Frederick Homer (1861–1891) A romancer of Oregon, Frederick Balch was born in Lebanon and raised in Portland and in Goldendale, Washington. Balch showed an early interest in Indians and in writing. He completed a novel with an Indian motif at age 21, but his conversion to Christianity caused him to destroy the manuscript. Balch studied for the ministry and became a Congregational pastor in the Hood River Valley; meanwhile, he also continued to write. The first result was the novel *The Bridge of the Gods*, published in 1890; it has been reprinted many times since then, and the title phrase has echoed down the Columbia River Gorge ever since. As poet Walt Curtis noted, Balch "claimed to have gathered real lore from the last informants of the vanishing natives" and wove them into a "story of warring Indian tribes seeking to establish a confederacy to drive whites from the Pacific Northwest." Integral to the story is a legend of a natural bridge that spanned the Columbia River, the **Bridge of the Gods**.

Seldom in good health, Balch died of tuberculosis in Portland on June 3, 1891, shortly after his book was published. He left behind another manuscript, completed in 1887, which was edited and finally published in 1932. *Genevieve: A Tale of Oregon* is partly autobiographical, and includes elements from his discarded first manuscript. The character Genevieve is based on Ginevra Whitcomb, a woman who was, according to Curtis, "the love of his life"; Ginevra died tragically of pneumonia, and Balch presided at her funeral. Frederick Balch, Ginevra Whitcomb, and, poetically enough, Balch's editor and biographer, Alfred Powers, all came to rest in the cemetery in Lyle, Washington, in the Columbia River Gorge.

> Wiley, Leonard. *The Granite Boulder: A Biography of Frederic Homer Balch, author of* The Bridge of the Gods. Portland, Oregon: Leonard Wiley, 1970.

Baldock, Robert H. "Sam" (1889–1968) Sam Baldock was born and raised in Colorado, and came to Oregon in 1915 with some training in civil engineering (he completed his University of Colorado degrees in the 1930s, having had to drop out of college in 1913). He began as a transit man for the Oregon State Highway Commission, and worked up through the department, innovating as he went. He was noted for innovations in asphalt paving techniques, calculating the monetary value of highway engineering, and "the concept of geometric highway design," which could result in "freeways driven with ruthless rectilinearity through narrow gorges," according to a tribute issued by his alma mater. Baldock retired in 1956, and his contributions were recognized when the name Baldock Freeway was given to the section of the new **Interstate 5** freeway between Salem and Portland. The name is only rarely encountered today, and is sometimes confused with the **Banfield Expressway**.

Baldock Freeway *see* **Robert H. "Sam" Baldock**

► **Bandon** This Coos County community is located at the mouth of the Coquille River in a region historically occupied by the Lower Coquille bands of the **Coos Indians**. The discovery of gold in coastal

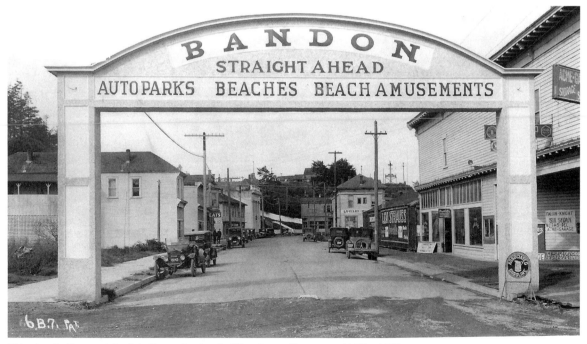

This view to the west depicts the main street of Bandon as it appeared in the 1920s. Steven Dotterrer collection.

sands in the 1850s brought many short-term prospectors to the area; the permanent settlement at Bandon, however, dates from the 1870s. Irish immigrant George Bennett, who arrived in 1873, bestowed the Irish name, and the post office opened in 1877. The townsite was platted in 1886 (with the name Averill, which did not stick), and Bandon was incorporated as a municipality in 1891.

The Coquille River harbor was somewhat navigable, as was the river itself, and steamboats plied upstream to Myrtle Point. The harbor was improved by jetties, on which construction began in 1884; the **lighthouse** was first lit in 1896. In 1903, work on the jetty demolished **Grandmother Rock**, a landmark and a sacred site of the **Coos Indians**. Coastal schooners brought supplies to Bandon and the Coquille River Valley from San Francisco, and lumber and dairy products—in the 1910s, there was a condensed milk plant on the waterfront—were shipped south. On September 26, 1936, a forest fire spread into the oily **gorse** brush (an imported shrub) that was common around the town. The fire spread into Bandon itself, becoming an inferno that consumed all but twenty houses, sent panicked crowds to the beach to escape the burning embers, and killed eleven residents. The 1940 census gave Bandon a population of 1,004—a decline of almost 50 percent from the previous decade.

The completion of the **Oregon Coast Highway** in the 1930s did much to boost Bandon as a coast resort, and this was apparent after the fire, as many cabins and motor courts—the forerunner of motels—went up along the highway. Bandon also became a center of cranberry culture (it had been carried on since the 1880s), an industry that has slowly grown until by 2005, the area produced about 5 percent of the nation's **cranberries**. The Bandon Cheese Company turned out a sharp, aged cheddar **cheese** that became locally famous from the 1960s, and won national awards in the 1990s. However, the company had financial problems more than once; the Tillamook County Creamery Association purchased it in

2000, and production ceased in Bandon in 2002. In the meantime, a new industry came to town: **golf**, in the guise of the Bandon Dunes golf resort, which opened its first links in 1999. The success of this sports resort has reshaped Bandon's economy and its icons. Bandon's population in 1970 was 1,832; in 2007, it was estimated at 3,235.

Beckham, Dow. *Bandon By-The-Sea: Hope and Perseverance in a Southwestern Oregon Town.* Coos Bay, Oregon, and Lake Oswego, Oregon: Arago Books, 1997.

Banfield Expressway The term "Banfield Expressway" or "Banfield Freeway" is used to describe a section of **Interstate 84** from Portland up **Sullivan's Gulch** to the city's eastern limits. This segment of the freeway was opened as the Banfield Expressway in 1955, named for Thomas H. Banfield (1885–1950), chair of the Oregon State Highway Commission from 1943 to 1950. Banfield was a civic leader and industrialist, the president of the Iron Fireman Manufacturing Company, which produced automatic-stoking furnaces (those made in Portland stoked sawdust, rather than the coal used in the East). While other local names for freeway sections, such as the Baldock Freeway and **Minnesota Freeway** have faded from popular usage, Portlanders still refer to "the Banfield."

Banks Located at the northern edge of the **Tualatin Plains** in Washington County, Banks is located in agricultural country that was settled in the mid-nineteenth century. A community developed in the early 1900s; a post office named Banks was established in 1902, and then was discontinued in 1904 only to be re-opened in 1907. A railroad was built through the town shortly thereafter, opening in 1911 and connecting Portland with Tillamook. Briefly, in 1911–12, Banks was the terminus of the United Railways, an interurban electric line that went east over Cornelius Pass to Portland. An extension of that line northwest to new lumber operations at Vernonia opened in 1921, and in the same year Banks was in-corporated. By 1930, with a population of 209, Banks was a small lumbering center; dairy farming and strawberry culture were the major agricultural activ-ities. The population reached 563 by 1990, and has since grown explosively; it was estimated at 1,435 in 2007; many residents commute to technology-related jobs in Hillsboro and Beaverton.

Bannock War One of the last armed conflicts between Native Americans and the U.S. Army took place on the heels of the **Nez Perce War** of 1877. In 1878, impoverished Bannock Indians in Idaho joined with a number of **Northern Paiute Indians** near Steens Mountain. Perhaps 1,500 Indians, families included, moved northward, pursued by troops under the command of General **Oliver Otis Howard**; a battle near Pilot Rock was followed by an Indian retreat toward the Umatilla Reservation; the Paiute leader **Egan** was killed, and both Indians and troops scattered. By later summer both Paiutes and Ban-nocks surrendered in the last white-Indian warfare in Oregon. The Bannock War ended seventy-eight Indian lives and those of nine soldiers and six white settlers.

Barber, Rex T. (1917–2001) Noted World War II Army Air Corps pilot Rex Barber was born in **Cul-ver**, and was educated at Linfield College and Ore-gon State. Barber participated in an attack on Japa-nese admiral Isoroku Yamamoto, commander in chief of the navy and the instigator of the 1941 raid on Pearl Harbor. Lt. Barber was one of four pilots who attacked and downed Yamamoto's plane on April 18, 1943, and has been credited with the fatal hit. Barber retired from the Air Force as a colonel in 1961 and returned to Culver with his family, where he sold insurance and was elected mayor of the town. In 2003, a new bridge carrying Highway 97 across the Crooked River near Culver was named the Rex T. Barber Veterans Memorial Bridge.

Barchus, Eliza (1857–1959) Eliza Rosanna Lamb was born in Salt Lake City, and moved to Portland in 1880 with her husband, John H. Barchus. In the early 1880s she began to study painting; the first painting she sold was a landscape view of Mount Rainier, and landscapes, especially of mountains, became her lifelong subject. Widowed in 1899 and with a family to support, Barchus turned her paint-ing from pastime to career. She exhibited at the 1905 **Lewis and Clark Centennial Exposition** in Port-land, and produced postcards and a catalog to pro-mote her artwork. Economic necessity caused her to churn out paintings, especially views of Mount Hood and Multnomah Falls, that were popular as parlor pieces and in hotel lobbies and business offices. She painted less after about 1920, and ceased in 1935, bowed by arthritis and failing eyes. Mid-twentieth-century art collectors did not especially favor her sentimental—and relatively common—landscapes, but by the 1990s, Barchus paintings were again cov-eted and prices soared. Barchus postcard views of Mount Hood are both iconic and ubiquitous.

Barchus, Agnes. *Eliza R. Barchus, the Oregon Artists, 1857–1959*. Portland, Oregon: Binfords & Mort, 1974.

barley Barley is and has long been a major live-stock feed crop in Oregon. It is grown primarily in Klamath County and in northeastern Oregon.

Barlow This tiny Clackamas County town was the Donation Land Claim of Thomas McKay. McKay sold the property to **Samuel K. Barlow** of Barlow Road fame, who in turn sold it to his son William. Wil-liam (1822–1904) and Martha Ann (1824–1901) Bar-low built a house there in the 1850s, which burned about 1883. In 1885, they erected on its site an Italianate-style house, at the end of a drive of black walnut trees—the first in Oregon—that were planted in 1859. The house is on the National Register of Historical Places, and some of the trees remain as well. The Oregon & California Railroad built through

Barlow in 1870, and a post office opened in 1871. The community was incorporated in 1903; by the 1910 census Barlow reported a population of sixty-nine. A 1915 publication states that Barlow is in the "center of [a] large agricultural section, the soil of which is adapted to intensified farming, especially small fruits and vegetables." Although it was along the Pacific Highway, Barlow did not develop as a commercial point; the post office was closed in 1975, and the estimated population in 2007 was 140. A small cast-iron fountain—providing fresh water suitable for dogs, horses, and people—stands at the corner of First and Main Streets, where it was placed in 1904 by the daughter of William and Martha Ann Barlow.

Barlow, Samuel Kimbrough (1795–1867) Samuel K. Barlow is the namesake of the **Barlow Road**, a segment of the **Oregon Trail** that carried wagons over one of its most arduous stretches around Mount Hood. Barlow was born in Kentucky in 1795, and he, his wife, Susannah Lee, and four children came west to Oregon over the trail in 1845. Beyond The Dalles, most overlanders made their way down the Columbia River, often by raft; Barlow decided to take his party south around Mount Hood. It was a difficult journey, and by the time the group reached a point west of today's Barlow Pass, the onset of winter caused them to stash their wagons and supplies and speed onward to the Willamette Valley.

After his road-building enterprise, Sam and Susannah purchased land near Oregon City in 1848 and took up farming; he sold the property to his son William in 1852; the town of **Barlow** marks the spot. Sam died in 1867.

Barlow Road This famous segment of the **Oregon Trail** extended about 150 miles from The Dalles around the southern edge of Mount Hood to the Philip Foster farm and then Oregon City. Until 1846, when the route was opened, overland travelers generally rode the Columbia River downstream from The Dalles, a treacherous experience that required portaging at the Cascades, and one that was often fatal, as in the case of the children of **Jesse** and **Lindsay Applegate**.

Samuel K. Barlow and his family, with the valued assistance of **Joel Palmer**, blazed the land route in 1845, and in 1846 he obtained the permission of the **provisional government** to build and operate it as a toll road, with Philip Foster as a partner. In the next few years, about three out of every four emigrant parties used the road, paying $5 per team and $1 per person or head of cattle. Still, it was not a profitable enterprise; Barlow and Foster turned over the road to other operators after 1848, and it remained a toll road until 1915, when the state of Oregon acquired title to the route. Extensively re-engineered, much of the western section of the road from Sandy to the summit is now part of **Highway 26**; the eastern section is largely abandoned. In 1992, the Barlow Road was placed on the National Register of Historic Places as a Historic District.

Basques in Oregon Immigrants from the Basque regions of Spain participated in the California gold rush of the 1850s, but it was not until the 1890s that Basques were drawn to the **Owyhee River** and **Treasure Valley** regions of Idaho and Oregon, where they engaged in sheep herding and often operated hotels and boarding houses. Immigration to this area reached its height in the 1900s and 1910s; most of the immigrants came from one Spanish province, Bizkaia. **Jordan Valley** has a strong Basque culture.

Munro, Sarah Baker. Basque Folklore in Southeastern Oregon. *Oregon Historical Quarterly* 76 (1975): 153–174.

Bay City The town of Bay City in Tillamook County was founded in 1888, an act said to have been committed by Winfield Cone, who was from Bay City, Michigan. Bay City post office was established in 1889, and the town was incorporated in 1910, a year before a railroad came through to link the town with Portland. In 1915, Bay City also had weekly steamship service to Portland, and residents engaged in lumbering, salmon fishing, and farming, and worked in a sawmill, a sash and door factory, a salmon cannery, and a sanatorium. Bay City's population has wavered over the years: 281 in 1910, 511 in 1920; 379 in 1940, then 761 in 1950. By 1990, it was 1,027, and it was estimated at 1,230 in 2007.

Bayocean The Bayocean Peninsula is a sandy spit that extends north from Cape Meares in Tillamook County, separating Tillamook Bay from the Pacific Ocean. Essentially a sand dune, the peninsula was partially timbered in the nineteenth century. A Kansas City-based developer, Thomas B. Potter, visited the area in 1906 and envisioned a future resort there. Through the agency of the Potter-Chapin Realty Company, fresh from developing the Arleta subdivision in southeast Portland, T. B. Potter and his son, Thomas I. Potter, began creating Bayocean in 1907. Bayocean was then a lengthy river-and-ocean boat trip from Portland (or, worse, a train-and-stagecoach ordeal), so it was a difficult proposition to sell lots for vacation homes. The company persevered, aided by the arrival of direct railroad service from Portland in 1911; in 1915 Bayocean was a place for "hunting, fishing, boating, deep-sea fishing, clam digging. Large natural park, tennis court and golf links. Natatorium." A post office was established in 1909; Bayocean had a hotel and a summertime tent city for camping out, and an assortment of beachside bungalows had been built by 1920.

The north jetty at the mouth of Tillamook Bay was completed in 1917, and the changes thereby wrought began to destroy the peninsula. The ocean cut through the southern end of the spit in 1939 and several times thereafter. The post office of the now-abandoned town closed in 1953, and the last house washed away in 1960. Although the completion of a south jetty in 1974 has stabilized the peninsula, Bayocean is long gone, consumed by the sea.

Webber, Bert, and Margie Webber. *Bayocean: The Oregon Town that Fell into the Sea*. Medford, Oregon: Webb Research Group, 1989.

Beach Bill *see* **McCall, Thomas Lawson "Tom"**

beans Green string beans, also called snap beans, were a staple for settlers and farmers in Oregon. A variety of these beans that proved to be popular for canning was developed in the Blue Lake area of California near Ukiah; it was introduced into Oregon about 1923, and newer strains have developed over time. **Stayton** became "the bean capital of the valley" and an important processing center. In 1937, the Blue Lake Producers Cooperative opened in Salem, specializing in canned and dehydrated fruit and vegetables. One of the company's labels was Jack and the Beanstalk. The 1952 production of a comedy version of the fairy tale starring Bud Abbott and Lou Costello gave the company's canned beans a good advertising tie-in; Costello is said to have had more than forty cases of Blue Lake beans sent to his friends in the media and advertising industries.

bear Many black bears, *Ursus americanus*, live in Oregon: an estimated 25,000 to 30,000 of them. They are usually black in color, but "they can also be brown, cinnamon or blond." Black bears are omnivorous and eat grasses and berries, fruit and small mammals, insects and amphibians. Oregon once had grizzly bears as well, *Ursus arctos horribilis*. One of the last of his kind was a fellow known in the Siskiyou Mountains of southern Oregon and northern California as Old Reelfoot. He was a reported terror to ranchers, whose stock he attacked, and he was finally shot in 1890 near Pilot Rock. He was said to have weighed about 1800 pounds, although this might be an exaggeration. The pelt was stuffed and mounted, and Reelfoot traveled about on exhibition for a few years; he disappeared before World War I.

▶ **Bear Creek Valley** The name is not distinctive, but the place is. The creek in Jackson County is a tributary of the **Rogue River**, and the **California-Oregon Trail** traversed the valley. The wide and level valley was reported in the 1840s to be covered by stands of native grasses as high as a horse. Gold miners and homesteaders came in the 1850s, the **Takelma Indians** were forcibly removed, and the Bear Creek Valley became an agricultural mecca, "the Italy of Oregon" in the 1880s. **Apple** and then **pear** orchards came early in the twentieth century, and during the Depression of the 1930s, the Bear Creek Orchards of **Harry and David** took the

name across the nation, giving a mundane place name a certain distinction that it still holds.

Beard, James Andrew (1903–1985) American culinary maven James A. Beard was born in Portland, the only child of Elizabeth and John Beard. In his autobiographical *Delights and Prejudices* (1964), Beard recounts a childhood shaped by food, for his mother ran a boardinghouse with the aid of a Chinese cook, Let. Summers were spent on the coast at **Gearhart**, where he delighted in crab feasts and wild berries. Beard accompanied his mother to the once-famous Portland **public market**, and honed his tastes at the city's Hazelwood Restaurant and the Georgian Room at **Meier & Frank**.

The young Beard aspired to a career as an actor

This view of the Hillcrest Orchard on the east edge of Medford was taken about 1917. Development of this land in the Bear Creek Valley for apple and pear orchards had begun in the 1890s. Reginald H. and Maude Parsons had acquired it in 1908, and developed Hillcrest into a model orchard property. Placed on the National Register of Historic Places in 1984, Hillcrest maintains its orchard status, but has been increasingly surrounded by urban development since the 1990s. In 1997, the Parsons family began planting vineyards on some of the property. Oregon Historical Society, OrHi 90976.

or singer; he attended **Reed College**, but the even-then-famously liberal school was not pleased with his sexual orientation. In 1923, he joined a theatrical troupe and spent a few years traveling and attempting to make it in the theater world. In the mid-1930s, Beard began catering for parties in New York City. In 1940, his first cookbook, *Hors D'Oeuvres & Canapés*, was issued, and it was followed by one of the first books on outdoor grilling. He worked in Navy canteens during World War II; after the war, the cookbooks proliferated, and he appeared on the infant television in a cooking show in 1946. Always having to scramble to make a living, Beard contributed articles to magazines, did consulting work with restaurateurs, promoted food gadgets and food products. In 1955 he founded the James Beard Cooking School.

Beard retained his Oregon connections, and the school strengthened them; for many years he taught cooking classes on the Oregon coast, usually at Seaside. Beard was among the first American food writers to document and encourage regional foods and recipes, most prominently in *American Cookery* (1972). Reed College gave Beard an honorary doctorate in 1976; Beard left the bulk of his estate to the college, including his New York City townhouse and his cookbook collection. The house is now the headquarters of the James Beard Foundation, which continues his efforts to promote the heritage and future of an American cuisine.

Beard, James. *Delights and Prejudices.* New
    York: Athenaeum, 1964.
Clark, Robert. *James Beard: A Biography.* New
    York: HarperCollins, 1993.

beaver The American beaver, *Castor canadensis*, is an aquatic rodent once widely distributed throughout northern North America. The lust for the **fur** of the beaver was the impetus behind much of the early European and American commercial activity during the nineteenth century in what is today Oregon. The fur of the beaver makes, in particular, very fine hats; with the disappearance of the European beaver in pursuit of hat-making materials, the **Hudson's Bay Company (HBC)**, the **Pacific Fur Company**, and other endeavors arose to supply beaver pelts from America. Changing fashions, new technologies, and the over-hunting of beaver all contributed to the demise of the industry and the near-demise of the animal. In the 1820s, the HBC attempted to create a "fur desert" in the American West, an area of "no beaver," to the east of their trapping areas in the Pacific Northwest.

The beaver is also the state animal of Oregon, as designated by the legislature in 1969. The animal appears on one side of the state flag, which was adopted in 1925. In addition, the beaver is the mascot of **Oregon State University**, the name of its yearbook and of its athletic teams.

Beaver was also the name of a very prickly character in the history of the HBC in the Oregon Country, the Rev. Herbert Beaver. Beaver was an Anglican cleric sent in 1836 to minister at Fort Vancouver at the behest of HBC's chief factor (director) there, **John McLoughlin**, who became a Catholic; the HBC incorporated a polyglot lot of many ethnicities and religions. Beaver's self-righteous views, especially concerning (in opposition to) intercultural marriages and those not blessed by his church, eventually brought the two men to blows in 1838; Rev. Beaver left for London on furlough and did not return.

The American beaver should not be confused with the mountain beaver, *Aplodontia rufa*, a rascally rodent that thrives in the Coast Range and the Cascades, making tunnels and burrows and eating tree seedlings, although it prefers to eat ferns. Residents of these areas who try to maintain lawns consider mountain beavers to be pests.

► **Beaver** This is a small rural community in Tillamook County where one of the numerous Beaver Creeks meets the Nestucca River. The Beaver post office was established in 1889. It was the site of an early **cheese** factory.

Ike Hiner, cheesemaker, and his helper, Elizabeth Foland, at the cheese factory in Beaver. This was the first cooperative cheese factory in Tillamook County, and was organized in 1892. The photograph was taken in 1893. Tillamook Pioneer Museum. Oregon Historical Society, OrHi 38421.

Beaver The **Hudson's Bay Company**, transnational seekers of beaver pelts, brought the steamship *Beaver* to the Oregon Country in 1836 from England, basing her at first at **Fort Vancouver**. For many years this small sidewheeler carried on the company's business along the Pacific Coast. She wrecked at Victoria, British Columbia, in 1881.

Beaver Creek Settlement in this rural agricultural area southeast of Oregon City in Clackamas County began in the 1850s. A post office named Beaver was established in 1868, and a variety of other names—and somewhat different locations—were used for the area's post office over the next few decades; the names included Mink, Shubel, Beaver Creek, and Hoff. In 1915, the area was described as active in dairying, poultry raising, fruit growing, and lumbering; it was also suggested that the area

was rather religious, if a bit split on the matter: "near by are 8 churches, including a Welsh church." The latter refers to the still-active Bryn Seion Welsh Church, established in 1884. The post office name was finally settled in 1922: Beavercreek. This spelling has persisted with the USPS, but Beaver Creek is usually found on maps.

beaver money In 1849, the legislature of the **provisional government** authorized the minting of coins to supplement the short supply of federal coinage; however, the arrival of new territorial governor **Joseph Lane** brought that plan to a halt, for Oregon was, since 1848, a federal territory, and such activities were illegal. But there was a need, and some of the original promoters of the idea joined with **George Abernethy** to form the Oregon Exchange Company, which proceeded to issue gold coins in denominations of $5 and $10, to the sum of some $58,500. The gold content was very high, thus people held onto them. They were in use until about 1854, when the San Francisco mint opened and began to supply the needed coinage for commerce on the West Coast. The beaver money coins are scarce and highly collectible.

Beavers (baseball team) Baseball was a popular amateur sport throughout Oregon from the 1860s, with local teams in cities and towns from Portland (the Pioneers, 1867) to Jacksonville (the Gold Bricks). Professional baseball in Portland dates from the Portland Gladiators in 1890. The construction in 1901 of a large baseball park on NW Vaughn Street by two streetcar companies helped propel the establishment that same year of the Pacific Northwest League and the Portland Webfooters team. The Webfooters became the Portland Beavers in 1906, and played at Vaughn Street ballpark until its closure in 1955; subsequent games were played in **PGE Park**. Beginning in the 1960s, the Beavers were a farm team for a succession of major-league teams, and left Portland for Salt Lake City in 1994. The Beavers returned after 2001, when the Albuquerque Dukes moved to Portland and adopted the venerable name.

Andresen, Paul, and Kip Carlson. *The Portland Beavers.* Charleston, South Carolina: Arcadia, 2004.

Beavers (OSU) The **Oregon State University** (OSU) athletic teams are know as the Beavers; the football Beavers meet the football **Ducks** at the annual **Civil War.** Back in its days as State Agricultural College, ca. 1892, the athletic mascot was a coyote. A beaver crops up now and then in the next few decades, but it is not until 1933 that "Billy" Beaver is the official mascot—and Billy was a real, live beaver. In the early 1940s, Billy morphed into Benny, and Benny has remained. In 1999, a newly designed "angry" beaver was introduced, and became the official mascot in 2001. It is still Benny, however.

Beaverton The rich soils and open aspect of the **Tualatin Plains** attracted American settlers in the 1840s. The Washington County community of Beaverton began to take shape when the townsite was laid out in 1869; the Oregon Central Railroad arrived from Portland in 1872, and a post office began operations the same year. The name refers to the presence of **beaver** in the area; their dam building resulted in expanses of what was referred to as beaver-dam soil, a deep silt perfect for vegetable growing, and Beaverton was a farm-centered town.

Beaverton was incorporated as a municipality in 1893, and the 1900 census gave it a population of 249. The arrival of the **Oregon Electric Railway** in 1908 and the 1914 electrification of the former Oregon Central line made Beaverton a suburban commuter town. The local industries in 1915 were lumbering, fruit growing, gardening, and brick and tile manufacturing; Beaverton was "celebrated" for its onions, asparagus, rhubarb, horseradish, and celery, all of which were marketed in Portland. Beaverton's population in 1920 was 580.

In 1929, Rose Biggi began processing horseradish in her Beaverton basement; that enterprise grew into Beaverton Foods, purveyors of a wide assortment of horseradish and mustard products. Beaverton's population reached 1,052 in 1940; post–World War II suburban development boosted that to 2,512 in 1950. With the opening of new tract housing and shopping areas such as **Cedar Hills** in the 1950s, Beaverton's area and population grew rapidly. The new **Sunset Highway** and the siting of the headquarters of **Tektronix** in Beaverton in 1956 fostered the growth of the electronic-related **Silicon Forest**. Beaverton's population in 1970 was 18,577. Commuter train service to Beaverton, which had died by 1929, was suddenly revived in 1998 with the opening of **MAX**, connecting the city with Hillsboro,

Portland, and Gresham. By 2007, Beaverton claimed 85,560 residents.

beer and brewing Beer was once a very local commodity, one that in the absence of refrigeration had to be served fresh. Consequently, in nineteenth-century Oregon, every sizeable community from The Dalles to Jacksonville to Baker City had a brewery or two. The first commercial brewery appeared in Portland in 1852, in Salem in 1862. The Salem establishment grew into the Salem Brewery Association, brewers and bottlers of Salem Beer. Alas, Salem voted in local option **prohibition** in 1913, ahead of the statewide act. The company revived after the national repeal and was operated by Sick's Brewery from 1943 until it closed in 1955; by then, **Blitz-Weinhard Brewing Company** in Portland was the single remaining brewery in the state: refrigeration, volume production by national brewers, improved transportation—and the prohibition experience—had eliminated all the others.

Finally, changes in state law permitted, and economic and social changes encouraged, the establishment of new breweries, which started in 1980. The first long term success began with BridgePort Brewery in Portland in 1984, founded by Dick Ponzi, also a pioneer in the revived Oregon **wine and winemaking** industry. Oregon has since experienced a widespread growth in both small microbreweries and in brewpubs, which produce beers for only a single retail outlet; the chain of McMenamins pubs combined those models. By 2006, there were some sixty brewing companies with more than eighty plants; more than half the operations were in the Portland area.

beeswax Large chunks of beeswax have been found at various points along the Oregon Coast, particularly on the sands at the mouth of the **Nehalem River** below **Neahkahnie Mountain**. The wax is believed to have been the principal cargo of a Spanish sailing ship en route from the Philippines to Mexico; either the vessel *Santo Christo de Burgos* (1693) or the *San Francisco Xavier* (1705) are the likely prospects. Bees native to Mexico did not produce wax suitable for making candles, which were heavily used by the Spanish emigrants there. The wax has given rise to legends of a treasure ship; examples can be viewed at the Tillamook Pioneer Museum in Tillamook.

Belluschi, Pietro (1899–1994) Born in Italy, Pietro Belluschi studied engineering in Rome and at Cornell University; he immigrated to the United States in 1923. After a stint as a mining engineer in northern Idaho, Belluschi arrived in Portland in 1925 with a letter of introduction to the office of architect **A. E. Doyle**. By 1927, Belluschi was the chief designer in the office, where he worked on the new Pacific Building and on a remodeling of Portland Union Station. His first major commission for the firm was for the **Portland Art Museum** (1931–32), a sleek modern design in brick and marble that won him wide attention. Belluschi became a partner in the Doyle firm in 1933, and took control of it under his own name in 1943. In that period, he designed an addition to the museum, and also undertook a number of residential commissions that displayed not only his interest in the clean lines of the International style, but also in Asian motifs, and in the use of regional traditions and native woods. He designed a number of churches in the 1940s and 1950s, and in 1945–48 produced the Equitable Building in downtown Portland: the nation's first curtain-wall skyscraper in aluminum and glass; it was placed on the National Register of Historic Places in 1976. Other major designs included a square-block office for the *Oregonian* and the Federal Reserve Bank in Portland, and the Marion County Courthouse in Salem.

Belluschi left Portland in 1950 to head the school of architecture and planning at the Massachusetts Institute of Technology. He continued to practice architecture, designing such structures as Saint Mary's Cathedral in San Francisco (with others;

1963–70) and many others across the nation and abroad. He retired from MIT in 1965. Back in Portland, he had a hand in the design of another round of churches and residential projects.

Clausen, Meredith L. *Pietro Belluschi: Modern American Architect.* Cambridge, Massachusetts: MIT Press, 1994.

Belmont neighborhood, Portland The newly platted lots of Sunnyside Addition were the reason for the construction of the Willamette Bridge Railway Company line along Morrison and Belmont Streets in East Portland in 1888. The new Morrison Street Bridge provided a route to the city center, and the new railroad served suburban commuters. It first extended to SE Thirty-fourth Avenue, then beyond to **Mount Tabor**. A post office named Sunnyview operated from 1890 to 1894; the name Sunnyside was already being used for another post office in Clackamas County. The post office and streetcar line became the nucleus of a retail district along SE Belmont Street between Twenty-ninth and Thirty-seventh that persisted through the end of streetcar service in 1948 to a revival in the late 1990s.

▶ **Bend** The county seat of Deschutes County, Bend was a place on the Deschutes River, a crossing that was known as Farewell Bend, the last place road travelers saw the river. The name was used for a post office in the vicinity as early as 1886; it was closed in 1902. In 1904, the post office name was revived, at the Pilot Butte Development Company's townsite near **Pilot Butte**. Development was in the air, as the Tumalo Irrigation Project promised to make the arid land productive with water from the Deschutes, and two railroads were heading south from the Columbia River to Bend, opening markets for its pine timber resources. Bend was incorporated in 1905; the 1910 census recorded 536 residents.

The railroads arrived in 1911, and in 1915, Bend

The rustic Pilot Butte Inn is pictured about 1930, sited above the banks of the Deschutes River and the Newport Avenue Bridge, which was also given a rusticated look. Steven Dotterrer collection.

had a brickyard and a flour mill. Two immense lumber mills—Shevlin-Hixon and Brooks-Scanlon—opened in 1916; the 1920 census showed 5,415 people, and by 1930, the population was 8,848. The Pilot Butte Inn opened in 1917, a rustic inn for well-heeled sportsmen. Another railroad extension to the south opened in 1928; Bend was a city of workers' bungalows and prosperity. In 1950, the Shevlin-Hixon mill was sold to Brooks-Scanlon as the pine woodlands diminished; Brooks-Scanlon began dealing in resort properties such as **Black Butte** Ranch by 1970, and their mill closed in 1982. Bend's population in 1980 was 17,260.

As resource industries declined, outdoor recreation and retirement living brought a new influx of residents. Bend's population reached 52,029 in 2000, and an estimated 77,780 in 2007.

Hatton, Raymond. *Bend in Central Oregon*. Portland, Oregon: Binfords & Mort, 1978.

► **Benson, Simon** (1851–1942) Born in Norway, Simon Berger Iversen moved to the United States with his family when he was sixteen. The surname changed to Benson; in Wisconsin, Simon learned English, married, and in 1879 brought his wife and child to Oregon, hoping to find work in a logging camp. He gradually bought logging lands in Washington and Oregon, and during the 1890s became an active proponent of new logging techniques: building logging railroads into the woods, using steam engines to yard logs, developing ocean-going rafts that sent logs to California sawmills by sea. He sold his holdings in 1909, and dedicated time and money to a variety of other civic and business affairs: the building of the Benson and Columbia Gorge Hotels, promoting the **Columbia River Highway**, benefiting Benson Polytechnic High School for boys in Portland, giving land in the Columbia Gorge for parks, building a bridge at **Multnomah Falls**. In 1912, Benson gave Portland money for public drinking fountains: made of handsome bronze with four ever-bubbling bowls, the Benson fountains have

"MEMORIES, MEMORIES!"

This cartoon was distributed as a postcard, and depicts a citizen leaning on one of the public drinking fountains donated to the city of Portland by philanthropist and temperance advocate Simon Benson. The citizen contemplates the steins of beer he once drank before prohibition was enacted in Oregon in 1914; it went into effect on January 1, 1916. Steven Dotterer collection.

proliferated throughout the city. Benson ostensibly hoped that with water freely available, loggers would quench their thirst there rather than in a saloon, to the benefit of the loggers' employers, including Benson. Benson moved to California in 1920, where he engaged in land development. Benson's philanthropy has its legacy in a high school, a state park, and a hotel; one of his Portland residences, built in the Queen Anne style, was rescued from the wrecker's ball, moved a few blocks in 2000, and restored to become a feature of the **Portland State University** downtown campus.

Benton County The Oregon provisional legislature established Benton County in 1847, naming it for the Missouri senator, Thomas Hart Benton (1782-1858), who had been a longtime congressional advocate for United States control of the **Oregon Country**. Benton County was carved from Polk County and initially extended south to the California border and west to the Pacific Ocean. Subsequent partitions pared it down to its present 679 square miles in the center of the Willamette Valley. The population in 1860 was 3,074; by 1910, it reached 10,633.

The **Kalapuyan Indians** lived in this portion of the valley, notably the Marys River band. The tribe was decimated by malaria and other illnesses during the 1830s. Emigrant American settlers appeared in numbers in the 1840s. The townsite of Marysville, which grew to become **Corvallis**, developed in the late 1840s, and it became the county seat in 1851. A courthouse was erected in 1854; it was replaced in 1889 by an Italianate-style building that is the oldest courthouse in continued use in the state.

The economic underpinnings of Benton County have long been agriculture, **Oregon State University**, and lumber and wood products; high technology has joined the list since the 1980s. The presence of the college, with its agricultural emphasis, has contributed to a diverse agricultural history for the county; the early dependence on wheat gave way to hops, grass seed, nursery stock, grapes for wine production, dairying, and Christmas trees. Benton County's population in 1950 was 31,570; the estimate for 2007 was 85,300.

berries A number of berries are native to Oregon, going by such common names as salmonberries, elderberries, huckleberries (blue and red), thimbleberries (red and blue), snowberries, and wild **blackberries** and wild strawberries and high bush cranberries; salal has berries, and so does Oregon grape. All are edible (red elderberries are not recommended). Also, non-native berries have gone wild, notably two species of blackberries. Many introduced berries are commercially grown in Oregon, including **blackberries**, **boysenberries**, **marionberries**, **loganberries**, **strawberries**, and **raspberries**.

Berry, Don (1931-2001) Born in Minnesota but a longtime Oregonian, Don Berry attended **Reed College**, where he began to delve into Asian metaphysical ideas. Berry melded those interests with regional history and Native American spiritual concepts in his first novel, *Trask* (1960). The central figure was based on Elbridge Trask, the namesake of the **Trask River** and a restless man who came to the **Tillamook** area in the 1840s. *Trask* was followed by *Moontrap* (1962) and *To Build a Ship* (1963). Berry also wrote *A Majority of Scoundrels*, a history of the Rocky Mountain **fur trade**. Berry was an early user of cyberspace, and much of his work remains there in *Berryworks*, "an eclection of fiction, nonfiction, poetry, essays, etc., by Don Berry," at www.donberry.com.

Berry, Rae Selling (1881-1976) A horticulturist and a plant collector, Rae Selling Berry developed a nine-acre garden south of Portland that became the Berry Botanical Garden. Rae Selling was the daughter of a prominent Portland businessman, Ben Selling, and his wife, Matilda. Rae married an Englishman, Alfred Berry, and the family moved in 1908 to the **Irvington neighborhood**, where Rae's interest in plants developed. Over the next thirty years she expanded her horticultural knowledge through reading. She financially supported plant expeditions and did her own gardening, often from seeds supplied by the colleagues she financed; she also traveled extensively in the West on plant excursions, specializing in primulas and rhododendrons, but exhibiting wide interests.

In 1938, the Berrys moved to a new house in the **Dunthorpe** district north of Lake Oswego, where nine acres of forest with a ravine and meadow allowed Rae to expand her collection and to experiment with growing plants that were "difficult" for the region, such as alpine plants. After her death, a group formed to preserve her gardens, and in 1978 the Berry Botanical Garden was opened, its mission the promotion of Pacific Northwest native plants, the maintenance of special plant collections such as rhododendrons and primula, and preservation and education activities.

▶ **bicycles and bicycling** Bicycles were a popular form of transportation and recreation in Oregon in the 1890s and early 1900s. A map of roads suitable for cyclists in the Portland area was published in 1896. City planners have helped develop an extensive network of bicycle lanes and separate paths in Portland, Eugene, and other urban areas since the 1980s. *See also* **Cycle Oregon**.

blackberries Nearly the nation's entire commercial blackberry crop is grown in Oregon, most of it in Marion County on some 5,000 acres. The native California blackberry or Pacific dewberry *(Rubus ur-*

sinus), juicy and very sweet, grows in the wild. These have been largely overrun by naturalized commercial vines known as Evergreen (bland berries) and Himalayan (juicy, tasty), which since the 1930s have blanketed creeksides and fields west of the Cascade Range. The Evergreen variety *(Rubus lacianatus)* was introduced to the state from England about 1850. The Himalayan *(Rubus armeniacus)* appears to be of Armenian origin, but came to the West Coast via India and Luther Burbank's California plant experimenting in 1885. Commercial blackberry production in Oregon stems from the discovery in 1926 of a thornless form of the Evergreen blackberry by Philip Steffes of Sublimity. The thorny imported blackberries are notably dominating; in **Ken Kesey**'s novel of logging on the Oregon Coast, *Sometimes a Great Notion*, they are described as smothering a building virtually overnight. *See also* **boysenberries**; **loganberries**; **marionberries**; **raspberries**.

A half-dozen adventuresome bicyclists prepare to go on the road in Lake County about 1900. Dalph Schmink (second from right) courted Lula Currier by bicycling from Lakeview to Summer Lake, a round trip of 120 miles. The couple wed in 1901. Schminck Memorial Museum.

Black Butte The area around Black Butte in Deschutes County was range and timber land in the early 1900s. A subsidiary of the Brooks-Scanlon Lumber Company of **Bend** purchased some of the land near **Sisters** in 1970 to add to their existing holdings and proceeded to pursue the development of what was considered to be a new niche in real estate, the second, or vacation, house. A targeted advertising campaign went to well-to-do Oregonians, and lots were available by the summer of 1970; the resort had a golf course, lodge, swimming pool, and tennis courts. In the 1980s the developers withdrew from Black Butte Ranch, leaving it in charge of an organization of the property owners. The resort helped to inaugurate what became a succession of second-home developments in Central Oregon in the next three decades.

blackcaps *see* **raspberries**

black cottonwood *see* **cottonwood**

blacks in Oregon The path to full citizenship in Oregon has been difficult for Indians, for Asians, for those of mixed races; it has been especially so for blacks. Aside from a few sojourners, blacks were not present in Oregon until American emigrants came to the still-disputed **Oregon Country** in the 1840s; some brought their black slaves with them. In 1844, **slavery** was made illegal by the **provisional government**—but so was the very presence of black people, free or slave, who were encouraged to leave by the provision of whipping twice a year "until he or she shall quit the territory." Though unenforced, the law was chilling, as was the 1848 exclusion law. After the creation of the American-governed **Oregon Territory** in 1848, the federal **Donation Land Act** of 1850 accorded free land to "whites and half-breed Indians" only. Oregon's exclusion law was repealed in 1854, but in the late 1850s, as statehood was considered and the nation was on the brink of civil war, slavery issues tangled with exclusion, and Oregon's 1859 constitution prohibited slavery, but also prohibited blacks from living in the state. During the **Civil War**, pro-slavery and pro-Confederate voices were heard—a large segment of Oregon's recent emigrants were from slave-holding states—and the **Knights of the Golden Circle** held militia training. An 1862 law banned interracial marriage and placed a tax on non-white residents.

In 1883, an attempt was made to remove the ban on black suffrage from the state constitution; despite its being a legally moot point, the effort failed. Similar efforts in 1895 and 1916 also failed, but in 1927, intensive efforts by the state's black community, including journalist **Beatrice Morrow Cannady**, succeeded in deleting the language. It was 1951 before Oregon repealed its law prohibiting interracial marriage, and 1959 before the voters of the state ratified the fifteenth amendment.

Despite the ostensible legal barriers they faced, African-Americans lived and worked in Portland, Salem, Jacksonville, and Astoria. Oregon's 1880 census counted 487 black residents; in 1900, the figure was 1,105. The arrival of the railroads brought a substantial black workforce to Portland; blacks were employed as waiters, cooks, and sleeping car porters aboard passenger trains and at Union Station, and in the **Union Pacific Railroad** shops in the **Albina neighborhood**. For several decades, the fashionable Portland Hotel maintained an all-black waitstaff; while the jobs were reasonably well-paying, they emphasized that blacks were suitable only for servants' work. Some Portland subdivisions excluded blacks from land ownership, and by the 1930s Portland real estate agents agreed to sell housing to blacks only in the Albina district—a policy that caused great tensions during World War II, when thousands of blacks moved to Portland for employment in the shipyards and other war work. Portland's black population increased from 1,931 in 1940 to 9,529 in 1950. Racial strife marked the 1960s as **urban renewal** projects ripped into the Albina district. Local activists such as **DeNorval Unthank** worked to mend the breaches, and racial barriers to property ownership eventually fell; blacks moved into other parts of Portland—even into suburbia and smaller cities and towns. In 1940, African-Americans comprised 0.2 percent of the state's population—about 2,000 persons; by 2000, 3.7 percent of the population was identified as of black or African-American heritage.

McLagan, Elizabeth. *A Peculiar Paradise: A History of Blacks in Oregon, 1788–1940*. Portland, Oregon: Georgian Press, 1980.

black walnuts *see* **walnuts**

Blaine, James G. (1830–1893) *see* **Holbrook, Stewart Hall**

Blanchet, François Norbert (1795–1883) Father Blanchet was from Quebec, ordained in 1819, and working as a missionary near Montreal when he was called to lead a small group of Catholic religious to the Oregon Country in 1838. With the Rev. Modeste Demers, Blanchet traveled overland to **Fort Vancouver**; they came as the result of requests for priests made by **Hudson's Bay Company** employees, some now retired and farming on **French Prairie**, others still in the company service. Blanchet immediately went to **Saint Paul**, where in 1839 he held the first Catholic mass in the Oregon Country. Blanchet also worked to convert local Indians to Catholicism. One of his tools was a pictorial Catholic history and catechism, commonly called the "Catholic ladder," that proved to be very effective and was emulated by other Catholic missionaries. It was copied, too, by the Protestants in the Oregon Country; a hand-drawn version by the Rev. Henry and Eliza Spalding survives, which makes an especial point of depicting the Roman pope toppling into the flames of hell. In 1844, the pope established three new ecclesiastical provinces in the area, and Fr. Blanchet became the first archbishop of Oregon City. He wrote several historical works and a dictionary of the **Chinook jargon**. His nephew, François Xavier Blanchet (1835–1906), founded the Catholic Church in **Jacksonville**; his brother Augustin Magloire Blanchet (1797–1887), first archbishop of Walla Walla, is the namesake of a Seattle school. The Catholic charity for the homeless in Portland, Blanchet House, remembers him, as does a school in Salem.

Nichols, Marie Leona Hobbs. *The Mantle of Elias; the Story of Fathers Blanchet and Demers in Early Oregon*. Portland, Oregon: Binfords & Mort, 1941.

White, Kris A., and Janice St. Laurent. Mysterious Journey: The Catholic Ladder of 1840. *Oregon Historical Quarterly* 97, no. 1 (Spring 1996): 70–88.

Blitzen River *see* **Donner und Blitzen River**

Blitz-Weinhard Brewing Company From 1955 until 1984, the Blitz-Weinhard Brewery was Oregon's only producer of **beer**. Its antecedents go back to 1856, when Henry Weinhard (1830–1904), a German-born brewer, arrived in Portland and began a small brewing operation. Weinhard's City Brewery operations grew rapidly on West Burnside Street, where the major plant was located in the 1860s. One of Weinhard's civic gestures was to offer to pipe beer through the **Skidmore Fountain** at its inauguration in 1888. Weinhard's City Brewery continued to flourish after his death in 1904, housed in an imposing brick complex. The two oldest remaining buildings of the complex were built in 1908, designed by **William Whidden** and **Ion Lewis**. Prohibition came to Oregon early, in 1916, but the company survived by brewing near beer and soft drinks; in 1928; the company merged with the former brewery of Arnold Blitz in 1928, forming Blitz-Weinhard. The beer branded Blitz became their chief product after the repeal of prohibition in 1933; Blitz also produced a workingman's brand, Bohemian Club, and Olde English 800 malt liquor.

Heirs of Henry Weinhard controlled the brewery in the 1970s, and introduced Henry's ale, which had great success. Nonetheless, the impact of national brewery mergers came to Portland, and Blitz-Weinhard was sold to the Pabst empire in 1979; later, Heileman purchased Pabst; then Stroh purchased Blitz-Weinhard; finally, Miller bought the Henry brand. Production of Henry's and other products in Portland ceased in 1999. The Henry brand continues; despite the apparent long lineage, the Henry brand dates from the 1970s; one might rather have preserved the Blitz name. The brewery complex buildings became a major development in the **Pearl District** in the early 2000s.

Bloch, Ernest (1880–1959) The composer Ernest Bloch was born in Switzerland, studied the violin and music composition in Belgium and Germany, and came to the United States in 1916; that same year saw the completion of one of his best-known compositions, the cello rhapsody *Schelomo*. He directed the Cleveland Institute of Music and then the San Francisco Conservatory of Music in the 1920s, and became an American citizen in 1924. After returning to Switzerland in 1930, Bloch returned to San Francisco in 1938, lived with his son in Lake Grove, Oregon, in 1939, taught at the University of California at Berkeley, and finally moved to Agate Beach, near **Newport**, Oregon, in 1941. There he purchased a beach house formerly owned by Salem publisher **Asahel Bush**. He lived there until his death; Agate Beach became a place of reflection and connection with nature. Bloch is noted for his lush works for string instruments, and it was at Agate Beach that he composed the *Suite Hébraïque* for viola or violin and piano or orchestra (1951), and *Concerto Grosso No. 2 for Strings* (1952)—it was his most productive period, when he wrote more than a third of his works. The annual Ernest Bloch Music Festival at Newport began in 1990; efforts to preserve his Agate Beach house for use as a retreat or institute began in 2005.

Strassburg, Robert. *Ernest Bloch, Voice in the Wilderness: A Biographical Study*. Los Angeles: Trident Shop, California State University, Los Angeles, 1977.

blue heron The regional subspecies of the great blue heron, *Ardea herodias fannini* Chapman, is common in Oregon near bodies of water; fish are the major part of their diet, although they also eat amphibians and rodents, insects and shellfish. The blue heron is the official bird of the city of Portland, is the name of a popular brewing company, and is the name of a paper manufacturing company; and also a cheese company, a bed-and-breakfast inn, an herb nursery, and a chiropractic clinic. Oregonians are quite fond of blue herons.

Blue Mountains Located in the northeastern quadrant of the state, the Blues are uplift mountains; the grouping includes the Ochoco Mountains, Aldrich Mountains, the Strawberry Range, Greenhorn Mountains, and Elkhorn Mountains. The term dates back to the early 1800s. Geographic names historian Lewis L. McArthur quotes the Rev. Gustavus Hines describing the range as being of "indescribable beauty and grandeur," which "from its azure-like appearance, has been called the 'Blue Mountains.'"

Boardman This Morrow County community was laid out in 1916 on agricultural land along the Union Pacific Railroad by **Samuel H. Boardman**. It was incorporated in 1927; the 1930 census gave it a population of exactly 100 residents. The small town center moved southward in 1952 after a highway realignment, and then south again in 1964 after the construction of the John Day Dam. The population in 1970 was 192. Since then, development nearby on the former Boardman Naval Weapons Systems Training Facility site (1941) led to the construction of a coal-fired power plant (the coal comes from Wyoming) and of a huge dairy operation, Threemile

Canyon Farms; industrial potato production for frozen french fries and hash browns also boomed. Boardman's population in 1980 was 1,261; in 2007, it was estimated at 3,310.

Boardman, Samuel H. (1874-1953) Samuel H. Boardman was born in Massachusetts, and came to Oregon via Colorado. He and his wife, Anna Belle, took up a homestead in eastern Oregon in 1903, where, historian Lewis L. McArthur noted, the Boardmans "sniffed sand and worked to develop irrigated land" for the next dozen years. Boardman platted the townsite of **Boardman** in 1916, about the time he began to work for the state of Oregon on highway projects. This led to his interest in parks: Boardman became the first state parks superintendent in 1929, and went on to acquire and shape the state park system for the next twenty-one years. His forte was in recognizing and then acquiring land suitable for parks; among his notable acquisitions were parklands at **Cove Palisades** and **Silver Creek Falls**.

Bobbie the Wonder Dog Bobbie, a handsome mix of Scotch collie and English shepherd, became separated from his owners, the G. F. and Leona Brazier family of Silverton, while they were driving across Indiana in 1923. The distraught family searched and searched for Bobbie, but did not find him. Six months later, Bobbie appeared in the streets of Silverton, footsore and weary. Bobbie's miraculous journey made him an instant media celebrity, the subject of books, newspaper and magazine articles, and motion picture newsreels. Bobbie died in 1927 and was buried with great ceremony at the pet cemetery of the Oregon Humane Society. Rin Tin Tin (one of them; there were several over the years) laid a wreath on his grave a week later. Bobbie became a Silverton icon, memorialized in an annual parade honoring pets, in a town mural, and in a replica of his doghouse; many Silvertonians, however, remained skeptical of the incident.

Alexander, Charles. *Bobbie, a Great Collie*. New York: Dodd, Mead and Company, 1926.

Bohemia mining district The **gold mining** district known as Bohemia is located in the Calapooya Mountains of Lane County, at the headwaters of the Row River. Gold discoveries were made in the area after the Civil War, and **Cottage Grove** became the gateway to the area after the arrival there of the Oregon & California Railroad in 1872. This was a hard-rock mining area, and stamp mills were used to break up the ore brought out from the mineshafts. Another flurry of activity occurred with the development of the Musick and Champion mines beginning in 1889, and again after the Oregon & Southeastern Railroad was built up the Row River toward the Bohemia mines in 1902-03. Things quieted down again, but revived slightly in the Depression years of the 1930s. The Bohemia Mineowners Association operate a museum about the gold-mining past in Cottage Grove. The Bohemia district is ever hopeful of a major revival.

Bonanza At the north end of the Langell Valley in Klamath County is Bonanaza, named not for a golden mineral discovery, but for water. A rural post office was opened in 1875 to serve a recent influx of livestock ranchers. The community was incorporated in 1901; by 1915, Bonanza was located in an irrigated agricultural district where residents carried on general farming, stock raising, and dairying. The 1920 census credited Bonanza with seventy-seven residents; in 1950, there were 259. The estimated population in 2007 was 445.

Bonneville Dam The building of Bonneville Dam across the Columbia River in 1933–37 was an epochal event in Oregon and the Pacific Northwest. It is located about forty miles east of Portland near the head of tidewater on the river and just below the **Cascades**, the immense rapids that marked the entrance to the Columbia River Gorge and the site of the legendary **Bridge of the Gods**. The dam is named for an early military explorer of the American West, Brig. Gen. Benjamin L. E. Bonneville (1795–1878). Construction of the dam obliterated the rapids, flooded the locks at **Cascade Locks**, and greatly altered native fish runs on the river.

Bonneville Dam was built primarily to generate hydroelectric power, and secondarily to improve navigation. The Army Corps of Engineers, who operate the facility, built the dam. The Bonneville Power Administration (BPA) generates and markets the electrical power; its rates have historically favored some large users such as public utility districts (PUDs) and industrial users, a fact that contributed to the development of the **aluminum industry** despite the lack of local bauxite ore. In 1941, BPA hired songwriter **Woody Guthrie** to compose a series of songs celebrating the dam and its impact, as part of a publicity motion picture effort. A second powerhouse was built between 1974 and 1981, increasing the dam's electrical output.

The world's largest single-lift lock opened at Bonneville Dam in 1938. An ocean-going freighter, the SS *Charles L. Wheeler Jr.*, passed through and docked upriver at The Dalles; that proved to be a one-time event, and the river is dominated by local barge traffic. A new, larger lock was opened in 1993.

Bonneville Dam was built with fish ladders, which permit the passage of migrating **salmon** and steelhead trout. Although they move freely below Bonneville, native white **sturgeon** cannot use the ladders, which has isolated the sturgeon populations above and below the dam. A fish hatchery, and a display pool of sturgeon, is located where Tanner Creek enters the Columbia River, just below the dam.

Bonneville Power Administration
see **Bonneville Dam**

Boones Ferry *see* **Wilsonville**

Boring Sited in Clackamas County on the North Fork Clackamas River, Boring, "The most exciting place to live," was platted as Boring Junction in 1903. The Oregon Water Power & Railway Company was then building a railroad and power line through the townsite en route to hydroelectric projects on the upper Clackamas River, and the post office of Boring opened the same year. The name derives from that of longtime local resident W. H. Boring.

Bottle Bill *see* McCall, Thomas Lawson "Tom"

Bowerman, William J. "Bill" (1911–1999) Bill Bowerman was born in Fossil and attended school there and in Medford and Seattle; a minor Medford high school football player, he went on to the University of Oregon, graduating in 1934 with a degree in business administration and experience in track and basketball. After a few years of high school teaching and coaching, Bowerman returned to the University of Oregon in 1948 as the freshman football coach. However, he soon made his mark as a track coach; between 1948 to 1972, Bowerman trained some thirty-three Olympics contenders and a number of NCAA champions and record-holders, among them **Steve Prefontaine** and Phil Knight. Bowerman was also noted for his innovations not only in his training programs, but in equipment such as athletic footwear and track surfacing. With his former student Knight, Bowerman in 1964 founded a company to distribute athletic shoes, Blue Ribbon Sports, which later became **Nike**.

Bowmer, Angus L. (1904–1979) Angus L. Bowmer was the founder and longtime guiding light of the **Oregon Shakespeare Festival**. Born in Bellingham, Washington, Bowmer was exposed to Shakespeare when studying at the University of Washington with noted English actor and teacher B. Iden Payne. In 1931, Bowmer came to Ashland to teach English at Southern Oregon Normal School (now

Southern Oregon University), and soon became involved in local theater efforts. The remains of the long-abandoned **chautauqua** building became the site of an experiment in 1935, when the city sponsored both boxing matches and the performance of two Shakespearean plays as part of July 4 festivities. Perhaps oddly, Shakespeare was more popular, and the ensuing Oregon Shakespeare Festival became a foundation of the city's economy. Bowmer continued to teach until 1970, and was active with the festival until his death. The principal indoor performance building at the festival is named the Angus Bowmer Theatre, opened in 1970.

Bowmer, Angus. *As I Remember, Adam: An Autobiography of a Festival.* Ashland, Oregon: Oregon Shakespearean Festival Association, 1975.

boysenberries These blackberry variants were the result of experiments in California in the 1920s by Rudolph Boysen, involving cross-pollinating of raspberries, blackberries, and loganberries. He abandoned his project, but tales of his large, reddish-purple berries came to the attention of others, including Walter Knott of California, who managed to acquire a few plants and nursed them into production. By 1935, he was selling boysenberries, named by him in honor of their creator, at Knott's Berry Farm in Buena Park. Mrs. Knott's boysenberry preserves helped build the farm's fame. By 2000, about three quarters of the nation's boysenberries were grown in the Willamette Valley of Oregon.

▶ **Breitenbush Hot Springs** These hot mineral springs are located in Marion County on the Breitenbush River, a tributary of the North Santiam River. The springs were well known in the nineteenth century; the land around them was homesteaded in 1904. In 1927, Merle D. Bruckman, whose father had made a small fortune by inventing a machine to make ice cream cones, purchased the area. Bruckman built a lodge and other buildings and was the first postmaster at the Breitenbush post office,

which opened in 1928. He operated the resort for some twenty years before retiring and selling the property in the mid-1950s; the post office closed in 1952.

The resort changed hands several times and was damaged by floods, and it closed in 1972. It was purchased in 1977 by Alex Beamer, who guided the project that transformed the springs into a retreat and conference center, a "worker-owned cooperative and

Sheltered beneath a rustic wooden shelter, a family dips their toes in the foot bath at Bruckman's Breitenbush Hot Springs about 1940. It appears, however, that all of them are wearing shoes. Clarence I. Christian photograph. Steven Dotterer collection.

intentional community" that offers a year-around series of workshops and conferences supported by vegetarian cuisine and a wilderness setting.

Bridal Veil Falls One of a series of waterfalls along the south face of the Columbia River Gorge, Bridal Veil Falls in Multnomah County is one of countless like-named features around the country. The falls do have an appropriately misty, veiled quality. With the coming of the **Union Pacific Railroad** through the gorge in the 1880s, a sawmill and **company town** were established below the falls, with the timber coming from the headwaters of Bridal Veil Creek on Larch Mountain. In decline after 1960, the mill closed in 1988. It has been demolished, along with most of the former worker houses of the town, but the post office, open since 1887, still sits on a knoll overlooking the river and postmarks wedding invitations for weddings all over the Pacific Northwest.

Bridge of the Gods The sketchily documented "Indian legend" of the Bridge of the Gods involves Mount Hood (Wy'east), Mount Adams, and Mount Saint Helens, coyote, fire, and volcanic eruptions, culminating in the collapse of a natural bridge across the Columbia River at the place known as the **Cascades**. A huge landslide once blocked the river at that point; the remnants of the slide were visible to members of the Lewis and Clark Expedition and it formed the rapids that are the Cascades. **Frederick Homer Balch** used the term as the title of a romantic novel, and it is the name of the spindly steel cantilever highway bridge at **Cascade Locks**, which opened as a private toll crossing in 1926.

➤ **bridges** The techniques and practices of constructing wooden bridges arrived in Oregon with emigrant builders in the 1840s; Howard McKinley Corning's *Dictionary of Oregon History* reported the construction of the first bridge in Washington County in 1846, a log structure across Dairy Creek. Very

likely other structures preceded this one, but it is always helpful to have a beginning point. Wood was the principal component of bridge structures until the era of railroad construction in the 1880s, which brought iron and steel to the forefront. Wooden bridges spanned the Yamhill River near Lafayette in 1851 and Marys River at Corvallis in 1856. It was not until the 1880s that bridges crossed the Willamette River at Portland and Albany.

The Interstate Bridge over the Columbia River in 1917 connected Portland with Vancouver; it was followed by Columbia crossings in the 1920s at Cascade Locks (the **Bridge of the Gods**), Hood River and Longview, and in 1966 at Astoria. The work of

This was the longest single-span steel bridge in Oregon when it opened in 1893. It crossed the Willamette River at Albany. The sign cautions against riding or driving across the bridge at any pace faster than a walk, and against taking more than twenty head of horses, cattle, or mules, or more than a hundred head of sheep across at a single time. Oregon Historical Society, OrHi 106093.

C. B. McCullough set a tone for highway bridges throughout the state in the 1920s and 1930s, especially a series of handsome concrete arches across coastal estuaries. Wooden **covered bridges** were widely built west of the Cascade Range through the 1930s on less-traveled highways. The dramatic Saint Johns Bridge in **Portland** (1931) was another bridge that approached being sculpture. The freeways of the 1950s through the 1970s brought little that was sculptural to bridge-building, although the Fremont Bridge in Portland boasts a graceful arched span and the **Glenn Jackson** Bridge is gently sinuous. Notable Oregon railroad bridges include the single span crossing of the Crooked River gorge on the Oregon Trunk Railway some 320 feet above the river (1911); it is parallel to a new highway bridge named for **Rex T. Barber**.

Smith, Dwight A., James B. Norman, and Pieter T. Dykman. *Historic Highway Bridges of Oregon*. 2nd rev. ed. Portland, Oregon: Oregon Historical Society Press, 1989.

Wortman, Sharon Wood, and Ed Wortman. *The Portland Bridge Book*. 3rd ed. Portland, Oregon: Urban Adventure Press, 2006.

Britt, Peter (1819?–1905) This Swiss-born portrait artist came to the United States in 1845, joining his father in Highland, Illinois. He learned the new trade of photography in nearby Saint Louis, and headed west in the spring of 1852 with some other adventuring Swiss men. After a short stop in Portland, he reached the raw gold-mining camp of **Jacksonville** in November, on foot, with "an odd two-wheeled cart laden with camera equipment, a yoke of oxen, a mule, and five dollars in cash." Over the next half-century, Peter Britt documented Jacksonville: the people, the buildings, the funerals and weddings, the surrounding landscape. Britt took the first photograph of **Crater Lake** in 1874.

Peter Britt built a Gothic Revival–style house on the hillside above the town, enlarging it over the years to include a greenhouse and wide porches.

Fascinated by horticulture, Britt attempted to grow many semi-tropical plants, planted a pear orchard, and established a vineyard that produced its first wine in 1858; it was sold locally under the Valley View label until the 1890s.

None of the three Britt children married; after their deaths, the Britt property came to the state of Oregon. Alas, the house burned—twice—in the 1950s, but the photographic equipment, negatives, studio props, paintings, and other contents had been sequestered by the new Jacksonville Museum. The grounds surrounding the house site—watched over by the towering Sequoia redwood Peter Britt planted on the birth of his son in 1862—became the site of the **Peter Britt Music Festival** in 1963. Britt Hall on the **Southern Oregon University** campus is also named for Peter Britt.

Miller, Alan Clark. *Photographer of a Frontier: The Photographs of Peter Britt*. Eureka, California: Interface California, 1976.

► **Brookings** The town of Brookings in Curry County was founded about 1908 as a **company town** of the California and Oregon Lumber Company, headquartered in San Francisco. The mill and townsite were isolated, reached only by ship; no real port existed at the mouth of the Chetco River, but one was improvised. Noted California architect Bernard Maybeck was hired by the Brookings investors to plan the town, and at least one remnant remains: Maybeck's Chetco Inn, designed to house visiting executives, eventually became a nursing home. Brookings post office opened in 1913. The mill first cut virgin Douglas-fir, and in the early 1920s began cutting redwood as well. The remoteness of the operation caused the company to solicit workers from afar, and a number came from Mexico, and then from Arkansas. The company failed in 1925, and Brookings took an immediate dive in population from an estimated 1,500 to about 200.

The development of the **Oregon Coast Highway** helped give the town new life in the form of tourism;

for a time, the growing of lilies for the bulb industry was also important. Brookings had a population of about 3,000 in 1951, when it was incorporated. The population declined in the 1960s, but reached 4,400 in 1990 and an estimated 6,455 by 2007, when Brookings was well established as a popular retirement town.

broom *see* **Scotch broom**

Brother Jonathan The side-wheel steamship *Brother Jonathan* sank during a summer storm on July 30, 1865, on Saint George's Reef near Crescent City, California. She had been built in 1850 and rebuilt in 1861, and was en route from San Francisco to Portland with 190 passengers and a crew of fifty-four. Among the passengers, many of whom were prominent in Oregon affairs, were Anson G. Henry, surveyor general of Washington Territory, and Brig. Gen. George Wright, en route to take command of the Army's Department of the Columbia. There were only nineteen survivors of one of the most notable **shipwrecks** on the Pacific Coast.

Brothers *see* **Three Sisters**

Broughton, William, Lt. *see* **Vancouver, George; Columbia River**

Brown, Tabitha Moffatt (1780–1858) Born in Massachusetts, Tabitha married the Rev. Clark Brown in 1799. They raised four children; he died in 1817, and Tabitha supported the family by teaching. They moved to Maryland, then to Missouri. In 1843, her son Orus went to Oregon; he returned in 1845 and convinced a number of family members to emigrate west. Tabitha was among the party, which set forth in April 1846 via the **Southern Emigrant Road**; it was a difficult trek, and the party arrived in the Willamette Valley on Christmas Day. Tabitha

This photograph was taken in the late 1910s, and depicts the Chetco Inn, designed by Bernard Maybeck and built to house business visitors to the California and Oregon Lumber Company operations at Brookings. The yard is covered with bracken fern, common in open coastal areas that have been logged or burned. Steven Dotterer collection.

settled in Forest Grove, where she and Harvey Clark founded an orphanage; she worked with Rev. George H. Atkinson and Clark to establish Tualatin Academy, the forerunner of **Pacific University**. Brown was designated **Mother of Oregon** by the state legislature in 1987.

Brownsville In the Cascade Range foothills of Linn County, along the Calapooia River, is Brownsville, sited in an area that was settled by emigrant farmers in the 1840s. A post office named Calapooya was established in 1850; the name was changed to Brownsville in 1859. In 1853, James Blakely laid out the townsite and named it for Hugh L. Brown; both had settled there in 1846, and Blakely had built the first house. The river supplied power for a flour mill in 1859, and a sash and door factory followed. In 1863, the second mill in Oregon's fledgling **woolen industry** opened in Brownsville. The city was incorporated in 1876; in 1880, a narrow-gauge railroad arrived from the north, and the 1880 census showed 143 residents. The town had 919 residents in 1910, and a 1915 report indicated the presence of a woolen mill, flour mill, tannery, fruit cannery, and creamery in the city. The population declined in the next few decades, but reached 1,175 in 1950 and an estimated 1,755 in 2007. A landmark in the town is the house of John M. and Elizabeth Moyer, an Italianate villa built in 1881 and now a museum; Elizabeth was the daughter of Hugh L. Brown.

Bryant, Louise (1885–1936) Born in Nevada, Louise Bryant spent some formative years in Oregon. She graduated from the University of Oregon and moved to Portland, where she met and, in 1909, married a prominent and well-to-do dentist, Paul Trullinger. For a time the couple lived in a notable bohemian enclave, a houseboat colony on the Willamette River near Sellwood. Bryant was interested in writing, in leftist politics, and in issues such as women's suffrage, and contributed articles to the Portland *Spectator*. Noted artist John Trullinger, the uncle of her husband, Paul, painted her portrait in 1913. In 1915, she met **John Reed** in Portland; the following year, she left Trullinger and moved in with Reed in New York City. There she became part of the rising journalist's wide circle of literary and artist friends. Reed and Bryant married in 1917 and traveled to revolution-torn Russian in 1917. Bryant continued to work as a journalist on her own account, and she made a brief trip back to Portland in 1919 to give a lecture about the Russian revolution. Reed died in 1920, and Bryant in 1923 married a well-known American diplomat, William Bullitt; that marriage ended in divorce in 1930. Bryant's last years were bleak; financial and health problems plagued her until her death near Paris in 1936. Her life is treated with high drama in the film *Reds* (1981), where she is portrayed by Diane Keaton.

Dearborn, Mary V. *Queen of Bohemia: The Life of Louise Bryant*. Boston: Houghton Mifflin, 1996.

buckaroo The term "buckaroo," derived from the Spanish *vaquero*, is commonly used in eastern Oregon to designate a cowboy or ranch hand; it is a term of respect and position.

➤ **Buena Vista** The small Polk County community is a few miles south of Independence on the Willamette River. Reason B. and Martha Hall took a donation land claim in the area in 1847, and Reason Hall apparently bestowed the name—"pleasant view"—about 1850, in recognition of family members who participated in the 1847 Battle of Buena Vista in the Mexican-American War. Hall began operating a ferry across the river in the early 1850s, and in the 1860s, clay deposits at Buena Vista began to be used to produce crocks, flower pots, vases, and similar pottery, an enterprise undertaken by the Freeman Smith family. A post office was opened in 1866, and the clay enterprise branched into producing sewer and drain tile in the 1870s, shipping its product downriver by steamboat.

By 1880, Buena Vista was a small but busy town

with hotels, a druggist, a sawmill, and the pottery works, which employed about fifty people, including some **Chinese**. Buena Vista was not, however, on the railroad, and the Smith clay operation moved to Portland in 1886, incorporated as the Oregon Pottery Company, and concentrated on producing sewer tiles, then in great demand in Portland and the growing towns nearby. The town declined; the post office closed in 1935, and "Buena Vista drifted into a somnolence that some lamented but none openly protested," according to Howard McKinley Corning in *Willamette Landings*. The ferry continues to operate, one of three **ferries** remaining on the Willamette River.

Bull Run The community named Bull Run is located in Clackamas County (with a post office from 1893 to 1939, which used the form Bullrun, which saves space but looks odd), as well as Bull Run Lake and Bull Run River, extending into Multnomah County. Since "run" means "river," the term "Bull Run River" is likewise a bit odd. The probable source of the names is an event in 1862 involving the pursuit of a stray bull into the river; this happened shortly after the arrival of news of the Civil War battle of the same name. The area surrounding Bull Run Lake was set aside as a protected forest reserve by presidential proclamation in 1892. In 1895, the first water arrived through the system of dams, pipelines, and reservoirs that serve Portland and many nearby communities. An interurban electric railway terminated at Bull Run in 1913, part of an abortive but ambitious attempt both to connect Portland with the mountain by train and to exploit the hydropower resources of Bull Run River, a tributary of the **Sandy River**; the line was abandoned by 1930.

Portland's legendarily clean and pure water supply is commonly referred to as Bull Run water.

The very quiet settlement of Buena Vista as it looked on August 18, 1939. T. J. Edmonds photograph. Federal Writers' Project. Oregon Historical Society, OrHi 58879.

► **Bumble Bee Seafoods** Cans of **salmon** and tuna emblazoned with a cheery bumblebee were associated with **Astoria** for most of the twentieth century. The brand was one of many salmon brands marketed in the 1910s by the Columbia River Packers Association (CRPA). CRPA was formed in 1899 by a group of seven Astoria fish canneries, which primarily canned salmon. In the 1910s, tuna also began to be canned in Astoria. By 1940, tuna surpassed salmon as CRPA's major pack, and by the 1950s, Bumble Bee tuna was the leading West Coast brand of a kitchen staple that filled countless sandwiches and casserole dishes.

Major changes in the 1960s removed Bumble Bee from local control. Tuna availability off the Oregon Coast declined, and Bumble Bee tuna came from widespread sources in the Pacific Ocean, and even in the Caribbean. The last Bumble Bee canning operations in Astoria occurred in 1984, and ownership of the brand shifted several times thereafter; the apian emblem began to appear on other seafood products. Bumble Bee remained on the shelves, but its manufacturing and resource ties to Oregon ceased in the 1980s.

The cover of a recipe booklet for using Bumble Bee Seafoods, published about 1965. The "Love Story" of the salmon briefly tells of the life cycle of the fish, including the heroic efforts they make to return to the spawning grounds of their birth. Bonneville Dam is described as "a giant gray wall" blocking upstream migration, and the calm, warm waters behind each dam are "unnatural." The story, however, fails to mention the peril to salmon from fishermen. Author's collection.

Bunce, Louis (1907–1983) One of the state's major artists of the twentieth century, Louis Bunce was born in Wyoming. He came to Portland, where he studied at the Museum Art School in 1925–26 before heading east to the Art Students League in New York City. In New York, he was exposed to many currents of modern art and many artists, including Jackson Pollock. During the Depression, Bunce was involved with the **Works Progress Administration** in New York and Oregon; two of his murals from that period are found in the post offices of Grants Pass and Portland's Saint Johns branch. Bunce taught painting and printmaking at the Museum Art School in Portland from 1946 until 1972. In 1949, Bunce and his wife, Gloria, opened the Kharouba Gallery, the first in Portland to showcase contemporary art.

An artist who tried his hand at abstract expressionism, surrealism, expressionism, and even cubism, Bunce hit a public nerve in 1958 when his design for an abstract mural at the new Portland airport terminal—solicited by the port commission—was leaked to commissioners and the media before Bunce had a word in the matter. The ensuing brouhaha exposed many Portlanders to "modern art," and exposed Bunce to the wrath of many who were more than a little uncomfortable with non-representational art. The mural was completed and installed, and has remained in the terminal ever since; Bunce subsequently did other commissioned public works in the abstract vein.

Bunyan, Paul *see* **Stevens, James**

Burlington Northern Santa Fe Railway (BNSF) One of the two major railroad companies operating in Oregon, BNSF was formed in a 1996 merger of Burlington Northern Railroad and the Atchison, Topeka & Santa Fe Railway. The company's principal Oregon lines extend north and east from Portland to Canada and the Midwest via Washington state; south from Portland to Eugene (built as the **Oregon Electric Railway**), and north-south line from the Columbia River through Bend and Klamath Falls to California and the Southwest (in part originally the **Oregon Trunk Railway**). All of these lines were included in the Burlington Northern Railroad, itself formed in 1970 from a merger of a number of smaller carriers, including the **Spokane, Portland & Seattle Railway**. Since the merger, BNSF has spun off some branch lines to regional carriers.

Burns The county seat of Harney County, Burns is located at the northern edge of the Harney Basin, a region that became dominated by cattle interests after the **Bannock War** of 1878. George McGowan came to the basin from the Willamette Valley in 1882, opening a mercantile business the next year with partner Peter Stenger near the present site of Burns. McGowan proposed the name as a tribute to Scottish poet Robert Burns, and as a counter to a name honoring his partner, Stenger. The Burns post office was established in 1884, with McGowan as postmaster. Harney County was created in 1889, and Burns was incorporated as a city in 1891, when its population was about 300. Burns was remote, and supplies were hauled by wagon from Ontario or Huntington on the main railroad line. The town was a regional supply point from its inception, and the 1900 census showed 574 residents. During the years between 1905 and 1918, several factors pushed activity in and around Burns: the anticipation of a railroad (not satisfied until 1924), abnormally high rainfall for several successive years, homestead fervor, and land speculation that was fueled by the first three factors. Burns's population reached 1,022 in 1920. The arrival (finally) of the railroad brought with it a huge new industry, the Edward Hines Lumber Company, which built a mill and town adjacent to Burns at **Hines** in 1928; the city's population in 1930 was 2,599.

Burns prospered quietly through World War II and beyond, primarily because of the lumber mill at Hines. The population in 1970 was 3,293. The Hines mill was sold to Snow Mountain Pine in 1983; the flooding of **Malheur Lake** closed the railroad connection to Burns in that year, and mill operations shrank, further exacerbated by reduced logging in the Blue Mountains. The last timber-related enterprise in the area closed in 2007. The estimated population of Burns in 2007 was 3,020.

Burns Paiute Tribe and Reservation Descendants of the Wadatika band of the **Northern Paiute Indians** are the principal enrollees of the Burns Paiute Tribe. Under the Indian Reorganization Act of 1936, the tribe was able to hold elections and to purchase 760 acres of land, and twenty-seven houses were built there in 1938. Tribal government was not fully established until 1968, and in 1972 the Burns Paiute were granted federal tribal recognition. The tribe has acquired additional allotment lands, and operates a small casino at Burns.

Burnt River Rising in the Blue Mountains of Baker County, Burnt River flows east and southeasterly to join the Snake River near Huntington. The origin of the name is unclear, but it was used during the fur-trapping era of the 1820s and 1830s.

Bush, Asahel (1824–1913) Asahel Bush was a printer, a wielder of political influence, and a banker, who left a significant legacy to the city of Salem. Bush was born in Massachusetts and was apprenticed to a printer in his youth, and he also studied law. He came west to Oregon in 1850 and settled in Oregon City the next year, where he established the *Oregon Statesman* newspaper as a voice for the Democratic Party. When the territorial capital moved to Salem in 1853, Bush and the paper moved there, too. In 1854, Bush married Eugenia Zieber. In the heady years preceding the Civil War—when the issue of Oregon's future statehood and its status with regard to slavery were boiling topics in Salem—Bush was a voice for the Union, despite his overt racism and support for slavery (but not in Oregon—somewhere else). His acerbic editorials were legendary and earned him the nickname "Bushy Bush."

Bush sold the *Oregon Statesman* in 1861, served as state printer, and then in 1867 partnered with Portland banker **William S. Ladd** to found the Ladd & Bush Bank in Salem, which quickly grew to prominence. Bush bought out Ladd in 1877 and continued to run the bank as sole owner. The ornate cast-iron façade of the Ladd & Bush bank was erected in 1869; in 1955, the bank—by then a branch office of United States National Bank—was enlarged with the use of nearly identical cast iron that had been removed from the 1868 Ladd & Tilton Bank in Portland; the bank has remained in use ever since.

Eugenia Bush died in 1863, leaving Asahel with four small children. The Bush family bought 100 acres on the south edge of Salem in 1860, and in 1877–78, Asahel built a large new residence in the Italianate style. The house and outbuildings remained in family hands until 1953. The properties subsequently became Bush's Pasture Park, and the Salem Art Association has maintained the house as a museum; the barn, which burned in the 1960s, has been rebuilt and is used as the Bush Barn Art Center.

bus transportation Intercity passenger transportation by motorbus in Oregon began as early as about 1910, when automobiles were available to transport travelers in Central Oregon from the new railroad stations of the **Oregon Trunk Railway** to interior towns such as Prineville and Burns over roads that were wholly unimproved. At first, horse-drawn stages often offered competing service: they were slower, but more reliable and considerably less expensive. The development both of major highway projects such as the **Columbia River Highway**, and of reliable gasoline and (later) diesel buses, introduced scheduled bus routes in the post–World War I years.

The 1920s saw a proliferation of such routes. In 1922, sixty-five different operators ran intercity bus lines in Oregon. In 1925, Pickwick Stages of California extended their operations up the **Pacific Highway**. The motorbuses were seen as a threat by railroad operators, and by the late 1920s, three of them also went into the motorbus business. **Southern Pacific Company** purchased several companies and merged them into Oregon Stages in 1928; the **Union Pacific Railroad** began Union Pacific Stages in 1928, operating east up the Columbia River; the **Spokane, Portland & Seattle Railway (SP&S)** founded the SP&S Transportation Company in 1924; it ran routes to Astoria and throughout north-western Oregon. All eventually merged into Greyhound Lines.

Minor feeder routes operated all over the state in the 1920s and 1930s, not only taking away local business from the railroads but reaching many places—especially remote logging camps and mill towns—that lacked railroad service. During World War II, with rubber and gasoline rationed, buses provided essential transportation. Postwar prosperity brought rapid cutbacks in intercity bus service. Greyhound spun off suburban Portland routes to other operators; these eventually became part of the TriMet system. Greyhound gradually cut services in the 1980s; some routes were taken over by small operators. In 2004, Greyhound, by then the only significant operator of intercity buses in the state, ceased service along the Oregon Coast and in Central Oregon.

Butte Falls Located northeast of Medford in Jackson County, the rural post office of Butte Falls on Butte Creek (opened in 1906) took on more urban prospects in 1911. That was the year the Pacific & Eastern Railway arrived from Medford. Butte Falls was the temporary terminus of a line that appeared to have the financial backing of **James J. Hill** and was aiming to cross the Cascade Range to a connection with the **Oregon Trunk Railway**. Butte Falls incorporated as a city in 1911. But the railroad stopped right there, and it never amounted to much.

Butte Falls had a population of 166 in the 1920 census. The railroad became a logging line, and Butte Falls was a small logging town. Its population climbed to 358 by 1970, fell to 282 in 1990 after major logging operations ceased in the area, and was estimated in 2007 at 445.

butterfly fleet *see* **mosquito fleet**

C

Calapooia River This stream originates in the Cascade Range of Linn County southeast of Albany, where it empties into the Willamette River. A rushing river through the foothills, it became a meandering slough when it reached the valley floor, bordered by numerous wetlands and marshes. The mills at **Brownsville** took early advantage of the waterpower of the Calapooia. The rich bottomlands were drained and converted to agricultural use beginning in the 1840s, extensively altering the landscape. The river's name refers to the **Kalapuyan Indians** who inhabited the Willamette Valley.

    Boag, Peter G. *Environment and Experience: Settlement Culture in Nineteenth-Century Oregon.* Berkeley: University of California Press, 1992.

Calapooya Mountains A westward extension of the Cascade Range, the Calapooya Mountains are the divide between the watersheds of the Willamette and Umpqua Rivers. They also mark the southernmost lands of the **Kalapuyan Indians**.

California black oak *see* **oak**

California laurel *see* **Oregon myrtle**

California-Oregon Trail A land trail has existed for many centuries that roughly parallels the route of **Interstate 5** in Oregon. Sometime called the Siskiyou Trail or the Oregon-California Trail in historic times, the route was used by Indians of many tribes and by Euro-American trappers and explorers from the 1820s onward. Trails connected with water routes at several points. From points in the north, such as the Hudson's Bay Company fur post at **Fort Vancouver**, canoes could be used to travel south on the Willamette River to the head of the valley. Trails also crossed the **Tualatin Mountains** over Cornelius Pass and the adjacent Logie Trail and across the **Tualatin Plains**, reaching the Willamette River at a point nearly opposite **Champoeg**. A west side trail followed the edge of the valley to avoid marshy lands near the river; in places this trail is approximated by Highway 99W, and in Lane County by Territorial Highway. An east side trail similarly skirted the foothills, which also made it easier to ford major rivers on the side, such as the Santiam; Highway 99E very roughly parallels this trail. South of Cottage Grove, the route is very similar to that taken by the **Pacific Highway**, the forerunner of Interstate 5. The trail was part of the **Southern Emigrant Road**, sometimes called the Applegate Trail, and it was the chief land route to California from Oregon during the gold rush there, which attracted many early Oregon emigrants. The first railroad connection between the states, completed in 1887, also followed the same route; like the later roads and freeways, the railroad was able to build directly down the Willamette Valley, bridging rivers and marshy lands such as **Lake Labish**.

    Dillon, Richard H. *Siskiyou Trail: The Hudson's Bay Company Route to California.* New York: McGraw-Hill, 1975.

California poplar *see* **cottonwood**

camas *Camassia* is a plant genus of North America, found in wet meadowlands and prairies. Camas are sometimes called Indian hyacinth; they are perennial plants that emerge in the spring with a stem topped by six-petalled flowers which are various shades of blue or blue violet, and sometimes lilac or white. Four species occur in Oregon, in virtually every county. Camas roots were a popular food with many Native peoples, and are still eaten. The bulbs were harvested in autumn after the flowers withered, and could be roasted or boiled. Dried bulbs could be made into flour. Although agricultural uses and development have vanquished many camas fields, the swaths of blue flowers can still be seen in many places in the Willamette Valley, northeastern Oregon, and southern Oregon. A similar plant, which grows in the same areas, is the death camas; it is of a different genus, *Zigadenus*, but has white flowers similar to those of *Camassia*.

▶ **Camp Abbott** Camp Abbott was a World War II military engineering training camp built in Deschutes County south of Bend. Opened in 1943, it was active for about a year. Most of the facilities were demolished after the war, but the officer's club building survived. The site became the nucleus of the resort development **Sunriver** in the 1960s and 1970s, and the club building was remodeled to become the resort's Great Hall.

Camp Adair This immense World War II troop training camp in Benton County was named for Lt. L. Henry Rodney Adair (1882?–1916), who was born in Astoria and was a descendent of Astoria's (and Oregon's) first U.S. postmaster, John Adair. More than 50,000 acres of private farm and forest land was acquired for the cantonment, which at its height accommodated more than 40,000 troops and support staff. After the war, much of the land was returned to the farmers from whom it was taken in 1942. The camp was decommissioned in 1946; some of it persists in **Adair Village**.

Campbell, Prince Lucien (1861–1925). Grandiloquently named Prince Lucien Campbell was the son of Thomas Franklin and Jane Eliza Campbell, Campbellite Christians who came to **Monmouth** in 1869 when Thomas was asked to head the new Christian college being established there (its descendent is **Western Oregon University**). Prince Lucien Campbell was named president of the University of Oregon in 1902, when it had perhaps 250 students. By the time of his death in 1925, the school enrolled 3,000 students and had achieved some stability and a good reputation. A man of oratorical skills and personal charm, he used those gifts on behalf of the school. Campbell hired **Ellis F. Lawrence** for the faculty; Lawrence founded the school of architecture and allied arts and used his own architectural skills to shape the appearance of the campus. Ironically, the chief memorial to Prince Lucien Campbell is a pugnaciously ugly eight-story semi-skyscraper office building. He deserved better.

Camp White A World War II military training camp that opened in 1942, Camp White was located on the Agate Desert in Jackson County, about seven miles northeast of Medford. It was named for George A. White, a journalist for the *Oregonian* newspaper who became Oregon adjutant general in 1915; he remained in the military until his death a major general in 1941. The camp also served as a prisoner-of-war (POW) camp for captured German soldiers. Covering nearly seventy-seven square miles and encompassing about a thousand buildings, Camp White housed as many as 40,000 army troops in training. The camp was deactivated in 1946. The hospital remained, to become the White City Domiciliary of the Veterans Administration in 1949; it has been renamed the Southern Oregon Rehabilitation Center & Clinics and continues to offer residential care to military veterans. *See also* **White City**.

Canby The town of Canby is in Clackamas County on Baker Prairie above the Molalla River. This is a rich agricultural area and was settled farmland in the 1850s. The community formed around the station on the **Oregon & California Railroad**, which came through from Portland in 1870; the Canby post office was opened in 1871. The name honors Maj. Gen. Edward R. S. Canby (1817–1873), a well-known Union figure in the late Civil War. Canby was posted to Oregon in 1870, and achieved something close to martyrdom for the time when he was assassinated in 1873 while heading a delegation treating with the Modoc Indians in the **Modoc War** in northern California. Canby was incorporated as a municipality in 1893, and the 1900 census reported a population of 392. In 1915, Canby was reported to be "surrounded by [a] rich and extensive agricultural area and the principal industries are farming, dairying, sheep raising and fruit growing, especially the rais-

ing of berries. Many of the large farms are being cut up into small home tracts in this vicinity."

The **Pacific Highway** came through the town, and by 1940, Canby's population reached 988; it doubled by 1950, and continued to spiral upward, reaching an estimated 15,140 by 2007. Despite the growth, agriculture, especially of berries, flowers, and vegetables, remains important in the area. The Clackamas County Fair has been centered at Canby since 1907. The Canby ferry crosses the Willamette River about three miles from the city center; in operation since 1914, it is one of three **ferries** still operating on the river.

Canemah This Clackamas County townsite at the upper end of **Willamette Falls** was established in the 1850s as a portage point for river traffic. It was also a place for the construction of river steamboats from the 1850s through the 1870s, such as the

The gateway to Camp Abbott was made of peeled logs and is based on the logo of the U.S. Army Corps of Engineers. The photograph was taken about 1943. Steven Dotterrer collection.

Gazelle (*see* **shipwrecks**). Canemah was the terminus of the East Side Railway, an **interurban railway** from Portland to Oregon City that opened in 1893, and picnic grounds and a baseball field made it a destination for Sunday excursionists. The riverfront gives no clues to the town's origins, but a cluster of wood-frame houses remains, some in the Gothic and Greek revival styles, that date from the 1850s and 1860s. Canemah is now part of **Oregon City**, and the houses are included in the Canemah Historic District, placed on the National Register of Historic Places in 1978.

Cannady, Beatrice Morrow (1889–1974) Born, raised and educated in Texas, Beatrice Morrow came to Portland in 1912, where she married Edward Cannady, the editor of the city's African-American newspaper publisher, *The Advocate*. Living in a city with a population of **blacks** that numbered but a thousand, Beatrice Cannady became involved in civil rights issues almost immediately, protesting the showing of D. W. Griffith's racist but immensely popular motion picture, *The Birth of a Nation*, in 1915. Cannady graduated from the Northwestern College of Law in 1922, worked on *The Advocate*, and gave hundreds of talks and presentations. Cannady worked to remove racist language from the Oregon constitution, finally having some success in 1927. Cannady was a vocal force of support in the African-American community of Portland and Oregon through the 1930s, when she moved to California.

Mangun, Kimberley. "As Citizens of Portland We Must Protest": Beatrice Morrow Cannady and the African-American Response to D. W. Griffith's "Masterpiece." *Oregon Historical Quarterly* 107, no. 3 (Fall 2006): 382–409.

► **Cannon Beach** Located in Clatsop County opposite the monolith called Haystack Rock (235 feet high), Cannon Beach is a seaside resort with a long history. Tillamook Indians had villages there, and members of the **Lewis and Clark Expedition** came to the beach in 1806 to witness the dissection by the Tillamook of a beached whale. They arrived too late to witness much of the process, but bartered for some oil and blubber. The **Chinook jargon** term for whale is ékoli, or ecola, and is the source for the name of Ecola Creek (known as Elk Creek until 1974), Ecola Point, and Ecola State Park at Cannon Beach.

The name Cannon Beach derives from a shipwreck. In 1846, the U.S. Navy sent the schooner *Shark* from Honolulu to Fort Vancouver on an investigative trek to the Oregon Country. Returning seaward, the *Shark* hit a shoal at the mouth of the Columbia on September 10 and was destroyed in the breakers; the crew was saved, but the ship was a total loss. Not long after the event, a portion of the wreckage with three cannons was found by several Indians and navy midshipman and cached nearby; the beach got its name thereby, although the cannons disappeared for many years.

Settlers came to the area in the 1890s, when a toll road was cut through from Seaside; a post office opened in 1891, although it was closed in 1901. Some homesteaders filed claims, but as Terence O'Donnell said, "If any in fact had intended to farm in a serious manner, the violent winds and sandy soils would have soon discouraged them." But some tourists came, attracted by the scenery, and small hotels served them. One of the *Shark's* lost cannons was found again in 1898, some prominent Portlanders purchased property, and the post office was reopened in 1910 (it was named Ecola until 1922, when it once again became Cannon Beach). In 1913, Governor **Oswald West** cannily contrived to pre-empt most coastal property from private development by declaring the ocean beaches to be public highways; in 1913, West built a splendid cabin at Cannon Beach overlooking Haystack Rock. Virtually destroyed by fire in 1991, the cabin was rebuilt in 1993–95.

Cannon Beach was not an easily reached resort in the early twentieth century. Until 1940, it was on a virtually dead-end road from the north. A precarious trail led south over Neahkahnie Mountain, a route finally opened in 1940 to allow the **Oregon Coast Highway** to come directly through the town. In 1941, the **Sunset Highway** opened a shorter route to Portland. Cannon Beach incorporated as a city in 1956; its population was reported in 1957 to be 516. The estimated population in 2007 was 1,680. The two other guns from the *Shark* were uncovered in 2008.

> O'Donnell, Terence. *Cannon Beach: A Place by the Sea.* Cannon Beach, Oregon: Cannon Beach Historical Society/Oregon Historical Society, 1996.

► **Canyon City** The county seat of Grant County, Canyon City had its beginnings in the early 1860s as a gold-mining camp on Canyon Creek, a tributary of John Day River. A post office was established in 1864, the same year in which the county was created. The itinerant miner and poet **Joaquin Miller** also moved to Canyon City in 1864. The 1880 census reported a population of 393, a figure that was not topped until 1950, when it reached 508. Saint Thomas Episcopal Church, built in 1876, is an eclectic wooden structure in a Gothic Revival style which has survived all of the city's three major fires: 1878, 1898, and 1937. The city and its residents were documented photographically in the late nineteenth century by **George I. Hazeltine**. Canyon City was incorporated in 1891. County government has long been the main economic support of Canyon City; nearby cattle ranching and lumbering operations have contributed to the economy as well. Canyon

The rustic appeal of the Cannon Beach Hotel at Cannon Beach is apparent in this photograph taken by Benjamin A. Gifford in the 1910s. It took a tortuous drive over a toll road from Seaside to reach Cannon Beach at this time. Oregon Historical Society, Gi 7765.

The modest quarters of Grant County official and litterateur Joaquin Miller in Canyon City, as seen about 1922. The building is part of the Grant County Museum. Mason collection.

City's population was 639 in the 1980 census, and an estimated 670 in 2007.

canyon live oak *see* **oak**

Canyonville Northbound travelers on the **California-Oregon Trail** breathed a sigh of relief when they reached the point that became Canyonville, where Canyon Creek opens into the valley of the South Umpqua River. The tortuous, aptly designated canyon made a descent of some 1,300 feet, and was frequently strewn with fallen trees and washouts. A post office was established in 1852 in the small community that grew up at the canyon mouth (its name was North Canyonville, shortened in 1892). Canyon City was incorporated in 1901; its population in the 1910 census was reported at 364. Although the railroad avoided the Canyon Creek route, the **Pacific Highway** wound through it; it was still a famously difficult route. The construction of the **Interstate 5** freeway in the 1960s and subsequent changes virtually obliterated the canyon and most traces of the earlier transportation routes through it. The Seven

Feathers casino and resort opened in 1992, operated by the **Cow Creek Band of Umpqua Tribe of Indians.** Canyonville's population in 2007 was estimated at 1,590.

► **Cape Arago** Located in Coos County just south of the mouth to Coos Bay, Cape Arago was named in 1850 for Dominique François Jean Arago (1786-1853), a French physicist who was a friend of the explorer and naturalist Alexander von Humboldt (1769-1859). Humboldt Bay was named at about the same time, and that was apparently on the mind of William P. McArthur of the U.S. Coast and Geodetic Survey; Cape Arago appeared on a map he prepared in 1850. Capt. James Cook applied the name Cape Gregory to the headland when he sighted it on March 12, 1778, Saint Gregory's Day. *See also* **lighthouses.**

Cape Blanco The most westerly point in Oregon, Cape Blanco—White Cape—is in Curry County. The name was in use by Spanish navigators by 1600, although it is not clear exactly what point they were referring to (most likely one some distance to the south); little at Cape Blanco suggests whiteness. Capt. **George Vancouver** applied the name Cape Orford, a portion of which designation survives nearby at **Port Orford.** *See also* **lighthouses.**

Cape Falcon Cape Falcon is directly north of **Neahkahnie Mountain** and **Short Sand Beach** in Tillamook County. The Spanish maritime explorer **Bruno de Heceta** gave the name on August 18, 1775—the day of Santa Clara de Montefalco. The point has been known as False Tillamook Head. *See also* **Tillamook Head.**

Cape Ferrelo The name Cape Ferrelo was applied to this rugged headland in Curry County by **George Davidson** of the U.S. Coast and Geodetic Survey in 1869. Bartoleme Ferrelo was a pilot with the Portuguese explorer (for the Spanish) Juan Rodriguez Cabrillo. While their 1542 expedition up the coast probably reached no farther north than Point Arena, California, Davidson felt it deserved some geographic recognition.

Cape Foulweather Meeting very bad weather shortly after making this landfall, Capt. **James Cook** gave this name to the point he saw, located in present-day Lincoln County. It was the first sighting of land Cook made in this 1778 voyage to the North Pacific. Some accounts state that the Yaquina Head **lighthouse** was supposed to have been built on Cape Foulweather, but this is not true; the lighthouse is properly located.

Cape Kiwanda This Tillamook County promontory is north of Nestucca Bay near Pacific City. Fish-ermen began launching wooden dories into the ocean through the surf from the beach at Cape Kiwanda about 1910. In 1926, the Nestucca River was closed to commercial gillnet **fishing**, and ocean fishing increased. The early boats were double-ended, a point at each end, and powered by oars. Motorized boats required modifications, including a square stern; such designs were common by the 1960s, but they continued to be launched from the beach. Into the 1970s, hundreds were launched each day, in search of rockfish or coho salmon; in 1976, Pacific City was reputedly the second largest salmon fishing port in the state. Since then, fishing restrictions on both salmon and coho, the result of greatly diminished runs, have reduced the dory fleet; fewer than two hundred were in use by 2005.

Located just south of Cape Arago was the spectacularly sited estate of Louis B. Simpson, a son of Asa Simpson. The first house, built about 1910, is pictured about 1915. The estate was known as Shore Acres; it has been part of Shore Acres State Park since the early 1940s. Jack L. Slattery/Jack's Photo Service. Oregon Historical Society, OrHi 106094.

Cape Lookout "Cape Lookout bears its present name in error, which will doubtless never be corrected," stated Lewis L. McArthur in *Oregon Geographic Names*. One of the most dramatic headlands on the Oregon Coast, Cape Lookout is some ten miles south of **Cape Meares** in Tillamook County, to which the name Cape Lookout was first applied—by the English adventurer and explorer John Meares, in 1788.

Cape Meares Situated in Tillamook County just south of Tillamook Bay, Cape Meares was originally tagged **Cape Lookout** by John Meares in 1788. One of the coast's most notable **lighthouses** is situated on Cape Meares, and the lighthouse, too, has sometimes said to have been built on the wrong cape. However, it was in fact firmly intended to be on Cape Meares, and that is where it was built in 1890.

Cape Perpetua This Lincoln County headland was sighted by Capt. **James Cook** in 1778, and was so named because the sighting was on Saint Perpetua's Day, March 7. *See also* **Cape Foulweather**.

Cape Sebastian The Spanish explorer Sebastian Vizcaino noted a "high, white bluff" on the coastline at about what he thought was the forty-second parallel, on January 20, 1603. He named the point for Saint Sebastian, whose day it was. We do not know that this was the point he saw; his measurements were, understandably, a bit off. **George Davidson** of the Coast Survey applied the name to this Curry County feature in the *Coast Pilot* of 1869.

Carlton Near the North Yamhill River in Yamhill County is the small town of Carlton, which in the twenty-first century is increasingly associated with the wine industry and fine meats. Farmers settled the region in the 1840s. The town developed after the arrival of the Oregon Central Railroad in 1872, with a station named for local landowner Wilson Carl. Carlton was incorporated in 1899, and the

1900 census showed a population of 145. The town had a long interlude as a timber town between its agricultural present and its similar beginnings. A sawmill was built in 1906 and the river dammed to provide a log pond; the Carlton & Coast Railroad began building west into the Coast Range timber in 1910. A 1915 report indicated that the town was supported by "dairying, fruit growing, hops, sheep raising, walnut growing and lumbering," with major livestock operations and plant nurseries as well. Timber was an economic mainstay into the 1950s, with the last major mill leaving in 1962. The former log pond is now the nucleus of the Carlton Lake State Game Refuge. Agriculture has reawakened, notably through specialty meat producers Carlton Farms (established in 1956) and several vineyards; the station of the now-abandoned railroad is a vineyard tasting room. The population in 2007 was estimated at 1,755.

Carnation *see* **dairy industry**

Cascade Locks The **Cascades** of the Columbia River were an obstruction to navigation, requiring a portage; a plank road and then a rail portage was built here, operating between 1855 and 1863; after that date, the portage was shifted to the Washington state side of the river. The federal government in 1875 authorized a set of locks to permit boats to pass the Cascades, and construction began in Oregon in 1878; the work was not completed until 1896. However, in 1883 a railroad line extended up the river, reducing the need for the locks. A post office with the name Cascade Locks was established in 1878, and a town grew up around it. The construction of the **Bridge of the Gods** in the 1920s and of **Bonneville Dam** in the 1930s prompted the incorporation of the town in Hood River County in 1935; the 1940 census reported 703 residents. The locks were submerged in 1938, replaced by locks at the dam itself. The remnants of the 1896 locks can be viewed from the city park, as can the locomotive named the *Oregon Pony*, which once pulled trains on the portage railroad line. The population of Cascade Locks was estimated at 1,075 in 2007.

Cascade Mountains *see* **Cascade Range**

Cascade Range The Cascade Range, or Cascade Mountains, extends from southern British Columbia south to Mount Lassen in northern California. The portion within Oregon is virtually all of volcanic origin, and includes **Mount Hood**, the **Three Sisters**, and Mount Mazama, the cradle of **Crater Lake**, among other peaks. The range derives its name from the **Cascades**, the rapids that mark a point where the Columbia River emerges from the gorge carved through the basalt that underlies the region.

Case, Robert Ormond, and Victoria Case. *Last Mountains, the Story of the Cascades.* Garden City, New York: Doubleday, Doran, 1945.

Harris, Stephen L. *Fire & Ice: The Cascade Volcanoes.* Rev. ed. Seattle: The Mountaineers/Pacific Search Press, 1980.

Cascades The Cascades of the Columbia River were created, probably about the year 1450, by a massive earth slippage known as the Bonneville Landslide from Table Mountain on the Washington side of the river. The event blocked the river entirely, and is the genesis of the tale of the **Bridge of the Gods**. There were both Upper Cascades and Lower Cascades, and they were obstacles to navigation—however, they could be navigated downstream under certain conditions, such as that of the *Oneonta* in 1870 and some notable traversals occurred by steamships before the completion of the **Cascade Locks** in 1896.

Cascades Indians *see* **Wasco and Wishram Indians**

Cascadia The term "Cascadia" has been bandied about since the 1980s to refer to a geopolitical concept or region: essentially, the **wet side** of the **Cascade Range**, from Vancouver, British Columbia, south to Eugene, or perhaps farther. The idea is that this area—moist, urban, with a liberal and well-educated populace—is distinctly different from the **dry side**. Therefore, one could erase the east/west divisions (between Oregon, Washington, and [a little part of] British Columbia), and instead draw a line down the spine of the **Cascade Range**. The result would be a region with a certain political homogeneity. As the Cascadian Independence Project posited it in 2007, "Cascadia is the unique coastal-mountain bioregion between San Francisco and the Alaskan panhandle in which the dominant culture is one of respect and honor for the environment and a strong tradition of democracy and social justice". That may be a bit much. The idea owes something to Ernest Callenbach's *Ecotopia* (1981), as well as to earlier movements such as that advocating the **State of Jefferson**.

cascara The cascara buckthorn, *Rhamnus purshiana*, also known as chittam or chittum or cascara sagrada, grows widely in western Oregon as a shrub or small tree, especially in damp areas or in the understory of evergreen forests. The bark is harvested and used as an ingredient in laxatives; stripping cascara bark and selling it was long a common household income supplement for coastal families.

Cathlamet Indians *see* **Lower Chinookan Indians**

cattle industry While some cattle came to the Oregon Country with the **Hudson's Bay Company** in the 1820s, the first major influx came in 1837 when **Ewing Young** and others drove several hundred head up from California. Cattle were also driven overland on the **Oregon Trail**, and most settlers raised them for meat, allowing them to forage in the

Willamette Valley grasslands. More commercial cattle ventures began in the 1870s and 1880s, when the lands of southeastern Oregon were opened to white ranchers such as **Bill Hanley** and **Pete French**. Cattle ranching has been widespread east of the Cascade Range on both private lands and on public lands leased for grazing purposes. Portland's **Kenton neighborhood** developed around new meat packing plants in the 1910s.

> Simpson, Peter K. *The Community of Cattlemen: A Social History of the Cattle Industry in Southeastern Oregon, 1869–1912.* Moscow: University of Idaho Press, 1987.

Cave Junction Located in Josephine County on the **Redwood Highway** and in the Illinois River Valley, Cave Junction acquired a presence when a post office was opened with that name at the turnoff to the **Oregon Caves**. Cave Junction soon developed as a commercial center as well, serving nearby gold mining and ranching operations, and several small lumber mills were established. Lumbering increased during the 1950s, only to fall precipitately until by 1990, but a single mill remained in a valley where some thirty had once operated. In the 1980s, grape production and wineries began to contribute to the town's economy. Cave Junction was incorporated as a municipality in 1948; its estimated population in 2007 was 1,685.

Cavemen *see* **Grants Pass**

Cayuse Indians The Cayuse people are associated with the **Umatilla** and the Walla Walla Indians through their historic proximity and through the signing of treaties in 1855 that placed the three tribes on the **Umatilla Reservation**. The historic homeland of the Cayuse people was in the upper courses of the Umatilla, Grande Ronde, and Walla Walla Rivers in northeastern Oregon and the most southeastern corner of Washington state. Typical Cayuse housing consisted of mat lodges that might be up to sixty feet in length, with several households within. Summer rounds in pursuit of game, berries, fish, and other foodstuffs usually meant temporary camps of small mat huts. The Cayuse had horses by the late eighteenth century and were noted for them; indeed, a short-legged breed is known as the Cayuse. The mission of **Marcus and Narcissa Whitman** was located in Cayuse territory near Walla Walla in 1836, and it was Dr. Whitman's failed attempt to treat a measles epidemic among the Cayuse that led to their deaths in 1847. The epidemic was the proximate cause of the **Cayuse War**. The Cayuse by the 1850s had suffered a disastrous population loss through disease and war. Their descendants are among those enrolled in the **Confederated Tribes of the Umatilla Indian Reservation**.

Cayuse War The Cayuse War of 1847–50 in the Oregon Territory was ignited by the deaths of **Marcus and Narcissa Whitman** and others at the Whitman Mission near present-day Walla Walla by **Cayuse Indians**. The killings caused the Willamette Valley settlers to raise volunteers to avenge the act. The result, after numerous skirmishes and forays, was the surrender of five Cayuse who were summarily tried and executed at Oregon City in 1850, although their exact roles in the event are still undetermined.

CCC *see* **Civilian Conservation Corps**

cedar The western red cedar, *Thuja plicata*, is a large evergreen tree with a thin and fibrous, reddish-brown bark and wood that is rot-resistant and very easy to split. The trees can reach from 100 to 175 feet in height and grow in single stands as well as with other conifers. They like moisture, and are found along the entire Oregon Coast and in lower elevations west of the Cascade Range. Natives used cedar to build plank houses and to construct canoes, which could be hollowed from the trunks; the inner bark made rope, fishing nets, roof thatching, and blankets and cloaks. White settlers prized cedar for its ease of splitting, making it easy to obtain shakes for roofing. Commercially, cedar is logged to produce siding and roof shingles, fence posts, interior paneling, outdoor decking, and for boatbuilding. *See also* **Port Orford-cedar**.

Cedar Hills Cedar Hills in Washington County was one of the first post–World War II suburbs, located along the **Sunset Highway** west of Portland and south of the old settlement of **Cedar Mill**. It included single-family residences on curvilinear streets, a complex of rental apartments, and a very controlled shopping center: one store of each kind, all lined up in a row with identically sized neon signs: SHOES, DRUGS, etc.

Cedar Mill This Washington County suburb was centered near the intersection of SW Barnes Road and Cornell Road, where a small falls provided the power for an equally small sawmill. This was built in 1855 by Justus Jones and his son, who sold it in 1869 to J. Q. A. Young and W. R. Everson; in 1874, Young was designated the first postmaster at Cedar Mill, which he also named; the mill cut primarily cedar. While the post office closed in 1904, the area in 1915 was said to have a population of about twenty-five, who engaged in dairying, truck gardening, fruit raising, general farming, livestock and poultry raising. The area has been thoroughly suburbanized since the 1960s; however, the falls on Cedar Mills Creek survived, as did the J. Q. A. Young house (and onetime post office), owned by the Tualatin Hills Park and Recreation District.

Dodds, Linda S., and Nancy A. Olson. *Cedar Mill History*. 2nd ed. Portland, Oregon: L. S. Dodds and N. A. Olson, 1986.

Celilo Falls These falls on the Columbia River were the first in a succession of falls, rapids and chutes—collectively known as **The Dalles**—that extended west through Tenmile Rapids (also known as

Little Narrows and Short Narrows), then Fivemile Rapids (also known as the Long Narrows) to the Big Eddy and Threemile Rapids. Celilo Falls was roughly forty feet in height, and by volume of water it was the sixth largest falls in the world. The falls and the rapids above were major **salmon** fishing points, and Celilo was a trading center that brought Natives from hundreds of miles to "the great emporium or mart of the Columbia," said explorer Alexander Ross. The region was the homeland of the Upper Chinookan **Wasco and Wishram Indians**, and the Klickitat Indians of the north shore, as well as the **Sahaptin Indians** to the east; Celilo also was very close to the lands occupied by the **Molala Indians** and the Yakamas. While the spring and summer runs of salmon were attractions to traders—the fish were dried and smoked to preserve them for traveling—the proximity to other tribes with trade goods greatly increased the attraction of the area.

Celilo Falls retained its appeal as a fishing point long after its trading advantages had been disturbed by the influx of white settlers. Whites viewed the falls as an impediment to navigation, forcing goods and travelers to portage around the obstructions. The **Oregon Steam Navigation Company** operated a portage railroad from 1862 until 1880, after which the line was incorporated into the transcontinental route being constructed down the Columbia River. Not until 1915 was the Celilo Canal completed, permitting through navigation to upriver points.

The demand for inexpensive hydroelectric power as well as concerns about **floods** such as that of 1948, and a desire for water for irrigation, drove the decision to build **The Dalles Dam**—despite the fact that this would utterly destroy tribal fisheries protected by the 1855 Middle Oregon treaty. Construction was completed in 1957, completely inundating Celilo Falls.

Barber, Katrine. *Death of Celilo Falls*. Seattle: Center for the Study of the Pacific Northwest in association with University of Washington Press, 2005.

► **Celilo Village** This unincorporated Wasco County community is located near the site of **Celilo Falls**. Its residents are tribal members, from the Yakama Nation, the **Confederated Tribes of Warm Springs**, the Nez Perce Tribe, or the **Confederated Tribes of the Umatilla Indian Reservation**. The historic fishing sites at Celilo Falls are gone, but the Army Corps of Engineers was required to provide alternate fishing access, in recognition of rights granted by treaty in 1855.

Central Oregon Normal School
see **Drain**

Central Point The Jackson County agricultural community of Central Point grew from a small post office, established in 1872 at a major crossroads a few miles northeast of Jacksonville. The Oregon & California Railroad reached the area in 1884 and finally connected with California in 1887. Central Point was incorporated in 1889, and the 1890 census reported a population of 534. By 1915, it was reported that the "principal crops are peaches, apples, pears, apricots, berries, grapes, alfalfa, potatoes, onions, melons and all varieties of garden truck." Rogue Creamery was founded in Central Point in 1935, producing butter, cheddar **cheese** and other products; the company became widely known in the early 2000s for its blue cheese. Central Point's population in 1950 was 1,667; in 1970, it was 4,004, and it has since exploded as a commuting suburb of Medford. The estimated population in 2007 was 17,025.

Century Drive The scenic automobile route was initiated by the Bend Commercial Club in 1921 as a 100-mile—hence "century"—loop drive from Bend back to Bend through Deschutes National Forest and past numerous mountain lakes including Elk Lake, Lava Lake, and Cultus Lake; there are a few reservoirs, as well: Crane Prairie and Wickiup. Even as

Indian Village near The Dalles Ore-

P-385 Smith

Strung along the Columbia River Highway adjacent to the Celilo Canal, Celilo Village was a traditional community that housed Indians of several tribes during the salmon runs. The photograph is from about 1950. Mason collection.

a single-lane gravel road, it was a popular excursion in the 1920s. Various highway alignment changes and extensions have occurred over the years, and the reason for the name has become unclear as a result. The first twenty-odd miles are the approach to the ski resort at **Mount Bachelor**.

Century Farm and Ranch Program The program to recognize Oregon families that have continuously farmed or ranched on the same land for more than a century, had its beginnings in 1958, in anticipation of the 1959 centennial of Oregon statehood. The initial sponsors were the state department of agriculture and the **Oregon Historical Society**; since 2000, the Oregon Farm Bureau and the state parks department have added support. A program to identify family farms and ranches that have survived for 150 years or more was announced in 2007.

Champoeg One of the resonant place names in Oregon history, Champoeg was a village along the Willamette River in Marion County, located near the site of a historic crossing of the river by the north-south **California-Oregon Trail**. The name is probably of Indian origin with a touch of French orthography; the town was at the north end of **French Prairie**, where former fur trade workers had settled in the 1820s. As early as 1813, the North West Fur Company had a small establishment near Champoeg, called Willamette Post; the area had also held a village of the Ahantchuyuk band of **Kalapuyan Indians**. The **Hudson's Bay Company** established a warehouse at Champoeg, primarily for shipping wheat. Champoeg was the site of the **Wolf Meetings** in the 1840s, which led to the meeting that formed the **provisional government** in 1843. Champoeg persisted as a landing and shipping point for **river transportation** into the 1850s, and small mills on Champoeg Creek and Case Creek sawed lumber and ground grain. On December 2, 1861, however, the town was virtually wiped off the map by the tremendous Willamette River **floods** of that year. There was a Champoeg post office from 1850 until 1905; from 1864 to 1880, it was named Newellsville, for local squire Robert Newell. In 1901, the **Oregon Historical Society**, in one of its first official actions, placed a monument at Champoeg to mark the site where the provisional government developed. Much of the property where Champoeg once stood was acquired by the state of Oregon and has been developed as a state park; nearby is also the Robert Newell house, operated as a house museum by the Daughters of the American Revolution. Champoeg was also long the site of the Veteran Steamboat Men's Association annual reunion, an event which began about 1922, and which brought sternwheel steamboats once again to the Champoeg shore. The last such reunion by water was in 1952, aboard the steamboat *Claire*.

> Hussey, John A. *Champoeg: Place of Transition; a Disputed History*. Portland, Oregon: Oregon Historical Society, 1967.

Champooick District One of the four original governmental districts (counties) established in 1843 by the **provisional government**, Champooick District included present-day Marion County, as well as all of present-day Oregon east of the Willamette River south to the border with California, and directly east clear to the Rocky Mountains. Champooick is a variant spelling of Champoeg. The three other districts were **Clackamas District**, **Twality District**, and **Yam Hill District**.

Charbonneau, Jean Baptiste (1805–1866) Jean Baptiste Charbonneau was the son of Toussaint Charbonneau (1767–before 1843) and **Sacajawea**. He was born in present-day North Dakota while his father was acting as an interpreter for the **Lewis and Clark Expedition**, and his mother accompanied the party. In ensuing years, William Clark assisted the young man in his education; Jean Baptiste traveled to Europe, returning about 1829, then engaged in the western **fur trade** and settled in Mexican California, where he was a businessman and gold miner. The gold rush in Montana called to him in 1866; on the way, he died of pneumonia, near **Jordan Valley** in eastern Oregon, where he is buried. The community of Charbonneau in Marion County is named for him.

Charleston This unincorporated community in Coos County is a noted port for sports and commercial ocean fishing. Although white settlers were in the area in the 1850s, the Charleston post office—named for one of those settlers—was not established until 1924; it was discontinued in 1959.

Chatham see **Vancouver, George**

chautauqua Chautaquas were a popular cultural experience nationwide from the 1880s into the 1920s. The chautauqua "movement" began in the New York town of that name in 1874. Chautauquas were summer institutes, open to a wide public that included entire families, and provided education, entertainment, and physical culture in a quasi-Christian environment. Activities included lectures, sermons, concerts, physical exercise classes, Bible study, jugglers and magicians, and poetry readings: it was a wide stage. Political and moral topics were popular; **Eva Emery Dye** and suffragist **Abigail Scott Duniway** presented, and William Jennings Bryan was a favorite speaker. Oregon had several recurring chautauquas: a one-year attempt in Canby in 1885 was followed by long-lived programs in **Ashland** and in **Gladstone**, both of which started in 1893. La Grande, Albany, The Dalles, Corvallis, and Gearhart are among other places in Oregon where chautauqua programs took place. One of the principal booking agencies for the Pacific Coast was headquartered in Portland, the Ellison-White Chautauqua System.

Since the early 1980s, the Oregon Council for the Humanities has sponsored a series of statewide traveling speakers and presenters under the rubric Oregon Chautauqua.

Chávez, César *see* **Mexicans in Oregon; Mount Angel**

cheese The perishability of dairy products often induced farmers in remote areas to market them as butter and cheese, which lasted longer and brought good prices. The dairy farmers of remote Tillamook County in the 1890s created a network of cooperative creameries along that part of the coast early in the twentieth century; ten of them banded together in 1909 as the Tillamook County Creamery Association, which has since developed into a major national producer of cheddar and jack cheeses. Creameries—which processed milk from a number of farmers into bottled milk, butter, cheese, ice cream, and other products—were found in almost all agricultural Oregon towns by the 1910s. Cheddar cheese—"rat cheese" or brick cheese—was the most common product, but some creameries developed specialties. **Bandon** became known in the 1950s for its extra-sharp, aged cheddar; a distinctive blue cheese was developed in **Langlois**. The Rogue Creamery in **Central Point**, opened in 1935, was noted in the 1950s and 1960s for its blue and cheddar cheeses; in the late 1990s, the company was revivified by the growing interest in artisanal cheeses. The growth of **farmers' markets** in the 1990s helped encourage small-scale cheese making, sometimes using goat or sheep milk, and cottage cheese industries have taken hold in the Willamette Valley, along the Alsea River, in Redmond, and elsewhere in Oregon since the mid-1990s. *See also* **Beaver**.

Chehalem Mountains A small uplift outcropping in Yamhill and Washington Counties, the Chehalem Mountains are just north of the Dundee Hills, and are capped by Bald Peak, elevation 1,629 feet. Like the Dundee Hills, the slopes of the Chehalems have a history of orchard use in the early twentieth century—walnuts, filberts, plums—that is now shifting to grape growing. The Chehalem Mountains American Viticultural Area (AVA) was designated in 2006.

► **Chemawa** This community in Marion County is the site of the Chemawa Indian School. The school traces its history to 1880, when federal philosophy toward the Native populace was leaning toward removing children from their family and tribal setting and training them in farming, manual arts, and (for young women) household duties. The Carlisle Indian School in Pennsylvania was the model for this approach. The original site chosen for such a school in the Pacific Northwest was at Forest Grove.

In 1885, a permanent site was selected north of Salem. The school had 453 students by 1900, from the first through the tenth grades. Students came from throughout the West, including Alaska, and lived at the school in dormitories.

The school eventually dropped the early years of schooling and Chemawa became an accredited high school in 1927. The campus, once a complex of red brick, was changed in the 1970s with new buildings on a new site; the old structures were razed. The Indian boarding school experience was not always popular with parents or students, as it deliberately stripped students of native language and culture and trained them for occupations that were often either inappropriate or menial or both. Despite such

OREGON–INDIAN TRAINING SCHOOL, CHEMAWA.

The new Indian training school at Chemawa is pictured in an 1887 lithograph from the Portland illustrated magazine *West Shore*. Students are shown arrayed in military formation just behind the locomotive of the Oregon & California Railroad train, while workers in the foreground attack a tree stump. University of Washington Libraries, Special Collections, NA4017.

problems, the school has survived, the oldest continuously operating Indian boarding school in the nation.

Chemult Named for a Klamath Indian chief, this community was established with the 1926 opening of a new railroad line connecting Oregon and California; the post office opened in 1928. It soon became a major service station and stopover point along **Highway 97**, especially after the completion of the Willamette Pass highway from Eugene. In recent years it has been the station stop for Amtrak's *Coast Starlight* for Sunriver and Bend.

cherries The Pacific Northwest is one of America's major cherry producing regions; Oregon and Washington state combined produce some 60 percent of the nation's crop. Noted nurseryman **Henderson Luelling** brought cherry seedlings overland from Iowa in 1847. The Luelling farms in the Milwaukie area had producing orchards in the 1870s, and developed several important varieties of cherries. The Bing—Oregon's famous sweet cherry—is named for the Chinese foreman at the nursery. Joseph H. Lambert, another horticulturist who had purchased some of the Luelling holdings, developed the Lambert variety there in 1870. Nearly all of the region's commercial cherries today are of the Bing, Lambert, and Rainier varieties, although Royal Annes and others are also used.

Cherries grow well in the Willamette Valley, and were extensively planted in the hills surrounding **Salem**; the Salem Canning Company was canning them for shipment in 1890. Salem held a Cherry Fair in 1903 (it had a King Bing), and in 1907 announced that it was, in fact, the Cherry City. Prof. Ernest Weigand at **Oregon State University** (then Oregon Agricultural College) developed a method of brining cherries that was introduced in 1927; brined cherries become maraschino cherries. The maraschino trade grew during the Depression years, and the college named a hall after Weigand.

After World War II, canning was gradually replaced by freezing as a method to preserve cherries, and production also shifted to orchards in Wasco and Hood River Counties. Housing subdivisions have replaced many cherry orchards in the Salem area, and the spring blossom tours have been suspended. The Salem transit system, however, still calls its bus fleet the Cherriots.

Chetco Indians *see* **Athapaskan Indians**

Chetco River The Chetco River is located in Curry County, draining a portion of the northern Klamath Mountains along a course of about fifty-five miles. It empties into the Pacific at **Brookings**. Logging along the river and its tributaries began in earnest in the 1920s, with the lumber milled at Brookings and shipped from the perilous port at the mouth of the Chetco by coastal lumber schooners. Most of the river was designated in 1985 as Wild and Scenic River, time having eased the scars of logging.

Chiloquin Situated on the Williamson River near its junction with the Sprague River, Chiloquin is a community created by the construction of the **Southern Pacific Company** railroad line across the Klamath Indian Reservation in 1911. The new station was named for the local Chaloqin family, and a post office was opened in 1912. Allotments of reservation land in the townsite were made to whites beginning in 1918, and the development of lumber mills, a box factory, and ranching set off a building boom in the 1920s. Chiloquin was incorporated in 1926; its population in 1940 was recorded as 741. During the height of lumber operations, following the termination of the Klamath Indian Reservation in 1955, the town had a population of about 900. The last lumber mill closed in 1988; Chiloquin's estimated population in 2003 was 720.

Chinatown/Japantown Historic District, Portland *see* **New Chinatown/Japantown Historic District, Portland**

▶ **Chinese in Oregon** Chinese sojourners came to California in the 1850s to seek gold, and in the 1860s to build railroads. The term "sojourners" indicates that their intention was to come, make money, and then return to China—but that did not always happen. Chinese came from California to **Jacksonville** and other southern Oregon gold camps, and they found their way to the Blue Mountain gold fields in the 1860s. Almost entirely young men, they formed a distinct ethnic group that was not always appreciated by the white majority. Chinatowns formed in several Oregon towns, including Jacksonville, **Portland**, **John Day**, and **Pendleton**. Anti-Chinese agitation in the 1880s, inflamed by

accusations of job-stealing and low wages, drove some Chinese to refuge in Portland, such that by 1890, the city's population was one-tenth Chinese. Prejudice was evident in the conduct of Oregon governor **Sylvester Pennoyer**, and in the unprosecuted massacre of more than two dozen Chinese miners in **Hells Canyon** in 1887.

Portland's Chinese business district in the late nineteenth century centered on SW Second Avenue near Oak Street; a small community of market farmers also lived and worked near Tanner Creek and the future site of **PGE Park**. In the 1920s and 1930s, many Chinese businesses moved into the historic North End, which also included many **Japanese** firms and residents; this is now known as the **New Chinatown/Japantown Historic District**. The Chinese-American population has not been extensively replenished by new immigration from China,

One of the employment niches open to Chinese in Oregon was in salmon canneries, where they labored to cut the fish for canning. This scene in a cannery at Astoria was photographed in the early 1900s. Keystone View Co. Author's collection.

but the population of those of Chinese heritage has grown. Chinese moved out of the traditional downtown living quarters, to **Ladd's Addition** and other southeast Portland neighborhoods. Since the 1980s, Chinese businesses have increasingly appeared along SE Eighty-second Avenue.

Portland State University and Chinese Consolidated Benevolent Association. *Dreams of the West: A History of the Chinese in Oregon, 1850–1950*. Portland, Oregon: Ooligan Press, 2007.

Wong, Marie Rose. *Sweet Cakes, Long Journey: The Chinatowns of Portland, Oregon*. Seattle: University of Washington Press, 2004.

► **Chinook Indians** The Chinookan Indians were established on both sides of the Columbia River from its mouth upriver to the vicinity of The Dalles, and up the Willamette River to Willamette Falls. The term "Chinook Indians" here refers to those bands at the mouth of the Columbia and in the vicinity of Shoalwater Bay in Washington state, including the Chinook and the Clatsop Indians; *see* **Lower Chinookan Indians** regarding the Cathlamet, Multnomah, and Clackamas Indians, and **Wasco and Wishram Indians** for those tribes.

The Chinook and Clatsop had available a tremendous fishery, with the Columbia River hosting five species of **salmon** as well as **sturgeon**, eulachon or **smelt**, and steelhead trout. Other common foods included elk, deer, bear and a variety of small animals, and numerous berries, ferns, **wapato**, and **camas**. Permanent villages held family dwellings built of split cedar planks; there were also temporary villages at sites for fishing and gathering wapato, for instance. Travel was on foot or by canoe.

This engraving of a cedar-plank longhouse of the Chinook Indians was made in 1841 from a sketch by Alfred T. Agate, an artist with the Wilkes Exploring Expedition. The central hearth is used for cooking, heating, and smoking fish and meats. Sleeping quarters are arrayed along the sides on elevated platforms. Oregon Historical Society, OrHi 4465a.

The Chinook and Clatsop began trading with European and American mariners in the 1790s. By the time of the **Lewis and Clark Expedition**, which reached their country in 1805, they were experienced in commerce, a fact that rather disappointed and annoyed the leaders of that group. The secondary chief known as **Concomly** raised his position in the tribe through his dealings with the whites at **Fort Astoria**. The high visibility of the tribes was, however, swiftly compromised by their early exposure to diseases, most especially smallpox, brought by white traders and mariners, which decimated the population early in the nineteenth century. By the 1840s, few Chinook and Clatsop remained; many had married into or otherwise melded with the **Tillamook Indians** or with Salishan bands in the Willapa Bay region.

The Treaty of Tansy Point in 1851 was unratified by the U.S. Senate, leaving the Chinook and Clatsop tribes in a legal limbo. In the late twentieth century, efforts were made to form a tribal organization. The Chinook Nation, which is not federally recognized, is headquartered in Chinook, Washington, across the Columbia River from Astoria; the Clatsop-Nehalem Confederated Tribes, similarly unrecognized, operate from Seaside.

Chinook jargon This language was the commercial tongue used by Natives and European and American traders, trappers, and missionaries from at least the late eighteenth century through much of the nineteenth century. It is also called Chinook or Chinuk wawa, from the word for "talk." It has no definitive form, as it was used—and constantly modified and added to—from Alaska south to the Oregon Coast as well as inland in the Pacific Northwest. The name is derived from that of the **Chinook Indians** who lived at the mouth of the Columbia River; the jargon has some basis in the Chinookan tongue, but the vocabulary mixes a variety of Native words with others from English, French, Hawai'ian, and various Scandinavian languages.

In nineteenth-century Oregon, a polyglot region with many immigrants and transients as well as Natives, use of the Chinook jargon was fairly common in industries such as logging and fishing. It was also kept alive, in print and in colloquial use, by many Oregon **pioneers** of the 1840s and 1850s as a quaint reference to their arrival at a time when the social fabric was less smooth and shiny than they imagined it to be by, say, 1890. *Klahowya* was a greeting that might be heard on the streets of Portland; a man might be a *tyee*, an important person; someone strong or genuine was *skookum*; a "Boston man" was an American, while a "King George man" was from England; *Memaloose* referred to death or dying, so that Memaloose Island (there is more than one) is an island of the dead, a cemetery; something bad or worthless was *cultus*.

The jargon passed from daily use, but survives in some Native communities with a diverse population, such as the **Confederated Tribes of Grand Ronde**, as Chinook wawa, usually with the addition of words from other Indian languages and a less Anglicized pronunciation.

Chinook salmon *see* **salmon**

Chinook wind In western Oregon, a Chinook wind is a warm and wet winter wind coming from the southwest. When someone says there is a Chinook headed this way, she is speaking not of a salmon, but of a blustery blow.

Chinuk wawa *see* **Chinook jargon**

chittum *see* **cascara**

Christmas trees Oregon is the nation's leading producer of Christmas trees, an agricultural product that is notable for its inedibility. While Oregonians were bombarded with advertising in the 1950s and 1960s extolling the idea that **tree farms** were going to be the solution to the problem of forests denuded of their trees by logging, they were not so aware of the growth of a new industry, growing trees for Christmas. The industry is concentrated in the foothills of the Cascade Range and the Coast Range, especially in the Willamette Valley. The crop was Oregon's eighth most valuable agricultural commodity in 2007, with a value of $114 million.

Christmas Valley The odd land of Tinsel Street, Snowflake Road, and Candy Lane is located in Lake County, not far from Christmas Lake, from which comes its name. (However, the origin of the name Christmas Lake, according to geographic names historian Lewis L. McArthur, "is one of the puzzles in Oregon nomenclature.") Christmas Valley is more than a hundred miles from most anywhere else, a remote, unincorporated rural community that is noted for producing alfalfa, and for having bitterly cold winters and hot and dusty summers: it is a desert landscape. In the early 1960s, it became the site of one of Oregon's more noted real estate scams, when some 72,000 acres were sold to the Penn Phillips Company of California. Penn Phillips laid out and named the roads, built a golf course and airstrip, and marketed lots and parcels, many of twenty acres, to retirees and those seeking vacation retreats. Many purchased, but few moved and stayed there, such that by 1972, only an estimated 150 people lived in a development that was advertised to accommodate some 5,000. Christmas Valley still has a small golf course, and supported a population of perhaps 800 by 2005.

Cinnamon Bear *see* **Lipman, Wolfe & Company**

▶ *City of Portland* The *City of Portland* was the **Union Pacific Railroad**'s crack streamlined train between Portland and Chicago, running through the Columbia River Gorge and the Blue Mountains, Cheyenne, and Omaha. Built in the depths of the Depression as railroads strove to bol-

ster sagging passenger-train travel, the *City of Portland* was a sleek yellow-and-brown, caterpillar-shaped speedster, powered by a diesel engine, then very new to the industry. Inaugurated in 1935, the first train had a front grille that resembled that of an automobile, and it included sleeping accommodations, coaches, meal service, and that wondrous new invention, air conditioning. The *City* ran on a schedule of thirty-nine and three-quarter hours, or two nights and one day from Portland to Chicago—but it "sailed" from each terminal only six times a month. With new equipment, the *City* became a daily train in 1947, and remained the premier Union Pacific train in the Pacific Northwest until the creation of Amtrak in 1971.

Civic Auditorium *see* **Keller Auditorium**

Civic Stadium *see* **PGE Park**

Civilian Conservation Corps (CCC) The Civilian Conservation Corps was created as part of the New Deal in 1933 to provide employment relief during the Depression years, with young men engaged on conservation work for the public benefit. The CCC operated in every state; Oregon was a major location, with some sixty-one camps and more than 2,000 men in 1940. CCC workers worked on public lands, building trails, roads, bridges, and other improvements in campgrounds and parks.

Among the many notable legacies of CCC projects in Oregon are the development of the state park at **Silver Creek Falls** and the lodge and facilities at the **Oregon Caves**. The CCC did the rockwork on the winding road to the top of Rocky Butte in Portland; they labored on the Deschutes irrigation project and on firefighting crews. Much of their work survives, often characterized by heavy masonry work and vernacular wooden buildings that evoke a woodland rusticity. Many CCC enrollees stayed in Oregon.

Civil War, 1861–65 No battles were fought in Oregon during the Civil War, but Oregon was affected by it nonetheless. In fact, the national politics that led to the war also led to Oregon's statehood in 1859, for Oregon was admitted as a non-slaveholding state. The new state's constitution, however, explicitly forbade blacks from living in the state: one approach to avoid the slaveholding question was, apparently, to ban the presence of those who might be enslaved. It was not a workable approach.

The conflict itself affected U.S. military operations in the District of Oregon, as federal soldiers were sent eastward. In response, the army post at Fort Umpqua was abandoned in 1862, and volunteers were recruited, especially to staff posts at the borders of the **Coast Reservation** and in eastern Oregon. **Fort Stevens** and two other posts on the Washington state shore were built to protect the mouth of the Columbia River from possible Confederate attack. But, as historian Stephen Beckham noted, "For many of the soldiers the Civil War in Oregon was a monotonous, numbing assignment."

The Southern cause had numerous supporters and sympathizers in Oregon, where many recent emigrants were from Missouri, Tennessee, Kentucky, and Virginia. **Joseph Lane**, former Oregon territorial governor and its first U.S. senator, was the running mate of Democratic presidential candidate John C. Breckenridge in 1860; their defeat, and their unpopular pro-slavery platform, sent Lane back

The Union Pacific Railroad invented the sleek trains called "streamliners" in the 1930s. The number M10002, pictured here with its striking automotive-influenced grille, was the engine that powered the first streamliner *City of Portland* in 1935. This publicity photograph was shot at Celilo Falls in 1940, with Celilo Village chief Tommy Thompson (far left), his son and daughter, Henry Thompson and Ida Thompson. Son-in-law Jimmy George hands a salmon to engineer Tom Rumgay; Tommy Thompson's wife Flora is to the right of Jimmy George. Everett Olmstead/Elite Studio photograph. Historic Photo Archive, 9305-A4311-A.

to his Douglas County farm, retired from political life. A number of Oregon newspapers were denied the use of the U.S. mail for expressing pro-Southern views. The **Knights of the Golden Circle** practiced military maneuvers, at least once virtually in sight of the state capitol building. In Jacksonville, a Confederate flag was found flying one morning; Mrs. Zany Ganung chopped down the pole and dragged the flag off to stoke the stove. Union sentiments also ran strong, and volunteers joined the First Regiment, Oregon Cavalry, which provided troops for regional army posts and engaged in skirmishes with the **Northern Paiute Indians**.

Edwards, G. Thomas. Six Oregon Leaders and the Far-Reaching Impact of America's Civil War. *Oregon Historical Quarterly* 100, no. 1 (Spring 1999): 4–31.

Johannsen, Robert Walter. *Frontier Politics and the Sectional Conflict: The Pacific Northwest on the Eve of the Civil War.* 1955. Reprinted as *Frontier Politics on the Eve of the Civil War.* Seattle: University of Washington Press, 1966.

LaLande, Jeffrey M. "Dixie" of the Pacific Northwest: Southern Oregon's Civil War. *Oregon Historical Quarterly* 100, no. 1 (Spring 1999): 32–81.

Civil War (football game) The Oregon Civil War is an annual football game between the Oregon State University **Beavers** and the University of Oregon **Ducks**. The game has taken place since 1894, although the term "Civil War" is much more recent. Newspaper articles began using it in 1929, and it appeared in the Oregon State University yearbook in 1938. The pitting of teams from the two large state schools, located but fifty miles apart, has spread from football to most sports and a variety of other activities in which both schools participate.

Clackamas County In 1843, Oregon's **provisional government** established four districts, the predecessors of today's counties. One of these was named **Clackamas District**: it included parts of what are now four states and the province of British Columbia. Inevitably, some shrinkage occurred, particularly after treaty negotiations with Great Britain. By 1854, Clackamas County in Oregon Territory attained the dimensions it has had since, containing 1,879 square miles. The name derives from that of the Clackamas, a band of **Lower Chinookan Indians** who lived principally along the lower reaches of the **Clackamas River**.

The attractions of **Willamette Falls**—water power and water transportation—inspired the establishment of settlements there, and **Oregon City** quickly emerged as the dominant townsite in the early 1840s. It became the seat of county government, and of the provisional and territorial Oregon governments as well; the territorial capital moved to Salem in 1852. A formal Clackamas County courthouse did not rise until 1884, a hulking structure that was demolished after a new building was erected in 1937.

Clackamas County's economy has been based on agriculture, timber, and manufacturing since the mid-nineteenth century. Prairie lands south of Canby and along the **Pudding River** were settled in the 1840s, when wheat was a major crop; it was milled into flour at numerous mills in Oregon City, **Aurora**, **Mulino**, and other towns. General farming, dairying, and the cultivation of **berries** have been mainstays since 1900, and nurseries have been important since the 1940s. The falls at Oregon City have supplied power for mills producing pulp and paper, woolen goods, flour, and lumber; timber has come from the forest lands in the Cascade foothills and along the **Clackamas River**.

The county's population was recorded in 1860 as 3,466; in 1900, it was 19,658, and in 1950, 86,716. Since 1950, there has been explosive growth in the westernmost part of the county near Oregon City, Milwaukie, and Gladstone, and especially West Linn, as these areas become part of the Portland metropolitan area. The eastern part of the county, most of it in national forest ownership, is still largely unpopulated. The estimated population in 2007 was 372,270.

Clackamas District This was the name of one of the four districts (counties) established by the **provisional government** in 1843. It included much of what is now northern Oregon, most of British Columbia and Idaho, a piece of western Montana, and Washington state east of the Cascades. The three other districts were **Champooick District**, **Yam Hill District**, and **Twality District**.

Clackamas Indians *see* **Lower Chinookan Indians**

Clackamas River Rising in the Cascade Range in eastern Marion County, the Clackamas River flows westward about eighty-five miles to enter the Willamette River north of Oregon City. It has been a popular stream for sports fishing since the late nineteenth century, especially for **steelhead trout**. Its once-strong runs of Coho and spring and fall Chinook **salmon** were decimated after the construction of the Cazadero Dam for hydroelectric power near Estacada in 1905; a sequence of additional hydroelectric dams extends farther upriver.

Clark, William (1770–1838) *see* **Lewis and Clark Expedition**

Clatskanie White settlers came to this area where the Clatskanie River meets the Columbia River about 1852; it is in Columbia County, and the name is taken from the **Clatskanie Indians**. The Bryant family were among those settlers, and the name Bryantville was used for a while. A post office was established with the name Clatskanie in 1871, and steamboats came up the Clatskanie River to the center of the town; the steamer *Novelty* was built there in 1878, and other steamboats were built there in the late 1800s. Extensive logging operations were carried out in the Coast Range south of Clatskanie,

including those of **Simon Benson** and O. J. Evenson. Clatskanie in the first half of the twentieth century lived on logging and lumber mills, fishing, dairy farming, and mink farming. The town was incorporated in 1891; the Astoria & Columbia River Railroad linked it to Portland in 1898, and river traffic began to decline. In the 1910s, Clatskanie held an annual rose festival, and in 1918, the Columbia River Highway arrived. The town had a population of 311 in the 1900 census; this jumped to 1,171 in 1920 when logging operations were at their height, and declined to 708 by 1940. It was 1,286 in 1970, and an estimated 1,710 in 2007. Only a few fishing and recreational boats still use the Clatskanie River, but the manually operated railroad bridge still swings open, wide enough to allow a river steamer to reach the center of town. Author Raymond Carver (1938–1988) was born in Clatskanie and affected by it, though he moved to Yakima in his childhood.

Clatskanie Indians The Clatskanie were of Athapaskan language stock, and lived south of the Columbia River in what became Clatsop and Columbia Counties, along the interior drainage of the Nehalem River; seasonally, they apparently also at times occupied lands along the south shore of the Columbia. A small band, they are little documented ethnographically; their living situations were very similar to that of the **Chinookan Indians**. They were represented by only a few people at the 1851 Treaty of Tansy Point, which was never ratified, and as early as 1844 they were described as "very nearly extinct." The term—which is from the Chinookan language; we do not know what the Clatskanie called themselves—has persisted as the name of a town and a river; the Klaskanine River in Clatsop County is derived from the same word.

Clatsop County The **provisional government** created Clatsop County on June 22, 1844, carving it from the western and northern sections of **Twality District**. Part of this was north of the Columbia

River, so on June 27, 1844, that portion was designated Vancouver County in what would later become Washington state. Adjustments were made to the Clatsop County boundaries in 1845 and 1853; it now has an area of 873 square miles located at the very northwestern corner of the state. The name reflects that of a band of **Chinook Indians** who lived on the south shore of the Columbia River and along the northern Oregon coast.

Euro-American settlement in the **Oregon Country** began at **Fort Astoria** in 1811, and a few people lived at **Astoria** when the county was formed. Many early county government activities took place in private homes, first at Lexington and then at Astoria. Lexington was a settlement at the northern end of **Clatsop Plains** on the **Skipanon River**; it vanished before 1860. In 1854, electors chose Astoria as the official seat of the county. A wooden two-story courthouse was erected there, and the first county court sat in 1856. In 1908, the courthouse was replaced by a brick structure in an Italian Renaissance Revival style, which still serves county government.

The **fur trade** built Fort Astoria; Clatsop Plains was an agricultural area beginning in the 1840s (not always very successfully). Fishing, and the canning of fish, propelled the county's economy from the 1880s through the 1950s. Logging and milling lumber has been practiced since the 1840s; it was the second major industry from the 1890s until the 1980s. Virtually all of the virgin timber in Clatsop County has been logged. Dairying and general farming were long practiced on Clatsop Plains, and in the valleys of the Lewis and Clark, Youngs, Klaskanine, and Wallooskee Rivers, and near Brownsmead. Dairy farming, a major industry through much of the twentieth century, nearly vanished in the 1990s. Tourism has also been a long-standing activity. **Seaside** flourished as a seashore resort beginning in the 1870s; other vacation sites developed at **Gearhart** and **Cannon Beach**, and since its conversion from military base to state park, at **Fort Stevens**. Although very much a workaday city for most of its existence, Astoria has increasingly become a tourist destination, noted for its Victorian architecture, maritime-related history, and scenic setting. Reflecting its economic ups and downs, Clatsop County's population has ebbed and flowed: 498 in 1860 (not including Indians); 7,222 in 1880; 23,030 in 1920, but fewer in 1930, and then 24,697 in 1940. It climbed to 28,437 in 1970, and was estimated in 2007 at 37,440.

Clatsop Indians *see* **Chinook Indians**

Clatsop Plains The grass-covered coastal sand ridges extending from the Columbia River south to Seaside were perceived as fertile future farmland in the 1840s. A Presbyterian missionary group, headed by Dr. William H. Gray, came in 1846 and settled on the Plains. Alas, grazing cattle and sheep quickly exposed the sand, and the ridges became moving dunes. Waterways, that once made it possible to travel nearly the entire length by canoe, became choked with introduced water lilies. Efforts to stabilize the sands in the 1930s with imported **Scotch broom** and other plantings superficially succeeded. A 1940 guidebook noted of the **Oregon Coast Highway** in this area, "In spring this section of the route is banked with Scotch broom. Sometimes fifteen feet high and bearing long sprays of golden pea-like flowers, it is constantly spreading farther south along the coast."

In the wetlands areas, **cranberry** raising was tried, beginning in 1911; it was successful during the 1940s and 1950s, but declined to a handful of acres by 2000. Dairying, bulb culture, and stock raising continued on Clatsop Plains through the twentieth century, but they likewise declined and had virtually vanished by 2000. Much of the Plains has gradually developed as rural residential property.

Hanson, Inez Stafford. *Life on Clatsop*. [Eugene, Oregon?]: privately printed, 1977. Reprint 2004.

clearcut Nineteenth-century logging practices involved felling and removing the trees desired for milling; undergrowth, trees too small for use, and trees of undesired species, were left, though they were often crushed or uprooted by the logging. Such areas were allowed to regenerate on their own, a haphazard process, but one that eventually scabbed over most of the visible damage and eventually reconstituted a forest. Beginning in 1929, legislation encouraged reforestation; the law was strengthened in 1971. In the mid-twentieth century, with the development of **tree farms** and in the wake of the disaster of the **Tillamook Burn**, the technique of clearcutting took hold: all vegetation was removed from a logged tract, clearing the land for replanting of only the desired species of trees. It is a visually ugly process, one that is apparent on both private and public lands throughout northeastern and western Oregon. *See also* **hoedad**.

Cloud Cap Inn This is a rustic lodge high on Cooper Spur, on the north slope of Mount Hood in Hood River County. It was built of logs in 1889, designed by the noted architect **William Whidden**. The instigators were Portland banker **William S. Ladd** and attorney **C. E. S. Wood**; Wood's wife, Nannie, supplied the picturesque name. Ladd and Wood created a stage line to serve the inn from Hood River, reached by train and riverboat from Portland. The inn failed as a commercial venture in 1890, but James and Sarah (Tansana) Langille ran a more modest operation beginning in 1891, and they succeeded, running a guide service for climbers and hikers. In the late 1920s, a mammoth resort was planned for the area, an inspiration set off by the Mount Hood Loop Highway, then being planned. The Depression killed those plans, and it shut the inn also for a time; World War II was no help, either, and Cloud Cap was sold to the U.S. Forest Service in 1942. They considered demolishing the now-ramshackle inn in 1950; instead, the Crag Rats, a climbing club from Hood River, rescued it. Cloud Cap Inn was placed on the National Register of Historic Places in 1974.

► **coal mining** Coal has been found at scattered sites throughout western Oregon and stabs were made at mining it, for example in Clatsop County in the 1890s and near Medford in the 1910s. But the quality was exceedingly low, and the deposits spotty. The one area where coal was commercially mined with success was in the **Coos Bay** region. The Beaver Hill mine, the Newport-Libby mine, and others exported coal to San Francisco by the shipload in the 1870s, despite its poor quality—it was still preferable to the Mount Diablo coal that was available in California. Although better-quality imports from Australia in the 1880s reduced the demand for Oregon coal, the enterprise held on, sometimes stubbornly, for many years. According to historians Alfred Powers and Emil Peterson in *A Century of Coos and Curry*, the Henryville mine on Isthmus Slough was "the most colossal coal mining venture in Coos County to hang on for many years with never a penny of profit." The industry was moribund by the 1920s, although one mine was still operating in 1953. Periodic voices have been raised since then to resume coal mining, particularly with regard to holdings at Eden Ridge in Coos County.

Beckham, Dow. *Stars in the Dark: Coal Mines of Southwestern Oregon.* Coos Bay, Oregon: Arago Books, 1995.

Coast Range Mountains The Coast Range parallels the Pacific shore from the Columbia River south into Coos County; to the south lie the Klamath Mountains. Rugged and pierced by a succession of short westward-flowing rivers, the Coast Range is an old range, with portions estimated at more than sixty million years. It averages about 1,500 feet in elevation, punctuated by several notable peaks that yet do not reach any great heights: landmark **Saddle Mountain** (3,283 feet, but sharply defined) in the north part of the range in Oregon, and **Marys Peak**

The crew stands on the tracks outside the entrance to the Beaver Hill mine in Coos County, where coal mining was a major economic activity for several decades. Oregon Historical Society, OrHi 38865.

(a rounded 4,097 feet) in the central part of the range. On the eastern slope of the range, Coast Range rivers flow into the Willamette River at the northern end of the range; farther south, the **Umpqua River** cuts through the Coast Range from its headwaters in the Cascades, the only river to do so. The Coast Range is heavily timbered with Sitka spruce, Douglas-fir, hemlock, and western red cedar; it was extensively logged from the 1890s through the 1980s, and still contributes timber to mills along the coast and in the Willamette and Umpqua River valleys.

Coast Reservation The Coast Indian Reservation was established in 1855, essentially as a remote refuge for the beleaguered treaty survivors of the **Rogue River Wars** of the 1850s: **Takelma, Coosan**, and **Siuslaw Indians**, and various **Athapas-** kan Indians: Chasta Costa, Galice, Chetco, Upper Coquille. It also included the resident **Alsean Indians** (Alsea and Yaquina) and some **Tillamook Indians** (Siletz, Salmon River, Nestucca). The reservation extended from Cape Lookout south to the Siltcoos River, and inland about twenty-two miles—an area nearly the size of Delaware. It included lands where Indian title had not been dealt with; more troubling was that the inhabitants were expected to farm in this dank and remote area that was unlike their homeland. It soon began to shrink, as well. In 1865, the Yaquina Bay area was opened to white settlement, dividing the reservation into northern and southern portions, headquartered at **Siletz** and near **Yachats** respectively. In 1875, both northern and southern sections were thrown open to white entry due to the machinations of Oregon's redoubtable senator **John H. Mitchell**. What remained was the **Siletz Reservation**.

> Schwartz, E. A. Sick Hearts: Indian Removal on the Oregon Coast, 1875–1881. *Oregon Historical Quarterly* 92, no. 3 (Fall 1991): 228–264.

Coast Starlight This is the name of Amtrak's principal West Coast long-distance passenger train, operating from Seattle to Los Angeles via Portland, the Willamette Valley, and the Cascade Range. It was inaugurated with the creation of Amtrak in 1971. The name of the train is derived from the history of the **Southern Pacific Company (SP)**, which operated passenger trains between Oregon and California from 1887 until Amtrak's inauguration. The *Coast Daylight* was an SP train on the scenic coast route between San Francisco and Los Angeles; in the 1950s, a night train on this run was called the *Starlight*. Extending this train to the Pacific Northwest resulted in *Coast Starlight*. The *Coast Starlight* is one of Amtrak's most popular long-distance trains, noted for its views of Klamath Lake, Willamette Pass, and the Willamette Valley.

Coburg A small agricultural town at its inception, Coburg in Lane County was named in 1865 for a local stallion that had been imported from the Coburg district of Bavaria. In 1882, the community became—by financial exigency, not sound planning— the temporary southern terminus of the ill-fated narrow-gauge Oregonian Railway. The Coburg post office opened in 1884, and the town was incorporated in 1893; it proceeded to lead a quiet rural life. Never on a major highway, Coburg was deprived of its branch line railroad, which was torn up in 1976. The central section of the town was placed on the National Register of Historic Places in 1986, which has encouraged tourism. Although Coburg was also bypassed by **Interstate 5** in the 1960s, the freeway is but a mile away and inspired two major enterprises: Monaco Coach, which moved its headquarters and a recreational vehicle factory to Coburg in

the early 1990s, and Marathon Coach, founded in 1983, which built a Coburg plant in 1994 to produce luxury motor coaches. Coburg had a population of 270 in 1920; that climbed to 693 by 1950, to 763 in 1990, and to an estimated 1,070 in 2007.

> Nolan, Edward W., and Susan K. Barry. *Coburg Remembered*. Eugene, Oregon: Lane County Historical Society, 1982.

Coburn, Catherine Scott *see* **Scott, Harvey Whitfield**

► **Coe, Henry Waldo** (1857–1927) Dr. Henry Waldo Coe was born in Wisconsin, attended school

Dr. Henry Waldo Coe is pictured before a painting of one of his heroes, Theodore Roosevelt. The photograph was probably taken in Chicago in 1912, when Coe was there as a member of the Republican Party's national convention; the convention nominated William Howard Taft over Roosevelt as their presidential candidate. *Chicago Daily News* photograph. *Chicago History Museum*, DN-0063748.

in Minnesota, graduated from Long Island College Hospital in New York in 1880, and moved to North Dakota. He served briefly in the Dakota territorial legislature and as mayor of Mandan before moving to Portland in 1891. Specializing in "nervous and mental diseases," Dr. Coe was the proprietor of Morningside Hospital, served a term as a state senator, and founded a medical journal, *The Pacific Medical Record*, in 1893.

When he lived in the Dakotas, Coe met and formed a friendship with Theodore Roosevelt, whose ranch was in Coe's legislative district. In his later years, Dr. Coe commissioned a series of statues, which he donated to Portland. The first of these was a bronze of Roosevelt, titled "Rough Rider," by A. Phimister Proctor in the Park Blocks in 1922. This was followed in 1924 by a gilded statue of Joan of Arc, cast in 1924 by French sculptor Emmanuel Frémiet and erected to honor those who served in World War I; it stands in a traffic circle in the **Laurelhurst district**. Two final statues were erected after Coe's death: of George Washington by Pompeo Coppini (1927), on SE Sandy Boulevard; and of Abraham Lincoln, by George Fite Waters (1928), in the Park Blocks.

coho salmon *see* **salmon**

Colegio César Chávez *see* **Mount Angel**

Columbia City This small town in Columbia County on the banks of the Columbia River once had great ambitions, dating from its founding in 1867 by brothers Jacob and Joseph Caples as a seaport and the terminus for a railroad to California, projected by **Ben Holladay**; alas for the Caples, Portland became the terminus. The Columbia City post office opened (as Columbia) in 1870 when hopes were high, and has continued ever since, though Columbia City remained but a minor logging and mill community. River steamers provided transportation, and in 1883 the town did get a railroad from Portland and the

rest of the world. Columbia City was incorporated in 1926; it had a population of 310 in the 1930 census. In 2007, the population was an estimated 1,955, having doubled in the previous two decades. The Italianate house of Dr. Charles Green Caples, son of Joseph Caples, was built in 1870. It has been a house museum since 1959, a remnant of Columbia City's days of aspiration.

▶ **Columbia County** Named, quite apparently, for the Columbia River that forms its northern and eastern boundaries, Columbia County was created by the territorial legislature in 1854. Its boundaries have remained unchanged since; it has an area of 657 square miles. The county court met at the now-vanished community of Milton from 1854 to 1857, when it moved downstream a few miles to **Saint**

The general store and post office at the crossroads town of Mist was a Columbia County landmark from its construction in the early 1900s until it burned in 2001. The post office operated from 1888 until 1975. The photograph was taken in 1966. At the time, the store was buying cascara bark from enterprising foragers. Mel Jughans photograph. *Oregon Journal* collection. Oregon Historical Society, OrHi 106095.

Helens. The stone courthouse was built in 1906. The recorded population in 1860 was 532, and in 1880, 2,042.

The Multnomah band of **Chinook Indians** inhabited the riverine areas of Columbia County, with major villages along Multnomah Channel and near Deer Island. Inland on the headwaters of the Klaskanine and Clatskanie Rivers were the **Clatskanie Indians**, an Athapaskan-speaking group.

Columbia County's economic mainstay has been logging and lumbering. In 1915, it was reported that "with the exception of a few cleared and cultivated spots, some marsh lands and a considerable area that has been logged over, Columbia County is one vast, solid forest." The Northern Pacific Railway supplemented river transport in 1883, and sawmills were active in Saint Helens, **Rainier**, and **Clatskanie**. Beginning in the 1920s, the interior town of **Vernonia** was the center of a large lumbering enterprise. Columbia County's population reached 10,580 in 1910, and 20,971 by 1940. Old-growth timber vanished by the 1950s, and mills have since operated using second- and third-growth timber. Agriculture was also important, especially dairying near Clatskanie and **Scappoose**. Natural gas fields were identified near the town of Mist; they were mildly productive after their development in 1979, and the then-emptied domes became the site of underground storage for natural gas imported from elsewhere. Columbia County's estimated population in 2007 was 47,565.

▶ *Columbia Rediviva* This was the name of the ship captained by **Robert Gray** when he entered the mouth of the Columbia River in 1792, along with the sloop *Lady Washington*. Details about the ship are sketchy. She was probably built in Massachusetts in 1773 as the three-masted merchant vessel *Columbia*. After a rebuilding in 1787, she took the name *Columbia Rediviva*, signifying that she was the rebuilt, reconditioned, renewed *Columbia*. The vessel was eighty-three feet long, and twenty-four feet wide,

and carried a crew of thirty-one on this voyage. The *Columbia Rediviva* is the namesake of virtually all the many Columbias in the Oregon Country.

Nokes, J. Richard. *Columbia's River: The Voyages of Robert Gray, 1787–1793*. Tacoma, Washington: Washington State Historical Society, 1991.

Columbia River The Columbia River is 1,243 miles long, flowing from Columbia Lake in British Columbia through Washington state and along the Oregon-Washington boundary to the Pacific Ocean at Astoria. The river takes its name from the ship *Columbia Rediviva*, captained by **Robert Gray**, who entered the river in 1792. Other Euro-American explorers who encountered the river include **Bruno de Heceta**, Capt. **George Vancouver** and Lt. William Broughton, and members of the **Lewis and Clark Expedition**. David Thompson (1770–1857) of the North West Company was the first Euro-American to follow the entire course of the river from its source to its mouth, a feat he accomplished in 1811.

The Columbia River is the path to Oregon's largest port, **Portland**, and has been an artery of both international and local travel from canoes to flat-

The ship *Columbia Rediviva* of Capt. Robert Gray is shown "in a squall" by the artist George Davidson, drawn in 1793. Oregon Historical Society, OrHi 984.

boats to sternwheel steamboats to diesel-powered barges. The Columbia River Gorge also provided a passage for **river transportation**, railroads, the **Columbia River Highway**, and **Interstate 84**. The waters of the Columbia supported immense fisheries, including five species of **salmon**, **sturgeon**, **smelt**, and **lamprey**. The potential hydroelectric power of the river instigated the construction of some fourteen dams, producing a revolution in the region's industrial capabilities, irrigation possibilities, and navigational parameters, but also causing immense damage to fisheries and permanently changing the flowing river into a series of sluggish lakes.

Dietrich, William. *Northwest Passage: The Great Columbia River.* Seattle: University of Washington Press, 1996.

Holbrook, Stewart Hall. *The Columbia.* New York: Rinehart, 1956.

McKinney, Sam. *Reach of Tide, Ring of History: A Columbia River Voyage.* Corvallis: Oregon State University Press, 2000.

White, Richard. *The Organic Machine.* New York: Hill & Wang, 1995.

Columbia River Highway The Oregon Department of Transportation has characterized the Columbia River Highway as "the pinnacle of early-20th-century rural highway design." This roadway was constructed between Portland and The Dalles during the years from 1913 to 1922, with the initial grand opening in 1916; it was soon also extended west to Astoria. The idea of a scenic motorway to and through the Columbia River Gorge was developed by Washington state's good roads advocate **Sam Hill**, an attorney and the creator of Maryhill Museum; **Samuel Lancaster**, an engineer with an artist's eye; and a number of Portland-area civic leaders including **John B. Yeon**, **Simon Benson**, **Henry L. Pittock**, **Julius L. Meier**, and **C. S. Jackson** of the *Oregon Journal*. Their inspiration came from Europe, in particular the coastal corniche, or "edge" roads, of the Riviera. Lancaster designed the road with easy grades, scenic overlooks, such as **Crown Point**, and careful engineering to preserve and enhance the natural features of the Columbia River Gorge. The road became part of **Highway 30**, and was replaced by **Interstate 84**. Much of the original highway was closed, damaged, or simply neglected after World War II: the famous Mitchell Tunnel, with windows, was demolished when the freeway was widened; the Oneonta Bluff tunnel was closed and bypassed; in 1982, the largest bridge on the original route, at Hood River, was destroyed. Preservation advocates managed to have the highway placed on the National Register of Historic Places in 1983, and in 1984 it was recognized as a National Historic Civil Engineering Landmark. Since then, the Oregon Department of Transportation has spearheaded a reconditioning and repair of the highway, which has included reopening closed portions, either as roadway or as bike and pedestrian trails.

Bullard, Oral. *Lancaster's Road: The Historic Columbia River Scenic Highway.* Beaverton, Oregon: TMS Book Service, 1982.

Lancaster, Samuel Christopher. *The Columbia: America's Great Highway through the Cascade Mountains to the Sea.* Portland, Oregon: S. C. Lancaster, 1915.

Columbus Day storm In a state that lacks hurricanes and significant tornadoes, the Columbus Day storm of October 12, 1962, was a landmark event. The "remnants of a tropical storm" that smashed the West Coast took forty-six lives (twenty-four of those in Oregon), downed billions of board feet of standing timber, and cost an estimated $230 million. Wind speeds reached a sustained 130 miles per hour at Mount Hebo south of Tillamook, and gusts of at least 145 miles per hour at Cape Blanco. The storm toppled the tower of a building on the Western Oregon University campus in Monmouth, blew the doors off a massive World War II hangar at Astoria, and caused electrical power outages that took months to repair.

Lucia, Ellis. *The Big Blow: The Story of the Pacific Northwest's Columbus Day Storm*. Forest Grove, Oregon: News-Times Publishing Co., 1963.

► communal colonies and communes

Driven by philosophical or religious constructs, intentional communities are an American phenomenon; familiar examples include New Harmony, Indiana, and Amana, Iowa, along with numerous cases in California: Kaweah, Point Loma, Holy City. Some such experiments occurred in Oregon; most notable was the **Aurora** Colony of **William Keil** in the Willamette Valley, a Christian communist farming group that lasted from 1855 until 1883, after Keil's death in 1877. New Odessa was an agricultural community of Russian immigrant Jews located near **Glendale** in Douglas County from about 1882 to 1887. In the late nineteenth century, several small colonies briefly appeared, inspired by Edward Bellamy's novel *Looking Backward*, including one in Lincoln County named Bellamy. New Era in Clackamas County was a Spiritualist group. In the twentieth century, the counterculture movement of the 1960s and 1970s propelled several communal groups near **Wolf Creek**, as well as in Lane County, associated with the **Oregon Country Fair**, and in rural Jackson County. In the 1980s, all Oregon experienced the impact of **Rajneeshpuram** and its inspiration, the **Bhagwan Shree Rajneesh**.

Kopp, James J. Documenting Utopia in Oregon: the Challenges of Tracking the Quest for Perfection. *Oregon Historical Quarterly* 105, no. 2 (2004): 308–320.

company towns A company town is one in which a single company operates the principal (and, usually, only) industry, and also owns and operates

One of Oregon's small communal colonies and communes was this farming settlement in Polk County known as Socialist Valley. Inspired by *Looking Backward*, the loosely organized group coalesced in the 1890s near Falls City, where some of the members had a sawmill. William L. Jones photo. Steven Dotterer collection.

all of the town's housing and retail businesses, acting as employer, landlord, and merchant. Company towns were not rare in Oregon, but they were not so common, either. Most of them were isolated communities engaged in lumbering, such as **Valsetz**, **Gilchrist**, **Hines**, **Seneca**, **Westfir**, and Bridal Veil.

Carlson, Linda. *Company Towns of the Pacific Northwest*. Seattle: University of Washington Press, 2003.

Concomly (1770s-ca. 1830) A prominent headman of the **Chinook Indians**, Concomly was known to Euro-American traders at the mouth of the Columbia River from at least 1795. He is mentioned in the journals of the **Lewis and Clark Expedition**, and he worked with the **Pacific Fur Company** post at **Fort Astoria**, trading salmon and beaver pelts for American goods. Several of Concomly's daughters married fur traders; one was the mother of **Ranald MacDonald**. Concomly worked with British traders after the Fort Astoria experience, and was a frequent dinner guest of **John McLoughlin** at **Fort Vancouver**. He died in 1829 or 1830, perhaps of malaria, a disease brought to the region by Euro-Americans. In a bizarre turn of events, some five years later a **Hudson's Bay Company** physician disinterred Concomly, removed his head, and sent it to England for scientific study. It remained at the Royal Naval Hospital Museum until 1952, when it was sent to Astoria; it was there displayed in a local museum. At last, it was returned to Concomly's descendants in 1972, and was re-interred near Chinook, Washington.

Concordia University Part of the Concordia University System of the Lutheran Church-Missouri Synod, Concordia University is located in northeast Portland. It began as a training academy for churchmen in 1905. It became a junior college—Concordia College—in 1950, and began admitting women in 1954; in 1977, it became an accredited four-year college. University status came in 1995 with its incorporation into the Concordia University System of ten Lutheran schools across the nation.

Condon The county seat of Gilliam County had its beginnings in the 1880s. The townsite was laid out in 1883, and the owners began selling town lots in 1884, the same year a post office was established. The name comes from that of Harvey C. Condon of nearby Arlington, who was a nephew of Dr. **Thomas Condon**. In 1885, Gilliam County was created. The surrounding countryside held wheat and cattle ranches. Condon was incorporated in 1893, and the 1900 census showed a grand total of 230 residents. A branch line of the Union Pacific Railroad reached Condon in 1905, and by 1915, the town boasted that it had shipped some 3.35 million bushels of wheat in one season. The population jumped to 1,109 in 1910, and wavered around that figure for the next century. From 1929 until 1976, Condon was also the terminus of the Condon, Kinzua & Southern Railroad, which extended south some twenty-four miles to a sawmill and **company town** called Kinzua. Condon's population in 1970 was 973; in 2007, it was estimated at 775. In 1998, Condon's historic downtown commercial district was placed on the National Register of Historic Places, and the Hotel Condon, a three-story brick traveler's hotel built in 1920, was restored; Condon is looking to historic tourism to bolster its economy. It also boasts a nine-hole golf course sited in the shadow of a grain elevator.

Condon, Thomas (1822–1907) Born in Ireland, Thomas Condon immigrated to New York in 1833, and graduated from the Auburn Theological Seminary in 1852. He then sailed for Portland, where in 1853 he was ordained as a Congregational minister. Condon served as pastor in Saint Helens, Forest Grove, Albany, and, from 1862 to 1870, at The Dalles. It was while he was at The Dalles that he was able to exercise his interest in fossils and the geological development of the Oregon Country, making forays into the fossil beds of the John Day country; his article, "The Rocks of the John Day Country," was published in *Overland Monthly* in May 1871. By 1872, he was teaching geology at **Pacific University**, and was named state geologist. After the opening of the **University of Oregon** in 1876, Condon received appointment as professor of geology; he taught and served as chair of the department of natural sciences until his death in 1907. His groundbreaking book, *The Two Islands and What Came of Them* (1902), laid the foundation for the study of the state's historical geology. Condon's fossil collections are at Pacific University and at the University of Oregon's Museum of Natural and Cultural History, which has a permanent exhibit about Condon. Condon Hall on the campus is also named for him, as is the visitor center at the John Day Fossil Beds National Monument. The town of **Condon** is named for his nephew, Harvey C. Condon.

Clark, Robert Donald. *The Odyssey of Thomas Condon: Irish Immigrant, Frontier Missionary, Oregon Geologist*. Portland, Oregon: Oregon Historical Society Press, 1989.

Confederated Tribes of Coos, Lower Umpqua, and Siuslaw Indians
see **Coos Indians**

Confederated Tribes of Grand Ronde
When the **Grand Ronde Reservation** near the community of **Grand Ronde** was terminated in 1956, so was federal recognition of the tribes represented there. Those tribes reorganized in 1974 as the Confederated Tribes of Grand Ronde, and federal status was restored to them in 1983; a reservation of 9,811 acres was established in 1988. The confederation website calls out the Umpqua, Molalla (Molala), Rogue River, Kalapuya, and Chasta tribes; anthropologists make fine divisions of these, but it is apparent that the Willamette Valley confederation includes members whose tribes historically lived in southwest Oregon. Their presence here is the result of the forced removal after the **Rogue River Wars**,

and the subsequent shrinking and then abolishment of the **Coast Reservation**. The Confederated Tribes established Spirit Mountain Casino in 1995, and its financial success has funded the Spirit Mountain Foundation and an active reconstruction of the tribal community.

Confederated Tribes of Siletz
The Confederated Tribes of Siletz are based on the **Siletz Reservation**, which is a small remnant of the **Coast Reservation**. Members of some twenty-seven tribes and bands are included in the confederation; most are from western Oregon but some are from southwest Washington and northwest California. The Siletz area itself is in the homeland of the Siletz **Tillamook Indians** and the Yaquina **Alsean Indians**, but the history of the Coast Reservation is that many other tribes were moved there in the aftermath of the **Rogue River Wars** and several treaties of the 1850s. The present tribal organization occurred after the federal government imposed termination on the Siletz Reservation in 1955. In November 1977, the Siletz became the first Oregon tribe—and only the second in the United States—to be restored to federal recognition, as the Confederated Tribes of Siletz. The tribes gained self-governance in 1992. In 1995, they opened the Chinook Winds casino at Lincoln City.

Confederated Tribes of the Umatilla Indian Reservation
The three tribes that constitute the confederation are the Walla Walla, **Umatilla**, and **Cayuse Indians**. They are headquartered on the **Umatilla Reservation**. The tribal organization dates from 1949. In 1951, the tribes began legal proceedings involving the 1855 treaty fishing rights, an effort that has continued since that time and included the tribes' participation in the founding of the Columbia River Intertribal Fish Commission in 1972. The tribes avoided termination, and have established programs to restore fisheries, preserve and teach native languages, and acquire additional

tribal lands. The tribes developed Wildhorse Casino in the 1990s, and in 1998 opened a stunning museum and cultural center, the Tamástslikt Cultural Institute.

> Karson, Jennifer, ed. *Wiyaxayxt/Wiyaakaa'awn: As Days Go By: Our History, Our Land, and Our People—the Cayuse, Umatilla, and Walla Walla*. Pendleton, Oregon: Tamástslikt Cultural Institute; Portland, Oregon: Oregon Historical Society Press, in association with the University of Washington Press, Seattle, Washington, and London, England, 2006.

Confederated Tribes of Warm Springs

The confederation, based on the **Warm Springs Reservation**, includes **Northern Paiute**, **Wasco**, and Tenino or Warm Springs **Sahaptin Indians**. The tribes organized in 1937 and were federally chartered in 1938. The Warm Springs Lumber Company, still an economic mainstay of the tribes, was established in 1942. The tribes participate in the Columbia River Intertribal Fish Commission, founded in 1972, the same year they opened the Kah-Nee-Ta resort. The Museum at Warm Springs opened its doors in 1993, and in 1996, Indian Head Casino was inaugurated.

Cook, James (1728-1779) The English navigator, cartographer and explorer Capt. James Cook did not set foot in Oregon, but on his third Pacific Ocean voyage, in 1776–79 aboard the naval vessel HMS *Resolution*, Cook sailed up the coast en route to examine the possibilities of a **Northwest Passage**. He paralleled the Oregon shore in the spring of 1778, mapping and naming as he went. The legacy names include **Cape Foulweather** and **Cape Perpetua**. In 1931, a headland just south of Cape Perpetua was given the name Captain Cook Point; at the end of the point is a defile known as Cooks Chasm.

Coos Bay (body of water) The **Coos River** and a number of substantial sloughs—Isthmus, South, Kentuck, Catching, Pony—drain into Coos Bay, whose estuary presents one of the few decent natural ports between San Francisco and Vancouver Island. Even so, substantial dredging, jetties, and other works have been needed to create a port there. Docks and mills at **Coos Bay** and **North Bend** made it one of the largest lumber shipping ports in the world from the 1940s through the 1970s, as well as a major center of both commercial and sports ocean fishing, especially from **Charleston**.

► **Coos Bay (city)** The city of Coos Bay had its beginnings about 1854, with the founding of the townsite of Marshfield. Surprisingly, considering the expanse of tide flats in the vicinity, the name is a reference not to marshes but to the town of Marshfield, Massachusetts, though the reason for the reference is still debated. Marshfield developed as a **shipbuilding** and lumbering center beginning in the 1850s when Californian **Asa Mead Simpson** began those enterprises. By the 1870s local **coal mining** operations were also shipping fuel to San Francisco. The Marshfield post office opened in 1871, and a wagon road connected the region to Roseburg in 1872. The town was incorporated in 1874, and the 1880 census recorded 642 residents.

Not until 1916 was Marshfield connected by railroad with the outside world. World War I brought a sudden growth in the wooden shipbuilding industry, but the end of the war brought an immediate collapse. The population of Marshfield in 1920 was 4,034. The economy was bolstered by the completion of the **Oregon Coast Highway**, especially the completion in 1936 of the spectacular bridge across the bay designed by **C. B. McCullough**. In 1944, residents voted to change the city's name to Coos Bay; the post office enacted the change the next year. A prominent legacy of the old name is the main high school, which is still named Marshfield.

Timber remained the largest industry in the Coos Bay region until the early 1980s, by which time all of the large, **old-growth** timber had been cut. The industry virtually collapsed in the 1990s; the waterfront, once a hive of industry with lumber mills, docks and wharves, and shipyards, grew silent. Coos Bay's 1970 population was 13,466; despite economic woes, the estimated figure for 2007 was 16,210.

Robbins, William G. *Hard Times in Paradise: Coos Bay, Oregon.* Rev. ed. Seattle: University of Washington Press, 2006.

➤ **Coos County** This county was created in 1853 by taking lands from parts of Umpqua and Jackson Counties, the impetus being the influx of gold seekers to this part of the territory. The name is from the **Coos Indians**. Assorted boundary adjustments were made with Curry County in 1855 and 1872, and then with Douglas County in 1882, 1951 and 1983; the present area of Coos County is 1,629 square miles. The population in 1870 was 1,664. **Empire** was the first county seat, and so remained until an election in 1896 resulted in the selection of **Coquille** as the new government center. A new courthouse was built there in 1898, with an addition in 1916; subsequently, the first courthouse was demolished in 1951, and additions were made to the 1916 addition; the result is unimpressive.

The original inhabitants of the area now Coos County were the Coos Indians; among the Coosan were the Hanis, Lower Umpqua, and Miluk, including the Lower Coquille. The language of the area's **Athapaskan Indians** differed from that of the Coos; the Upper Umpqua and Upper Coquille are among that group.

In the 1850s, Coos County was the site of gold excitement, as gold was found in beach sands north of the Coquille River mouth. The port possibilities of **Coos Bay** soon brought logging and lumber mill-

A small part of the Coos Bay fishing fleet, most of them salmon trollers, is pictured in port in about 1940. Frank Patterson photograph. Steven Dotterer collection.

The sternwheel steamboat *Alert* is tied up along the Milli-coma River, a tributary of Coos River, at the landing for the community of Allegany, which has had a post office since 1893. The *Alert* was built in Bandon in 1890, and served in the Coos Bay mosquito fleet until she was wrecked in 1919. Oregon Historical Society, CN 021039.

ing, as well as **shipbuilding**, to the area, and in the late nineteenth century, **coal mining** was added to the economic pillars. Coal did not last, and wooden shipbuilding declined after World War I, but lumber kept the economy booming. The county's population reached 10,324 in 1910; in 1920, it was 22,257, and by 1950, 42,265. In 1980, at the final shaky peak of lumber production, the count reached 64,047; the estimate in 2007 was 63,050.

Coos Indians The Coos Indians include members of two Coosan language groups, the Hanis, who lived around Coos Bay and on its tributary rivers and sloughs, and the South Slough and Lower Co-quille Miluk, whose territory was, respectively, on South Slough and lower Coos Bay, and on the coast near the mouth of the Coquille River. Salmon were a major subsistence food, along with **lamprey**, **smelt**, and other fish; the Coos also ate shellfish, sea lions and seals, and deer and elk. A variety of berries, **camas**, fern, and **wapato** supplemented their diet. Like most coastal tribes, the Coos lived in familial cedar lodges, and traveled on foot and by canoe. The Coos encountered whites during the gold-mining rushes of the 1850s. While the Lower Co-quille had some involvement with the **Rogue River Wars**, other Coos did not; still, they were greatly impacted by it. The U.S. Senate never ratified a treaty signed in 1855; nevertheless all Coos were removed to reservations to the north. The closing of the Alsea Reservation in 1875 induced many to re-turn to their homeland near Coos Bay or to join the **Siuslaw Indians** near Florence. The Confederated Tribes of Coos, Lower Umpqua, and Siuslaw Indians were given federal recognition in 1984, and opened Three Rivers Casino in Florence in 2004.

Coos River Draining into **Coos Bay**, Coos River heads in western Douglas County and flows west-ward about sixty miles. The Coos and its tributary, the Millicoma River, were served by vessels of the Coos Bay **mosquito fleet** in the later 1800s and early 1900s.

► **Copperfield** This vanished community in Baker County was the site of a legendary event in the political career of Governor **Oswald West**, an outspoken foe of vice and liquor. Copperfield was a small mining town in the canyon of the Snake River; the post office opened in 1899, and by 1913, was an incorporated municipality. The governor had been troubled for some time by reports that illicit liquor was common and gambling and prostitution ram-pant in Baker County, particularly at **Huntington** and Copperfield; the county sheriff was not inclined to take any action. On December 31, 1913, West declared martial law in effect in Copperfield and sent his secretary, Fern Hobbs (1883-1964) to Copperfield by train, along with a detachment of five men from the Oregon National Guard. The group arrived in Copperfield in the early afternoon of January 2, 1914. Miss Hobbs presented the declaration to city officials—most of them engaged in the saloon business—and called upon them all to resign. Upon their refusal, the Guard arrested them. Miss Hobbs was five feet four inches in height and weighed under a hundred pounds, and she carried out her duties with aplomb before she left town on the afternoon train. In a state where women had just won the right to vote, this was an empowering episode. The Guard stayed; an additional contingent of twenty-six arrived shortly and stayed for several months. Gov. James Withycombe finally revoked martial law January 21, 1915. Copperfield has been very quiet ever since.

Coquille The city of Coquille has been the county seat of Coos County since 1896. The settlement of Coquille was granted a post office in 1870, as farmers began to settle the **Coquille River** Valley. Coquille was incorporated in 1885; the 1890 census recorded a population of 494. Nearby **coal mining** activities helped induce the construction of the Coos Bay, Roseburg & Eastern Railroad from **Coos Bay** south to Coquille and Myrtle Point in the 1890s, but the line never managed to make it to Roseburg. Coquille prospered as the county seat and a lumber town. The census noted 1,642 residents in 1920, and 3,523 in 1950. The estimated figure for 2007 was 4,215.

Coquille Indian Reservation The Coquille Indian Reservation consists of a number of parcels of land in Coos County held by the Coquille Indian Tribe. The tribe had been terminated by the federal

The wide-open town of Copperfield is pictured as it appeared about 1910, not long before Governor Oswald West toppled its city government. The new Homestead branch of the Union Pacific Railroad cuts across the townsite. *Oregon Journal* collection. Oregon Historical Society, CN 007127.

government following the Termination Act of 1954, but regained federal recognition in 1989. The Upper Coquille Indians, an Athapaskan-speaking tribe, inhabited the drainage of the Coquille River; the Lower Coquille or Miluk were a Coos Indian band occupying villages near the river's mouth. Since restoration, the tribe has engaged in a variety of economic and social programs, including The Mill casino and hotel, and Coquille organic cranberries. *See also* **Coos Indians**; **Athapaskan Indians**.

Coquille Indians *see* Athapaskan Indians; Coos Indians

Coquille River Extending about thirty-six miles south and east from its confluence with the Pacific Ocean at Bandon, the Coquille River in Coos County traverses a valley that has supported a major dairy industry since the 1890s and penetrates deep into timber country to the east. The river was long a highway for water travel, with small sternwheel steamboats connecting Bandon with Coquille and Myrtle Point from the late 1870s through the 1930s; gasoline launches were also used, particularly to supply dairy farms and to take milk to creameries and **cheese** factories in Coquille and Myrtle Point. The Bandon harbor was improved with jetties in the 1880s, and a lighthouse began operating in 1896. *See also* **Grandmother Rock**; **lighthouses**.

Corbett, Henry Winslow (1827–1903) Henry W. Corbett was born in Massachusetts and went to New York City in 1843 to engage in business. He was sent to Portland by sea in 1851 with a cargo of merchandise to sell, and his quick success brought him west again in 1853, bringing with him his bride Caroline. Building on his New York connections, Corbett rapidly built a successful career in Portland, benefitting from the **gold** excitements of the 1860s and investing in local transportation projects such as the **Oregon Steam Navigation Company**. With Henry Failing, Corbett took the reins of the First National Bank of Portland in 1869; Failing also became a partner with Corbett in the hardware business.

After the death of Caroline in 1865, Corbett in 1867 married Emma Ruggles; the couple built a handsome mansion on a city block south of the **Pioneer Courthouse**. Corbett served a term in the U. S. Senate beginning in 1866, a Republican who concentrated on economic issues. In Portland, he became a prominent supporter of schools and the public library. In the 1920s, Corbett's widow achieved notoriety for maintaining a milk cow at her downtown residence, by then surrounded by office buildings and theaters. A street and a school in Portland are named for H. W. Corbett, as is the town of Corbett in eastern Multnomah County, where he had purchased a farm in 1885.

corn Sweet corn was a major component of the nineteenth-century family farm, but it has become a major commercial crop since World War II. It is grown in western Oregon valleys for market sale. It is also a major Oregon crop for freezing and canning; the state is the nation's fourth largest grower of sweet corn. *See also* **Aumsville**.

Cornelius The city of Cornelius arose on land in Washington County that was settled by emigrant families in the 1840s. One of those farming families was that of Benjamin Cornelius; they arrived in 1845. The townsite was the result of the construction of a railroad from Portland, which arrived in the area in 1872; the post office had opened in 1871. The community was incorporated in 1893, and the 1900 census show a population of 246. By 1915, Cornelius was reported to be an agricultural center noted for nursery stock, hop growing, dairying, and stock raising; the town had a lumber mill and a creamery. The population in 1950 reached 998.

After World War II, Cornelius began to assume a suburban aspect, as a bedroom community to Portland and the expanding **Silicon Forest** to the east.

The population rose to 4,402 in 1980, and to an estimated 10,895 in 2007.

Cornucopia One of Oregon's **ghost towns**, Cornucopia is located high in the Wallowa Mountains of Baker County. **Gold** was the drawing card; it was discovered and mines and mills were developed in the 1880s. The Cornucopia post office opened in 1885, and a tortuous road from Baker City served the remote camp, at an elevation of 4,700 feet. This was hard-rock mining, with tunnels driven into the mountainside and the gold-bearing quartz ore processed by nearby mills. Like many gold-mining operations, the activity fluctuated widely, influenced by the quality of the ore, operating costs, the national economy, and gold prices. In 1915, Cornucopia had daily stage service and three quartz mills, but the town's most prosperous times actually were during the 1920s and 1930s. World War II shut down the mines in 1942, and the post office closed. In the 1950s and 1960s, Cornucopia was a notable ghost town destination with numerous cabins and abandoned mill buildings. By 2000, little remained to mark the camp.

Corvallis The county seat of Benton County, Corvallis is located in a part of the Willamette Valley that was settled in the 1840s. The townsite developed from about 1847, when Joseph C. Avery platted the first lots and streets; Avery also operated a ferry across **Marys River**. The Marysville post office was established in 1850, and was renamed Corvallis in 1854. In the 1850s, Corvallis was an agricultural shipping center, located at the usual head of navigation on the Willamette River; it was incorporated as a city in 1857. The Southern Methodist Church established Corvallis College in 1865; in 1869 the legislature designated the school as its land grant agricultural college and supplied some money. It became wholly a state institution in 1886 and has developed into **Oregon State University**. Railroad service from Portland reached Corvallis in 1880, and during the following decade, Corvallis was subjected to "railroad fever," as lines were built connecting the city to **Yaquina Bay** and were projected eastward across the Cascade Range to the Midwest. The fever collapsed during the nationwide financial travails of the early 1890s. During that heady period, Corvallis built a new courthouse—the oldest courthouse in Oregon still in use—as well as a city hall, a new flour mill and electric light plant, a brick hotel, and the first building on the present Oregon State University campus.

Corvallis had a population of 1,819 in the 1900 census, a figure that grew to 5,752 by 1920. By that time, Corvallis was also a lumbering center, and local farmers engaged in dairying and raised fruit; the city had a fruit and vegetable cannery and a prune dryer as well as several creameries. The city's population reached 16,207 in 1950, 40,960 in 1980. The growth of the university and the development of high technology industries has supported the city's economy as lumbering waned. The population of Corvallis was estimated at 54,890 in 2007.

Cottage Grove Sweetly named Cottage Grove is located at the confluence of the Coast Fork Willamette River and the Row River in Lane County. The name was given to a rural post office in the vicinity in 1855. The exact location of the town and the post office (and of a nearby office, Lemati, which operated in the 1890s) skipped about a bit, as detailed in Lewis L. McArthur's *Oregon Geographic Names*, but the town eventually solidified around the railroad station on the **Oregon & California Railroad**, which arrived in 1872. In the late 1880s, Cottage Grove became the outfitting and supply point for the **Bohemia mining district**, when **gold** was discovered some thirty miles to the east. Cottage Grove was incorporated in 1887. In the early 1900s, a railroad was built up the **Row River** toward the mines; the mines soon lapsed, but logging increased, and more sawmills were built. Cottage Grove had a population of 1,834 in 1910, and in 1915, it was reported that there were twenty-five lumber mills tributary to the city. Hollywood excitement came to town in 1926, when silent film comedian Buster Keaton and a crew arrived to film a Civil War comedy (yes) based on the famous chase of the locomotive called *The General*; and that was the name of the film. The railroad up the Row River had a starring role, and the climatic scene involved tumbling the pursuing locomotive into the river from a flaming trestle.

Lumber mills carried the economy into the 1970s but have declined in importance since. The railroad up the Row ran out of logs to carry, and for a time in the 1980s it carried tourists, but it was abandoned in 1993. The late Victorian architecture of Cottage Grove's retail district was placed on the National Register of Historic Places in 1994, and the area has become noted for its antique shops. The estimated population in 2007 was 9,345.

cottonwood The black cottonwood, *Populus trichocarpa*, also known as the California poplar, is the tallest of native North American hardwoods, reaching from sixty to 120 feet in height; the tallest specimen, in Yamhill County, is 147 feet high. It is found along the Pacific Coast and the interior West from Alaska into northern Mexico, favoring moist or even wet soils in river valleys and flood plains, and also on upland slopes. It grows in stands of cottonwood alone, as well as mixed with willows and red alder. Commercially it is used to make crates and boxes, excelsior (shredded packaging), and as pulpwood for **papermaking**.

Couch, John H. (1811–1870) John Couch was born in Massachusetts and early showed an interest in sailing; as a boy, he shipped off to the East Indies. His first command was the *Maryland*, which he took from Newburyport, Massachusetts, to the Columbia River in 1840, but the trip was not a trading success. His backer gave him next the brig *Chenamus*, which he brought to Oregon City in 1842. Couch established a store there, sent the ship home, and re-

mained in Oregon. The captain continued to make trading trips between the East and Oregon, formed a partnership with his brother-in-law, Capt. George H. Flanders, and engaged in trade in Portland. The area of his land claim included a seasonal lake that became Couch Lake; much of it was platted as Couch's Addition and became part of the North End district of the city, including Union Station.

Couch was a stalwart citizen, and his name appears on a street, school, and park in Portland; his partner Flanders has a paralleling street. Couch Park was once the property of Cicero Hunt Lewis, who married Couch's daughter. The streets were part of Couch's Addition and were initially labeled A Street, B Street, etc.; the names were applied to the letters during the great street re-naming of 1894.

cougar The wild cat known as the cougar, *Felis concolor*, has a ferocious reputation in Oregon. Also known as puma, mountain lion, and sometimes panther, the cougar is found in the Cascades, Coast Range, and Blue Mountains. Oregon's **provisional government** arose out of the Wolf Meetings of 1843, which were called to deal with controlling predator animals in the Willamette Valley farming settlements. Bounties were set on several animals—and the highest bounty was set on the cougar. That practice continued for more than a century, and by the mid-1960s, according to the Oregon Fish and Wildlife Commission, the cougar population had reached "near extirpation." Cougars were declared game animals in 1967, and the population has subsequently recovered, which has resulted in calls to again suppress them. They occasionally kill livestock and have been known to attack humans, but there are no documented human fatalities from cougars in Oregon.

Council Crest Council Crest, elevation 1,074 feet, is the highest point in the range of hills to the west of downtown Portland, commonly known as the West Hills, and officially as the **Tualatin Mountains**. As the result of a national Congregational

Church conference in 1898, when some of those attending hiked to the summit, the name Council Crest was applied in recognition of the conference. A streetcar line reached up and looped around the top of the hill in 1906, and the streetcar company built an amusement park there the next year. The park—a scenic railway (roller coaster), an observatory, a water ride, a funhouse—lasted until 1929; a remnant of the observatory survived until 1941. The city acquired the property for a public park in 1936, and the streetcars themselves continued to run until 1950. For a number of years thereafter, one of the streetcars was on ceremonial view there, until vandalism prompted its removal; it is one of two Council Crest cars that survive in the collections of the Oregon Electric Railway Historical Society in Brooks. The cars used on the Council Crest line were the models for the replica Portland **streetcars**, four of which were built in 1991 for operation as tourist attractions on the new **MAX** system. Council Crest and adjacent Healy Heights has also, since the 1920s, been the site of numerous radio and television broadcasting towers.

Cove Nestled in a corner of the Grande Ronde Valley in Union County, the town of Cove dates from the 1860s, when it was known as Forest Cove. Forest Cove post office was opened in 1863, but confusion with Forest Grove resulted in the shortened form of the name in 1868. The Ascension Episcopal Church chapel and rectory, built of wood in a rendering of the Gothic Revival style, have been Cove landmarks since their construction in the early 1870s.

Cove was incorporated as a city in 1904, and a short-line railroad connected Cove with the town of Union and the main line Union Pacific Railroad about 1907. Cove was an agricultural trading center: in 1915, it boasted a flour mill, two box factories, three fruit-packing houses, and, each July, it celebrated a Cherry Fair. Cove's population in 1910 was reported at 433. It has remained a small town; the population reached 480 by 1980 and was estimated

at 620 in 2007. By the end of the twentieth century, Cove had become a center for the bottling of artesian water for Wal-Mart; cherries were still an important crop, and grapes for winemaking were a recent introduction.

▶ **Cove Palisades** The Crooked River joins the Deschutes River in a deep canyon in western Jefferson County, and beneath the sheer basaltic cliffs is "one of the most marvelous and spectacular settings in the state." So said **Samuel H. Boardman**, head of state parks, regarding their acquisition of some 4,000 acres of property at The Cove about 1940. Round Butte Dam was completed in 1965, creating Lake Billy Chinook, which submerged The Cove to produce hydroelectric power and irrigation water. The fish ladders never worked. Efforts began in 2006 to rework the fish passage system.

covered bridges In the relatively damp environment of Oregon west of the Cascade Range, the deterioration of wooden **bridges** was a problem that was often addressed by covering the trusses with a housing for protection, also made of wood, a technique

A fisherman and his travel trailer posed beneath a small waterfall at the state park at Cove Palisades about 1956. Oregon State Highway commission photograph. Oregon Historical Society, CN 008097.

that had been in use throughout the East and Midwest for many decades. Covered bridges were common. The development of an extensive road system in the state, which was vigorously pursued in the 1910s and 1920s, resulted in many new concrete and steel bridges, but also induced a spurt of growth in covered wooden bridges on secondary roads. Road commissions in several counties—Lane, Jackson, and Marion among them—built dozens of such bridges through the 1930s. The late spurt of wooden bridge building left Oregon with a legacy of about four dozen covered bridges by 2005. They range from the 1938 Goodpasture Bridge across the McKenzie River in Lane County, at 165 feet the longest in the state, each side pierced by ten windows, to the 1918 Hayden bridge over the Alsea River, ninety-one feet long and the oldest standing covered bridge in the state.

> Nelson, Lee H. *A Century of Oregon Covered Bridges, 1851–1952: A History of Oregon Covered Bridges, their Beginnings, Development and Decline, Together with Some Mention of the Builders and Techniques.* Portland, Oregon: Oregon Historical Society, 1976.

covered wagon The iconic artifact representing the experiences of thousands of overland emigrants—the **pioneers**—who came to Oregon in the 1840s and 1850s is the covered wagon: a four-wheeled conveyance with a canvas top, hauled by a team of oxen and containing a family's encapsulated prior lives and future hopes. Covered wagons—indeed, wagons and conveyances of all kinds and sizes, covered and uncovered, pulled by oxen, horses, mules, dairy cattle, humans—traveled more than 2,000 miles over the **Oregon Trail** and its various branches and permutations, and when they arrived, they were usually immediately converted to other uses or cannibalized for parts for other vehicles. The majority were originally farm wagons, and they were returned to that use. For that reason, few authentic, "original" covered wagons exist today: like the clothes and tools the emigrants brought with

them, they were usually put to work and "used up" in short order.

The imagery of the covered wagon has trumped its reality. While the vast majority of the emigrants from the United States to the contested country of Oregon in the 1840s indeed traveled in groups and carried their possessions in wagons, those wagons were not all of uniform size, and did not always have snowy white canvas covers carried on hoops. The Conestoga wagon was not found on the Oregon Trail; it was a freighting wagon of an earlier period. *See also* **Meeker, Ezra.**

Cow Creek Band of Umpqua Tribe of Indians This is the existing tribal entity of the Cow Creek band of the **Athapaskan Indians,** also known as the Upper Umpqua Indians. The band is headquartered at Canyonville in Douglas County. The area was also homeland to the **Takelma Indians** before the **Rogue River Wars.** The wars and the treaty negotiations that were part of them created the Cow Creek Reservation; however treaties were not ratified. A 1982 federal recognition led to a settlement with the Cow Creek Band.

crab Since World War II, the offshore Oregon crab fishery for the Dungeness crab, *Cancer magister*, has become the largest single species seafood take in the state. The crab is named for a small town on the Olympic Peninsula in Washington state, but the crab is found along the North Pacific shore into Alaska. **James Beard** wrote well about the joys of individual crab harvesting on the **Gearhart** beach in the early years of the twentieth century.

Crag Rats *see* **Cloud Cap Inn**

cranberries A native bog cranberry, *Oxycoccus oxycoccus* (there is some disagreement on the designation), occurs in coastal areas. Native tribes ate the berries fresh, cooked, and dried. Cultivated cranberries in Oregon date back to at least 1885, when

Charles D. McFarlin of Massachusetts came to Coos County and planted a variety he had developed there. These berries were larger than the native species; growing and harvesting was done in flat, low-lying fields. The fields were flooded to protect the berries from frost, and to aid in the harvest of the ripe berries (cranberries float). Cranberry growing developed on a small scale in Coos and Tillamook Counties in the 1890s; by the mid-1920s, Clatsop County was also producing cranberries.

Cranberry growing declined during the Depression years, but revived after World War II when the cooperative marketing group Ocean Spray was expanded into Oregon. Since then, growing declined substantially in Clatsop County, but remained strong in Coos County near **Bandon**; by 2005, Oregon was the fourth largest cranberry-producing state in the nation; much of that is still with the McFarlin variety of cranberry.

Crane The Harney County community of Crane, named for the sandhill crane, was a rural post office from 1895 to 1903; it was re-established in 1916 when it became the temporary end-of-the-line for a railroad that extended west from Ontario. Crane then became a major shipping point for cattle from the Harney Basin ranches, and a supply point; it declined when the railroad went farther west to Hines and Burns in 1924. The Crane Union High School is one of the nation's few and oldest (1923) public boarding high schools. The students—about eighty of them—are drawn from an area of 7,500 square miles; some travel well over a hundred miles to school, and so spend their weeknights in a school dormitory and travel home only on weekends.

Crater Lake Crater Lake is a deep (1,943 feet) and very blue lake situated in the crater or caldera of an extinct Cascade Range volcano, **Mount Mazama**. The mountain—which is named for a mountain-climbing club, the **Mazamas**—was active some 7,700 years ago. The activity culminated in an explosive eruption and collapse that blew the top off a peak that was once about 11,000 feet high; the highest point on the mountain today is 8,159 feet. The caldera subsequently filled with water from rain and snowmelt.

The lake was known to the **Klamath Indians** but was not seen by white explorers until 1853, when three gold prospectors stumbled upon it and forthrightly named it Deep Blue Lake. **Peter Britt** of Jacksonville, whose images helped publicize the lake, took the first photograph in 1874. The lake's major publicist was the redoubtable naturalist and activist **William Steel**, who saw the lake in 1870 and subsequently initiated or participated in many surveys of the lake and its surroundings. It was Steel who named many of the features, such as Wizard Island, and who, for better or worse, advocated establishing fish in the originally fishless lake. Stocking with rainbow trout, kokanee salmon, and others was first done in 1888; those two species have survived. No fish stocking has occurred since 1941.

Steel succeeded in his efforts to have Crater Lake declared a national park, which occurred in 1902; Steel was the park's first superintendent. Crater Lake Lodge, a grand pile in the national park rustic style of architecture, opened in 1915; on the National Register of Historic Places, it was renovated and restored between 1990 and 1995. The automobile road circling the lake was completed in 1918.

Deur, Douglas. A Most Sacred Place: the Significance of Crater Lake among the Indians of Southern Oregon. *Oregon Historical Quarterly* 103, no. 1 (Spring 2002): 18–49.

Harmon, Rick. *Crater Lake National Park: A History.* Corvallis: Oregon State University Press, 2002.

Creffield, Franz Edmund *see* **holy rollers**

▶ **Cressman, Luther Sheeleigh** (1897–1994) Luther Cressman was born in Pennsylvania and first pursued an academic path that led him through studying English poetry and classics to becoming an Episcopalian priest to earning a doctorate from Columbia University (1925) in sociology, with a minor in anthropology. Cressman married Margaret Mead, later to become a major figure in American anthropological studies, in 1923; they divorced in 1927, and shortly after that he married Dorothy "Cecelia" Loch. In 1928, Cressman left the church and in 1929 took a position in the sociology department at the **University of Oregon** in Eugene. Beyond his work in sociology, he helped develop the university's anthropology department and headed it from 1935 to 1963. He was also instrumental in founding in 1936 what became the Museum of Natural and Cultural History at the university.

Cressman worked extensively on the prehistory of Oregon peoples. His most renowned work stemmed from his discovery in 1938 of a number of well-crafted sandals, made of sage, which dated back some 9,000 years at a cave-dwelling site near **Fort Rock**. Previously, human habitation in western North American was not thought to go back more than about 4,000 years. His best-known writing was his account of this discovery and its repercussions, *The Sandal and the Cave* (1962); he also wrote *Prehistory of the Far West: Homes of Vanished Peoples* (1977) and many other monographs and articles.

Cressman, Luther S. *A Golden Journey: Memoirs of an Archaeologist.* Salt Lake City: University of Utah Press, 1988.

Creswell The Oregon & California Railroad built through the site of Creswell in 1872, about ten miles south of Eugene in Lane County. O&CRR promoter **Ben Holladay** gave the name to the station, which was also applied to the new post office the same year; the honoree was the U.S. postmaster general at the time, John A. Creswell. Creswell grew into a small agricultural trading center and timber mill town, and was incorporated in 1909; the census of 1910 reported 367 residents. Creswell came to na-

Anthropologist Luther S. Cressman is shown in 1938 at the cave in the Fort Rock Valley where he located sandals made some 9,000 years earlier. *Oregonian* photograph. Oregon Historical Society, OrHi 80013.

tional attention in the aftermath of the Korean War when local residents **Harry and Bertha Holt** began an adoption service for the Korean offspring of U.S. servicemen. Since the 1970s, Creswell's population has increased tremendously as the town became a commuting suburb of Eugene. The population was estimated to be 4,650 in 2007.

crimp One who practices the activity known as crimping; *see* **crimping**.

crimping During the era of sailing ships, crews were usually hired by the captain by contract, and did as they were told. It was common for merchant sailors to jump ship at a port city (San Francisco was a favorite during the gold rush era of the 1850s). Men engaged in crimping, called crimps, worked with sea captains to return the men to their ships— or, failing that, to supply a replacement. Crimping was a quasi-legal activity in **ocean transportation** worldwide until the 1900s, when the rise of steamships, international maritime law, and labor unions combined with the decline of captain-owned sailing ships to effectively eliminate the trade. Crimping took place in such ports as Portland, Astoria, and Coos Bay; in Portland, Joseph "Bunco" Kelly was a noted crimp on the Portland waterfront and **skid road** district in the 1880s and 1890s.

The outright kidnapping of a crewmember was often known as shanghaiing. Crimping and shanghaiing was usually a matter of getting a likely prospect drunk and delivering him to a ship about to sail; when sober, the victim found himself at sea and began his career in the merchant marine. The practice was most active at attractive port cities that were also close to the open sea, such as San Francisco and Victoria. River ports such as Portland were more problematic (it could take a day or two to reach the mouth of the Columbia), since a now-sober recruit might have opportunities to jump ship and swim ashore, or to encounter the watchful eyes of river pilots and customs officials.

Stories that allege that Portland had a network of tunnels with holding cells for a shanghai trade, and that the practice caused the disappearance of thousands of Oregon's young men, are unsupported by historical evidence. They have arisen since 1970 and constitute some remarkable urban folklore.

Alborn, Denise M. Crimping and Shanghaiing on the Columbia River. *Oregon Historical Quarterly* 93, no. 3 (Fall 1992), 262–291.

► **Crook County** This Central Oregon county was established by the legislature in 1882, the 8,600 square miles taken from the southern portion of Wasco County. The creation of Jefferson County in 1914, and Deschutes County in 1916, reduced its size, and the boundaries were not finalized until 1927; its current area is 2,991 square miles. The county seat has always been at **Prineville**, where government offices are based in the county courthouse built in 1909. The 1890 census gave the county a population of 3,244, Indians not included; the smaller county of 1920 was recorded with 3,424 residents. Population climbed substantially after World War II with the expansion of lumbering operations in Prineville, reaching 8,991 in 1950 and 9,985 in 1970. The exploding development of retirement and recreational living in Central Oregon since 1990 contributed to a 2007 population estimated at 25,855. The territory now encompassed by Crook County was once part of the homeland of the **Northern Paiute Indians**.

Crook County's economy has long been based in agriculture and timber. Irrigation projects, begun in the early 1900s, have made it possible to grow hay, potatoes, seed crops, mint, and grains. Cattle grazing on both private and public lands has endured since the 1880s. After the construction of the **Oregon Trunk Railway**, the city of Prineville in 1918 built a connecting railroad that fostered the development of a sizeable lumber industry, based on ponderosa pine timber from the nearby Ochoco National Forest. Reduced timber harvesting since the 1980s

This photograph shows a wooden flume of the Pilot Butte and Central Oregon canal of the Central Oregon Irrigation Company, located in Crook County in about 1905. Deschutes County was formed out of part of Crook County in 1916. Oregon Historical Society, OrHi 25619.

has closed mills in Prineville. The county has had an influx of retirees in the last years of the twentieth century, and has seen a rise in tourism with the growth of new leisure activities such as rock climbing, which has made Smith Rocks State Park a destination attraction.

Crooked River The Crooked River heads in the Ochoco Mountains of eastern Oregon, and in the Blue Mountains of Grant County, heading north and west some 130 miles to join the Deschutes River at **Cove Palisades**. Its descriptive name dates from the **fur trade** period of the 1820s. Historically the Crooked River hosted runs of anadromous fish such as Chinook salmon and lamprey, which migrated to and from the Pacific Ocean, but the runs have been eliminated by irrigation diversion of the waters and the construction of dams. Redband trout can still be found in the stream.

► **Crown Point** A crown jewel of the Columbia River Gorge is this high basaltic point in eastern Multnomah County, a featured scenic overlook on the **Columbia River Highway** since its completion. The viewpoint is capped by a remarkable structure designed by Portland architect Edgar M. Lazarus in 1915, described as "an example of German 'Art Nouveau' architecture." Columbia River Highway engineer **Samuel Lancaster** made the suggestion that Crown Point should have "an observatory from which the view both up and down the Columbia could be viewed in silent communion with the infinite." It would also memorialize "the trials and hardships of those who had come into the Oregon country" and "serve as a comfort station for the tourist and the travelers of America's greatest highway."

The Vista House opened in May 1918. The building includes floors and stairs of Alaskan marble, and an interior of Kasota limestone. The interior of the

VISTA HOUSE, CROWN POINT
COLUMBIA RIVER HIGHWAY, ORE.   638   © Cross & Dimmitt

This postcard view depicts the Vista House at Crown Point on the Columbia River Highway shortly after its completion.
Cross & Dimmitt photo. Steven Dotterrer collection.

dome is painted to simulate the marble and bronze that was intended to be used in its construction, but was not, because of cost. Green tiles originally covered the exterior of the dome; they were replaced by a copper sheath that, though it remained in place for some five decades, leaked abominably. In 2002, the roof was replaced with, again, glazed green tile, now underlain with a protective membrane.

Crown Zellerbach "Crown Z" was a San Francisco-based paper-manufacturing firm that was formed in 1928 by the merger of the Zellerbach Corporation and the Oregon paper company Crown Willamette. In Oregon, Crown Z owned the **paper-making** plant at Lebanon, which began in 1889, as well as plants at Oregon City and at Camas, Washington. By the 1930s it was the second largest paper company in the nation and the largest on the West Coast; it came to own twelve production plants and

more than 500,000 acres of timberland. In the 1950s, Crown Z began to develop a line of agricultural sprays, insecticides and other chemicals derived from wood. Crown Zellerbach was acquired in 1968 by the James River Company, which became Fort James Corporation in 1997 and was acquired in 2000 by **Georgia Pacific**.

Culver This Jefferson County community was established as a rural post office in 1900. The first postmaster, O. G. Collver, bestowed a former spelling of his ancestral name on the office, which was several miles east of the community that is situated along the line of the Oregon Trunk Railway, which arrived in 1911. Culver was incorporated as a city in 1946. The 1950 census reported a population of 301; in 2007, the estimate was 1,315, a more-than-doubling since 1990. Col. **Rex T. Barber** served as mayor for a time.

Curry County Situated in the southwestern-most corner of Oregon is Curry County. The county was first established in 1855, when gold mining was of more than passing interest in this coastal region, and it was named for the territorial governor, George Law Curry. The area of the county was originally about 1,500 square miles; adjustments with adjacent Josephine County (1880; 1927) and Coos County (1872; 1951) brought it to its current 1,640 square miles. The initial designated county seat was **Port Orford**; in 1859, residents voted to establish the county government seat at Ellensburg (renamed **Gold Beach** in 1891).

The region now included in Curry County was once part of the homeland of a number of Athapaskan-speaking Indians. These **Athapaskan Indians** included the Chetco, Chasta Costa, Upper Coquille, Upper Umpqua, Tututni, and other bands. Although there were early encounters with fur traders and explorers in the 1820s, such as **Jedediah Smith**, it was not until the gold rush influx of the 1850s that many whites entered the region. The conflicts were immediate and tragic, culminating in the **Rogue River Wars** and the forced removal of most of the remaining Indians to the **Coast Reservation**; however, a number stayed on along the interior Rogue River and in other remote locations.

The gold rush was short-lived. The 1860 census showed a grand total of 393 residents in the county, Indians not included. By 1910, the figure had reached 2,044. The county had exceedingly poor transportation connections with the rest of the state: there were minor port facilities at Gold Beach, Port Orford, and, later, Brookings, but no railroad ever reached Curry County. Road connections were primitive until the completion of the **Oregon Coast Highway** in the 1930s. In 1915, Curry County was described in a state publication as "one of the roughest and most mountainous counties of the State of Oregon, almost entirely a forested wilderness; it is the wildest and least explored county in Oregon and one of the wildest on the continent of the United States . . . Little is known concerning the resources of the county except as the most casual inspection reveals almost limitless timber wealth and great mineral and water power possibilities." Lumber production at **Brookings** beginning in the 1910s brought some industry, and specialty woods such as Oregon myrtle and Port Orford-cedar have a market—but the timber stands are much diminished. Curry County has also produced blueberries and nursery stock, and, rather surprisingly, a huge portion of the nation's Easter lily bulbs. Tourism—the spectacular coastal and river scenery draw many visitors—has been a key economic component since the 1930s; retirement residence has been a growth industry since the 1970s. Curry County's population in 1940 was 4,301; in 1970, 13,006; and in 2007 was estimated at 21,475.

Cutler City *see* **Lincoln City**

Cycle Oregon This long-distance bicycle touring of scenic Oregon byways began in 1988, and is held during the second week of September. The route usually covers about 400 miles.

Czechs in Oregon *see* **Malin**

D

dahlia Dahlias grow exceptionally well on the Oregon Coast and in the Willamette Valley. In the Willamette River at Portland is Swan Island, which in the 1920s was reformed by dredging a new river channel; the island became the site of the city's first airport. There too, Portland Dahlia Gardens began growing dahlias in 1927. In the 1940s, now named Swan Island Dahlias, the company moved to acreage near Canby. The firm has become the nation's leading grower of dahlia bulbs.

dairy industry Dairy cattle have been part of the Oregon Country since **John McLoughlin** brought them to Fort Vancouver in the 1820s. Early American settlers of the 1840s customarily kept dairy cattle for home use. Making butter and cheese were two ways of preserving milk products, but it took later processes such as pasteurization to create a wide production and distribution of fresh milk. An interim step was condensed milk, which was perfected by the 1890s; a number of Oregon towns had milk condensaries by the 1910s. One railroad station, near Forest Grove, was named for the company that owned several condensed milk plants, Carnation (founded in Carnation, Washington). In the early 1920s, a Nestlé condensed milk plant in Bandon produced canned milk from Coos County cows for shipment to Asia. As the dairy industry grew, farmer-owned cooperatives emerged as a common way to pool production and market products such as **cheese**. Co-ops were formed in such dairy-strong counties as Clatsop, Tillamook, and Coos; other co-ops, such as the Mount Angel Creamery, were more local. Farmers Cooperative Creamery of Carlton, formed in 1931, expanded over the years; it purchased the Mount Angel co-op in 1969, and today markets Rose Valley butter, a former Mount Angel brand. Darigold, begun in 1918, is a regional brand

that emerged from a merger of a number of cooperatives. Other dairy companies such as Alpenrose contract to purchase milk from farmers.

As mega-dairies developed from the 1970s, many cooperatives closed or merged, and many small farmers went out of the dairy business. By 2000, counties such as Clatsop and Coos, where dairies once dominated agriculture and the local economy, had but a single dairy remaining. **Tillamook County** remained a stronghold, and the valleys of the Willamette, Umpqua and Rogue Rivers had dairies, but huge new operations were underway in the irrigated regions of Morrow County and other eastern Oregon locations, far from the lush meadows of the Oregon Coast.

Dallas The county seat of Polk County is located in an area that was settled by American emigrants in the 1840s. A community existed in the vicinity with the name Cythiana, after a town in Kentucky— or perhaps it was Cynthiana, or perhaps Cynthia Ann, after the wife of **Jesse Applegate**, or perhaps Cynthian. Place names historian Lewis L. McArthur posits them all, but cannot resolve the discrepancies. No matter: by 1852, it was Dallas, with a U.S. post office of that name, honoring George Mifflin Dallas, former vice president (1845–49) under James K. Polk, for whom the county is named. The townsite moved south a mile or so in the mid-1850s, and the community remained a small county seat for some years. Dallas was incorporated in 1874, and the 1880 census recorded 670 residents. The narrow gauge Oregonian Railway meandered into town from the north in 1880, helping to resolve a dispute over the location of the county seat. That honor was heartily desired by the town of **Independence**, some ten miles distant, which got a standard gauge railroad the same year; however, inertia prevailed.

The population of Dallas reached 1,271 in 1900, and shortly thereafter the character of the town changed with the development of major lumber processing facilities. In 1906, George Gerlinger and other investors began buying timber tracts in the Coast Range to the west, extending rail lines to **Falls City**, and then east to Salem. The population rose to 2,701 in 1920, and 4,793 in 1950. While the timber industry in the area declined and then collapsed after 1970, Dallas has retained an appeal as a residential area and increasingly is a bedroom community for Salem, some fifteen miles away. Its population in 1980 was 8,530; the estimate in 2007 was 15,065.

Dalles *see* **The Dalles**

Daly, Bernard (1854–1920) Bernard Daly was born in Ireland and came to the United States at the age of five. He studied medicine in Ohio and Kentucky, and came to Lake County as a newly minted physician in 1887. Dr. Daly established a practice that extended well beyond the borders of Lakeview, quickly acquiring a reputation for answering any call for help. Daly was elected to the state house of representatives in 1892, and to the senate in 1896. He served three terms as a Lake County judge (a term for commissioner); he also passed the Oregon bar and was appointed a (real) circuit judge in 1914. Daly served for twenty-six years on the county school board, owned the 7-T Ranch at Plush in the Warner Valley, and in his later years went into banking, helping to found the Bank of Lakeview in 1908 and serving as its president at the time of his death.

For all of his civic good works, Daly is best remembered for two things. The first was his heroic response in the aftermath of the catastrophic **Silver Lake** fire in the frigid winter of 1894, a disaster that killed some forty-seven people and injured scores of others. Daly slogged his way to the town, some hundred miles from Lakeview, stayed for three days, and charged no one a penny. The second was the establishment in his will of the Bernard Daly

Educational Fund, which since 1922 has given scholarships to graduates of the county's high schools to attend college.

Cooper, Forrest E. *Introducing Dr. Bernard Daly.* Lakeview, Oregon: Lake County Historical Society, 1986.

Damascus The Clackamas County city of Damascus was once a rural post office that opened in 1867; the origin of the name is not known. The post office closed in 1904, and the community in 1915 was described as having two sawmills, two churches, and a creamery; nearby, lumbering and logging took place, and farmers engaged in dairying, fruit growing, and general farming. In 1962, Damascus was briefly in the news when townspeople announced that they were holding the Little World's Fair, in competition with the Century 21 fair in Seattle. Oregon's land use regulations eventually put Damascus in the path of urbanization east of **Happy Valley**. Subdivisions supplanted berry fields with amazing speed, and in 2004, the town was incorporated; the population was estimated at 9,775 in 2007. In 2007, Damascus was reinstituted as a post office name.

Danes in Oregon Danes are well known in **Junction City**, due to an unusual immigration from the Midwest in the early 1900s. Danes also migrated to **Astoria** from the late nineteenth century into the twentieth, attracted by the fishing and logging opportunities there that also appealed to other Scandinavian nationals. A small community in Curry County is named Denmark, apparently in honor of the family of Capt. N. C. Lorentzen, which settled there in 1878.

Darigold *see* **dairy industry**

Davenport, Homer (1867–1912) The once-famous editorial cartoonist Homer Davenport was born in the Waldo Hills near **Silverton**. He moved to Silverton in 1874, where he did drawings, raised chickens, tended store. He set down recollections of his youth in *The Country Boy: The Story of his Own Early Life* (New York: Dillingham, 1910). After brief flings at business college and an art school, Davenport found work in 1889 with the Portland *Mercury* and the *Oregonian*, but did not stay long. In 1892, he got a job as cartoonist with William Randolph Hearst's *San Francisco Examiner*, from which he was booted straight to New York to Hearst's *New York Journal* in 1895. There he quickly made a name for himself lampooning capitalists and Tammany politicians.

To Oregonians, Davenport was a "local boy makes good" figure, a status that he enhanced both with his book and with his efforts at importing and raising Arabian horses: he had an exhibit of his horses at the **Lewis and Clark Centennial Exposition** in Portland in 1905. Davenport died of pneumonia in 1912, at the age of forty-five; he is buried in Silverton.

> Huot, Leland, and Alfred Powers. *Homer Davenport of Silverton: Life of a Great Cartoonist.* Bingen, Washington: West Shore Press, 1973.

Davidson, George (1825–1911) Born in England, Davidson came to the United States with his family in 1832. He was educated in Philadelphia, studied surveying, and got a desk position with the U.S. Coast Survey in Washington in 1845. By 1850, Davidson was in the field, on the Pacific Coast. His "Directory for the Pacific Coast of the United States" was issued in the *Coast Survey Report* in 1858, was re-issued separately in 1862, and formed the basis for the *Coast Pilot* series throughout the nation. As the National Oceanic and Atmospheric Administration has stated,

> His 1889 edition of the 'Coast Pilot of California, Oregon, and Washington' became the authoritative list of sailing directions for the west coast mariner, traced the origin of many of the names of features on our west coast, delineated the tracks of early explorers and navigators,

and contained over 400 sketches of pristine coastal views prior to the encroachment of civilization. This document is considered one of the great historic works detailing the geography and early exploration of our Pacific margin.

In his later years, Davidson concentrated on mapping in California, where he achieved even greater fame; the highest point in San Francisco, Mount Davidson, is named for him. He taught at and was a regent of the University of California, presided over the California Academy of Sciences, and garnered honors and appointments aplenty. Davidson's Oregon connection lies in his work charting the coastline, documenting its topography, and with his USCGS colleague Cleveland Rockwell, establishing the sites for its **lighthouses**.

Davis, Harold Lenoir (1894–1960) H. L. Davis was, rather briefly, the *enfant terrible* of Oregon literature. He was born in Douglas County in the then-declining town of Nonpareil. His father, a teacher, moved often, and the family was later in Antelope and The Dalles, east of the Cascade Range. Davis graduated from high school in The Dalles, and held a variety of short-term jobs; he also wrote poetry. His first publication was in the prestigious national magazine, *Poetry*, in 1919. He continued to write and publish poetry, and was encouraged by H. L. Mencken to try his hand at prose as well. In 1926, Davis and **James Stevens** issued a caustic appraisal of the state of literature in the Pacific Northwest, titled *Status Rerum*, which effected a dustup between those appraised and those appraising. Davis and his wife, Marion, moved to Seattle in 1928, and he began to turn out word sketches and stories for periodicals, including "A Town in Eastern Oregon" in Mencken's *American Mercury*: another caustic piece. Davis went to Mexico to work on a novel, which was issued in 1935 as *Honey in the Horn*. The book was a coming-of-age story set in eastern Oregon in pioneer times, and it was lavished with praise, won a Harper Prize, and then was awarded a Pulitzer Prize. The Davises moved to Napa, California, and he continued to write short stories and novels. None came up to the notoriety of his earlier pieces, though he was a successful writer. He died in Texas. *Honey in the Horn* is something of an Oregon classic: it the Oregon pioneer story, but lacking the warm glow and sugar coating and triumphalism of the pioneer stories laid down by the actual **pioneers**. The novel exhibits a realism that reflects the Depression period of its writing, and the experiences of its writer. While *Honey in the Horn* has often been reprinted, Davis still lacks a good biography.

Day, John (1771–1820) For someone who accomplished very little, John Day left an indelible imprint on the Oregon landscape—in the form of a slew of geographic names. Day was a professional hunter who was a member of Wilson Price Hunt's overland contingent of fur trappers and traders, sent west from Saint Louis in 1811 by **John Jacob Astor** to establish a fur post at the mouth of the Columbia River. Day and another member of the party, Ramsay Crooks, became separated from the group along the Snake River, and made a truly horrific and mad dash westward on their own, being robbed of even their clothes along the tortuous way. Day was literally driven mad by the experience, but he arrived at the new Fort Astoria in May 1812, some three months after the Hunt party. The geographic names include the **John Day River** (Day's rescue occurred near its confluence with the Columbia River) and the town of **John Day**; oddly, another John Day River can be found near Astoria, and a former railroad station at its mouth is also named John Day. Secondary place names include **Dayville** and the **John Day Dam**, both named for the (easternmost) river.

Dayton The Yamhill County town of Dayton is located on the Yamhill River a few miles upstream from its confluence with the Willamette. It was settled in 1848 by Andrew Smith and **Joel Palmer**, and had a post office in 1851. The town was a rural commercial center, where farmers brought their wheat and produce for shipment downriver to Portland and other markets. In 1878, a narrow-gauge railroad opened, running twenty-three miles to Sheridan and connecting the steamboat landings at Dayton with farmers upriver; this became the nucleus of a small rail system through the Willamette Valley in the 1880s, although a re-alignment soon cut Dayton off the line entirely. Dayton was incorporated in 1880, when the census reported its population as 368; by 1900, it was down to 293. Agriculture thrived, however, especially filberts and walnuts, hops, and livestock raising and dairying. In 1911, a blockhouse from long-abandoned **Fort Yamhill** was placed in the town square, where it has resided ever since. By 1915, Dayton had a fruit cannery, factories making boxes and tool handles, and a creamery. The population reached 506 in 1940 and 949 in 1970. Substantial residential growth has occurred since 1970, with commuters who work in McMinnville and Newberg. Grape growing and winemaking have made inroads into the economy since 1980, and the Joel Palmer house emerged in the 1990s as a notable restaurant with a menu that emphasized local mushrooms. Dayton's population in 2007 was estimated at 2,495.

Dayville A post office was established in 1868 about three miles west of the present community, which is located on the **John Day River** at its confluence with the South Fork. Stock raising was joined in the early 1900s by the irrigated farming of alfalfa and some fruit, and the town was incorporated in 1914 when its population was about 100. Dayville positions itself as a "gateway" to the John Day Fossil Beds National Monument, although that might be a conceit. Several nearby guest ranches and tourist accommodations are available for those who visit the fossil beds or hunt. The population in 2007 was about 175.

Deady, Matthew Paul (1824–1893) Born in Maryland, schooled in West Virginia and Ohio, trained as both a blacksmith and a lawyer, Matthew Paul Deady arrived in Oregon in 1849, where he taught and practiced at **Lafayette**. He was elected to the territorial legislature in 1851 and served on the territorial supreme court from 1853 to 1859. In 1857, Deady presided over the convention that drafted the constitution for Oregon's future statehood, which came in 1859. He was appointed U.S. District Judge for Oregon in 1859, and moved to Portland, where he was instrumental in the founding of the Library Association of Portland. From 1873 until his death, he was president of the board of regents of the **University of Oregon**, which alone explains why the university's first building, designed by W. W. Piper and constructed in 1873–76, is named Deady Hall.

Deady was a prolific diarist, writer, and commentator, and his impact on the social and political life of Oregon lasted for four decades; his codification of Oregon laws, which he undertook between 1859 and 1866, was the handbook for lawyers for many decades longer, until it was replaced by the Oregon Revised Statutes in 1953.

Deady, Matthew P. *Pharisee among Philistines: The Diary of Judge Matthew P. Deady, 1871–1892.* Ed. Malcolm Clark, Jr. Portland, Oregon: Oregon Historical Society, 1975.

deer Deer are common wildlife in Oregon, and have been an important source of food for millennia. Mule deer occur in two subspecies: *Odocoileus hemionus hemionus*, found scattered throughout open woodlands in eastern Oregon, and *Odocoileus hemionus columbianus*, the black-tailed deer of western Oregon, which favors clearcuts and brushy areas. There are also small bands of Columbia white-tailed deer, *odocoileus virginianus*, which were once common in western Oregon wetlands and the grassy prairies and oak groves of the Willamette and Umpqua River Valleys. Decimated by loss of habitat and over-hunting, they are confined to a few islands in the lower Columbia River and in woodlands near Roseburg. *Odocoileus virginianus ochrourus*, the yellow-tailed subspecies of the white-tailed deer, was also once found along the eastern edge of the Cascade Range; it is still found in the Blue Mountains of eastern Oregon.

Delake *see* **Lincoln City**

Depoe Bay The community of Depoe Bay takes its name from a Siletz Indian, William Charles DePoe, and his wife, Matilda, who owned the land from the 1890s. Their heirs sold the property in the 1920s to the Sunset Investment Company, which platted the townsite. The **Oregon Coast Highway** reached the area in 1927, bridging the narrow gap that is the entrance to the small harbor and bringing vacationers and residents to the region. One of the Sunset investors, Harvey L. Collins, opened an aquarium that year, and the post office was established in 1928. The Whale Inn opened in 1930. Inspired by a seafaring tragedy that took place in 1936, an annual festival to honor those lost at sea began on Memorial Day in 1945, now known as the Fleet of Flowers. The small harbor has hosted commercial fishing boats, but primarily serves pleasure craft and sports fishing charter boats. Depoe Bay was incorporated in 1973, and the 1980 census reported a population of 723; in 2007, it was estimated at 1,355. The quaint aquarium, upstaged by **Newport**, closed in 1998.

Deschutes County In 1916, a chunk of western Crook County was sliced off to form Deschutes County, named for the river. The county has 3,055 square miles; in 1920, 9,622 residents were counted. The county seat is **Bend**; the first county offices were held in rented rooms, and the county court met in an office building until 1935. In that year, the county decided to purchase the former high school to use as the courthouse; though built of brick, the building was destroyed by fire in 1937, along with most of the county records. A new courthouse opened in 1940.

The western portion of Deschutes County was part of the homeland of the **Molala Indians**, a tribe that was active on both sides of the Cascade Range for much the length of the state. To the east were the **Northern Paiute Indians**. The Molala had small winter settlements, and tended to spend warmer months hunting for elk, deer and other game, salmon and steelhead trout, camas, nuts, and berries. The Molala were severely impacted by diseases brought to the area by white explorers and traders, and the population was greatly reduced by the 1830s. Descendants of the Molala are enrolled among the **Confederated Tribes of Grand Ronde** and the **Klamath Indians**. The Northern Paiutes ranged from the south and east to the Deschutes River, where they obtained salmon and traded with other groups.

The impetus for the creation of Deschutes County was in great measure the quick impact of the arrival of the **Oregon Trunk** and **Union Pacific** railroads in 1911. This led to the construction of two immense lumber mills at Bend in 1916, and stimulated the development of agricultural irrigation projects. A 1915 promotional booklet noted that "From any eminence in the [Deschutes] valley is viewed an extent of timber so vast that the giant trees in the distance look like the grass of the rolling meadow." These pine forests were ripe for the plucking, and the work went on until the 1970s. The irrigation projects were troubled, but did lead to the raising of potatoes, alfalfa, mint, and other crops. Tourism was an early draw: sports fishermen came to cast lines in the Deschutes, and after World War II, activities such as **skiing** and whitewater rafting became popular. Major destination resorts such as **Sunriver** were developed beginning in the 1970s. By 2000, Bend and vicinity were in the midst of huge population growth and development pressures, exacerbated by an influx of retirees and telecommuters. The county's population reached 21,812 by 1950,

and then jumped to 30,442 in 1970, 74,958 in 1990, and an estimated 160,810 in 2007.

► **Detroit** In the twenty-first century, Detroit is a small Linn County tourist town that caters to boaters and other users of the still waters of the North Santiam River behind **Detroit Dam**. In the 1890s, Detroit was a projected waypoint on a transstate railroad, the Willamette Valley & Coast, which linked Yaquina Bay to Albany en route to Boise and points east. A post office opened in 1891, but in 1893, financial troubles made Detroit the end of the overly ambitious railroad line; it was extended to its final terminus four miles east at **Idanha** in 1895. In 1915, the population was reported to be fifty, supported by "general farming, lumbering, fruit and stock raising." Detroit also hosted tourists who fished in the North Santiam or took the waters at the nearby **Breitenbush Hot Springs**, which became popular in the 1920s. The construction of Detroit Dam required moving the townsite to higher ground in 1952; the same year brought municipal incorporation. Detroit had a population of about 265 in 2007.

Detroit Dam Willamette River Valley business owners worked in the 1930s to promote a plan for the management of regional water resources, intending to reduce seasonal flooding as well as provide hydroelectric power and improve navigation and irrigation. The U.S. Army Corps of Engineers provided the Willamette River Project plan in 1937 and began its implementation in the 1940s. Detroit Dam on the North Santiam River, completed in 1952, is one of the most prominent of some dozen dams in the project, and the reservoir behind the dam is popular for recreational boating.

Diamond Craters The Diamond Craters in Harney County is an area of about five square miles where a series of volcanic events took place an estimated 6,000 to 25,000 years ago. The blasted land is pocked with craters, fissures, lava flows, and cinder cones. The name is taken from the nearby settlement of Diamond, a rural post office established in 1887 and itself named for the diamond-shaped brand of rancher Mace McCoy.

Discovery *see* **Vancouver, George**

Donald Donald is located in Marion County at the northern end of **French Prairie**. It was established in a long-settled farming area as a station on the **Oregon Electric Railway**, which was opened across the prairie in 1908. Robert L. Donald, chief engineer of the Oregon Electric, was the honoree for whom the station was named. A post office opened in 1910, and the town was incorporated in 1912. The railway constructed an electric substation in Donald, which has stood, abandoned, since electric traction was

discontinued in 1945. A 1915 booklet described the area's agricultural endeavors: "Grains, grasses, hay, clover, hops, fruits, berries, potatoes, vegetables and dairying; hogs, sheep, goats and poultry."

Situated off the Pacific Highway and Interstate 5, Donald remained a small rural shipping point for many decades; the population in 1915 was estimated at 160. It hovered near that figure until 1970, when 231 residents were reported, and has since climbed with increasing suburban development; in 2007, the estimate was 995 residents.

Donation Land Act The Donation Land Claim Act of 1850 (the "Claim" is often dropped) was enacted by Congress both to give an avenue to legitimize the de facto claims of settlers already in the new **Oregon Territory**, and to authorize new claims. Its enactment presaged the later Homestead Act,

This panorama was taken about 1912, showing the town of Detroit along the North Santiam River. The railroad tracks lead upstream another four miles to Idanha. William L. Jones photo. Oregon Historical Society, OrHi 75633.

and it helped swell the ranks of American emigrants to Oregon, despite the enticements of the California gold rush. Oregon's **provisional government** had provided for land claims of up to 640 acres for each married couple, and 320 acres for single persons; the 1850 law voided the provisional government act, but was so worded as to legitimize existing claims. The act of September 27, 1850, granted 160 acres to unmarried white males aged eighteen or older, and 320 acres to every married couple, provided the claimants arrived in the Oregon Territory before December 1, 1850. An unusual provision of the law was that in the case of claims by married couples, each owned half of the claim in their own name; this was one of the first instances of married women being explicitly permitted to hold property individually. The law also permitted claims by those who were half of Indian descent; this provision legitimized claims by the many children of early settlers who had an Indian parent. Those who arrived after the December 1, 1850 deadline but before December 1, 1854, could stake claims of 160 acres for a couple or 80 acres for an individual. A total of 7,437 patents—that is, titles to the land—were issued by the end of 1855. Claims were filed through offices in Oregon City, Roseburg, and The Dalles. The nature of the procedure also demanded the surveying of the lands claimed, work which commenced very quickly; the establishment of the **Willamette Stone** was part of that process.

Following the end of the original claim period, land was no longer available free in the Oregon Territory, but it could be purchased from the federal government for $1.25 per acre for up to 320 acres; the price later increased, and the acreage was reduced. In 1862, the Homestead Act was passed, which had a tremendous impact in the Great Plains region but was also applicable in Oregon. The donation land claims have had a significant impact on Oregon's landscape; maps and land records make frequent reference to donation land claim, or DLC, boundaries.

Donner und Blitzen River Commonly called Blitzen River, this drains the west slope of **Steens Mountain** in Harney County and flows north to empty into landlocked Malheur Lake. The name is from the German for "thunder and lightning," and was applied during a thunderstorm experienced by Oregon volunteers under Col. George B. Currey, who were patroling the area in 1864.

► **Dorchester Conference** This annual spring gathering and of Oregon's Republican party began with a meeting called by State Representative (later U.S. Senator) Robert Packwood in 1964. It was held at the Dorchester House in Oceanlake (now **Lincoln City**), a noted seashore restaurant and inn beginning in the 1930s. The conference has continued to meet on the Oregon coast, usually at Seaside. From its inception, it has been considered to be a forum for "moderate" Republicans with a commitment to the political process, which caused the conference to be marginalized through much of the 1980s and 1990s.

Double O Ranch The Double O Ranch in the Warm Springs Valley near **Harney Lake** was established by Amos W. Riley and James A. Hardin about 1875. It was purchased about 1895 by **Bill Hanley**, who expanded it into Harney County's largest cattle ranch, with some 25,000 acres, and a showplace where he brought guests to experience the wildlife as well as ranch life. The ranch became part of the Malheur National Wildlife Refuge in 1941, and is listed in the National Register of Historic Places. The town of Riley remembers one of the founders; also a rural public school is named the Double O.

Douglas, David (1799-1834) Scotsman David Douglas studied math and science, and worked with the botanical gardens in Glasgow. The Horticultural Society of London intended to send him to China as a plant collector, but diplomatic difficulties sent him instead to the eastern United States in 1823. The success of that venture paved the way for the Society and the **Hudson's Bay Company** to send him on a collecting trip to the Columbia River region, which he began in 1824. He was the first botanist to explore the region with some rigor. He arrived at **Fort Vancouver** in 1825, and over the next two years covered almost 4,000 miles, traveling at first with trapping parties, and later alone with an Indian guide. He studied and gathered specimens, and was responsible for introducing a number of Pacific Northwest plants to Europe. Douglas returned to England in 1827, but later visited California and Hawai'i; he was again at Fort Vancouver in 1833. In 1834, Douglas fell into a wild cattle trap while in Hawai'i and was fatally gored. The **Douglas-fir** is named for him, as is a Portland-area school district.

Douglas, David. *The Oregon Journals of David Douglas.* Ed. David Lavender. 2 vols. Ashland, Oregon: Oregon Book Society, 1972.

Morwood, William. *Traveler in a Vanished Land-scape; the Life and Times of David Douglas.* New York: C. N. Potter, 1973.

► **Douglas County** Douglas County was created in 1852, carved from the doomed **Umpqua County** of 1851. It was named for Senator Stephen A. Douglas of Illinois, an advocate of Oregon statehood. It was added to in 1856 and further amended in 1915, to arrive at its present area of 5,071 square miles. The first meeting of the county commissioners was held at Winchester in 1853; an 1854 election designated Deer Creek, now **Roseburg**, as the county seat. There has been a succession of courthouses, built in 1855, 1870, 1891, and 1929; the last is still in use. The area now included in Douglas County was in the past the homeland of several Indian tribes, including the **Takelma Indians** to the south, the Upper Umpqua bands of **Athapaskan Indians**, and the Lower Umpqua bands of the **Siuslaw Indians**. The **Cow Creek Band of Umpqua Tribe of**

The "Cape Cod inspired" Dorchester House at Oceanlake (now part of Lincoln City), as it appeared about 1945. *Oregon Journal* photograph. Oregon Historical Society, CN 005419.

Indians was federally recognized in 1982, and is headquartered at Canyonville.

Douglas County outside of the valley of the Umpqua River is heavily forested, and logging and lumbering have been economic mainstays since the 1880s, when railroads made it feasible to ship lumber products. Virtually every Douglas County community has or had a lumber mill, with large mills at Roseburg, Winston, and Sutherlin. Agriculture has also been important, especially fruit orchards, livestock, and, for many decades, **turkeys**. Nickel mining and refining was carried on at **Riddle** from the 1950s. Douglas County's population was 9,596 in 1880, and 19,674 by 1910. It reached 94,748 in 1980; timber harvest reductions slowed the growth for several years, but by 2007, Douglas County had an estimated population of 104,675.

Douglas-fir The hyphen is a clue (at least to those trained in botany) that this tree, the state tree of Oregon and a ubiquitous driver of the state's economy, is not, really, a fir tree: it is a false hemlock, which might not be too helpful a clarification. Nevertheless, *Pseudotsuga menziesii* (that Latin term honors Archibald Menzies, a Scots naturalist who first described the tree to the scientific community in 1791, rather than the other Scotsman, **David Douglas**, whose 1820s explorations also contributed to knowledge of it and gave it its common name) is a tree to be reckoned with. When Euro-Americans first encountered the Oregon Country, stands of Douglas-fir, usually mixed with western hemlock and other conifers, blanketed the foothills of the western slope of the Cascade Range and the eastern slope of the Coast Range Mountains, and were found throughout the westernmost third of the state.

The raising of poultry, such as the chickens seen here, but most especially of turkeys, was once a major industry in Douglas County. The poultry yard of the Franz family near Sutherlin is pictured in this 1911 photograph, which was taken for the Southern Pacific Company to promote agricultural settlement in the county. Oregon Historical Society, OrHi 106087.

Economically, Douglas-fir has dominated Oregon's **wood products industry** from its inception in the 1850s. Douglas-fir has been used to make dimensional lumber, masts for sailing ships, plywood, furniture, and laminated wooden beams; pulp and paper; and it has been farmed for **Christmas trees**. The trees easily grow 200 feet in height and, historically, they frequently exceeded 300 feet in height. Douglas-firs can live 350 to 750 years. Most of the privately held Douglas-fir forests in Oregon were systematically logged during the period between 1890 and 1940; **forest fires**, often tied to logging activities, also wiped out much old-growth Douglas-fir, such as in the **Tillamook Burn** in the 1930s.

downwinders The people known as downwinders are those who lived in the path of prevailing winds that passed over the Hanford Nuclear Reservation in southeastern Washington from 1944 until the 1970s. In that period, activities at Hanford released a variety of radioactive isotopes into the atmosphere, including iodine-131 and airborne particles of plutonium, ruthenium, strontium, and cesium. Iodine-131 has a brief half-life of eight days, but large quantities were released, especially in 1945 and 1949. These activities were clandestine for many years, but came to public attention with evidence of excessive radiation ingestion in "downwind" areas, appearing especially in milk from cows or goats that had foraged on contaminated plants. Affected humans—affected both by damages to crops and livestock and by long-term personal health problems—have been engaged in legal actions with the federal government over the Hanford situation since 1990.

► **Doyle, Albert Ernest** (1877–1928) The work of architect A. E. Doyle had a major impact on the shape of downtown Portland in the first quarter of the twentieth century. Born in Santa Cruz, California, Doyle was a child when his family moved to Portland. At the age of fourteen he began to work as an apprentice in the architectural offices of **Wil-**

liam Whidden and **Ion Lewis**; he continued there for a dozen years. In 1903, Doyle went east to study architecture at Columbia University. He worked briefly in the New York City office of Henry Bacon, architect of the Lincoln Memorial, and he traveled to Athens in 1906 to study classical architecture. In 1907, Doyle returned to Portland, where he established a practice with William B. Patterson. They were almost immediately successful, garnering a

The sleek form of the new Equitable Building, designed by A. E. Doyle, rises behind workers engaged in demolishing in 1950 the former headquarters building of the *Oregonian* building, which had been built in 1894.
Oregonian collection. Oregon Historical Society, CN 009023.

commission for a new building for the **Meier & Frank** department store. Patterson left the firm in 1915, and Doyle carried on his office alone.

Between 1909 and 1918, Doyle's hand was on the designs for the **Lipman, Wolfe & Company** department store, a number of downtown office buildings, the master plan and major buildings for **Reed College**, the U.S. National Bank Building, and Central Library. In the 1920s, there were more banks, more office buildings, and several large residences; Doyle also did work in the Seattle area. His work was usually in the Renaissance revival and Classical revival styles, with extensive use of brick and glazed terra cotta. Doyle was also fluent in other styles; he designed rustic beach cabins and the lodge at **Multnomah Falls**. In the mid-1920s, Doyle's health began to fail; in 1925 he took on **Pietro Belluschi** as an assistant. Doyle died in 1928; the firm carried on with Belluschi and colleague William Hamblin Crowell. In 1943, A. E. Doyle & Associates was reorganized as Pietro Belluschi, Architect. According to architectural historian Richard Ellison Ritz, Doyle left "an indelible mark on Portland architecture" in both buildings and protégés.

► **Drain** The site of this Douglas County community was settled in 1847, and was purchased by Charles C. and Anna Drain in 1861. The construction of the Oregon & California Railroad through the area prompted the Drains to plat the townsite in 1872. The Methodist Church established a school to train teachers in 1883; two years later, the state legislature named it Central Oregon Normal School; "in its palmy days it had 12 teachers." Funded initially by both church and state, the school finally closed in 1908. Fires swept through the downtown district in 1903, and again in 1914. Drain was incorporated in 1887, and the 1900 census showed a population of 193.

Lumbering and agriculture supported the town, and by 1940, the population reached 637. Increased lumber mill activity boosted that to 1,204 in 1970;

the estimated population in 2007 was 1,075. The elaborate Queen Anne style residence of Charles and Anna Drain, built in 1893–95, is on the National Register of Historic Places, as is the Charles Hasard house; both were designed by Tennessee architect George F. Barber, who sold the plans by mail.

Drake, Sir Francis (ca. 1540–1596) The connection of the English privateer and globe-girdler with the state of Oregon is tenuous at best. Sir Francis Drake reported encountering "the most vile, thicke and stinking fogges" along the Pacific Coast, and it is quite possible that he briefly viewed landfall near Cape Blanco in 1578. The *Golden Hind* turned south and was beached for repairs at what is today Drakes Estero north of the Golden Gate. Assertions that Drake landed at Whale Cove, Boiler Bay, or any other Oregon point lack evidence.

Drake, June D. (1880–1969) His given name was somewhat unusual, and his middle initial was just

The ill-fated Oregon Normal School at Drain is pictured about 1905. Markham Studio photograph. Oregon Historical Society, OrHi 82067.

that: an initial, no name. June Drake was born in Marquam, Marion County, and moved with his family to **Silverton** in 1889; his father, Charles, came to own the Commercial Hotel in town, and served a term as mayor. With his brother Emory, June founded the Drake Brothers photography studio, buying out the business of William L. Jones. They ran the studio until 1908, when Emory left; shortly thereafter, the studio burned, with the loss of thousands of negatives. June rebuilt the business, and operated it until his retirement in 1960.

Drake's photography business was grounded in portraits, town scenes, and scenic views. He also used his business to advocate for the preservation and development of a scenic landscape that he came to treasure, located a few miles from his home town: **Silver Creek Falls**. Beginning about 1902, he photographed the falls and produced booklets and brochures to raise awareness of them, urging the state to acquire the land to protect it from loggers, who had already skimmed the trees from much of the surrounding hills. The efforts of Drake and other citizens succeeded in 1931. State parks head **Samuel H. Boardman** was pleased to see the park officially open in 1933. Drake erected many of the original signs in the park, and Drake Falls is named for him.

▶ **D River** This exceedingly short (120 feet) river with the exceedingly short name links Devils Lake with the Pacific Ocean at **Lincoln City**. It is sometimes reputed to be the world's shortest river, but this is one of those dubious and ultimately inane distinctions that is widely contested by advocates for the claims of other watercourses. Its name is its greatest distinction.

dry side The term refers to Oregon east of the **Cascade Range**; to the west is the **wet side**.

duck potato *see* **wapato**

The mouth of the D River at Delake (now Lincoln City) as it appeared in the mid-1950s. *Oregon Journal* photograph. Oregon Historical Society, OrHi 106089.

Ducks The mascot of the **University of Oregon** athletic teams is a duck. Since the time of a legendary handshake in 1947 between Walt Disney and athletic director Leo Harris (an agreement not formalized in writing until 1973, some time after Mr. Disney's death and well after the rise of litigiousness in such matters of copyright), the duck has very much resembled Donald Duck. The origin of the symbol appears to go back to the idea that Oregonians—at least those on the **wet side**—have webbed feet. Thus the term "**webfoot**" was sometimes used in the early 1900s to refer to a University of Oregon student, as it had earlier been applied to any Oregonian. In the 1920s, sports supporters at the university were known to bring a real, wild duck, named Puddles, to events; however, there was concern for the animal's welfare in this wild fraternity-boy environment, and the practice was halted. Then came Disney. Alumni should be grateful that a silly goose did not become the mascot, apt though it might be for characterizing many fans. *See also* **Civil War (football game)**.

Dufur The Wasco County town of Dufur is located on the Columbia Plateau south of The Dalles, an area where white settlement occurred with the development of stock ranches in the 1850s and 1860s. Brothers Andrew J. and E. Burnham Dufur purchased a farm in the area in 1859. A rural post office named for them opened in 1878, and the community that grew around it was incorporated in 1893; the 1900 census counted 336 residents. The grandiloquently named Great Southern Railroad arrived from The Dalles in 1905, bringing a new outlet for the wheat, barley, oats, and other crops grown in the area. In the early 1900s, fruit—apples, pears, and cherries—was the coming crop. The three-story brick Balch Hotel, now on the National Register of Historic Places, opened in 1907, and the railroad was extended a few miles farther to the now-vanished town of Friend in 1912. Dufur's population peaked in 1920 at 533 people.

The Great Southern faded fast, and was abandoned in 1936 as roads improved throughout the region. Dufur endured a period of somnolence. Its population was 493 in the 1970 census, but the introduction of an annual Threshing Bee in 1971 perhaps spurred a renewed appreciation of Dufur's heritage. Dufur's population was estimated at 655 in 2007.

Dundee The name Dundee is a tangible link to the town's origins as a railroad center in Yamhill County. Although the area had been settled by emigrant farmers beginning in the 1840s, the community came into being with the investment of Scotch financiers, led by William Reid (1844–1914), who came to Oregon from Dundee, Scotland, in 1874. In 1880, Reid's cash infusion saved the faltering Oregon Railway, a narrow-gauge line that was planned to connect Willamette Valley farmers with Portland. Reid's plans called for Dundee to be the nerve center of a network of lines that extended south to McMinnville and Airlie, north to Portland, and across the Willamette and along the east side of the valley to Coburg, with a massive bridge at Fulquartz Landing near Dundee and railroad shops in the town itself. With prosperity in view, the Dundee post office was opened in 1882.

But plans faltered again, and by the early 1890s, the Southern Pacific Company had acquired the fragmented narrow-gauge lines, converted them to standard gauge, and merged them into their network of Willamette Valley rail lines. Dundee settled down as a small agricultural center, and was incorporated in 1895. In the early decades of the twentieth century, the nearby Dundee Hills and **Chehalem Mountains** became a noted center for nut culture, especially walnuts ("Walnut groves said to be among the largest in the United States") and then hazelnuts. Prunes were also popular for many years, and fruit and nut dryers and packing plants were signatures of Dundee and its vicinity. Since the 1970s, grape growing and winemaking have replaced fruits and nuts in Dundee's economy, and residential growth has burgeoned. Dundee had a population of 124 in the 1900 census, and 308 in 1950; 1980 reported 1,223, and the estimate in 2007 was 3,040.

Dunes City This coastal community in Lane County was created by residents who were concerned they might be adversely impacted by proposals to establish a national park in the nearby sand dunes. Dunes City was incorporated in 1963; it is not a post office address. The national park concept did not come to pass, but the Oregon Dunes National Recreation Area was finally created in 1972. The focus of activity in Dunes City has subsequently been to provide rental sites and facilities to support dune buggy rides, whereby people may career over the once-spectral dunes with much noise and enthusiasm. The population of Dunes City in 1970 was 976; the estimated population in 2007 was 1,360.

► **Duniway, Abigail Jane (Scott)** (1834–1915) Born in Illinois, Abigail accompanied her family on the overland trek to Oregon in 1852; her mother and a young brother died en route, events she recorded in her journal. Abigail taught school near Salem before marrying Benjamin C. Duniway in 1852. Benjamin was injured in 1862, and Abigail had to return to teaching to help raise their children; she took up millinery work and operated a hat shop in Albany for several years. Abigail had also begun writing; her first novel, *Captain Gray's Company; or, Crossing the Plains and Living in Oregon*, was published in 1859.

In 1871, the Duniway family moved to Portland, where her brother, **Harvey W. Scott**, edited the *Oregonian* newspaper. Duniway began a weekly newspaper, *The New Northwest*, which advocated equal rights for women, a cause she had good reason to champion. The same year, she organized the two-month tour of the Pacific Northwest of national suffragist leader Susan B. Anthony. In 1873, she was one of the founders of the Oregon State Women Suffrage Association, and she began to tour and talk on behalf of the cause. She wrote editorials for her newspaper, as well as serial novels that helped boost the readership. Duniway's approach to the suffrage issue differed from that of many of her East Coast allies, who frequently were also in favor of the **prohibition** of liquor. Duniway preferred moderation to prohibition, and cautioned that tying the issues together alienated many otherwise supportive men—who often expressed concern that giving women the vote could mean the end of certain "masculine" practices.

Publication of *The New Northwest* ceased in 1887, and Duniway turned her attentions to Idaho, where she and her family lived on a ranch in the Pahsimeroi Valley. She returned to Portland in 1894. Idaho granted women the right to vote in 1896, the fourth state to do so; Washington did so in 1910, and Oregon, finally, voted for equal suffrage in 1912. Among those she never convinced was her influential brother, Harvey Scott. Abigail wrote, and signed, along

Suffragist and author Abigail Scott Duniway is pictured marking her ballot at the first non-local election in Oregon where women could cast a vote, in Portland in 1912. *Oregonian* photograph. Oregon Historical Society, OrHi 4601a.

with governor **Oswald West**, the proclamation, and she was the first woman in the state to officially register to vote. Her autobiography was published a year before her death: *Path Breaking; an Autobiographical History of the Equal Suffrage Movement in Pacific Coast States.*

Edwards, G. Thomas. *Sowing Good Seeds: The Northwest Suffrage Campaigns of Susan B. Anthony.* Portland, Oregon: Oregon Historical Society Press, 1990.

Moynihan, Ruth Barnes. *Rebel for Rights, Abigail Scott Duniway.* New Haven, Connecticut: Yale University Press, 1983.

Dunthorpe An enclave of expensive residences on Palatine Hill, Dunthorpe is an unincorporated community just south of Portland in Multnomah County. It was developed in the 1920s.

Durham This Washington County community was known since the 1870s as Durhams Mills, centered on the sawmill and flouring mill built on Fanno Creek by Alonzo A. Durham. The Oregon Electric Railway built through the area in 1908 and named the station Durham; it is not a post office address. With the construction of Interstate 5 nearby in the 1960s, Durham experienced suburban growth. The area was incorporated as a city in 1966; the 1970 census reported a population of 410, which had increased to an estimated 1,395 by 2007.

Dye, Eva Emery (1855–1947) Eva Dye and her physician husband came to Oregon in 1890 with their family, settling in Oregon City. Dye had been educated at Oberlin College in Ohio, and brought with her interests in education—she frequently spoke at **chautauquas**—as well as temperance and woman's suffrage. And she was a writer and a poet. She quickly took an interest in the history of her new homeland, and in the early 1900s produced several works of historical fiction that were notable not only for their historical grasp and drama, but also for their impact on popular views of history. Dye had a romantic flair, and she saw Oregon's history in terms of America's manifest destiny. In *McLoughlin and Old Oregon* (1900) Dye wrote of the fur trade, and she gave to McLoughlin a stature that he has retained; the 1909 preservation of McLoughlin's Oregon City house, now part of the Fort Vancouver National Historic Site, owes much to Dye. In *McDonald of Oregon* (1906), Dye set forth the dramatic life of **Ranald McDonald**. Dye's most influential book was published in 1902: in *The Conquest: The True Story of Lewis and Clark*; Dye admitted that she waxed expansive on the role of **Sacajawea** in the **Lewis and Clark Expedition**. The results included the entwining of Sacajawea with the idea of woman's suffrage and the perception that she literally guided the Corps of Discovery to the Pacific shores; they also inspired the erection of a statue of Sacajawea at the **Lewis and Clark Centennial Exposition**. Dye's view of Indians swung from doomed savage to romantic remnant of a dying race; in writing of Sacajawea, she almost managed to make her "white"; as historian Katrine Barber has noted, "Her characterizations of conquest are as troubling as they are lasting."

Browne, Sheri Bartlett. *Eva Emery Dye: Romance with the West.* Corvallis: Oregon State University Press, 2004.

E

Eagle Creek The post office at Eagle Creek in Clackamas County was opened in 1867. It is near the Philip Foster farm, a pioneer landmark on the **Barlow Road** section of the **Oregon Trail**. The construction of a hydroelectric project on the upper Clackamas River in the early 1900s brought an electric **interurban railway** through Eagle Creek in 1906; by 1915, it was described as a village with a population of about 200, where "lumbering, general farming, fruit and berry raising, poultry and live stock raising, dairying," was carried on; there were flour and sawmills in the vicinity. The area is still a rural community.

Eagle Point Situated on Butte Creek in the Cascade Mountain foothills of Jackson County, the Eagle Point area was settled by farmers in the 1850s. A water-powered gristmill was erected on the creek about 1872; it has operated, off and on, since that time. The post office dates from the same year, named for a nearby cliff where eagles soared. In 1911, a railroad reached Eagle Point from Medford; the ambitious plans called for it to reach over the Cascades to eastern Oregon and beyond, and the plans encouraged Eagle Point to incorporate as a city that same year. By 1920, that dream had died; Eagle Point had a population of 128; the railroad became a logging line that for the next forty years carried logs to Medford mills. Eagle Point remained a rural agricultural town, where (in 1915) the principal crops were reported to be "apples, strawberries, blackberries, onions, wheat, corn and poultry products." After World War II, Eagle Point increasingly became a residential area for workers in the industries of nearby **White City**, and for Medford, a dozen miles to the south. The population of 607 in 1950 grew to 3,008 in 1980, and to an estimated 8,565 by 2007.

Eastern Oregon Normal School
see **Eastern Oregon University; Weston**

Eastern Oregon University With the demise of the Eastern Oregon Normal School in **Weston** in 1909, Oregon east of the Cascade Range was left without any state-supported institution of higher education. The legislature finally dealt with this situation in 1929 with the establishment of the (new) Eastern Oregon Normal School in La Grande. The name was changed to Eastern Oregon College of Education in 1939, and in 1941 it became a four-year, degree-granting school. In 1952, a master's program was added, and the name was changed, again, to Eastern Oregon College, in 1956. Although teacher training remained a key program, the school developed into a full liberal arts college in the 1960s, and in 1973 another name change produced Eastern Oregon State College. The addition of doctoral programs impelled yet another name change in 1997, when the school became Eastern Oregon University. Enrollment has remained modest for several decades at about 3,000 students.

Eastmoreland neighborhood, Portland
Eastmoreland is a purely residential neighborhood in Southeast Portland that was developed on lands that were part of **William S. Ladd**'s Crystal Springs Farm. The Ladd estate began breaking up this property in the early 1900s, when it sold a portion for the creation of **Reed College** and platted Eastmoreland immediately to the south of the new campus. A streetcar line reached the area in 1911, but lot sales went on slowly through the 1920s and 1930s. The neighborhood has no commercial district, but the Eastmoreland Grocery has maintained a precarious presence on the eastern edge of the subdivision since 1924.

east wind When "the east wind" blows, it has a major impact on residents in the Portland metropolitan area. In distinction from the prevailing winds, which come from the west or southwest over the Pacific Ocean, the east winds come through the Columbia River Gorge, bringing (in summer) hot, dry air from the Columbia Plateau. In winter, east winds bring bitterly cold air from the same region; if this collides with rainy weather in the Portland area, it brings not just freezing temperatures, but freezing rain. *See also* **Chinook wind**.

Echo Echo is a small rural trade center on the Umatilla River in Umatilla County, situated at a point where the **Oregon Trail** crossed the river in the 1840s and 1850s. Fort Henrietta was located near there during the Yakima War, 1855–56; a replica of the fort is in Echo. In anticipation of the opening of the **Union Pacific Railroad**'s transcontinental line, a post office was established at Echo in 1881, named for Echo Koontz, daughter of residents James H. and Cynthia Ann Koontz. A small town grew around the railroad station, and Echo was incorporated in 1904. Irrigation brought a new agricultural prosperity to the area in the early 1900s, and alfalfa, clover, fruit, and vegetables were added to the earlier livestock raising activities. Sheep and wool remained important products, and Echo once had a large wool scouring plant. Echo's population was 400 in 1910; it fell to 280 in 1940, rose to 500 in 1980, and was estimated at 710 in 2007.

Ecola *see* **Cannon Beach**

Ecotopia The novel *Ecotopia: The Notebooks and Reports of William Weston* was published in 1975, written by Ernest Callenbach. It describes an ideal future (1999) society situated along the North Pacific Coast, an area that broke away from the United States in 1980 to pursue an ecologically sustainable lifestyle. The novel had a tremendous impact in northern California and the Pacific Northwest, giving a push to the creation of "green" movements, to transit development, and to the notion of **Cascadia** as an identifiable bioregion.

Ecotrust *see* **C. Howard and Jean Vollum**

eels *see* **lamprey**

Egan (d. 1878) Egan, or E-He-Gant, was a headman among the **Northern Paiute Indians** in the 1860s and 1870s, a signer of the 1868 treaty that the U.S. Senate did not ratify and which created the Malheur Reservation. The continued influx of settlers and miners into southeast Oregon led to further armed conflict, culminating in the **Bannock War**. Egan was killed by Umatilla Indian scouts assisting the U.S. Army in 1878. There was a rural post office from 1882 to 1884 a few miles southwest of **Burns** that was named for Egan, and the name was also attached to a tavern in the vicinity in the late twentieth century.

Egan, H. Chandler (1884–1936) *see* **golf**

electric railways *see* **interurban railways; streetcars**

▶ **Elgin** The town of Elgin is located in Union County at the northern margin of the Grande Ronde Valley. The valley itself was extensively settled by farming families in the 1870s and 1880s. Elgin post office opened in 1885, and the town was incorporated in 1891, the same year that a branch railroad from La Grande arrived, connecting it with transcontinental service. The railroad line was extended to Joseph in 1908. Elgin's population was a reported 603 in 1900. Sawmills and agriculture, especially the production of potatoes and apples, bolstered Elgin's economy in the early years of the twentieth century. The population rose to more than a thousand people, served by a weekly newspaper and hosting an annual apple show each fall. The Elgin Opera

House opened in 1912, designed with the "improbable role" of housing both city offices and a theater.

The Depression years closed sawmills, and Elgin's population declined. It rebounded in the 1950s; lumber and plywood production have continued to support the town. The Elgin Opera House is on the National Register of Historic Places and is a tourist attraction, featuring weekly movies and a historical museum. Elgin's estimated population in 2007 was 1,685.

Eliot, Thomas Lamb (1841–1936) Born and raised in Saint Louis, Thomas Lamb Eliot was the son of a clergyman, and he was in the first graduating class (1862) of Washington University, which his father organized and administered. He subsequently attended Harvard Divinity School, married Henrietta Robins Mack (1865), and in 1867 received a call through the American Unitarian Association for a minister to serve in Portland, Oregon. Eliot went. In Portland, his liberal leanings and community activism made him a prominent citizen. Eliot served as the county public school superintendent in 1872–75, and presided over the Children's Home, the Oregon Humane Society, and an association of charities; he served on the board of directors of the Portland Art Association and the Library Association of Portland, of the American Unitarian Association and the Pacific Theological Seminary at Berkeley. After the death of a member of his congregation,

The students of Couch's high school perch on the porch above the store of Daniel Sommer and Company in Elgin in **1896.** Oregon Historical Society, OrHi 59777.

Simeon G. Reed, Eliot counseled his widow, Amanda, on the creation of **Reed College** with the monies he left. The first classroom building at the college was designated Eliot Hall. Eliot was also interested in mountaineering, and Eliot Glacier on Mount Hood near Cloud Cap Inn is also named for him.

elk The elk, *Cervus elaphus roosevelti*, is a four-footed ungulate of North America. It is sometimes called wapiti, derived from a Plains Indian term; in Oregon it is also known as the Roosevelt elk, while the same animal on Washington state's coast is called the Olympic elk. The elk is widely found in the Coast Range and Cascade Range, at higher elevations in the summer and coming down to lower fields during the winter. It was a favored meat of most Oregon Indians, and is hunted yet as a food source.

Elkton The community of Elkton is situated on the Umpqua River in Douglas County, very close to the historic site of the Hudson's Bay Company post of **Fort Umpqua** (1836–54). Elkton is on the Umpqua River, and the river was a historic trade route through the Coast Range for Indians and trappers, and by the 1850s, for gold miners and merchants involved in the mining excitement in southern Oregon. A post office was established at Elkton in 1851. **Umpqua County** was created in 1851, and the new county government first met in Elkton in 1852. But only once. In the early 1900s, plans were made for a railroad from Drain to the Coos Bay region via Elkton and the Umpqua River route, and construction began. The 1907 financial depression, as well as progress on another line to Coos Bay from Eugene, stopped the project. Just east of Elkton, a tunnel for the unbuilt railroad was converted to highway use in the early 1930s.

Elkton has been a waypoint for most of its existence, the site of small sawmills and dairy farms; in the 1910s, it had a creamery and a factory that made wooden handles. Since World War II, Elkton has been a resort area, and since the 1980s, vineyards and winemaking have come to town. Elkton was incorporated in 1948, and the 1950 census reported a population of 201. The estimated population in 2007 was 245.

Ellensburg *see* **Gold Beach**

Empire Grandly named Empire City was once a notable community on Coos Bay in Coos County. Its beginnings were with a company of adventurers from Jacksonville in the gold rush days of the 1850s, formed as the Coos Bay Company. The object was to use Coos Bay as a landing point for carrying supplies shipped from San Francisco to the interior mining towns. A townsite was established in 1854, and Empire City became the seat of the new **Coos County** in 1855. The post office opened in 1858 (the name was shortened to Empire in 1894).

Empire paled later in the century; the county seat went to Coquille in 1896, and North Bend and Marshfield (now the city of **Coos Bay**) came to dominate the area economy. While it was an incorporated municipality, it had a population of but 252 in the 1890 census, falling to 147 by 1910. It reached 665 by 1940, and wartime growth in the Coos Bay region made it 2,261 by 1950. Its post office was abolished in 1957, and in 1965 Empire voted to merge with the city of Coos Bay. The traces of its former separate existence have been almost obliterated.

Empire Builder The phrase "empire builder" has had many applications, but in the Pacific Northwest, it was widely used to characterize railroad magnate James Jerome Hill (1838–1916), who, without federal land grant assistance, built the transcontinental **Great Northern Railroad** line west from Saint Paul, Minnesota, to the Pacific Coast. The Great Northern reached Puget Sound in 1893; in 1908, the Hill-supported **Spokane, Portland & Seattle Railway** connected Portland with the Great Northern line at Spokane. The premier passenger train from Seattle and Portland to Saint Paul and Chicago, via the Great Northern, was the *Oriental Limited*, which began service in 1905 in connection with Hill's trans-Pacific steamship service from Seattle to Asia. In honor of Hill, a new train named the *Empire Builder* was placed in service in 1929. The train of that name has continued to the present over the same basic route, since 1971 under the operation of Amtrak, the national passenger railroad system.

The Oregon state song, "Oregon, My Oregon," written by J. A. Buchanan in 1920, refers to the Euro-American immigrants to the Pacific Northwest and their creation of an economic "empire" that displaced the Indian nations. *See also* **"Land of the Empire Builders."**

emus In the 1980s, some Oregon ranchers began experimenting with raising Australian emus for food. Oregon State University began a research program in 1995 regarding the raising of ratites: emus, ostriches, and rheas. After a flurry of interest in the 1990s, interest has subsided but a number of farmers raise emus, especially in the Willamette Valley.

Enterprise The city of Enterprise is on the Wallowa River at the base of the Wallowa Mountains and is the county seat of Wallowa County, which was formed in 1887. The Wallowa Valley was homeland for many Nez Perce Indians, until white settlers came to the area about 1871. Gold seeker and miners reached the area in the 1860s. In 1877, those Nez Perce allied with chief **Joseph** (ca. 1840–1904) declined to be forced to move to Idaho, precipitating the **Nez Perce War**.

Located in a remote valley, Enterprise formed around the cattle ranching that developed in the valley, and Enterprise post office opened in 1887. A railroad was expected to arrive from La Grande, and Enterprise was incorporated in 1889; the 1890 census gave it a population of 242. Railroad construction, however, stopped at Elgin in 1891, more than fifty miles shy of Enterprise.

The railroad finally arrived in 1908, and by 1910, the population had jumped to 1,242, and to 1,895 in 1920. In 1909, the town finally erected a county courthouse, too, having lacked such a facility for more than twenty years. The Wallowa Valley was then a prosperous area of farms, dairies, and livestock ranches. The railroad brought new lumber mills while some gold and silver mining continued; for a time quarries produced marble, granite, and other building stone.

Enterprise has remained a small trading center and seat of county government. Timber operations have continued, though the scale declined dramatically in the 1980s. The population of Enterprise has wavered over the years; in 2007, it was estimated at 1,990, a very slight increase over that in 1920.

Estacada Located on the Clackamas River in Clackamas County, Estacada was established as a townsite as a result of a hydroelectric power project. In 1903–05, the Oregon Water Power & Railway Company constructed a railroad up the Clackamas from Portland to supply materials for dam construction at what was known as the Springwater project. Estacada post office was founded in 1904 and the town was incorporated in 1905. By 1907, the project was producing power and sending it to Portland along transmission lines that followed the railway. The railway itself was powered by electricity, and Estacada quickly became a popular spot for day trips from the big city, for fishing, picnicking, and eating chicken dinners at the Hotel Estacada. Estacada's population was 405 in 1910.

The electric **interurban railway** also provided frequent service that gave rise to small farms supplying city markets. By 1915, Estacada was "surrounded by fertile uplands devoted to fruit raising, general farming, dairying and poultry raising." There were also several nearby sawmills, and lumber production continued through the 1960s. The foothills around Estacada are also used to grow **Christmas trees**, a major crop since the 1950s. Since 1980, Estacada has seen increased population from retirees and from workers who commute to jobs in the Portland suburban areas. The estimated population in 2007 was 2,965.

▶ **Eugene** The city of Eugene is the county seat of Lane County and the site of the **University of Oregon**, situated on the Willamette River near the confluence of the Coast and Middle Forks and the McKenzie River. It is named for its founder, Eugene Franklin Skinner (1809–1864), whose surname is attached to the butte that overlooks the city center from the north end of Willamette Street. Skinner erected a cabin at the site in 1846. A post office named Eugene City was established in 1853 (the "City" was dropped in 1889), and during the 1850s and 1860s, during high water, river steamboats served Eugene occasionally; it was also located near the **California-Oregon Trail**. The city of Eugene was incorporated in 1862, and the census of 1870 credited it with 861 residents. The **Oregon & California Railroad** reached Eugene from Portland in 1871, and connected it to California in 1887. The **University of Oregon** was established in Eugene in 1872, and opened in 1876. The city's population reached 1,117 in 1880 and 3,236 in 1900. Initially the trading center for an agricultural country, Eugene developed industrially in the early 1900s, and its population by 1910 was 9,009. Lumber and planing mills joined a woolen mill, flour mill, creamery, fruit and vegetable cannery, and an excelsior factory. Local farms were engaged in dairying and poultry raising, livestock raising, and growing fruits and

A view looking north toward Skinner's Butte on Willamette Street, the main commercial street of Eugene, in 1936. "Rhythm on the Range" with Bing Crosby and Frances Farmer is playing at the Rex Theatre, along with Mickey Rooney in "Down the Stretch." Seymour's Café was a city institution into the 1970s. Author's collection.

nuts such as **filberts**. Truck farming for local markets was also popular. The **Oregon Electric Railway** opened its interurban electric line to Portland in 1912.

The completion of the Natron Cutoff of the **Southern Pacific Company** in 1926 opened a new rail route over the Cascade Range to California, and made Eugene a major freight distribution center and railroad maintenance site. Lumber mills expanded again in the 1940s and 1950s, and the city became the nexus of the Oregon lumber industry during the mid-century years. During the 1970s and 1980s, the city was noted as a center of counterculture activities, the home of the **Oregon Country Fair** and the Hoedads (*see* **hoedad**), and just next door to **Springfield**, home of **Ken Kesey**. With the rapid shrinkage of logging operations beginning in the late 1970s, Eugene's economy relied more on the university, agriculture and food processing, and cultural tourism in the late twentieth century. Eugene's estimated population in 2007 was 153,690.

F

Fairview A rural Multnomah County community that has burgeoned into a residential suburb of Portland in recent decades, Fairview had its beginnings about 1855. The arrival of the railroad in 1882 resulted in a station by that name. In 1883, a post office named Cleone opened there, since the Fairview name was already in use elsewhere; Cleone was finally exchanged for Fairview in 1914. The town was incorporated in 1908, a year after the arrival of an electric **interurban railway** connecting Troutdale with Portland; Fairview became the location of a machine shop for the interurban line. In 1915, dairying, fruit growing, and truck farming were the principal activities, bolstered by a cheese factory. The 1910 census reported a population of 204; by 1950, it reached 438, and is estimated at 9,695 in 2007.

Falls City The rather modest but picturesque falls of the Little Luckiamute River gave rise to the name of this Polk County town. Located at the western edge of Willamette Valley agricultural lands, Falls City was endowed with a post office in 1889, and was incorporated as a municipality in 1893 (although the city website dates its inception to 1891). The town's pastoral quietude was disrupted in 1903 when a railroad was opened from **Dallas**, about ten miles to the east, to reach a rich timber belt in the Coast Range Mountains. Lumber mills followed and prosperity came with them; the population of 269 in 1900 mushroomed to an estimated 1,200 in 1915, but plummeted to 494 by 1930. It has been a quiet community since; the railroad left in the early 1960s, and the last of the mills shortly thereafter. The population in 2007 was estimated at 965.

farmers' markets The term "farmers' market" is used to refer to a (usually) seasonal, periodic (such as weekly), open-air (in most cases) marketplace where farmers have the opportunity to sell their products at retail, direct to the consumer. The market is usually organized by a local community group, or as a business enterprise, and often takes place in a public park or a private parking lot, with space (sheltered with tents, or not) rented to the farmers. Often other vendors, especially food-related merchants, can also rent space. In Oregon, the farmers' market movement dates from at least 1979, when the Lane County Farmers' Market began, which traces its origins to the Eugene public market that closed in 1959.

Farmers' markets have two main antecedents: roadside stands, and **public markets**. Individual roadside farm stands could be found along rural and suburban roads from the 1910s into the 1980s; some have survived beyond that time, and there has been a minor resurgence since the 1990s. All three options provide a way for farmers to bypass the "middle man," the wholesale dealer or broker, and thus increase the farmer's margin of profit, and all offer consumers fresher merchandise at competitive prices. Very different things are the crafts-centered affairs known as **Saturday Market** in Eugene and Portland.

Father of Oregon As officially designated by the state legislature in 1957, Dr. **John McLoughlin** is the father of Oregon. *See also* **Mother of Oregon**.

Fealy, Barbara (1903–2000) Born in Utah, raised there and in California, educated in Florida and Illinois, Barbara Fealy studied landscape architecture in the 1920s, one of the first women to venture into this field. She came to Oregon from Utah in 1947, quickly adapting to the Northwest's climates and plant life. Fealy was noted for her quality control and perfectionist inclinations, and her work, as noted by landscape architect Carol Meyer Reed, "was characterized by its simplicity of form, casual elegance and timeless quality." Two of her best-known projects were done in (often stormy) collaboration with architect John Storrs (1920–2003): the seashore resort of **Salishan** at Gleneden Beach for developer John Gray (1965), and a new campus for the **Oregon College of Art and Craft** in the late 1970s. She also did a master plan for the Leach Botanical Garden in Portland and designs for a Portland garden located in the sister city of Sapporo, Japan. Fealy's plans were widely published, including in popular publications such as *Sunset* maga-

zine, and she was a noted mentor to women entering the field of landscape architecture.

ferries The arrival of Euro-American settlers in the 1840s also brought wheeled wagons and muddy roads, and where roads met rivers, ferries were established. Among the earliest was one built by **Jesse Applegate** about 1843 for Alanson Beers, who had a land claim along the Willamette River not far from the early Methodist mission established by **Jason Lee** in 1834. Daniel Matheny established another ferry nearby in the 1850s; Matheny's ferry, also known as the **Wheatland** ferry for a now-vanished town on the west bank. A ferry has operated at that location continuously every since. Each successive vessel has been named for Daniel Matheny, with the most recent incarnation being the *Daniel Matheny V*, built in 2002.

Numerous ferry routes crossed the Willamette until bridges began to be erected in the 1880s. Among the major crossings were the Stark Street ferry in Portland, which began operating about 1855 and continued even after the construction of bridges across the river beginning in 1887. The Stark Street ferry ceased in 1895 when the toll was removed from the Morrison Street bridge. At Saint Johns and at Sellwood, ferries operated until the completion of major bridges in 1931 and 1925, respectively. The Oregon & California Railroad ferried railroad cars across the Willamette from 1870 until the completion of the first Steel Bridge in 1888. Boones Ferry crossed the river at **Wilsonville**, operating from about 1847 until 1954 with the opening of the Interstate 5 bridge, now named the Boone Bridge. Near Champoeg, a historic river crossing on the **California-Oregon Trail** was served by ferry from about 1850 to 1857, operated by Michel Laframboise. Numerous other places once hosted ferries: among them were Milwaukie, Oregon City, Independence, Albany, Corvallis, and others. Two Willamette River ferries have continued to operate, in addition to that at Wheatland: the **Canby** ferry near the town of that name, which began operations in 1914, and the **Buena Vista** ferry, which has operated (with interruptions) since the 1850s.

On the Columbia River, the crossing to Vancouver, Washington, where a ferry operated as early as 1846, was the first location to be bridged in 1917. Ferries once crossed the Columbia from Rainier, Goble, Hood River, Biggs, Arlington, and Umatilla. At the mouth of the Columbia, a network of small boats—a **mosquito fleet**—connected Astoria with various points on the Washington shore beginning in the 1880s. Regular ferries connected Astoria with Ilwaco (later, Megler) to provide direct access to the narrow-gauge railroad that ran on the Long Beach peninsula from 1888 to 1930. These vessels began carrying automobiles in the 1910s, and evolved into a major highway ferry system until it was replaced by a bridge in 1966. The one remaining ferry on the Columbia River connects Westport with Puget Island in Washington state. A **Northern Pacific Railway** train ferry crossed the Columbia from Goble to Kalama, Washington, from 1884 until a railroad bridge opened at Vancouver in 1908. The ferry, the *Tacoma*, could carry twenty-seven railroad cars on each crossing; this was an essential link in the railroad route between Portland and Seattle.

Along the Oregon Coast, ferries crossed virtually all the major rivers. In 1929, there were ferries at Yaquina Bay, Alsea Bay, Siuslaw River, Umpqua River, Coos Bay, and the Rogue River. The completion of the **Oregon Coast Highway** bridged all of these estuaries by 1936.

Ferries were also to be found on the Rogue, Umpqua, Santiam, Yamhill, Umatilla, and Snake Rivers. Road and street names often refer to now-vanished ferries. In the Portland area one will find Boones Ferry Road (from southwest Portland to **Wilsonville**), Scholls Ferry Road, Taylors Ferry Road, Grahams Ferry Road, and Bakers Ferry Road. Similar vestigial names can be found around the state.

"Fifty-four forty or fight" This phrase was a political slogan of James K. Polk's presidential campaign in 1844. It refers to the position that the appropriate boundary between the western United States and British territory (Canada) should be drawn at latitude 54° 40', at about the present southernmost point of the Alaska panhandle. Polk was elected, and the boundary issue was settled, but at a line that was rather to the south of his campaign call. Latitude 49° was established as the boundary by the Oregon Treaty of 1846.

filberts Hazelnuts, commonly called filberts in Oregon, exist as a wild shrub, *Corylus cornuta* var. *californica*, but it is the cultivated variety, *Corylus avellana*, which is best known today. The wild California hazelnut is found in coastal areas and was a favored foodstuff of local Indians, easily harvested and traded; shrub patches were periodically burned to improve the yield. The largest specimen of the wild hazelnut is found near Otis on the Oregon coast. The early Oregon nurseryman **Henderson Luelling** brought *C. avellana* to the state in the late 1840s, and specimens from the 1850s still grow in **Scottsburg**. The nation's first commercial filbert orchard, listed on the National Register of Historic Places, had its beginnings in 1892 near **Springfield** where George and Lulu Dorris bought farm property. In 1903, the Dorris family planted their first filbert orchard, which in the next fifty years grew to more than 9,000 trees. Filberts were widely planted in the Willamette Valley over the next few decades. After declining in the years after World War II, filberts increased in national popularity beginning in the 1980s. Oregon produces nearly all of the nation's commercial crop of filberts. The Dorris Ranch, now part of the Springfield park system, is still a working orchard as well.

Finley, William L. (1876–1953) Born in California and raised there and in Oregon, William Finley took an early interest in the natural world, and birds in particular. In 1894, he and his neighbor, Herman Bohlman, founded the North Western Ornithology Foundation, and the two young men took up photography to document their interests and their discoveries. Their photographs of the birds on Three Arch Rocks on the Oregon coast were instrumental in President Theodore Roosevelt's 1907 creation of the West Coast's first bird refuge there. Finley's conservationist impulses and documentary photographs led him and his wife, Nellie, into a career of writing, lectures, and motion pictures about wildlife and in support of wildlife preservation. Finley served as president of the Audubon Society, helped create the Oregon Fish and Game Commission, and worked to form wildlife refuges centered on the **Klamath Lake** marshes and the **Harney Lake** basin. After his death, a new habitat for wintering and resting dusky Canada geese in the Willamette Valley was acquired in the 1960s; it is named the William L. Finley National Wildlife Refuge in his honor.

Mathewson, Worth. *William L. Finley, Pioneer Wildlife Photographer.* Corvallis: Oregon State University Press, 1986.

Finns in Oregon The Pacific Northwest proved to be an attractive locality for Finnish immigrants to America in the late nineteenth century. As in Finland, many could find work fishing or working in the woods. The first wave of immigrants in the 1870s came to **Astoria**, and most of them came from Finnish immigrant communities in Pennsylvania and Ohio; their favorable accounts soon encouraged other Finns. Many of those who came from Finland directly were from a few communities. Finns could be found along the Columbia River and in Portland as well; historian George Hummasti has said a popular riddle in the early twentieth century was, Why is the Columbia River like a salmon? The answer is that it has Finns on both sides. The heavily Scandinavian population of Astoria in the 1920s was most heavily Finnish, with about a quarter of the residents of Finnish heritage. The Uniontown-Alameda Historic District encompasses such landmarks as Soumi [Finland] Hall.

fires Fires have been defining disasters in many Oregon communities. A substantial portion of Portland's downtown commercial district was wiped out by fire in December of 1872, and on August 2, 1873, another fire wiped out some twenty-two additional blocks of businesses. Help came from Vancouver, Washington, by steamboat, and from Salem via the recently completed railroad. There were no fatalities. Jacksonville suffered from large fires in 1873 and 1874, which led to a city ordinance requiring the use of brick for commercial buildings, thought to be resistant to fire; such requirements were often made following (only rarely preceding) major conflagrations. Fires often also precipitated a professionalization of firefighting, which usually began with volunteer cadres that frequently acted more as social clubs (such was the case in Portland) than as rescue operations. Other incendiary events took place at **Silver Lake** in 1894, in **Astoria** in 1922, and in **Bandon** in 1936. *See also* **forest fires**; **Tillamook Burn**.

fishing, commercial Fishing was a source of livelihood for most of Oregon's Indians into the mid-nineteenth century. It also became an industrial product for Euro-Americans beginning in the 1860s. (There were earlier attempts, most notably by the ill-fated **Nathaniel Wyeth**.) George and William Hume, who had been canning **salmon** on the Sacramento River, brought their operation to the Columbia River in 1866, at Eagle Cliff east of Cathlamet, Washington. The Humes—there were altogether four brothers, and all became involved in the industry—were major players in the commercial salmon-canning industry, which grew along the Columbia River in the 1870s and 1880s, with headquarters in the Astoria area. Commercial salmon packing took place at other locations as well, such as on Tillamook Bay at Bay City, on the Nestucca and Umpqua Rivers, on Coos Bay, and on the Rogue River. On the Columbia, salmon were caught near the mouth by gillnet fishing (*see* **mosquito fleet**) and by seining nets, drawn in by horses from sandbars and shoals. Farther up the Columbia, where Indians caught salmon with spears and dipnets in traditional fashion, industrial-strength **fishwheels**, mounted over channels or on floating barges, scooped up salmon by the thousands. By 1883, there were thirty-nine salmon canneries on the lower Columbia River, with 1,700 boats; they shipped 629,400 cases of fish, with forty-eight one-pound cans in each case. Most cannery workers were **Chinese**, while those doing the fishing were often of Scandinavian lineage: **Finns** and **Swedes** dominated, but there were also Germans and Croatians, Danes and Icelanders. The fish runs began to decline in the 1880s while demand for canned salmon rose—by the 1910s and 1920s, it was a staple food in the Midwest. Canneries responded by canning not only the favored spring Chinook salmon, but also canning coho and chum salmon and fall chinook—all once considered inferior fish. Despite attempts to improve runs through hatchery spawning, runs declined due to overfishing, habitat destruction, and, after the mid-1930s, dam construction. The decline closed and consolidated canning operations; the Columbia River Packers Association came to dominate the field with its **Bumble Bee Seafoods** brand; other major canners included Barbey Packing and Union Fishermen's Cooperative. The industry collapsed in the 1970s; in 1977, only 2,547 cases were packed, fewer than in the inaugural year 1866, and the Bumble Bee plant closed in 1980. As the Northwest Power and Conservation Council put it, "From humble beginnings, salmon canning grew to become the major industry of the Columbia River and then, with the decline of salmon and steelhead, fell into near oblivion, all in the space of 114 years."

Salmon dominated the Oregon commercial fisheries scene for many decades, overshadowing other fishing enterprises. Commercial harvesting and cultivation of oysters took place in **Yaquina Bay** beginning in the 1860s, and has continued; Coos Bay, Tillamook Bay, and Nestucca Bay have also produced oysters. Coastal fish runs have changed over the decades, and at various times Astoria canneries have also processed albacore tuna, smelt, crab, and shrimp. Since the 1970s, commercial fishing has concentrated on products for regional fresh or flash-frozen markets, taking crab, shrimp, and various groundfish as well as limited amounts of salmon. An Indian fishery also supplies local markets.

Tetlow, Roger T., and Graham J. Barbey. *Barbey: The Story of a Pioneer Columbia River Salmon Packer*. Portland, Oregon: Binfords & Mort Publishers, 1990.

Fishtrap This is a writers' gathering at **Wallowa Lake** that began in 1988 and that conducts summer writing workshops and other gatherings. The Nez Perce term for a fish trap is the basis of the word Wallowa.

fishwheels Fishwheels were immense structures that resembled water wheels and that literally scooped fish—salmon, in particular—from the river in wholesale lots. Built over or beside narrow waterways, or anchored on scows along the main stream, fishwheels were embraced by operators of fish canneries soon after their first appearance in 1879. They were used principally along the Columbia River, where they incurred the wrath of Indian fishers (whose traditional and treaty-guaranteed sites were often affected), sports fishermen, and, of course, of those who fished by other means such as gillnetting. Although gillnets took far more fish in total, the fishwheels became visible symbols of overfishing, which had precipitated a decline in salmon fisheries since the 1880s. Oregon outlawed fishwheels in 1926, and Washington state followed suit in 1934.

Seufert, Francis. *Wheels of Fortune*. Ed. Thomas Vaughan. Portland, Oregon: Oregon Historical Society, 1980.

Flanders, George H. (1821–1892)
see **Couch, John H.**

Flavel, George (ca. 1824–1893) A legendary seaman whose specialized maritime knowledge made him wealthy, Capt. George Flavel was a pilot who guided thousands of vessels over the treacherous bar of the Columbia River in the late nineteenth century. Flavel and his wife, Mary Christina (Boelling), constructed a grand house in **Astoria** in 1886 in the Queen Anne style and designed by Carl W. Leick. The house came to the city from the family in 1934, and after a series of vicissitudes, became a museum in the 1950s. It is today an architectural landmark in a city of architectural delights; Mary Boelling's childhood house in the Greek Revival style sits across the street from the Flavel house, still in use as a residence. The name Flavel is also attached to a now-vanished community (the post office operated from 1897 to 1918) on Tansy Point opposite Astoria, which had ambitions of becoming both a fashionable resort and a bustling seaport. Neither outcome was achieved, although in 1915–17, Flavel was the northern terminus of the Great Northern Pacific Steamship Company, which sped travelers from San Francisco to Flavel and thence by fast train to Portland on a schedule that equaled the all-rail route.

flax industry The conversion of flax fiber into linen was an early Oregon enterprise, and one that came and went fitfully for a century. The first flax was reported to grow in Oregon in 1844, but it was 1867 before efforts were made to commercially deal with a product from the flax. Joseph Holman's Salem plant pressed oil from flaxseed, which was used for cattle feed, while the fiber was used to make upholstery; it did not last long. Other efforts in the early 1900s were thwarted by fires of suspect origin, perhaps inspired by Eastern capitalists of the "linen trust," likely an apocryphal institution. In 1915, the state penitentiary began using inmate labor to produce linen; fire again disrupted the enterprise. Growing and processing of flax in the Willamette Valley continued through the 1920s with moderate success, and **World War II** gave a sudden impetus to the industry, which could no longer depend on European supplies. The products were not so much table linens, however, as "such unglamorous products as ropes, twines, thread, nets, fishing tackle, mops, rugs and toweling, and defense materials." After the war, Oregon State University aided in developing the industry locally, turning to using flax fibers mixed with other fabrics to create rugs. By the mid-1950s, the penitentiary operation ceased, as had all other facilities.

Wyatt, Steve M. Flax and Linen: An Uncertain Oregon Industry. *Oregon Historical Quarterly* 95, no. 2 (Summer 1994): 150–175.

Fleet of Flowers *see* **Depoe Bay**

floating houses *see* **houseboats**

floods The Ice Age Missoula floods of some 13,000 years ago dramatically shaped the basic contours of Columbia River gorge. Since the nineteenth century, many floods of lesser dimensions have had a pronounced impact on Oregon. The Columbia River is susceptible to flooding during times of heavy winter rains, but the most severe flooding has occurred during the spring, when western Oregon rains are joined with snow melt waters that come from throughout the huge Columbia River basin. The list of years of significant Columbia River flooding is long and tedious: in one century, 1842, 1844, 1853, 1859, 1862, 1863, 1866, 1870, 1871, 1872, 1880, 1882, 1894. The construction of **Bonneville Dam** and others upriver have largely tamed the flooding, but major floods still occurred in 1948 (destroying the wartime city of **Vanport**), 1964 (the "Christmas Flood," which affected all of western Oregon, lasted twenty days, and took at least thirty-two lives), and 1996, another February incident of warm rains on snow packs throughout the Northwest.

Flooding of the Willamette River most often occurs during the winter rains. Major flooding occurred in 1813 and 1844, and a disastrous flood in December of 1861 washed away the pioneer settlements of **Champoeg**, Orleans, and Linn City. Property damage was severe; the number of lives lost is not known. The Willamette River floods of January and February 1890 washed out bridges and allowed steamboats to reach heretofore unimagined landing sites. The lower reaches of the Willamette have often backed up to the flood stage during the Columbia's spring freshets, causing severe flooding in the Portland area. This phenomenon was apparent in the 1894 flood, which was a roiling torrent at The Dalles, but only a sedate rising of the waters in downtown Portland (the high water mark can be seen in the doorway of the Haseltine Building on SW Second Avenue).

More localized floods have been common in Oregon. Bridge Creek, for example, has sent floodwaters through the town of **Mitchell** in 1884, 1904, and 1956. The most disastrous flood in terms of lives lost was the **Heppner** flood of June 14, 1903, when a storage dam failed and sent a wall of water into the town; about 247 residents died.

Laskin, David. *Rains All the Time: A Connoisseur's History of Weather in the Pacific Northwest.* Seattle: Sasquatch Books, 1997.

Florence Florence is situated in Lane County where the Siuslaw River enters the Pacific. The area was the site of a number of villages of the Siuslaw Indians, and was part of the Coast Reservation until it was opened for American settlement in 1875. The name of the community is probably derived from the wreck of the sailing vessel *Florence* in 1875. A post office opened in 1879, the town was incorporated in 1893, and the 1900 census reported a population of 222. The harbor hosted small coastal steamships, thanks to the construction of the first jetty in 1893 and, in 1894, the Heceta Head **lighthouse** north of the river mouth. An annual festival celebrating the native coastal rhododendron has been held since 1908. By 1915, there was some industry in the form of salmon fishing and canning, logging and lumbering, and dairy and other farming.

The completion of the Siuslaw River bridge at Florence in 1936 was one of the last links in the creation of the **Oregon Coast Highway**. Florence is located at the northern edge of the Oregon Dunes National Recreation Area, a stretch of coastal dunes within the Siuslaw National Forest that was established in 1972. In the 1990s Florence increased its tourist appeal by fixing up and promoting its Old Town harborside. In 2004, the Confederated Tribes of the Coos, Lower Umpqua and Siuslaw Indians opened Three Rivers Casino; in 2007, the Chamber of Commerce noted that "Logging, farming and fishing are no longer the major industries; in fact, they have all but disappeared." The population of Florence in 2007 was about 8,270.

flour mills *see* **wheat**

Flumgudgeon Gazette and Bumble Bee Budget By some accounts this was the first newspaper in the Oregon Country, albeit the multiple copies were produced by hand copying rather than printing, and it was issued only during the sitting of the legislature of the **provisional government** at Oregon City in 1845. Virtually all the "news" was political commentary, hence the satiric nature of the name. The first newspaper issued from a real printing press came out on February 5, 1846, the *Oregon Spectator*, also of Oregon City.

flying saucers *see* **unidentified flying objects**

Forecourt Fountain *see* **Keller Fountain**

forest fires Fires in the forest were once a common occurrence. In the dry eastern Oregon ponderosa forests, natural fires burned through quickly every decade or two but did little damage to the thick-barked trees. On the west side of the Cascade Range, where conditions were much more moist, raging infernos apparently took place at long intervals, perhaps about every 150 years. Many Indian bands used fire to burn the lands annually to encourage seed and nut growth and enhance browsing plants for game; this practice developed the "natural" prairies of the Willamette and Umpqua Valleys, with their stands of fire-resistant oak.

But white settlers saw timber as wealth, and were greatly disturbed at the massive fires they witnessed. Among those were burns in the Coast Range west of Corvallis in 1853, a huge conflagration in the Cascade foothills east of Silverton in 1865, and forest fires near Mount Hood and north of Vancou-

ver, Washington, in 1902. The sequence of three major groups of fires in the Coast Range, beginning in 1933, called the **Tillamook Burn**, incited major efforts to avoid and suppress forest fires. That practice has continued and has grown into a major industry, despite doubts in recent years as to its efficacy or desirability. The "Keep Oregon Green" program began in 1942, publicizing efforts to prevent forest fires.

► **Forest Grove** At the western edge of the immensely fertile **Tualatin Plains** in Washington County is Forest Grove, which was among the earliest areas settled by American emigrants in the Oregon Country. Stalwart Congregationalists Alvin T. and Abigail Smith arrived in the area of what is

Wagons loaded with cans of milk from nearby dairies are lined up outside the condensary of the Pacific Coast Condensed Milk Company plant in Forest Grove, producing under the Carnation label. Located at the south edge of the town in the early 1900s, the plant had its own railroad station. The dairy industry was a key part of the Washington County economy. Burlington Northern collection. Oregon Historical Society, CN 018751.

now Forest Grove in the fall of 1841. The Smith house, built in 1854 and on the National Register of Historic Places, still stands at the southern edge of the city. The nucleus of the community was the Tualatin Academy, founded by the Congregational Church in 1849 but with antecedents going back to 1842; the academy's descendant, **Pacific University**, still dominates the city. The use of the name dates from 1851; the post office opened in 1858. Forest Grove was incorporated in 1872, the same year the Oregon Central Railroad arrived from Portland; the 1880 census gave it a population of 547.

The Oregon Electric Railway provided another route to Portland in 1908, and in 1910 the population was recorded as 1,772. By 1915, Forest Grove boasted a Carnation condensed milk factory, a fruit cannery, flour and feed mills, a brick and tile factory, a woodwork and planing mill, and a gopher trap factory. An imposing home for the elderly opened in 1922, conducted by the Masonic lodge. After World War II, despite its distance from Portland, it shared in some suburban population growth, increasingly so after 1990 as the **Silicon Forest** stretched westward from Beaverton. Forest Grove recorded 4,343 residents in 1950, 8,175 in 1970, and an estimated 20,395 in 2007. The Masonic home was converted to a brewpub and resort in 2000.

Forest Park The genesis of Portland's Forest Park was visible in the 1903 master parks plan by John C. Olmsted. The park stretches for some seven miles along the crest of the **Tualatin Mountains** in the northwestern section of the city. A 1939 land donation started the actual acquisition process, which by 1948 enabled the city to dedicate a 4,200-acre park. The lands had been logged early in the twentieth century, but second-growth timber covered the hills, and the name was once again an apt one. The park is now 4,718 acres, one of the largest natural areas within the limits of a U.S. city.

Fort Astoria Founded by the **Pacific Fur Company** of **John Jacob Astor**, Fort Astoria became the nucleus of the future city of **Astoria**. A group aboard the ship *Tonquin* arrived at the site on the Columbia River in March 1811, and built a log stockade enclosing a store, blacksmith shop, and other buildings. The Astor overland party arrived to reinforce the group in February 1812. The mission of those at Fort Astoria was to trap and trade for furs, especially beaver and sea otter.

The company was a vulnerable American asset during the War of 1812 between the United States and Great Britain. In 1813, the Pacific Fur Company was sold to the British North West Company. Before the news reached the Pacific Coast, the British warship HMS *Raccoon* seized the fort, without opposition, on December 12. The post was immediately renamed **Fort George**. The year 1818 began a period of "joint sovereignty" of the **Oregon Country** by the United States and Britain, a situation not resolved until 1846. The fort was restored to U.S. control, but it was a moot point. The North West Company was subsumed by the **Hudson's Bay Company (HBC)** in 1821, which found it to be an awkward headquarters post in an area of few furs. In 1825, HBC moved their main operations upriver to the new **Fort Vancouver**.

Fort Clatsop Named for the Clatsop band of the **Chinook Indians**, Fort Clatsop was the winter headquarters of the **Lewis and Clark Expedition** in 1805–06. The fort was sited on the west bank of what is now the Lewis and Clark River in Clatsop County, several miles southwest of Astoria.

Fort Dalles The creation of the Oregon Territory as an American domain brought troops of the U.S. Army to **The Dalles** in 1850, where they established Camp Drum. In 1850, a crude log fort was built there, which was replaced in 1858 under the command of Col. George Wright. Clerk Louis Scholl, who had studied drafting and engineering, drew up the plans for the buildings, guided by Andrew Jackson Downing's popular designs for Gothic revival-style "cottages." The picturesque application of the style to officers' houses, a guardhouse, and stables gave the fort a most unusual aspect. The Yakima War of 1856–57 was a reason for manning Fort Dalles, and it also drove the construction of Fort Simcoe in Washington Territory, which similarly had (and has) buildings designed by Louis Scholl. Fort Dalles was reduced to a quartermaster's depot in 1861 and abandoned in 1867. The surgeon's quarters at the fort have remained standing, a brooding Gothic revival edifice in weathered wood that is now a museum.

Knuth, Priscilla. *"Picturesque" Frontier: The Army's Fort Dalles.* 2nd ed. Portland, Oregon: Oregon Historical Society Press, 1987.

Fort George In 1811 the **Pacific Fur Company** had established **Fort Astoria**, which in 1813 was purchased by the North West Company. The British military took control late in 1813, and changed the name of the post from Fort Astoria to Fort George. The fort was returned to American hands in 1818, but in actuality it remained under British control; the North West Company itself was taken over by the **Hudson's Bay Company** in 1821, and Fort George/Astoria remained a trading post until after 1826.

Fort Henrietta *see* **Echo**

Fort Hoskins Along with **Fort Yamhill** and **Fort Umpqua**, Fort Hoskins was established in 1856 to keep a watch on the Indians of the **Coast Reservation**. It was located along the western edge of Kings Valley in Benton County, overlooking the **Luckiamute River**. Lt. **Phil Sheridan** was involved in building a road from the fort to the Indian agency at **Siletz**. Fort Hoskins was decommissioned in 1865. The nearby community of Hoskins served for many years as the operations center for the Valley & Siletz Railroad, a lumber road that connected the mill town of **Valsetz** with the outside world from

1918 to 1979; the Hoskins post office operated from 1891 to 1958. A picturesque covered bridge crossed the Luckiamute from 1938 until it was destroyed by the **Columbus Day storm** of 1962; the equally picturesque Hoskins general store stood adjacent. The site of Fort Hoskins is now a Benton County park.

Bensell, Royal A. *All Quiet on the Yamhill: The Civil War in Oregon: The Journal of Corporal Royal A. Bensell, Company D, Fourth California Infantry.* Ed. Gunter Barth. Eugene: University of Oregon Book, 1959.

Hilleary, William M., Herbert B. Nelson, and Preston E. Onstad, eds. *A Webfoot Volunteer: The Diary of William M. Hilleary 1864–1866.* Corvallis: Oregon State University Press, 1965

Fort Klamath This army post northwest of Klamath Falls was established by the Oregon Volunteers in 1863 to watch the **Klamath**, **Modoc**, and **Northern Paiute Indians** in the vicinity. The Klamath ceded a large territory in 1864 and the Klamath Reservation was created at that time; the Modoc were also expected to live on that reservation, despite historic rivalries. Fort Klamath was the site of the military execution of four Modoc leaders in 1873, the culmination of the disastrous **Modoc War**. Fort Klamath post office was established in 1879. The military presence was no longer important by the mid-1880s, and the fort was closed in 1890. The site was placed on the National Register of Historic Places in 1971, and Klamath County maintains a museum there.

Fort Rock Located in Lake County, northwest of **Christmas Valley**, Fort Rock is a small, unincorporated community that formed around a rural post office established in the valley in 1908, during a homesteading period that also saw the blossoming of nearby **Silver Lake**. The town is named for a prominent geological feature, Fort Rock, that is the result of volcanic activity that took place below water, emerging as a giant tuff ring that resembles a fortress. Numerous similar rings and cones can be found in the region. The natural feature also gave its name to Fort Rock Cave, a nearby archaeological site where, in 1938, **Luther S. Cressman** found and identified sandals made by human inhabitants of the cave some 9,000 to 10,000 years earlier—a find that markedly changed perceptions of the length of time that humans had lived in North America. The town of Fort Rock is also the site of a museum dedicated to remembering the homesteading period of the 1900s and 1910s, when a few years of above-average rainfall encouraged hundreds of families to attempt dry-land farming in a near-desert region.

Hatton, Raymond. *Pioneer Homesteaders of the Fort Rock Valley*. Portland, Oregon: Binfords & Mort, 1982.

Fort Stevens The fort at the mouth of the Columbia River is named for Gen. Isaac Stevens (1818–1862), who was the first governor of Washington Territory, the instigator of numerous military clashes with Indians, and the formulator of a series of disastrous treaties with Native peoples in the Northwest; he died in battle during the **Civil War**. Fort Stevens was established in 1863 to guard the mouth of the river from attack by naval forces, either of the Confederacy or of their allies, the British. Across the river, Cape Disappointment was armed in 1862; in 1875 it became Fort Canby. A third protective post was established in Washington state in 1896 at Fort Columbia.

The major coastal batteries—disappearing guns—were built after 1897. Fort Stevens was a bustling installation during the Spanish-American War and World War I, but reached its height during **World War II**, when about 2,500 men were stationed there. On the night of June 21, 1942, an offshore Japanese submarine fired several rounds toward the fort, landing on the beach; the commander of the fort did not return fire. Fort Stevens was thus the only mainland military installation in the United States to be fired upon during the war. Fort Stevens was deacti-

vated after the war, its guns removed in 1947 and the site given over to the Corps of Army Engineers. Much of the fort was acquired by the state in 1975, and has been developed as part of Fort Stevens State Park. Included in the park are some of the fortifications, such as Battery Russell, and the noted shipwreck, the *Peter Iredale*. Some of the 1890s officers' houses still stand as well.

Fort Umpqua The **Hudson's Bay Company** established a trading post on the Umpqua River near the later site of the town of **Elkton** in 1836. The post traded with **Siuslaw** and **Coos Indians**, who brought furs to exchange for tools, blankets, and other merchandise. The post was closed in 1854. There was also a U.S. Army post named Fort Umpqua; it was located near the mouth of the Umpqua River, opposite the later town of Winchester Bay. The fort operated from 1856 to 1862, intended to monitor Indians on the **Coast Reservation**. "In 1862 the paymaster reported that he had found all the officers and men out hunting on his visit to the fort, and because of this, and that there were no Indians left in the country, it was abandoned," reported Howard McKinley Corning in the *Dictionary of Oregon History*.

► **Fort Vancouver** Situated on the Columbia River in what is today Clark County, Washington, Fort Vancouver was the economic and political nerve center of the **Oregon Country** from its inception in 1825 until its abandonment by the **Hudson's Bay Company (HBC)** in 1860. When the HBC moved its regional headquarters there from **Fort George**, Fort Vancouver was located in territory that was jointly claimed by Great Britain and the United States, a situation not resolved until the Treaty of 1846. In the absence of any official political structure, the emigrant fur trappers, explorers, and early farming settlers of the area looked to HBC for guidance; similarly, HBC had a strong hand on the economy of the area as its sole land-based trading entity, with auxiliary forts and communities at such points as Fort Boise, **Fort Umpqua**, and Nisqually. The first chief factor—the term used for the regional manager of HBC—at Fort Vancouver was the redoubtable **John McLoughlin**, who reigned from 1825 until his retirement in 1845. McLoughlin sited the fort, directed the establishment of its farming operations, and supervised the construction of a stockade some twenty feet high and 750 feet long, 450 feet in width. About forty buildings were constructed inside the fort: warehouses for furs, a house for the chief factor, a blacksmith shop, a school. Beyond the pale was more housing, a small shipyard, a sawmill (the region's first), gardens, and orchards; McLoughlin famously brought to Oregon in his pocket the seeds of the first **apple** trees. The diverse populace at the fort reflected the international nature of the HBC trading operations: there were Scots, French-speaking Québécois and Métis from Canada, Kanakas from Hawai'i, Irish, and Cree and Iroquois and Chinookan Indians—among others. The fort became the center of regional fur-trading commerce, where furs were collected and shipped and where supplies and trade goods arrived from Europe. During the 1840s, the fort was also a place where American emigrants, intent on settling in the disputed but fertile Willamette Valley, could buy or barter needed goods and foodstuffs.

The 1846 treaty with Great Britain clearly put Fort Vancouver in American territory, and the era of the fur trade was rapidly dwindling. At its height, Fort Vancouver supervised a regional enterprise with some six hundred employees, a number of ships, and more than two dozen outpost operations. After 1846, HBC operations at Fort Vancouver shrank, and the company moved its headquarters to Fort Victoria in British Columbia in 1849 and closed Fort Vancouver in 1860. Meanwhile, the U.S. Army had established Vancouver Barracks adjacent to Fort Vancouver. With the establishment of the **Oregon**

Artist Gustave Sohon made this sketch of Fort Vancouver as it appeared in 1850, looking eastward toward Mount Hood. This lithograph from his drawing was published in the Pacific Railroad Surveys volume on the northern route to the Pacific Coast. University of Washington Libraries, Special Collections, NA4171.

Territory in 1848, and after the departure of HBC, the Army occupied the site, eventually naming their own facilities Fort Vancouver. The Army's Department of Oregon (1858–61 and 1863–65) and Department of the Columbia (from 1865) supervised Army operations in the Pacific Northwest from this location. Vancouver Barracks was decommissioned in 2001. Vancouver National Historic Reserve includes elements from the HBC and Army activities on the site of Fort Vancouver.

Fort Yamhill The area along the South Yamhill River in Yamhill County where this fort was established in 1856 was the homeland of the Yamhill band of the **Kalapuyan Indians**. The Kalapuyans had been decimated by disease in the 1830s, and the valley was settled by emigrant farmers in the 1850s. The **Rogue River Wars** in southern Oregon resulted in the forced resettlement of many hundreds of Indians from diverse tribes to the remote and dreary

Coast Reservation. Three forts were established to monitor access; the other two were **Fort Hoskins** and **Fort Umpqua**. Fort Yamhill included a sentry box, barracks, blacksmith and carpenter shops, a hospital, stables and a barn, and other structures; the construction was in part supervised by Lt. **Phil Sheridan**. The fort was maintained through the Civil War and abandoned in 1866. The blockhouse was sold—for $2.50—and finally, in 1911, was moved to the town square of Dayton, where it still stands. The site of the fort was converted to farmland. In the late 1980s, the site, including one building from the fort, slightly emended, was acquired by the **Confederated Tribes of the Grand Ronde** and the Oregon State Parks and Recreation Department. It is being developed as a state park.

► **Fossil** The discovery of a number of fossils after a landslide on the Thomas B. Hoover ranch prompted the name of the post office of Fossil, which

A panoramic view of the town of Fossil as photographed about 1895 by Martin M. Hazeltine. Oregon Historical Society, OrHi 39236.

opened in 1876. The community was incorporated in 1891, when it had a population of about 150. **Wheeler County** was created in 1899, and Fossil became the county seat; the present courthouse was erected in 1902. By 1915, Fossil had an ice plant and a small sawmill and flour mill. Fossil's population peaked in the 1950s at more than 600; in 2007, it was approximately 465. One can still find fossils in Fossil.

fossils *see* **Condon, Thomas**

Fred Meyer Stores This is a retail store chain founded in the 1920s by **Fred G. Meyer**. The first store was a grocery, located in the Portland **public market** at SW Fifth Avenue and Yamhill Street in 1922. Meyer proceeded to open stores at other sites, such as the Astoria Public Market, and to add other merchandise; he established a self-service drugstore in 1928. In 1931, Meyer opened a "one stop" shopping center in the **Hollywood neighborhood**, where he had earlier had a grocery. Fred Meyer stores sprouted throughout the Portland area in the 1940s and 1950s, stores that combined groceries with drugs, apparel, hardware, and free parking. Eve's Buffet, named for Fred's wife, provided food service at some stores; at least one location in the 1970s featured an Eve's Lounge, where martinis were served to shoppers, backlit by a stained glass panel with a silhouette of Eve and a scattering of suggestive apples. The chain expanded into Washington state in the 1960s and to Alaska in the 1970s. Meyer died in 1978, setting the stage for a more impersonal approach to merchandising after the company was the victim of a leveraged buyout in 1982. The name was extended to operations in Montana, Utah, Arizona, and Idaho; the company took over other chains in Washington and California, but kept the names (among those was the QFC grocery store chain). In 1999, Fred Meyer merged with the eastern grocery giant Kroger. Fred G. Meyer ran his stores with a homespun straightforwardness that made him as popular personally as his stores were. The

later owners have not kept that spirit; the now-lapsed advertising campaign to call the store Freddy's was woefully misdirected. Fred Meyer still sells a lot of, well, everything.

Freewater *see* **Milton-Freewater**

Frémont, John C. (1813–1890) Born in Georgia, Frémont joined the U.S. Army's Topographical Engineers in 1838. In 1841, he married Jessie Benton, the daughter of a powerful U.S. senator, Thomas Hart Benton of Missouri. Senator Benton was a vocal proponent of the idea that it was the "manifest destiny" of the United States to extend across the American continent, a position that made him an ally of those who favored American control of the **Oregon Country**. (In gratitude, Oregon named **Benton County** for the senator from Missouri.) The marriage eventually aided John Frémont's own professional and political ambitions. Between 1842 and 1846, Frémont led a group of military engineers and explorers on three expeditions into the non-American West. Frémont encountered the 1843 **Great Migration** of Oregon-bound emigrants, and reached The Dalles and **Fort Vancouver** before going south into Mexican California and returning to the East. He revisited California on his third expedition in 1845–46, where he caused a good deal of trouble and carried out some stunningly cruel behavior, in addition to helping to incite the so-called Bear Flag Revolt. In a foray north into the Klamath Lake country, he massacred a party of **Klamath Indians**. After playing a leading role in the California segment of the Mexican War of 1846, Frémont purchased land there, which proved valuable after the gold discoveries of 1849. Frémont was one of the first two senators of the new state of California in 1850, and was then a Republican presidential candidate in favor of the abolition of slavery in 1856 (Buchanan was nominated) and again in 1864. Frémont suffered financial reverses in the early 1870s, was appointed governor of the territory of Arizona in 1878, and died in New York state. The name Frémont is found throughout the American West; in Oregon, marking his experiences east of the Cascade Range, there is the Fremont National Forest (reconstituted in 2002 as Fremont-Winema National Forest), Fremont Meadow, and Fremont Canyon in Deschutes County, and NE Fremont Street in Portland; the latter gave rise to the dramatic arched Fremont Bridge of **Interstate 405** across the Willamette River. The Fremont Highway (Oregon 31) extends from La Pine to Lakeview.

Nevins, Allan. *Frémont, Pathmarker of the West.* New York: Longmans, Green, 1955. Reprint. Lincoln: University of Nebraska Press, 1992.

French, John William "Pete" (1849–1897) Born in Missouri and raised in California, Pete French got a job with Hugh Glenn, one of the state's biggest wheat growers. In 1872, Glenn sent young French north with some 1,200 head of cattle to establish a ranch in the **Harney Lake** Basin. French bought a small existing ranch, and from his base at the **P Ranch** expanded the French and Glenn holdings until they encompassed the valley of the **Donner und Blitzen River**, and all or part of the Happy, Diamond, and Catlow Valleys. During the 1880s, French fenced thousands of acres of public lands and was involved in fraudulent land claims by his employees for his benefit. In the same period, new settlers to the area conflicted with French's cattle ranges. In 1894, when drought lowered the level of water in **Malheur Lake**, French tried to keep settlers from claiming the "new" land; though his ploy failed, it exacerbated tensions.

Settler Ed Oliver was one of those who crossed paths with French. Oliver needed a road easement over French's property to reach his own, and French opposed it despite the county court's granting Oliver permission to survey the road. It was a final straw in a ten-year feud; on December 26, 1897, Ed Oliver rode up to French aggressively, and French responded with a whip. Oliver drew a gun, and as French

turned to ride away, he shot him. Oliver was acquitted of murder; the episode was seen by the jury, and by many other settlers, as one of self-defense. Much of French and Glenn's land holdings became part of the Malheur National Wildlife Refuge, including the P Ranch and two sites on the National Register of Historic Places: Sod House Ranch with its complex of bunk house, office, corrals, barn, and stone storage warehouse, and the Round Barn, an immense circular wooden structure built as a training space for horses. The town of **Frenchglen** also marks French's impact on southeastern Oregon.

Gray, Edward. *Life and Death of Oregon "Cattle King" Peter French, 1849–1897.* Salem: Edward Gray, 1995.

Frenchglen This tiny Harney County community is located near the site of **P Ranch**. A rural post office named Somerange (a name derived from "summer range," the summer pasturage for cattle) was established on the west flank of Steens Mountain in 1923. In 1926, it was moved west a few miles and re-designated Frenchglen, a name created by combining part of **Pete French** with the name of his business cohort, Dr. Hugh James Glenn. The landmark Frenchglen Hotel was also built in the 1920s, and the store that was formerly at the P Ranch moved to Frenchglen, too. The post office closed in 1943, but was re-opened in 1947. The hotel is on the National Register of Historic Places and is owned by the Oregon Parks and Recreation Department; it is leased for operation as a hotel and restaurant.

▶ **French in Oregon** The **fur trade** in the early days of the Oregon Country brought many French Canadians to the area beginning in the 1820s. Those leaving the service or retiring often took up farms, particularly in the area known as **French Prairie** and also in Douglas County, where a group settled in the 1850s in an area known as French Settlement, northwest of Roseburg. A number of French immigrated to the United States in

Jeanne DeRoboam was born in France and was in Jacksonville in the 1860s, where she operated the Franco-American Hotel. In 1873, she married brick maker George Holt, who completed the construction of the United States Hotel for her in 1881. In September 1880, she hosted U.S. President Rutherford B. Hayes and his party in the partially finished hotel. Peter Britt photograph. Author's collection.

the wake of revolutionary upheavals in 1848. Many were attracted to the gold fields of California and southern Oregon; accordingly, both Yreka, California, and Jacksonville, Oregon, had prominent hotels named the Franco-American.

French Prairie This prairie-like expanse in Marion County is located between the Willamette and Pudding Rivers north of **Lake Labish**. Located in the homeland area of the **Kalapuyan Indians**, the area had been systematically burned over many decades, leaving open grasslands interspersed with stands of **oak**. Beginning in the 1820s, as the **fur trade** expanded in the **Oregon Country**, some trappers retired or chose to step away from the trade in favor of farming, and some of those chose to settle on French Prairie. The reasons included the fact that, by the 1830s, disease had decimated the native peoples, leaving the land relatively available; that the soil was of excellent quality for general farming; and that the area was in close proximity to the trading post of **Fort Vancouver**. The name French Prairie reflects the fact that the preponderance of those who settled there before the 1840s were of French-Canadian descent, most of them former employees of the **Hudson's Bay Company (HBC)**. By 1843, about a hundred families of French descent lived in the area. The settlers were among those who pressed the HBC to have Catholic priests sent to the area; the first came in 1838, when **François Norbert Blanchet** arrived from Quebec. The towns of **Saint Paul**, Saint Louis, **Gervais**, and Butteville reflect the French impress on the land, as do the names of **Lake Labish** (Lac la biche) and **Pudding River** (Riviére au boudin).

fruit growing *see* **apples; cherries; pears; peaches; prunes**

Fulton neighborhood, Portland This area along the west Willamette shore south of downtown Portland was a residential streetcar suburb of the 1890s, platted as Fulton Park in 1888 by George, James, and **William Steel**. There was a Fulton post office from 1883 until 1906. A number of industries were also located along the waterfront and the paralleling railroad, including lumber mills, shipbuilders' yards, and furniture factories. In the early 1970s, a transformation of a former furniture factory into a shopping mall led to a northern portion of Fulton becoming known as the **Johns Landing neighborhood**. The Fulton name survived in but a few places;

a former speakeasy and beer parlor, lately the Home Tavern, was renovated in 1988 and reopened as the Fulton Pub and Brewery by the McMenamins organization, and the city maintains Fulton Park.

fur trade The Euro-American connections with the North Pacific Coast of North American derived in large part from the international fur trade, first in **sea otter** pelts, and later **beaver** furs. Other furs were part of the enterprise, but those two animals were the core of the commerce. Sea otter were highly prized in China in the late eighteenth and early nineteenth centuries, and they were found all along the Pacific Coast, south to Baja California. Russian, British, and American traders were active in the business of acquiring furs—usually by trade with coastal Indians—and exchanging them in China for goods wanted in their respective home countries, such as tea and chinaware. The sea otter was rapidly depleted, and tastes changed in China, as well, such that the trade expired by the 1820s. Meanwhile, in Britain, the pelt of the beaver (and there is, or was, a European beaver) became popular for hats, cloaks and other luxury clothing. The **Hudson's Bay Company (HBC)**, chartered in 1670, became one source of furs from North America; along with the North West Company and the American **Pacific Fur Company** (both of which HBC eventually subsumed), HBC operations dominated the trade in the **Oregon Country** through the 1840s.

Vaughan, Thomas, and Bill Holm. *Soft Gold: The Fur Trade & Cultural Exchange on the Northwest Coast of America.* 2nd ed. Portland, Oregon: Oregon Historical Society Press, 1990.

Galice Indians *see* **Athapaskan Indians**

► **Garden Home** A Multnomah County suburban district with a "mildly sentimental" name, Garden Home gained a post office in 1882, and an interurban electric railroad to Portland in 1908. Garden Home became the junction point for the Oregon Electric Railway's lines west to Forest Grove and south to Salem and Eugene. By 1915, with a population estimated at 350, it was reported that "many Portland office men make this place their home. Dairying, farming, fruit growing, poultry raising and gardening." The Portland Hunt Club and the Portland Golf Club were nearby. Garden Home's exclusive cachet has diminished, the trains went in 1933, the post office closed in 1954, and the area is engulfed in a more generalized suburbia.

The post office and general store at Garden Home about 1910, with postmaster Nichols by the fence. Oregon Historical Society, OrHi 19798.

Gardiner This onetime port city is located on the northern side of the Umpqua River estuary in Douglas County. Unassuming today, it was an important if remote settlement in the 1850s. Named for Boston merchant Gardiner Chism, the community had its beginnings with the wrecking of Chism's ship *Bostonian* in 1850 at the river's mouth. Impelled by the disaster, the salvaged goods became stock for a store. Gardiner became a trading point where ships from San Francisco met trails leading to the interior gold fields of southern Oregon in the 1850s. Gardiner was a customs port in 1851 and the Gardiners City post office operated from 1851 to 1858; as Gardiner, it reopened in 1864. Gardiner was the major port city at the **Umpqua River** mouth through the nineteenth century. In 1915, it was still boasting that it was the "business and transportation center of Western Douglas County," and it was said that it contained a number of "unusually attractive and well-painted homes, serving for Gardiner the title, 'The White City.'" Its collection of 1870s residences and business buildings was designated a district on the National Register of Historic Places in 1994. A later development at Gardiner was the construction in the early 1950s of a large paper mill by the International Paper Company. The mill dominated the city until its closure in 1999.

Garibaldi The oddly named town of Garibaldi is located in Tillamook County. One of the first white settlers in the area at the north end of Tillamook Bay was one Daniel Bayley, who arrived in the late 1860s. Bayley was an admirer of the Italian patriot Giuseppe Garibaldi (1807–1882), which prompted him to use the name for the post office—of which he was the first postmaster, in 1870. Not until a railroad arrived from Portland in 1911 did Garibaldi see major development; prior to that event, small coastal vessels were the only alternative to trails to reaching the outside world. By 1915, the town had an estimated population of 200, who engaged in salmon fishing, stone quarrying, and working in a cheese factory and a salmon cannery; the nearby lowlands held a number of dairies. A lumber mill was built in 1918; enlarged in the 1920s, it was said to be among the world's largest mills. In 1930, residents erected the prominent wooden *G* on the hillside behind the town; it is still a landmark. The mill faltered in the Depression and closed, but production revived in 1947; lumber production, signaled by the immense smokestack that towered over the waterfront, supported the town. Garibaldi was incorporated in 1946, and the 1950 census counted 1,249 residents. But the mill closed for good in 1974. The mill site was converted to a campground for visitors coming for fishing and hunting; the smokestack was demolished. Garibaldi has been working since the 1970s to convert itself into a tourist stop, with some success. The population in 1980 was 999, and 899 in 2000; the estimate in 2007 was 895.

Huckleberry, E. R. *The Adventures of Dr. Huckleberry: Tillamook County, Oregon.* Portland, Oregon: Oregon Historical Society, 1970.

Garry oak *see* **oak**

Gaston The community of Gaston in Washington County is named for Joseph Gaston (1833–1913), a lawyer, editor, and by the 1860s, a railroad investor. One of those investments—a rocky one—was the Oregon Central Railroad, which reached west from Portland through Forest Grove and got as far as the townsite of Gaston in 1872. A post office opened in 1873, as did a Congregational church. In 1880, Joseph Gaston began draining shallow Wapato Lake east of Gaston to convert it to farmland. Gaston grew as a farming community, and was incorporated in 1914—that was the year that the railroad was electrified, offering frequent trains to Portland, Forest Grove, and McMinnville. Logging was carried on in the Coast Range foothills to the west, and in 1915 it was reported that "the piling industry is quite important." So was dairying and general farming. The census of 1920 gave Gaston a population of 221, which climbed to 368 in 1950, 471 in 1980, and an estimated 650 in 2007. Grape growing and wine making are supplanting dairying.

Gates High in the North Santiam River canyon of Marion County lies Gates, a community that formed about 1888, when the Oregon Pacific Railroad reached the area; a post office opened in 1892. The rail line never made it over the Cascade Range to the east, and Gates was a somewhat somnolent town. It was described in 1915 as a small center of lumbering, mining, stock raising, and general farming; however, the gold, silver, lead, and copper mines that were said to be "near" Gates were largely imaginary. The town was incorporated in 1950 (population 422), when **Detroit Dam** was under construction a few miles up the canyon. The estimated population in 2007 was 505.

► **Gearhart** A seashore and golfing community in Clatsop County, Gearhart was established in the 1880s and named for a local settler who had arrived in 1850, Phillip Gearhart. Marshall Kinney purchased the property about 1889 and platted the townsite of Gearhart Park in 1890. Not coincidentally, that was the same year that the Astoria & South Coast Railway arrived, in which Kinney was an investor. Some say that as early as 1888 there were visitors knocking **golf** balls around at Gearhart; certainly by 1892, the Hotel Gearhart (1890) had a three-hole course, and Kinney developed a full 9-hole course in 1901. After through train service from Portland was inaugurated in 1898, Gearhart thrived with the development of numerous large, cedar-shingled seaside summer homes. Noted food authority **James Beard** wrote a vivid account of Gearhart summer life in the early twentieth century, when families came for the season while father stayed in the city to work, rushing shoreward each weekend for a quick family reconnection.

Gearhart post office opened in 1897, and the town was incorporated in 1918; in 1920 it had a

Gearhart was a seashore resort for the well to do in the early 1900s, when a number of large, Craftsman-style summer houses were erected on the dunes facing the Pacific Ocean. Among the regular visitors were the family of James Beard. Benjamin A. Gifford photograph. Oregon Historical Society, Gi 7745.

population of 127. The Hotel Gearhart burned in 1913, and was replaced by a monumental shingled hostelry that perched on the foredune like a huge Cape Cod cottage. It, too, burned, and was replaced in 1923; that structure was demolished in 1972. Meanwhile, the golf course was altered and enlarged several times; the present 18-hole course is one of the oldest on the West Coast. Gearhart remains a town with many sequestered private summer homes strewn across the once-grassy dunes. The population in 2007 was estimated at 1,185.

George Fox University George Fox University is the descendent of Friends Pacific Academy, founded in Newberg in 1885 by the Society of Friends, often known as Quakers. In 1891, a collegiate-level school became Pacific College; the plethora of similarly named institutions (for example, **Pacific University**) eventually prompted changing the institution to George Fox College in 1949, honoring the founder of the Society of Friends. George Fox merged in 1996 with the graduate-level Western Evangelical Seminary, leading to the designation George Fox University. The school has grown considerably in size in recent years, with the enrollment in 2007 of about 3,185, and off-campus classes in Portland, Salem, Eugene, and Boise. Its athletic teams are known as the Bruins.

Georgia-Pacific (GP) In post–World War II Oregon, the Georgia-Pacific Company had a brief but high-impact presence. The company was founded in Atlanta in 1927, and moved west after the depletion of the Southern pine forests. GP bought existing plywood mills in Washington state and in Springfield in 1947–48, then purchased the huge C. D. Johnson lumber mill in **Toledo** in 1951. Company headquarters were moved from Atlanta to Portland in 1954, and additional mill properties and timberlands were acquired in **Coos Bay**, Springfield, and other points. In the early 1970s, a court-ordered breakup resulted in a spinoff company, Louisiana Pacific (LP); the LP offices were also in Portland, from 1973 until they moved to Tennessee in 2004. GP opened its grandiose Portland headquarters in 1970, a bland white tower that had three notable features: a museum of logging history; a sculpture created from an immense tree trunk, pierced by metal rods (the martyred tree in popular parlance); and a dazzlingly white stone sculpture of writhing horizontal nudes in a fountain (popularly Family Night at the Y or Three Groins in a Fountain, but officially named The Quest, by Count Alexander von Svoboda).

Having taken what they could from their forest lands, GP moved back to Atlanta in 1982; The Quest remained, but the martyred tree has vanished.

Germans in Oregon In the late nineteenth and early twentieth centuries, German-speaking immigrants were one of the largest foreign groups in the Oregon populace. One influx came as a result of revolution in Germany in 1848; others were attracted to the gold fields of California and southern Oregon, such as the Swiss-born **Peter Britt**. Merchants and brewers as well as many farmers were among the immigrants; they included Aaron Meier, one of the founders of the **Meier & Frank** department store in Portland and father of future governor **Julius L. Meier**, and Henry Weinhard, founder of the **Blitz-Weinhard Brewing Company**. In the 1860s German communalist farmers settled in **Aurora**, and in the 1880s German Catholics and German-speaking Swiss congregated in and around the town of **Mount Angel** in the Willamette Valley. Portland had a Turnverein Hall for German athletic and social affairs, and a chapter of the Arion Society, promoting German classical music; there were German language newspapers such as the *Oregon Deutsche Zeitung*, which began publishing in 1867; the *St. Joseph's Blatt* was issued in Mount Angel from 1896 to 1991. Some distinct anti-German activity occurred during World War I, symbolized by the changing of several street names in Portland: in the Brooklyn neighborhood, Frankfurt became Lafayette (for the French general who aided the American revolution), Karl became Haig (for a British general), Frederick became Pershing (for the American general). Germantown Road might have become Libertytown Road, but the war ended before the name was changed. Historian Eugene Snyder told the sad tale of Liebe Street, which "patriots" wanted renamed; it honored an early German-born settler, Carl G. Liebe. "Sad to say, Mr. Liebe was still living . . . which seems to make the proposal rather unfeeling," especially since liebe means love or charity in the German language. The city council had the good sense to reject the proposal in light of Mr. Liebe's long and faithful American citizenship.

Gervais Gervais in Marion County is a creation of the Oregon & California Railroad, which built south through this part of the Willamette Valley in 1870. The rich farmland in this section, **French Prairie**, had been settled in the 1830s; among the earliest white settlers was Joseph Gervais (1777–1861), a French-Canadian fur trapper who came west with **John Jacob Astor**'s Pacific Fur Company in 1811. Gervais was also prominent in the formation of the **provisional government** in 1843, and was a successful farmer. The new railroad town was named for Gervais, being located a few miles from his lands. A post office was opened in 1871 and the town was incorporated in 1874; the 1880 census gave Gervais a population of 202. Early in the twentieth century, Gervais was a center for "fruit, hops, hay, oats, wheat, hogs, poultry and dairying." Schreiner's **iris** nursery was founded near Gervais about 1925. The town's population reached 332 in 1940, and 992 by 1990; residential growth driven by the town's nearness to Salem boosted the count to an estimated 2,250 in 2007.

ghost towns Some Oregon towns have vanished, for reasons many and varied. **Champoeg** washed away in a flood; **Wheatland** dwindled to dust when riverboats ceased to be the major highway for wheat; mining towns like **Copperfield** and **Granite** dwindled when the mines failed to produce; cutting all the timber killed **Valsetz**, **Westfir**, **Seneca**, and Bridal Veil. Changing agriculture doomed **Shaniko**; lack of rain dried up **Fort Rock**.

Erickson, Kenneth A. *Lumber Ghosts: A Travel Guide to the Historic Lumber Towns of the Pacific Northwest.* Boulder, Colorado: Pruett, 1994.

Florin, Lambert. *Oregon Ghost Towns.* Seattle: Superior Publishing Co., 1970.
May, Keith F. *Ghosts of Times Past: A Roadtrip of Eastern Oregon Ghost Towns.* 2nd ed. Pendleton, Oregon: Drigh Sighed Publications, 1998.

Gilbert, Alfred Carlton (1884–1961) A. C. Gilbert was born in Salem, and attended Tualatin Academy and **Pacific University** in Forest Grove. A powerful athlete, Gilbert transferred to Yale in 1905. He did not come back to Oregon. He completed Yale with a degree in medicine, and he garnered a gold medal in the pole vault at the 1908 Olympics in London. Forsaking medicine, Gilbert went into the toy business, where the Erector set (1913), American Flyer trains, magic sets, and chemistry sets made the A. C. Gilbert Company famous. A. C. Gilbert's Discovery Village is a children's museum in **Salem** that started in 1989; it includes the Victorian house of Gilbert's uncle, Andrew T. Gilbert.

➤ **Gilchrist** The Gilchrist Timber Company, founded in Wisconsin in the 1880s, moved its operations to Mississippi after the northern woods were gone. In the early 1900s, they looked again, this time to the pine forests of northern Klamath County, where they acquired some 85,000 acres of timber by 1925. The Depression forestalled a westward move, but in 1937, construction began on the town of Gilchrist, the last **company town** built in Oregon. By 1938, the company-owned Klamath Northern Railroad was opened to the Southern Pacific line to the south and the sawmill and pine logging operations commenced. The company sold its mill in 1990 to another operator; the town's buildings were also sold to private individuals in 1997.

Fisher, Jim. *Gilchrist: The First Fifty Years.* Gilchrist, Oregon: Gilchrist Timber Co., 1988.

The very modern retail shops at the company town of Gilchrist, pictured shortly after construction was completed in 1938. Gilchrist was the last company town built in Oregon. The roofs were built to prevent snow buildup. Mason collection.

Gilliam County The eastern third of Wasco County was taken to create Gilliam County in 1885. It is named for Col. Cornelius Gilliam, a participant in the **Cayuse War** who was accidentally shot and killed in 1848. The temporary county seat was placed at **Arlington**, then named Alkali. A permanent county seat was not decided until 1890, when the county's voters selected **Condon**. However, those voters were, as the Oregon State Archives noted, "reluctant to provide a courthouse in Condon," so county government functioned within the walls of a two-room house until 1903. The courthouse burned in 1954, and a replacement was erected in 1955. Gilliam County has an area of 1,223 square miles.

The region now Gilliam County was part of the homeland of the **Sahaptin Indians**, who had villages along the Columbia River and traveled inland seasonally to gather food. The Middle Oregon treaty of 1855 created the Warm Springs Reservation; many of the descendants of the Sahaptin belong to the **Confederated Tribes of Warm Springs**.

Euro-American settlement waited for some time, despite the fact that the **Oregon Trail** crossed the county; the land did not appeal to those emigrants. Eventually some of them returned to the east side of the Cascade Range. The transcontinental railroad crossed the county through Arlington in 1883, but it was not until 1905 that a branch line was built up Alkali Canyon to Condon. The county is in the heart of the Columbia Plateau **wheat** region, and the chief products have long been wheat, barley, and beef cattle. Some irrigation at the northern end of the county has enabled the planting of apple orchards and vegetable crops. The county's population in 1890 was about 3,600; aside from a brief peak in 1920 when the figure reached 3,960, it has never been so great since. The census of 1950 showed 2,817 residents; the estimate in 2007 was 1,885.

Gladstone The area where Gladstone sits in Clackamas County was settled in the mid-nineteenth century, but a community came rather later. A post office with the name Gladstone opened in 1890, and an electric interurban railroad connecting Portland with Oregon City opened in 1893, rolling right down the main street. A **chautauqua** was established in 1893 on wooded grounds of ninety acres, and became the leading summer occasion for the town for many years. The distinctive beehive wooden building was demolished in 1954. Gladstone was incorporated in 1911; in 1915, it was reported that the population of the city "is made up of Portland and Oregon City office and business men, employees of the Oregon City Woolen and Paper Mills, and retired farmers. Onions and celery are quite extensively raised here." The 1920 census showed 1,069 residents; thirty years later, the figure was 2,434. The re-routing of the **Pacific Highway** via Gladstone in the 1930s began a long period of strip retail development along the city's western edge. Since the 1960s, this has been "auto row." The town's population has grown as it has merged into the Portland conurbation; the 1970 population was 6,254; in 1990, it was 10,152; the estimate in 2007 was 12,200.

One of Gladstone's landmarks is the Powwow tree, a bigleaf **maple** that began growing about 1780 and which has presided over the first Clackamas County Fair (1860), the first state fair (1861), and a variety of local festivities. It was designated a state heritage tree in 2004.

Glendale Located on Cow Creek in southern Douglas County, Glendale began to develop in 1883 as a station on the new Oregon & California Railroad; a post office opened the same year. Glendale station was near New Odessa, a short-lived communal colony of Russian Jews who farmed and provided wood for the railroad for fuel and crossties. The milling of lumber soon became—and has remained—the mainstay of the town's economy. Glendale was incorporated as a municipality in 1901, and the 1910 census reported a population of 646. Situated several miles from the Pacific Highway and the succeeding freeway, Glendale has been relatively isolated for most of its existence. A fire burned out the business district in 1928; things were fairly quiet until an arson fire at the Superior Lumber Company in 2001, attributed to the Earth Liberation Front. Glendale's estimated population in 2007 was 955.

Glenesslin see **shipwrecks**

gold The 1848 gold discoveries in California sent swarms of fortune seekers west—or, in the case of Oregon settlers, south. Hundreds, indeed thousands, of Oregonians rushed for the gold fields. Some came back, others stayed; some returned and began growing provisions for California miners, or producing lumber for them. By 1851, gold discoveries were being made in southern Oregon: along the **Illinois** and **Applegate Rivers** and its tributaries, including Rich Gulch at **Jacksonville**; on the coastal sands north of **Bandon**, and at **Gold Beach**. The excitements of the 1850s are entwined with troubles over land and Indians, characterized by the **Rogue River Wars**. Gold discoveries in Idaho and Montana in the 1860s impacted Oregon because Portland became the entry for supplies, sent from San Francisco by ship and then up the Columbia River via the **Oregon Steam Navigation Company** boats. Gold discoveries were made in the 1860s in Oregon in **Baker** and **Grant Counties**, site of the camps of Auburn and **Canyon City**. Another rush in northeastern Oregon occurred in the early 1900s, and in the Calapooya Mountains in the **Bohemia mining district** in the 1870s, with later recurrences. Gold has been found and mined at a variety of other places including **Ashland** in the Siskiyou Mountains, **Cornucopia** in the Wallowas, Golden near Wolf Creek, and Quartzville on the upper reaches of the North Santiam River.

Brooks, Howard C., and Len Ramp. *Gold and Silver in Oregon*. Portland, Oregon: Oregon

Department of Geology and Mineral Industries, 1968.

Gold Beach Romantically named Gold Beach began its life as mundane Ellensburgh, although it is also rather sweet that its namesake was Sarah Ellen Tichenor, daughter of Capt. William (1813–1887) and Betsy Tichenor, founders of **Port Orford**. **Gold** was indeed found in the sands of the beach here, near the mouth of the Rogue River, in the 1850s. This excitement gave rise to the creation of **Curry County** in 1855; Port Orford was the first seat of county government, but that moved to Ellensburgh in 1859. Flooding of the Rogue River in 1861 brought a virtual end to the beach mining, and in 1863, remote Ellensburgh was given a post office. The post office department in 1877 dropped the *h*, and the name was changed to Gold Beach in 1890. A few years later, in 1895, Gold Beach became the terminus of a mail route that has persisted ever since and has become a major tourist attraction: **mail boats**—first a rowboat, later gas and then "jet" boats—began ferrying the mail on the wild **Rogue River** between Gold Beach and Agness, a settlement some thirty-two miles upriver. Although the route today is seen as one carrying the mail from "civilization" (Gold Beach) to the remote interior, in the original scheme Gold Beach was at the end of a tortuous route from the railhead via pack train (or pack man, on foot) and boat to the remote seashore.

Gold Beach was the site of the first **salmon** cannery in Oregon, established by Robert D. Hume in 1876. Salmon canning peaked in the early 1900s; by 1935, the depletion of salmon had become so severe that commercial fishing was ended. Gold Beach also became a center of sports fishing, both on the Rogue, beginning in the 1890s, and at sea. The completion of **Conde B. McCullough**'s bridge across the Rogue River in 1932 marked the completion of the **Oregon Coast Highway**, although there were still some amendments yet to come. While small sea-going steamships made landings at Gold Beach, the har-

bor was poor; the new bridge and highway ended Gold Beach's isolation. The city of Gold Beach was not incorporated until 1945, and the 1950 census counted 677 souls living there. The growth in tourism and retirement living has gradually boosted its population; the 1970 census recorded 1,554 residents; the estimated population in 2007 was 2,445.

Gold Hill Place names historian Lewis L. McArthur wrote, "There is now some controversy as to the exact location of the hill so known, but, from what evidence the writer has seen, it is quite certain that the original Gold Hill was on the south bank of Rogue River opposite the present community of Gold Hill." Jackson County was awash in minor gold discoveries in the mid-nineteenth century. One of the successful miners was Thomas Chavner (1814–1888), who in middle age made a modest financial success of a gold mine he operated at Gold Hill. Thomas and his wife, Margaret (1827–1880), had five children between 1862 and 1877, and Thomas planned to build a large house for his family. He died in 1888, and his surviving children completed the house shortly after. The Chavner house is on the National Register of Historic Places, a Victorian extravaganza designed by the East Coast firm of Palliser & Palliser, which published plan books of house designs. The Oregon & California Railroad reached the area in 1883, and the Gold Hill post office opened in 1884. Gold Hill was incorporated in 1895, and the 1900 census showed a population of 385. By 1915, Gold Hill had two lumber planing mills, a box factory, a machine shop, and a cement factory, and five gold mines with mills in the area. One of those, on Sardine Creek, in the 1930s became the site of the **House of Mystery**. The town's growth was slow; the population reached 619 in 1950, and 603 in 1970. Since then, the town has become a residential suburb of Grants Pass; the estimated population in 2007 was 1,080.

golf Golf may have had its beginnings in Oregon

at **Gearhart** about 1888; or perhaps the game there came a bit later in 1892. The antecedents of Portland's Waverley Country Club were enthusiasts who played on a course set up in 1890 on the unsold lots of the Waverly subdivision, located in the vicinity of SE Twenty-seventh Avenue and Powell Boulevard—a street is still there named Waverleigh Boulevard (yes, there are three spellings; all derive from the series of novels by Sir Walter Scott). In 1899, the group arranged to remove to a new site on the Willamette River north of Milwaukie; they added an *e* to Waverly and in 1900 began developing a large course. In Medford, the Rogue Valley Country Club, with a membership of wealthy, sporting Easterners who were engaged in the booming fruit industry, began in 1910; among them was a college, amateur and Olympic golfing champion, H. Chandler Egan (1884–1936). Egan went on to a career designing gold courses, beginning in the 1924 with the Medford club, and including courses at the Eugene Country Club, Eastmoreland in Portland (public), and Oswego Lake Country Club, among others. In 1929, he co-designed the renovation of the course at Pebble Beach, California. Courses have developed throughout the state, ranging from the nine holes in the wheat country in Condon, in the shadow of the Archer Daniels Midland grain elevator (built 1967), to the almost absurdly posh courses near **Bandon** known as Bandon Dunes (opened 1999).

Good Government Congress An unusual political movement in Jackson County during the Depression evolved into a series of events that has been, rather melodramatically, referred to as Jackson County's Civil War. The Good Government Congress was the creation of **Medford** newspaper publisher and activist Llewellyn A. Banks, with the support of Earl Fehl, another publisher and a county commissioner (they were called county judges at that time). The Congress broadly assailed local government, calling them the Gang, and in 1933 they physically interfered in a county sheriff election; for that, Fehl among others was arrested. Inquiries by the Oregon state police led to Medford officer George Prescott knocking on the front door of the Banks residence. Banks shot the officer dead. The senseless shooting destroyed the Congress, but for strong investigative reporting and editorializing, Robert W. Ruhl, editor and publisher of the Medford *Mail Tribune*, won a well-deserved Pulitzer Prize.

LaLande, Jeff. The "Jackson County Rebellion": Social Turmoil and Political Insurgence in Southern Oregon during the Great Depression. *Oregon Historical Quarterly* 95, no. 4 (Winter 1994–95): 406–471.

Goose Hollow neighborhood, Portland This neighborhood is situated in the vicinity of SW Jefferson Street and Eighteenth Avenue. The genesis of the name is said to be the fact that in the 1890s, Tanner Creek, which came out of the **Tualatin Mountains** at that point to wend north and east to the Willamette River, provided common watering holes for several families that raised geese. A dispute arose over whose geese were whose; the press reported that the squabble occurred in Goose Hollow. The area was the site of a cable car powerhouse in the 1890s; the cable car line ran on Jefferson and turned south on Eighteenth to climb a rickety trestle to Portland Heights. The area name was revived in 1967 by the Goose Hollow Inn, operated by noted tavern-keeper Bud Clark, who lost his previous establishment, the Spatenhaus, to **urban renewal** (it was located on the block now comprising the **Keller Fountain**). Clark later served as mayor of Portland (1985–1993). The Goose Hollow neighborhood was noted in the 1950s and 1960s as a location for inexpensive housing for artists and Portland State University students; the construction of the Interstate 405 freeway and a connection to the **Sunset Highway** demolished the majority of the area's small Victorian workers' houses.

Goose Lake *see* **Lakeview**

Gorge, The This is a common term for the section of the **Columbia River** extending from near Biggs downriver about eighty miles to the vicinity of Troutdale. This stretch of the river is characterized by high, vertical cliffs, with many waterfalls on the south bank, and, until the completion of **Bonneville Dam** and **The Dalles Dam**, a succession of turbulent places: **Celilo Falls**, **The Dalles**, and the **Cascades**.

gorse The common European gorse, *Ulex europaeus*, is said to have been introduced about 1893 in the vicinity of **Bandon** on the Oregon Coast. The Oregon Department of Agriculture, which classifies gorse as a noxious weed, describes it as a "stiff, spiny, much-branched shrub, often forming dense thickets," and growing from one to nine feet in height. It is also a "persistent, spiny, pioneer species" that grows rapidly in a wide range of circumstances. It contains a good deal of natural oils in its spines and is highly flammable; indeed, gorse fueled the ferocious fire that burned Bandon to the ground in 1936. It is found west of the Cascade Range, especially in coastal Coos and Lane Counties.

government *see* **politics and government; provisional government**

► **Government Camp** The Clackamas County community of Government Camp owes its name to an incident involving a contingent of the U.S. Mounted Rifles, which took the **Barlow Road** in 1849. A snowstorm wiped out many of the animals, and some forty-five wagons were abandoned on the road.

The Skiway was a bizarre aerial tramway that opened in 1951 between Government Camp and Timberline Lodge. Passengers were carried in wheelless city buses suspended from the overhead cables. The system was a financial bust and operated for only a few winter seasons. Sawyer's photograph. Steven Dotterrer collection.

The community had a small hotel and various summer cabins in the early years of the twentieth century, but did not develop much until a winter road was opened in 1926. Winter sports—ski jumping, downhill **skiing**—soon developed. Government Camp post office opened in 1931; the construction of **Timberline Lodge** on the slopes of Mount Hood above gave added impetus to Government Camp, as did work by the **Civilian Conservation Corps** to clear snags from ski trails.

► **Grande Ronde River** The valley of the Grande Ronde River was historically part of the homeland of the **Nez Perce** and **Cayuse Indians**. It extends about 180 miles from headwaters in the Blue Mountains, and traverses Union and Wallowa Counties to empty into the Snake River in Washington state. The valley north of La Grande is excellent agricultural territory and was settled for farming in the 1880s. A large stretch of the Grande Ronde is a designated Wild and Scenic River noted for its wilderness experience. It was once a major salmon stream; dams have reduced the runs to near extinction.

► **Grandmother Rock** This landmark rock was located at the mouth of the **Coquille River** in Coos County, and was a sacred site to the **Coos Indians**; the name is translated from the Miluk Coos language. White settlers called it Tupper Rock, naming it for Bandon hotelier John P. Tupper. Most of Grandmother Rock was demolished and used in jetty construction in 1903. The seal of the Confederated Tribes of the Coos, Lower Umpqua, and Siuslaw

The highly productive valley of the Grande Ronde River is viewed from the top of Mount Emily, about 1949. Oregon State Highway Commission photograph. *Oregon Journal* collection. Oregon Historical Society, OrHi 105353.

J. P. Tupper's Ocean House hotel and Grandmother Rock as they were pictured in A. G. Walling's *History of Southern Oregon*, **1884.** Oregon Historical Society, OrHi 106096.

Indians depicts the rock, whose site remains sacred to the Coos.

Grand Ronde The town of Grand Ronde was originally the settlement that grew up around the Bureau of Indian Affairs headquarters for the **Grand Ronde Reservation**, established in 1855; the town was known as Grand Ronde Agency. In 1915, when most of the reservation land had been allotted to individual Indians, the town was described as having a population of "30 (white); over 300 Indians in former GRIR." Stock raising, dairying, fruit growing, and hog raising were the agricultural activities, and some logging was done. Grand Ronde Agency had both Roman Catholic and German Methodist churches, and there was an "eighteen piece Indian band."

In 1922, a railroad was extended from Willamina, about nine miles east and the terminus of a branch of the **Southern Pacific Company**, to "New Grand Ronde," which was located about two miles south of Grand Ronde Agency in Yamhill County. By 1924, the Spaulding-Miami Lumber Company had built a sawmill, a rather elaborate two-story railroad station, and a very imposing hotel that resembled a Swiss chalet. For the next fifty years, this was a lumber town.

The re-establishment of the Confederated Tribes of Grand Ronde in 1983 began another round of changes in the town. Grand Ronde is the headquarters for the **Confederated Tribes of Grand Ronde**, which opened nearby Spirit Mountain Casino in 1995. The railroad station survives as tribal offices; the railroad itself ceased to operate about 1980. The lumber company's once-grand hotel was converted to a bed and breakfast inn.

Grand Ronde Reservation The Grand Ronde Reservation was created in 1855 as a result of treaties signed that year by a number of western Oregon tribes, negotiated by Indian agent **Joel Palmer**. It also came to include Indians from the Oregon Coast after the closure of reservations there in 1865 and 1875. The reservation was ended with the Termination Act of 1954, but the Confederated Tribes of Grand Ronde persisted, and succeeded in accomplishing restoration; the tribes were granted a 9,811–acre reservation in 1988.

Granite This picturesque former gold-mining community in Grant County began in 1862 and prospered sporadically into the 1870s. A post office opened in 1878. City government was established in 1901, when about 250 people lived there; the count was forty-five in 1930, and forty in 1950; the 1970 census reported a mere four residents, and the post office was closed in 1957. By 2007, **ghost town** tourism had helped the count rebound to thirty.

Grant County Named most honorably for the commander of the Union Army, Gen. Ulysses S. Grant, Grant County was established on October 14, 1864. The land for the county was taken from Wasco and Umatilla Counties; the later establishment of Lake, Harney, and Wheeler Counties reduced its size to the present 4,528 square miles. **Canyon City**, then a gold rush center, was the first and permanent county seat. The 1870 census—for a rather larger county—showed 2,251 residents, Indians excepted.

The southern portion of what is now Grant County was once the northern extent of the homeland of the **Northern Paiute Indians**. In the mid-nineteenth century, the Paiutes tended to keep farther to the south, and **Umatilla** and **Cayuse Indians** moved into some of those lands. The northwestern areas of the county were part of the seasonal homeland of the **Sahaptin Indians** of the Columbia River, who ranged into the upper drainage of the John Day River seeking roots, camas, trout, and lamprey. Descendants of these tribes might be members of the

Confederated Tribes of the Umatilla Indian Reservation, **Confederated Tribes of Warm Springs**, or the **Burns Paiute Tribe**.

The first economic activity by white emigrants was gold mining, which took place in the 1860s on Canyon Creek in Canyon City, in John Day, and in camps to the north in the vicinity of Susanville. Placer gold mining persisted for some years, but ceased to be the mainstay of the economy; it was replaced by livestock raising and the growing of alfalfa and hay in the **John Day River** valley, and lumbering. Much of the county is national forest land in the Blue Mountains, which has supplied mills in John Day as well as timber that was shipped east to Baker City over the **Sumpter Valley Railway**. Many **Chinese** miners were in Grant County, especially in the 1880s; some stayed to form a small Chinese community in **John Day**. For many years, the community was anchored by Ing "Doc" Hay and Lung On, who were business partners until Lung On's death in 1940; Doc Hay continued to do business until 1948, and died in 1952. Their business was selling goods of all kinds to the Chinese community, but especially dealing in prescribing and selling traditional Chinese herbal remedies, to all who asked. The store and its contents remained intact, and the store is on the National Register of Historic Places; it was named a National Historic Landmark in 2005. Grant County's population was 5,610 in 1910, the year the Sumpter Valley Railway reached **Prairie City**. In 1950, with a minor post–World War II lumber boom, the population was 8,329; in 1970, 6,996; and the estimate in 2007 was 7,580.

Grants Pass This is the county seat of Josephine County. The name Grants Pass was apparently given to a location along the **California-Oregon Trail** to honor the Civil War victories of Gen. Ulysses S. Grant. It was applied when a post office was established in 1865. Grants Pass was a small community until the arrival of the **Oregon & California Railroad** in 1883. A county boundary change shifted

Grants Pass from Jackson to Josephine County, and the Josephine county seat was moved from the old gold-mining town of Kerby. Grants Pass was incorporated in 1887, and developed as a lumber-milling center; the 1890 census reported 1,432 residents. The establishment of the nearby **Oregon Caves** National Monument in 1909 helped establish tourism as an economic force, further enhanced by recreational fishing in the Rogue River and the development in the 1920s of the **Redwood Highway** to and along the California coast. A group of pelt-clad businessmen formed the Grants Pass Cavemen in 1922 to promote the city, and the caveman theme is still prominent in the area. A fiberglass statue of a caveman was erected in 1971, and the high school mascot, too, is a caveman. The city's population in 1930 was 4,666; it reached 8,116 in 1950 with increased post–World War II logging. Recreation, especially boating and rafting on the **Rogue River**, has grown since the 1950s as well, and Grants Pass has prospered since the 1990s with an influx of retirees. The population in 1970 was 12,455; in 2007, it was estimated at 31,740.

grapes *see* **wine and wine making**

Grass Valley "Pioneer settlers, without ever changing countenance, tell newcomers that in early days the rye-grass was so tall in this part of Oregon that it was well over a man's head. They even state that this was so when the man was on horseback. This accounts for the name." So said geographic names historian Lewis L. McArthur. Grass Valley is in Sherman County, in wheat country. The rural Grass Valley post office opened in 1882, but the community formed around the station of the Columbia Southern Railroad, which began building south from the Columbia River toward **Shaniko** in 1897; it reached that point in 1901. Grass Valley was incorporated the same year, and the 1910 census reported 342 residents. By 1915, the town had three large grain warehouses, a bank, and a weekly newspaper.

The 1950 census showed 195 residents; the estimated population in 2007 was 170.

Graveyard of the Pacific There is more than one. One is near the entrance to the Strait of Juan de Fuca, the southern and western coast of Vancouver Island, where hundreds of vessels have been lost. A *Wikipedia* entry in 2007 stated, clumsily, that the term referred to a "coastal region in the Pacific Northwest Coast from Oregon northward to the tip of Vancouver Island." In Oregon, the "graveyard" is specifically the mouth of the Columbia River, where a treacherous bar, shifting sand islands and alternate channels, dense fog, strong currents, and heavy rains have contributed to some 2,000 **shipwrecks** and to the loss of more than 700 lives. It has also been called the River of Lost Ships.

Gibbs, Jim. *Pacific Graveyard: A Narrative of Shipwrecks where the Columbia River meets the Pacific Ocean.* 4th ed. Portland, Oregon: Binfords & Mort, 1993.

Gray, Robert (1755–1806) Although thousands of Indians lived along its shores, the Columbia River is said to have been discovered in 1792 by Robert Gray, an American sea captain from Rhode Island. During the Revolutionary War, young Gray served in the Continental Navy, and he worked afterwards for a trading company in Massachusetts. Gray and Capt. John Kendrick sailed in 1787 on a trading expedition to the North Pacific Coast, Gray commanding the *Lady Washington* and Kendrick the **Columbia Rediviva**. Gray entered Tillamook Bay in 1788, where one of his crew was killed. After trading for furs and switching ships, Gray took the furs to Canton, China, and proceeded back to Boston, arriving in 1790 and completing a circumnavigation of the globe, the first by an American merchant ship.

The success of that voyage led to a second trip beginning but two months later, again with the *Lady Washington* and the *Columbia Rediviva*. While sailing north up the Oregon Coast, Gray noticed a strong steam of muddy water swirling out from the shore, and he investigated, crossing the dangerous bar and entering the river on May 11, 1792. He named the river for his ship, the Columbia. Gray continued his trading expedition, and went around the world again, arriving in Boston in July 1793. On October 19, 1792, Lt. William Broughton, under the direction of the British Capt. **George Vancouver**, also entered the river, traveling much farther upstream than did Gray. The United States later made use of Gray's incursion as a basis for American claims to the Oregon Territory. Gray continued to sail in the merchant marine along the Atlantic seaboard until his death in 1806.

> Howay, Frederic William. *Voyages of the "Columbia" to the Northwest Coast, 1787–1790 and 1790–1793*. Ed. Frederic W. Howay. Boston: Massachusetts Historical Society, 1941. Reprint. Portland, Oregon: Oregon Historical Society in cooperation with the Massachusetts Historical Society, 1990.
>
> Scofield, John. *Hail, Columbia!: Robert Gray, John Kendrick, and the Pacific Fur Trade*. Portland, Oregon: Oregon Historical Society Press, 1993.

Great Migration The first large contingent of American emigrants to the Oregon Country took place in the spring of 1843. The Great Migration traveled in two large groups, totaling about 875 persons. Among these **pioneers** were **Jesse** and **Lindsay Applegate**, **Asa L. Lovejoy**, and **James W. Nesmith**.

Great Northern Railroad (GN) The Great Northern Railroad extended from Saint Paul, Minnesota, west to Seattle, completing its main line in 1893. Its founder and longtime leader was James J. Hill, known as the *Empire Builder*. The Great Northern acquired a route into Portland from Seattle in 1910, and it also constructed a line from Bend south to Klamath Falls and into California in 1928–30. In the 1910s, GN and the **Northern Pacific Railway** formed the Great Northern Pacific Steamship Company, which built fast ocean steamships to run between Flavel, near Astoria, and San Francisco. The **Astoria Column** was primarily financed by the Great Northern, which ran a special transcontinental train to its dedication ceremonies. The Great Northern was also the half-owner, with the Northern Pacific Railway, of the **Spokane, Portland & Seattle Railway**, the **Oregon Electric Railway**, and the **Oregon Trunk Railway**. *See also* **Burlington Northern Santa Fe Railway**.

Great Reinforcement The term is used to describe a group of Methodist missionaries who came to the **Oregon Country** in 1840 in response to entreaties to the church made by the Rev. **Jason Lee** in 1838. Lee's plea for Methodist settlers was in part intended to counter the influence of the British **Hudson's Bay Company** and increase the American presence. The group of forty-nine emigrants arrived at Fort Vancouver aboard the ship *Lausanne* and included several future local luminaries in the region, including **George Abernethy**.

Green, Edith Starrett (1910–1987) Edith Green was born in South Dakota, and moved to Oregon with her parents in 1916. She graduated from the University of Oregon and began a career in education and politics: teaching school, doing radio commentaries, working for the Oregon Education Association, running for the office of secretary of state, and serving as a delegate to Democratic national conventions. A Portland resident, Green was elected to the U.S. House of Representatives in 1954 (she defeated the Republican candidate, **Tom McCall**, a future governor), and was re-elected nine times. She was Oregon's second woman representative (after **Nan Wood Honeyman**), a liberal Democrat and one of seventeen women in the House in 1955. Green devoted her attentions to education and issues of women's rights, proposing the Equal Pay Act in

1955; it was finally enacted in 1963. She promoted rural library service, and she worked hard for the passage of what became known as Title IX, which prohibits sex discrimination in federally funded schools; among other things, the law helped promote athletic opportunities for college women. After retiring from politics at the end of 1974, Green taught government at Warner Pacific College and served on the Oregon Board of High Education. A federal office building in Portland is named for her and Wendell Wyatt, her Republican colleague who served in the House from 1963 through 1974.

▶ **Greenhorn** Now a **ghost town** on the border between Baker and Grants Counties, Greenhorn was a gold-mining camp in the 1860s and 1870s. It was incorporated in 1903, when mining was still going on; the post office operated from 1902 until 1919. It has had no permanent population for several decades, but still exists as an incorporated entity with an estimated population in 2007 of two.

▶ **Gresham** Given the name of the then-postmaster general in Washington, DC, Gresham post office opened in 1884 in a rural section of Multnomah County. The town was linked to Portland by electric **interurban railway** in 1903, and it was incorporated in 1904. By 1915, its population of 1,200 was supported by agriculture, especially berries and fruit, dairying, poultry raising, and truck gardening, supplying the Portland market. Gresham also had a brickyard and sawmills, and was the headquarters of the Oregon State Grange. In 1907, the local granges sponsored the first Multnomah County Fair; Gresham was the site for the fair until 1970. Interurban commuter service ceased prior to 1950, at which time the town's population was 3,049. Suburban residential growth came soon thereafter; while Gresham's population in 1950 was 3,049, it reached 33,005 in 1980. Commuter rail service returned with **MAX** in 1986; the population in 2007 was estimated at 99,225. Berries are still grown—barely—at the city's eastern edges.

Grey, Zane (1875–1939) The popular writer of Western adventure fiction was also a noted outdoorsman who was fond of fishing on the **Rogue River**. Grey acquired a cabin on a former mining claim at

MAIN STREET IN GREENHORN, ONCE A THRIVING CITY OF 500 PEOPLE

The main street of Greenhorn as it appeared in November of 1929. Located at an elevation of 6,257 feet, Greenhorn was a nineteenth-century gold-mining town that had a revival in the early 1900s, but was deserted by the time of World War I. *Oregon Journal* collection. Oregon Historical Society, OrHi 83020.

Winkle Bar, and wrote and fished there; among the products were *Tales of Freshwater Fiction* (1909) and *Rogue River Feud* (1929).

Guilds Lake district, Portland Guild or Guilds Lake was once a swampy, low-lying body of water in northwest Portland, a prime habitat for **wapato** and game birds. In the late nineteenth century, Chinese woodcutters lived nearby, and there were several dairies on its shores. The lake's moment of glory came in 1905, when the shores were cleared, the water level was raised, and the fabulous **Lewis and Clark Centennial Exposition** was held there. In succeeding years, the lake was filled in with dredge spoil and soil sluiced from the hills above, to create railroad yards and industrial plants and warehouses. During World War II, emergency housing was erected in the Guilds Lake area.

Guthrie, Woodrow Wilson "Woody" (1912–1967) The noted American folk musician and song-writer Woody Guthrie spent one month in the spring of 1941 in Oregon and Washington state. He was there working on behalf of the beleaguered Bonneville Power Administration (BPA) to produce a music track for their promotional motion picture, *The Columbia*, produced to promote the use of public hydroelectric power. Brief though it was, Guthrie's visit produced several songs that have become iconic to the region. This is particularly true of "Roll on, Columbia, Roll on," which in 1987 was designated the official Washington state folk song. Countless cruise line and bus tourists have been handed the lyrics and forced to sing it en route to visit **Bonneville Dam** and the Columbia River Gorge. *The Columbia*, produced by Stephen Kahn, was not completed until 1948; in 1953, newly empowered Republicans in the BPA ordered copies of the film and its songs destroyed, to prevent Guthrie's populist lyrics from being further disseminated. A copy survived, and it was reissued on videocassette in 1993.

Carriker, Robert C. Ten Dollars a Song: Woody

The retail district of downtown Gresham in the 1930s. Wesley Andrews photograph. Oregon Historical Society, OrHi 15675.

Guthrie Sells His Talent to the Bonneville Power Administration. *Columbia* 15, no. 1 (Spring 2001).

gyppo A gyppo or gypo logger is a contractor, an independent operator who sells logs to a mill and does the hauling. The rise of the log truck and the sales of timber in lots on federal lands made it possible for small-scale loggers to engage in business, and gyppo logging operations rose in the 1930s and blossomed in the late 1940s and early 1950s in Oregon. The life of the gyppo operator was at the center of **Ken Kesey**'s novel *Sometimes a Great Notion*. The term is derived from the small contractor's ability to cut the price of work by cutting various corners, such as by working long hours, and thus "gyp" a regular contractor of his prospects. As Walter F. McCulloch noted in *Woods Words*, "So many one time little gypos have grown into medium sized or big operators that the term has become more respectable today, [and] does not mean gypping."

▶ **Gypsies in Oregon** Gypsies or Rom or Romani people were reported in Oregon in the late nineteenth century, itinerants noted for colorful dress, fortune-tellers, and shrewd bargaining over horses. In the 1940s and 1950s, many Romani families settled in the Portland area; a number of used-car dealerships in southeast Portland were Gypsy-owned, and retail storefronts in older downtown Portland buildings were often family homes.

These Gypsy children are cooling off in the David P. Thompson Memorial fountain—better known as The Elk—on SW Main Street in Portland, on July 9, 1952. Romani families lived in former retail storefronts near SW Second and Third Avenues in this vicinity. Oregon Historical Society, OrHi 106088.

H

Haines A community began in Baker County's Powder River valley in 1883; the next year the railroad reached the area and a post office was opened, named for local landowner I. D. Haines. A townsite was platted in 1885, and municipal government was formalized in 1901. The population in 2007 was about 435. Since the 1960s, Haines has been noted for its Eastern Oregon Museum of History and for the Haines Steak House. The area is agricultural, producing hay, grain, and cattle.

Halfway Located in Baker County, Halfway is (broadly speaking) halfway between the ghost gold-mining town of **Cornucopia** and the near-vanished community of Pine. The Pine Creek Valley was an established cattle-ranching area when the Halfway post office opened in 1887. A small town grew up, a supply point for the gold mines to the north and the surrounding farmers and ranchers. Halfway was incorporated in 1909, and a few years later could boast of a bank, a high school, a weekly newspaper, and three churches. Halfway's moment of quirky fame came in 2000 when, as a publicity stunt for the Internet firm Half.com, the town made that its name. The moment passed, and Halfway has returned. It counted about 355 residents in 2007.

Hall, Hazel (1886–1924) Born in Minnesota, Hazel Hall and her family moved to Portland when she was a young girl. When she was twelve, an incident— scarlet fever? a fall?—left her an invalid, wheelchair-bound. She lived with her mother and sister in a house in Northwest Portland, where she did fine needlework to help the family income. As her eyes began to fail, Hall turned to writing poetry when she was in her twenties, poems often occasioned by the sights from her second-floor window, and intro-spections about loneliness, isolation, and the work

of women. "To an English Sparrow" was her first published poem; it ran in the Boston *Transcript* in 1916. In the next few years, Hall was a literary sensation, with her poetry published in numerous national publications, including *Harper's* and the *Yale Review*. A collection of poems, many dealing with sewing, was issued in 1921 as *Curtains*; *Walkers* was issued in 1923. Her career was brief; Hall died in 1924.

The annual poetry honors of the Oregon Book Awards are named for Hazel Hall. The house where she lived and wrote, the window from which she viewed her world, is on the National Register of Historic Places.

Halsey The rural community of Halsey developed along the Oregon & California Railroad, which built through the area in 1871. The area had been thickly settled from the 1840s, and Halsey became the shipping point for agricultural produce, which had previously gone through the Willamette River landing of Peoria some six miles west. The town plat was that year filed by William L. Halsey, and incorporation followed in 1876. Farming, especially of grains and fruit, and in recent years the raising of grass seed, has been the principal industry. In 1968, Halsey became the site of a large pulp mill. Halsey's population in 2007 was about 780.

Hammond Hammond was once an incorporated town in Clatsop County; it is still a postal address, although it was subsumed within the boundaries of **Warrenton** in 1991. Located on Point Adams at the mouth of the Columbia River, Hammond was initially platted as New Astoria, and was adjacent to **Fort Stevens**. The fort and Hammond were connected to Astoria and Portland by railroad in 1898; the railroad was owned and developed by lumberman A. B. Hammond (1848–1934), who also built a large lumber mill at Astoria. The Hammond post office opened in 1897, and incorporation followed in 1899. A 1915 promotional booklet noted that Hammond had a salmon cannery, and alleged that there was "good farming country tributary" to it; this was a distinct exaggeration.

The 1910 census reported a population of 957; this fell to 244 by 1930, and rose to 522 in 1950. Hammond remained a small town dependent on fisheries-related industry.

Hanis Indians *see* Coos Indians

Hanley, William "Bill" (1861–1935) Born on a family farm near Jacksonville, Bill Hanley grew up with livestock, and in 1879 went into ranching with his brothers when they purchased land in far-distant Harney County. Bill Hanley acquired the **Double O Ranch** at Harney Lake, and made it a legendary center of rangeland hospitality and the largest cattle ranch in the county; closer to Burns, he built up the Bell A Ranch, where he hosted local luminaries such as **C. E. S. Wood** and Wood's friend, the nationally famed artist Childe Hassam. Hanley was a congenial man with political aspirations. In the pre-World War I years, when Oregon politics bubbled with populist ideas, Hanley ran for governor, but lost; he was the unsuccessful candidate for U.S. senator in 1914 on the Progressive Party ticket. Hanley was long a proponent of development; he owned the Harney Valley Improvement Company and pushed the construction of the **Oregon Trunk Railway** into Central Oregon. But, as historians Jeff LaLande and Cain Allen have written, he "came to see the government's policy of encouraging small-scale homesteads in the arid region as folly." Hanley became an ardent spokesman for the conservation of wildlife. But he remained a booster of the region he loved. Hanley was attending "Bill Hanley Day" at the Pendleton Round-Up on September 15, 1935, when he died.

Monroe, Anne Shannon, and William Hanley.

Feelin' Fine!: Bill Hanley's Book. Garden City, New York: Doubleday, Doran & Co., 1930.

Happy Valley Happy Valley in Clackamas County was settled by farming families in the 1850s, and it was thoroughly rural until suburban developments began in the 1950s. The community was incorporated in 1965; the 1970 census reported 1,392 residents. Since the 1990 count of 1,519 residents, residential growth has been explosive in Happy Valley, which in 2007 had an estimated population of 10,380.

Harney County In 1889, the southern two-thirds of Grant County was sliced off to form Harney County, named for Gen. William S. Harney, who was commander of the U.S. Army's Department of Oregon in 1858–59. It is Oregon's largest county in area, with 10,228 square miles. The county seat is **Burns**, where the first seat of county government was in the Smith and Young building, erected there in 1890. The building was purchased by Burns citizens to give to the county, an inducement to pick Burns over rival Harney City for the county seat. The present courthouse was built in 1942. The region was long part of the homeland of the **Northern Paiute Indians**, and the **Burns Paiute Tribe and Reservation** is located just outside Burns.

The end of the **Bannock War** in 1878 brought cattle ranchers such as **Pete French** and **Bill Hanley** into the area. Much of the county was available for homesteading, but the opposition of ranchers was coupled with the area's harsh climate. A series of years with relatively higher rainfall in the early 1900s, coupled with a common but mistaken belief that "rain follows the plow" (that is, plowed lands actually were thought to attract higher rainfall levels), helped inspire a rash of homesteading in eastern Oregon. Homesteads were claimed throughout the Harney Basin and the Catlow Valley and farm settlers planted wheat and other grains with high hopes. The homestead boom went bust before 1920, leaving behind numerous agricultural **ghost towns** and abandoned farms. Harney County's population in the 1890 census was 2,559; in 1920, after a peak a few years earlier, it was 3,992. The railroad arrived in Burns in 1924 and the construction of the large Edward Hines mill complex at **Hines** brought a new era of lumber prosperity. The population in 1950 was 6,113, and in 1980 it reached 8,314. The last timber products mill closed in 2007. Alfalfa raising and cattle ranching continue. Tourism has been encouraged by the appeal of the Malheur Wildlife Refuge, **Steens Mountain**, and other natural features. Harney County's estimated population in 2007 was 7,680.

Brimlow, George Francis. *Harney County, Oregon, and Its Range Land*. Portland, Oregon: Binfords & Mort, 1951.

Harney Lake This shallow alkali lake in Harney County is in the Malheur National Wildlife Refuge. During normal water years, it is less than four feet in depth, but it has been known to dry up in drought times. The Harney Basin is fed by the Silvies and **Donner und Blitzen Rivers**, which empty into **Malheur Lake**. When the water level is high enough, the water passes through the Narrows into Mud Lake and then into Harney Lake. During the extraordinary high water levels of the 1980s and the late 1990s, all three lakes merged. The only life form in the lake is a form of brine shrimp.

➤ **Harrisburg** The Linn County town of Harrisburg is located on the Willamette River in an area that was settled by farming families in the 1850s. The post office of Harrisburg opened in 1855; in times of high water, river steamboats could reach upriver as far as Harrisburg, and the community was incorporated in 1866. The **Oregon & California Railroad** passed through the town in 1871, and the 1880 census showed a population of 442 residents. Through World War II, Harrisburg remained a supply center for the area's farmers, its population growing slowly; it reached 862 by 1950, and 1,939 in 1980; the estimated population in 2007 was 3,400.

Main St Harrisburg Oregon.

The Linn County town of Harrisburg did not present a prosperous appearance when photographer J. G. Crawford took this picture, probably in the mid-1870s. Oregon Historical Society, CN 016033.

Harry and David The Fruit-of-the-Month Club company known as Harry and David grew out of an orchard in the **Bear Creek Valley** that Seattle hotelier Samuel Rosenberg acquired in 1910: he traded his new Sorrento Hotel for 240 acres of pears and apples. After his death in 1914, his sons Harry and David took over the business; educated at Cornell University, noted for its agricultural training, the brothers began to specialize in pears, especially Comice dessert pears, which they called Royal Riviera pears. The "club" idea originated in the Depression of the 1930s, when the company promoted pears as gift boxes from corporations to their customers. The Fruit-of-the-Month Club came about in 1938, playing off the popularity of the Book-of-the-Month Club. The company has expanded beyond pears and apples, but still bases its business on prime fruit for gift purposes.

hay Grass, alfalfa, and clover that is dried for animal feed is known as hay, and has long been a major Oregon crop. It is produced around the state, but in recent decades southeastern Oregon has been the major production region, in addition to Morrow County in the north. Since the climate in this area often requires irrigation, alfalfa production is often problematic and controversial.

Haycox, Ernest (1899–1950) Ernest Haycox was born and raised in Portland, briefly attended Reed College, and majored in journalism at the University of Oregon, where he began writing fiction. He suffered numerous rejections before finally selling a story to San Francisco's *Overland Monthly* magazine, and made the first of many sales to the national magazine *Collier's* in 1930. In the next two decades he churned out short stories and novels, most of them set in the American West. Several were turned into major motion pictures. The short story, "Stage to Lordsburg," published by *Collier's* in 1937, became the John Ford epic *Stagecoach* (1939) with John Wayne, and the novel *Trouble Shooter*

(1937) was worked into Cecil B. DeMille's *Union Pacific* (1939). In the 1940s he wrote several works that had a more particularly Oregon background, such as *Canyon Passage* (1945; filmed in 1946, partly in Jacksonville and southern Oregon, with Susan Hayward, Brian Donleavy and Dana Andrews), with the Rogue River, Crater Lake and gold mining as the setting, and the posthumously published *The Earthbreakers* (1952), a novel of the Oregon **pioneers** of the 1840s in the Willamette Valley.

Haycox lived in Portland, and made a very comfortable living as a writer, one noted for his knowledge of and attention to the details of Western history and landscape, and for his characters' self-reliance, industry, pluck and luck. About the protagonists of *The Earthbreakers* he wrote, "There is no escape, no golden land, no security; it is a timeless illusion. We must sweat and cry."

Haycox, Ernest, Jr. *On a Silver Desert: The Life of Ernest Haycox.* Norman: University of Oklahoma Press, 2003.

hazelnuts *see* **filberts**

Hazeltine, George Irving (1836–1918) George Hazeltine came to California in 1853 with his older brother **Martin M. Hazeltine**; the two operated a daguerreotype photography gallery in San Francisco until 1855. George took off for Red Bluff, California, for a few years, and then went to the gold-mining town of **Canyon City** in Oregon, where he practiced photography until 1891. His work was primarily portrait photographs, and scenic views of and mining activity in the John Day region. He became a major businessman and investor in Canyon City, served as a judge and as the treasurer of Grant County, and was the city recorder for two decades.

Hazeltine, Martin Mason (1827–1903) Martin Hazeltine was born in Vermont, and went west to California in search of gold in 1850. He returned to the East to study photography, and came west again in 1853 to San Francisco with his younger brother **George I. Hazeltine**, with whom he operated a studio until 1855. He did a great deal of photography for railroad companies, and also sold scenic landscape views and stereopticon slides depicting scenes throughout the West, including Alaska. Like his contemporary, **Carleton E. Watkins**, he took photographs of Yosemite, and reached into Yellowstone. He was headquartered in Boise, Idaho, between 1882 and 1884, and then in Baker City from 1885 until his death. His scenes along the rail lines of the **Southern Pacific Company** and the **Union Pacific Railroad** were familiar throughout the West. *See also* **Fossil**; **Sumpter Valley Railway**.

Heceta, Bruno de (1744–1807) The Spanish mariner Bruno de Heceta (or Hezeta) y Dudagoitia headed an expedition that departed from San Blas, Mexico, in 1775, seeking evidence of Russian incursions along the coastline. Heceta located the mouth of the Columbia River on this voyage, but was not able to enter it. As the Spanish were notoriously close-mouthed about their activities, his discovery was not shared with other mariners; general European and American knowledge of the Columbia awaited the voyages of Capt. **George Vancouver** and Capt. **Robert Gray** in 1792.

Heceta Head Named for the Spanish explorer **Bruno de Heceta**, Heceta Head in Lane County is renowned as one of the most photogenic points on the Oregon Coast. Its distinctive **lighthouse** is complemented by a picturesque light keeper's cottage in the Queen Anne style. Conveyed to the U.S. Forest Service, the cottage was placed on the National Register of Historic Places in 1973, and became a bed and breakfast in 1995.

Helix The rural post office of Helix opened in 1880. The odd name is said to derive from an incident involving an infection in the helix of the ear of W. B. Henderson, according to geographic names historian Lewis L. McArthur. To add to the aura of oddness, the tiny town has streets named Vesper, Aurora, and Solar. Helix was incorporated in 1903, and the 1910 census counted 109 residents. By 1915, the town claimed the "distinction of having [the] largest wheat warehouse station in the state, [with the] farms tributary to the station producing 1,200,000 bushels of wheat annually." The population in 1950 was 182; the estimate for 2007 was 230. Wheat stills grows there.

Hells Canyon This term has been used, apparently since the 1930s, for a stretch of the Snake River bordering Baker and Wallowa Counties—from Oxbow Dam near the site of the vanished town of **Copperfield** downstream to the mouth of the **Grande Ronde River** in Washington state. The term was popularized by, among others, **Richard Neuberger**, who penned pieces in *Harper's Magazine* ("Hell's Canyon, the Biggest of All," April 1939) and the *Saturday Evening Post* ("The Mail Carrier of Hells Canyon, October 24, 1942). What Hells Canyon is, is deep and steep and rugged: a mile deep in places, up to ten miles wide. Some mining was done in the canyon—not only copper, but also gold, though not with major success. A notorious massacre of more than two dozen **Chinese** gold miners occurred near the mouth of Deep Creek in 1887 and lends a sobering note to the canyon's history and name.

Nokes, R. Gregory. "A Most Daring Outrage": Murders at Chinese Massacre Cove, 1887. *Oregon Historical Quarterly* 107, no. 3 (Fall 2006): 326–353.

hemlock The western hemlock, *Tsuga heterophylla*, is a native evergreen tree found in a coastal belt from Alaska to northern California; it is common in the Coast Range Mountains and generally on the west side of the Cascade Range. Hemlocks grow from 160 to 200 feet or more in height, and up to eight feet in diameter; they are long-lived, with specimens dated at more than 1,200 years of age.

Hemlock trees cast a dense shade, and often grow among and beneath Douglas-fir and Sitka spruce only to eventually become dominant in the climax forest. The western hemlock was not initially favored for timber—"not worth cutting" was the evaluation into the 1930s. Since then it has been employed in pulp and paper manufacturing, the production of rayon fiber, and to make lumber, usually used for doors, windows, staircases, and wooden trim. Western hemlock is the state tree of Washington state.

Also found in Oregon is the mountain hemlock, *Tsuga mertensiana*. It is found generally at higher elevations than the western hemlock, above 5,000 feet in the Cascade Range, and in the Siskiyou Mountains.

Heppner Heppner's beginnings stem from a general store opened in 1873 by Henry Heppner; a post office of that name opened the same year. Morrow County was established in 1885, and Heppner was designated the temporary county seat. In 1886, an election favored it remaining there over moving it to Lexington some nine miles away, and in 1887 Heppner was incorporated as a city. The developing wheat- and sheep-raising country of Morrow County brought a branch railroad line to Heppner in 1888. Heppner was a prosperous agricultural trade center by 1900, when the census recorded a population of 1,146.

On the evening of June 14, 1903, a sudden summer thunderstorm broke over the city, followed by the collapse of a dam at a storage reservoir. A forty-foot wall of water smashed down Willow Creek into the unsuspecting city, destroying most of the residences and much of the retail district and leaving at least 247 persons dead—the worst disaster in Oregon history in loss of life. The city recuperated, and by 1915 could be proud of its creamery and flouring mill and the warehouses for wool and wheat; but the 1910 census showed only 880 residents. The population rebounded to 1,324 in 1920, and has changed little since that time. The estimated population in 2007 was 1,415. A new dam on reservoir on Willow Creek was completed in 1983.

DenOuden, Bob. "Without a Second's Warning": the Heppner Flood of 1903. *Oregon Historical Quarterly* 105, no. 1 (Spring 2004): 108-119.

Hermann, Binger (1843-1926) Born and reared in Maryland, Binger Hermann came to Oregon in 1859 as part of a group known as the "Baltimore Colony," Marylanders who came intending to settle in the Coquille River Valley of Coos County. Hermann taught school as a young man, studied law, and was admitted to the Oregon state bar in 1866; he then commenced to practice law in Oakland. He quickly stepped into politics, serving in the state legislature and then the state senate in the 1860s, accepting minor federal appointments with the internal revenue and the land office in Roseburg in the 1860s and 1870s, and serving as a colonel in the state militia in the early 1880s. Hermann was elected as a Republican to the U.S. House of Representatives in 1884, and was in that office until 1897, when President McKinley appointed him to head the General Land Office, which dealt with various federal **land grants**. He resigned from that post in 1903, again held a congressional seat from 1903 to 1907, and then retired to practice law and to "engage in literary pursuits." It was a wise move, for Hermann was embroiled in land fraud accusations and entanglements, well publicized by **S. A. D. Puter**, and accused of destroying public documents and of collusion. The jury could not decide; but Hermann's once-promising career came to an abrupt end.

Hermiston Located in Umatilla County, Hermiston is situated in the Umatilla River Valley, which became the site of an extensive agricultural irrigation project in the early 1900s. Hermiston post office opened in 1905, and the town was incorporated in 1907; the 1910 census gave it a population of 647. The principal industries in the area in the 1910s were dairying and fruit and bee culture. The construction of McNary Dam (1947–1954) boosted Hermiston's population, and irrigation received another boost. The population reached 4,893 in 1970, and jumped to an estimated 15,780 in 2007. Railroad operations and access to **Interstate 84** and Interstate 82 have made Hermiston an agricultural distribution and processing center, and made Wal-Mart the biggest employer in town, hiring some 850 Hermistonians. Irrigation has made it possible to grow water-dependent crops in the area, and Hermiston watermelons and other melons are featured in Pacific Northwest markets.

heron *see* **blue heron**

Hezeta, Bruno de *see* **Heceta, Bruno de**

Highway 26 Federal Highway 26 crosses Oregon from Ontario on the east through John Day, Prineville, Government Camp, Portland, and Seaside to Astoria on the coast. The segment from Portland to Seaside is popularly known as the **Sunset Highway**.

► **Highway 30** This federally designated highway essentially follows the route of the **Oregon Trail** from Ontario over the Blue Mountains and down the Columbia River to Portland, and then continues to Astoria. The section from between Portland and The Dalles was built as the **Columbia River Highway** in the 1910s, and was then extended downriver to Astoria.

► **Highway 97** U.S. Route 97 is a major south-to-north highway connecting from **Interstate 5** in northern California through Klamath Falls and Bend to the Columbia River and connections to **Interstate 84** and north into Washington state. In

The Boiling Point service station on Emigrant Hill, pictured about 1930, illustrates the transition from oxen to automobile along Highway 30, the route of the Oregon Trail. It was still a rough climb, but the outcome of the struggle was a boiling-over radiator rather than an exhausted or dying animal. Wesley Andrews photograph. Oregon Historical Society, OrHi 15239.

Biggs Junction is located at the junction of Highway 97 with Highway 30. The photograph was probably taken in the late 1940s. A ferry crossed the Columbia River from here to Maryhill, Washington, until 1962. Clarence I. Christian photograph. Steven Dotterrer collection.

Oregon it is often referred to as The Dalles-California Highway.

Highway 99 This major north-south highway basically follows the route of the original **California-Oregon Trail** and the **Pacific Highway** of the 1910s and 1920s; the **Interstate 5** freeway replaced it in the 1960s.

Highway 101 *see* **Oregon Coast Highway**

highways and roads *see* **Baldock, Robert H.; Banfield Expressway; Barlow Road; bridges; California-Oregon Trail; Columbia River Highway; covered bridges; ferries; Highway 26; Highway 30; Highway 97; Highway 99; Hill, Samuel; Interstate 5; Interstate 82; Interstate 84; Interstate 205;** **Interstate 405; Lancaster, Samuel C.; Minnesota Freeway; Mount Hood Freeway; Oregon Coast Highway; Oregon Trail; Southern Emigrant Road; Sunset Highway**

Hill, James Jerome *see* **Empire Builder**

Hill, Samuel "Sam" (1857–1931) Sam Hill was born to a Quaker family in North Carolina, but Sam grew up in Minneapolis. After attending Haverford College and Harvard University and emerging with a law degree, Sam went to work in 1886 for James J. Hill and his **Great Northern Railroad** in Minneapolis. In 1888, Sam Hill married Jim Hill's daughter Mary Frances; the marriage was a rocky enterprise. Sam Hill came west to Seattle on behalf of the railroad, and in 1899 he helped to found, and became first president of, the Washington Good Roads

Association; good roads became his passion. He began to build a house in Seattle in 1902, and in 1907 he purchased 6,000 acres of land at what is now Maryhill, named for his wife. He planned a Quaker community, orchards, and a grand villa on a bluff overlooking the gorge. He had **Samuel C. Lancaster** build test roads at Maryhill (they remain there), and in 1910 he headed the **Pacific Highway** Association. In 1913, Hill helped Lancaster, **John B. Yeon**, and others promote the **Columbia River Highway**. A replica of Stonehenge was erected in 1918 to memorialize those killed in World War I, and in 1919 Hill began to turn the grand villa of Maryhill—in which his wife refused to live—into a museum of art. Queen Marie of Romania (a friend of the gregarious Hill) dedicated the museum in 1926. Hill died in Portland in 1931. Hill's many and wide-ranging enthusiasms have helped support the idea that the phrase, "What in the Sam Hill?!" is a reference to him; however, it is not.

Tuhy, John E. *Sam Hill: The Prince of Castle Nowhere*. Portland, Oregon: Timber Press, 1983.

Hillsboro Located on the **Tualatin Plains**, Hillsboro is the county seat of Washington County. White settlement occurred in the area from the 1840s, with David Hill farming at the future site of Hillsboro in 1845. The area was called Columbia or Columbus in the late 1840s, and a post office named Hillsborough opened in 1850 (changed to Hillsboro in 1892). A permanent county building was built in 1852 and the town grew as a government center and trading town. A railroad arrived from Portland in 1871 and Hillsboro was incorporated in 1876. Hillsboro's population in the 1880 census was 402; by 1910, it was 2,016. By 1915, Hillsboro had two electric interurban railways to Portland and boasted a fruit-preserving plant, a planing mill, a sawmill, a flour mill, a milk condensary, and a sash and door factory. After the end of World War II, Hillsboro began to experience suburban development, paralleling the growth of the **Silicon Forest** to the east.

The 1950 population was 5,142; in 1970, it was 14,675. By 1990, there were 37,598 residents, and by 2007, an estimated 88,300. Interurban commuter trains, discontinued by 1931, in effect returned in 1998 with the opening of the **MAX** light-rail line from Hillsboro to Portland.

Hillsdale district, Portland This was a rural community along the Oregon Central Railroad, which built through the area from Portland en route to Forest Grove and points south in 1871. The railroad used the name Summit to avoid confusion with Hillsboro on the same line, but locally a Hillsdale school and Hillsdale community church were founded. Hillsdale post office was established in 1886. In 1892, the railroad changed the station name to Bertha, since the new owner, the **Southern Pacific Company**, had another station named Summit on its lines; Bertha was the given name of Mrs. Richard Koehler, a railroad official. By 1915, the Hillsdale area was noted for it horticulture, dairying, poultry raising, and fruit growing, and the railroad line had been electrified to provide frequent commuter service. The construction of Capitol Highway in the 1920s improved access to Portland; the highway bridge over the railroad is still in use, but the tracks were removed in the 1930s to build the Beaverton Highway. Hillsdale post office closed in 1935, but the small town core has persisted and grown around a shopping center built in the 1950s.

Himes, George H. (1844–1940) George Himes, "the Printer," was a professional documentarian of the Oregon **pioneer** experience. He himself crossed the plains on the **Oregon Trail** at the age of nine. Himes was trained as a printer and worked in several newspaper offices before establishing his own printing and publishing firm in Portland. Though it was a financial quagmire for him, the business enabled Himes to pursue his endless efforts to document and exalt the Oregon pioneers. He was one of the founders, and for many years the voice and pen of, the Oregon Pioneer Society, which from its founding in 1873 held yearly conferences and published an annual book of reminiscences. In 1875, Himes compiled a set of letters between himself and **Matthew P. Deady** and published it as *Wallamet or Willamette*, a discussion on the proper spelling of the river name. Himes also was on hand at the founding of the **Oregon Historical Society** in 1898, and served for many years as its secretary and de facto curator.

Laugeson, Amanda. George Himes, F. G. Young, and the Early Years of the Oregon Historical Society. *Oregon Historical Quarterly* 101 (2000), 18–39.

► **Hines** This Harney County community was established by the Midwest-based Edward Hines Lumber Company beginning in 1928 as the site of a huge lumber mill, using ponderosa **pine** from the Blue Mountains north of Burns. Situated near a warm springs at the northern edge of the Harney Basin, Hines was incorporated in 1930 and continued as a mill town until the mid-1990s. The ghostly concrete walls of the unfinished Ponderosa Hotel, erected at the beginning of the Depression, are a town landmark, as is the smokestack of the now-abandoned sawmill. The last remnant of the lumber industry in Hines ceased operations in 2007. Hines has become a residential suburb of Burns, with a population in 2007 of 1,825.

Hirsch-Weis Manufacturing Company *see* **White Stag**

Hobbs, Fern (1883–1964) *see* **Copperfield**

Hobson, Dorothy Anne *see* **Valsetz**

hoedad A hoedad is not a hodad. There are two kinds of hoedads, and a hoedad is not the same as

This 1941 photograph shows the Edward Hines Lumber Company mill at Hines, just east of Burns. The wigwam burner at the left burned wood waste from the mill; the smokestack is at the powerhouse, generating steam to run machinery and generate electricity. Ponderosa pine logs for the mill came by train from the Blue Mountains some fifty miles to the north. J. H. Eastman photograph. Steven Dotterer collection.

a Hoedad, but connections exist between them. First, hoedads are forest imps of folklore, creatures seen and invented by loggers in the conifer forests of the Midwest. As the logging industry moved westward late in the nineteenth century, the legendary hoedads came west, too. Second, hoedads are tools, used by forest workers to quickly dig the hold to plant tree seedlings. Finally, Hoedads (with a capital H) are tree planters, members of a cooperative group that was formed in Eugene in 1971 and lasted into the 1980s. They contracted with timber companies to plant tree seedlings on logged-over, **clearcut** lands. The Hoedads won a reputation for turning commercial reforestation from a nasty job done by untrained people to respected (and paid-for) work done by dedicated people who hoped they were also improving their environment. Hoedads were often seen as members of the counterculture.

> Cox, William T. *Fearsome Creatures of the Lumberwoods, with a Few Desert and Mountain Beasts.* Washington, DC: Judd & Detweiler, 1910.

Hoffman, Julia Christianson (1856–1934) A leading figure in the arts and crafts movement in Oregon, Julia Hoffman was a photographer, sculptor, and worker in ceramic and metal. Hoffman's chief legacy is the **Oregon College of Art and Craft**, which grew from the Arts and Crafts Society that she founded in Portland in 1907. One of her children, **Margery Hoffman Smith**, was also a noted artist and designer; Margery was also a frequent and often unwilling subject of her mother's photography.

> *Julia E. Hoffman: A Family Album.* San Francisco: San Francisco Museum of Modern Art, 1977.

Hogg, T. Edgenton, Col. *see* **Santiam Pass; Yaquina Bay**

Holbrook, Stewart Hall (1893–1964) For several decades Stewart Holbrook was one of the most nationally visible Oregonians. Journalist, lumberjack, historian, raconteur, and all-around character, the Vermont-born Holbrook first arrived in Portland in 1923, thirty years old, wanting to write, though he lacked even a high school diploma. Holbrook had worked in the woods in New England, but he quickly took on, or invented, the persona of a native Oregonian (with a New England accent). Within a few years he was regularly contributing features to the *Oregonian*, such as a series on shanghaiing in Portland that appeared in 1933. His career with the newspaper spanned thirty-six years. When his book *Holy Old Mackinaw: A Natural History of the American Lumberjack* achieved success in 1938, he moved back East, writing five more books of what he described as "low-brow history" before returning to Portland in 1943. He wrote a succession of popular histories on a variety of topics, many of them tied to Oregon and the Northwest, including *Burning an Empire: The Story of American Forest Fires* (1944), *Far Corner, a Personal View of the Pacific Northwest* (1952), and *The Columbia* (1956). Holbrook was also an early conservationist, seeing the adventure and even romance of logging while arguing that logging was destroying a once-forested empire. In the early 1960s, Holbrook created the James G. Blaine Society, named for a perennial presidential hopeful of the late nineteenth century. The society was intended to discourage emigration to Oregon, a harbinger of the pleas soon to come from governor **Tom McCall**; the name was selected because Blaine had the good sense not to visit Oregon. Holbrook also had an alter ego, one Mr. Otis; Mr. Otis painted, and was thus an artist, of the primitive-moderne school. Paintings by Mr. Otis were often reflective of some of Holbrook's literary themes: logger legends, Western legends, and the perils of modern life, and they usually took a poke at contemporary art movements such as abstract impressionism and surrealism. In the 1950s and 1960s, Holbrook was an ambassador for Oregon, with articles and books that reached a national audience.

Wildmen, Wobblies & Whistle Punks: Stewart Holbrook's Lowbrow Northwest. Ed. Brian Booth. Corvallis: Oregon State University Press, 1992.

► **Holladay, Benjamin "Ben"** (1819–1887) Ben Holladay, the "Stagecoach King" of Western legend, was born in Kentucky in 1819, went west to Missouri and engaged in supplying the Army during the Mexican-American War (1846–48). Holladay moved west again to California, where he engaged successfully in operating stagecoach and express companies. Among his investments was in the famed Pony Express, which he ran for a few months in 1861, and the Butterfield Overland Stage Company, which had lucrative mail contracts in the Southwest. The Civil War was most profitable to Holladay, and

This photograph was intended to convey the firm impression that Ben Holladay was a man of substance. He was indeed physically imposing, and he had a way with money and political influence, but true substance eluded him.
Oregon Historical Society, OrHi 49501.

he sold his enterprises for $1.5 million in 1866 to the rising Wells, Fargo & Company and moved to Oregon.

Holladay now plunged into railroad investment, putting money into the Oregon Central Railroad in 1868. His machinations pushed the **Oregon & California Railroad** from Portland south through the Willamette Valley via Eugene and Ashland, to a California connection at Sacramento. Construction was halted at Roseburg in 1873. **Henry Villard** succeeded to the railroad property in 1876, but the California connection was not made until 1887. Meanwhile, Holladay had also invested in river transportation, real estate, and the construction of a resort at **Seaside**. Holladay built a grand house in Portland, a house in Washington, DC (he vainly hoped to become a U.S. senator; money changed hands in the attempt), and even one near White Plains, New York.

Holladay was a brash and uncouth fellow, qualities that did not serve him well in Oregon. Historian Malcolm Clark, Jr., described Holladay as an "arrogant, aggressive and wholly unscrupulous man, with a genius for promotion unbalanced by any sound understanding of financial realities." His last years involved retrenchment and a series of lawsuits over his financial affairs, some of them quite tangled indeed. His name is attached to a street and a real estate subdivision in Portland: Holladay's Addition is the site of **Lloyd Center**. Seaside also has Holladay Drive, its principal north-south commercial street, as well as a now-vanished railroad station, the absolute end-of-the-line terminus of the railroad from Portland to the seashore. Ben Holladay died, little mourned or even much noticed, in Portland in 1887, two years before his young second wife, Portlander Lydia Esther Campbell (1849–1889).

Lucia, Ellis. *The Saga of Ben Holladay, Giant of the Old West.* New York: Hastings House, 1959.

Hollywood neighborhood, Portland The Hollywood business district grew up on NE Sandy

Boulevard near Forty-second Avenue in the 1920s, and took its name from the Hollywood Theatre, a grand extravaganza of a movie palace that opened there in 1926. Sandy Boulevard was a long-established road leading to the Sandy River, and streetcar service began along this section in the 1910s. Retailer **Fred Meyer** opened a grocery in the Hollywood **public market** in the late 1920s, and in 1931 his first "one stop" shopping center was established there.

Holt, Harry (1904–1964) **and Bertha Holt** (1904–2000) Bertha and Harry Holt lived in Creswell, where Harry was a successful lumberman and farmer. During and after the Korean War (1950–53), the Holts became concerned with the plight of GI babies: children fathered by American soldiers with Korean women. Stigmatized in Korea, the children were treated as orphans and faced a daunting future. In 1955, the Holts began a program to adopt eight of these children, despite legal impediments that had to be addressed by a special act of Congress. The Holts, who were evangelical Christians, began to advocate for the adoption of these children by American families through what was called proxy adoption: arranged by agents, the adoptions resulted in thousands of babies being flown in "baby lifts" from Korea to the United States, where they first met their adoptive parents. The plan was criticized by many child advocates of the time, and to some people it was shocking because it resulted in households of mixed races.

Harry Holt died in 1964, but Bertha continued their work, which evolved into Holt International Children's Services, headquartered in Eugene.

holy rollers The term "holy rollers" has been current in colloquial language since the nineteenth century to refer to Pentecostal Christians whose worship involves an active component, such as speaking in tongues or acting out encounters with spiritual adversaries. In western Oregon during much of the twentieth century, the term "holy rollers" was spe-

cifically used to describe the followers of Franz Edmund Creffield (1867?–1906) and his Church of the Bride of Christ, which surfaced in **Corvallis** in 1903 and was also active for a time near Yachats on the Oregon Coast. Over the course of the next three years, Creffield and his followers—most of them women—were the center of a series of scandalous allegations and episodes that mixed religious fervor with communal living, family feuds, alienated affections, property destruction, incarceration for insanity, and potent journalism. Creffield was finally assassinated in Seattle by George Mitchell, the brother of one of the followers, Esther Mitchell; George was found innocent of the act, only to be gunned down by Esther in the waiting room of King Street Station. Esther later committed suicide, as did Creffield's wife, Maude Hurt. The Creffield scandal rocked Corvallis and for several decades provided a topic for whispered discussions.

Baldasty, Gerald J. *Vigilante Newspapers: A Tale of Sex, Religion, and Murder in the Northwest.* Seattle: University of Washington Press, 2005.

McCracken, Theresa, and Robert B. Blodgett. *Holy Rollers: Murder and Madness in Oregon's Love Cult.* Caldwell, Idaho: Caxton Press, 2002.

Homestead Act The earliest land claims in Oregon were made under the **Donation Land Act** of 1850. After that act terminated, a similar process was used under the Homestead Act of 1862. Claimants could receive up to 160 acres of undeveloped federal land, providing they had lived on the land for five years and had built a house that was at least twelve feet by fourteen feet in size.

Honeyman, Nan Wood (1881–1970) The daughter of **C. E. S. Wood** and Nanny Moale Wood, Nan Wood was born in West Point, New York, moving to Portland with her parents in 1884. She graduated from Saint Helens Hall and later attended Finch School in New York City. Nan married David Honeyman, an official with the large Honeyman Hardware

Company of Portland, in 1908. Though she was raising a family of three children, Wood took an active interest in civic affairs, serving in the 1920s as president of the League of Women Voters and working with the state Democratic Party. She also worked to repeal prohibition, and in 1933 presided over the state convention that ratified the repeal amendment. Nan Honeyman was elected to serve a term in the Oregon house of representatives in 1934, and in 1936 was elected to the U.S. Congress—the first woman from Oregon to hold that position. Her re-election attempts in 1938 and 1940, however, failed. Honeyman worked for the U.S. Price Administration during World War II, and she also briefly served in the Oregon senate to fill a vacancy. From 1942 to 1953, Nan Honeyman was the U.S. collector of customs at Portland. In later years she moved to California, where she died in 1970.

Hood River Hood River has had its name since the 1850s, descriptive of waters flowing from the slopes of **Mount Hood** north to the Columbia River. The town of Hood River, located at that confluence in Hood River County, can be reckoned from the establishment of a post office there in 1858. It was a small river landing until the transcontinental railroad came through in 1883, connecting the town with Portland as well as all points east. By 1900, Hood River was a lumbering center, and the construction of the Mount Hood Railroad south into the upper river valley between 1906 and 1909 increased that trade. Hood River was incorporated in 1901, and the 1910 census reported 2,331 residents. Hood River County had been created in 1908, with Hood River the county seat. The upper valley developed rapidly as a center of fruit culture in the years before World War I, and the town was the headquarters of the nationally distributed trade magazine, *Better Fruit* (1906-72). In 1915, the town boasted an annual **chautauqua**, three cold-storage warehouses for the Hood River Apple Growers' Union, and an annual apple fair. Related to the fruit business were

two ice plants, three box factories, and a vinegar factory. After the repeal of **prohibition**, Hood River Distillers was formed to make use of the area's fruits in the production of alcoholic beverages; the company has prospered, and in the 1990s, after years of being known primarily for the production of affordable local vodka, it began building up a line of premium products, again looking to local fruit. Hood River's population increased to 3,701 by 1950, and to 4,329 in 1980. In the 1980s, Hood River rather quickly became the center of a new recreational industry, wind surfing, done on the impounded but far from placid waters of the Columbia River. The city's estimated population in 2007 was 6,710.

Hood River County The growth of fruit growing and lumbering prompted a desire for people in the Hood River area to form a separate county. This occurred in 1908 when a statewide initiative vote created Hood River County from Wasco County. It is the second-smallest Oregon county, with 533 square miles. Hood River has always been the county seat. The area is part of the homeland of several villages of **Wasco** and **Wishram Indians**.

The Mount Hood Railroad was built into the upper Hood River valley in 1906–09 to tap traffic from the orchards and lumber mills. Fruit culture developed rapidly along the Pacific Coast in the years before World War I, development that was fueled by moneyed Eastern emigrants; the Hood River area and Rogue River's **Bear Creek Valley** were especially affected. In 1915, the county's apple orchards were

a scene of beauty, especially in spring time when thousands of acres of apple blossoms scent the air with their fragrance. In the fall these trim trees are heavy with their load of fancy fruit. The orchards are well kept and well cultivated; the homes are modern and the living conditions are such as have attracted a citizenship that ranks second to none in the United States in education and culture. Hood River

County is a rare blending of scenic beauty, highly specialized industry and social advantages. . . . Hood River apples and Hood River strawberries are celebrated throughout the world for quality.

A small but significant group of **Japanese** came to the county to work in the orchards and fields, and a number of them eventually became major growers. Strong prejudice against Japanese-Americans occurred during and shortly after World War II in Hood River County, resulting in lingering postwar wounds. Timber production fell considerably in the 1970s, and fruit culture shifted from apples and strawberries to pears; agriculture was threatened by rapid residential growth. The Mount Hood Railroad became a tourist-hauling line after 1984, and tourism—revolving around the railroad, the orchards, windsurfing, winemaking and beer brewing, and the region's history—has become a major industry. The county's population in 1910 was 8,016, increasing slowly until about 1980, when it reached 15,835; the estimated figure in 2007 was 21,470.

Hoover, Herbert Clark (1874–1964) Herbert Hoover was born into a Quaker family in Iowa; his father died in 1880, his mother in 1884, and the children were sent to relatives. Herbert stayed with an uncle for a year in Iowa, and in 1885 went to **Newberg**, Oregon, to stay with his uncle, Dr. Henry J. Minthorn. He worked on the family farm, attended Pacific Academy where he did well in mathematics, and after his graduation moved to **Salem** to help open a real estate office with his uncle and several partners. An ambitious chap, he learned to type and to do bookkeeping, and spent his evenings attending business school. His mathematical talents and interest in engineering led him to attend the new Stanford University in California, and he left Oregon for Palo Alto in 1891. From there, Hoover went on to a career in mining engineering, followed by a political life that included the U.S. presidency and international peace efforts. The National Society of the Co-

lonial Dames in America maintains the Minthorn family house in Newberg as a museum.

Hopkins, Sarah Winnemucca
see **Sarah Winnemucca**

hops Hops, an important flavoring agent in many beers, was first grown commercially in Oregon in the Willamette Valley, beginning in the 1860s near Silverton and Eugene. It quickly became an important export crop, and in the early 1900s the state was the nation's chief producer of hops, with some 14,000 acres in production. The hop harvest in late summer was labor-intensive; entire families from Portland and other cities would camp near the hop fields to participate in the picking. **Prohibition** (1916 in Oregon; nationwide by 1919) destroyed most of the American market for hops, and although it revived somewhat in the late 1930s with the repeal of the 18th Amendment, Oregon production dropped due to a blight. In 1910, Polk County had about 4,000 acres in hops; by 1974, this had fallen to 400 acres. The rise of craft breweries beginning in the 1980s helped to fuel a revival of the industry, although it waned again in the late 1990s.

horseradish *see* **Beaverton; Malin**

horses Horses were imported to North America by the Spaniards in the sixteenth century, and they quickly made their way into Indian hands, such that by the early nineteenth century the **Nez Perce** and **Cayuse Indians** and other Plateau tribes had them and had become accomplished breeders and riders; the Nez Perce were noted for their development of the Appaloosa horse. Coastal and river-oriented tribes tended to adopt the horse at a later date. Additional horses came into Oregon during the 1840s for use by farmers in the Willamette Valley. Horses came west on the **Oregon Trail**, too, but as stock; they were not suitable for hauling the overland wagons used in that trek. Horse racing was a sport common among the Indians and among early settlers, many of whom were from states such as Kentucky with a long history of the sport. Silvertonian **Homer Davenport** was a fan of Arabian horses, being among the first breeders to import them into the United States; Davenport exhibited them at the 1905 **Lewis and Clark Centennial Exposition** in Portland. *See also* **Steens Mountain**.

Hoskins *see* **Fort Hoskins**

► **Hot Lake** A large hot springs in Union County was developed into a health sanitarium early in the twentieth century. The Hot Lake Hotel was built in 1907, located along the main line of the Union Pacific Railroad. After several successful years, the building burned in 1934; the rebuilt enterprise has had a checkered history as a sanitarium, nursing home, and hotel. The complex of buildings was listed on the National Register of Historic Places in 1979, and has endured at least two failed resuscitations since then.

► **houseboats** The distinctive residence known as a houseboat was once common on the more placid waterways of Oregon: it was a raft, usually of logs, surmounted by a small wood-frame dwelling which could be moved upstream or down, which paid no property tax and was beholden to no one. Houseboats were often occupied by those who worked on rivers, such as log drivers and fishermen and their families. In the first half of the twentieth century, they could be found along the lower Columbia River and in tributary rivers and sloughs, and in coastal bays and rivers as well. A well-known photographer, Lily White, traveled the Columbia on a houseboat and floating studio, and the bohemian journalist **Louise Bryant** lived on one in the Willamette

HOT LAKE SANATORIUM

On the main line of the O. R. & N. Co., 314 miles east of Portland. Special round-trip excursion tickets from all O. R. & N. points. The largest, hottest and most curative spring known; best bathing facilities, most courteous attendants; first-class medical and surgical conveniences; finest operating room in the West; steam heat, electric lights; hot and cold water throughout the building. For further information write the Hot Lake Sanatorium Co., Hot Lake, Ore. Dr. W. T. Phy, Medical Superintendent and Manager.
Form O-22—8-18-09—5M
RYDER BROS. PTG & STAT'RS BAKER CITY OR.

A postcard view from 1909 shows the facilities at Hot Lake and notes its easy access by train. Steven Dotterer collection.

River. By the 1950s, most remaining houseboats were stationary, but problems were apparent: sewage and garbage were commonly discharged directly into waterways, and many houseboats lacked such amenities as electricity and piped water. The ensuing cleanup of houseboating has left but a remnant of the fleet; because of the costs of dealing with sewage, water, and garbage, they are often the sanctuary of the well to do. Houseboats can be found on the Willamette River near Oaks Park, along the Multnomah Channel opposite **Sauvie Island**, and on Hayden Island in the Columbia River; they can also be found in a few offbeat places such as along the shores of the **John Day River** in Clatsop County.

House of Mystery Located near **Gold Hill** in Jackson County on the banks of Sardine Creek (named for the canned variety) at an abandoned gold-mining site, the House of Mystery—also known as the Oregon Vortex—is the odd creation of John Litster (1886–1959), a reputed "geologist, mining engineer, and physicist." Litster apparently acquired the property in the 1920s, and in the abandoned and tilting structures he perceived visual and phenomenal mysteries: things tilted oddly, tall people seemed to shrink, water appeared to run uphill. In 1930, he opened his site to the public, and it has been open ever since. Litster and his wife, Mildred, were tireless promoters. John wrote a number of pamphlets attempting to explain the "mysteries," but the explanations have remained opaque to generations of visitors; many simply see optical illusions. Litster had a shadowy past that included prison time; he also had a penchant for writing poetry. Among his works is *A Vagabond's Testament*, privately printed in Medford in 1939.

This sylvan scene by photographer Benjamin A. Gifford depicts a houseboat somewhere along the Columbia River. Drawn up to the bank, this working houseboat can easily be towed to another site. Oregon Historical Society, Gi 2169.

Howard, Oliver Otis (1830-1909) Born and raised in Maine, Oliver Howard graduated from West Point Military Academy in 1854. Howard married Elizabeth Anne Waite in 1855, and in 1857 went to Florida during the Seminole Wars. There he experienced a conversion to an evangelical Christianity that influenced all of his later life. Howard returned to West Point as an instructor, and served with distinction during the Civil War. From 1865 to 1874, Howard headed the Bureau of Refugees, Freedmen, and Abandoned Lands, the reconstruction-era agency that tried to help the newly freed slaves, and which proved to be another soul-forming activity. In 1874, he took command of the Department of the Columbia at **Fort Vancouver**, though he resided in Portland. His most noteworthy experience was his leadership of the Army against the band of Indians represented by **Joseph** during the **Nez Perce War**. Howard failed to display much respect for his adversaries, a failing that Joseph noted and deplored, as did Howard's sometimes-wayward aide, **C. E. S. Wood**. However, Howard also displayed sympathy with the Indians' position, despite his determination to force their acceptance of the federal stance that they could not return to their ancestral lands in the Wallowa Mountains. Howard also later directed forces in the **Bannock War**. He then returned east, where he was superintendent of West Point for a few years and where he retired as a major general in 1894. Howard is remembered through Howard University in Washington, DC, the descendant of an institution founded in 1867 to educate African-Americans; he served as its president from 1869 to 1874. Howard also founded Lincoln Memorial University in Tennessee in 1895, to help educate "mountain whites." Mount Howard and Howard Spring in Wallowa County are named for him, as is Howard Valley in Harney County, traces of his experiences in those areas.

Howell, Thomas Jefferson (1842–1912) This pioneer Oregon botanist came west with his family in 1850. Benjamin and Elizabeth Howell took up a donation land claim on **Sauvie Island** in 1854; two of their five children, Joseph and Thomas, became interested in botany, an avocation that Thomas converted to a lifelong passion that took him around the state and the Pacific Northwest. Thomas and Joseph located a pond plant in 1878 that noted Harvard botanist Asa Gray named *Howellia aquatilis*; thereafter "Thomas lost all interest in farming," noted Jack Cleaver in *Island Immigrants*. Thomas first published a catalog of regional plants about 1881. His travels and research led him to compile and print *A Flora of Northwhst [sic] America: Containing brief descriptions of all the known indigenous and naturalized plants growing without cultivation north of California, west of Utah, and south of British Columbia*, a massive work of 816 pages published in segments between 1897 and 1903. Some thirty Northwest plant species and varieties are named *howellii*.

Thomas's brothers Joseph and John in 1873 purchased the James and Julia Bybee property, adjoining that of their parents. The Bybee house (built ca. 1858) still stands there in Howell Territorial Park, which also includes meadows, wetlands, and the remnants of an orchard of representative **apples** and other fruits that were cultivated in nineteenth-century Oregon. Thomas married Effie McIlwane in 1892; in his later years he left Sauvie Island and was the proprietor of several grocery stores in the Portland area.

Hubbard The Marion County community of Hubbard is located on **French Prairie**, which was long-settled farmland when the Oregon & California Railroad came through in 1870. Charles Hubbard, a pioneer of 1847, donated land for the station, and he platted a townsite. The Hubbard post office opened in 1871. Hubbard was incorporated as a municipality in 1891; the 1900 census showed it to have a population of 213. The area around Hubbard has long been producing hops, berries, poultry, and dairy products. Mineral Springs Road passes the site of

Hubbard's once-noted Wolfer Mineral Springs, named for George Wolfer, who came to join the **Aurora** Colony in 1863; the mineral springs operated as a sanitarium and resort in the 1920s and 1930s. Hubbard had an estimated population of 3,095 in 2007.

Hudson's Bay Company (HBC) Founded in 1670, the Hudson's Bay Company is the oldest commercial enterprise in North America, a British corporation with tentacles that extended around the world. The HBC impact in the **Oregon Country** is related to its longtime interest in the **fur trade** and to the fact that it was virtually a government, and a British one. HBC was a powerful Canadian company in the early 1800s, and in 1821 it took over one of its major rivals, the North West Company. From the 1810s, HBC had posts in the Oregon Country, in present-day northern Washington and Idaho. Taking over **Fort George** from the North West Company, the HBC made it their Columbia region headquarters, though it was an unsatisfactory post far from the fur-bearing areas. New chief factor **John McLoughlin** established **Fort Vancouver** in 1825 and moved the chief operations there. From the 1820s into the mid-1840s, this was the nerve center of Euro-American activity in the Oregon Country, and McLoughlin was its personal representative. The HBC had posts at **Fort Umpqua** and Fort Boise, and a post and agricultural enterprise at Fort Nisqually in Washington state. The settlement of the agreement of joint occupancy of the Oregon Country between Great Britain and the United States in 1846 put Fort Vancouver on American soil. The HBC withdrew its headquarters to Victoria, British Columbia, in 1849. A post remained at Fort Vancouver until 1860.

Hume, George and William *see* fishing, commercial

Huntington The former railroad town of Huntington lies near the confluence of Burnt River with the Snake River in a parched section of Baker County. Brothers J. M. and J. B. Huntington settled here in 1882 near the route of the Oregon Trail at a former stage stop, and a post office named for them opened the same year (J. M. Huntington, postmaster). Huntington very soon became the junction point of two segments of the **Union Pacific Railroad** system, the Oregon Railway and Navigation Company and the Oregon Short Line; when they joined there in 1884, it opened Oregon's second transcontinental railroad connection.

In the next few decades Huntington became the site of large railroad maintenance and repair shops, yards, and refueling facilities. It also became a warehouse point for goods destined to the ranching country to the south and west, and some imposing commercial buildings were erected in the 1890s. It was incorporated in 1891, and by 1900 had a population of 821. Along with Baker County in general and **Copperfield** in particular, Huntington had a reputation for wide-open drinking and other sinful activities.

By 1915, Huntington boasted a bank, a weekly newspaper, a high school, and three churches. Improvements in railroad technology shut the Huntington facilities beginning in the 1950s, and the Interstate 84 freeway bypassed the town in the 1970s. Its population in 2007 was estimated at 560.

hydroelectric power *see* Bonneville Dam; Clackamas River; John Day Dam; McNary Dam; The Dalles Dam; West Linn; Willamette Falls

I

I-5 *see* **Interstate 5;** *similarly, see* **Interstate 83; Interstate 84; Interstate 205; Interstate 405**

Idanha Situated on the North Santiam River in Marion and Linn Counties, Idanha was the end of the line for an abortive trans-Cascade railroad project; the last few miles from **Detroit** to Idanha were completed in 1895, which is also the year the post office opened. The construction of **Detroit Dam** precipitated the incorporation of the community in 1949, and the removal of the railroad in 1950. The census of 1950 gave Idanha a population of 442; by 1972, the figure was 382; and the estimated population in 2007 was 230. The name derives from a bottled mineral water from Idaho; a once-prominent Boise hotel was also named the Idanha. The reason for its use in Oregon is obscure.

Illinois River The Illinois River rises in the Siskiyou Mountains of Josephine County and flows north about seventy-five miles to join the Rogue River west of Grants Pass. It was apparently named for the three Althouse brothers—Samuel, John, and Phillip—who were from Peoria, Illinois, and who mined for gold along the Illinois during the boisterous rushes of the early 1850s. The naming of the tributary Althouse Creek and the ghost town of Althouse also reflect their impact.

Imbler A rural agricultural town in Union County, Imbler developed after a railroad arrived from La Grande in 1890. The post office opened the next year, and by 1915, Imbler, population about 300, shipped approximately "500 cars of grain, flour and feed, 100 cars of apples, 100 cars of potatoes, 25 cars of hogs, 10 cars of hay, [and] 50 cars of lumber"

annually. The town was incorporated in 1922, and had a population in 2007 of about 295.

Independence Independence is situated on the Willamette River in Polk County, an area settled by American farmers in the 1840s. The name commemorates Independence, Missouri, one of the jump-off points used by **Oregon Trail** emigrants. While Polk County can be envisioned as the nexus of the idea of Oregon as Eden, and while it is a locale that was greatly favored by early settlers, it is a very recent conceit that Independence, Oregon, was "the end of the Oregon Trail." A post office was opened in 1852, and the town of Independence was incorporated in 1874. Local crops such as wheat and hops were shipped by riverboat; the arrival of the railroad in 1880 provided other travel options. The 1880 census showed 691 residents. The downtown historic district contains numerous commercial structures highlighting the properous 1890s and 1900s. Independence often served as the font of libations for residents of **Monmouth**, a town some two miles to the west. Monmouth went dry by local option; Independence did not, and a local railroad conveniently connected the two towns. Since the 1960s, Independence has become a residential suburb for Salem, some twenty miles away, and it now abuts Monmouth, which finally went "wet" again in 2002. The population of Independence in 2007 was about 7,905.

Indian potato *see* **wapato**

Industrial Workers of the World (IWW) The IWW was founded in 1905 in Chicago, the idea being to counter the work of the American Federation of Labor (AFL)—which organized its members by their occupation—with a single union that would represent all workers: One Big Union. Among the early organizers were Eugene V. Debs, later Socialist party candidate for president, and Mary Harris Jones, better known as Mother Jones. The IWW, also known as Wobblies, acquired a reputation for radicalism: their motto was "An injury to one is an injury to all"; its constitution emphasized that "the working class and the employing class have nothing in common." Aiming to improve the lot of workers worldwide, the IWW found itself at odds with the ruling business class in the first decades of the twentieth century. In Oregon, the tens of thousands of logging and lumber mill workers were prime candidates for IWW membership: they were mainly itinerant men at the mercy of employers who often provided filthy lodgings, bad food, dangerous working conditions, and erratic paychecks. The "little red card" of membership in the IWW was a signal of solidarity with other workers; to employers, it was the sign of a malcontent and possible saboteur, and holders of the card were not well treated. In 1917, workers in the **wood products industry** around the state agitated for change, and both the AFL and the IWW were seen as enemies by management. Their efforts were countered by a management-sponsored organization, the Loyal Legion of Loggers and Lumbermen (the 4L). Wartime concerns over saboteurs and "disloyal" Americans made it difficult for workers to advocate change, and the Wobblies' influence waned in the postwar years—when some of their changes were achieved, in fact. In Washington state, the IWW was involved in several dramatic and even shocking events related to labor questions, such as the Everett massacre, the Spokane free-speech fight, and the martyrdom of a Wobbly in Centralia; while Oregon workers were spared the drama, they participated in the struggle.

Tyler, Robert L. *Rebels of the Woods: The I.W.W. in the Pacific Northwest.* Eugene: University of Oregon Books, 1967.

▶ **Interstate 5** Paralleling the former **Pacific Highway** and its predecessors, the **Oregon & Cali-**

fornia Railroad and the **California-Oregon Trail**, Interstate 5 is a four- to six-lane freeway that extends from the Columbia River on the north, via Portland, Eugene, and Medford, to the California border south of the summit of the Siskiyou Mountains. The portion from Portland to Salem was known as the **Baldock Freeway** shortly after its construction in the late 1950s. One of the last segments of I-5, which opened in 1966, was the Marquam Bridge over the Willamette River in Portland, which linked I-5 to I-84, but was originally intended to connect to the unbuilt **Mount Hood Freeway**; the off-ramp stubs are still apparent. The last section, also opened in 1966, was a rebuilding of the route through Canyon Creek south of **Canyonville**, a construction project that virtually obliterated the creek and its canyon, once the most formidable section of the California-Oregon Trail.

Interstate 82 This freeway heads north from a point on I-84 just west of Heppner across the Columbia River into Washington state and connects with I-90 near Ellensburg. The route was completed in 1989.

The Interstate 5 interchange with Van Duyn Road, Exit 199, east of Coburg, as it appeared shortly after construction was completed in the mid-1960s. The interchange is now the east edge of Coburg and a center for motorhome sales. Oregon Department of Transportation; Oregon Historical Society, OrHi 100045.

Interstate 84 Stretching across the northern section of Oregon to the Idaho border at Ontario, I-84 replaced the **Columbia River Highway** and **Highway 30** as the main route to the east. The route also parallels that of the **Union Pacific Railroad** and the **Oregon Trail**. The water-level section of the route from Portland to The Dalles was built in the 1950s and early 1960s; it was completed to interstate standards by 1969. East of The Dalles, the highway was improved in the 1950s, but rebuilding to freeway dimensions did not begin until after 1966, with the last upgraded section, near Baker City, being put in service in 1980. The first few miles of I-84 east from Portland were opened as the **Banfield Expressway** in 1955, before interstate standards were adopted. The freeway was initially designated as Interstate 80N, an offshoot of the route to San Francisco; it was changed to Interstate 84 in 1980. Initial planning was that a new segment through southeast Portland, known as the **Mount Hood Freeway**, would replace the Banfield Expressway route. This exceedingly unpopular proposition was finally squelched, requiring an upgrading of the former Banfield Expressway.

Interstate 205 A partial ring road that parallels I-5 to the east through the outer Portland metropolitan area (its counterpart on the west side is the much shorter **Interstate 405**), I-205 was a controversial construction project. An initial segment was a bridge across the Willamette River at Oregon City, which opened in 1970. The connection from the bridge west to I-5 was completed in 1974. The routing of the section through Multnomah County encountered stiff opposition, resulting in the formation of a new city, **Maywood Park**, specifically to influence the route and reduce its adverse impacts. Transportation commission chair **Glenn Jackson** eventually brokered a deal that permitted construction to resume in 1978 after a five-year hiatus. The agreement included provisions for a future light-rail line; construction of this **MAX** route began in 2006.

Most of the I-205 route was completed with the opening of the Glenn L. Jackson Bridge across the Columbia River in 1982; Washington state's link of I-205 back to I-5 was finished in 1983.

Interstate 405 This freeway is located in Portland, and in a deep cut slices through an area just to the west of the retail core. It was built between 1964 and 1969, and is sometimes referred to as the Stadium Freeway for its proximity to **PGE Park**. The final segment at the north end included the Fremont Bridge, completed in 1973.

➤ **interurban railways** This term refers to railway lines that connect towns and cities with frequent, rapid trains, usually powered by electricity. Interurban railways were developed in the 1890s; many died in the 1920s with the rise of good highways and affordable automobiles, but some lasted longer. Oregon has the distinction of having built what is often considered the nation's first interurban railway, the East Side Railway, which opened in 1893 from Portland through the Sellwood neighborhood, Milwaukie, and Gladstone to Oregon City; it

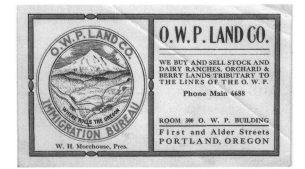

This real estate advertising card, issued about 1905, is from the O. W. P. Land Company—connected to the Oregon Water Power & Railway Company (OWP&R). The OWP&R had recently built hydroelectric plants and electric interurban railways connecting Portland with Gresham, Troutdale, and Estacada. Many people were eager to buy lands where they could carry on small farming and orchard enterprises, and still be quickly and inexpensively connected to the city for marketing—and perhaps even for commuting to city work. Mason collection.

was powered by electricity generated at **Willamette Falls**. This line remained in continuous operation through World War II, and finally ceased in 1958 after access to downtown Portland was cut by road construction. Other interurban lines radiated from Portland to Estacada and Troutdale, and to Linnton and North Plains; another line went from Oregon City to Molalla and Mount Angel. The **Oregon Electric Railroad** built an extensive system extending as far as Eugene, and the **Southern Pacific Company** turned several of its Willamette Valley lines into interurban railway services. Only the Oregon City line and an affiliated route to Gresham survived to and through World War II.

Ione This tiny Morrow County town grew up around a rural post office that opened in 1884. A railroad came through in 1888, and the town was incorporated in 1903, the same year it was struck by the crashing waters of the **Heppner** flood. The 1910 census gave Ione a population of 239. In 1915, it was reported that Ione "ships more poultry than any other town on the Oregon-Washington Railroad & Navigation system," and that general farming, wheat raising, and dairying were also carried on nearby. Ione's population has wavered only slightly over the years: 439 in 1920, 262 in both 1940 and 1950, 255 in 1990, and an estimated 345 in 2007.

iris The growing of iris bulbs is a significant agricultural activity in the Willamette Valley, where two of the nation's largest bulb dealers are located. Schreiner's was established north of Salem about 1925, while Cooley Gardens in Silverton began operations in 1928.

Irish in Oregon Many Irish came to Oregon in the nineteenth century. In Portland, they were the largest ethnic group in the 1870s, and helped to build and populate Saint Patrick's Catholic Church in the **Slabtown neighborhood** and Saint Mary's Cathedral nearby. The Irish were prominent in the

livestock industry in Lake County in the 1870s. The Ancient Order of Hibernians had a lodge in Lakeview, and one in Portland. One of the most noted Irish in Lake County was not in the sheep business, but was a physician, Dr. **Bernard Daly**. Many Irish were also engaged in the sheep and wool business of Morrow County.

Kilkenny, John F. *Shamrocks and Shepherds: The Irish of Morrow County.* 2nd rev. ed. Portland, Oregon: Oregon Historical Society, 1981.

iron production The discovery in the 1850s of iron ore deposits on Iron Mountain south of Portland inspired dreams of an industrial empire. In 1862, some six tons of ore from land near Sucker Lake (now **Lake Oswego**) was sent to California for assaying, with encouraging results. **William S. Ladd** was one of the backers of the Oregon Iron Company in 1865, along with John and Henry Green. The investors had high hopes that iron would be needed to build the railroads being projected in Oregon. The first iron ingots were produced in a smelter by the Willamette River at present-day Lake Oswego in 1867, and iron was manufactured for railroad cars and storefronts, but steel rails never came from the plant. It operated intermittently, at its early height employing nearly 300 workers. From 1881 to 1885 the Oregon Iron & Steel Company operated at the site; in 1888, a new plant was built, producing primarily cast sewer pipe for Portland. Production peaked in 1890; the plant closed for good in 1919. A stone furnace from the early iron works stands in George Rogers Park near downtown Lake Oswego; to the east, SW Iron Mountain Boulevard wends among expensive residences.

Goodall, Mary. *Oregon's Iron Dream: A Story of Old Oswego and the Proposed Iron Empire of the West.* Portland, Oregon: Binfords & Mort, 1958.

irrigation Early examples in Oregon of the use of irrigation to improve agricultural production include ditches dug by the brothers Courtney across the

Umatilla Meadows near today's Hermiston in 1857–58, and another 1850s ditch near The Dalles carrying water from Mill Creek some fifteen miles. But major irrigation projects came in the first decades of the twentieth century, with Federal Reclamation Act projects in the **Umatilla** area, 1904–08, and the Klamath Project beginning in 1903 and continuing for some years. The private, but state-endorsed, Tumalo Project in Central Oregon began with high hopes about 1902, but slid into a fiscal and operational morass in the 1920s and 1930s. The federal Owyhee project, built in the 1920s and 1930s, brings Owyhee River water to the **Treasure Valley** area. The completion of **McNary Dam** adds more Columbia River water to irrigate lands in the **Hermiston** vicinity in the 1960s. Irrigation is practiced in the Willamette and Rogue River Valleys as well. *See also* **Crook County.**

Irrigon The promise of irrigation from the Umatilla Project prompted the establishment of the town of Irrigon in Morrow County. A post office was opened in 1902. In 1915, it was reported that the West Umatilla Project was underway; already the area was producing alfalfa, apples, peaches, strawberries, cherries, and berries. Irrigon was not incorporated until 1957, in the wake of the **McNary Dam** construction; its population then was 261. The 1970 census showed the same figure, but by 1980, there were 737 residents. The estimated population in 2007 was 1,850. The largest employer in the mid-2000s was Western Alfalfa, which prepared livestock feed from alfalfa.

Irvington neighborhood, Portland This Portland residential neighborhood was platted in 1884, as the east side of the river began to develop. By 1890, with bridges and streetcar lines extending to the west side downtown, Irvington lots began to sell. The subdivision was named for the original donation land claim settler, Capt. William Irving. Irvington residential lots had restrictions that dic-

tated relatively expensive houses and prohibited commercial buildings. The neighborhood was built up primarily in the early 1900s; the Irvington Club was founded in 1898 and still has an impact in the community.

Island City This Union County community is northeast of La Grande, situated on what was an island formed by the Grande Ronde River and a branch, Mulholland Slough. The area was long devoted to farming and livestock, and the town once had a flouring mill. The Island City post office opened in 1873 and closed in 1972; by that time, the town was virtually part of La Grande. It was incorporated in 1904 and has retained its own municipal government. The population in 2007 was estimated at 980.

Italians in Oregon The Italian presence in Oregon was strongest in Portland, where in the years between 1900 and 1917, the Italian immigrant population went from about 1,000 to about 10,000. Many immigrants settled first in the **South Portland neighborhood** where they built the Catholic Saint Michael the Archangel Church, while others located in and near **Ladd's Addition** (the location of Saint Philip Neri Catholic Church, founded in 1913) and in **Milwaukie**, where they were able to make a living doing market gardening. A newspaper, *La Tribuna Italiana*, began publishing in Portland in 1911, soon putting out a daily edition; it lasted until 1932. The Italian Gardeners and Ranchers Association built a distribution building in 1922 on SE Union Avenue. Italians became entrenched in the produce business; traces of that long association are still visible in business names such as Rinella and Rossi.

Gould, Charles F. Portland Italians, 1880–1920. *Oregon Historical Quarterly* 77 (1976): 239–260.

Toll, William. Ethnicity and Stability: The Italians and Jews of South Portland, 1900–1940. *Pacific Historical Review* 54 (1985): 161–190.

IWW *see* **Industrial Workers of the World**

J

Jackson, Charles Samuel "Sam" (1860–1924) Born in Virginia, Sam Jackson came west in 1880, settling in Pendleton where he worked with the *East Oregonian* newspaper, eventually becoming its publisher. He built it into a politically and economically influential regional paper, which also helped involve Jackson in other business ventures. In 1902, Jackson was approached by several influential Portlanders who hoped he might work with them to save a new daily newspaper, the *Evening Journal*, which was trying to compete with the entrenched, powerful, and Republican *Oregonian*. Jackson accepted the challenge, bought the paper, renamed it the *Oregon Journal*, and conducted it as an independent paper that championed the downtrodden and the powerless. Journalism historian George Trumbull reported that Jackson made the "frequent" remark that "If the time ever comes when the *Journal* cannot be free and fearless and independent, I will throw it into the river." It remained free, although it was a number of years before it was profitable. Jackson fought for pure milk, improved harbors, bridges across the Willamette, and good roads, including the **Columbia River Highway**. After Jackson's death, his son Philip L. Jackson became publisher. The paper remained independent until its acquisition by the competing *Oregonian* in 1961. It continued publication until 1983, for most of that time ostensibly still independent of the *Oregonian*'s editorial control.

Jackson, Glenn L. (1902–1980) A native of Albany, Oregon, Glenn Jackson went on to graduate from Oregon Agricultural College in 1925. From there he went to Wyoming and sold electrical appliances from door to door. His boss for that stint was selected president of the California-Oregon Power Company (COPCO), and he took Jackson to the Med-

ford headquarters with him, where he became a sales manager. Jackson served in the Army Air Corps in World War II, briefly operated a lumber mill, and then returned to COPCO, where he swiftly rose to executive heights. COPCO merged with the Pacific Power and Light Company (PP&L) in 1971; soon he was chairman of PP&L; he became "a businessman's businessman." In that position he also had a potent political impact. As businessman, Jackson ranched, developed a golf course, owned a number of newspapers, helped found and operate **Air Oregon**, and was a board member of banks, **Fred Meyer**, and an insurance company. Among his most influential positions (1959–1979) was as chair of the Oregon Highway Commission and its successor, the Oregon Transportation Commission. His tenure there was marked by the construction of the **Interstate 5, 84**, and **205** freeways, the development of a system of highway rest areas, and the bridging of the Columbia River at Astoria, closing the last **ferry** operation on the **Oregon Coast Highway**. The Interstate 205 bridge across the Columbia River is the Glenn L. Jackson Memorial Bridge.

Jackson County The territorial legislature established Jackson County in 1852, from the southwestern portion of Lane County "and the unorganized area south of Douglas and Umpqua Counties," said the *Oregon Blue Book*. Numerous boundary changes occurred as other counties were created in the southwestern quadrant, resulting in a final area of 2,801 square miles. Most of the shaping had occurred by the time of the 1870 census, when the county had a population of 4,478. Jackson County's creation was the result of the influx of miners as the California gold rush crossed the line to pan for gold in the **Illinois** and **Applegate River** valleys. The area was accessible via the **California-Oregon**

Trail, and gold discoveries at Jacksonville in 1852 were almost adjacent. The region that is now Jackson County was home to the **Takelma Indians** as well as to a few bands of isolated **Athapaskan Indians** along the Applegate River. The trail over the Siskiyou Mountains also brought in Modoc, Shasta, and Umpqua Indians. The rapid influx of miners brought quick and painful encounters between whites and Natives that led to the **Rogue River Wars** in the 1850s and to the swift removal of most of the Native inhabitants by the end of the decade. Settlers intent on farming soon occupied the fertile **Bear Creek Valley** in the late 1850s and the 1860s. **Jacksonville** became the county seat in 1853.

While gold mining continued on a small scale in the Jacksonville and Ashland areas after 1870, agriculture rose in importance as wheat fields replaced native grass prairies along Bear Creek. A railroad reached the valley in the 1880s and by 1887 linked it to Portland and to California. **Peter Britt** was producing **wine** at his Valley View Vineyards in the 1880s. In the early 1900s, fruit orchards, apples and then pears, began to cover the valley floor as refrigerated railroad transportation provided access to distant markets. A promotional brochure in the 1910s noted that "Vineyards, hillside orchards and gardens will, it is believed, ultimately bring a large part of this hillside land into productive use." Jackson County's population reached 20,405 in 1920. By this time, **Medford** was the dominant city in the county, and in 1927 voters chose to move the county seat there. Logging operations in the Cascades brought lumber mills to valley towns, and lumbering was a major industry from the 1920s into the 1980s. Wine grapes and winemaking returned to the area in the early 1980s. Jackson County's population reached 58,510 in 1950, and 132,586 by 1980. The estimated population in 2007 was 202,310.

Dunn, Joy B., ed. *Land in Common: An Illustrated History of Jackson County, Oregon.* Medford, Oregon: Southern Oregon Historical Society, 1993.

Jacksonville Jacksonville in Jackson County came about as the result of the discovery of gold by James Cluggage and James Poole in Rich Gulch, a tributary of Daisy Creek, probably in the early days of 1852. Rich Gulch was only one of many gold strikes in the region, but it soon mushroomed to become the major settlement. It was first called Table Rock City for the landmark **Table Rock**s several miles to the north. It was named the county seat of the new Jackson County in 1853, and brick store buildings were erected on the main thoroughfares, California Street and the intersecting Oregon Street. Jacksonville was incorporated in 1860, and the census of that year credited it with 892 residents. Through the 1860s and 1870s, Jacksonville prospered as county seat and a local agricultural and mining trade center, documented by town photographer **Peter Britt**. However, when the **Oregon & California Railroad** came to the valley in the 1880s, geography caused it to bypass Jacksonville, and the rival city of **Medford** arose a few miles to the east. Jacksonville responded by building an elegant new brick courthouse in 1884, and constructing a short connecting railroad to Medford in 1890, but decline was inevitable. The 1880 population of 839 fell to 489 by 1920, and in 1927 the county seat was transferred to Medford. The final event in the Jacksonville courthouse was the dramatic trial of the three young D'Autremont brothers—Ray, Roy, and Hugh—for a 1923 train robbery in which four men died.

Jacksonville was somnolent in the 1920s; during the 1930s, many residents turned again to gold mining to make ends meet. The town's population rose to 1,193 by 1950, and in the 1950s and 1960s its history and architecture were discovered by a wider public. The Jacksonville Museum opened in the old courthouse in 1947, and historic preservation efforts brought the town national attention. For its collection of nineteenth-century small-town commercial and residential buildings, much of the city of Jacksonville was placed on the National Register of Historic Places as a national landmark district in 1966. Since that time, tourism and the **Peter Britt Music Festival** have been the city's economic engines. The population reached 1,896 in 1990, and an estimated 2,635 in 2007.

> Engeman, Richard H. *The Jacksonville Story.* 2nd ed. Medford, Oregon: Southern Oregon Historical Society, 1990.

James G. Blaine Society *see* **Holbrook, Stewart Hall**

Jantzen Beach Jantzen Beach was a popular amusement park that opened in 1928 adjacent to the Interstate Bridge (1918) crossing the Columbia River to Vancouver, Washington. The park was named for Carl Jantzen, one of the investors; Jantzen was a founder of Portland Knitting Mills (1910), which became Jantzen, Inc., a once-noted manufacturer of sportswear and swimsuits. The company logo of a woman diving—and wearing a Jantzen suit—also adorned the amusement park. Jantzen Beach was noted for the Big Dipper, a wooden roller coaster, and for its carousel, which survives in the shopping mall that replaced the park in 1970; its future was in doubt in 2008.

Japanese in Oregon The first Japanese immigrants to Oregon came in the 1880s, with a major influx in the early 1900s. Portland was a center for many Japanese, who established a Nihonmachi or Japantown in Portland's North End, now the **New Chinatown/Japantown Historic District**. Other Japanese immigrants settled near Salem, some of them doing market gardening in the **Lake Labish** area, while others farmed and owned business firms in Independence, Salem, and Keizer. Another group in the early 1900s settled in **Hood River County**, where they worked in and later owned orchards and strawberry farms; still other families headed for the irrigated farmlands of the **Treasure Valley** near Ontario. During **World War II**, Japanese in western

Oregon were sent to internment camps; most Oregon Japanese went to Minidoka, in Idaho. Anti-Japanese sentiment was especially strong in the Hood River area, and many Japanese did not return there after the war. Trade connections with Japan in the late twentieth century helped inspire the construction of a classical Japanese garden in Portland's Washington Park (1967), and Sapporo was Portland's first sister city, a link established in 1959.

> Azuma, Eiichiro. A History of Oregon's Issei, 1880-1952. *Oregon Historical Quarterly* 94, no. 4 (Winter 1993-94): 315-367.
>
> Tamura, Linda. *The Hood River Issei: An Oral History of Japanese Settlers in Oregon's Hood River Valley.* Urbana: University of Illinois Press, 1993.

Japantown/New Chinatown Historic District, Portland *see* **New Chinatown/ Japantown Historic District, Portland**

Jefferson Emigrant settlers occupied land in this part of Marion County by the 1840s. In 1851, Jacob Conser established a ferry across the Santiam River near the future Jefferson, and he had his hand in two other erstwhile communities on the river, Syracuse and Santiam City. Meanwhile, the residents of the area began a private academy that they named the Jefferson Institute in 1856. A town coalesced; Jefferson post office was established in 1861. In 1870 the Oregon & California Railroad built southward through Jefferson toward Roseburg, and the town was incorporated in the same year. The Jefferson Institute lasted until a public school was established in Jefferson in the 1890s. In the 1900 census, 273 residents were found in Jefferson. By 1915, a creamery, a flouring mill, and two sawmills were operating in Jefferson, and the farmers nearby grew wheat, hops, potatoes, and fruits, and engaged in dairying. Jefferson's population hovered around 400 from 1910 through World War II; it rose to 636 in 1950, to 936 in 1970, and to an estimated 2,590 in

2007. Jacob Conser's Greek Revival–style house of 1854 is still a landmark in Jefferson, listed on the National Register of Historic Places.

Jefferson, State of *see* **State of Jefferson**

Jefferson County Created in 1914 from territory once part of Crook County, Jefferson County is named for Mount Jefferson. The county seat is **Madras**, and the county has an area of 1,791 square miles. About half of the **Warm Springs Reservation** is located in Jefferson County, and the region is part of the homeland of the **Sahaptin Indians**. The population of Jefferson County in the 1920 census was 3,211; the **Oregon Trunk Railway** had just been completed through Madras and into Central Oregon in 1911, fostering agricultural development. Irrigation projects in the 1930s upped the agricultural prospects of Jefferson County, and potatoes, alfalfa, mint, and seed crops are grown; in the dryer eastern portion of the county, wheat farming and cattle grazing were carried on. Forest products have been part of the economy of the county since the 1910s as well. Jefferson County's population in 1950 reached 5,536; in 1980 it was 11,599; the estimate in 2007 was 22,030.

Jennings Lodge The Clackamas County community of Jennings Lodge was platted as a townsite in 1905 along the route of the Portland-Oregon City electric **interurban railway**. Named for Berryman Jennings, who had settled in the area in 1847, Jennings Lodge was given a post office in 1910 (first called simply Jennings). In 1915, it was described as having a population of about 800; it was "a suburban residence section of garden farms. Many summer homes are located along the banks of the Willamette river. Good salmon fishing." Many suburban commuters raised chickens and other poultry. With the completion of the four-lane Highway 99E through Jennings Lodge in the 1930s, a retail strip developed through the community; however, many older bungalows remain in the wooded areas west of the highway.

Jews in Oregon Revolution in Germany induced a migration of many German Jews to America in the late 1840s, and the California gold rush brought some of them to the Pacific Coast. Jewish merchants such as Aaron Meier, one of the founders of the **Meier & Frank** department store, came to Portland, Jacksonville, The Dalles, and Salem in the 1850s. Congregation Beth Israel was formed in Portland in 1858, and in 1859 it built the first synagogue north of San Francisco on the Pacific Coast; rabbi Stephen Wise served at Beth Israel from 1900 to 1906 before going on to a distinguished career in New York City. A rural Russian Jewish commune was attempted in the 1880s near **Glendale**. The early twentieth century brought another influx of European Jews to Oregon, many of whom first settled in the **South Portland neighborhood**. During the 1920s, the influential **Ku Klux Klan** in Oregon was hostile toward Jews and Catholics as well as blacks, but in 1930, the state elected its first Jewish governor, **Julius L. Meier**. Oregon's Jewish population has been concentrated in the Portland area. The disruptions of **urban renewal** and freeway construction contributed to a dispersal of the city's Jewish population into the western suburbs in the 1960s, and since World War II Jewish communities have also formed in cities such as Ashland and Eugene.

Lowenstein, Steven. *The Jews of Oregon, 1850–1950.* Portland, Oregon: Jewish Historical Society of Oregon, 1987.

Toll, William. *The Making of an Ethnic Middle Class: Portland Jewry over Four Generations.* Albany, New York: State University of New York Press, 1982.

John Day Named for the **John Day River** that flows through it, this small ranching community is the largest town in Grant County. It began during the gold rush of the 1860s, when nearby **Canyon**

City was the center of activity. John Day City post office was established in 1865, and closed in 1871; another office named John Day opened in 1879 and has continued. After Canyon City's Chinese section burned in 1885, many **Chinese** moved to John Day, where a large population lived in what was called Tiger Town. The Kam Wah Chung Company store in John Day is a remainder of that community, an herbal shop that was operated by Ing Hay and his business partner Lung On during the first decades of the twentieth century. John Day was incorporated in 1901; the 1910 census reported 282 residents; that figure reached 708 by 1940. Timber operations boosted the population to 1,597 in 1950; although the mills have closed since 2000, the population estimate for 2007 is 1,850.

John Day Dam The John Day Dam, the last constructed on the lower Columbia River, was built between 1958 and 1971, and is maintained by the U.S. Army Corps of Engineers. It was built to generate hydroelectricity, and includes a navigation lock and fish ladders. The dam impounds the river upstream for more than seventy-six miles to **McNary Dam**.

John Day River This river rises in the Strawberry Mountains of Grant County and flows west and north for about 281 miles before entering the Columbia River. Its northern stretch is the boundary between Sherman and Gilliam Counties. Some 147 miles was designated the John Day Wild and Scenic River in 1988, and is especially popular for whitewater rafting and for fishing for steelhead, bass, and salmon. For a brief period from 1889 to 1899, a small sternwheel steamboat, the *John Day Queen*, was operated by Charles Clarno on a section of the river near the present town on Clarno. The river is named for **John Day** of the **Pacific Fur Company**. A John Day River also flows in Clatsop County, a tidal stream that is home to a number of **houseboats** and fishing vessels.

Johns Landing neighborhood, Portland
The **Fulton neighborhood** immediately south of the area known today as Johns Landing was platted as a residential subdivision in the late 1880s. The waterfront at Fulton and to the north included a number of industries from the 1880s until the mid-1900s; many of them such as the B. P. John Furniture Company were wood products firms. When B. P. John closed its operations and moved to California, the John family worked with developer John D. Gray and architect John W. Storrs in the early 1970s to convert the former industrial buildings to new uses. The project took the name Johns Landing; the Watertower at Johns Landing opened in 1973 as an early prototype of mall-style retail shops located in a recycled industrial building.

Johnson City Delbert Johnson built a trailer park in a suburban area of Clackamas County in 1959. Failing to get the park annexed to neighboring Gladstone in 1968, Johnson succeeded in incorporating it as a city in 1970. State law has since changed, making similar municipalities an unlikely creation. Johnson City had a population of about 675 in 2007.

Jones, Nard *see* **Weston**

Jordan Valley The Malheur County town of Jordan Valley had a post office as early as 1867, located on the road connecting the **Treasure Valley** area of Idaho with northern Nevada and the trail to California. The community was incorporated in 1911, at a time when sheep raising was popular in the area, and many **Basque** immigrants came to the region as sheepherders. One of Jordan Valley's features is a pelota fronton, a walled field to play this ball game favored by the Basques, who built it about 1915. Irrigation in the valley permitted raising some crops. Jordan Valley's population in 1920 was 355; in 1950, 236; the estimate in 2007 was 230.

Joseph (ca.1790–1870) This famous leader of a group of the **Nez Perce Indians** is sometimes referred to as Joseph the Elder. He replaced his given name, Tuekakas, with Joseph when the Presbyterian missionary, Rev. Henry Spalding, baptized him in 1839. Joseph maintained cordial relations with the incoming whites, and his son **Joseph** the Younger was sent to a mission school. In 1855, Washington territorial governor Isaac I. Stevens embarked on a round of treaty signings east of the Cascades, and a Nez Perce reservation was created with Joseph's collaboration. Only eight years later, in 1863, after a gold rush into the Nez Perce country set off numerous incidents, the federal government unilaterally slashed the size of the reservation by nearly 90 percent. Betrayed, Joseph renounced Christianity, destroyed his American flag, and declined to sign the treaty that would ratify the new boundaries. Joseph had not signed the original 1855 treaty; his band remained in the Wallowa Valley. Joseph died in 1870, and is buried outside the town named for him overlooking **Wallowa Lake**.

Joseph (ca. 1840–1904) This Nez Perce leader was born in the Wallowa Valley; his given name was Hin-mah-too-yah-lat-kekt (Thunder Rolling Down the Mountain). He was widely known as Joseph, or Joseph the Younger to distinguish him from his father, also **Joseph** (ca. 1790–1870). The younger Joseph was educated at a mission school. The fate of the Wallowa band of the **Nez Perce Indians** was set by the actions of his father and other leaders who did not sign the 1855 treaty; after the elder Joseph's death in 1870, the younger took a place as one of those leaders. He resisted the moving of the group from the Wallowa Valley, but the pressures of white miners and cattlemen to enter the valley were insistent, and in 1877 Gen. **O. O. Howard** threatened a cavalry attack to force the holdouts onto the Idaho Nez Perce Reservation. Initially Joseph prepared to bow to the threat and move, but a raid by several Nez Perce warriors that led to the deaths of some

white settlers caused the federal troops to pursue the Wallowa band. The ensuing **Nez Perce War** ended with the surrender of the group in Montana; Joseph's surrender speech was transcribed by Lt. **C. E. S. Wood**; in Wood's phraseology, Joseph proclaimed, "Hear me, my chiefs; my heart is sick and sad. From where the Sun now stands, I will fight no more forever." Joseph and the Wallowas were sent to Indian Territory (Oklahoma), where many sickened and died. They were allowed to move to the Colville Reservation in eastern Washington state in 1885. Joseph spoke of Indian rights with President Theodore Roosevelt, and he maintained a warm relationship with C. E. S. Wood. Wood's son Erskine twice spent time with Joseph and his family at Nespelem, and Joseph was a guest at Wood's Portland residence, where the noted sculptor Olin Warner made a bronze medallion of his face (Warner also sculpted the **Skidmore Fountain**).

Gidley, Mick. *Kopet: A Documentary Narrative of Chief Joseph's Last Years.* Seattle: University of Washington Press, 1981.

Greene, Jerome A. *Nez Perce Summer, 1877: The U.S. Army and the Nee-Me-Poo Crisis.* Helena, Montana: Montana Historical Society Press, 2000.

Joseph (city) Naming itself for the Nez Perce chief **Joseph** (ca. 1790–1870), the city of Joseph acknowledged the fact that Joseph was banished and the homeland of the Wallowa Nez Perce was in white hands. The Joseph post office was established in what was then ranching country in 1880, and the town was incorporated in 1887; the 1890 census reported a population of 249. The valley was productive, and by the 1910s was producing crops of alfalfa and other forage, wheat and oats, apples and pears, and even strawberries. The railroad arrived from La Grande in 1908, and Joseph was the terminus; there was a creamery and flour mill and a brickyard. Recreational cabins and lodges along the shore of **Wallowa Lake** were built in the 1910s and 1920s, and Joseph's population reached 770 in 1920. The figure fell to 666 by 1950, rising to 999 in 1990. The annual Chief Joseph Days rodeo has been a town fixture since the 1940s. In 1982, a bronze foundry opened in Joseph, the first of a small wave of metal-sculpture-related art foundries and galleries that have located in Joseph. Joseph's estimated population in 2007 was 1,100.

Josephine County The county of Josephine, named for an early white settler, Josephine Rollins, was created from the western half of Jackson County in 1856. Its boundaries have shifted a little over the years; its current area is 1,641 square miles. Sailor Diggings was named the first county seat; it is gone, an ephemeral gold-mining camp that was probably near Waldo. The next year, the voters chose Kerbyville in the Illinois River valley as the county seat. The territorial legislature imperiously changed the name of Kerbyville to Napoleon in 1858, but popular usage prevailed; the post office has used the name Kerby since 1856. In 1886, in recognition of the fact that the railroad had reached Grants Pass, the county seat was moved to that new city. A courthouse was built in 1887, which was replaced in 1917. Josephine County was a center of violence during the **Rogue River Wars** of the 1850s, and the native **Takelma** and **Athapaskan Indians** were exterminated or removed to the **Coast Reservation** by the end of the 1850s.

The early economy of gold mining shifted to agriculture in the Rogue River and Applegate River valleys, and to logging and lumbering. Josephine County's population in 1860 (no Indians were counted) was 1,623; by 1890, that had increased to 4,878. In the early 1900s, fruit culture and grape growing increased; the 1930 population was 11,438. Increased logging operations and tourism, such as whitewater rafting on the Rogue and Illinois Rivers, increased the population to 26,542 by 1950, and 58,855 by 1980. High tech industries moved to Grants Pass in the 1980s, and grape growing and winemaking came to the Illinois River valley in the same period. Josephine County's estimated 2007 population was 82,390.

Hill, Edna May. *Josephine County Historical Highlights*. 2 vols. Grants Pass, Oregon: Josephine County Historical Society [and] Josephine County Library, 1976–79.

▶ **Jumpoff Joe** In the nineteenth century, Jumpoff Joe was a landmark on the Oregon Coast at Nye Beach in **Newport**. A large rocky formation known as a sea stack, Jumpoff Joe was shaped like a shoe, with an open arch at the heel. Jumpoff Joe was, however made of softer stuff—namely, concretionary sandstone—and it has eroded away to near-nothingness. In 2006, it was a small lump described as looking "like a seal sunning himself."

Junction City The Lane County city of Junction City was expected to be a railroad junction point. The **Oregon & California Railroad** built through the town in 1871, the Junction City post office opened in 1872, and Junction City was incorporated in 1872. But there was no junction; the town developed as a supply and shipping center for agricultural products. In 1880, the census showed 482 residents; in 1900, 506. In 1902, A. C. Nielsen of Minnesota

The slipper-like rock formation called Jumpoff Joe was a landmark on the beach at Newport. In the background at the left is the Yaquina Head lighthouse—Cape Foulweather does not have a lighthouse, and is in any case some six miles farther north. Steven Dotterer collection.

bought 1,600 acres of land east of Junction City and advertised in a Danish-language Midwestern newspaper for **Danish** people to come and make a new life in Lane County. Some forty families of Danish heritage responded to the call, bought small farming parcels, and established a Lutheran church. By the 1910s, Junction City had a fruit cannery and two grain elevators, a flour mill and two creameries; the population in 1920 reached 687.

The building of the **Pacific Highway**, officially U.S. 99, in the 1910s and 1920s put Junction City on the main road, which continued north to Albany and Portland. In the 1930s, an alternate route from Junction City via Corvallis to Portland was designated U.S. 99W, and the original highway U.S. 99E— and Junction City was, at last, a major junction. The population in 1950 was 1,475. The construction of the new **Interstate 5** freeway in the late 1950s, however, left Junction City several miles off the map. In 1960, local activists led by Dr. Gale Fletchall developed the idea of making something of the Danish settlement of the early 1900s, and the annual Scandinavian Festival began in 1961. Junction City's estimated population in 2007 was 5,135.

Kah-Nee-Ta *see* **Confederated Tribes of Warm Springs**

Kaiser, Henry John (1882–1967) Henry J. Kaiser never lived in Oregon, but he had a significant impact on it. Born in New York State, he came to Vancouver, British Columbia, early in the twentieth century; by 1912, he was engaged in the new business of road paving, taking contracts in Cuba and California, among other places. Kaiser set up his headquarters in Oakland, California, and his business prospered; by the early 1930s he was partnering with other contractors in some major public works projects, notably the building of Hoover Dam, **Bonneville Dam**, and Grand Coulee Dam, and the foundations of the San Francisco-Oakland Transbay Bridge. Kaiser also became involved in shipbuilding; during World War II, Kaiser built new shipyards in Portland and in Vancouver, Washington. He engaged in innovative **shipbuilding** methods, and he was an instigator of the wartime community of **Vanport** and its efforts to provide childcare and education benefits for war workers. His interest in health care led to the formation of Kaiser Permanente (KP), a leading health-maintenance organization on the Pacific Coast and in the Washington, DC, area. KP had its beginnings in California in 1933 and evolved into a prepaid medical program with its own clinics and hospitals. KP came to Oregon in 1942.

Kaiser Permanente *see* **Kaiser, Henry John**

Kalapuyan Indians The Kalapuyan people lived in the Willamette Valley and its foothills and in the upper drainage of the Umpqua River. Kalapuyan is a language group; anthropologists have identified some thirteen bands or tribes—that is, distinct dialects—but the exact number of distinct groups that once existed is unknown. The Tualatin or Atfalati, Yamhill, Ahantchuyuk or Pudding River, Luckiamute, Marys River, Santiam, Mohawk, and Yoncalla tribes of Kalapuyans are among those that are better known. The Willamette Valley provided a life of abundance in terms of food resources; the Kalapuyans relied on the very abundant fields of **camas**, and also used **wapato**, tarweed seeds, berries, and hazelnuts. Game included birds, deer and elk, bear and small mammals, and grasshoppers; the river provided salmon and **lamprey**. The Kalapuyans were noted for their annual autumn burning of the valley, a practice that created and maintained the open grasslands, such as **French Prairie**, for better game forage and for the harvesting of seeds and grasshoppers.

The Kalapuyans lived in winter villages with multi-family houses built of cedar planks, while during the summer, temporary camps were used while making the rounds of gathering berries and other foods. The first recorded contacts with Euro-Americans occurred in the 1810s when fur trappers entered the valley; the Pacific Fur Company established the Willamette Post near the later town of **Champoeg** in 1813. But aside from a few former fur trappers, there was no Euro-American settlement in the valley until the arrival of Methodist missionaries with **Jason Lee** in 1834. The several thousand Kalapuyans suffered several catastrophic waves of introduced diseases, the most deadly being an epidemic of malaria in the early 1830s that left only a small population by 1840. Treaties that encompassed all the Kalapuyans were ratified in 1855, and the remaining populace was removed to a reservation at **Grand Ronde** in 1856. The **Confederated Tribes of Grand Ronde** include descendants of the Kalapuya. The name survives in several spellings in the **Calapooia River**, the **Calapooya Mountains**, and Calapooya Creek. The names of the various bands also figure prominently in Willamette Valley place names.

Mackey, Harold. *The Kalapuyans: A Sourcebook on the Indians of the Willamette Valley.* 2nd ed., with a new afterword from the Confederated Tribes of Grand Ronde and an updated bibliography. Salem, Oregon: Mission Mill Museum Association; Grande Ronde, Oregon: The Confederated Tribes of Grand Ronde, 2004.

Kane, Paul (1810–1871) The Canadian artist Paul Kane was largely self-taught; he traveled to Europe to study and copy art. His particular interest was in depicting Native peoples, and he took two treks in the Canadian Northwest during the 1840s to do this, being supported on his second trip by the **Hudson's Bay Company**. That lengthy excursion took him to the Pacific Coast, to Fort Victoria and **Fort Vancouver**, where he arrived late in 1846. Kane stayed in the **Oregon Country** until the spring of 1847, doing extensive sketching all the while. Returning to Toronto, he produced more than a hundred oil paintings derived from his travel sketches. His work—including the voluminous sketches—has become a national treasure to Canadians, and it includes a number of works that are not only art but are also part of the historical and ethnographic record of Canadian and American Indians and of the fur-trapping and missionary period in the Oregon Country. Among his works are a vivid if slightly fanciful rendition of an eruption of Mount Saint Helens in 1842 or 1843 (Kane was not present, of course), a rare detailed interior view of a lodge of the **Chinook Indians** and numerous other scenes of Chinook life and Chinook peoples, and sketches of the missionaries **Marcus and Narcissa Whitman**.

Kay, Thomas L. *see* **woolen industry**

"Keep Oregon Green" *see* **forest fires**

Keil, William (1812–1877) William Keil was born in Prussia and immigrated to the United States in 1836. Stepping westward, he was in Missouri in 1844, where he led the formation of a communal Christian colony called Bethel; its adherents were known as Bethelites. Still the West pulled him, and he sent scouts to locate land in the Oregon Country; the place selected was near Willapa Bay in Washington Territory, and toward that point Dr. Keil led his family and followers in 1855. Among the party was his son Willie, who was nineteen years of age; tragically, Willie died four days before the party departed for the Pacific Coast, and a saddened father decreed that Willie should come regardless.

Sealed in his coffin in alcohol—whiskey, it is said—Willie reached Willapa Bay with the party, and was buried; the grave has remained there since.

The Bethelites soon found the country too damp and unproductive for farming, and Keil sought better lands. He found them near the **Pudding River** in the Willamette Valley, and he and other members of the group purchased extensive lands and established the soon-thriving Aurora Colony (named for one of Keil's daughters) at **Aurora**. Keil was a strong leader of the communal colony, which sought to live cooperatively rather than competitively and to sacrifice personal desires if needed for the community good. Keil died in 1877, and the colony continued, precariously, until 1883, when the lands and other assets were distributed to individuals who had participated in the colony. At its height, there were nearly 400 people in the colony, and they controlled about 15,000 acres of farmland in addition to business properties in Aurora.

Keizer The city of Keizer is located on rich Willamette River bottomlands north of Salem, an area that was settled for farm use in the 1840s, by among others Thomas D. and J. B. Keizer, emigrants to Oregon in 1843 who took up donation land claims in the area that was long known as Keizer Bottom. Residential and then commercial growth began after World War II, although floods in the 1940s also somewhat dampened the growth rate. The Keizer branch post office opened in 1948, and agitation for a separate city occurred beginning in the 1960s. Municipal government was attained in 1982. Keizer is a Salem suburb with little to suggest a coherent community, although valiant efforts have been made by the Keizer Historical Society and city government to promote the concept. The 1990 census credited Keizer with 21,884 residents; the estimate in 2007 was 35,435.

▶ **Keller, Ira** (1899–1978) Ira Keller was born in Portland, Maine, and educated at Rensselaer Poly-

technic Institute in New York State. He had a varied career with a number of national corporations such as Westinghouse and Container Corporation of America, and retired in 1953. Keller and his wife, Lauretta, moved to Portland, Oregon.

Retirement did not suit Keller, and he proceeded to found a paper products company in 1954. In 1958, he began a fourteen-year stint on the then-new Portland Development Commission (PDC). The PDC was established to revitalize "blighted" or declining urban areas, initially through the federal program known as **urban renewal**. Portland's first urban renewal area was in the South Auditorium area and the **South Portland neighborhood**, where blocks of small older houses, apartment houses, residential hotels, and retail buildings, most built of wood, were razed to create "superblocks" thought to be more suitable for development. The project in effect razed a transition area that was home to many Jewish and Italian immigrants, raised a good deal of controversy, and for some years brought little redevelop-

At the beginnings of the urban renewal project for what was called the South Auditorium Redevelopment, San Francisco landscape architect Lawrence Halprin (right) points out to Ira Keller (left) and mayor Terry Schrunk his firm's design for a public fountain in 1968. Oregon Historical Society, CN 012280.

ment. Although Keller was criticized for not being amenable to citizen input, he worked hard to refine the urban renewal process and was committed to building a new and urban Portland. The projects brought controversy and some notable public art to Portland, including the **Lovejoy Fountain** and the **Keller Fountain** that faces the renovated **Keller Auditorium**—recognition of Keller's positive contributions to the city.

Keller Auditorium Portland's Civic Auditorium opened in 1917 at the southern edge of the downtown area, a city-owned facility that over the next forty years hosted concerts, public lectures, political rallies, opera, and the library and museum of the **Oregon Historical Society**. The area around the Auditorium was part of the South Auditorium Renewal Project, a 1960s urban renewal project of the Portland Development Commission. The Auditorium received a severe facelift in 1968, its classically detailed exterior stripped and replaced by a strikingly white box with a vestigial portico of thin white columns. A gift from Richard B. Keller caused Civic Auditorium to be renamed Keller Auditorium in 2000, in honor of Richard's father, **Ira Keller.** *See also* **Keller Fountain.**

Keller Fountain Situated directly facing the entrance to **Keller Auditorium** in Portland is the Keller Fountain, a full-block park erupting with racing brooks that shoot off concrete ledges into a sunken pool. The fountain—originally known as the Forecourt Fountain—was part of the artwork for the South Auditorium Renewal Project; the design was entrusted to San Francisco landscape architect Lawrence Halprin, who in 1966 designed the **Lovejoy Fountain** and Pettygrove Park in the project area. Angela Danadjieva designed the fountain for Halprin's office; she went on to a major career as a landscape architect in the Bay Area. Forecourt Fountain opened in 1971, and was renamed for **Ira Keller** in 1978.

Kenton neighborhood, Portland The Kenton neighborhood was a real estate subdivision platted in 1905 by George F. Heusner, intended to house workers in the developing industrial area to the north. The Swift meatpacking firm opened a Portland processing center on Columbia Slough in 1909, and Kenton became Cowtown for packing-plant workers. **Cattle** sellers brought herds to market by train, and stayed in the Hotel Kenton as they transacted business with Swift or the new Pacific International Livestock Exposition ("the PI") nearby. The PI started as a cattle show in 1910, and was incorporated in 1918 as one of the nation's five leading livestock shows. In 1942, the PI was used as an assembly center for Japanese-Americans being sent to inland detention camps. The meatpacking business declined and virtually disappeared in the 1950s and 1960s; the PI declined, holdings its last fairs in the early 1980s. The site was used for the Multnomah County Fair from 1970 into the 1990s, and the Expo Center developed on the site beginning in the 1960s.

Kerby *see* **Josephine County**

Kerns, Maude Irvine (1876–1965) Maude Kerns, born in Portland, was schooled at the University of Oregon, the California School of Fine Arts, and Columbia University. She exposed herself to modern European nonrepresentational art and studied widely, only to return to Eugene, where she taught art and was head of the university art department until her retirement in the 1940s. From the 1930s through the 1950s, Kerns was a prominent Oregon artist in the abstract arena. She was one of a group of Eugene-area artists who formed a community center for visual arts in 1950; this developed into the Maude Kerns Art Center.

Kesey, Ken (1935–2001) Born in Colorado, raised on the family farm in Springfield, Oregon, Ken Kesey was a high school wrestler who became a wrestler of words. He graduated from the University of Oregon in speech and communications, and received a fellowship to a creative writing program at Stanford University; there he earned pocket money by engaging in certain experiential episodes with hallucinogenic drugs such as LSD and mescaline. His writing was fruitful, and *One Flew Over the Cuckoo's Nest* was published in 1962; it incorporated elements from Kesey's psychotropic experiences into a story set in an Oregon mental institution. This was followed in 1964 by *Sometimes a Great Notion*, a sprawling account of a family-owned logging outfit and its misfits, or, as one writer phrased it in the *Oregon Blue Book*, "the conflicts between West Coast individualism and East Coast intellectualism." It also contained vivid accounts of how rapidly things rust in the Oregon rain, and how fast the blackberries can overwhelm the works of man. Kesey also ran with the Merry Pranksters, a group of LSD enthusiasts who performed "acid tests"; Tom Wolfe wove that into his *The Electric Kool-Aid Acid Test* (1968). Kesey was arrested on a marijuana possession charge and moved to Pleasant Hill, outside Springfield, in 1965. He published a third novel in 1992 and numerous short works over the years; in 1995, *Last Go Round* was published, a novel centered on the history of the **Pendleton Round-Up**.

King City King City in Washington County is a planned adult suburban community, a real estate development with regally named streets that was incorporated in 1966. In 2007, its estimated population was 2,700.

Kiger mustangs *see* **Steens Mountains**

Kingsmen, The *see* **music and musicians**

Kinzua *see* **Condon**

Kiser, Fred H. *see* **Pacific Crest Trail**

Klamath County The state legislature created Klamath County in 1882, taking the land from the western portion of Lake County to the amount of 6,135 square miles. Linkville—renamed **Klamath Falls** in 1892—was and is the county seat. Government transactions were carried out in rented quarters until a courthouse was purchased in 1888. When the county determined that larger quarters were needed, in 1912, it set off more than a decade of rancorous and costly disputes. A monumental building resembling the Parthenon was erected, but in the wake of recall elections and lawsuits, it was not completed. Construction began in 1918 on another building; although injunctions were sought to stop it, the work was completed within a year. It was not occupied until 1923, after the settlement of the legal questions; the unfinished Greek temple version was finally demolished in 1927. The 1918–19 courthouse was severely damaged by earthquakes in 1993 and has been replaced.

The census of 1890 gave Klamath County a population of 2,444. That increased steadily, reaching 11,413 in 1920. In the next decade, the completion of several railroad projects helped to stimulate lumber production and agriculture, and the population reached 32,407 in 1930 and 42,150 in 1950. In 2007, it was estimated at 65,815.

The county's economy has long been formed on agriculture and timber. The 1870s and 1880s were a time of extensive cattle ranching. In the early twentieth century, the work of the Klamath Project changed the landscape and hydrology of much of the southern part of the county, draining Lower Klamath Lake, irrigating dry lands and introducing new cash crops such as potatoes, barley, and horseradish. Timber production reached a new peak in the late 1950s after the termination of the Klamath Reservation, a disastrous episode that amounted to timber theft from the **Klamath Indians**. By the 1980s, timber had peaked, and mills closed abruptly. Klamath County has also endured fallout from the Klamath Project, as conflicts between the water needs of agriculture on the one hand and native fish and wildlife, especially birds, on the other, reached high levels early in the twenty-first century.

► **Klamath Falls** The county seat of Klamath County was founded with the name of Linkville, derived from its position on the Link River that connected Upper **Klamath Lake** with Ewauna Lake. The town began about 1867, as ranchers moved into the Klamath Basin. The post office of Linkville opened in 1871; with the establishment of Klamath County in 1882, Linkville became the county seat. The post office name was changed to Klamath Falls in 1892, and in 1893 the city of Klamath Falls was incorporated. The 1900 census showed it had 447 residents. With the arrival of a railroad branch from San Francisco in 1909, and the beginnings of the Klamath Project, the city expanded rapidly as lumber mills sprang up and retail business boomed. The population reached 4,801 in 1920; in 1930, immedi-

ately after new railroad connections had opened to Portland, Spokane, and Nevada, the population reached 16,093. An Air Force base was established during World War II, and after the war the Oregon Institute of Technology brought a new enterprise to town, but lumber reigned supreme with **Weyerhaeuser** and other major operations until the 1980s. The city's population was 15,775 in 1970; despite mill closures, it climbed to an estimated 20,110 by 2007.

► **Klamath Indians** The Klamath and their neighbors, the **Modoc Indians**, shared a similar language but differed somewhat in their culture. Both tribes occupied lands in the Klamath Basin on the east side of the Cascade Range in southern Oregon (the Modocs extended into northern California) and shared similar practices. The Klamath people lived in the Klamath Marsh area, around Upper Klamath Lake, and along the Klamath, Sprague, and Williamson Rivers, and fish—particularly suck-

The elegant four-story White Pelican Hotel was built in 1911, and was the first major use of geothermal heating in Klamath Falls, which has several hot springs and is underlaid with a geothermal aquifer. The photograph was taken in the mid-1920s, shortly before the hotel burned in 1926. Steven Dotterer collection.

er, but also salmon and trout—were a mainstay of their diet. Fishing was a year-around activity, but spring brought runs of sucker and salmon. During spring and summer, other foods were gathered and processed, including waterfowl eggs, **camas**, and the seeds of the yellow pond lily (*Nuphar polysepalum*) known as wokas (the origin of the name Wocus Bay on Klamath Lake); hunters sought waterfowl, deer, and elk. Fall brought huckleberries and other berries, pine nuts, and another run of suckers. The Klamath lived in lodges; winter lodges, half-buried, were of wooden poles and planks covered with tule mats and earth. The more temporary summer lodges were mat-covered poles, or small wickiups of bowed branches and mats.

Hudson's Bay Company trappers crossed Klamath country in the 1820s, and the Klamath acquired horses and were trading along the Columbia River in the 1830s. In the 1860s, American ranchers eyed the Klamath territory as rangeland, and in 1864 a treaty that included the Modocs was signed, which created the Klamath Reservation for both tribes. The reservation was heavily forested with pine, which led to enclaves of white mill towns such as **Chiloquin** where the business was cutting Indian timber. Ponderosa pine made the Klamath tribe self-sufficient and economically well off by the 1950s, a situation that derailed with the 1954 federal termination act; their success was a tool to end their status. Termination resulted in claims of several millions of dollars being paid to the Klamath in 1964 and 1969; however, treaty rights of hunting and fishing were not terminated. Tribal government was reconstituted as the Klamath Tribes, including the Klamath, Modoc, and the Yahooskin band of the **Northern Paiute Indians**. Federal recognition of the tribes was granted in 1986.

Haynal, Patrick. Termination and Tribal Survival: The Klamath Tribes of Oregon. *Oregon Historical Quarterly* 101 (2000): 270–301.

Tule mat lodges of the Klamath Indians as depicted in an 1855 engraving from the Pacific Railroad Surveys. University of Washington Libraries, Special Collections Division, NA 4177.

Stern, Theodore. *The Klamath Tribe: A People and their Reservation*. Seattle: University of Washington Press, 1966.

► **Klamath Lake** Klamath Lake, the largest body of fresh water in the state, ranges up to eight miles in width and is about twenty miles long. It is located in **Klamath County**, fed by the Williamson and Sprague Rivers and drained by the Link River at Klamath Falls, into the Klamath River. Officially, this is Upper Klamath Lake, to distinguish it from Lower Klamath Lake, located south of the city of Klamath Falls and extending into California. The distinction is no longer apparent, for Lower Klamath Lake has been drained and the land put to agricultural use; common usage has dropped "Upper" from Klamath Lake. Klamath Lake is shallow and its water level has been maintained since 1917 by the Bureau of Reclamation. The extensive marshlands, which once supported tremendous migratory bird populations, have largely been drained, although efforts have been made since the 1990s to preserve and restore that habitat. The Lost River and shortnose suckers, once a common food fish for the **Modoc** and **Klamath Indians**, have also declined precipitously due to reclamation projects. The lake was navigated by freight and passenger steamboats in the late nineteenth and early twentieth centuries, and logs were floated to mills at Klamath Falls.

Most, Stephen. *River of Renewal: Myth and History in the Klamath Basin*. Portland, Oregon: Oregon Historical Society Press in association with University of Washington Press, 2006.

Klamath Mountains *see* **Siskiyou Mountains**

Klamath Reservation *see* **Klamath Indians**

"LOG STORAGE" IN UPPER KLAMATH LAKE, OREGON   J.H.EASTMAN. T-1042

A boom corrals logs in Upper Klamath Lake in 1940. The logs will be floated to a mill on the lake shore, probably at Klamath Falls. J. H. Christian photo. Steven Dotterrer collection.

Knights of the Golden Circle The Knights were a **Civil War**-era organization of pro-Southern sympathizers. On the Pacific Coast, they were accused of advocating the creation of a Pacific Republic, and they were rumored to conduct military exercises. In fact, they did so: in Salem, for example, a group practiced maneuvers within blocks of the capitol building.

kokanee *see* **salmon**

Korean War, 1950–53 Some 60,000 Oregonians participated in the Korean War, and memorials stand in Portland and in Wilsonville to those who fought in this United Nations theater. Another legacy is the work of the Holt International Children's Services founded by **Harry and Bertha Holt**.

Krause, LaVerne (1924–1987) This Eugene artist was raised during the Depression in a variety of rural and urban homes, where, she said, "I was always the resident artist all through school." She won a scholarship to the University of Oregon, where she studied art, graduating in 1946; during the war years, she worked during the summer in Portland shipyards. Krause married and had children, but she continued to paint at home, and her work was presented in a four-woman show at the Portland gallery of **Louis Bunce** in 1951. By 1959, her painting had moved from representations of the built environment to abstractions from them, and she began to teach at the Museum Art School and the Arts and Crafts Society (**Oregon College of Art and Craft**) in Portland. In 1966, she began a teaching career at the University of Oregon, and was a full professor by 1972. It was her teaching, her art advocacy, and her passion for art that made her a force in the Oregon arts community; she was given the Oregon Governor's Art Award in 1980. During her tenure, which lasted until 1986, she founded the printmaking program at the university; the LaVerne Krause Gallery is located in Lawrence Hall on the campus.

Ku Klux Klan (1915) The "new" Ku Klux Klan was formed in Georgia in 1915. Its members had to be Christian, white, and American-born; it was anti-Catholic, anti-communist, and anti-Semitic. Fueled by the popularity of D. W. Griffith's inflammatory motion picture, *Birth of a Nation*, the new Klan soon spread across the nation, with the first klaverns—the term for local chapters—forming in Oregon in 1921. Beginning with Medford, Klan organizers were active in La Grande, Portland, Ashland, Astoria, and many other communities—there were some fifty-eight klaverns by the end of 1922.

Very few **blacks** lived in Oregon in 1915; consequently, the focus of Klan activities in the state fell on the Catholic Church, whose members comprised about 8 percent of the population. In 1922, the Klan backed a ballot measure that was intended to close Catholic parochial schools: it mandated attendance by all children at public schools. The measure passed, but was eventually overturned by the U.S. Supreme Court, thanks to the fact that the law also affected private schools and schools run by other religious groups, such as the Lutherans. It was a very curious episode in the history of Oregon education. That same year of 1922 saw the election of Walter Pierce as governor, with the active support of the Klan. But it was a short-lived movement, both in Oregon and nationally.

Horowitz, David A. *Inside the Klavern: The Secret History of a Ku Klux Klan of the 1920s.* Carbondale: Southern Illinois University Press, 1999.

Toy, Eckard. The Ku Klux Klan in Oregon. In *Experiences in a Promised Land: Essays in Pacific Northwest History.* Eds. G. Thomas Edwards and Carlos A. Schwantes. MA Thesis, University of Oregon (1959): 269–286.

L

Ladd, William Sargent (1826–1893) William S. Ladd was born in Vermont and raised in New Hampshire, and made his way to Portland in Oregon in 1851, lured by the prospect of engaging in business. It was not a smooth path at first. According to *A History of the Pacific Northwest: Oregon and Washington*, "his affairs reached at one time so low an ebb, that he was glad to save paying his six dollars road tax by digging out and burning up a couple of fir stumps in the street in front of his store." Ladd dealt in liquor, as well as groceries and other merchandise. He erected the first brick building in Portland in 1853, and was elected mayor of the city in 1854, the same year that he married Caroline Ames Elliott, a cousin of his business partner, C. E. Tilton. In 1859, Ladd and Tilton formed the state's first bank, a most profitable and long-lived institution which became the U.S. National Bank of Oregon. Ladd partnered with **Asahel Bush** in 1867 to form the Ladd & Bush Bank of Salem.

Ladd had many interests, in both business and philanthropy. Farming and animal breeding were among those interests; on the east side of the Willamette River, Ladd had the Hazel Fern Farm and Crystal Springs Farms, later developed into, respectively, the **Laurelhurst district,** and **Reed College** and the **Eastmoreland neighborhood**. He also owned several farming properties with his colleague **Simeon G. Reed**. Ladd invested in local **iron production** facilities at Lake Oswego, in railroads, in flouring mills, and in land. He gave money to the Library Association of Portland, to churches of various denominations, and to **Willamette University**. The Ladd family's elaborate wooden carriage house, built in the 1880s, has survived at the corner of SW Broadway and Columbia Street, a city landmark; the house was sited on a full block just to the east.

Ladd's Addition, SE Ladd Avenue, and the Ladd & Tilton Branch of U.S. Bank in Salem remember William S. Ladd's contributions to the state.

Ladd's Addition district, Portland Like many neighborhoods in southeast Portland, Ladd's Addition was established on farmland once owned by **William S. Ladd**. Ladd himself directed the creation of this subdivision in 1891, shortly after the area was linked to downtown Portland by new bridges, and new streetcar lines on SE Hawthorne Boulevard and SE 11th Avenue, the north and west edges of the development. The plat is most unusual; historian Eugene Snyder described it as "a rectangle crossed by two diagonals, which divide the plat into four isosceles triangles. Those are further divided into smaller triangles, quadrilaterals, parallelograms, and trapezoids." Some accounts say that Ladd was inspired by Pierre L'Enfant's 1791 plan for Washington, DC, but a quick look demonstrates that this is wrongheaded. Although the plat was filed, few lots were sold at the time, perhaps because Ladd's death in 1893 led to the creation of the Ladd Estate Company, which fostered a number of real estate subdivisions in the early twentieth century. Many lots in Ladd's Addition sold in the 1910s and early 1920s, while sections at the southern edge of the plat remained leased for market gardening, primarily to **Italian** farmers, into the 1920s. Ladd's Addition was placed on the National Register of Historic Places in 1988, cited for its design and for the mixture of residential architectural styles. The district is also noted for the American elms that line many streets, and the four diamond-shaped rose gardens imbedded in the plan.

Lady Washington *see* **Gray, Robert**

Lafayette American emigrants settled along the California-Oregon Trail where it crossed the Yamhill River in the early 1840s. In 1846, Joel Perkins laid out a townsite near the small falls there, named for his hometown of Lafayette, Indiana. It was designated the seat of government for Yamhill County the same year, and by 1851 had a post office. One of Oregon's earliest major bridges was one that was erected across the Yamhill River in 1852. The river was navigable, and flatboats and then steamboats connected Lafayette to Oregon City until the 1880s.

Oregon's first circuit court met in Lafayette in 1847. The residence nearby of a number of educated men of an oratorical and judicial bent such as **Matthew Deady**, led to the creation of Lafayette Academy about 1852, and briefly helped Lafayette garner the moniker Athens of Oregon, though the distinction was short-lived.

Lafayette was incorporated in 1872, but in 1889, it lost the county seat to upstart McMinnville. Locks were installed around the falls in 1900 and operated until 1954, but the improvement failed to revive river transportation (the locks were helpful in floating logs to downstream sawmills, however). By 1915, Lafayette was a small farming town of about 400 people, occupied in growing hops and apples and dairy cattle. In the 1970s, it developed as a popular site for antique shops. The population by 2007 was about 3,730. The surrounding area is increasingly devoted to growing wine grapes.

La Grande The county seat of **Union County** since 1905 (and also 1864–74; the county seat location was a contentious issue), is situated at the eastern edge of the valley of the Grande Ronde River along the route of the Oregon Trail. The town was established in the 1860s, a time of great gold-mining excitement to the south and east of the valley. A post office was established in 1863, Union County was formed in 1864, and La Grande was incorporated in 1865. La Grande became a railroad town with the completion of the transcontinental Union Pacific

Railroad in 1884. By the first decades of the twentieth century, three industries supported La Grande: agriculture (farming, fruit raising, livestock), timber (four large lumber companies), and the railroad ("75 engine and train crews" were headquartered there). There were "2 creameries, 3 ice factories, cold-storage plants, meat packing plant, iron foundry, 3 machine shops and flour mill."

In 1929, **Eastern Oregon University** opened as Eastern Oregon College of Education, and has provided another economic base for the city. Lumber milling has declined considerably, and streamlined railroad operations have also reduced local employment. In 2007, La Grande's population was about 12,950. Downtown La Grande boasts a streetscape of brick commercial structures from the period of the city's initial boom, ca. 1885–1900; the district is on the National Register of Historic Places.

Lake County This county, which encompasses some 8,359 square miles, was established in 1874 by taking the southern part of Wasco County and the eastern section of Jackson County. Klamath County was created in 1882 from the western part of Lake County, but its area grew again slightly in 1885 with the annexation of a part of Grant County. The name is derived from the presence of many shallow lakes, although a number of them went west in 1882 to the new Klamath County. The initial Lake County seat of government was designated as Linkville (now Klamath Falls), but the voters chose to move it to **Lakeview** in 1876. A formal courthouse, built of locally produced brick with an imposing if awkward tower, was completed in 1909, but was replaced by a steel and concrete block in 1954.

The territory now embraced by Lake County was the homeland of the **Northern Paiute Indians**, comprised of a number of bands whose members spoke a common language. The territory did not support a large population, most of whom were dependent on hunting, fishing, and foraging over a large and unforgiving landscape. White incursions into the area were sporadic until the 1860s; the Army established Fort Bidwell in California's Surprise Valley, southeast of Goose Lake, in 1865, to monitor Indian activities.

Lake County's economy was initially based on livestock raising. An influx of homesteaders in the 1890s and early 1900s gave rise to such communities as **Silver Lake**, and to the irrigated farming of alfalfa and grain. The county's population in 1890 was 2,604; by 1930, it reached 4,833. Fremont National Forest has supplied logs for mills in Lakeview since the 1920s; lumber production has declined since the 1980s, however. Outdoor recreation has also been a mainstay of the county's economy, especially since World War II, bolstered by the establishment of the Hart Mountain National Antelope Refuge, established in 1936 as a sanctuary for **pronghorn antelope**. Lake County's population in 1970 was 6,343; the estimate for 2007 was 7,565.

Lake Labish This low-lying "beaver dam" land in Marion County once drained into the **Pudding River**. It was named by early settlers on French Prairie for *la biche*, the female elk or deer. In the 1860s, efforts began to control the lake and drain it to gain access to the rich soil. On November 12, 1890, a Southern Pacific Company train derailed on the trestle over Lake Labish, killing five passengers. A number of **Japanese** farmers settled in the Lake Labish area in the early 1900s, growing market vegetables. The lakebed is noted for its fragrant onion fields and for growing grass and flower seed.

▶ **Lake Oswego** The city of Lake Oswego descends from the community known as Oswego, which dates back to about 1850, when Alonzo A. Durham—an immigrant to Oregon in 1847 from New York State—established a sawmill on the banks of Sucker Creek, which drained a small lake into the Willamette River. Durham—who is also the namesake of the community of **Durham**—named the place for Oswego, New York, near his birthplace in Genesee County. The lake was known as Sucker Lake, which was changed in 1913 to Lake Oswego; Sucker

Oswego was a small industrial and suburban community when this photograph of the retail area was taken, looking south on State Street about 1952. The name of the town was changed to Lake Oswego in 1959. Clarence I. Christian photograph. Steven Dotterer collection.

Creek connecting it to the Willamette River was renamed Oswego Creek in 1927.

Oswego was the center of Oregon's short-lived **iron industry**, which first took hold in the 1860s with the discovery of iron ore on Iron Mountain. Local investors led by **William S. Ladd** built an iron works; local trees provided the charcoal, while the lime came from the San Juan Islands of Washington Territory.

In the 1880s, a narrow-gauge railroad linked Oswego with Portland and the western side of the Willamette Valley. In 1890, the **Southern Pacific Company** took over the line, converted it to standard gauge, and integrated it with its extensive Oregon lines. By the mid-1890s, this line offered frequent passenger train service between Oswego and Portland. When the route was converted to an electric **interurban railway** in 1914, Oswego quickly became a commuter suburb of Portland, a development assisted by the Ladd Estate Company which sold expensive suburban homes along the route. At the same time, Oswego was a blue-collar town that manufactured iron castings and cement and shunted logs around en route to mills upstream and down.

The town of Oswego, which had been incorporated in 1910, changed its name to Lake Oswego in 1959, reflecting in its nomenclature the transition from an industrial and commuting town to a high-toned suburb. Suburban electric train service ended in 1929, and the town continued to grow as a secluded and expensive residential area. Its 1950 population of 3,616 was double that of the 1940 census; by 2007, the city had 36,355 residents, nearly all of whom were distinctly unfamiliar with the city's gritty industrial heritage.

Lakeside The Coos County city of Lakeside is on the edge of Tenmile Lake and not too far from North Tenmile Lake. A community existed here early in the twentieth century, and the post office of Lakeside was opened in 1908. Lakeside was a quiet resort and residential center for many decades. The estab-lishment of the Oregon Dunes National Recreation Area in 1972 pushed recreational development in the Lakeside area, and it was incorporated as a city in 1974. The dunes are a spectacular natural phenom-enon, greatly altered in the past century by human intervention in the form of plantings that have "stabilized"—that is, made moribund—the dunes, and by the creation of a federal recreation area that recog-nizes the vociferous use of all-terrain vehicles (ATVs) as the highest and best form of recreation. ATVs effectively de-stabilize the dunes, and are therefore perhaps benign engines of the regeneration of the dunes; however, there is no ongoing evaluation of the effects. Lakeside's 2007 population is about 1,545.

Lakeview In the normal course of events, it is difficult to view Goose Lake from the town of Lakeview, even if one were to get up on the north hillside: the shore is about a half-dozen miles away. But the lake is elastic, and sometimes in times of high water the shore is closer. The region was populated by **Modoc Indians**, who signed a treaty in 1864 that removed them to the Klamath Reservation in 1871. Thereafter, white ranchers and settlers appeared in the Goose Lake area in numbers. A rural post office was opened on the M. W. Bullard ranch in 1876, with the name Lakeview, as proposed by one John A. Moon. And Lakeview became the county seat of **Lake County**, formed in 1874; the temporary county seat had been at Klamath Falls. Lakeview was incorporated in 1889; the 1900 census reported a population of 761.

Lakeview suffered a fire in 1900, and endured a tremendous influx of would-be settlers in the early 1900s, when attempts were made to undertake extensive dry-land farming in the region. Some rampant speculation and fraud in land dealings occurred in 1909, when lands granted for an early wagon road were sold, often to unsuspecting outsiders unaware of Lakeview's desert environment. The narrow-gauge Nevada-California-Oregon Railroad made it to Lakeview in 1911, having been stretching itself slowly northward from Reno since 1881. It proved to be the end of the line. The railroad was acquired by the **Southern Pacific Company** and converted to standard gauge in 1927. The railroad connection inspired the construction of some lumber mills; Lakeview's population reached 1,799 by 1930, and 2,831 in 1950.

After World War II, Lakeview was briefly excited by the discovery of uranium ore nearby, used in atomic bomb production. The White King and Lucky Lass mines impelled the construction of a mill to process uranium in 1958. The mill closed in 1960, and the mines followed in 1964. Lakeview's population in 1970 was 2,705; the estimate in 2007 was 2,730. The former uranium mines were declared Superfund pollution sites in 1995.

► **Lambert Gardens** These now-vanished private gardens were located in southeast Portland near Reed College. Beginning in the 1920s, nursery owner Andrew Lambert planted some ten special gardens on his thirty acres, eventually opening them to the public for a fee. The gardens were popular through the 1950s, but after Lambert was unable to sell them to the city, they were sold in 1968 for apartment development.

Lampman, Ben Hur (1886–1954) Ben Hur Lampman was first and foremost a newspaperman, who moved to Oregon from working in North Dakota as an editor, compositor, and printer. From 1912 to 1916, he edited and published the Gold Hill *News*, where his whimsical style came to the attention of the Portland *Oregonian*. He joined the *Oregonian* in 1916 as a reporter, but was soon doing editorial writing. Newspaper historian George S. Turnbull remarked on his human touch, leisurely style, and

750—SUNKEN GARDENS, LAMBERT GARDENS

PORTLAND, OREGON

A postcard view of the formal sunken gardens at Lambert Gardens in Portland, about 1950. Author's collection.

"feeling for the living things in the outdoors." His nature stories and essays were immensely popular, and were collected in several books, along with his poetry; among them are *How Could I Be Forgetting?* (1926); *The Tramp Printer, Sometime Journeyman of the Little Home-town Papers in Days that Come No More* (1934); and *At the End of the Car Line* (1942). Lampman was named poet laureate of Oregon in 1951. His writings over four decades set a conservationist ethic in motion that blossomed after his death. A scenic corridor along the Rogue River near Gold Hill is named for Lampman.

lamprey Small eel-like fish with a complex life cycle, lamprey live lives that are intertwined with those of **salmon**, the iconic fish of the Pacific Northwest. There are several varieties of the fish, of which the most noted is the Pacific lamprey, *Lampetra tridentata*. Like many salmon varieties, Pacific lamprey are born in freshwater, the eggs laid by parents who swim upstream from the ocean to spawn in upstream gravel bars. After several years of feeding on tiny plants and animals, Pacific lamprey morph and then migrate seaward for two to three years; as adults, they act as scavengers and parasites, or prey on larger animals such as salmon and marine mammals before returning upstream to spawn and die. Lamprey are historically a major food source for those Indians who lived along the Columbia River and its tributaries, and along many coastal streams such as the Siletz River. Their runs have dropped precipitously, more so than even salmon; for better or worse, there has been little support for lamprey hatcheries or lamprey recovery plans.

Lancaster, Samuel Christopher (1864–1941) Samuel Lancaster was the engineering genius behind the design and construction of the **Colum-**

The photograph depicts Billy Barnhart's camp on the bluffs overlooking the Umatilla River on the Umatilla Reservation. The two women stand beside a wooden rack on which lamprey are hung to dry. In the background is a canvas-covered tipi, and at the left a wagon draped in canvas. The photograph was taken in 1903 by Lee Moorhouse. University of Oregon, Special Collections and University Archives, PH036_5609.

bia River Highway between 1913 and 1922. He was born in Mississippi and educated in Tennessee. His work in building hard-surfaced roads in Tennessee brought him national attention, and he came to Oregon in 1908; **Sam Hill** hired him in 1909 to design his experimental roads at Maryhill. He did a campus plan for **Linfield College** before taking on the supervision of the Columbia River Highway in 1913. Though an engineer by training, Lancaster clearly had a romantic vision of what roads could and should do. Lancaster promoted **Crown Point** as the site of an observatory; the Vista House there became the highway's emblem and crowning glory. Lancaster wrote engagingly about the highway in *The Columbia: America's Great Highway through the Cascade Mountains to the Sea* (1915).

"Land of the Empire Builders" This is the first line of the Oregon state song, "Oregon, My Oregon," with words by John A. Buchanan, an Astoria attorney and poet, and music by Henry B. Murtagh of Portland. The song was officially adopted in 1927, but had been selected through a contest held by the Society of Oregon Composers in 1919 and 1920, when they solicited verse from Oregon citizens for a state song. A committee of judges selected three suitable "poems." These words were then made available to the state's composers, who set them to music in a separate contest. The music is pedestrian; the words are of their time and place. Buchanan had some sympathies for Oregon's original inhabitants, but was nonetheless able to write blithely about conquering heroes. *See also* **Empire Builder**. This is the text:

> Land of the empire builders,
> Land of the golden west;
> Conquered and held by free men,
> Fairest and the best.
> Onward and upward ever,
> Forward and on and on;
> Hail to thee, land of heroes,
> My Oregon.

> Land of the rose and sunshine,
> Land of the summer's breeze;
> Laden with health and vigor,
> Fresh from the Western seas.
> Blest by the blood of martyrs,
> Land of the setting sun;
> Hail to thee, land of promise,
> My Oregon.

land grants The federal government conveyed land from public ownership to private hands in a variety of ways during the nineteenth and early twentieth centuries. Among these were grants that produced funds to aid education (much of this was fraudulently used); grants for the construction of military wagon roads (five such grants were made in Oregon between 1864 and 1869; some of the lands were fraudulently used, but most eventually reverted to the public domain); and railroad construction grants (the major grant was embroiled in fraud; *see* **Oregon and California Revested Lands**). Oregon (and Minnesota) also had federal lands programs involving so-called swamplands, which in the 1880s were a prolific source of ill-gotten gains and wholesale chicanery. Land grant programs should not be confused with federal lands granted to settlers through the **Donation Land Act** or the Homestead Act.

Lane, Harry (1855–1917) Born in Corvallis and the grandson of **Joseph Lane**, Harry Lane received his medical degree from Willamette University in 1878, and eventually settled in Portland. He was superintendent of the Oregon State Asylum in Salem, 1887–91. A Democrat with reform tendencies, Lane was a white knight when he ran for mayor of Portland, a city that was, according to historian Gordon Dodds, "in the grip of business interests, gamblers and thugs." He served from 1905 to 1909, often obliged to suffer having his vetoes of pork-laden city legislation overridden by council members. He was later elected to the U.S. Senate, serving from 1913 until his death on May 23, 1917.

► Lane, Joseph (1801–1881) The namesake of Lane County was born in North Carolina and was raised in Kentucky and Indiana. Joseph Lane served in the Indiana legislature from 1822 to 1846, when he went off to serve in the Mexican War. He became a major general and received an appointment from President Polk as the first governor of the **Oregon Territory**. It was a brief term, from his arrival on March 3, 1849 until June of 1850, and was marked by Lane's efforts to bring about the hanging of the five Cayuse Indians who were charged with leading the 1847 raid on **Marcus and Narcissa Whitman**'s mission. From June of 1850, Lane served as the territory's delegate to Congress, and from Oregon's

Oregon's first territorial governor, Joseph Lane, as photographed about 1855. Oregon Historical Society, OrHi 1703.

statehood in 1859, as the state's first U.S. senator. He then ran as a Democratic candidate for vice president on the Breckenridge ticket in the 1860 election. Lane returned to Oregon after his Senate term, retiring to his land claim in the Umpqua River Valley and taking no further part in political life, which had been damaged by his pro-slavery sentiments. His son Lafayette Lane served a term in Congress in the 1870s, and one of his grandsons, **Harry Lane**, was elected to a U.S. Senate seat.

Hendrickson, James E. *Joe Lane of Oregon: Machine Politics and the Sectional Crisis, 1849–1861*. New Haven, Connecticut: Yale University Press, 1967.

Lane County Named for Oregon's first territorial governor, **Joseph Lane**, Lane County was established in 1851, taking land from the southern portion of Linn County and some from now-vanished Umpqua County—it originally extended east to the Rocky Mountains and south to the border of California. Numerous changes occurred subsequently. It was extended west to the Pacific Ocean in 1853 and the eastern boundary was cut back to the crest of the Cascade Range in 1854; other minor changes occurred until 1923. Its current area is 4,620 square miles. The county seat of Eugene was selected in 1853. A courthouse was erected in 1855, was replaced in 1898, and was replaced once more in 1959.

The land that is now included in Lane County has been the homeland of several Native groups: a number of bands of the **Kalapuyan Indians** were in the Eugene-Springfield area, while the **Siuslaw Indians** occupied lands along the coast and the Siuslaw River. The **Molala Indians** were found in the Cascade foothills.

In the 1860 census of Lane County, a population of 4,780 people, Indians not included, was recorded. The Willamette Valley floor was already fairly thickly settled by farming families by that time. Steamboats regularly came up the Willamette to Corvallis, in Benton County, and at high water periods they reached Eugene. Wheat, and flour from it, was already an export product in the 1860s. Eugene became the site of the nascent **University of Oregon** in 1872, and the Oregon & California Railroad connected the county with California in 1887. The population in 1900 was 19,604. The early 1900s were a time of tremendous growth for the timber industry in Lane County; by the 1950s, it was the center of the nation's production of building lumber. Agricultural products have included grass seed, **filberts**, fruit and berries, and dairy products. Lane County's population in 1950 was 125,776; the estimate in 2007 was 343,140.

Langlois This small Curry County town was named for a family that came to the area in 1854. The Langlois post office dates from 1881. By 1915, the region was dotted with dairy farms, and there were five cheese factories near Langlois. In the 1940s and 1950s, the Langlois Cheese Makers produced a blue vein **cheese** that achieved national acclaim, including good words from the *New York Times* and from **James Beard**. The factory burned in 1957 and was not rebuilt. The cheese is still remembered.

larch The western larch or western tamarack, *Larix occidentalis*, is a tall, narrow deciduous tree that ranges in height from eighty to 150 feet. It grows at fairly high elevations in the Blue Mountains and along the eastern slope of the Cascade Range in Wasco and Jefferson Counties, and is usually found mixed with other conifers. It often follows or survives forest fires, then is later replaced by other species. It is logged commercially and used for construction lumber, flooring, plywood, pulp, and utility poles.

Larch Mountain A volcanic peak of the Cascade Range in Multnomah County, Larch Mountain is 4,055 feet high. The name is a reference to the noble fir, *Abies procera*, the wood of which has been mar-

keted as **larch**. Larch Mountain has long been noted for its huckleberries. Multnomah Creek heads on Larch Mountain and flows north, cascading to the Columbia River at **Multnomah Falls**.

Laurelhust district, Portland Laurelhurst was a real estate subdivision, platted in 1909 by the Laurelhurst Company. **William S. Ladd** had purchased Hazelwood Farm from the Thomas Frazar family in 1869, changed its name to Hazel Fern Farm, and made it a showplace for horse and cattle breeding. Ladd died in 1893; his estate sold the property, which was now within the city limits, for development in 1909, save a portion sold to the city for a park. The developers had previously prospered with a land subdivision in Seattle, also named Laurelhurst. A streetcar line, built through the farmland in the 1890s, already served Portland's Laurelhurst. The curvilinear streets were built up with houses—Laurelhurst was exclusively residential—in the 1910s and 1920s. The traffic circle at SE Thirty-ninth Avenue and Glisan Street initially held the real estate office; it was subsequently turned into parkland and became the site of a statue of Joan of Arc, a civic contribution by Dr. **Henry Waldo Coe**.

Lawrence, Ellis Fuller (1879–1946) Ellis Lawrence was born in Massachusetts and educated at Phillips Academy and the Massachusetts Institute of Technology, where he received his master's degree in architecture in 1902. He worked for a Boston firm that sent him to a project in San Francisco, but he stopped over in Portland; the 1906 San Francisco earthquake persuaded him to remain there rather than continue south. In Portland, he was associated with several firms but was also deeply immersed in architectural education through his involvement with the **University of Oregon** in Eugene. In 1914, he helped to found the School of Architecture and Allied Arts, and served as its dean until his death. He served as campus architect and designed many major buildings, including the library and art museum and, in part, the Architecture and Art Building. He also did a tremendous amount of commercial work, including some 200 residences, the phantasmagoric Elsinore Theatre in Salem (1926) and the Art Deco public market building in Portland (1933). In an odd burst of irony, much of his Architecture and Art Building was demolished and replaced in 1957 with an un-Lawrence-like structure that was graciously named Lawrence Hall.

Lazarus, Edgar M. (1868–1939)
see **Crown Point; Morrow County**

Lebanon This area along the South Santiam River in Linn County was settled by farming families in the late 1840s. The Lebanon post office was established in 1851. The small town was incorporated in 1878. A branch line railroad reached Lebanon in 1880, the same year the census showed it had a population of 270 souls. Railroad connections brought lumber mills and the **papermaking industry** to town. Agriculture was celebrated in the Lebanon Strawberry Festival, which was first held in 1909. Lebanon's population reached 922 in 1900, and 2,729 in 1940. The postwar acceleration of lumbering operations boosted that figure to 7,277 in 1970. Residential growth has continued to expand as Lebanon increasingly is a bedroom community for nearby **Albany**. The estimated population in 2007 was 14,705.

Lee, Dorothy McCullough (1901–1981) Born into a Navy family that traveled widely, Dorothy McCullough completed high school in Rhode Island and by age twenty-two had completed a law degree at the University of California. Moving to Portland in the late 1920s, she was elected to the state legislature in 1928, where she served for fourteen years. She and Gladys M. Everett formed a partnership in 1931, the state's first woman-owned law firm. Lee was elected to a position on the Portland city council in 1943, from which position she aimed for the office of mayor in 1948, running on a reform platform that gave rise to the moniker No Sin Lee. Dedicated to the suppression of vice and corruption in a city that had plenty of it, Mayor Lee made inroads on the issues, but she also made enemies and did not succeed in her re-election bid in 1952.

Pitzer, Paul C. Dorothy McCullough Lee: The Success and Failure of "Dottie-Do-Good." *Oregon Historical Quarterly* 91 (1990): 5–42.

Lee, Jason (1803–1845) The first of a cadre of Protestant missionaries to the Oregon Country was that led by the Rev. Jason Lee. Lee was born in Quebec, educated in Massachusetts, and ordained in the Methodist Episcopal Church, which in 1833 sent him on a mission to the Flathead Indians. Lee arrived at **Fort Vancouver** in 1834, and headed, not to the Flatheads, but at the instigation of **John McLoughlin**, to the **Kalapuyan Indians** of the Willamette Valley. The site selected was a few miles north of Salem, not far from the future settlement of **Wheatland** at what is known as Mission Bottom; it is now within Willamette Mission State Park. The results were disappointing. In the first year, the mission school enrolled fourteen Indian children; five ran away, and seven died. Discouraged by the prospects for Christian conversions and education among the declining Indian populace, the mission group moved to the site of **Salem** in 1840, and refocused their efforts on ministering to the now-rapidly growing population of immigrant settlers. The Methodist educational ventures led to the Oregon Institute and **Willamette University**. Lee was a controversial figure in early Oregon, an expansionist who advocated for American control of the region and who sparred with Catholics as well as his co-religionists. His church objected to his expenditures and to his veering from the course of Indian education and conversion, and replaced him in 1843. He returned east seeking vindication, and died in Canada. His body was removed to the Lee Mission Cemetery in Salem in 1906. The Lee house survives in Salem at the

Mission Mill Museum. Lee was selected to represent Oregon in the National Statuary Hall in 1953, where he joined John McLoughlin, a Catholic who was cheated of his land by some Methodists.

Loewenberg, Robert J. *Equality on the Oregon Frontier: Jason Lee and the Methodist Mission, 1834–43*. Seattle: University of Washington Press, 1976.

Lents neighborhood, Portland Oliver (1830–1899) and Martha (1833–1905) Lent, immigrants from Ohio, settled in an area along Johnson Creek about 1852, where Oliver operated a sawmill for some years. They moved a few miles west in 1866 to the present Lents area, and Oliver developed into a citizen of solid repute, holding several public offices. A post office named Lents opened in 1886, and Oliver Lent platted a townsite in 1892, the same year that a suburban railroad line reached the area from downtown Portland. An electric-powered **interurban railway** connected with this line in 1903,

giving Lents an express route to Portland as well as links to other east Multnomah County suburbs. Lents grew into a suburban commercial district surrounded by residential tracts with many small houses on large lots. The expanding city quickly reached out, with Portland absorbing much of the area in 1912; the post office name was discontinued in 1917. The construction of **Interstate 205** in the late 1970s virtually destroyed the Lents business district; faltering attempts were made to resurrect it in the early 2000s.

▶ **Lewelling, Seth** (1820–1896) Seth Lewelling was born in North Carolina to a Quaker family engaged in the nursery business. The family moved to Indiana and then to Iowa, from where Seth's brother **Henderson Luelling** (family members differed in their spelling of the name) came to Oregon in 1847, with a good deal of nursery stock. In 1850, Seth and another brother, John, also came to Oregon. All three went south to the gold fields of California

In the 1930s, Walter Boychuk photographed the former house of Seth Lewelling, built in Milwaukie about 1847. Oregon Historical Society, OrHi 106107.

almost immediately, but returned to the **Milwaukie** area. Here Seth remained and went into the nursery business with vigor, specializing in fruit cultivars, especially apples, pears, peaches, and cherries. In the 1860s and 1870s, Seth Lewelling developed and introduced the Black Republican and Bing **cherries**; the Bing was named for the foreman of Lewelling's Chinese work crew, Ah Sit Bing. Other introductions included varieties of grapes, prunes, apples, and even an almond.

McClintock, Thomas C. Henderson Luelling, Seth Lewelling, and the Birth of the Pacific Coast Fruit Industry. *Oregon Historical Quarterly* 68, no. 2 (June 1967): 153–174.

Lewis, Ion (1853–1933) Architect Ion Lewis was born and educated in Massachusetts, where he worked for several prominent Boston firms. Lewis came to Portland in 1889 to visit his friend **William Whidden**, and he stayed, becoming a partner in the firm of Whidden & Lewis; some of their projects are noted in the entry for Whidden. The firm dominated the Portland architectural scene into the early 1900s, when their protégé **A. E. Doyle** began his rise to prominence.

Marlitt, Richard. *Matters of Proportion: The Portland Residential Architecture of Whidden & Lewis.* Portland, Oregon: Oregon Historical Society Press, 1989.

Lewis, Meriwether (1774–1809) *see* **Lewis and Clark Expedition**

► **Lewis and Clark Centennial Exposition** Portland's world's fair of 1905 was the Lewis and Clark Centennial and American Pacific Exposition and Oriental Fair. It may have been a bit pale in comparison with the 1904 Louisiana Purchase Exposition in Saint Louis, but it was a huge event for a young city, and one that left a mark on the entire region. The city's business elite began promoting the idea early in the century, with prompting

from the likes of **Harvey W. Scott**, editor of the *Oregonian* and first president of the **Oregon Historical Society**, Col. Henry Dosch, an avid fan of world's fairs, and **Henry W. Corbett**, bank president and former U.S. senator. The site selected was the marshy **Guilds Lake district** in Northwest Portland, which was turned into a real lake adorned with a U.S. government exhibition building, and surrounded by an array of confectionary-like structures of white, all brilliantly lighted at night by electricity. There was a carnival midway called The Trail. Statues of Meriwether Lewis and William Clark were recycled from the 1904 Saint Louis fair (so were many of the exhibits and entertainments). A statue

The Lewis and Clark Centennial Exposition gave Oregon a chance to promote and peddle its products. This is the Umatilla County exhibit at the fair. The man is holding three ears of corn and standing next to a bundle of corn stalks. The exhibit features wheat, visible in the background, and beer, presumably making use of Umatilla County barley. Image courtesy of Special Collections and University Archives, University of Oregon Libraries, PH037_0646.

of **Sacajawea** was unveiled; roses were planted in the city's gardens and parks, leading in the direction of the **Portland Rose Festival**. The nation's first transcontinental automobile race induced two Oldsmobile curved-dash runabouts, named Old Scout and Old Steady, to make the trek from New York City to Portland in forty-four days—it took Old Steady an additional eight days.

The fair was a financial and promotional success, and it caught the city and the state of Oregon at a moment of economic upswing. Portland's population increase and business advances in the period just before World War I justified the efforts that the business community had invested in the fair.

Abbott, Carl. *The Great Extravaganza: Portland and the Lewis and Clark Exposition*. 3rd ed. Portland, Oregon: Oregon Historical Society Press, 2004.

Lewis and Clark College Albany College was founded in 1868 by the Presbyterian Church in **Albany**, the outgrowth of an academy they had begun in 1858. The first college was site on land donated by the pioneer Monteith family. A small co-educational school in a single building, Albany College had an initial enrollment of eighty-six, equally divided between men and women. The college enlarged a bit in 1892 and moved to a site south of Albany in 1925. In an expansionist mode, Albany College started a junior college in Portland in 1934 and removed the entire college there in 1938. In 1942, the trustees managed to acquire the estate of one of the heirs of the **Meier & Frank** department store, Lloyd Frank's Fir Acres on Palatine Hill south of Portland. They then changed the college name to Lewis and Clark College as a "symbol of the pioneering spirit that had made and maintained the College," according to the college website. The Pirates had been the mascot of the college until in 1946; thenceforth they were the Pioneers.

Lewis and Clark's school of law descends from a state law school established in Portland in 1884, which was moved to the University of Oregon in Eugene in 1915. Dissident faculty elected not to move and formed the Northwestern College of Law; Northwestern became affiliated with Lewis and Clark College in 1965 and established a new facility on that campus in 1967.

Beckham, Stephen Dow. *Lewis & Clark College*. Portland, Oregon: Lewis & Clark College, 1991.

Lewis and Clark Expedition In the years 1803–06 of the new American republic, President Thomas Jefferson sent an Army expeditionary force west from Saint Louis to the Pacific Ocean, across territories not known to the nation at large. Part of the territory they crossed was included in the 1803 Louisiana Purchase, which added immensely to the nation's size, at least on paper. The westernmost part of the trip was into a land controlled by Native people; it was also land in which the Great Britain, Russia, Spain, and the United States had expressed interest. Headed by Capt. Meriwether Lewis and Capt. William Clark, the band consisted of twenty-six soldiers, two interpreters, one interpreter's wife and child (**Sacajawea** and **Jean Baptiste Charbonneau**), Clark's black slave, York, and a dog, Seaman. They left Saint Louis in the spring of 1804 and followed the Missouri River upstream; the group wintered at Fort Mandan in the Dakotas before setting forth again across Montana, Idaho, Washington, and Oregon in the spring of 1805. The group reached the Columbia River in the fall, descending in Indian canoes to the mouth; they spent the winter of 1805–06 at **Fort Clatsop**. The return trip began in March, and the Corps of Discovery reached Saint Louis before the end of September. Although it was a military expedition, it was constituted as a reconnaissance group that was instructed to gather information about the lands traversed. Records were kept of the flora, fauna, geology and natural features, economic prospects, and the Indian peoples and their characteristics. The aim was partly pure scientific inquiry, part diplomatic exploration, but withal peaceful. The impact on American life was negligible until after the publication of the first edited edition of the journals of the expedition in 1814; it influenced American diplomacy and the notion of America's "manifest destiny" to extend across the continent. **Eva Emery Dye** fictionalized the expedition's story in *The Conquest*.

> Ambrose, Stephen E. *Undaunted Courage: Meriwether Lewis, Thomas Jefferson, and the Opening of the American West*. New York: Simon & Schuster, 1996.
>
> *The Journals of the Lewis and Clark Expedition*. Ed. Gary E. Moulton. 13 vols. Lincoln: University of Nebraska Press, 1983–2001.

Lexington The small Morrow County town of Lexington began as a rural post office that opened in 1885 along Willow Creek. A branch railroad line was built through the area in 1888, and Lexington became a shipping point for an area that in 1915 was described as engaging in "diversified farming, stock raising, dairying, wheat and wool growing." The town was incorporated in 1903, the year of the **Heppner** flood upstream, which also tore through Lexington, though with less disastrous results. Lexington's population was 185 in the 1910 census; in the ensuing censuses, that figure has ranged up as high as 307 (1980); the estimated population in 2007 was 280. The town's elementary school closed in 1997.

► **lighthouses** Oregon has a rugged coastline with few large or accessible harbors and an abundance of offshore rocks. From north to south, this has resulted in the construction and operation of some nine lighthouses (one floating) since 1857. The sites for lighthouses were among the issues considered by **George Davidson** during his coast surveys.

At the mouth of the **Columbia River**, a stationary, manned lightship, the *Columbia*, was moored offshore from 1892 until 1979 when it was replaced by a large navigational buoy. The last lightship ves-

BOYER /261. Tillamook Light – Oregon Coast

The crag known as Tillamook Rock held one of the most forbidding lighthouses on the Pacific Coast. The photograph, probably taken in the 1930s, shows a supply vessel approaching the rock. Personnel and supplies had to be lifted from ship to rock by a derrick, which is visible at the right. Mason collection.

sel in service is maintained as an exhibit by the Columbia River Maritime Museum at Astoria.

The offshore protuberance of **Tillamook Rock** was crowned with a lighthouse, built in 1879–81, that was horrendously difficult to build and a continuing nightmare to operate. One life was lost in the construction; maintenance required putting on and taking off crews and supplies by breeches buoy from a ship hovering near the rock. Storms tossed small boulders through the roof and windows; a 1934 storm put out the light and destroyed the Fresnel lens. In 1957, the light at "Terrible Tilly" was extinguished for good. The lighthouse was empty until 1980, when a columbarium was established there, with remains flown out by helicopter; it has not been a lucrative enterprise.

Construction began on the **Cape Meares** lighthouse in 1886, and it commenced operations in 1890. An automatic beacon replaced it in 1963; the decommissioned lighthouse stood vacant until 1980. Since then it has been part of the state park and is available for viewing.

The tower of the Yaquina Head lighthouse north of **Newport** was built between 1871 and 1873 with some 370,000 bricks shipped up from San Francisco. It is the tallest Oregon lighthouse at ninety-three feet. The light was automated in 1966; it uses the original lens, and is in operation. Since 1993, it has been open to the public. Restoration work on the tower was completed in 2006. Contrary to some accounts, it was not intended that the lighthouse should have been built at **Cape Foulweather**, located several miles north.

The small wooden lighthouse at Yaquina Bay, in downtown Newport, was built in 1871 and operated only until 1874, when the Yaquina Head lighthouse effectively supplanted it. The building charted a perilous course for many years and it was nearly demolished several times, until the Lincoln County Historical Society saved it and in 1956 began to use it as a museum. In 1974, it was transferred to the Ore-gon state parks system. Finally, in 1996, the light was relit as a private aid to navigation.

The lighthouse at **Heceta Head** was built in 1892–94 and automated in 1963. It still has its original Fresnel lens; the lighthouse operation was stopped in 2000–01 for repairs to the lens and the rotating mechanism.

Funds were appropriated for the first lighthouse at the mouth of the **Umpqua River** (and the first in Oregon) in 1851, but mishaps delayed completion until 1857. The lighthouse was built on sand, and in 1864 it collapsed; a replacement was built at **Cape Arago** to the south. A second Umpqua River lighthouse was built in 1891–94. It was automated in the 1960s and repaired in the mid-1980s; the Fresnel light still shines, and the tower is available to the public through the Douglas County Museum.

The light at the **Cape Arago** lighthouse was first lit in 1866, atop an iron tower on an island reached by a rowboat. In 1896, the lighthouse tower was encased in bricks and stuccoed over, but erosion endangered the structure and a replacement was erected in 1909. The current concrete tower in turn replaced this in 1934. The light was de-activated on January 1, 2006.

The light at the mouth of the **Coquille River** was first lit in 1896, but in 1939, an automated beacon on the south jetty replaced it and the lighthouse was abandoned. It stood empty until the creation of Bullards Beach State Park in 1963, which included the lighthouse grounds. Restoration work took place in 1976, and in 1991 a solar-powered light was installed in the tower. Additional foundation repair work took place in 2007.

The lamp in the **Cape Blanco** lighthouse was first lit in 1870, atop a tower made partially of bricks manufactured on site; most of the brick, however, was shipped up from San Francisco. The light was automated in 1980; now in Cape Blanco State Park, the lighthouse has been open to the public since 1996 and underwent extensive restoration work in 2002–03.

There are also two oddities: Warrior Rock light, at the northwest tip of **Sauvie Island** on the Columbia River, had a small lighthouse from 1889; it was demolished by a barge in 1969. Lighthouse historian Jim Gibbs built a private, wooden lighthouse on **Cape Perpetua** in 1976, naming it Cleft of the Rock; it was made an official navigation aid in 1979.

Gibbs, James, and Bert Webber. *Oregon's Seacoast Lighthouses: An Oregon Documentary*. Medford, Oregon: Webb Research Group, 2000.

► **Lincoln City** In the 1920s, a string of towns extended along the Oregon Coast from Oceanlake in the north, south through Delake, Nelscott, Taft, and Cutler City—all popular resorts along the developing **Oregon Coast Highway**. By the 1960s, the area was a virtual commercial strip of motels, souvenir shops, and saltwater taffy stores, poorly served by the slogan **Twenty Miracle Miles**. Acrimonious discussions finally led to a vote in 1965 to consolidate the five communities into one, duly (and dully) christened Lincoln City for its location within Lincoln County. The names Delake and Oceanlake refer to the large freshwater Devils Lake, as does its outlet to the Pacific, **D River**. Nelscott was a resort real estate development begun in 1926, named for Charles P. Nelson and Dr. W. G. Scott. Taft was an older settlement: the post office opened in 1906, named for William Howard Taft, then the secretary of war. In the 1940s and 1950s, Taft was the location of the Redhead Round-Up, an annual beauty contest featuring red-haired young women. Cutler City was another resort town, begun in the 1920s by Mr. and Mrs. George Cutler. Lincoln City was blessed with an outlet mall in 1989, and with Chinook Winds Casino, opened in 1995 by the **Confederated Tribes**

The site of the Nelscott Beach Cottages was carved from the native Sitka spruce forest. The town of Nelscott was one of five that merged in 1965 to form Lincoln City. The office and gas station in the foreground appears to have been converted from a beached vessel. Auto camps of this kind proliferated along the Oregon Coast in the 1920s and 1930s. This photograph was probably taken in the early 1930s. Wesley Andrews photograph. Steven Dotterrer collection.

of Siletz. The population of Lincoln City in 1970 was 4,196; in 2007 it was estimated at 7,615.

Lincoln County Lincoln County was created by the legislature in 1893, slicing off the western portions of Benton and Polk Counties. A series of adjustments were made: 1923, 1925, 1927, 1931, 1949; since then it has remained stable with 992 square miles in area. The namesake is Abraham Lincoln. **Toledo** was designated the county seat, but it was 1899 before a courthouse was erected. Three times the residents voted on the question of removing the county seat from Toledo to **Newport**; the removal failed in 1928 and 1938, but it won in 1954. The **Coast Reservation** was established in 1855, and it included most of what became western Lincoln County. The area around Yaquina Bay was opened to white settlers in 1865 (the harvesting of oysters was a factor), and in 1875 the reservation was terminated, leaving as an inland remnant the **Siletz Reservation**. The area now included in Lincoln County was originally the homeland of the Salmon River and Siletz bands of the **Tillamook Indians** and the Yaquina and Alsea bands of the **Alsean Indians**. The establishment of the Coast Reservation brought Indians of many tribes from southwest Oregon and the southern Oregon Coast to the area; descendants are often members of the **Confederated Tribes of Siletz** or the **Confederated Tribes of Grand Ronde**.

The early economy of Lincoln County was based on the native oysters of Yaquina Bay, tiny morsels shipped in quantities in the 1860s and 1870s to San Francisco restaurants until they vanished from overharvesting. Oyster farming, using the Japanese Pacific oyster beginning in 1918, has since revived and extended the oyster business. Efforts to create a major port on the bay with a railroad connection to the Willamette Valley and the East began in the 1870s, faltered spectacularly in the 1880s, and collapsed by the early 1890s, but a scraggly railroad did connect Yaquina City (now a ghost town) and Toledo with Corvallis by 1884. Agriculture in Lincoln County was virtually all of the subsistence variety. The county's population in 1900 was 3,575. Growth came with the erection by the Spruce Division of the U.S. Army Signal Corps of a gigantic lumber mill at Toledo during World War I, designed to quickly produce lightweight spruce wood for airplane construction. The war ended before production began, but the mill was taken over by the C. D. Johnson Lumber Company and became the county's largest employer. The completion of the Salmon River Highway from Portland in the late 1920s and of the **Oregon Coast Highway** in 1932 paved the way for the **Twenty Miracle Miles** of north Lincoln County in the 1950s. Lincoln County's population reached 9,903 in 1930, and 21,308 by 1950. The estimated population in 2007 was 44,630.

Linfield College In 1849, the Oregon Baptist Educational Society was formed at Oregon City to establish a "school of high moral and religious character." Sebastian C. Adams began classes of this character in McMinnville in 1855, and in 1858 the Baptists obtained a charter from the territorial legislature for McMinnville College. The school received a donation of twenty-five acres of land in 1881, and built Pioneer Hall in 1883; by 1900, more than a hundred students were enrolled. The school was renamed Linfield College in 1922, in honor of George Fisher Linfield, following a substantial donation by his widow, Frances E. Ross Linfield. Linfield College was accredited in 1928. In 1982, the college took over the nursing school at Good Samaritan Hospital, giving it a Portland campus. The McMinnville campus grew from 78 acres to 193 acres with the 1998 acquisition of land and buildings from the Hewlett-Packard Company. Enrollment in 2005 was 2,674. *See also* **oak**.

Linn County The county of Linn was created by the provisional legislature in 1847 from a portion of Champooick District. The boundaries changed in

1851 and 1854 and Lane and Wasco Counties were established. Linn County was named for U.S. Senator Lewis F. Linn (1795–1843) of Missouri, who had been an advocate for American occupation of the Oregon Country and who is credited for the ideas underlying the later **Donation Land Act**. It was part of the homeland of the Santiam and Tsankupi bands of the **Kalapuyan Indians**. The county seat was established as Albany in 1851, though the first temporary courthouse was a school in **Brownsville**. The 1853 Albany courthouse burned in 1861; its 1865 replacement was twice remodeled before itself being replaced by the current courthouse in 1940. The area of Linn County is 2,297 square miles.

Immigrant farmers who grew wheat and general farm products and raised livestock settled the Linn County land in the 1840s. The rich soil has led to diversified agricultural production over the years, which has included beans and corn, berries, and common and perennial ryegrass for seed; the county is a leading national producer of seed crops. Linn County is also a major lumber and wood products producer, with paper mills in Lebanon and Halsey; Albany's Timber Carnival celebrated the industry. The construction of manufactured homes and the processing of rare and primary metals have been mainstays of Albany's industrial base since the 1960s. Linn County's population in 1860 was 6,772; by 1900, it reached 18,603, and in 1950, 54,317. The estimate for 2007 was 109,320.

Linnton neighborhood, Portland Named, liked Linn County, for a Missouri senator who died in 1843, Linnton was once an independent city. It was laid out in the mid-1840s by Morton M. McCarver and Peter H. Burnett as a likely future city; the premise was reasonable, but Portland won the prize. A community did not develop until later in the century; the Linnton post office was established in 1889, shortly after a railroad passed through the town. The Clark & Wilson Lumber Company established a sawmill in 1905, which grew to a huge en-

terprise in the next few decades. Linnton was incorporated as a city in 1910, and in 1915 was connected to Portland by an electric **interurban railway**. In 1915, Linnton was described as a city whose 1,400 residents engaged in "lumbering, manufacturing, tile works, foundries, dairying, poultry raising and truck gardening." In the same year, citizens voted to merge Linnton with Portland. The Linnton post office closed in 1936, and the Clark & Wilson mill burned in 1947. The Linnton Plywood Association built a plant on the Clark & Wilson property in 1951, which became the area's industrial mainstay until its closure in 2001. The Linnton commercial district was sliced in half in the early 1960s with the reconstruction of **Highway 30**. The Linnton school was converted to condominiums in 1992, and the community and the city have since engaged in a prolonged debate over the industrial or residential direction of future development in the area.

Lipman, Wolfe & Company Lipmans was once one of Portland's major department stores. The founders were Adolphe Wolfe and his uncle, Solomon Lipman, who had been successful merchants in California before coming to Portland in 1880. The store boasted a number of regional mercantile innovations such as the first elevator and the use of clearly marked prices: no haggling. By 1912, the firm was so successful that it opened in new quarters on Fifth Avenue, across the street from its chief competitor, **Meier & Frank** (M&F). Both stores were multi-storied edifices faced with gleaming white terra cotta, and both were designed by the city's leading architect, **A. E. Doyle**.

Lipmans catered more to the carriage trade than did the middle-of-the-road M&F or the third major department store, **Olds & King**. In 1937, the store began sponsoring a Christmas season radio show that many Portland residents thought was purely local: the Cinnamon Bear story, involving Judy and Jimmy Barton of Maybeland and their quest to find a missing silver star from their Christmas tree;

their adventures were accompanied by the (stuffed) Cinnamon Bear. Although the program originated in Hollywood and was syndicated nationally, it achieved near-cult status in Portland by the 1950s, and the bear was more popular than Santa.

The Lipman family sold the store to the Dayton-Hudson chain in the 1950s, and in 1980 it became part of the holdings of Marshall Field & Company, which changed its name to that of a Seattle chain, Frederick & Nelson; Frederick & Nelson closed the store in 1986. The classy Lipmans building was converted into a luxury hotel.

literature The iconic first bit of literature to come from the Oregon Country was a novel that poked into the soft underbelly of the **Jason Lee** Methodist mission community. Titled *The Grains; or, Passages in the Life of Ruth Rover, with Occasional Pictures of Oregon, Natural and Moral*, it was written by Margaret Jewett Bailey (1812?–1882) and published in Portland by the firm of Carter & Austin in 1854. **Abigail Scott Duniway**'s *Captain Gray's Company* was issued in 1859. The literary line has continued through the sentimental nineteenth-century poetry of **Sam Simpson**, the "Sweet Singer of Oregon's Beauty," and the roisterings of **Joaquin Miller**, "Poet of the Sierras" and county judge, while **Frances Fuller Victor** put Oregon history into literary form and **Sarah Winnemucca** wrote of the plight of America's Indians. Renaissance man **C. E. S. Wood** penned *The Poet in the Desert* about the beauty of southeastern Oregon. At the turn of the last century, **Frederic Homer Balch** and **Eva Emery Dye** romanced the past in novels with historical themes. In the twentieth century, **H. L. Davis** was the first Oregonian to win a Pulitzer Prize for his historical novel, *Honey in the Horn*, in 1936. Popular Oregon writers of mid-century who impacted the state included **Anne Shannon Monroe**, **Ernest Haycox**, **James Stevens**, and **Alfred Powers**, as well as journalist and politician **Richard Neuberger**. Another journalist and historian was **Stewart**

Holbrook, lionizer of loggers; **Ken Kesey** took another interpretation of loggers altogether. Later in the twentieth century, **Terence O'Donnell** wrote lyrically of Oregon as well as of his second home, Iran, and poet **William Stafford** wrote of the natural world.

Oregon Literature Series. 6 vols. Corvallis: Oregon State University Press, 1993–94.

Powers, Alfred. *History of Oregon Literature*. Portland, Oregon: Metropolitan Press, 1935.

Lloyd, Ralph B. (1875–1953) Ralph Lloyd lived in Portland for only a brief time, but his name is firmly planted on the city. Lloyd was born into a Ventura, California, ranching family, and first came to the Pacific Northwest in 1907. He apparently purchased a piece of real estate in Portland in 1910, and, driven by the conviction that Portland was on the verge of becoming a metropolis and that the east side of the river would be the site of most of the growth, he continued to buy more and more property. He was able to do so because, in 1920, oil came in—big—on the family's ranch. Lloyd bought extensively on both sides of **Sullivan's Gulch** and in Holladay's Addition, and made grand plans that were put off by the Depression and World War II; the Art Deco skyscraper hotel that he proposed in the 1930s did not come to pass. Lloyd died in 1953; for the sequel, *see* **Lloyd Center**.

Lloyd Center In the 1930s, **Ralph B. Lloyd** had proposed a grand development on property he owned on Portland's east side. The Depression quashed those plans, but they were resurrected after World War II. The development required public investment as well as private money, for it involved the closure or rebuilding of many city streets. After his death in 1953, the Lloyd family corporation deviated somewhat from his plans for a "self-sufficient region, with homes, stores and a residential hotel on some fifty acres," according to historian Bill Toll. What was built was one of the first large open-air shopping malls on the West Coast, designed by Seattle architect John Graham, Jr. It boasted free parking for some 8,000 automobiles, a branch of the **Meier & Frank** department store, huge Woolworth and Newberry variety stores, an outdoor ice rink, restaurants and specialty shops, and professional offices. In time, a Sheraton hotel and state and federal office buildings, as well as commercial office space, flanked the shopping center. The Lloyd Center was unusual for its location within an older city, and only a mile from the traditional downtown retail core; it was, however, easily accessible from new freeways. The Lloyd properties have undergone additional construction, including high-rise housing since the late 1990s, erasing the golf course that long marked the south edge of the properties, and **MAX** trains now supplement auto-oriented shoppers and workers. The shopping mall was renovated and fully enclosed in 1990.

lodgepole pine *see* pine

loganberries Reddish, tart, long, and lean, the loganberry (*Rubus loganobaccus*) is probably a cross between a red raspberry and a wild blackberry, developed in the 1880s by John H. Logan of Santa Cruz, California. Loganberries do not travel well as fresh fruit (and the berry is rather more tart than many people like), but in the 1890s commercial canning made it possible to process and ship canned loganberries, which made excellent pies. Loganberries were extensively planted in the Willamette Valley early in the twentieth century, and the Salem Fruit Union and other processors canned the berries and produced loganberry juice, dehydrated loganberries, jams and jellies. New berry varieties such as **boysenberries** reduced the demand for loganberries by mid-century, but they remain an important crop for preserves, pie-making, and sweet wine.

Anecdotal evidence suggests that loganberries were greatly favored for home winemaking after December 31, 1915, when prohibition took hold in Oregon.

logger *see* **lumberjack**

➤ **logging and lumbering** With extensive forestlands, Oregon has long been a land where trees were felled and used. The **Chinook Indians** and others used **cedar** for many purposes, including hollowing out the logs for canoes, and splitting them to produce planks for the walls and roofs of their lodges. Early merchant traders and fur trappers brought metal tools that made it possible to use other woods, and in other ways, such as log forts and trading posts. The first true sawmill came to the Oregon Country in 1827 at the **Hudson's Bay Company** post at **Fort Vancouver**, and from that time small mills sprang up on creeks around the region—water provided the power. Early mill sites included Oregon City (1829) and Hunt's Point (near Bradwood in Clatsop County), where in 1844 Henry H. Hunt built one of the first privately owned commercial mills, which shipped lumber to Hawai'i. By 1850, there was a steam-powered sawmill, and lumber was being shipped to Asia, to the gold fields of California and to the booming city of San Francisco. By 1870, 183 sawmills operated in Oregon, 138 of them powered by water and forty-five by steam. The principal wood was **Douglas-fir**.

The arrival of transcontinental railroad connections in 1883 opened new markets for Oregon lumber, and new resources as well in the form of the now accessible pine forests of the Blue Mountains in northeastern Oregon. In the 1890s and early 1900s, as it became clear that the federal lands in Oregon were not all suitable for farming, forest reserves were formed; these eventually became national forest lands. Railroads again brought new timber areas into production in the early 1900s, including much of the Coast Range mountains, the **pine** forests of Central Oregon near Bend and Klamath Falls, and the Blue Mountains north of Burns. The first plywood plant was built in **Saint Johns** in 1905. Logging itself transitioned to a mechanized operation, where steam donkey engines pulled the logs to steam-powered railroad trains, which hauled the logs to steam-powered sawmills. Loggers, once itinerant, usually single men who lived in bunkhouses and caroused on **skid road**, transitioned to family men who commuted from **company towns** to the woods by train.

By 1929, Oregon had some 608 lumber mills; sixty-four planing mills shaped the wood, forty-seven factories made wooden furniture, and there were five paper mills. The 1930s brought hard times, which were exacerbated by the **Tillamook Burn**, which devastated a huge swath of timberlands. Still, in 1938, Oregon for the first time led the nation in timber production; by 1947, there were 1,537 lumber mills. The 1940s and 1950s saw a shift to truck logging, and the chainsaw revolutionized the felling of trees: what once took two men two days now took one man an hour to accomplish. Operators became

larger and more diversified: **Crown Zellerbach** and **Weyerhaeuser** flourished in the 1940s and 1950s, followed by the introduction of **Georgia-Pacific** from the South. Large, old-growth timber rapidly vanished from private lands and diminished on federal lands, and mills converted to use smaller logs; log exports to Asia rose, closing mills while keeping loggers busy. New products such as plywood, veneer, particleboard, and laminated beams made use of smaller logs; paper mills used wood pulp.

By 1975, environmental concerns began to force changes in logging practices to reduce erosion (replanting was required in 1971) and to consider wildlife and fisheries resources. Statewide land-use planning began in 1973, and the **spotted owl** was designated a threatened species in 1989; both actions contributed to a slowing of a tree harvesting. Timber production has declined since 1980, and

A trainload of logs is on its way to the Silver Falls Timber Company mill at Silverton from the foothills of the Cascade Range. In the background are snags from an earlier forest fire. The photograph was taken in the 1920s by June Drake, who operated the studio as the Drake Brothers for many years after his brother Emory left in 1908. Author's collection.

many mills have closed. *See also* **papermaking industry; wood products industry**.

Lonerock Lonerock, "the oldest town in Gilliam County," was a small agricultural village. It still is, although it has been gradually shrinking in population for some decades. A rural post office named Lone Rock opened in 1875, the name taken from the still-prominent rock that looms over the townsite. (In the early 1900s, the post office department, in a misguided attempt at efficiency, pushed together many two-word post office names into streamlined, single-word names; Lone Rock was among the many victims of this practice.) R. G. Robinson and Albert Henshaw established the town in 1881, platting lots and streets in 1882. The town was incorporated in 1901. Gilliam County is wheat country, but in the early 1900s, the area around Lonerock also supported stock and poultry raising, dairying, and growing alfalfa and hay. The 1910 census reported a population of seventy, rising to a high of eighty-two in 1930; by 1970, it was twelve (the post office closed in 1963). It has hovered near this figure since, and was estimated in 2007 to be twenty.

▶ **Long Creek** A ranching town in northern Grant County, Long Creek grew up around the post office, which opened in 1880. A general store, saloon, hotel, and livery stables were in place in the early 1880s, and a water-powered flour mill was located nearby in 1885. Small and remote though it was, Long Creek achieved the status of an incorporated municipality in 1891, and the 1900 census credited it with 123 residents. Long Creek had its own newspaper, the weekly Long Creek *Eagle*, founded in 1886. This became the *Blue Mountain Eagle* in 1898, under which name the paper survived a flight to Canyon City in 1900 and later to John Day, where it

For a time, Long Creek was, like so many places in Oregon, a sawmill town. The photograph shows the stacked lumber and the wigwam burner of the Howell Lumber Company as it appeared in 1959. Logs for the mill came mostly from private forest lands some miles away. Dorys Crow photograph. *Oregon Journal* collection. Oregon Historical Society, OrHi 77490.

has continued to soar ever since. The weekly Long Creek *Ranger* began publication in 1900, and survived until 1930. Long Creek at the beginning of the twenty-first century is still a small ranching town, population 220 (2007 estimate).

William F. Willingham. *Starting Over: Community Building on the Eastern Oregon Frontier.* Portland, Oregon: Oregon Historical Society Press, 2005.

Long Tom River Winding east and north for about fifty miles from the Coast Range Mountains in Lane and Benton Counties, the Long Tom River drains into the Willamette River south of Corvallis. In the 1850s, much of its lower course wound lazily through wetlands and past oak-studded prairies. The town of **Monroe** is on the Long Tom, some half-dozen miles from the mouth of this small stream, and about 1868, the sternwheel steamboat *Ann* managed to twist its way upstream and load some flour from the mill there. This was, apparently, a one-time event.

Fern Ridge Dam was completed in 1941, creating a huge shallow reservoir upstream, accompanied by a channelized course below the dam; this did reduce flooding uncertainties, but it wiped out the wetlands. The **Oregon Country Fair**, situated on the Long Tom above the reservoir, has worked since the 1990s to restore some of the upstream portions of the river. The river's name is apparently the result of Euro-American efforts to pronounce the name of an Indian band; the resulting attempt replicates a term that is connected to nineteenth-century placer gold mining: a long tom is a wooden trough with a metal bottom and riffles, used to separate flecks of gold from river mud and gravels. Long toms were used in many places in Oregon, but not along the Long Tom.

Lostine The community of Lostine, apparently named for a now-vanished hamlet in Kansas, is in Wallowa County. A rural post office with this name opened in 1878, as white settlement came to the Wallowa Valley in the wake of the removal of **Nez Perce Indians** from their homeland. Lostine was incorporated as a municipality in 1903, and a railroad from La Grande arrived in 1908; the 1910 census showed Lostine with a population of 230. Residents of the area engaged in farming, dairying, stock raising, and lumbering; lime and marble were produced on occasion. The town's population has changed very little over the years, and was estimated at 250 in 2007.

Lot Whitcomb The first steamboat built on the Willamette River was the sidewheeler *Lot Whitcomb*, named for the founder of the townsite of **Milwaukie**, businessman Lot Whitcomb (1807–1857). Launched on Christmas Day in 1850, the vessel was 160 feet long; the first commander was Capt. **John C. Ainsworth**. She was operated between Milwaukie, Portland, and Astoria, but quickly proved to be expensive to operate; she was often used to tow sailing ships on the Columbia River. The *Lot Whitcomb* was sold off to California in 1854.

Louisiana Pacific *see* **Georgia-Pacific**

Lovejoy, Asa Lawrence (1808–1882) Asa L. Lovejoy was born in Massachusetts and was trained as a lawyer. He came overland to the Oregon Country and settled at Oregon City in 1843 to practice law, but also took up a land claim at the site of Portland with a partner, William Overton. There, in partnership with **Francis W. Pettygrove**, he laid out the original 16-block townsite. A flip of the **Portland Penny** named the town Portland, rather than Lovejoy's proposal of Boston, the capital of his home state. Lovejoy married Elizabeth McGary in 1845; he continued from law into politics, serving as mayor of Oregon City, a member of the legislature of the **provisional government**, first speaker of the house of the territorial legislature in 1849, and a member of the territorial senate in 1851. After participating in the state constitutional convention in 1857, Lovejoy's political activities receded. Lovejoy is buried in Lone Fir Cemetery in Portland, and is remembered in the name of a prominent street and in the **Lovejoy Fountain**.

Lovejoy Fountain Located in Portland's South Auditorium urban renewal area, the Lovejoy Fountain and nearby Pettygrove Park were designed by noted San Francisco landscape architect Lawrence Halprin. They were part of a sequence of works, which also includes the **Keller Fountain**, which came from Halprin's office in 1965; the Lovejoy Fountain and Pettygrove Park were built in 1966. Halprin said that the rocky reaches of the Sierra Mountains were his inspiration for the fountain; the idea behind the tree-capped rounded mounds of Pettygrove Park has received less analysis. The fountain is named for **Asa L. Lovejoy**; Pettygrove Park honors **Francis W. Pettygrove**; the two platted the future city of Portland in 1845. The **Portland Penny** that Lovejoy and Pettygrove used to select the name Portland, was used to determine which name was applied to the fountain and which to the park.

Lowell This Lane County community was settled in the 1870s, when Amos Hyland operated a ferry across the Middle Fork Willamette River. A rural post office named Cannon was opened in 1880; its name was changed to Lowell in 1883. Hyland platted a townsite in 1908, anticipating a railroad line that finally arrived in 1912 and became a through route to California in 1926. Lookout Point and Dexter Dams on the Middle Fork were built in the early 1950s as part of the Willamette Valley Project to control flooding. The **covered bridge** at Lowell, first built in 1907, was replaced with another wooden covered bridge in 1945; this was raised in 1953 to accommodate the reservoir. A concrete bridge supplanted it in 1981, but the wooden bridge was retained and refurbished as a pedestrian structure. The dams also relocated the railroad and the Willamette Pass Highway. Lowell was incorporated in 1954;

its population in 1957 was estimated at 575. The 1980 census showed 661 residents, and its estimated 2007 population was 995.

Lower Chinookan Indians The term "Lower Chinookan Indians" is used here to refer to a number of bands that are connected by a basic Chinookan language and live along the Columbia River and its tributaries. These include the Multnomah, Clackamas, and Cathlamet Indians. For the Lower Chinook Indians proper—the Chinook and Clatsop bands near the mouth of the Columbia River, *see* **Chinook Indians**; for Chinookan-speaking Indians living farther up the Columbia River, *see* **Wasco and Wishram Indians**. The Cathlamet band lived along both sides of the Columbia River from Cathlamet Bay, just east of Astoria, upstream to near Kalama, Washington. The Multnomah homeland was also on both sides of the Columbia from Kalama to the Sandy River, including Multnomah Channel and **Sauvie Island** and a short distance up the Willamette River. Clackamas Indians lived along both shores of the Willamette from the Portland area upstream to Willamette Falls and the lower reaches of the Clackamas River.

Like the Chinook and Clatsop, the Cathlamet, Multnomah, and Clackamas lived in cedar-plank lodges that held several families, sited in large permanent villages along the river. Fish were a basic food: salmon, sturgeon, lamprey, steelhead, and smelt were staples. Other foods included elk, deer, and bear, and other small animals; ducks and geese; a wide variety of berries and roots, and especially the **wapato**. These tribes were exposed to white traders and explorers from the late eighteenth century, with consequences: they had early access to trade goods and guns, and early exposure to introduced diseases such as smallpox, measles, and malaria. As anthropologist Michael Silverstein noted, the Multnomah and Clackamas "were thoroughly ravaged" by disease by 1850, with the survivors often intermarrying with other Indians and a consequent severing of tribal connections. Treaties were signed, but never ratified by the U.S. Senate; some Chinook ended up on the Grand Ronde Reservation, while others "formed an economic fringe in the local industries" of the region.

Silverstein, Michael. Chinookans of the Lower Columbia. In *Handbook of North American Indians*, vol. 7, Northwest Coast. Washington, DC: Smithsonian Institution, 1990: 533–546.

Loyal Legion of Loggers and Lumbermen *see* **Industrial Workers of the World**

Luckiamute Indians *see* **Kalapuyan Indians**

Luckiamute River This thirty-mile-long tributary of the Willamette River rises in western Polk County, is joined by the Little Luckiamute River from the northwest, and joins the Willamette just south of Buena Vista. The name is of Indian origin, but its derivation is not known; *see* **Kalapuyan Indians**.

Luelling, Henderson (1809–1878) Oregon's largest agricultural income producers in the twenty-first century are **nurseries**. The nursery industry can be traced to the historic activities of two brothers, Henderson Luelling and **Seth Lewelling**. Henderson Luelling was born to a Quaker family in North Carolina; in 1830, he married Elizabeth Presnall, and moved west, first to Indiana and then to Iowa, where he farmed and operated a small nursery. In 1847, Henderson, Elizabeth, and eight children packed an assortment of fruit cultivars in earth-filled wooden boxes and took the Oregon Trail. The Luellings settled on land near **Milwaukie** and laid out a nursery in 1848, going into business with their son-in-law William Meek. Henderson brought to Oregon varieties of apples, pears, cherries, and peaches, as well as quince, black walnut, shell-bark hickory, grape, currant, and gooseberry plants. Seth Lewel-

ling joined the operation in 1850, and by 1851, they had some 18,000 young fruit trees for sale. Henderson sold out his interest to Meek in 1854 and moved to California, where he also engaged in the nursery trade. A school in Milwaukie honors Henderson Luelling.

McClintock, Thomas C. Henderson Luelling, Seth Lewelling, and the Birth of the Pacific Coast Fruit Industry. *Oregon Historical Quarterly* 68, no. 2 (June 1967): 153–174.

lumber industry *see* **logging and lumbering; wood products industry**

lumberjack This was the common term in the nineteenth century and into the mid-twentieth century for a woods worker or logger, a man who worked in the woods to fell trees for lumber or pulp production. There were various specialized terms, such as a feller who cut trees down, and a bucker who sawed them up. Most lumberjacks were single men, and most were itinerant: that is, they moved around, from job to job, as the timber was cut and as better pay, working conditions, or camp food was offered at various outfits.

Holbrook, Stewart. *Holy Old Mackinaw: A Natural History of the American Lumberjack*. New York: Macmillan, 1938.

Lyons Located on the North Santiam River in Linn County, the rural Lyons post office opened in 1891. The Oregon Pacific Railroad arrived in the community in 1888 on its abortive thrust east over the Cascades from the Willamette Valley at Albany. In the late nineteenth and early twentieth centuries, lumber production, general farming, fruit raising, and dairying were the economic underpinnings of Lyons and vicinity. The construction of **Detroit Dam** in the early 1950s boosted the area's population, and Lyons was incorporated in 1958. Its population in 1970 was 645; the estimated population in 2005 was 1,105. A lumber mill is still there.

M

MacDonald, Ranald (1824–1894) Ranald Mac-Donald was born at the fur-trading post of **Fort Astoria** to Scotsman Archibald MacDonald and his wife, a daughter of **Concomly**. He was sent to Manitoba for an education and took a job as a bank clerk, but MacDonald had long heard tales of Japan and of the possible connections between Asian and Native American peoples. Japan was closed to foreigners; however, MacDonald signed aboard the whaling ship *Plymouth* in 1845, and in 1848 managed to land himself, alone, in a small boat on Japanese soil. Captured and imprisoned, he found himself teaching the English language to Japanese samurai, preparing for the eventual opening of Japan to other nations. In 1849, MacDonald was remitted and returned to the United States, where his account of Japan were conveyed to the U.S. Congress. MacDonald went to sea again, and then prospected the British Columbia gold fields in 1858. He spent the rest of his life in British Columbia, and died in Washington state while visiting a niece. Reportedly, his last words were to her: "Sayonara, my dear, sayonara." MacDonald's accomplishments were virtually unnoted in his lifetime; not until 1923 was an edited version of his notes and writings published. A monument to MacDonald stands in his birthplace, Astoria, as well as in Nagasaki, Japan; he is buried near Curlew Lake in Washington state.

Roe, JoAnn. *Ranald MacDonald: Pacific Rim Adventurer*. Pullman: Washington State University Press, 1997.

Schodt, Frederik L. *Native American in the Land of the Shogun: Ranald MacDonald and the Opening of Japan*. Berkeley, California: Stone Bridge Press, 2003.

▶ **Madras** The county seat of Jefferson County, Madras was once called The Basin, describing its location along Willow Creek. The name Madras is reputedly derived from the cotton cloth of that name; madras cloth is named for a city in India. A post office named Madras opened in 1902 to serve a rural ranching area. The town was incorporated in 1910 in anticipation of the arrival in 1911 of the **Oregon Trunk Railway**. Jefferson County was formed in 1914 with **Culver** as the first seat of county government, but the honor was wrenched away by Madras in 1917. The 1910 census showed Madras with a population of 364. Madras suffered a major fire in 1924, and its population remained stable until after the completion of the North Unit of the Deschutes irrigation project in 1946. The population was 412 in 1940, 1,258 in 1950, and 2,235 in 1980. Lumber production as well as growing peppermint and seed for such crops as onions, garlic, and carrots were economic supports after World War II. Since 1980, the residential vacationland impact of the Bend area has also impacted the Madras area. The estimated population in 2007 was 6,585.

madrona The madrone or madrone tree, *Arbutus menziesii*, is a broad-leafed evergreen with a distinctive smooth red bark that peels in strips. The madrone is found from British Columbia south to southern California along the coast and in interior valleys such as those of the Willamette, Umpqua, and Rogue Rivers. It is a common understory tree in oak groves and in stands of **Douglas-fir** and other conifers. The scientific name honors naturalist Archibald Menzies (1754–1842), who sailed with Capt. **George Vancouver** in the 1790s.

mail boats Railroad lines and scheduled steamboat routes were designated carriers of the U.S. mail, but small boats were also used in some circumstances, such as making rural deliveries on coastal lakes in Coos County. A mail route to **Gold Beach** developed in the 1890s from the railroad station of Dothan in Douglas County via pack train down the isolated canyon of the **Rogue River** to Angess, and then via boat to the river mouth. Muscle-powered at first, the mail boats on the Rogue were motorized in the 1910s and developed into a tourist excursion in the 1930s with the completion of the **Oregon Coast Highway**.

Malheur County Oregon's second largest county includes nearly 10 percent of the state's land area at 9,874 square miles. The county was established in 1887 by taking land from the southern section of Baker County. The name comes from the **Malheur River**. The initial county seat was **Vale**, where a courthouse was built in 1887. In 1888, an election was held to select a permanent seat from among Vale, Jordan Valley, and Ontario; again, Vale prevailed. The county's population in 1890, exclusive of Indians, was 2,601.

The region occupied by Malheur County was the homeland of the **Northern Paiute Indians**, comprised of a number of bands that spoke a common language. The population was concentrated along the **Owyhee River**, and the Paiutes often intermarried with the adjoining Shoshone Indians, sometimes known as Bannock or Snake Indians. The U. S. Army had posts such as Fort Harney to "pacify" Natives during this period. The Malheur Reservation was established in 1871, intended to hold "all the roving and straggling bands" in the region, but mismanagement coupled with land greed on the part of incoming settlers conspired to end the reservation in the year of the **Bannock War**, 1878 (it was not officially terminated until 1882).

The transcontinental **Union Pacific Railroad** crossed the northern tip of the county, connecting it with both Portland and the east in 1884. **Ontario** was the principal commercial town; a few branch line railroads penetrated the northern part of the county in the 1900s and 1910s. By the 1890s, sheep

This chilly looking photograph depicts the Jefferson County courthouse in Madras as it appeared about 1917. The county was brand new, having been created in 1914. *Oregon Journal* collection. Oregon Historical Society, CN 006981.

raising was a major enterprise, especially to the south along the tributaries of the Owyhee, where many sheepherders were **Basques**. In 1915, the county was described as advancing with the introduction of irrigation, and boasting of 1,600 miles of road, of which 5 percent were improved with gravel. Also, it was reported here that "thousands of coyotes are killed annually." The western portion of the **Treasure Valley** has developed into a prime agricultural area, irrigated with Snake and Owyhee water and producing potatoes, onions, and seed crops. Sugar beets were once a major output; the closure of several regional processing mills in the late twentieth century reduced that crop. Malheur County's population, always heavily concentrated in the vicinity of Ontario, was 8,601 in 1910, and 23,233 in 1950. It reached 26,896 in 1980, and was estimated in 2007 at 31,620.

Malheur Lake Located in the Harney Basin in Harney County, shallow Malheur Lake is fed principally by the **Donner und Blitzen River** and the Silvies River. It is an interior basin lake and has no outlet; when the water level rises, the lake drains westward through the Narrows to Mud Lake and thence to **Harney Lake**, the lowest in the chain. Water levels can change dramatically; the most recent high water occurred for several years in the 1980s and again in the late 1990s, which flooded out ranches, roads, and a railroad. At one time, the basin drained to the east via the Malheur River into the Snake River; the channel is still a visible landmark. Malheur and Harney Lakes and the marshes and sloughs along the rivers historically attracted huge flocks of migrating birds. The documenting work of naturalist and photographer **William L. Finley** led to the creation of the Malheur National Wildlife Refuge in 1908, encompassing the lakes and much of the wetlands, and including lands once part of the cattle empire of **Pete French**.

Langston, Nancy. *Where Land & Water Meet: A Western Landscape Transformed*. Seattle: University of Washington Press, 2003.

Malheur Reservation *see* **Malheur County; Northern Paiute Indians**

Malheur River The name of the Malheur River can be traced back to the journal of fur trapper **Peter Skene Ogden**, whose crews were there in 1825–26. An incident involving the disappearance of some furs they had earlier cached on its banks gave rise to calling the river *malheur*, an unfortunate place or a place of bad times. It rises in the Blue Mountains of Grant County and flows east and south past Drewsey through northern Harney and Malheur Counties to meet the Snake River near Ontario. Two major forks come from the north and the south, the latter once having been the outlet for **Malheur Lake**.

Malin The town of Malin is located in Klamath County on land that was reclaimed from Tule Lake, which was drained in the early 1900s. The community was established in 1909 with the arrival of some fifty families comprising the Czech Colonization Club of Nebraska. Malin post office was opened in 1910, with the name being derived from the Czech term for horseradish, then and now a major agricultural product of the area; approximately a third of the world's supply grows in the Tule Lake region of Oregon and California. Malin was incorporated in 1922, and recorded a population of 215 in 1930, and 592 in 1950; the estimated population in 2007 was 800.

"Czech Colonization Club." *Journal of the Shaw Historical Library* 1, no. 1 (1986).

manzanita The coastal shrub known as manzanita, *Arctostaphylos columbiana*, is a bushy evergreen plant with a notable reddish-brown bark that peels and flakes off. The name is derived from the Spanish, "little apple"; manzanita has small, red-brown fruits, though they are not among those considered to be edible, at least with pleasure.

Manzanita Named for the **manzanita** shrub found in the vicinity, Manzanita is a beach resort in Tillamook County north of Nehalem Bay. The townsite was platted in 1912, a year after the railroad arrived connecting the Tillamook beaches with Portland. A post office was established in 1914, and a number of beach cottages, many in the popular Craftsman style of the period and sheathed in weathered shingles, were built by 1920. The Manzanita Inn became a noted seaside respite, also in the Craftsman style. The town was incorporated in 1946, and the 1950 census counted 339 residents. The 1980 census showed a population of 443, since which time a large number of residences have been constructed; the estimated population in 2007 was 715.

maple Three varieties of the maple are found in Oregon. The bigleaf maple, *Acer macrophyllum*, is also known as the Oregon maple. It a handsome shade tree with large leaves and it occurs naturally throughout western Oregon valleys and foothills, and in the Columbia River gorge. Its propensity to produce vivid fall colors and its majestic height and canopy—it commonly ranges from thirty to seventy feet in height—have led to its wide use as an ornamental tree. Equally vivid in autumn is the vine maple, *Acer circinatum*, which is more of a shrub, although it can reach a height of twenty-five feet. The vine maple favors stream banks in western Oregon, and is often found in the understory of the coniferous forests of the Coast Range. The third maple is the Rocky Mountain, mountain or dwarf maple, *Acer glabrum*, a fairly short shrublike tree that is found in the canyons of the Cascade Mountains and the Blue Mountains.

Mapleton Mapleton is an unincorporated community in Lane County, situated on the **Siuslaw River** near the head of navigation, about fifteen miles upstream from Florence. The area was settled by farming families in the 1880s, and the rural post office of Seaton was re-named Mapleton in 1896, reputedly at the suggestion of the postmaster, Julian Ann "Grandma" Bean, and in recognition of an abundance of bigleaf **maple** trees in the area. Mapleton grew to rely more on logging and lumber production than agriculture during the twentieth century. A **covered bridge** was built across the Siuslaw in 1934 with two spans of 114 feet, each pierced by six Gothic-style windows on each side; the bridge also had a draw span to permit boats to continue upriver a short distance. Located on a major highway and subject to abuse by heavy loaded log trucks, the distinctive bridge was torn down in 1970 and replaced by an extraordinarily ugly concrete span. Davidson Industries, Mapleton's last operating sawmill, closed in 2004.

marionberries The marionberry is a cross between two blackberries, Chehalem and Ollalieberry, and is noted for its "aromatic bouquet and an intense blackberry flavor," according to a trade organization. It was developed in Marion County and introduced in 1956; the principal commercial production, for freezing and for jams and flavorings, is in Oregon.

Marion County Marion County is descended from the **Champooick District** created in 1843 by the provisional government. That immense territory was pared down by 1856 to the current county borders, encompassing 1,194 square miles in the heart of the Willamette Valley. The county was named in 1849 for a Revolutionary War hero, Francis Marion, "the Swamp Fox" (ca. 1732–1790), for reasons that remain obscure. **Salem** was designated the county seat, and the first courthouse was erected in 1854. This was replaced in 1873 by a most imposing Italianate structure designed by Portland architect William W. Piper, an iconic "wedding cake" extravaganza. It was demolished in 1952; "some felt it was replaced by a cake box." The stark lines of the mid-century building were disrupted in 2007 when a miscreant, pursued by police, drove a pickup into the front entrance, demolishing it.

The area now Marion County was historically occupied by bands of **Kalapuyan Indians**, those known as Santiam and Ahantchuyuk. The Kalapuyans practiced field burning, which established and maintained a prairie-like landscape dotted by groves of **oak** trees. While early Euro-Americans perceived this as a natural landscape, it was one created to make it easier to harvest tarweed seeds, a choice food, and to provide forage for game animals. Marion County was the focal point of early Christian missionary efforts to Pacific Northwest Indians. **Jason Lee** and the Methodists established Willamette Mission near **Wheatland** in 1834, moving their operations to the site of Salem a few years later after encountering both a lack of potential converts and a resistance to conversion. Catholic missionaries, whose services were requested by French-Canadian residents of **French Prairie**, arrived at **Saint Paul**, led by **François Norbert Blanchet** in 1839.

For early American settlers, the attraction of Marion County was its excellent agricultural land, land that was already partially cleared by the Native burning practices. It was densely settled in the 1840s and 1850s, wheat being the initial principal crop. Fruit trees, obtained from the nurseries of **Seth Lewelling**, grew into orchards of apples, peaches, and cherries. By 1915, Marion County was noted also for asparagus and celery, onions, hops, prunes, and loganberries; thoroughbred goats and sheep were raised, too. "The panorama of orchards, hop yards, gardens, clover fields, grain fields . . . studded with large, well-built barns and spacious homes, is one never to be forgotten." Crops have changed somewhat since then, and Marion County farms have produced fewer prunes and cherries, have abandoned **flax**, and have added green beans, blueberries, raspberries, and wine grapes to the list of agricultural products; nursery plants have also grown in importance, and lawn sod and **Christmas trees** are somewhat controversial recent agricultural products. The county's economy has also been sustained by lumber production since the 1840s, and most prominently by state government, which includes not only state offices but also the main penitentiary and mental health facilities. Marion County had a population of 7,088 in 1860, and 27,713 by 1900. The figure reached 47,187 in 1920 and 101,401 in 1950; in 1990, the count was 228,483, and was estimated at 311,070 in 2007.

markets *see* **farmers' markets; public markets; Saturday Market**

Marshfield *see* **Coos Bay (city)**

Martin, Charles Henry (1863–1946) Charles H. Martin was born in Illinois, and graduated from West Point in 1887. He was first assigned to Fort Vancouver, Washington; his subsequent military career took him to the Philippines, China, Mexico, Panama, Europe, and to various points in the United States; he attained the rank of major general by the time of his retirement in 1927. Martin married Louise J. Hughes of Portland in 1897, and he maintained an Oregon residence throughout his career. Though he had proclaimed himself a Republican, Martin ran for the House of Representatives as a write-in candidate on the Democratic ticket in 1930; he won, and won again in 1932. In 1934, he sought and obtained the nomination as Democratic candidate for governor; a three-way split vote that included a popular independent candidate gave Martin the seat. However, Martin opposed many of the New Deal programs of Franklin Roosevelt, and said so long and loudly and, said some, profanely. He proved to be an outspoken proponent of strict law and order, opposed to labor unions, appeared to be unsympathetic to the poor, and soon became a distinct liability to the Democratic Party. He remained popular with business leaders who supported his views on labor and his staunch patriotism. Martin failed to be re-elected in 1938.

Murrell, Gary. *Iron Pants: Oregon's Anti-New Deal governor, Charles Henry Martin.* Pullman: Washington State University Press, 2000.

Maryhill *see* **Hill, Samuel "Sam"**

Marylhurst University Saint Mary's Academy and College was established in Portland in 1893 to serve Catholic women. Founded by the Sisters of the Holy Names of Jesus and Mary, a teaching order that first came to Oregon in 1859, it was authorized to grant bachelor's degrees in 1898. In 1908, the Sisters purchased land along the Willamette River between West Linn and Lake Oswego, and there they established a Marylhurst Normal School, a teacher training institution, in 1911. In 1930, Saint Mary's College, now renamed Marylhurst College, moved to the new site (Saint Mary's Academy remained in Portland, serving students through grade 12). The normal school and college were combined in 1950. Marylhurst became co-educational in 1974 and began adding graduate level programs in the mid-1980s. It changed its name to Marylhurst University in 1998.

Marys Peak In Benton Count, Marys Peak is the highest point in the central section of the **Coast Range Mountains**, reaching 4,097 feet. At the summit, the surf at Newport is visible, about twenty-one miles away. Mount Rainier is visible to the north, while to the south Mount Thielsen in the southern Cascades can be seen.

Marys River This short Benton County river heads north of **Marys Peak** and flows east to the Willamette River just south of Corvallis. The origin of the name is swathed in obscurity. Some reference it in the 1830s as Riviére de Souris and the English equivalent, Mouse River; by 1846, Marys River is the common usage. The town of Marysville, now **Corvallis**, was laid out in 1847.

Maupin The city of Maupin is situated on the Deschutes River in Wasco County, one of two points of easy crossing of the river between its mouth and Bend. Howard Maupin operated the first ferry there in the early 1870s. A post office was established in 1909, and by 1911, the Oregon Trunk Railway connected Maupin to the outside world. A bridge replaced the ferry in 1912, and the town was incorporated in 1922; the 1930 census reported a population of 249. Since the 1970s, Maupin has grown as a recreation center, prompted by the popularity of sports fishing and then of whitewater river rafting. Maupin's population was 428 in 1970, and was estimated at 490 in 2007.

MAX This is an acronym for Metropolitan Area Express, and was devised to tag the light-rail project that is operated by the Portland-area TriMet transit system (TriMet is the short form for Tri-County Metropolitan Transportation District of Oregon). Light rail is a term that describes rail-based transit that operates both on reserved rights-of-way and in city streets, at moderate speeds, and is usually powered by electricity transmitted through overhead wires. It is basically an updated version of what were called, a century earlier, electric **interurban railways**. MAX was created in the aftermath of the debacle of the unbuilt **Mount Hood Freeway**, and funds diverted from that project helped build the light-rail line. The first route, built in 1982–86, connected Gresham with downtown Portland; it used portions of a long-abandoned interurban railway. Fifteen miles long, the route was one of the nation's first new-generation light-rail lines.

MAX was extended west eighteen miles to Hillsboro in 1998; a five-and-a-half mile line to Portland International Airport (PDX) opened in 2001, and a 5.8-mile extension on Interstate Avenue went into service in 2004; another line south to Clackamas

Town Center opens in 2009, and other projects are planned.

Maywood Park This Multnomah County town was created in the wake of the construction of a freeway in the hopes of minimizing its impact. Maywood Park is in Multnomah County. The developer of the wooded residential subdivision named it when he observed one winter night "how attractive the woods were in May." The area was platted in the late 1920s, but extensive residential building did not take place until the late 1930s. Planning for **Interstate 84** and **Interstate 205** prompted residents to incorporate as a city in 1967, in the hopes that they would thereby gain leverage to steer the freeways around rather than through their neighborhood. They were not fully successful, but the freeway is depressed as it passes Maywood Park, and the streets remain tree-lined and quiet. The town has no business section. Maywood Park's population in the 1970 census was 1,230; in 1980, reflecting the freeway impact, it was 845; the estimated population in 2007 was 750.

Mazamas The Mazamas are a Portland-based mountain climbing and outdoors club, named with the Spanish word for mountain goat. The club was founded in 1894 on the slopes of Mount Hood, with 105 charter members, among them **William Steel**. Membership is contingent on the applicant having climbed, on foot, a peak in the Cascade Range that has a living glacier. The club has been active in promoting wilderness conservation since its inception. A Seattle-based contingent of the club split off in 1907 to form the Mountaineers. The club's motto, in **Chinook jargon**, is *Nesika klatawa sahale,* or "We climb high." *See also* **Crater Lake**; **Mount Mazama**.

McCall, Thomas Lawson "Tom" (1913–1983) Though Tom McCall's parents had moved from Massachusetts to Oregon in 1909, Tom happened to

be born back East. Tom grew up partly in Massachusetts, partly on the family ranch, Westwold, on the Crooked River near Prineville. McCall graduated from the University of Oregon in 1936 with a degree in journalism, and took a job with a newspaper in Idaho. He married Audrey Owen in 1939, and by 1942, they were in Portland, where McCall worked for the *Oregonian* and as a news announcer on their affiliated radio station, KGW. McCall served in World War II, and after the war began to get involved in politics through the Young Republicans. In 1955, McCall stepped into television news, working with KGW from 1956 until his election as secretary of state in 1964.

From that platform, McCall ran for, and won, the governor's seat in 1966. He quickly forwarded a number of environmental issues, beginning with the Beach Bill that protected ocean shores through zoning. He pushed for the establishment of the Willamette River Greenway in 1967. He continued with the Bottle Bill (mandating a deposit on soft drink containers) and Senate Bill 100, which created the Land Conservation and Development Commission (LCDC) and set statewide planning goals that emphasized the conservation of farmland and open spaces. Protecting Oregon's once-much-vaunted "livability" was a refrain for McCall. In a blithe moment, McCall said "Come visit us again and again [in Oregon]. But for heaven's sake, don't come here to live." But it was taken by many as an enticement; the state's population increased by nearly 25 percent during the course of his two terms in office.

McCall left office in 1975; he continued to lend his voice to supporting land-use planning issues, especially under successor **Robert W. Straub**. He made another stab at the governorship in 1978, but failed to carry his campaign forward. He endured cancer for several years before his death in 1983. McCall's name is perpetuated in a waterfront park in Portland, a nature preserve in the Columbia River Gorge, and several public schools.

McCall, Dorothy Lawson. *Ranch Under the*

Rimrock. Portland, Oregon: Binfords & Mort, 1968.

Walth, Brent. *Fire at Eden's Gate: Tom McCall and the Oregon Story*. Portland, Oregon: Oregon Historical Society Press, 1994.

► **McCullough, Condé B.** (1887–1946) C. B. McCullough was born in the Dakota Territory and earned degrees in civil engineering at Iowa State College. He came to Oregon to teach structural engineering at Oregon Agricultural College (Oregon State University) in 1916, but soon moved to Salem as the state bridge engineer. In this capacity, at a time when the state's highway construction program was growing tremendously, McCullough made a mark with his innovative and esthetically compelling designs. They included a number of concrete arch structures for the **Pacific Highway**, such as Winchester bridge over the Umpqua River, and a succession of bridges along the developing **Oregon Coast Highway**. That highway was ostensibly open in 1932, but it included six ferry crossings; by 1936, McCullough-designed spans obviated five of those, replacing them with elegant structures with distinguishing Art Deco touches. The 1936 Coos Bay bridge was named for McCullough in 1947. His bridges have proven to be enduring as well, and when saltwater deterioration forced the replacement of his bridge across the **Alsea River** in 1991, the new span carefully echoed the old.

Hadlow, Robert W. *Elegant Arches, Soaring Spans: C. B. McCullough, Oregon's Master Bridge Builder*. Corvallis: Oregon State University Press, 2001.

The Art Deco-style drawbridge at Florence was designed by C. B. McCullough to carry the Oregon Coast Highway over the Siuslaw River. It opened in 1936. Frank Patterson photo. University of Washington Libraries, Special Collections, UW2760z.

McDonald, Ranald *see* **MacDonald, Ranald**

▶ **McKenzie Pass** The route connecting the Willamette Valley with Central Oregon via the McKenzie River and McKenzie Pass was used in the 1850s. It was established as a toll road in 1872 and operated until 1894. In 1921, it opened as an automobile road.

▶ **McKenzie River** The McKenzie River rises in the Cascade Range of eastern Lane County and flows west about eighty-five miles to join the Willamette River about five miles north of Eugene. The McKenzie has long been a noted fly-fishing stream, and fishing and hunting lodges and resorts line the river. One of Oregon's most noted **covered bridges**, the Goodpasture Bridge, crosses the McKenzie River near Vida. The McKenzie drift boat, a wooden craft built in several versions in the early 1900s by Prince Helfrich and Veltie Pruitt, was refined by Woodie

"Knoble" Hindman. Hindman's 1946 design became the official symbol of the city of **Springfield** in 1985.

▶ **McLoughlin, John** (1784–1857) Born of Irish and Scotch parents in Quebec, John McLoughlin was trained in medicine, but took a position in the fur trade with the North West Company. In 1821, when the North West Company was taken over by the **Hudson's Bay Company (HBC)**, McLoughlin was in charge of Fort William on Lake Superior. In 1824, his assignment was to the post of chief factor of the HBC's Columbia District. The headquarters was then at **Fort George** at Astoria; under McLoughlin, operations were moved in 1825 to the new **Fort Vancouver**. From then until his retirement in 1846, John McLoughlin was perhaps the leading figure in the economic, social and political life of the **Oregon Country**. McLoughlin earned a reputation as a stern but fair trader and mediator, a genial host, and an astute businessman; he was called the

The forbidding lava fields of McKenzie Pass are one of the features of the highway, which opened to automobiles in 1921. This photograph taken in the 1920s shows the lava beds as well as wooden snow fences, intended to minimize snow buildup on the road. The highway is still closed by snow every winter. Ralph Eddy photograph. Steven Dotterer collection.

"great white-headed eagle" in acknowledgement of his mane of white hair and his power. He was charged by HBC to monopolize the fur trade, to work equably with local Indians, and, in the interest of preserving the fur habitat, to discourage permanent settlers.

As time went by, McLoughlin came to see the future as based on something other than furs, and he assisted settlers and missionaries with supplies and seeds and advice. The 1846 treaty that established the boundary between the United States and British territory in Canada set his future course. McLoughlin had acquired property and built a sawmill at **Oregon City**. Retiring from HBC in 1846, he became a United States citizen in 1849 and lived in Oregon City until 1857. Despite his efforts on behalf of many Americans, certain prominent parties, in some part due to his adversaries' Methodist inclinations and to his own Roman Catholicism, cheated him out of much of his Oregon City property. McLoughlin's legacy is visible at Fort Vancouver

Looking every inch the determined businessman that he was, John McLoughlin was captured in a daguerreotype photograph, probably taken about 1849. Joseph Buchtel photograph. Oregon Historical Society, OrHi 248.

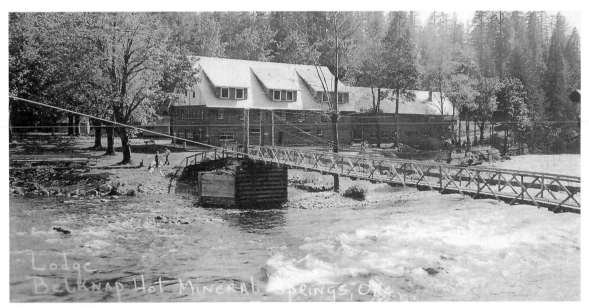

Frank and Helen Bigelow were the owners and managers of the lodge at Belknap Hot Springs on the McKenzie River when this photograph was taken about 1940. The springs had been a destination since R. S. Belknap had located them in 1869. By 1940, the resort included a hotel, a bathhouse and swimming pool, a ballroom, and a post office, all powered and illuminated by a small hydroelectric plant. Mason collection.

and at his Oregon City house, saved from destruction in 1909 through the efforts of **Eva Emery Dye** and other allies. McLoughlin's name is attached to schools, a prominent Portland street, and to **Mount McLoughlin**. A statue of McLoughlin by Gifford M. Proctor was placed in the National Statuary Hall in 1953, and in 1957, he was given the designation **Father of Oregon**.

Morrison, Dorothy Nafus. *Outpost: John McLoughlin and the Far Northwest*. Portland, Oregon: Oregon Historical Society Press, 1999.

McMinnville The county seat of Yamhill County grew around a post office established in 1855 as McMinville (with one *n*). William T. Newby, an emigrant to Oregon in 1843, settled near the site the next year, and built a gristmill; he also platted the townsite in 1853, naming it after his Tennessee birthplace. The Baptists established a small college there in 1858, which grew into **Linfield College**. The Oregon Central Railroad arrived within hailing distance in 1871, linking the area to Portland; the line was extended to McMinnville proper in 1879, and south to Corvallis in 1880. The town was incorporated in 1876, and the 1880 census showed it had a population of 670. In 1886, Yamhill County residents voted to move the county seat from **Lafayette** to McMinnville.

By 1915, McMinnville was the center of an agricultural district that raised fruit, poultry, dairy cattle, hops, sheep, and Angora goats; prunes and walnuts were produced, as was wool and mohair, and there was a milk condensary, a fruit evaporator, and a lumber-planing mill. McMinnville enjoyed frequent electric **interurban railway** service to Portland via two routes. The population reached 2,767 in 1920.

On June 9, 1950, the McMinnville *Telephone-Register* published a photograph of a purported unidentified flying object—a UFO—taken on a nearby farm by Mr. and Mrs. Paul Trent. The flying saucer incident eventually led to an annual UFO festival. The prominence of that festival was upstaged in the 1990s by the growth of the Oregon wine industry and the popularity of Oregon pinot noir wines, leading to an annual pinot noir festival in McMinnville. The city is the home of an aviation empire begun in 1960 by Delford M. Smith with Evergreen Helicopters; Smith also created the Evergreen Aviation Museum, the owner of Howard Hughes's Spruce Goose plane, as a tribute to his son. Increasingly a bedroom community of the **Silicon Forest** communities as well as a destination resort for oenophiles, McMinnville has seen its population rise from 6,635 in 1950 to 14,080 in 1980 and an estimated 31,665 in 2007.

McNary, Charles Linza (1874-1944) Born on a Marion County farm, Charles McNary graduated from Stanford University with a law degree. He moved to Salem to begin a law career, which quickly saw him serving as a deputy district attorney, as dean of the law school at Willamette University from 1906 to 1913, and then as an associate justice of the Oregon Supreme Court from 1913 to 1915. After the death of U.S. Senator **Harry Lane** in 1917, Republican McNary was appointed to complete his term, and served there until his death. McNary proved to be an advocate for irrigation and reclamation projects and farm support; as minority leader of the Senate from 1933, he supported much New Deal legislation although he sometimes clashed with President Roosevelt. McNary was the originator and sponsor of legislation to construct **Bonneville Dam**. In 1940, he was Wendell Wilkie's vice presidential candidate on the Republican ticket. McNary died in office in 1944, a national figure who had worked hard for Oregon interests. **McNary Dam** was named for him, most appropriately; a school in Keizer also recognized him.

Neal, Steve. *McNary of Oregon: A Political Biography*. Portland, Oregon: Western Imprints (Oregon Historical Society), 1985.

McNary Dam Constructed between 1947 and 1954 above the mouth of the Umatilla River, McNary

Dam is part of the Columbia River project to produce hydroelectric power, aid navigation, reduce floods, and to increase irrigation to nearby agricultural lands near **Hermiston**.

meadowlark The western meadowlark, *Sturnella neglecta*, was nominated as the state bird of Oregon by schoolchildren; their selection was ratified by the state legislature in 1927. The meadowlark is found widely across the state, particularly east of the Cascade Range, for it prefers a habitat of undisturbed grasslands or sagebrush, where it nests on the ground. The meadowlark is noted for its distinctive, melodious song and its equally distinctive appearance, characterized by a bright yellow chest and belly with a black V across the chest. Once a common sight on Willamette Valley fenceposts, the meadowlark is seen there with much less frequency since the 1970s; it has also been declining, less rapidly, in other inland valleys and in Central Oregon, impacted by development and pesticides. The Western meadowlark is found throughout much of western North America, and is also the state bird of Kansas, Montana, Nebraska, North Dakota, and Wyoming.

Medford The county seat of Jackson County is located in the **Bear Creek Valley**. It was created as a result of the construction of the **Oregon & California Railroad** through the valley, which had been settled by miners and farmers in the 1850s. The railroad bypassed the historic county metropolis of **Jacksonville**, which was sited against the foothills, when it built up the valley in 1884. Surveyor J. S. Howard laid out the townsite in 1883; the post office opened in 1884; and Medford was incorporated in 1885. It quickly became the chief trading center for the region. The 1890 census gave Medford a population of 967; it was 1,791 in 1900, and 8,840 in 1910 as the district experienced a real estate boom in orchard lands. In 1915, it was reported of Medford that the "city is well built and possesses the appearance of a metropolitan center."

Medford's economy lapsed in the 1920s as the land boom dissipated. In the Depression of the 1930s, the **Good Government Congress** disrupted local politics. Fruit culture and fruit-packing continued to anchor the economy, and companies such as **Harry and David** reached new markets. Lumber and plywood production increased in the 1940s and 1950s. Medford's population hit 17,305 in 1950, and 39,476 in 1980. The downtown area, increasingly deserted in the 1970s and 1980s as suburban shopping proliferated, rebounded somewhat during the 1990s with impetus from the successful restoration of the historic 1924 Craterian Theatre into the Craterian Ginger Rogers Theater as a community performance center. (The new name reflects the longtime association of actress Ginger Rogers with the area; she appeared on stage at the Craterian in 1926, and owned and operated a ranch north of Medford from 1940 to 1990. The name Craterian is derived from Crater Lake.) Medford's estimated population in 2007 was 75,675.

Meek, Joseph Lafayette (1810–1875) Joseph Meek was born in Virginia, and became a fur trapper in the Rockies from 1829 to 1840. A "mountain man," Joseph Meek traveled far and experienced great adventures. He settled down in 1840, taking up a land claim on the **Tualatin Plains** that year; he became active in the efforts to form a **provisional government** in 1843 and was elected the first sheriff—and tax collector; he also conducted the first census, in 1845, and served in the legislature. Meek's moment of national glory came in 1848 when he traveled to Washington, DC, to seek federal assistance following the deaths of **Marcus and Narcissa Whitman**. Meek famously described himself as "envoy extraordinary and minister plenipotentiary from the republic of Oregon to the court of the United States." The Oregon Country was since 1846 under American jurisdiction, and Meek argued for the establishment of an **Oregon Territory**. His petition was heard, Meek was appointed a U.S. marshal, and he accompanied the new territorial governor, **Joseph Lane**, back to Oregon in 1849. Meek retired to his Washington County farm in the late 1850s. In the late 1860s, historian **Frances Fuller Victor** interviewed Meek and crafted their talks into her book *The River of the West: Life and Adventure in the Rocky Mountains and Oregon* (1870).

► **Meeker, Ezra** (1830–1928) Ezra Meeker revived the **Oregon Trail** and helped boost it to legendary status. Meeker was born in Ohio and came west over the trail in 1852–53 to the Puget Sound country of Washington Territory with his new wife and child. The family settled near Puyallup in 1862, where Meeker was a very successful hops farmer. Late in his life, he became convinced that the Oregon Trail deserved recognition and preservation as an historical artifact and as a memorial to the **pioneer** American settlers. Meeker proved to be a most successful publicist: in 1906 he recreated his trek, eastbound, by ox cart, pulled by the team of Dave and Dandy, a lengthy event that was well covered by newspapers across the country. He eventually crossed the Missouri and continued until he reached the East Coast, met Theodore Roosevelt, and pushed the idea of marking the trail before Congress. After returning to Puyallup in 1908, he set off again in a **covered wagon** in 1910, this time from The Dalles, Oregon, on a similar adventure, even making a detour to San Antonio to pose in front of the Alamo; he returned in 1912. Indefatigable, Meeker subsequently covered the route by train, automobile, and, in 1924, by airplane. Along the way, he distributed postcards, thousands of which survive today. Meeker was a prolific author of books and pamphlets, about the Pacific Northwest, about the Oregon Trail, about growing hops, and about himself. Although a resident of Washington state for most of his life, Meeker was nonetheless the archetypal Oregon Country Pioneer. Dave and Dandy, preserved by taxidermy, can be seen at the Washington State Historical Museum in Tacoma.

Pictured at a farmhouse stop somewhere in Oregon, Ezra Meeker poses with his wagon tent in a photograph taken about 1913. Albert H. Barnes photograph. University of Washington Libraries, Special Collections, Barnes 1889.

Meier, Julius L. (1874–1937) Julius Meier was born in Portland to German Jewish immigrants Aaron and Jeannette (Hirsch) Meier; Aaron was a partner in the **Meier & Frank** department store. Julius Meier attended public school and graduated from the University of Oregon law school in 1895, and practiced law for several years before entering the family business. There he was the store's general manager until 1930 and subsequently its president. Meier engaged in a number of civic activities, heading the state commission for the 1915 Panama-Pacific Exposition in San Francisco and promoting Liberty Loan drives during World War I. Meier entered the political arena in 1930 after the death of his friend and former law partner George W. Joseph, who had just won the Republican nomination for governor. Meier entered the fray as an independent candidate favoring state involvement in the development of hydroelectric power from the Columbia River, a position that Joseph had espoused but which the official Republican replacement candidate opposed. It was a contentious issue; Meier won the election as governor, but had to witness federal rather than state development of the Columbia with **Bonneville Dam** as the first project; he came to support that approach. His election also seemed to override the recent appeal of the **Ku Klux Klan**, which had influenced elections in the 1920s. Meier's Depression-era administration improved the state's finances, regulated the liquor trade with the repeal of prohibition, established a state police system, and created a state unemployment commission and board of agriculture. Meier declined other political opportunities for health reasons and retired from office in 1935. His Columbia River gorge estate, Menucha, has become a favorite conference and retreat center.

Meier & Frank The full-block, thirteen-story, white terra cotta bulk of the Meier & Frank department store in downtown Portland spoke loudly of the company's large presence in retail trade. The company had its beginnings in 1857, when Aaron Meier (father of **Julius L. Meier**) began selling dry goods at a store on Front Street. Emil Frank became a partner in 1873, and the store expanded. Emil left in 1888, but his brother Sigmund (who had married Aaron Meier's daughter Fannie) joined the firm and the name remained, even after Aaron Meier's death in 1889. By 1898, the store was occupying the SW Fifth Avenue site that became their headquarters. Architect **A. E. Doyle** designed the signature building, which was erected in segments that opened in 1909, 1915, and 1930, when the entire block was occupied. From the 1910s through the 1950s, Meier & Frank, **Lipman, Wolfe & Company**, and **Olds & King** reigned as the three major shopping destinations in downtown Portland. Among the store's beloved features were the weekly Friday Surprise shopping sprees, the central information kiosk with its clock (the favorite "I'll meet you there" location in downtown), and the store window Christmas concoctions. Meier & Frank's banks of elevators were presided over by "starters": commanding women equipped with stentorian voices and clicking castanets who dispatched the crowded elevators to their various destinations. The store's Georgian Room restaurant, beloved of **James Beard**, served chicken salad to thousands of shoppers.

With downtown department stores faltering in the 1950s, Meier & Frank bought and demolished the venerable Portland Hotel to build a parking lot (it was later transformed into **Pioneer Courthouse Square**) in hopes of boosting sales. The company built its first branch store in Salem in 1955, and then one in the **Lloyd Center** in 1960. After a bitter battle, the Meier and Frank families sold the business to the May Company chain in 1966. While other stores were added, the Meier & Frank label declined over the years, and May sold it in 2005 to Federated Department Stores. Federated converted all the stores to their Macy's brand; the former flagship store was renovated and re-opened in 2007 as Macy's at Meier & Frank Square. The upper floors were converted to hotel use.

Memaloose Island Several islands in the Columbia River are named Memaloose, derived from the Chinookan word for "to die." The most prominent is in Wasco County between The Dalles and Mosier. Among the Wasco, Wishram, and other Chinookan tribes, after a period of mourning, the deceased were wrapped in a skin robe or finery and deposited with some personal belongings in a customary sepulchral structure on a bluff or island. Plank houses were common, and these islands of the dead were, unfortunately, considered by many whites to be curiosities for study or plunder in the 1870s and 1880s. Memaloose Island holds the grave of Victor Trevitt, who was buried there in 1883 with full Masonic honors. A former state printer, Trevitt is said to have declared that in the resurrection, "I'll take my chances with the Indians." The Indian graves, however, were removed to the mainland with the construction of **Bonneville Dam**. The graves from two other islands upstream were also moved before they were inundated by the waters backed up from The Dalles Dam.

Menzies, Archibald *see* **Douglas-fir; madrona**

Merrill The town of Merrill in Klamath County is named for Nathan S. Merrill who settled in the area in 1890, bought a ranch in 1894, and laid out part of the townsite. A post office named Gale was established in the area in 1890; the name was changed to Merrill in 1896. Merrill was incorporated in 1903 as the Lost River irrigation project was underway, and it developed as an agricultural center where farmers grew potatoes, alfalfa, oats, and barley. The population in 1910 was 237; by 1950, the count was 835. Merrill's estimated population in 2007 was 915.

Metolius The town of Metolius in Jefferson County is located on the **Oregon Trunk Railway**, whose construction prompted its establishment. The Oregon Trunk opened in 1911, and the Metolius post office opened in the same year. Metolius was incorporated in 1913, and the 1920 census showed a population of seventy-four. In 1940, the figure was forty, and ten years later, 157. Irrigation that came to the area in the 1940s brought in crops of mint, potatoes, and hay. The post office was discontinued in 1956, but the area began to attract residents commuting to Madras; the population reached 451 in 1980 and an estimated 850 in 2007.

Metolius River The Metolius River emerges from huge natural springs at the north base of **Black Butte** and flows north and east in Jefferson County to the Deschutes River. It is about forty miles in length.

Metro A public planning and service agency, Metro consolidates land-use planning and a variety of other regional enterprises for three counties and twenty-five cities in the Portland area. Metro began operations in 1979 with the combining of the Metropolitan Service District (MSD) with the Columbia Region Association of Governments. In 1992, a home-rule charter was approved that changed the MSD to Metro and clarified its mission to perform regional planning and policy development and provide services that enhanced the environment. Metro encompasses Clackamas, Multnomah, and Washington Counties and twenty-five incorporated cities. It is governed by an elected council. Metro operates a number of parks and historic cemeteries, deals with waste and recycling issues, and plans for sustaining fish and wildlife populations. It owns and operates the Oregon Zoo, the Oregon Convention Center, the Portland Center for Performing Arts, and Expo, an exposition center.

Mexicans in Oregon Spain once laid some claims to the **Oregon Country**, but it relinquished them by treaty in 1819. In 1821, Mexico declared its independence from Spain, with the northern boundary being the forty-second parallel, today's Oregon-

California boundary. With the end of the Mexican-American War in 1848, California became an American territory, but one with many residents of Mexican heritage. The California gold rush brought some of them north, even into Oregon, as miners and pack-train operators. Some of the terminology also came north, as the first official of gold rush **Jacksonville** was termed an alcalde, the term for mayor in Mexican California. The 1870s brought vaqueros or **buckaroos** from California and Mexico into the cattle country of southeastern Oregon. During World War I, Mexicans were recruited to come to the United States, especially for farm work; however, in 1924 the U.S. Border Patrol was formed and free travel between the nations ended. World War II brought another labor shortage, and again Mexican nationals were recruited under the bracero program, which extended into the 1950s; many Mexicans remained and an increasing number obtained citizenship. Mexican-Americans became residents in such areas as the **Treasure Valley** of eastern Oregon and western Idaho and in the Willamette Valley, particularly in Marion and Washington Counties. The Valley Migrant League formed in **Woodburn** in 1964 to improve conditions among farm workers, most of whom were Mexicans or Mexican-Americans. In 1973, Colegio César Chávez opened in **Mount Angel**. The enactment of the North American Free Trade Agreement in 1994 increased Mexican immigration. Cities such as Hillsboro, Cornelius, Woodburn, and Ontario have significant Mexican populations, and agricultural industries such as **nurseries** and fruit orchards employ thousands of Mexican-Americans in Oregon.

Gamboa, Erasmo. *Mexican Labor and World War II: Braceros in the Pacific Northwest, 1942–1947.* Austin: University of Texas Press, 1990.

Gamboa, Erasmo. Mexican Mule Packers and Oregon's Second Regiment Mounted Volunteers, 1855–1856. *Oregon Historical Quarterly* 92, no. 1 (Spring 1991): 41–59.

Meyer, Fred G. (1886–1978) Born Frederick Grubmeyer in Brooklyn, New York, in a family of grocers, Fred Meyer changed his name and went west in 1905. He adventured in Alaska for a few years, sold coffee by wagon and in Portland storefronts, and in 1922 opened a grocery store near the downtown **public market**. Meyer opened other grocery stores near public markets in Astoria and in the **Hollywood neighborhood** in the 1920s, and in 1931 opened the first of his one-stop shopping centers in Hollywood. A hard-working and plain-speaking man, Fred built **Fred Meyer Stores** into a retail empire in Portland and Oregon, with great support from his wife, Eve. Personally frugal, Meyer supported local community projects with his money, and he was known to finance new business ventures in problematic times. His estate founded the Meyer Memorial Trust, one of Oregon's first major family charitable trusts.

Mill City Located on the North Santiam River in Marion County, Mill City's name states its purpose and encompasses its history. A sawmill was opened there in 1887, and in 1888 a post office was established and a railroad arrived, connecting Mill City with the outer world. In 1915, Mill City was said to have a population of about 500 persons, who were engaged in "lumbering, general farming and fruit growing." Mill City was not incorporated until 1947, as construction began on **Detroit Dam** farther upriver. The 1950 census showed a population of 1,792. Mill City's population in 1970 was 1,451; the estimate for 2007 was 1,620.

Miller, Joaquin (Cincinnatus Hiner) (1837–1913) Joaquin Miller, the "Poet of the Sierras," lived an adventurous life, and as a writer he made sure that his public was aware of that fact. He was born to a Quaker family in Indiana; in 1852, they took the Oregon Trail, and settled on a farm near Eugene. Miller set off for the California gold fields in 1855; he mined and mingled (he married a young girl named Paquita) with the **Modoc Indians** in northern California, and, the *Oregon Blue Book* noted, "had several altercations with the law over matters relating to the ownership of livestock and gunplay." Returning to Eugene, he attended college and studied law, then carried express in the Idaho gold fields, and edited the Eugene *Democratic Register* during the Civil War. His editorial views appeared to defend the Confederacy, and the paper was barred from the U.S. mails, so Miller sold it and moved to **Port Orford**. There he met and married Theresa Dyer, daughter of a local politico and a competent poet who wrote under the pen name Minnie Myrtle. Ever footloose, Miller headed for another gold rush at **Canyon City** in 1864, driving a herd of cattle on the way, then setting up a law practice, writing his own poetry (*Specimens*, 1868), planting an orchard, and serving as a Grant County judge from 1866 to 1870. In 1870, he ditched Minnie Myrtle Miller and his three children and crossed the Atlantic, where he became a literary lion from the frontier American West and his book of poems *Songs of the Sierras* was published to great acclaim in 1871. He subsequently traveled widely in Europe and Asia, lived in San Francisco, New York City, and Washington, DC, and then settled in Oakland, California, from 1885 to 1897; then, as the *Oregon Blue Book* noted, "Oakland remained his home intermittently until his death in 1913." Among his works is *Life amongst the Modocs: Unwritten History* (London, England: R. Bentley, 1873).

Frost, O. W. *Joaquin Miller.* New York: Twayne Publishers, 1967.

Millersburg The town of Millersburg, incorporated in 1974, came into legal existence in order to prevent the adjacent city of **Albany** from placing some of the area's industrial plants within its city limits and thereby—egad!—taxing them. The Wah Chang Corporation—since owned by Teledyne—operated a zirconium processing plant there, and **Weyerhaeuser** had several wood-products plants, including a paper mill. Since the 1960s, travelers on Interstate 5 have known Millersburg for its foul odors and wafting industrial vapors. Its estimated 2007 population was 1,030. No postal address exists for Millersburg; Albany is the postal name.

Milton-Freewater This Umatilla County town is on the Walla Walla River, a few miles south of Walla Walla, Washington. It was created in 1950 with the merger of the two communities of Milton and Freewater; the visible nucleus of each has survived. Milton grew up around a rural post office, established in 1873 and named by the first postmaster, W. A. Cowl, for his New York state birthplace. Freewater, immediately north of Milton, derived from an 1889 townsite first named New Walla Walla, and changed to Freewater in 1890. Geographic names historian Lewis L. McArthur reported that both the town and its name may have been a response to a local liquor **prohibition** ordinance in Milton. The construction of a branch railroad line from Pendleton to Walla Walla in 1887 helped promote agricultural development in the area, and by 1915, Milton hosted a flouring mill and three fruit-packing plants, while Freewater boasted of its orchards of apples, peaches, and prunes; Freewater had a bank, while Milton had two banks. Since World War II, the area has been a center for growing **peas** for freezing and canning, and since the 1990s, growing grapes for **wine** has also advanced. In 1920, the two towns had a combined population of 2,411, with hourly electric **interurban railway** service to Walla Walla. By 1950, there were 3,851 residents; the 2007 estimated population was 6,550. A promotional slogan unveiled in 2003 designated the area as the Muddy Frogwater Country; this has led the town to become obsessed with frog motifs.

Miluk Indians *see* **Coos Indians**

Milwaukie Milwaukie, sited on the Willamette River in Clackamas County, was an early townsite rival of Portland. It was founded in 1847 by Lot Whitcomb (1807–1857), who came there with **Henderson Luelling**. At Milwaukie, Whitcomb built a sawmill and gristmill, and he built boats: coastal sailing ships and the first steamboat constructed on the Willamette, the eponymous *Lot Whitcomb*. Some 500 people were resident in Milwaukie by 1850, and a post office was established that year. But Milwaukie quickly faded as a major port, though it was noted in the late nineteenth century as the site of **Seth Lewelling**'s fabled nursery, where the Bing cherry was developed. It was also the home of another horticulturist, Joseph H. Lambert, developer of the Lambert cherry. Milwaukie's first step to suburbia came in 1893 with the opening of an electric **interurban railway** through Milwaukie, connecting Oregon City with Portland. The town was incorporated as a municipality in 1903; by 1910, its reported population was 860. In 1915, Milwaukie was reported to be a rich agricultural area of "small fruit culture and small farming," and the grange was an active enterprise. The town's population reached 1,871 in the 1940 census, after the development in the 1930s of Highway 99E, known locally as "the superhighway." After World War II, Milwaukie expanded dramatically in area and population, and agricultural pursuits diminished. Its 1970 population was 16,444; the 2007 estimate was 20,920.

Minam River Rising in the Eagle Cap Wilderness of the Wallowa Mountains, the Minam River flows about thirty miles northwesterly to join the Wallowa River near the town of Minam. Remote and roadless, the stream is a designated Wild and Scenic River.

Minnesota Freeway The section of the **Interstate 5** freeway extending from its intersection with Interstate 84 in Portland, north to the Columbia River, was known in its early phases in the 1960s as the Minnesota Freeway. This was not because its destination was Minnesota, but because the alignment followed that of N. Minnesota Avenue, and its route excised that street from the map.

Mist *see* **Columbia County**

Mitchell The rural community of Mitchell in Wheeler County developed around a post office established in 1873 to serve local ranchers. It is named for the infamous **John Hipple Mitchell**. Mitchell townsite was platted in 1885, and it was incorporated in 1891. Much of the town burned in 1899, and it was battered by two floods in 1904. By 1915, the area around Mitchell was devoted to "general farming (particularly hay and grain for home consumption), and livestock, cattle, horses, sheep (wool) and hogs. Three crops of alfalfa [are] raised on irrigated land. Fruits of the hardier varieties do well; also peaches and apricots in sheltered spots." Mitchell's population has been rather stable over the years: 210 in 1910; 219 in 1940; 196 in 1970; and an estimated 175 in 2007.

Mitchell, John Hipple (1835–1905) John H. Mitchell was born as John M. Hipple; he was educated in Pennsylvania, where he taught school, studied law, and was admitted to the bar in 1857. He left for California and Oregon, arriving in Portland in 1860 where he took up the practice of law. In Portland, he began a long and controversial political career that brought national attention to Oregon, much of it adverse. Mitchell, a Republican, was elected to the Oregon state senate, serving from 1862 to 1866 and as president of the senate in the last term. He was an unsuccessful candidate for U.S. Senate in 1866, but he tried again in 1872 and took the prize, serving from 1873 to 1879. Before he was seated, opponents charged Mitchell with bigamy, desertion, and living under an assumed name (he had indeed left a wife and child back East under the surname Hipple, but the Senate declined to investigate). He was not re-elected in 1882, but he picked up part of another term in 1885 and was then re-elected, serving until 1897, when again his re-election failed. In Portland, he resumed the practice of law, and then was again sent to the Senate from 1901 until his death. During this period Mitchell was implicated in the sale of fraudulent **land grant** properties. As the office of the Senate historian noted, "at the time of his death, [Mitchell] had been indicted and convicted of having received fees for expediting the land claims of clients before the United States Land Commissioner and an appeal was pending." It is worth remembering that at this time, it was not the electorate but the Oregon legislature that elected U.S. senators; it took **William S. U'Ren** to fix that problem.

Mitchell Point Tunnel *see* **Columbia River Highway**

Modoc Indians The homeland of the Modoc Indians was in the Klamath Basin, encompassing Lower Klamath Lake, Tule Lake, and the Langell Valley in Oregon and California. The patterns of life for the Modoc closely resembled those of the **Klamath Indians** to the north. Fishing was a more seasonal activity, since the Modoc depended on the suckers found in the lakes and marshes and did not have direct access to the runs of salmon on the Klamath River. Like the Klamath, the Modoc gathered **camas**, lily seeds, and the eggs of waterfowl, hunted for elk and deer, and harvested berries and nuts to supplement their diet. Housing was typically in semi-underground lodges topped by plank and mat roofs during the winter, and temporary summer lodges of mats and brush.

The Modoc met Euro-American trappers in the 1820s, and like the Klamath they soon acquired horses. The **Southern Emigrant Road** crossed their lands in 1846, and some altercations occurred with travelers. Ranchers coveted the Klamath Basin lands in the 1860s, and in 1864 the Modoc and the Klamath signed a treaty that created the Klamath Reservation. Many Modoc were not pleased with the

arrangement. An earlier treaty had granted them land in the Tule Lake region; though it was unratified, many Modoc believed it was, and should be, valid. The conflict led to the **Modoc War**. Those Modoc involved in the war were not allowed to return to Oregon until after 1909; their descendants are among the members of the reconstituted Klamath Tribes, which include the Klamath, the Modoc, and the Yahooskin band of the Northern Paiute Indians.

Modoc War The dissatisfaction of a number of members of the **Modoc Indian** tribes with life on the Klamath Reservation induced some of them to leave the reservation and attempt to return to their traditional homeland in the vicinity of Tule Lake, California. Negotiations failed to persuade a group of Modoc men and families under the leadership of Captain Jack to return to the reservation, and a brief armed conflict sent the group into the tortuous lava beds south of Tule Lake, where they formed a stronghold late in 1872. The U.S. Army attempted to remove them with a force of several hundred men in battle, but failed. Negotiations then ended in disaster with the assassination of Gen. E. R. S. Canby and the Rev. E. Thomas at a meeting to discuss a peaceful settlement; the army resumed its assault. In the end, the Modoc surrendered in the spring of 1873; Captain Jack and three other leaders were hanged, while two more were sent to federal prison. The remainder of the renegade band—thirty-nine men, sixty-four women, sixty children—were sent to Indian Territory (Oklahoma). After 1909, they were allowed to return to Oregon, although many stayed. In the course of the war, the Modoc had no more than fifty-three warriors; the army strength reached 530 troops. Seventeen Modoc died in the conflict, including those hanged; the army lost fifty-two troops. It was a costly and bloody war that came to a tragic conclusion.

Murray, Keith A. *The Modocs and their War*. Norman: University of Oklahoma Press, 1959.

Molala Indians The Molala or Molalla Indians occupied an extensive area in the foothills on both sides of the Cascade Range from Mount Hood in the north to Mount McLoughlin in the south. The Molala relied on elk and deer as primary food sources, and also hunted other small mammals and birds. They supplemented their diet with salmon and steelhead; **camas**, tarweed seeds, hazelnuts, and huckleberries. The Molala traded with the Klamath Indians to the south and with Chinookan tribes to the north. Winter villages at lower elevations consisted of semi-subterranean houses finished with bark walls and a gabled roof topped with poles and covered with bark slabs. The summer dwellings, temporary shelters, were often huts of bark and poles or shelter made of mats and boughs. The Molala had horses by the 1820s and 1830s, and occasional conflicts with white settlers occurred in the 1840s. Never a large tribe, they were much reduced by introduced diseases in the 1830s. Treaties in 1855 removed the Molala to the **Grand Ronde Reservation**; some, however, went to the Klamath Reservation and some others to Siletz or remained outside the reservation system. The Molala are a constituent of the **Confederated Tribes of Grand Ronde**.

Molalla The community is named for the Molalla River, which takes its name in turn from the **Molala Indians**. The Molalla Prairie area in Clackamas County attracted white agricultural settlers in the 1840s, and there was a rural post office named Molalla in 1850–51, again in 1868–74, and once more and continuing from 1875. Attracted by the timber resources, a branch railroad from Canby came to town in 1913, and the town was incorporated in the same year. The town's signature public event, the Molalla Buckeroo rodeo, dates its inception from that year as well, born in the celebration that welcomed the railroad; the Molalla Buckeroo Association was formed in 1923. (The Molalla event includes a word play on the term "**buckaroo**.") By the 1910s, the town's economy was based on "dairy-ing, clover seed, stock raising, lumbering and general farming. Pears, prunes and cherries." The railroad connections boosted timber production in Molalla in the 1920s and 1930s. Some timber operations continued, but since the 1970s, Molalla has been increasingly a residential city; its population in 2007 was estimated at 6,830.

▶ **Monmouth** A group of Disciples of Christ emigrants arrived in Polk County, Oregon Territory, in 1853 from Monmouth, Illinois, with the aim of establishing a college and a town. They set to their task. Monmouth College was initially funded from the sale of lots after a townsite was surveyed in 1855. A post office opened in 1859, and in the same year the town of Monmouth was incorporated. The college struggled to survive; in 1865 it merged with a similar nearby institution, Bethel College, to become Christian College. The college evolved into the public Oregon State Normal School in 1882; it has survived, sometimes precariously, as **Western Oregon University**, the chief industry of Monmouth. The college and its religious heritage contributed mightily to Monmouth's status as a **prohibition** town: no liquor allowed. That status began in the nineteenth century, continued through Oregon's statewide prohibition beginning in 1916, and continued beyond the national repeal of 1934. Monmouth was the last "dry" town on the Pacific Coast when it was ended by popular vote in 2002; previous efforts to repeal the law had failed more because of the perceived civic novelty of the situation than because it was effective at (or that it was thought desirable to effect) preventing anyone from buying liquor, which was easily available two miles away in **Independence**. Supported by the college and farming, and since the 1970s increasingly a bedroom community for Salem commuters, Monmouth recorded a population of 606 in 1900, 582 in 1920, rising to 1,956 in 1950; it jumped to 5,237 in 1970, and was an estimated 9,335 in 2007.

Jansson, Kyle R. The Changing Climate of Ore-

11. Oregon State Normal School. Monmouth, Or.

This panorama of Monmouth depicts Oregon State Normal School—later Western Oregon University—as it appeared in 1909. The central building is Campbell Hall; the tower collapsed in the Columbus Day storm of 1962. In the foreground is the small train of the Independence & Monmouth Railway, which connected the two towns from 1890 until 1918. Steven Dotterer collection.

gon's Driest Town. *Oregon Historical Quarterly* 102 (2001): 337–51.

► **Monroe** The town of Monroe lies in Benton County along the **Long Tom River** in a fertile area that was settled in the 1850s. A rural post office in the area called Starr's Point opened in 1852; the name was changed to Monroe in 1874, in honor of the former president. A farming town for many decades, Monroe was poised for greater things in the early 1900s, when railroads and logging operations came to town. A railroad from Corvallis to Eugene through Monroe was opened in 1913, preceded by several rail lines west of Monroe into the Coast Range timberlands. Monroe was incorporated as a city in 1914, when it had a population of about 400 people and could boast a weekly newspaper, a bank, a sawmill, flour mills, a creamery, a fruit and vege-table cannery, and a brick and tile factory. But great growth did not come; Monroe's population in the 1920 census was 191, and it reached 362 by 1950. The brick and tile works was a mainstay for many

years, but industry has left Monroe. Its estimated population in 2007 was 625.

Monroe, Anne Shannon (1877–1942) Journalist and author Anne Shannon Monroe wrote for newspapers in Tacoma, Washington, and in Chicago, and for magazines such as the *Saturday Evening Post*. At a time when this was a new and unsettling idea, she wrote advice on *Making a Business Woman* (1912), and in 1926 penned some uplifting thoughts that went through many editions in *Singing in the Rain: The Famous Heart to Heart Talks That Have Helped Thousands*. She wrote several books that speak to Oregon. Among them are a novel of romance and struggle on a water-starved homestead (*Happy Valley: A Story of Oregon*, 1916; reissued in 1991), and a rendition of **Bill Hanley**'s autobiography, *Feelin' Fine!* (1930). She lived in Lake Grove.

Montavilla neighborhood, Portland Montavilla is a real estate concoction, the name a blending of **Mount Tabor** and "villa." The community sprang up on marginal farmland east of Portland, land that in the 1890s was beginning to be subdivided for residential use. The construction of bridges across the Willamette River, beginning in 1888, was joined by the construction of suburban railroads in the service of this movement. Two such railroads reached the area in the vicinity of SE Eightieth Avenue and Stark and Glisan Streets in the early 1890s, each powered by small steam locomotives. The Montavilla post office was opened in 1891, and by 1899, both suburban lines were electrified and offered fast, inexpensive transit to downtown Portland. As the city expanded eastward, Montavilla was absorbed within it; the post office name was discontinued in 1902.

Monument The town of Monument is on the North Fork John Day River in Grant County. "It was named for a peculiar rock or mountain nearby, which resembles a pulpit or rostrum," said geographic names expert Lewis L. McArthur. This was initially a rural post office that opened in 1874 to serve local ranchers and stockmen, around which a small settlement grew. The town was incorporated in 1905, and the 1910 census gave it a population of 119. In 1950, it was 228, while the 2007 estimate is 135 residents. An unusually favorable microclimate has fostered commercial orchards of peaches and other fruit since the 1930s, especially near Kimberly, a few miles west of Monument.

Moorhouse, Thomas Leander "Lee" (1850–1926) A multifaceted character in eastern Oregon for several decades, Thomas Leander "Lee" Moorhouse was born in Iowa and came west with his family in 1861. Headquartered after 1874 in **Pendle-**

The kilns at the Monroe Tile Company in Monroe as they looked on September 3, 1961. The works were a major employer in the town for many decades. Robert L. Hacker photograph. Oregon Historical Society, OrHi 1300.

ton, Moorhouse was a businessman who indulged in retail trade, real estate, insurance, ranching, and mining, took a great interest in civic affairs (mayor of Pendleton, treasurer, surveyor), was agent on the Umatilla Reservation in 1889–91, and served as assistant adjunct general of the Oregon State Militia, which gave him the title Major, which he greatly appreciated. Most importantly, Major Moorhouse took up the practice of photography in 1897, and between then and 1916, he amassed some 9,000 images of eastern Oregon life, most especially of its Native people. Many of the images were made by other photographers, and appropriated by Moorhouse. A dedicated amateur of the art, he used dry plate glass negatives and large-format cameras; despite his amateur standing, Moorhouse photographs appeared on postcards and in publications, including souvenir books that he issued himself. His unstudied portraits of **Umatilla** and **Cayuse Indians** on and off the reservation constitute his most important legacy. Early in the twenty-first century, the University of Oregon—which holds the largest collection of Moorhouse photographs—began working with the **Confederated Tribes of the Umatilla Indian Reservation** to identify the hundreds of unnamed individuals photographed by Moorhouse.

Grafe, Steve L. Lee Moorhouse: Photographer of the Inland Empire. *Oregon Historical Quarterly* 98, no. 4 (Winter 1997–98): 426–477.

Moro The county seat of Sherman County; there should be no confusion with nearby Morrow County. The very name of Moro is frustrating to contemplate. McArthur's *Oregon Geographic Names* states: "There are several stories as to how the town got its name. One version is that Judge O. M. Scott, who formerly lived in that place, named it for Moro, Illinois. Another version is that it was named for [the] Moore Brothers, who were interested in the townsite. Still another story is that it was named Moro for the Moors, which seems unlikely to the compiler. The reader may choose."

The community arose from a trading post established by Henry Barnum about 1879, as wheat farming was beginning on the Columbia Plateau. Sherman County was split off from Wasco County in 1889, and the first county seat was the town of Wasco; by 1891, it was repositioned in Moro. The growing wheat traffic gave rise to a branch railroad south from the Union Pacific Railroad mainline, which reached Moro in 1899. This perhaps helped induce municipal incorporation, which happened the same year. The new courthouse opened in 1899, too. The weekly *Sherman County Journal*, founded in 1931, was the last Oregon newspaper printed by traditional letterpress printing, which ceased in 1997.

The railroad was abandoned in 1966, but Moro is located on **Highway 97**, which has developed since the 1970s into a major throughway connecting California with the inland Pacific Northwest. Wheat farming is still the major—now, virtually the only—enterprise in Sherman County. Moro's population in 1900 was 335; in 2007, it was 380.

Morris, Carl A. (1911–1993) Modern abstract impressionist painter Carl Morris was born in California and studied in Chicago and Paris. During the Depression, he headed the Federal Art Project office in Spokane, Washington; there he met his future wife, Hilda Grossman (Deutsch). Carl and **Hilda Morris** moved to Seattle in 1940, then to Eugene and finally Portland. Both had strong art connections in the East, but remained in Oregon. Carl Morris's abstract oil paintings, often of landscapes, especially of eastern Oregon and of the high desert country, can be seen in many museums; he also did a mural for the Eugene post office in 1941.

Johnson, Barry, and John S. Weber. *Carl Morris: Paintings 1939-1992.* Catalog of an exhibition at Portland Art Museum, September 28–November 14, 1993. Portland, Oregon: Portland Art Museum, 1993.

Morris, Hilda (1911–1991) Born in New York City, Hilda Grossman moved to Spokane, Washington in 1938, where she taught sculpture at the Federal Art Project Center. There she met and married **Carl Morris**; by the time of their sojourn in Seattle in 1940–41, Hilda had gained international recognition for her sculptures. In Portland, she worked in clay, in steel and cement, and in bronze, and also did watercolors and sumi-ink drawings. Art critic Sue Taylor has described her "monumental bronze," "Ring of Time" (1967), as a distillation from the study of a South Asian bronze in the Portland Art Museum that Morris reshaped into "the giant, craggy form of a Mobius strip" with connotations of Shiva, "a yawning vortex and potent metaphor, at once the mouth of the womb and the face of death." It is a compelling piece; it is sited at an insurance company building.

Guenther, Bruce, and Susan Fillin-Yeh. *Hilda Morris.* Catalog of an exhibition at the Portland Art Museum, April 15–July 16, 2006. Portland, Oregon: Portland Art Museum; Seattle: University of Washington Press, 2006.

Morrow County In 1885, the western portion of Umatilla County and a snip of eastern Wasco County were joined to create Morrow County. It has an area of 2,049 square miles. The name honors Jackson Lee Morrow, a settler in the area and a member of the Oregon legislature when the county was established. The temporary county seat was named as **Heppner**, and an election in 1886 confirmed that town over the rival town of Lexington. A frame building was erected to serve as the courthouse; this was torn down in 1902 and in 1903 was replaced by the still-standing structure, designed by Portland architect Edgar M. Lazarus and constructed of native-quarried bluestone with sandstone trim.

The area now Morrow County was in the resource territory of the **Sahaptin Indians** at the western portions, and part of the homeland of the **Umatilla** and **Cayuse Indians**. The Columbia River provided salmon and sturgeon; the high plains south of the river supported luxuriant fields of bunchgrass, useful for grazing horses.

The transcontinental railroad crossed Morrow County's northern edge in 1882; a branch line south to Ione, Lexington, and Heppner followed in 1888. Morrow County's population in 1890 was 4,205. Cattle grazing on the natural pasturelands was the first economic activity, but was supplanted by wheat ranching and other pursuits early in the twentieth century. By 1915, it was noted that "the broad wheat fields are the most interesting feature of Morrow County scenery." The county's population peaked in 1920 at 5,617; in 1970, it stood at 4,465. However, the developments of a coal-fired power plant and an industrial-sized dairy near **Boardman** have helped fuel population growth along **Interstate 84**. The population reached 7,625 in 1990 and an estimated 12,335 in 2007.

French, Giles. *Homesteads and Heritages: A History of Morrow County, Oregon.* Portland, Oregon: Binfords & Mort for the Morrow County History Committee, 1971.

▶ **Morse, Wayne Lyman** (1900–1974) Wayne Morse was born and reared in Wisconsin, where he was an academic standout in speech, economics, and law. In 1929, he received the JD from Columbia University Law School; he took a position at the University of Oregon Law School and within a year was dean of the school. Morse began practicing labor arbitration, earning the respect of both labor and management for his fairness. He held a number of positions on labor-related boards and commissions through World War II.

Morse was elected to the U.S. Senate as a Republican in 1944; he was re-elected as an independent in 1950, and then as a Democrat in 1956 and 1962. In the Senate, Morse was a tireless advocate of civil rights and a supporter of programs for education and international law. Morse was a loud and influential critic of the Vietnam War, one of the two

Senator Wayne Morse in a characteristic pose, about 1950. Oregon Historical Society, OrHi 65704.

senators who opposed the Gulf of Tonkin Resolution that authorized U.S. intervention. A maverick who announced his principles and stuck with them, he attracted both enmity and respect; he was tagged the Conscience of the Senate as well as the Loneliest Man in Washington. His relations with his Oregon colleague in the Senate in the 1950s, **Richard Neuberger**, were often stormy, despite their political alliances. Morse was defeated in the 1968 election by Robert Packwood; re-election eluded him, and he died during the campaign of 1974. The Wayne Morse Ranch Historical Park in Eugene—he and his wife, Mildred, raised horses at what they called Edgewood Farm—is on the National Register of Historic Places.

> Drukman, Mason. *Wayne Morse: A Political Biography*. Portland, Oregon: Oregon Historical Society Press, 1997.

Mosier The family of J. H. Mosier settled on a land claim about 1853–54 where Mosier Creek meets the Columbia River in Wasco County, and the valley to the south was settled in the 1850s as well. The construction of the transcontinental railroad along the river in 1882 led to the establishment of the Mosier post office in 1884. Mosier was incorporated in 1914, and a 1915 promotional booklet noted that the area grew apples, peaches, pears, prunes, and cherries, with the growers having the "advantage of early ripening and market conditions, due to low elevation and favorable climate." The **Columbia River Highway** passed through the town, and the Mosier Twin Tunnels were one of the engineering landmarks of the highway. Mosier counted 259 residents in the 1920 census; in 1990, the count was 244. Retirement dwellers have contributed to a population influx since 2000; the estimated count in 2007 was 470 residents.

mosquito fleet The term "mosquito fleet" can be found along many coastlines, referring to small boats in great quantity. In Oregon, it was used in the Astoria area, at the mouth of the Columbia River, to refer to the small, sail-powered gillnet vessels of the 1880s to the early 1900s, sometimes called the "butterfly fleet" from the shape of the two sails. It also was used to describe the collection of steam- and (later) gas- or diesel-powered, passenger and freight vessels that connected Astoria with isolated canneries, mills, and towns such as **Hammond** and the Washington communities of Altoona and Deep River; these operated from the 1870s into the 1930s.

A similar collection of passenger- and freight-carrying launches and steamboats operated in **Coos County** from North Bend and Coos Bay to Charleston, Empire, Allegany, and Isthmus Slough, as well as connecting the two towns. The fleet disappeared with extensive road development before 1930.

Mother Joseph of the Sacred Heart (1823–1902) In 1856, Mother Joseph and four other nuns of the Sisters of Providence arrived at **Fort Vancouver**. The sisters proceeded to open a school, hospital and orphanage in Vancouver, and soon spread their activities throughout the Pacific Northwest, under the direction of Mother Joseph—who was also a competent architect who planned the order's early buildings. The order opened Saint Vincent Hospital in Portland in 1875 (designed by Mother Joseph), and Sacred Heart Hospital in Medford in 1911, and eventually a number of other charitable institutions. Mother Joseph's efforts have evolved into the Providence Health System.

Mother of Oregon As designated by the state legislature in 1987: **Tabitha Brown**. *See also* **Father of Oregon**.

mountain beaver *see* **beaver**

mountain lion *see* **cougar**

Mount Angel Situated in a farming area of Marion County, the town of Mount Angel had its beginnings in the early 1880s. George Settlemire and Benjamin Cleaver held property at the base of Graves Butte; Settlemire platted a townsite called Frankfort in 1881, which Cleaver acquired and renamed Roy; the Roy post office operated in 1882–83. The narrow gauge Oregonian Railway was constructed through the area in 1880. Meanwhile, Father Adelhelm Odermatt, who had served several Catholic parishes in the Willamette Valley, built a pilgrimage chapel atop Graves Butte (also known as Lone Butte and by a few other names), which he called Mount Angel. The small community quickly adopted the name as well; Mount Angel post office was established in 1883, and in 1884 the Benedictine Sisters moved there and established the Queen of Angels monastery, still a landmark in the town. It should be noted that Father Odermatt had trained at a seminary in Engelberg, Switzerland; Engelberg means "Mount Angel." The butte itself became the site of other Catholic activities including Mount Angel Abbey and Mount Angel College, and it has its own post office, Saint Benedict, established in 1914.

The abbey library, designed by the noted Finnish architect Alvar Aalto, opened in 1970.

The town of Mount Angel developed as an agricultural center, with many of the nearby farmers being of German Catholic background. It was incorporated as a municipality in 1893; the 1900 census gave it a population of 537. By 1915, the area was noted for its fruit raising and dairying, and an electric interurban railway connected Mount Angel with Oregon City and Portland. Mount Angel Normal School developed in the 1920s to train women as teachers; in 1947 it became Mount Angel Women's College. The school became coeducational in 1957, but encountered enrollment and financial problems in the 1960s. In 1973, Mount Angel College transformed itself into Colegio César Chávez, the first accredited four-year Chicano school in the nation. The Willamette Valley near Mount Angel had become home to many Mexican-Americans after World War II. Colegio César Chávez was a brave experiment in educating Mexican-Americans in a college-without-walls environment. Chávez himself visited the school in 1974. It closed, again a victim of financial and enrollment problems, in 1983.

Mount Angel had an estimated population of 3,755 in 2007.

Mount Ashland Located in the Siskiyou Mountains in Jackson County, Mount Ashland has an elevation of 7,533 feet. Long known as Ashland Peak, Mount Ashland is the watershed for the city of Ashland. In 1963, a small ski area was developed with a lodge and lifts, heavily financed by local businessman **Glenn Jackson**. It remained a local facility until the early 1980s, when extensive chair lifts and night lighting were added; snow, however, was not always forthcoming, and the resort has since gone through several financial crises while continuing to expand, despite stress on the water supply and other responsibilities accruing to the owner of the property, Rogue River-Siskiyou National Forest.

Mount Bachelor Standing 9,065 feet in elevation in Deschutes County, Mount Bachelor is not far from the **Three Sisters**, and the name is a play on that. According to geographic names historian Lewis L. McArthur, it might once have been known as Brother Jonathan—which is itself a moniker for the United States. Until the 1970s, the peak was known as Bachelor Butte. A ski area was developed on the butte in 1957–58 by Bill Healy and others, and its success led to, as McArthur noted, the circumstances whereby "commercial interests succeeded in replacing a fine, old, euphonious name with a commonplace form."

> Lucas, Peggy Chesman. *Mt. Bachelor: Bill Healy's Dream*. Bend, Oregon: Maverick Publications, 1970.

Mount Hood (community) The rural community of Mount Hood is situated in Hood River County about three miles from the town of Parkdale. A post office with the name Hood River opened in 1890; the nearby Parkdale post office opened in 1910, after the completion of the Mount Hood Railroad from the city of Hood River. The post office department consolidated the post offices in 1976, resulting in the odd-looking official postal name of Mount Hood Parkdale. Using either name separately is not acceptable to the USPS, nor is it acceptable to place a hyphen between the two names. The ZIP code is 97041.

Mount Hood (landmass) The imposing summit of Mount Hood, the highest mountain in Oregon and the fourth highest in the **Cascade Range**, is 11,249 feet in height. The dormant volcano straddles Clackamas and Hood River Counties. The term "Wy'east" has often been applied to Mount Hood, with the assertion that this is an Indian name for it, but there is little to substantiate the legend; still, it has a pleasant ring to it, and The Dalles has chosen to use it to name a school. The mountain has been a beacon for climbers and hikers; **Joel Palmer** went up it in 1845. The first recorded successful ascent was on August 6, 1857; **Henry L. Pittock** was among the victorious group. The first major resort was **Cloud Cap Inn** on the northern slope, opened in 1889; other recreational hotels and cabins developed on the western slope above the town of **Sandy**, at **Government Camp**, and in the 1930s at **Timberline Lodge**, which was developed as a ski resort; several others have been created since. Mount Hood has twelve glaciers, and still exhibits signs of the volcanism that created it in several hot and foul-smelling vents near the summit.

Mount Hood Freeway The uproar over this proposed but unbuilt freeway was the proximate cause for the construction of Portland's **MAX** light-rail system. The freeway was intended to head east from **Interstate 5**'s Marquam Bridge along the route of **Highway 26** (SE Powell Boulevard) through Gresham to Sandy, with a connection to **Interstate 84**. The project, formally proposed in 1962 but discussed in the 1950s, would have smashed through several well-established residential neighborhoods and removed about 1 percent of the city's housing stock. Portland mayor Neil Goldschmidt and governor **Robert Straub** were instrumental in not only canceling the freeway but also in getting federal funds shifted to transit—then a revolutionary accomplishment. The legacy of the aborted freeway includes MAX as well as a series of odd parking lots along Powell Boulevard (the result of early land acquisitions) and some bizarre protrusions from the Marquam Bridge (the leads to the unbuilt connecting ramps).

Mount Howard *see* **Howard, Oliver O.; Wallowa Lake**

Mount Jefferson Mount Jefferson is the second-highest peak in Oregon at 10,497 feet in elevation. It is located in the **Cascade Range** in Linn County, and is one of the oldest volcanoes in the region. It is a difficult peak to climb, with a 400-foot rocky pinnacle at the top. It was first ascended in 1888. Meriwether Lewis of the Lewis and Clark Expedition applied the name on March 30, 1806.

Mount Mazama This Cascade Range mountain in Klamath County is but a fragment of its original self, albeit a magnificent fragment. **Crater Lake** fills the caldera of this now-extinct volcano, which exploded with tremendous force about 7,700 years ago (estimated at 5677 BCE, give or take 150 years). Members of the mountaineering club known as the **Mazamas**, who were on their annual group trek, named the vanished mountain on August 21, 1896.

Mount McLoughlin One of the volcanic peaks of the **Cascade Range** in Jackson County, Mount McLoughlin was named for Dr. **John McLoughlin** in 1905. It is 9,495 feet in elevation, and is a prominent landmark from the **Bear Creek Valley**. A variety of names have been applied to the peak, including Big Butte, Snowy Butte, and Mount Pitt. Longtime southern Oregon residents often persist in calling it Mount Pitt, a name which apparently derives from the presence of pits used by local Indians to trap large game; the extra *t* adds a note of class.

Mount Saint Helens Located in Washington state, this Cascade Range volcano erupted explosively at 8:32 a.m. on May 18, 1980, after months of activity suggested an eventual event. Fifty-seven people died, and the ensuing storm of volcanic ash blanketed much of the Pacific Northwest. An almost perfect conical form, the mountain had an elevation of 9,677 feet; after the eruption, the somewhat craggy remains reached but 8,363 feet in height.

Mount Tabor neighborhood, Portland Mount Tabor, elevation 612 feet, is a small extinct volcanic cinder cone in southeast Portland. A forest fire burned through the surrounding countryside in 1846, and Dr. Perry and Elizabeth Prettyman established a land claim on the west side of Mount Tabor

about 1849; their son David Prettyman took a claim to the east. The cinder cone received the name Mount Tabor in 1853 from Plympton Kelly, the son of Rev. Clinton Kelly, another neighbor to the south. These families were among those who established the Mount Tabor Methodist Episcopal Church in 1853. The area was one of orchards and farms through the 1880s. Mount Tabor post office was opened in 1879, and the opening of the Morrison Street bridge connecting to downtown Portland in 1887 began the period of suburbanization of Mount Tabor. Steam-powered commuter railroads extended east to the slopes of the butte in 1889, and farmers responded by carving their lands into numerous residential subdivisions. The commuter railroads became city **streetcar** lines along SE Belmont and Yamhill Streets and Hawthorne Boulevard, where retail stores developed beginning in the 1890s. The independent post office closed in 1901, and the area was annexed into Portland in 1905.

► **Mount Vernon** Located along the John Day River in Grant County, Mount Vernon is a ranching

The post office at Mount Vernon about 1950, many miles from an airport with air-mail service. The sign at the lower left of the window advises, "Don't touch blasting caps." Author's collection.

community that had its beginnings in the 1870s. According to Lewis L. McArthur in *Oregon Geographic Names*, the name is derived from that of a "prize black stallion" owned by local settler David W. Jenkins. Jenkins built a stone stable for his steed, which reputedly sheltered settlers during the **Bannock War** of 1878. Mount Vernon post office was opened in 1877. By 1915, the town was reported to have a population of sixty, and was "surrounded by good stock and farming country." There were hot springs two miles north of the town with a good hotel. Mount Vernon was incorporated as a municipality in 1948, and the 1950 census credited it with a population of 451; the estimated population in 2007 was 600.

Mount Washington This craggy peak in the northern Cascade Range is the remnant of a volcanic plug; the surrounding softer material was eroded away during the last ice age by glaciers. The first ascent of the 7,794-foot peak was made in 1923; as for the first ski descent, an online extreme skiing guide states that it is "probably not skiable from [the] summit." Certainly not.

Mulino The Spanish word for mill is appropriate for this Clackamas County community, which formed around a sawmill (1848) and flour- and gristmill (1851) powered by the water of Milk Creek. A post office opened in 1888; in 1915 it was reported that the population in the neighborhood was about 200, and Mulino had a "flour mill, green house, shingle mill and saw mill" as well as a grange hall. The mill quit producing flour in 1924, but the founding Howard family continued to mill poultry and dairy feeds until 1958. The mill building was placed on the National Register of Historic Places in 1981.

Multnomah Athletic Club (MAC) This Portland social and athletic club was founded in 1891 as the Multnomah Amateur Athletic Club. In 1893, the club acquired the site of Multnomah Stadium. It sold the stadium in 1966; it is now **PGE Park**. Known to Portlanders as the MAC, the club is one of the largest indoor athletic clubs in the nation, with nearly 20,00 members.

Multnomah County The county of Multnomah was established in 1854, the area taken from parts of Clackamas and Washington Counties. The present boundaries are little changed from the date of establishment. The area of 465 square miles makes it the smallest county in the state. It is also the largest county in terms of its population. The census of 1860 recorded 4,150 residents in Multnomah County; in 1900, the figure was 103,167; in 1950, 471,537; and the estimate in 2007, 710,025. **Portland** is the county seat. The first courthouse was erected in 1866, and expanded several times before being replaced by the current courthouse in the same location in 1914. The name is derived from that of a band of **Lower Chinookan Indians** whose homeland extended on both sides of the Willamette and Columbia Rivers from the Portland area westward to the vicinity of Kalama, Washington. A number of villages were located on **Sauvie Island** and along the Multnomah Channel to the west side of the island. There was not a person named Multnomah, and images of Chief Multnomah are imaginary.

The principal economic engines of the county have included transportation, especially related to the port of Portland, such as the transshipping of goods from barge and train to seagoing vessels; wholesale and retail trade, based on Portland's development as a transportation center for water, rail, and road transport; and manufacturing. Much of the manufacturing, until after World War II, was related to wood products, and included not only lumber, but also sash and door manufacturing, shingle making, and furniture making. Since the war, woodproducts manufacturing has declined dramatically; metal fabrication, silicon chip manufacture, aluminum production (until the 1990s), and food preparation have risen in its stead.

▶ **Multnomah district, Portland** This southwest Portland neighborhood and commercial center has only recently been known as Multnomah Village, a term that blossomed in the 1990s. Multnomah began as a stop on the **Oregon Electric Railway**, which built through the area in 1907 and made it an appealing suburban location for commuters. A post office named Multnomah was established in 1912, and it operated until 1940, when the area took on Portland addresses. In 1915, truck gardening, floriculture, and dairying were listed as the principal enterprises in the area.

▶ **Multnomah Falls** Multnomah Creek rises on **Larch Mountain** and flows north to plunge 611 feet over the rim of the Columbia River Gorge at Multnomah Falls in eastern Multnomah County. The highest of the many waterfalls on the south side of the Columbia River Gorge, Multnomah Falls is also the second-highest year-around waterfall in the United States. The first falls are of 542 feet; the concrete arch bridge that spans the lower falls of sixty-nine feet was built in 1914, a gift of **Simon Benson** as an adjunct to the **Columbia River Highway**. A log bridge was in place at the same site as early as the 1880s. The Multnomah Falls lodge, designed by **A. E. Doyle** in rustic fashion, opened in 1925 as a restaurant and overnight lodgings; it was enlarged in 1927 and 1929 and underwent other changes in the 1960s. It was placed on the National Register of Historic Places in 1981. Of course, the waterfall has a legend of an Indian maiden sacrificing herself to save her tribe from sickness by plummeting from the top of the cliff, the misty falls

A three-car train of the Oregon Electric Railway is shown departing from Multnomah station for Portland about 1915. At that time, about forty passenger trains a day passed through Multnomah, bound for Salem, Eugene, Forest Grove, and Portland. The tracks were removed after freight service ended in 1944, and the right-of-way became SW Multnomah Boulevard. Author's collection.

4009 Multanomah Fall Oregon.

This stereocard view of Multnomah Falls was taken about 1900. The wooden bridge was replaced by a concrete structure donated by Simon Benson as part of the project to build the scenic Columbia River Highway. Author's collection.

appearing afterward to commemorate her selfless gesture. The tale is recounted in *Indian Legends of the Pacific Northwest* (1953) by Ella E. Clark, who prefaced her version by noting that had been set down by an unnamed woman who, with "two other pioneers" had written it up; "What changes in the Indian tradition may have resulted from the influences of white man's culture, probably no one can now determine," wrote Clark. One may infer, however, that they were substantial.

Multnomah Indians *see* **Lower Chinookan Indians**

Multnomah Stadium *see* **PGE Park**

Multnomah Village *see* **Multnomah district, Portland**

music and musicians Formal choral and orchestral music in Oregon revolved around activities in Portland until the twentieth century. Concerts were performed as early as the 1860s and 1870s, and the city's **Germans** formed a chapter of the Arion Society to promote German music. The **Oregon Symphony** had its genesis in the 1890s as the Portland Symphony Society, while the Portland Junior Symphony, founded in 1924, evolved into the present-day **Portland Youth Philharmonic**. Oregon has fostered a number of annual music festivals such as the **Peter Britt Music Festival** in Jacksonville, the **Ernest Bloch** Festival in Newport, and the Oregon Bach Festival in Eugene, which began in 1970.

The history of popular music leads to Portland's jazz years during World War II and continuing through the 1950s, when many **blacks** moved to Portland for wartime work in the shipyards and other industries. They brought music with them, and it attracted interracial audiences; the players were both local musicians and luminaries from out of town such as Charlie Parker. In 1963, two local bands, The Kingsmen and Paul Revere and the Raiders, both recorded—at the same Portland studio, and within days of one another—a rather trite composition called "Louie Louie," which quickly rose to national popularity. Part of the reason for its popularity was due to uncertainty about some of the lyrics, which *could* be heard to be rather unsavory, though in fact they are not.

Dietsche, Robert. *Jumptown: The Golden Years of Portland Jazz, 1942–1957.* Corvallis: Oregon State University Press, 2005.

myrtle *see* **Oregon myrtle**

Myrtle Creek Situated in Douglas County on the South Umpqua River, Myrtle Creek is also on the route of the California-Oregon Trail. The gold-mining excitement in southern Oregon in the early 1850s also brought white settlers to the area; James B. Weaver settled at the site of Myrtle Creek in 1851. A post office opened in 1854, and in 1862 John Hall bought the site and laid out a townsite; the name refers to the presence of **Oregon myrtle** trees. The Oregon & California Railroad came through in 1882, finally connecting to California in 1887, and the city of Myrtle Point was incorporated in 1893. The census of 1900 showed a population of all of 189 persons; by 1940, that had climbed to 441 persons. In 1915, the town had a prune-packing plant and lumber mills, and it was noted that the "poultry industry is important and is in flourishing condition." Increased logging and lumbering after World War II also increased the city's population: 1,781 in 1950, 3,365 in 1980. Population declined in the next decade as the lumber industry stagnated, but had risen again to an estimated 3,630 in 2007.

Myrtle Point The town of Myrtle Point, named for the **Oregon myrtle** trees to be found nearby, is located in Coos County near the head of navigation on the **Coquille River**. It was laid out as a townsite by Henry Meyers in 1861; he preferred the name Meyersville, but that did not prevail. The river valley developed as farmland, especially for dairying. Coal mining developed nearby in the 1870s, and in 1872 a post office named Ott was established near the townsite. Ott post office closed in 1876, and Myrtle Point post office opened that year. The town was incorporated in 1887, and the 1900 census recorded a population of 530. A railroad arrived from **Coos Bay** in 1893, headed for Roseburg, but because of the financial troubles of the 1890s, it ended at Myrtle Point. Connections were made there with river steamboats for **Bandon**, and until the 1920s, Myrtle Point was a transfer place between rail and water transport. By 1915, the town had a railroad connection north to Eugene, boasted of two cheese factories and a fruit drying plant, and had a planing mill and a sawmill. The population rose to 934 in 1920 and to 2,033 in 1950; lumber production spiked the population up to an estimated 3,202 in 1957. It has since fallen and stabilized; the estimate for 2007 was 2,540. The town's glory since 1912 has been the extravaganza of the Coos County Fair.

N

Naito, William S. "Bill" (1925–1996) Bill Naito was born in Portland, worked as a Japanese-language translator during World War II, and graduated from **Reed College** in 1949 (he served as a trustee from 1974 to 1996). He was then involved with his brother Sam Naito in the family business, the importing firm of Norcrest China Company. He was instrumental in new enterprises such as Import Plaza, which built on the craze for imported Asian goods in the 1970s, and the renovation of the former **Olds & King** department store into a retail emporium called the Galleria. Naito was very interested in history and historic preservation, and the family renovated a number of historic buildings in the **Old Town/Chinatown neighborhood** beginning in the late 1960s. Naito also promoted the development of Pioneer Courthouse Square, the construction and operation of replica Council Crest **streetcars** on the new MAX line, and the creation of the Japanese American Historical Plaza in Tom McCall Waterfront Park by landscape architect Robert Murase in 1990. Naito was an ebullient man who loved his city; SW and NW Front Avenue was renamed Naito Parkway in remembrance of his contributions.

Neahkahnie Mountain The prominent headland in Tillamook County overlooks the town of **Manzanita**. A trail over the precipitous western face connected the homelands of the Clatsop **Chinook Indians** and the Nehalem **Tillamook Indians**. The periodic discovery in beach sands below the mountain of lumps of **beeswax** have been traced to the wreck of a Spanish galleon in the eighteenth century, en route from the Philippines to Mexico; but legends persist of golden treasures and pirates, and amateur treasure hunters have periodically dug holes on and around the mountain. A landing by Capt. **Robert Gray** in 1788 resulted in the death of his black servant by local Indians, an incident that has added elements to some of the tales. Another **shipwreck** occurred in 1913 when the *Glenesslin* came ashore at the base of the mountain in full daylight. The **Oregon Coast Highway** along this route was not completed until 1940.

Needles, The *see* **Rooster Rock**

Nehalem Located on the Nehalem River in Tillamook County, this town developed in the 1880s. A post office with that name operated in the area since 1870, but it moved about; it was settled at the site of today's town in 1884. Nehalem was incorporated in 1889; the 1900 census gave it a population of all of fifty-nine residents. The community grew in the early years of the twentieth century as farmers settled in the lower Nehalem River valley and some commercial logging and fishing occurred in the area, shipped out by water. While the bay was a small harbor, it was not one of the finest on the coast. Nehalem was a few miles away from the railroad line that was built through the valley in 1911. Its population was 192 in 1920, 270 in 1950, an estimated 240 in 2007. The lumbering, shingle manufacturing, fishing and canning, general farming, and cheese making reported in 1915 have faded away; Nehalem is a small retail community along the **Oregon Coast Highway**.

Nehalem Indians *see* **Tillamook Indians**

Nehalem River The Nehalem River rises in Tillamook County and wends its way north, west, south, and west through parts of Washington, Columbia, and Clatsop Counties for about 115 miles, before emptying into Nehalem Bay and the Pacific Ocean. The major tributary is the Salmonberry River. The sand spit at the mouth of the river has produced a number of lumps of **beeswax**, associated with Spanish trade between Mexico and the Philippines.

Nelscott *see* **Lincoln City**

Neskowin The coastal resort community of Neskowin in Tillamook County dates from the establishment of a rural post office in the area in 1886. It was a hardscrabble farming and dairying area until a road was crookedly constructed from **Otis** in 1923, and Sarah and Henry Page remodeled their 1890s house to accommodate travelers. This became the Neskowin Hotel, a small shingle-covered inn that was a landmark in the town until it burned in 1968. The completion of the **Oregon Coast Highway** in 1932 helped boost the success of a golf course. The town has grown slowly since as a residential enclave in the shadow of Proposal Rock, a monolith on the shore at the mouth of Neskowin Creek.

Nesmith, James Willis (1820–1885) Born of a Maine family while they were visiting Canada, James W. Nesmith grew up in New Hampshire and Ohio. He farmed and received some legal training, and then emigrated to the Oregon Country in 1843 where he took up a donation land claim in Polk County. In Oregon, Nesmith was elected a judge of the provisional government in 1845, led volunteers against Indians in the **Cayuse** and **Rogue River Wars**, and served as U.S. marshal for the Oregon Territory in 1853–55. Nesmith and his wife, Pauline, purchased a flour mill on the banks of Rickreall Creek near Dallas; his nearby farm became his home until his death. He was appointed superintendent of Indian affairs, 1857–59, and then was elected as a Democrat to the U.S. Senate, 1861–67. Nesmith was a Democrat whose political views diverged from those of his good friend (and the namesake of his first son), **Joseph Lane**, and he was an ardent supporter of the Union cause, a position that placed him at odds with many Oregon Democrats. Nesmith also served a partial term in the U.S. House, 1873–75,

but did not seek re-nomination. A high promontory in the Columbia River Gorge, Nesmith Point, remembers this vaunted pioneer.

Nestucca River The Nestucca River and its tributary, the Little Nestucca River, rise in the **Coast Range Mountains** of Yamhill County; the Nestucca flows west about fifty miles to Nestucca Bay and the ocean, near Pacific City. In 1926, the Nestucca was the first coastal river closed to the use of gillnets in commercial salmon fishing, an early indication of the future crisis with the iconic **salmon**. The Nestucca Spit, separating the bay from the sea, was also the scene of a desperate wrangle between state highway engineers and state treasurer (later governor) **Robert Straub**. In 1966, the highway department proposed a realignment of the **Oregon Coast Highway** that would have zipped over dairy pastures and down the magnificent dunes of Nestucca Spit, sacrificing them to the gods of the straightaway. Straub and the cause of conservation finally triumphed; the dunes are now a state park, named for Straub.

Neuberger, Maurine (1907–2000) Born in Cloverdale, Oregon, Maurine Brown attended college at Oregon College of Education and the University of Oregon, as well as the University of California at Los Angeles, and served as a teacher in Oregon public schools from 1932 until 1944. She married **Richard Neuberger** in 1945, and served in the Oregon house of representatives from 1951 to 1955, serving at the same time that her husband was in the state senate. Maurine was a writer and photographer, and she became an advocate for the United Nations. After the death of Richard Neuberger in 1960, she filled his unfinished U.S. Senate term and was elected to a full term in that election; she was not a candidate for re-election in 1966. In the Senate, she promoted consumer and health causes—she sponsored bills to put warning labels on cigarette packages—and, like her husband, conservation issues. Her teaching background stayed at the forefront after 1966 as she taught classes on consumer affairs, the status of women, and political science at Boston University, Reed College, and other institutions.

Neuberger, Richard Lewis (1912–1960) Born in Oregon, Richard Neuberger graduated from the University of Oregon, where he studied journalism, in 1935. He was a correspondent for the *New York Times* from 1939 to 1954, and wrote numerous articles for the popular press, frequently about the Pacific Northwest and its natural resources and natural beauty. His book *Our Promised Land* about this Edenic region was published in 1938. Neuberger's articles about the Snake River and its hydroelectric power potential helped to popularize the name **Hells Canyon** for the Snake River gorge. Neuberger was elected to the state house of representatives in 1941; he served in World War II, commissioned a lieutenant and then a captain in the Army; he married Maurine Brown in 1945. Elected to the state senate in 1949, Neuberger then ran for and won a seat in the U.S. Senate, serving from 1955 until his death in 1960. In the Senate, he was a noted liberal Democrat, as was his fellow Oregon senator, **Wayne Morse**. The two had an uncomfortable relationship dating back to Neuberger's college days, despite similar views on major political issues. Neuberger was a conservationist who valued wildlife and the region's scenic assets, albeit one who was also an advocate for economic and population growth. He died unexpectedly while campaigning for a second term; his wife, **Maurine Neuberger**, was appointed to complete his term, and she won the following election.

> Neal, Steve, ed. *They Never Go Back to Pocatello: The Selected Essays of Richard Neuberger*. Portland, Oregon: Oregon Historical Society Press, 1988.

Newberg Situated in Yamhill County in the shadow of the **Chehalem Mountains** on the Willamette River, Newberg had its beginnings with the establishment of a rural post office in 1869, named for the postmaster's German hometown of Neuberg. The area had been settled by farming families in the 1840s, and was located very near to the site of a historic crossing of the Willamette on the **California-Oregon Trail**. The community began to grow with the promise of a railroad in the early 1880s, a promise that did not amount to much until the early 1890s, due to the company's financial and construction troubles. Dr. John Minthorn was one of the newcomers of 1885, and his nephew **Herbert Hoover** joined him there; both were members of the Society of Friends, which came to have many followers in the area. The Friends established an academy in 1885 (which Hoover attended for a brief time), and then Pacific College in 1891, which has since become **George Fox University**. Newberg was incorporated in 1889; by 1900, the census recorded a population of 945. In 1915, Newberg was the center of an agricultural center known for dairying, livestock raising, orchards of prunes and walnuts, fields of strawberries and loganberries, and for lumbering and the manufacturing of tile and brick. There was a large sawmill, a milk condensing plant, a fruit drier and two flour mills, and a cooperative canning association. Frequent interurban electric trains connected Newberg with McMinnville and Portland. The city's population was 2,566 in 1920, and 3,946 in 1950. Since World War II, Newberg has prospered with a large newsprint paper mill and a redirection of agriculture into grape growing and wine making. Newberg's population in 2007 was estimated at 21,010.

Newberry Crater Located in Deschutes County, Newberry Crater is the center of the group of volcanic peaks known as the Paulina Mountains, capped by Paulina Peak with an elevation of 7,985 feet. The crater area itself encompasses some seventeen square miles, including Paulina Lake and East Lake. Newberry Crater is in the Newberry National Volcanic Monument, created in 1990, which also holds hundreds of cinder cones and miles of flows of basalt and obsidian.

New Carissa Heading for Coos Bay to load a cargo of wood chips, the Japanese freighter *New Carissa* ran aground north of the entrance to the bay in February of 1999. A fairly straightforward mishap turned into a disastrous oil spill, an oil fire that split the ship, and the towing to sea and sinking of the ship's bow. The stern remained on shore to become one of Oregon's more horrific-looking **shipwrecks**; in 2008, the stern was removed. Artist Henk Pender documented the wreck in a series of immense oil paintings.

New Chinatown/Japantown Historic District, Portland This National Register of Historic Places district is a part of an area known in the late nineteenth and early twentieth centuries as the North End; by the 1920s a section near West Burnside Street was often known as **skid road** or skid row. The district, designated in 1989, extends from Burnside north to NW Glisan Street between NW Third and Fifth Avenues. Since the 1860s, the North End was a district near the waterfront that hosted a number of seasonal workers, immigrants, and sojourners from a variety of backgrounds. Among those have been **Japanese** immigrants who came to Portland in the early 1900s; here they operated hotels and boarding houses, restaurants, and laundries, and established a small Nihonmachi, or Japantown. Beginning in the 1920s and 1930s, a number of **Chinese** residents and businesses migrated to the same district from "old" Chinatown, centered on SW Second Avenue and Oak Street. The internment of Japanese residents during World War II depopulated the area, and the Japanese presence did not rebound. Although most residents left the area for east side suburbs by the 1970s, the Chinese business community did continue in place, including the language school of the Chinese Consolidated Benevolent Association and several tongs, or family groups. Recent "revitalization" efforts have included an elaborate Chinese gate on SW Fourth Avenue at Burnside Street, erected in 1986, and the Chinese Classical Garden, opened in 2000.

New Era *see* **communal colonies and communes**

New Northwest, The This weekly newspaper was founded in Portland in 1871 by noted suffragist and writer **Abigail Scott Duniway**. Duniway was its editor until 1876, and thereafter a frequent contributor; her contributions included serialized (and moralistic) novels such as *Edna and John: A Romance of Idaho Flat*. The paper was directed at a general audience, but its editorial stance favored the vote for women and exalted the contributions of women to Western American society. The paper ceased operations in 1887.

"*Yours for Liberty*": *Selections from Abigail Scott Duniway's Suffrage Newspaper*. Eds. Jean M. Ward and Elaine A. Maveety. Corvallis: Oregon State University Press, 2000.

New Odessa *see* **Glendale**

▶**Newport** Located "at the entrance to the famous, beautiful **Yaquina Bay**," Newport is "the year-round health and pleasure resort," said a 1915 booklet. The townsite in Lincoln County developed as a rustic seashore resort around Samuel Case's Ocean House hotel, which opened in 1866, and the Abbey House of 1871. Newport was then an undeveloped port; the land around the bay was first opened to white settlement in 1865 with the reduction of the **Coast Reservation**. The Newport post office opened in 1868. A wooden lighthouse was built at the mouth of the bay in 1871; it was decommissioned in 1874 after the opening of Yaquina Head lighthouse to the north in 1873; the **lighthouses** were an initial step in improving access to Newport. The city of Newport was incorporated in 1882, and by 1910, it had a population of 721.

It was through the efforts of Col. T. Edgenton

The waterfront of the resort and fishing town of Newport looked like this about 1900. The Ocean House Hotel stands on the hillside at the center, top. Steven Dotterrer collection.

Hogg and his magnificently conceived but disastrously executed railroad and steamship enterprise focused on **Yaquina Bay** that Newport became a viable resort, albeit still not all that easily reached. The first jetty construction began in 1881 to improve the harbor. In 1884, Col. Hogg's railroad finally began to bring Willamette Valley vacationers to his port of Yaquina City, where they were carried by steam launch the few remaining miles to the Newport bay front. Just over the hill from the bay another area of resort hotels and cottages developed, beginning about 1890, at Nye Beach, in the shadow of a rocky shoreline landmark called **Jumpoff Joe**. A wooden boardwalk was built in 1891 to connect the two areas. Dr. Henry J. Minthorn, uncle of **Herbert Hoover**, built a hot water sea-bathing facility at Nye Beach in 1902. In 1912, two large hotels went up at Nye Beach, including the New Cliff House, operated in recent years as the Sylvia Beach Hotel.

In the 1920s, the coastal areas around Newport began to be extensively logged. Some commercial fishing as well as lumber exports buoyed the economy, while the opening of the **Oregon Coast Highway** in 1932, followed by the Yaquina Bay Bridge in 1936, designed by **C. B. McCullough**, also boosted tourism. Newport's population reached 1,530 in 1930, and 3,241 in 1950. The Lincoln County seat was moved from Toledo to Newport by popular vote in 1954. The opening of the Oregon Coast Aquarium in 1992 brought a new round of tourism to the city, exacerbated by the aquarium's hosting of Keiko the orca, star of the motion picture *Free Willy*, from 1996 to 1998. Newport's population reached 7,519 in 1980, and in 2007 was estimated at 10,455.

Price, Richard L. *Newport, Oregon, 1866–1936: Portrait of a Coast Resort*. Newport, Oregon: Lincoln County Historical Society, 1975.

newspapers and journalism The press came to Oregon in the 1840s. Its first incarnation was written, not printed, in the form of the *Flum-gudgeon Gazette and Bumble Bee Budget* of Oregon City. Oregon City also launched the first printed newspaper, the *Oregon Spectator*. The Portland *Oregonian* had its beginnings in 1850 and developed as a major voice for Republican politics in the Pacific Northwest; associated with the *Oregonian* were its longtime editor **Harvey W. Scott** and publisher **Henry L. Pittock**; its staff in the twentieth century included writer **Ben Hur Lampman**, historian **Stewart Holbrook**, and future governor **Tom Mc-Call**. The Salem *Oregon Statesman*, led by its prominent editor **Asahel Bush**, also influenced Oregon politics, particularly on the eve of the **Civil War**.

Among other influential Oregon newspapers are the Pendleton *East Oregonian* (founded 1875); the Bend *Bulletin* (1903), and its editors George Palmer Putnam and Robert W. Chandler; the Astoria *Astorian* (1873), founded by DeWitt Clinton Ireland; the Medford *Mail Tribune* (1909), whose editor, Robert W. Ruhl, won the paper a Pulitzer Prize for its coverage of the shenanigans of the **Good Government Congress** in 1933; and the Eugene *Register-Guard* (1930).

Portland journalism has been dominated by the *Oregonian* since 1850, but a worthy (and Democratic) rival was the *Oregon Journal* (1902–1983), headed for many years by **C. S. Jackson**. Portland was also the headquarters of the monthly—and later weekly—illustrated news and literary magazine *West Shore* (1875–1891) and of *The New Northwest*, edited by **Abigail Scott Duniway** and a promoter of literature and the rights of women. Newspapers were published in foreign languages for immigrant Japanese, **Germans**, and **Italians**, and African-Americans read papers such as *The Advocate*, edited for a time by **Beatrice Cannady**.

Nez Perce Indians

At the beginning of the nineteenth century, the Nez Perce peoples lived over a wide territory that included part of northwestern Idaho, the southeast corner of Washington state,

and the northeastern corner of Oregon. The Nez Perce were already noted for their fine horses, and they fed and tended horses for the **Lewis and Clark Expedition** members during the winter of 1805–06. The Nez Perce homeland provided abundant game, including deer, elk, bear, moose, and mountain sheep, as well as smaller mammals and a variety of birds. Fish were also abundant: salmon, trout, suckers, sturgeon, and lamprey. Camas, bitterroot, wild carrot and wild onion, berries, nuts, and seeds supplemented their diet. The Nez Perce typically lived in villages in the winter in mat-covered longhouses; mat-covered, cone-shaped tents—tipis—were used while traveling, such as during rounds to collect food in the summer and autumn.

The Nez Perce worked with fur trappers in the area in the 1810s through the 1830s, and Catholic and Presbyterian missionaries were ministering to them in the 1830s and 1840s. Treaties were made with the United States in 1855, 1863, and 1868, and the Nez Perce Reservation was created. Not all Nez Perce were parties to the treaties, such as the band of **Joseph** the Younger in the Wallowa Valley of Oregon; the **Nez Perce War** was a consequence. The Nez Perce Tribe, headquartered in Lapwai, Idaho, is the continuing representation of the Nez Perce people; some lands have also been acquired in **Wallowa County**.

Josephy, Alvin M. *The Nez Perce Indians and the Opening of the Northwest*. New Haven, Connecticut: Yale University Press, 1965. Reprint. Boston: Houghton Mifflin, 1997.

Nez Perce War

Nez Perce War Several bands of the **Nez Perce Indians** signed the 1855 treaties negotiated by Washington's territorial governor, I. I. Stevens, but the band headed by **Joseph** the Elder did not. Joseph's band had long lived in the Wallowa River Valley, and they continued to do so. Joseph died in 1871; his successor was **Joseph** the Younger. Beginning in 1873, the federal government, pressured by white miners and settlers, pressed these Indians to leave the valley for the Nez Perce or **Umatilla Reservation**s; the group resisted. In the spring of 1877, the U.S. Army, led by Gen. **O. O. Howard**, set forth to collect the Wallowa band. About 700 members of the Wallowa Nez Perces, led by Joseph the Younger and Looking Glass (Allalimya Takanin, ca.1832–1877), set forth across the Snake River into Idaho and Montana in an attempt to reach what they hoped would be asylum in Canada. The Army pursued them, culminating in the Bear Paw Battle on October 5, 1877, with the group's surrender forty miles from the border and after an exhausting trek and excoriating clashes. The Indian survivors were sent first to Indian Territory (Oklahoma), and in 1885 were re-settled on the Colville Reservation in northeastern Washington state.

Lavender, David S. *Let Me be Free: The Nez Perce Tragedy.* New York: HarperCollins, 1992.

nickel *see* **Riddle**

Nike *see* **Bowerman, William J.; University of Oregon**

Nob Hill neighborhood, Portland In the late nineteenth century, as Portland was rapidly growing into a port city of some wealth, those who had some wealth often sought to build their homes away from the bustle of commerce. But not too far. The rising slope of land in a newly platted area northwest of the central district became, in the 1880s, a most desirable place for merchants and professional men with names like Glisan and Flanders to build their mansions. The area between West Burnside Street and NW Marshall Street, and from NW Seventeenth to NW Twentieth Avenues, became Nob Hill, the place where the nabobs of commerce went home for the night. The term has stretched a bit over the years, west to Twenty-third Avenue at least. Much of the neighborhood is within the Alphabet Historic District on the National Register of Historic Places. The district name derives from the

fact that their original plat had streets labeled A, B, C, etc.; in 1891, the letters were converted to names, remaining in alphabetical order.

Marlitt, Richard. *Nineteenth Street.* Rev. ed. Portland, Oregon: Oregon Historical Society, 1978.

Nordstrom The Nordstrom clothing store chain had its origins in Seattle in 1901, as a shoe store. Nordstrom opened a shoe store in Portland in 1950, and in 1966 opened a combined store selling both shoes and clothing under the name Nordstrom Best. The name reverted to Nordstrom in 1973, and the chain built a new full-block downtown Portland store in 1977.

North Bend The Coos County city of North Bend is adjacent to the city of **Coos Bay** and shares much of its history. The post office of North Bend opened in 1872, and the community was incorporated in 1903; the census of 1910 shows it with a population of 2,078. In 1915, North Bend boasted a sash and door factory, a box and veneer plant, two sawmills, and a shingle mill: it was a lumber town. North Bend went through a slump after 1926, when part of the town's largest mill burned. During the Depression, North Bend gained some fame for issuing and redeeming "coins" made of **Oregon myrtle** as a way to ease a local bank crisis.

The population reached 6,099 in 1950, and an estimated 9,830 in 2007. The long-abandoned five-story hulk of the North Bend Hotel, built in the 1920s, is the unfortunate heart of downtown North Bend. Periodically, efforts are made to merge North Bend and Coos Bay; in 2004, for the sixth time in sixty-one years, voters nixed the idea.

North End district, Portland *see* **New Chinatown/Japantown Historic District, Portland; skid road**

Northern Pacific Railway (NP) The first transcontinental line from the Midwest to the North

Pacific Coast was that of the Northern Pacific, which extended from Saint Paul, Minnesota, via the Columbia River Gorge to Portland, a route that opened in 1883. A connecting line extended north from Portland to Puget Sound. Building the Northern Pacific was a lengthy effort that began in the 1860s, and it was completed with the considerable financial machinations of **Henry Villard**. In pursuit of his aims, Villard in 1880 acquired the **Oregon Steam Navigation Company** and, for a time, a portion of the **Union Pacific Railroad** in order to complete his transcontinental route. Before the end of the 1880s, the Northern Pacific completed a direct line to Puget Sound via Yakima, Villard was toppled, and the NP route to Portland detoured via Tacoma rather than down the Columbia River. The Northern Pacific was instrumental in the construction of the Portland Hotel and of Portland Union Station. In the early 1900s NP became the co-owner of the **Spokane, Portland & Seattle Railway**, which again gave the NP a direct route into Portland via the Columbia River Gorge. The NP was also one of the major recipients of federal **land grants** to aid in its construction. Much of that land in the Pacific Northwest came into the hands of **Weyerhaeuser** and other major timberland holders. The NP disappeared in the 1970 creation of the Burlington Northern, later **Burlington Northern Santa Fe Railway**.

Northern Paiute Indians The term "Northern Paiute" describes peoples who, at the time of the first Euro-American contact, spoke related languages but were still distinct in cultural and political ways. The Northern Paiute homeland ranged over approximately 70,000 square miles of arid, basin-and-range lands in southeastern Oregon, southwest Idaho, and northwestern Nevada, as well as a corner of California. Within present-day Oregon, Northern Paiute groups were concentrated along the Deschutes River near its confluence with the Crooked River, in the Harney Basin and the headwaters of the Malheur River, along the Owyhee River, and in the Warner Lakes Basin. The groups were semi-nomadic, needing to travel to hunt, fish, and gather food from often-widespread localities. Among the common foods were deer, pronghorn antelope, hares and rabbits, squirrels, a variety of waterfowl, seeds and berries; the Owyhee and Malheur Rivers provided salmon and **lamprey**.

The Northern Paiutes of Oregon were impacted by white incursions later than the Indians near the Columbia and Willamette Rivers. The **Oregon Trail** touched an edge of their territory, but the main overland trail to California, across northern Nevada, bisected it. Horses were introduced to some Northern Paiutes by the 1820s, and to most by the 1850s. In the 1860s, gold miners and stock ranchers swarmed into the Malheur River country, and numerous clashes arose between Indians and whites. U.S. Army troops established local posts such as Camp Harney—later Fort Harney—and efforts were made to make treaties and establish reservations. But treaties were not always ratified or honored; the Malheur Reservation (1871–78) was a tragic failure and a bureacratic boondoggle; Indian leaders such as Winnemucca and **Egan** were mistreated: Egan was killed, Winnemucca found himself and his family, which included his daughter **Sarah Winnemucca**, sent on a forced march to the Yakama Reservation in Washington Territory. Some bands participated in the **Bannock War** of 1878, and the Northern Paiute history thereafter is fragmented among the families and bands that survived. The **Burns Paiute Tribe and Reservation** dates from the 1930s; other Oregon Northern Paiutes went to the Fort McDermitt Reservation on the Oregon-Nevada border, to the **Warm Springs Reservation** or the **Umatilla Reservation**, or remained outside the reservation system. *See also* **Malheur County**.

North Plains The Washington County community of North Plains is named for its location, on the northern edge of the **Tualatin Plains**, a fertile agricultural area that was settled in the 1840s. The

North Plains post office was opened in 1911, the same year that the United Railways opened an interurban electric line to Portland. North Plains in 1915 was a farming town, "noted for its splendid agricultural development and advantages for horticulture. General farming, dairying, grain growing and fruit raising." The town was bypassed by the **Sunset Highway**, and was not incorporated until 1963; the 1970 census recorded its population as 690. Since the 1990s, it has expanded as a bedroom community for **Silicon Forest** commuters; the estimated population in 2007 was 1,890.

North Powder Named for its location on the North **Powder River**, this Union County town was a stagecoach stop in the 1860s along the route of the Oregon Trail. The post office was opened in 1866, and the **Union Pacific Railroad** built through the town in the early 1880s. North Powder was incorporated in 1903; its population in the 1910 census was 455, rising to a high point of 613 in 1920. At that time, it was a lumber mill town, with general farming and stock raising on nearby ranches and some gold mining in the hinterlands. Located today on **Interstate 84**, North Powder remains a small agricultural community; its estimated population in 2007 was 500.

North West Company see **Hudson's Bay Company**

Northwest Passage The Northwest Passage was a mythical water route connecting the Pacific Ocean with the Atlantic. Numerous European expeditions—especially Spanish, British, French, and Russian—sought such a waterway from the sixteenth through the eighteenth centuries.

> Williams, Glyndwr. *Voyages of Delusion: The Quest for the Northwest Passage.* New Haven, Connecticut: Yale University Press, 2003.

nuclear power see **Trojan**

nurseries The propagation of nursery stock is big business in Oregon. It is a business that had its beginnings with two brothers, **Seth Lewelling** and **Henderson Luelling** in the 1840s, who specialized in trees and fruit stock. In the late nineteenth century, the J. A. Settlemier nursery in **Woodburn** was a major supplier of fruit and berry stock. By 1900, one of the nation's largest such firms was the Oregon Nursery Company of Salem, founded in 1867; in 1906 it moved to **Orenco** in Washington County. Specialized floral nurseries, such as those for **dahlias** and **iris**, developed in the 1920s. Since the 1950s, nurseries have flourished in the Willamette Valley, supplying a national market with ornamental trees and shrubs and perennial and annual plants. By 2007, the nursery business was the largest sector of Oregon's agricultural industry, bringing in more than one billion dollars.

Nye Beach see **Newport**

Nyssa The Malheur County city of Nyssa is located on the Snake River in the **Treasure Valley** area. The main line of the transcontinental **Union Pacific Railroad** crossed the Snake at Nyssa and opened to through traffic in 1884, and the post office at Nyssa opened in 1889; the origin of the name is clouded in speculation. The city was incorporated in 1903, and the 1910 census gave it a population of 449. In 1915, the area was noted for its artesian water supply and to the prospects for irrigation; farmers nearby raised stock, dairy cattle, and poultry, and grew alfalfa, apples, prunes, and grain. Irrigation water came from the **Owyhee River** in the late 1920s, and agricultural production adapted: potatoes, onions, mint, sugar beets, and corn became major crops. The Amalgamated Sugar Company, producer of White Satin sugar, built a large sugar beet processing plant that became the city's chief employer. The population reached 2,525 in 1950 and 2,629 in 1990. The Amalgamated plant closed in 2005; the population estimate in 2007 was 3,220.

O

oak Three major species of oak are found in Oregon. The Garry or Oregon white oak, *Quercus garryana,* grows throughout interior western Oregon. The tree is dense and rounded in form, grows from thirty to seventy feet in height, and has a diameter of from one to two and a half feet, with light gray bark. Its nuts are edible acorns; it grows on hillside slopes and in valleys, often in pure groves or with other oaks. Stands of Garry oak once dotted the Willamette Valley and can still be found. The wood is suitable for cabinetry work, interior finishes, and furniture.

The California black oak, *Quercus kelloggii,* has similar characteristics but a thick and dark brown bark; it can be slightly taller than the Garry oak with a thicker trunk. This is the common oak of southwestern Oregon foothills, and grows both in oak stands and in forestlands mixed with conifers.

Canyon live oak, or canyon oak, *Quercus chrysolepis,* is found in canyons and on gravelly soils and

This majestic white oak stands on the campus of Linfield College in McMinnville. The photograph was taken about 1890; the tree is thought to have sprouted about 1750. The tree stands near the school's Pioneer Hall, and has figured in college legend and song. In 2007, it was being accorded "geriatric care," but it finally succumbed and fell in 2008. Alvord photograph. Oregon Historical Society, CN 003449.

slopes in southwestern Oregon. It has a short trunk and large and spreading horizontal branches with a rounded, sometimes shrubby, crown. It may be short and stubby, ranging from twenty to a hundred feet in height with a light gray bark.

Oakland The Douglas County town of Oakland formed around a rural post office on a prairie with many oak trees nearby. The post office was established in 1852, with routes to **Scottsburg** (and thence San Francisco and the outside world), Jacksonville, and north to Eugene and Corvallis. The townsite moved a few miles to accommodate the construction of the Oregon & California Railroad in 1872, and Oakland was incorporated in 1878; the 1880 census credited it with a population of 369.

By 1915, Oakland and vicinity was the "largest **turkey** shipping center on the Pacific Coast," and sheep and fruit were also raised nearby. The town also had a sawmill, a planing mill, and a creamery. The town declined somewhat in the 1920s and 1930s, upstaged by nearby **Sutherlin**, but rebounded after World War II; the population in 1950 was 829, and 1,010 in 1970. Oakland had been on the **Pacific Highway**, but was several miles off of **Interstate 5**. The town's historic commercial core and residential section, much of it dating from the post-railroad prosperity of the 1880s, was placed on the National Register of Historic Places in 1979, and Oakland has profited from the appeal of historic tourism. The estimated population in 2007 was 940.

Oakridge High in the timber country of eastern Lane County, Oakridge began as a country post office named Hazeldell in 1888. A branch of the **Southern Pacific Company** railroad reached the area in 1912, and at the company's instance, the post office name was changed to Oakridge. The railroad was not completed beyond Oakridge until 1926, when the Natron Cutoff was opened and Oakridge was on the new main line to California. The railroad provided an outlet for timber production, and Oakridge was

incorporated as a city in 1935; the 1940 census showed a population of 520.

The Pope & Talbot Lumber Company opened a large new mill in Oakridge in 1948, eventually employing some 500 workers; the population of Oakridge was 1,562 in 1950, and 3,422 in 1970. During the 1970s, mill modernization resulted in downsizing, and in 1985, Pope & Talbot announced plans to close the mill. Employee efforts kept the plant going, but final closure came in 1990; a 1991 fire consumed most of the remnants of the mill structures. In 1990, the population was 3,063, and the town was in the economic doldrums. Efforts to attract retirees and commuters from the Eugene area, some forty miles away, have helped boost the population to an estimated 3,700 in 2007.

Oaks Amusement Park The Oregon Water Power & Railway Company built the large Springwater hydroelectric project on the Clackamas River in the early twentieth century. The project included an electric-powered **interurban railway** from downtown Portland, which skirted the Willamette River's east bank and crossed Oaks Bottom near the **Sellwood district**. Here the company built an amusement park, which opened on May 30, 1905, just before the opening of the **Lewis and Clark Centennial Exposition**. It featured a giant water slide, bathing in the Willamette River, a roller coaster, and other rides and concessions, and was immensely popular both during the exposition and for many summers thereafter. In 1925, the park was sold to Edward H. Bollinger; in 1943, Bollinger bought the land as well. Bollinger's son Robert operated the park until 1985, when it was turned over to a nonprofit corporation formed to perpetuate the enterprise. The park includes groves of oak trees with picnic facilities, a huge roller-skating rink that has operated continuously since 1905, a ca. 1920 Herschell-Spillman carousel, and a variety of other rides, which have changed over the years. Admission has been free since opening day.

Aalberg, Bryan. Oaks Amusement Park. *Oregon Historical Quarterly* 104, no. 2 (Summer 2003): 252–267.

oats For animal feed and for human consumption, red and white oats are grown in Oregon. Major production is in Klamath County and the Willamette Valley, especially Washington County.

Oceanlake *see* **Lincoln City**

ocean transportation With few good ports, Oregon has not seen an extensive coastal water transportation network. Some coast Indian tribes did use seagoing canoes along the Oregon coast, but the geography did not encourage this. From the 1820s, when the **Hudson's Bay Company** supplied its posts and shipped its furs by sea from Fort Vancouver, however, ocean navigation has been essential in importing goods and exporting products. Since the 1840s, **Portland** has been the major port and distribution center, a position that was solidified when connecting railroads met the ships beginning in the 1870s. The **Oregon Steam Navigation Company**'s monopoly on Columbia River travel was dependent on connections by steamship with San Francisco. The Portland–San Francisco trade developed very early as a mainstay of passenger and freight travel. The awarding of a mail contract to the Pacific Mail Steamship Company in 1850 led to frequent service aboard the steamships *California* and *Oregon*. The company passed into the hands of transportation magnate **Ben Holladay** in 1862. In the early twentieth century, the steamships *Bear, Rose City*, and *Beaver*, operated by a subsidiary of the **Union Pacific Railroad**, gave leisurely travelers a coastal trip between Portland and San Francisco. The export of wheat and lumber brought trans-Pacific shipping by the 1870s; in the 1880s, fleets of sailing vessels sailed for Liverpool and other European ports with wheat. The transition from individual sailing vessels to fleets of steam-powered ships made it hard to find crews for sailing ships, and **crimping** was an occasional practice in Astoria, Coos Bay, and Portland until World War I. Coastal passenger service to California lasted until the mid-1930s, the last ships in that service being those of the Admiral Line.

Coastal ports such as those on **Coos Bay, Yaquina Bay**, Tillamook Bay, and at the smaller ports such as Brookings, Port Orford, Gold Beach, Bandon, Florence, **Gardiner**, and Waldport, usually were served by smaller vessels with light draft, and carried canned fish and lumber to San Francisco, returning with needed goods and supplies. **Astoria** was usually a stop for Portland-bound passenger ships, giving it a higher level of service, but its freight shipments were primarily local. The rapid rise of container shipping in the 1970s changed port activity radically, making Portland the only major port in the state, handling both bulk grain and lumber cargoes and container traffic.

O & C lands *see* **Oregon and California Revested Lands**

O'Donnell, Terence (1924–2001) This Portland writer, boulevardier, and "consummate storyteller and friend of Persians" was born in the city, educated at the University of Chicago, and spent some fifteen years in Iran during the 1960s and 1970s. His Iranian years, when he farmed and lectured, are somewhat mysterious, and resulted in two books, *Garden of the Brave in War* (1980) and *Seven Shades of Memory* (1999). O'Donnell returned to Portland in 1972, did research and writing for the **Oregon Historical Society**, and taught at Portland State University. He was the author of a Portland historical handbook with Thomas Vaughan, a history of the town of Cannon Beach, and a biography of **Joel Palmer**. He was a noted urban walker, a friend of trees and the Portland Park Blocks, and a tireless promoter of **Pioneer Courthouse Square**.

Ogden, Peter Skene (1794–1854) A Canadian fur trapper and explorer who worked for the North West Company and the **Hudson's Bay Company (HBC)** in the Oregon Country beginning in the 1820s. A rather headstrong and hard-nosed fellow, Peter Ogden was not looked upon favorably by HBC when they took over the North West Company in 1821, but he was given responsibility for exploring the Snake River drainage and to carry out the company's "fur desert" policy: that is, to "trap out" the beaver so thoroughly that westward-moving American fur trappers would be discouraged from continuing farther. His expeditions covered much of present-day Idaho, Utah, western Montana, Nevada, California, and Oregon between 1823 and 1830. A colleague of the chief HBC factor at Fort Vancouver, **John McLoughlin**, Ogden succeeded him as factor in 1845, guiding the post during the period of tran-

sition to American occupation. Ogden retired to Oregon City in August 1854, and died there a month later. Ogden, Utah, is named for him; very likely SE Ogden Street in Portland is, also.

Cline, Gloria Griffen. *Peter Skene Ogden and the Hudson's Bay Company.* Norman: University of Oklahoma Press, 1974.

LaLande, Jeffrey M. *First over the Siskiyous: Peter Skene Ogden's 1826–1827 Journey through the Oregon-California Borderlands.* Portland, Oregon: Oregon Historical Society Press, 1987.

Old Believers The Old Believers are separated from the Russian Orthodox Church as a result of a schism that grew out of reforms introduced in the seventeenth century by Patriarch Nikon. The reforms primarily affected liturgical practices, but have also impacted the dress and mode of life of the adherents. Some 10,000 Old Believers are believed to reside in Oregon in the early twenty-first century; most of them came during the post–World War II period with help from Christian charities that helped them migrate from the Soviet Union. Yavhori Cam spearheaded a community in the vicinity of **Woodburn** in the 1960s, which has formed the nucleus of the Oregon group; it is thought to be the largest concentration of Old Believers in the United States. Old Believers do not eat meat on Wednesdays or Fridays; men do not shave their beards; traditional dress is worn. Several churches, with distinctive Russian-style domes, have been erected in the Woodburn vicinity. *See also* **Russians in Oregon.**

old-growth timber The phrase refers to standing trees in an area that has never been logged; that is, the stand is naturally occurring and among the trees are those at the natural extent of their life span. It is also known as virgin timber. Prior to Euro-American logging, virtually all the standing timber in Oregon was old growth. No old-growth timber remains on privately held lands; on federal lands, the old-growth timber that remains is esti-

A daguerreotype view of Peter Skene Ogden, probably taken about 1852. Oregon Historical Society, OrHi 707.

mated to be about 10 percent of the original acreage. Timberlands that were cut and have re-grown in forest are said to hold **second-growth timber**; there might also be third- and even fourth-growth timber.

Olds & King Once one of the Big Three department stores of Portland, Olds & King was founded in 1851 by W. P. Olds and S. W. King; they later took in another partner, and for some years the firm was known as Olds, Wortman & King. A full-block, four-story emporium of white glazed terra cotta was erected in 1910 at SW Tenth Avenue and Morrison Street. The interior was notable for a full interior atrium and grand staircase. In the early twentieth century hierarchy of Portland department stores, **Lipman, Wolfe & Company** attracted the affluent carriage trade, and **Meier & Frank** the middle class; Olds & King sold less expensive goods. The Schlessinger chain bought out the partnership in 1926, although the Olds & King name persisted until 1960,

when it became Rhodes department store; that name came from a Tacoma store owned by the same holding company. As department stores waned, Rhodes briefly became Liberty House and expired in the early 1970s. The building was subsequently purchased by Sam and **Bill Naito**, who renovated it as a shopping mall, the Galleria. This was successful for several years, followed by a period of decline in the 1990s; another renovation was undertaken in 2005.

Old Town/Skidmore historic district, Portland *see* Skidmore/Old Town Historic District, Portland

➤ *Oneonta* A side-wheel steamboat built at Celilo on the Columbia River in 1863, *Oneonta* was operated by the **Oregon Steam Navigation Company** on the leg of their operations known as the Middle River, from the Cascades to The Dalles. Put into service during the eastern Oregon gold rush of the 1860s, the *Oneonta* was the company's first

The sidewheel steamboat *Oneonta* of the Oregon Steam Navigation Company is shown at the Upper Cascades Landing in an 1867 photograph by Carleton E. Watkins. Oregon Historical Society, OrHi 1458.

attempt at something like elegance in riverboat construction, modeled after steamboats on the Mississippi. She proved expensive to operate, however, and in 1870 Capt. **John C. Ainsworth** took her downriver, through the turbulent **Cascades**, to operate on the Lower River, from Portland to the Cascades. In 1877, she was converted to a barge. Oneonta Bluff and Oneonta Gorge in the Columbia River Gorge keep her name in mind. The name comes from a city in New York state.

onions Oregon grows fresh and storage onions, and processes them for sale in bulk, frozen, and dehydrated. Major producing areas have been in Marion County, especially on the lands of **Lake Labish**, Washington County, Morrow and Umatilla Counties, and the **Treasure Valley** area of eastern Oregon.

Ontario The imminent arrival of a transcontinental railroad propelled the platting in 1883 of a townsite on the Snake River in Malheur County, named for the Canadian home province of one of the developers. The railroad came in 1884, along with a post office, and the town soon became a supply point for southeastern Oregon. It was incorporated as a city in 1899; the 1900 census reported 445 residents. By 1915, Ontario was a center of a developing agricultural region bolstered by irrigation. General farming, livestock raising (especially sheep for wool production), and fruit raising were the principal pursuits. A branch railroad west to the county seat of Vale opened in 1907, and was extended farther to Crane in 1916 and Burns in 1925, solidifying Ontario's trade with the region.

The success of the Malheur Irrigation Project boosted the agricultural production of Ontario and the **Treasure Valley** during the 1930s, with a heavy production of potatoes, mint, sugar beets, and onions. Ontario's population reached 3,551 in 1940, and 6,523 in 1970. The industrial and residential growth in the vicinity of Boise, Idaho, spilled west

into Ontario in the late twentieth century. The city's estimated population in 2007 was 11,325.

OO Ranch *see* **Double O Ranch**

Opal *see* **Whiteley, Opal**

opossum The Virginia opossum, *Didelphis virginiana*, is found throughout western Oregon and in the irrigated areas of northeastern Oregon as well. Southern men who came to Oregon in the **Civilian Conservation Corps** are reputed to have brought opossums with them as pets and then released them into the wild, and this quite likely did happen. However, the opossum was introduced earlier, about 1910–12, and has thrived ever since. The CCC boys probably helped the transplantation succeed.

►**Oregon** The state of Oregon joined the Union on February 14, 1859. Before statehood, there was the **Oregon Territory**, and before that, the **Oregon Country**. The origin of the name Oregon has been a topic of speculation and contention for about two centuries; a history of the discussion is found in *Oregon Geographic Names* by Lewis L. McArthur (7th ed., 2003). Since then, two articles have appeared that extend the conversation; that by Goddard and Love traces it to Maj. Robert Rogers' 1765 reference to "the River called by the Indians Ouragon," and that in turn to Algonquian languages and a term for the Ohio River. It is a convoluted tale.

Bryam, Scott, and David G. Lewis. Ourigan: Wealth of the Northwest Coast. *Oregon Historical Quarterly* 102, no. 2 (Summer 2001): 126–157.
Goddard, Ives, and Thomas Love. Oregon, the Beautiful. *Oregon Historical Quarterly* 105, no. 2 (Summer 2004): 238–259.

Oregon The construction of the battleship USS *Oregon* was authorized in 1890, along with sister ships USS *Indiana* and USS *Massachusetts*. She was built by the Union Iron Works of San Francisco, where her hull was launched in 1893, and she was commissioned in 1896: "the U.S. Navy had its first full-fledged modern battleship in Pacific waters," said historian Ken Lomax. She was just in time for service in the **Spanish-American War**. Her first task in that war was to reposition from her base in San Francisco to Key West, Florida, via the Strait of Magellan around South America; she made the trip in sixty-six days, a record for the period. The USS *Oregon* fired the first shot in the Battle of San-

AND ALL PRODUCTS OF THE
TEMPERATE ZONE

The natural resources and major products of the state of Oregon about 1907 are depicted on this promotional card in the form of an elaborate hat for a fashionable woman. Dairying, manufacturing, livestock, grain, apples, potatoes, salmon, flour, gold, prunes, walnuts, hops, wool, and timber are noted; also pictured are strawberries and cherries. The crown of the hat is "Portland, money center of the Northwest." The slogan of the Oregon Development League, which issued the card, was "More people on farms." Mason collection.

tiago, and the combination of her 'round-the-Horn voyage and her battle service earned her the nickname, Bulldog of the Navy.

The *Oregon* continued to serve, carrying troops to China during the Boxer Rebellion in 1900, but she was decommissioned in 1903. Variously re-commissioned and then placed on reserve in the next few years, she returned to full commission in 1917 during **World War I**, when she was the flagship of the Pacific Fleet and escorted troop transports to Siberia. After the war, she was finally retired and, in 1925, became a floating memorial in Portland, where she was used by veterans' groups and served as a military museum. The outbreak of **World War II** imperiled her retirement; in 1943, in the name of military need, she was gutted and stripped to become a floating ammunition magazine. Despite widespread public protest of the move, only a few pieces remained in Portland: a mast and a stack, both displayed on the Portland waterfront. The hull of the *Oregon* survived the war, but was scrapped in Japan in 1956.

> Lomax, Ken. A Chronicle of the Battleship *Oregon*. *Oregon Historical Quarterly* 106, no. 1 (Spring 2005): 132–145.

"Oregon, My Oregon" *see* **"Land of the Empire Builders"**

Oregon Agricultural College *see* **Oregon State University**

Oregon & California Railroad (O&C) With Oregon closely tied by commerce to San Francisco in the nineteenth century, there was a strong desire for a railroad connection. After many political and financial machinations, construction got underway in 1869, and by 1870, the road, now controlled by **Ben Holladay**, reached Salem. Construction continued south to Roseburg, but in 1873 the money ran out. It did not resume until 1881, after an 1876 reorganization under the hand of **Henry Villard**. The rails reached Ashland in 1884, and the link over the Siskiyou Mountains was completed on December 17, 1887—Oregon and California were finally connected by rail. The **Southern Pacific Company** leased the O&C in July 1887, and although the company continued its legal existence until 1927, it was a paper corporation. One legacy was the **Oregon and California Revested Lands**, the result of Southern Pacific's misuse of the terms of the land grant to the O&C. *See also* **Chemawa**.

Oregon and California Revested Lands

In 1866, a federal land grant was promulgated to subsidize the construction of a railroad connecting Oregon and California. The grant was of twenty sections, each a mile square, for every mile of railroad completed; the idea was that the railroad could raise construction and operation money by selling the land to settlers—farmers, essentially—whose products would also eventually travel by train. The contest took many turns as two companies vied for the prize, and the winning **Oregon & California Railroad** was not completed until 1887. The railroad—by now the **Southern Pacific Company**—began in 1894 to sell some of the lands, which were valuable for their timber, but not for farming; however, the grant specified that only "actual settlers" could purchase the land. The ensuing troubles, laid out in **S. A. D. Puter**'s book *Looters of the Public Domain* (1906), affected senator **John Hipple Mitchell** and former congressman **Binger Hermann**. Eventually, Congress took back most of the land, but because the anticipated tax revenues from private landholding did not occur, the affected counties were promised revenues from the sale of timber on the lands, now part of the national forest system. For many years, these "O&C counties"—Lane, Douglas, Jackson, and Josephine were the prime beneficiaries—had a revenue stream from this arrangement. The stream shrank in the 1980s as overharvesting and environmental regulations reduced timber sales, and ended in the early 2000s.

► **Oregon Caves** The Oregon Caves are located in the Siskiyou Mountains of Josephine County. Limestone caves, the domain of stalagmites and stalactites, are common in Missouri, Virginia, and other sections of the country, but are not so often found in the West, and their discovery in 1874 by Elijah Davidson—the story is he was hunting a bear and pursued it into the cave opening—was a source of regional awe and wonder. Remote and undeveloped, the Josephine Caves or the Marble Halls of Oregon, as they were referred to, were seldom visited until after President Theodore Roosevelt designated them a National Monument in 1909.

The opening of the **Redwood Highway** and a connecting access highway to the caves improved their accessibility, and that was shortly followed by the construction of the Oregon Caves Chateau in 1934, along with other improvements by the **Civilian Conservation Corps**. The Chateau was designed in the National-Park-rustic architectural style by local contractor Gust Lium (1884–1965); one of its endearing features is Cave Creek, which wends through the dining room. The Chateau was placed on the National Register of Historic Places in 1987.

► **Oregon City** Situated at **Willamette Falls** in Clackamas County, Oregon City was the site of much of the region's early human history. The falls were a major salmon and lamprey fishing site of the **Kalapuyan Indians** and other tribes, and the falls attracted the attention of white explorers who saw the potential for waterpower. In 1829, **John McLoughlin** of the **Hudson's Bay Company** built a sawmill and a gristmill powered by the falls of the river, and established the city's industrial future. In the 1840s, Oregon City grew to a sizeable settlement for the time and place, where **George Abernethy** established a store, emigrants from the **Oregon Trail** recuperated and restocked before heading up the Willamette Valley seeking land to farm, and the Oregon **provisional government** established their capital. Capt. **John Couch** thought it might be the

A postcard view of the striking "new chalet" at the Oregon Caves. Opened in 1942, the chalet was, like the chateau, designed by Gust Lium. Sawyer's photo. Steven Dotterrer collection.

This photograph of Oregon City and Willamette Falls was taken by Carleton E. Watkins in 1867. The four-story Imperial Mills building is a flour mill; the brick building with a tower is the Oregon City Woolen Mills. The falls have already been partially reconstructed to accommodate industry and river traffic. Oregon Historical Society, OrHi 21591.

head of navigation and the future port city of the region; he re-thought the matter and moved down-river to Portland. Oregon City was the site of the region's first two newspapers, the *Flumgudgeon Gazette and Bumble Bee Budget* and the *Oregon Spectator*. It saw the first fraternal lodge (Masonic), and when the **Oregon Territory** was created in 1848, it remained the capital city.

Oregon City was incorporated in 1851, and steamboats soon plied the river, transferring their passengers and freight around the falls. Several boats were built at the adjacent town of **Canemah**, at the top of the falls. The territorial capital moved to Salem in 1855. In the 1860s and 1870s, the falls were harnessed to provide power for a woolen mill and a paper mill, and the **Oregon & California Railroad** came through from Portland in 1870 (though it did not connect to California until 1887). The first generation of electrical power from the falls came in 1889, and by 1893, an electric **interurban railway**, one of the nation's first, connected

Oregon City and Portland. Oregon City's population in 1880 was 1,263; by 1900, it reached 3,494. In 1909, John McLoughlin's historic house was moved from the downtown area to the bluffs above to become a museum. During the first half of the twentieth century, Oregon City was an industrial town with an agricultural hinterland, and a government center, the seat of Clackamas County. The population by 1950 was 7,682.

Since World War II, Oregon City expanded well beyond its early form, with housing developments spreading over the farmland on the plateau east of the city. The construction of the **Interstate 205** freeway in the 1970s led to shopping malls and other expanded development, and the city's population climbed to 14,698 in 1990 and to an estimated 30,060 in 2007.

► **Oregon Coast Highway** The idea of an Oregon Coast Highway may have been in the air when governor **Oswald West** proclaimed the wet-

C 13 616 Coast Line, South Toward Humbug Mt., Oregon Coast Highway.

Looking south toward Humbug Mountain in Curry County on the Oregon Coast Highway about 1930, before the road was paved. Sawyer Scenic Photos. Author's collection.

sand beaches to be public highways in 1913, and in fact the beaches had been de facto highways for hundreds of years. But the rugged coastline, indented by dozens of estuaries, rivers, and creeks, made a highway a difficult proposition. The highway was initially conceived in 1919 as the Roosevelt Military Highway; however, scenery and commerce soon trumped military concerns and the name Oregon Coast Highway came into general use. The route began to take shape in the 1920s, when the Salmon River Highway reached **Otis** from Portland, and a tortuous through route connected Astoria and Tillamook. In the late 1920s and early 1930s, state highway engineers worked with **C. B. McCullough** to connect the isolated road segments and replace the numerous **ferries** with substantial **bridges**. The opening of the bridge across the Rogue River at Gold Beach in 1932 marked the formal completion of the route. However, it was 1940 before the inland section between Wheeler and Seaside was replaced with the spectacular coastline route over **Neahkahnie Mountain** and through the Arch Cape tunnel.

Oregon College of Art and Craft The Arts and Crafts Society was founded in Portland in 1907 by **Julia Hoffman**, known for her work in photography, metal work, and other arts. The arts and crafts movement, which promoted the creation and use of objects that were both functional and beautiful, was the inspiration for the school, which began by holding classes in member's houses. The school found a downtown Portland home in 1934, and moved to a larger site in Northwest Portland in 1952. The name was changed in 1978 to Oregon School of Arts and Crafts, and with an initial donation from the founder's daughter **Margery Hoffman Smith** a new campus was developed by architect John Storrs; the landscape design was done by **Barbara Fealy**. The school became a degree-granting college in 1994, and in 1996 changed its name to reflect that achievement.

Oregon Country The term was widely used in the early nineteenth century to refer to a portion of North America that roughly encompassed the Columbia River drainage system. During the 1820s and 1830s, as the European nations and the United States exercised expansionist ideas and colonial empires, the area was contested, on paper and in whole or part, by Great Britain, the United States, Russia, and Spain. The Treaty of 1818 established the United States and Britain as the serious claimants and proclaimed a joint occupancy of the region; international diplomacy resolved the main boundaries in the Oregon Treaty of 1846. The term "Oregon Country" is still occasionally used to refer to the U.S. holdings established in the 1846 treaty, which encompasses the states of Oregon, Washington, and Idaho and a portion of western Montana as well as a tip of southwestern Wyoming.

Oregon Country Fair The Oregon Country Fair had its beginnings as a "Renaissance Faire," a neighborhood fund-raising event for the Children's Community School, held in Eugene on November 1 and 2, 1969. With the slogan "Come in costume," the fair featured booths for the sale of crafts and artwork, musicians, and food; the theme reflected the then-growing counterculture movement. The fair soon acquired what became their permanent site near **Veneta** on the **Long Tom River**, where an annual assemblage of vaudevillians, musicians, craftsmen and -women, food booths, and theater events takes place. The fair is noted for its adherence to such principles as recycling, cooperation, environmental awareness, use of local materials, and artistic expression. It has also been noted for fostering the Flying Karamazov Brothers and nudism, for creative smoking materials, and for being very laid back. It is held annually in July.

Oregon Electric Railway The short-lived Oregon Electric Railway was conceived as a system of **interurban railways** in the Willamette Valley that would provide speedy, inexpensive, frequent passenger and freight service. The initial segment from Portland to Salem opened in 1908, and by 1912, the system served Albany, Corvallis, Eugene, Hillsboro, and Forest Grove. The **Southern Pacific Company** electrified a number of its Willamette Valley lines in competition with the Oregon Electric; the paint colors of the cars resulted in the Oregon Electric being known as the "green electric" and the Southern Pacific as the "red electric." Automobiles decimated the suburban traffic, and the Oregon Electric reduced its service in the late 1920s and discontinued passenger trains in 1933. Most of the trackage remains to serve freight customers; much of the Forest Grove line now hosts **MAX** light-rail trains, while the right-of-way out of Portland was used to construct Multnomah Boulevard and the **Interstate 5** freeway. The **Spokane, Portland & Seattle Railway** owned and operated the Oregon Electric for most of its existence.

Oregon Garden *see* Silverton

Oregon Health and Science University (OHSU)

This massive medical and research facility, headquartered on Marquam Hill in Portland, had some of its beginnings at **Willamette University** of Salem, which established a medical education program in 1867 and moved it to Portland in 1877. The University of Oregon in 1887 established a medical school, also siting it in Portland rather than in Eugene with other university programs. Meanwhile, the Oregon College of Dentistry began in Portland in 1898; in 1900 it merged with the Tacoma College of Dental Surgery to form North Pacific Dental College (later North Pacific College of Oregon). In 1913, Willamette University and the University of Oregon merged their medical-related Portland programs to become the University of Oregon Medical School. Construction began on the Marquam Hill campus in 1917, opening two years later; part of the land was a donation from the estate of **C. S. Jackson**. Mult-

nomah County opened a hospital on the hill in 1923; Doernbecher Memorial Hospital for Children joined the parade in 1926 (it was taken over by the medical school in 1928). The North Pacific Dental College joined the fold in 1945.

Since the end of World War II, the Marquam Hill complex has grown ever larger and more complex, adding nursing education, taking over the county hospital functions, and collaborating with the adjoining Veterans Administration Hospital. In 1974, the University of Oregon Health Sciences Center became an institution independent of the University of Oregon; in 1995, it cut its ties with the state system of higher education. The Oregon Health and Science University incarnation came in 2001 in conjunction with a merger with the Oregon Graduate Institute of Science and Technology. OHSU began to develop a second Portland campus at the South Waterfront in 2003, which was linked to Marquam Hill by an aerial tram in 2007.

Oregon Historical Society

The nonprofit society was founded in 1898 in Portland by a group of local businessmen; the first president was **Harvey W. Scott**. It received financial support from the state legislature beginning in 1899, and has published the influential *Oregon Historical Quarterly* since 1900. Printer and amateur historian **George H. Himes** was the de facto curator of the society in its first three decades; at the same time, he was also the major figure at the helm of the Oregon Pioneer Society, formed in 1873, which memorialized the early Euro-American **pioneers** in the Oregon Country. From 1917, the society was headquartered in what became **Keller Auditorium**. Thomas Vaughan came to the society in 1954 as its first professional director; during his 35-year tenure, a new headquarters building was opened in 1966 and the society built a national reputation for its research library and publications. In 2001, the society abruptly lost its state funding, precipitating staff reductions and the loss of programs in book publishing and oral history. Some state funding was restored in 2007.

Oregonian The state's major daily newspaper had its beginnings on December 4, 1850. **Henry L. Pittock** joined the staff in 1860, and was the publisher until his death in 1919. **Harvey W. Scott** was the Republican editor who set the newspaper's tone as the conservative voice of the Pacific Northwest. Scott served from 1865 until 1910; heirs of the Pittocks and the Scotts owned the paper until 1951. The paper was originally a weekly, but a daily edition began in 1861; the first Sunday edition appeared in 1881. The *Oregonian* building on SW Broadway, built in 1948 and designed by **Pietro Belluschi**, originally had a block-long window frontage displaying the whirring presses. A morning newspaper, the *Oregonian* also published the daily afternoon *Telegram* from 1877; it passed into other hands before dying during the Depression. The chief competitor was the afternoon *Oregon Journal*, established in 1902 and published by **C. S. Jackson**. The *Orego-nian* purchased the *Journal* in 1961 and published it until 1982.

Oregon Journal *see* **Jackson, Charles Samuel "Sam"**

➤ **Oregon myrtle** This handsome globular evergreen tree is better know outside Oregon as the California laurel, *Umbellularia californica*; it is also called California bay and pepperwood. It grows about eighty feet high and up to four feet in diameter in the southern Oregon **Coast Range Mountains** and in the **Siskiyou Mountains**. When growing somewhat apart from one another, the Oregon myrtle has a thick trunk and low and large limbs; in a forest situation, it develops a straight, clean trunk. It has a distinctive camphor-like aroma, and the leaves are sometimes used like bay leaves to flavor stews and soups. The wood has long been prized for woodworking and cabinet making, and since the 1920s has been extensively used to produce beautifully grained wooden bowls, lamp stands, plaques,

A grove of Oregon myrtle trees along the Oregon Coast Highway, about 1940. Frank Patterson photograph. Steven Dotterer collection.

key rings, salt and pepper shakers, clocks, frames, seagulls, whales, cowboy boot bookends, crucifixes, and salad bowl sets. One can often find the statement that "The Myrtlewood Tree is unique to two places in the world—The Holy Land and a small section of the Pacific Northwest": but the Mediterranean myrtle is *Myrtus communis*, a very different plant.

Oregon Railway and Navigation Company *see* **Union Pacific Railroad**

Oregon Shakespeare Festival A regional repertory theater company with a national reputation, the Oregon Shakespeare Festival has been an **Ashland** institution since 1935. It was the creation of college instructor **Angus L. Bowmer**, who saw possibilities for an Elizabethan outdoor performance theater in the shell of the old **chautauqua** building, which had been torn down in 1933. Using Depression-era public funding, Bowmer put on a production of *Twelfth Night* on July 2, 1935. It was a quick success, and the Oregon Shakespearean Festival Association was created in 1937 to continue the summer productions. World War II interrupted things, but the theater was rebuilt in 1947 and again in 1959. Plays outside the Shakespearean repertoire were added beginning in 1960, and in 1970 an indoor theater, named for Bowmer, was opened, permitting the season to expand into spring and fall months. A third theater was added in 1977; from 1988 to 1994, the group tried to operate a Portland company, but it was unsuccessful. The Oregon Shakespeare Festival has become one of the chief economic supports of the city of Ashland.

Oregon Spectator The first American newspaper to be published on the Pacific Coast was the *Oregon Spectator*, which pulled its first issue from the press in **Oregon City** on February 5, 1846. The collaborators on the project included **George Abernethy**, **John Couch**, William G. T'Vault, Robert Newell, and others. The first edition was of four pages, and was printed on a hand press that had been shipped around Cape Horn. Oregon City was the seat of both government and commerce when the *Spectator* began publication, but Salem soon became the territorial capital, and Portland eclipsed Oregon City as the commercial center. As a result, the paper ceased publication in 1855.

▶ **Oregon State University** The state's third largest public institution of higher education grew out of the local Corvallis Academy that began in 1852. Initially non-denominational, in 1865 it came under the auspices of the Methodist Episcopal Church, South, when it also first began to offer a college-level curriculum. Now Corvallis College, the school was designated in 1870 as the state's land-grant college despite its church affiliation; the name was changed in 1872 to Corvallis State Agricultural College. The state assumed actual control of the college in 1885, naming it the State Agricultural College of Oregon; in 1890, it became Oregon Agricultural College. Orange was named the official school color in 1893, and students were known as Aggies or Orangies. The first fraternity arrived on campus in 1905.

The university expanded continuously in the following decades, developing major programs in agricultural sciences, forestry, oceanography, chemistry, and botany. The name became Oregon State College in 1953, and Oregon State University in 1961. A campus in Bend opened in 1999. The school's athletic teams are known as the **Beavers**; an annual football clash with the University of Oregon is known as the **Civil War**.

Oregon Steam Navigation Company (OSN) Oregon's first local monopoly enterprise was the Oregon Steam Navigation Company, an enterprise organized in 1860 by a group of businessmen who had interests in transportation on the Columbia River; among them were **Robert R. Thompson**, Capt. **John C. Ainsworth**, and **Simeon G. Reed**.

The enterprise required assembling three fleets of river steamboats and two portage railroads in order to offer direct transport from Portland to **Umatilla** and Wallula, the major landings serving the booming gold rushes of western Montana, northern Idaho, and northeastern Oregon. (The **Celilo Falls** and associated rapids, and the rapids at the **Cascades**, required portaging freight and passengers around them.) The investors were wildly successful, and their steamboats, such as the sidewheeler *Oneonta*, were symbols of commercial conquest. OSN was a major factor in making Portland a major port city. Ainsworth, who headed the company for all but one of its years of operation, foresaw the company's eventual demise and sold it to the Oregon Railway and Navigation Company in 1880. The opening in 1883 of the paralleling railroad line through the Columbia River gorge greatly reduced river traffic. The OSN investors retired in great comfort.

Oregon Symphony During the nineteenth century, Portland hosted a succession of musical enterprises, ad hoc concerts or performances by traveling troupes. One of the earliest recorded symphonic concerts occurred at Oro Fino Hall in 1866, and an orchestral society was formed in 1875. The Portland Symphony Society was formed in 1896, the first such group in the West, and W. H. Kinross conducted the first concert at the Marquam Grand Theatre. An annual concert series began in 1899, and the group toured the state in 1902. In 1911, the society began transitioning to a professional organization. Carl Denton was the first music director, and conducted the symphony's performance at the 1918 dedication of Civic Auditorium (now Keller Auditorium). Willem van Hoogstraten conducted the orchestra from 1925 to 1938 to critical acclaim, but the Depression sank the symphony from then until its reorganization in 1947. It became the Oregon Symphony in 1967, and in 1980 hired James DePriest as musical director. During DePriest's reign, the symphony moved into the Arlene Schnitzer Concert Hall and undertook a number of recording contracts and touring performances. DePriest retired in 2002.

The imposing Mines Building at Oregon Agricultural College (now Oregon State University) was erected in 1913, the same year that the department of mines was established at the college. The department was discontinued in 1932. The building is now Batcheller Hall, part of a complex of structures for various engineering programs. Mason collection.

Oregon System During the Progressive Era of the early 1900s, Oregon was one of the states that managed, with the encouragement of political leaders such as **Harry Lane, Oswald West**, and **William S. U'Ren,** to reformulate some basic American political processes, in an effort to make government, as historian Stephen Dow Beckham noted, "more efficient, honest, and responsive to human need." The elements of the "system" included the citizen-driven initiative (to create laws outside of the legislative process) and referendum (referring laws enacted by the legislature to a popular vote), the ability to recall elected officials, the presidential primary election, and the popular election of U.S. senators (rather than having them elected by the legislature).

Oregon Territory As organized in 1848 after the Oregon Treaty of 1846 with Great Britain, the Oregon Territory comprised the present states of Oregon, Washington, and Idaho, and small pieces of western Montana and southwestern Wyoming. In 1853, the territory was divided horizontally into Washington Territory and Oregon Territory; Oregon Territory consisted of Oregon, southern Idaho, and the bit of Wyoming. With the creation in 1859 of **Oregon** the state, that part of Oregon Territory east of the Snake River was added to Washington Territory. An earlier and unofficial name for the region, and which included western Canada, was the **Oregon Country**.

Oregon Trail This overland land route from the Midwest to the **Oregon Country** was not a well-defined roadway but rather a succession of trails and paths that expanded over time to accommodate **covered wagons** and herds of farm animals. By the 1820s, fur traders were regularly walking and riding from the Missouri River to trapping areas in Wyoming and Idaho, and missionaries, adventurers and military expeditions followed in the 1830s. The first large and organized group of American emigrants came in 1843 to settle in the disputed Oregon Coun-

try and take up farms. They were followed in 1843 by a group of about 800 emigrants known as the **Great Migration.** The 1,900-mile route crossed what are today the states of Kansas, Nebraska, Wyoming, Idaho, and Oregon, through the trading posts of Fort Hall and Fort Boise. Emigrants often traveled in groups, but some families set off on their own; the jump-off points were usually Missouri River points such as Independence, Westport, or Saint Joseph, Missouri. The stream of wagons and families continued through the 1840s; after 1849 a new stream of Americans took the trail west as far as Fort Hall or its vicinity and then proceeded via the California Trail to that land of gold.

The trail within Oregon generally crossed the Snake River from Idaho in the **Treasure Valley** area, proceeded northwest over the **Blue Mountains**, and then cut across the Columbia River plateau south of the river to **The Dalles**. There, emigrants had to decide whether to try to navigate and portage down the river to **Fort Vancouver,** or to take the **Barlow Road** around Mount Hood to Oregon City and the Willamette Valley.

The number of **pioneers** who used the overland trail to Oregon can only be estimated; and some emigrants came by sea, as well. The figures range up to 4,000 in 1847, 3,600 in 1851, 10,000 in 1852 (despite the attractions of California gold), and about 5,000 in 1859. The total between 1840 and 1859 was about 52,000 people. It was a difficult experience, and nearly 10 percent of those who started out died along the way, from cholera, the perils of childbirth, and accidents such as drowning. Many turned back. A study by historian John Unruh concluded that between 1840 and 1860 about 362 emigrants and 426 Indians died as a result of violence on the Overland Trail (including the Oregon, California, and Mormon Trails).

The **Union Pacific Railroad** followed the general route of the Oregon Trail across Oregon in the early 1880s, as did **Highway 30** in the 1920s. An alternate route that followed the California Trail into Nevada and then veered northwest through the Klamath Basin to meet the **California-Oregon Trail** was the **Southern Emigrant Road**, also called the Scott-Applegate or Applegate Trail. *See also* **Meeker, Ezra**.

> Unruh, John David, Jr. *The Plains Across: The Overland Emigrants and the Trans-Mississippi West, 1840–60*. Urbana: University of Illinois Press, 1979.

Oregon Trunk Railway Without railroad service, the vast pine timber resources and the newly irrigated farmlands of Central Oregon could not be economically developed. The lure of timber and the prospect of a new inland rail route from the interior Pacific Northwest to California precipitated a railroad "war" in the early 1900s. Harney County rancher **Bill Hanley** was one of those who pushed the idea on **James J. Hill** to build into Central Oregon. Hill was the financier behind the Oregon Trunk, which began construction from the Columbia River up the Deschutes River canyon toward **Bend** in 1909. At the same time, E. H. Harriman, head of the **Union Pacific Railroad**, began construction of the Des Chutes Railroad from the same point up the same canyon—on the other side. By 1910, a truce was declared in the risky and expensive war, and the two lines arrived in Bend in 1911 over the same (shared) set of tracks. The route was eventually extended to Klamath Falls and into California in 1930 by another one of James Hill's lines, the **Great Northern Railroad**. The Oregon Trunk was owned and operated by the **Spokane, Portland & Seattle Railway** through most of its history.

Oregon Vortex *see* **House of Mystery**

Oregon-Washington Railroad & Navigation Company *see* **Union Pacific Railroad**

Orenco The Oregon Nursery Company in Salem was founded in 1867, and by the turn of the century boasted that it was the largest in the West, and was perhaps even one of the nation's largest **nurseries**. In order to further expand, the company in 1906 set about establishing a new operation, and a new town along with it, in Washington County. The **Oregon Electric Railway** came through in 1908, and the Orenco post office opened in 1909. The nursery eventually covered some 1,200 acres, but it did not survive the business downturn of the Depression. The town was incorporated in 1913, when it could boast a Civic Improvement League as well as the Farmers' Cooperative Marketing Association. The town government was dissolved in 1938, and the post office closed in 1955. The original townsite remains, now surrounded by suburbia. The Oregon Electric Railway tracks, which saw their last passenger trains in 1932, were used for the **MAX** light-rail system, resulting in the opening of a new station at Orenco in 1998 and a subsequent commercial and residential development north of the old townsite, called Orenco Station.

ostriches *see* **emus**

Oswego *see* **Lake Oswego**

Otis The hamlet of Otis began as a rural post office in Lincoln County a few miles from the mouth of the Salmon River. Otis was named for Otis Thompson, the nephew of Archibald S. Thompson, the first postmaster. With the completion of the Salmon River Highway (Oregon 18) from the Willamette Valley in the 1920s, Otis post office became the introduction to a string of coastal resort communities that developed south to Newport along the **Twenty Miracle Miles**. In the early 1930s, the **Oregon Coast Highway** (U.S. 101) was built north from what soon became known as Otis Junction, and the post office became the nucleus of several service stations and eating places, among them the Otis Café and, in the 1960s, Pixieland, a spinoff from the **Pixie Kitchen**. A rebuilding of U.S. 101 in the 1970s left Otis sidelined on Oregon 18, but the Otis Café has persisted, as has the post office.

Otis, Mr. *See* **Holbrook, Stewart Hall**

otters *see* **sea otters**

Owens-Adair, Bethenia Angelina (1840–1926) Oregon's first woman medical doctor was born in Missouri, and came overland as a child in 1843 on the same wagon train with **Jesse Applegate**. The family settled in Clatsop County, then moved to Roseburg, where at the age of fourteen she married Legrand Hill. He was not a gentleman; by legislative act, she was divorced in 1859, pursued her education and that of her son George, and in 1867 returned to Roseburg and went into the millinery business. She was successful at that, but early experiences doing nursing impelled her to seek medical training. She sought advice from Jesse Applegate and others, and went east to study in Philadelphia; she obtained her MD in 1880 from the University of Michigan. She married John Adair, the amiable but ne'er-do-well scion of a prominent Astoria family, in 1884. Bethenia Owens-Adair practiced in Portland in the 1880s, then in Yakima, Washington, and finally from the farm she bought in Clatsop County, Sunnymead, overlooking the Columbia River. She was noted for her stamina and her commitment to her patients, often traveling alone in abysmal weather. An ardent advocate for woman suffrage, Owens-Adair in later years took a great interest in the possibilities of eugenics in reducing mental illness and criminal behavior, and was a strong advocate for the sterilization of the criminal and the insane. She wrote an influential book on the subject in 1922; Oregon passed a sterilization statute in 1925. She also wrote a fascinating, if self-serving, autobiography.

> Owens-Adair, Bethenia. *Some of Her Life Experiences*. Portland, Oregon: Mann & Beach, 1906. Reprinted as *Gleanings from a Pioneer Woman Physician's Life*, s.l.: s.n., 1922.

owl *see* **spotted owl**

Owyhee River A tributary of the **Snake River**, the Owyhee is about 200 miles long, with its headwaters in northeastern Nevada. It flows northward into Idaho and Malheur County, Oregon, joining the Snake near Nyssa. The name derives from the death of three natives of the Sandwich Islands, also known as Hawai'i; Owyhee is simply another spelling. The Hawai'ians were part of a fur trapping party for the North West Company in 1819–20. The Owyhee Project of 1927–32 brought irrigation water to the **Treasure Valley** area.

oysters *see* **fishing, commercial; Lincoln County; Yaquina Bay**

Pacific Coast Survey Congress authorized coastal surveys beginning in 1807. The Pacific Coast got its first true survey as a result of the work of **George Davidson** and others in the Coast Survey Report of 1858.

Pacific Crest Trail The notion of a trail tracing the high point of the **Cascade Range** originated early in the twentieth century; it is said that what was first called the Skyline Trail was blazed from Mount Hood to Crater Lake in 1919 by Fred H. Kiser; Kiser had the photographic concession at

Crater Lake and was a noted landscape photographer. Kiser's photographs illustrated a 1922 book by Walter P. Eaton titled *Skyline Camps* that promoted the idea. In the late 1930s, a border-to-border trail along the spine of the West Coast was proposed, but only sections were implemented. The Pacific Crest Trail was designated a component of the National Trails System that was authorized in 1968, and was dedicated in 1993.

Pacific Fur Company This American fur company was established in New York City in 1810 primarily with the financial backing of **John Jacob Astor**, and it intended to compete with the well-established **Hudson's Bay Company** in the Western American **fur trade**. The company sent two parties west to found and supply **Fort Astoria** at the mouth of the Columbia River, one by land and one by the ship *Tonquin*; both groups had their misadventures.

The fort and the company's Oregon Country assets were sold in 1813 to the North West Company as a result of the War of 1812 between the United States and Great Britain.

> Irving, Washington. *Astoria, or Anecdotes of an Enterprise beyond the Rocky Mountains*. Philadelphia: Carey, Lea & Blanchard, 1836.

►**Pacific Highway** The term "Pacific Highway" was applied in the 1910s to the developing major roadway from the Canadian border at Blaine, Washington, to the Mexican border south of San Diego. As it took shape in Oregon, it followed the route of the **California-Oregon Trail** and the **Oregon & California Railroad**. One of its prime promoters was regional good roads enthusiast **Sam Hill**. The Oregon State Highway Department was created in 1913, completed a plan in 1914, and by 1917 shifted primary road-building responsibilities

This is a view of the Pacific Highway in the 1920s, looking north across Sunny Valley as the road descends from Sexton Mountain. While the sinuous curves and the Radio Park Auto Camp have been obliterated by Interstate 5, the Grave Creek covered bridge still stands. Steven Dotterer collection.

from the counties to the state. But it was a succession of county roads, mostly gravel, that made it possible for motorists to drive to the San Francisco world's fair of 1915, the Panama-Pacific International Exposition. During the 1920s, the route, now semi-officially designated the Pacific Highway and given the official federal designation **Highway 99**, received a number of handsome bridges designed by state engineer **C. B. McCullough**.

The initial route went from the Columbia River (the Interstate Bridge opened in 1917) via Portland, Lake Oswego, Oregon City, Albany, Eugene, Grants Pass, Ashland, and over Siskiyou Summit. In the 1930s, a four-lane road was built to Oregon City via Milwaukie (SE McLoughlin Boulevard in Portland, the "superhighway" in general parlance) supplanting the Lake Oswego route; this became Highway 99E between Portland and Eugene. An alternate Highway 99W was designated from Portland via SW Capitol Highway (and later SW Barbur Boulevard), via Tigard, McMinnville, and Corvallis to Eugene. Highway 99 was supplanted by **Interstate 5**, which was completed in 1966. The name Pacific Highway remains in use locally over many sections of the former thoroughfare.

> Livingston, Jill. *That Ribbon of Highway III: Highway 99 through the Pacific Northwest*. Klamath River, California: Living Gold Press, 2003.

Pacific International Livestock Exposition (PI) *see* Kenton neighborhood, Portland

Pacific Mail Steamship Company
see ocean transportation

Pacific Railroad Surveys A series of surveys was conducted between 1853 and 1855 by the U.S. War Department of possible transcontinental railroad routes from the Midwest to the Pacific Coast over three basic routes: south, central, and north. Made under the supervision of Secretary of War Jefferson Davis, the surveys noted not only the topographic problems and opportunities of different routes, but also their adjacent natural resources, terminal possibilities such as ports, and the flora, fauna, and existing inhabitants of the areas traversed. The surveys were published in twelve volumes between 1855 and 1860, with illustrations and detailed maps. The central survey became the basis for the first transcontinental line from Omaha to San Francisco, completed in 1869; the **Union Pacific Railroad** completed an offshoot of that route to Portland in 1884. The northern survey laid out the route taken by the **Northern Pacific Railway**, completed to Portland in 1883. The **Oregon & California Railroad**, opened in 1887, also made use of the surveys, as did the **Oregon Trunk Railway** to Central Oregon.

▶ **Pacific University** Pacific University was founded by leaders of the Congregational Church in Oregon, especially the Rev. George H. Atkinson, in Forest Grove in 1849. In that year the territorial legislature chartered Tualatin Academy; the phrase "and Pacific University" was added in its 1854 charter. The first actual baccalaureate degree was not given until 1863; the recipient was **Harvey W. Scott**. Another notable alumnus was **A. C. Gilbert**. Pacific carried on as a small liberal arts college for many decades, shedding the Tualatin Academy in 1915 and absorbing the Pacific Northwest College of Optometry. By the mid-twentieth century the school was noted for its eyes and ears: its optometry program and its music education offerings. Notable campus buildings include Old College Hall (1850) with a museum about the university, and Marsh Hall (1895), named for the university's first president (1853–79), Sydney Harper Marsh. The school's athletic teams were known as the Badgers until 1968; since then, they have been the Boxers, named for a sixty-pound bronze statue of a creature that is half dog and half dragon. The statue came from China with the Rev. Joseph Elkanah Walker in 1898 and was given to the University by his mother. It was initially named College Spirit, but in 1908, it was renamed Boxer in reference to the Boxer Rebellion that occurred in China in 1900. Boxer disappeared in the 1970s; a replica was cast in 1982.

> Miranda, Gary, and Rick Read. *Splendid Audacity: The Story of Pacific University*. Seattle: Documentary Book, 2000.

Pacific yew *see* **yew**

Paisley The town of Paisley is located in Lake County where the Chewaucan River flows into the Chewaucan Marsh before draining into Lake Abert. The area was being used for cattle ranching in the 1870s, and the Paisley post office, named for a town in Scotland, opened in 1911. The community developed in the homesteading period just prior to World War I, and was incorporated in 1911. In 1920, it had a population of 257; the estimated population in 2007 was 250. Paisley is the home of an annual Mosquito Festival.

Paiute Indians *see* **Northern Paiute Indians**

Palmer, Joel (1810–1881) Born in Ontario, Canada, to Quaker parents, Joel Palmer moved about in his younger days, to Pennsylvania and to Indiana, where he served in the Indiana legislature in the early 1840s. He headed west on the **Oregon Trail** in 1845; his diary became the basis of a guidebook for emigrants, *Journal of Travels over the Rocky Mountains* (1847). After going back to Indiana for his family, Palmer returned to Oregon and participated in the **Cayuse War** and as a negotiator with other tribes. Palmer's brief foray to the California gold fields was followed by his permanent settlement at **Dayton**, where he laid out the townsite, filed for a donation land claim and took up farming, and built a sawmill. He became superintendent of Indian affairs for the Oregon Territory in 1853, and immersed himself in attempting to conclude treaties with a number of Oregon tribes, enduring a particularly difficult involvement in the **Rogue River Wars**.

Bird's Eye View of Campus, Pacific University, Forest Grove, Oregon.

Science Hall   Herrick Hall   Academy Building   Marsh Hall

The stark campus of Pacific University in Forest Grove is shown as it appeared about 1905. Science Hall is now Old College Hall and was built in 1850. Herrick Hall was built in 1881 and burned in 1906. The Academy Building had housed the Tualatin Academy and was a contemporary of Old College Hall; it burned in 1910. Marsh Hall was built in 1895; it burned in 1975, but was rebuilt and restored. Steven Dotterrer collection.

Palmer's perceived leniency toward the Indians was the cause of his removal as superintendent in 1857.

Palmer retired to his Dayton farm and engaged in other business ventures. In 1862, he was elected to the state house of representatives, where he was speaker of the house; he served as a state senator from 1864 to 1868. He ran for governor on the Republican ticket in 1870 but lost the election. Palmer earned a reputation as a man of principle and a man of fairness. Palmer Creek remembers him, as does Palmer Glacier on **Mount Hood** (he climbed much of the way up the peak in 1845); his house, much remodeled, has since 1996 housed a restaurant that specializes in dishes that feature Oregon mushrooms.

> O'Donnell, Terence. *An Arrow in the Earth: General Joel Palmer and the Indians of Oregon.* Portland, Oregon: Oregon Historical Society Press, 1991.

papermaking industry Papermaking in Oregon on an industrial scale began at Oregon City in 1866, powered by the waters of **Willamette Falls**. Paper has been made there ever since, with two major mills since the 1890s. A mill to produce newsprint for the Portland *Oregonian* was built nearby on the Clackamas River in 1868, backed by publisher **Henry L. Pittock**. Other early mills developed at Lebanon in 1890 (straw was the basis at first, rather than wood pulp; it was converted in 1902). Other pulp and paper mills have been erected near Astoria (1884–1904), Newberg, Springfield, Halsey, and Gardiner.

Paul Bunyan *see* **Stevens, James**

Paulina (d. 1867) The war leader known as Paulina was affiliated with the Hunipuitöka, a **Northern Paiute** group that historically lived in northern Central Oregon. In the 1850s and 1860s, an influx of Euro-American miners and settlers interrupted the usual living and food-gathering activities of tribes such as the Northern Paiute. Leaders such as Winnemucca (the father of **Sarah Winnemucca)** looked for resolutions, while others such as Paulina reacted to white incursions by stealing horses and livestock and raiding white settlements. As historian Melinda Jetté has noted, in this period "All the resident groups—settlers, Native communities at Warm Springs and Umatilla, and the Northern Paiute—engaged in retaliatory actions that resulted in the deaths of dozens of people, including women and children." After finally agreeing to sign a treaty in 1865 (forced by the U.S. Army taking some Paiute hostages, including Paulina's wife and son), Paulina left the Klamath Reservation in 1866; he was killed in 1867 ("while eating a roasted ox," said Lewis L. McArthur) during a retaliatory raid. The name Paulina is common in Central Oregon: there is a town, the Paulina Mountains and Paulina Peak, a marsh, a creek, a prairie, a cove (where he was killed), and Paulina Lake in **Newberry Crater**.

> Griffin, Dorsey. *Who* Really *Killed Chief Paulina?: An Oregon Documentary.* Netarts, Oregon: C&P Press, 1990.

Pauling, Linus C. (1901–1994) Born in Portland and raised in Condon and Portland, the son of a pharmacist, Linus Pauling graduated from Oregon Agricultural College (now Oregon State University) with a BS in chemical engineering in 1922. In 1925, he received his PhD from the California Institute of Technology (Caltech) in chemistry, with minors in physics and mathematics. Early on, Pauling demonstrated an interest in crossing disciplinary boundaries in the sciences, a trait that continued and widened over the years. After several years in Europe studying with such noted physicists as Neils Bohr, Pauling returned to Caltech to teach and to chair the division of chemistry and chemical engineering, staying until 1964. In 1939, he published an influential textbook, *The Nature of the Chemical Bond and the Structure of Molecules and Crystals*, and his research at Caltech advanced the study of the molecular structure of living tissue and the nature of vitamin C, among other topics. During World War II, Pauling consulted for the National Defense Research Commission and served on the Research Board for National Security; for that he received the Presidential Medal of Merit in 1948. In 1954, Pauling was awarded the Nobel Prize in chemistry.

World War II and the atomic bomb changed Pauling's research interests. In 1958, he published *No More War!*, which decried not only nuclear weapons and their testing, but also the concept of war between nations. He also presented to the United Nations a petition signed by thousands of scientists from around the world who were opposed to nuclear testing. On October 10, 1963, Pauling was named a Nobel Peace Prize recipient for his work. The first nuclear test ban treaty went into effect on the same day. Pauling became a research professor for the Center for the Study of Democratic Institutions during 1963–67, and from 1969 until his retirement in 1973 was a professor at Stanford University. He then established the Linus Pauling Institute of Science and Medicine, a biomedical research group that carries on his interests in nutrition and disease processes. It is headquartered at Pauling's alma mater, Oregon State University.

Paul Revere and the Raiders *see* **music and musicians**

peaches Peaches were prominent on Oregon farmsteads from the 1850s, and commercial orchards were planted in Jackson County in the early 1900s. Peaches do not travel well as fresh fruit, do not ripen off the tree, and are prone to blight. Nevertheless, there is a local market for them, and they are grown in Jackson, Wasco, and Hood River Counties, on Sauvie Island, and in a microclimate near Kimberly in Grant County for sale at U-pick farms, farmers' markets, and supermarkets.

Peacock *see* **Wilkes Exploring Expedition**

Pearl District, Portland One of Portland's newest neighborhoods is the Pearl District, centered on land in Northwest Portland that once held railroad freight yards and maintenance facilities and regional warehouses for department stores, hardware retailers, and similar firms. High-rise residential structures have replaced most of the tracks, while former warehouses have been converted to lofts and condominiums. Extensive development began in the early 1990s as art galleries began moving into the then-low-rent spaces in the neighborhood. In 1996, the North Bank Station freight house buildings of the **Spokane, Portland & Seattle Railway** were placed on the National Register of Historic Places and renovated as stylish condominiums. Development was pushed further with the construction of the Portland streetcar line through the district in 2001.

The name is derived from a remark by a local art gallery owner, Thomas Augustine, that "the buildings in the warehouse district were like crusty oysters, and that the galleries and artists' lofts within them were like pearls," which was then spread through an article in Alaska Airlines' in-flight magazine. That observation was in turn based on a 1982 prediction by Augustine's visiting friend, Pearl Marie Amhara, that the area would someday develop into an arts district. The presence of the **Blitz-Weinhard Brewing Company** in the neighborhood suggested another name, Brewery District, but that had not the appeal of a pearl. The brewery buildings themselves have since been repurposed and Pearlized.

pears We know that pear trees may have come to the Oregon Country as early as 1825, when fruit trees were planted at **Fort Vancouver**. The brothers **Henderson Luelling** and **Seth Lewelling** brought pears west and sold orchard stock to farmers throughout the Willamette Valley. It was not until the development of effective refrigerated storage and refrigerated railcars in the early 1900s that extensive pear orchards were planted, growing pears for shipment to East Coast markets. The **Bear**

Creek Valley and the **Hood River** valley quickly became the focal points of the industry, and remain so in the twenty-first century. Oregon grows about one quarter of the nation's pears with a value of $84 million in 2007. The pear was named the Oregon state fruit in 2005.

peas Fresh green peas, which were grown for canning in the mid-twentieth century, have become primarily a crop for freezing. Oregon peas were planted during the first growing season at **Fort Vancouver** in 1825, and have been a common garden and market crop ever since. Umatilla County has been the center of green pea production since the early 1930s.

Pendleton The county seat of Umatilla County, Pendleton is located on the Umatilla River along the route of the **Oregon Trail.** Dr. William C. McKay established a trading post in the vicinity in 1851. The 1855 treaty with the Cayuse, Umatilla, and Walla Walla Indians resulted in the 1860 creation of the **Umatilla Reservation** immediately east of the future townsite. Umatilla County was created in 1862, with Marshall Station, not far from present-day Pendleton, designated the county seat; that honor moved to the city of **Umatilla** (then Umatilla Landing) in 1865. A town to the east of Marshall Station was platted by M. E. Goodwin and G. W. Bailey; when a subsequent election made their townsite the Umatilla county seat, the name Pendleton was selected, honoring the 1864 Democratic Party nominee for vice president, George H. Pendleton of Ohio. A post office named Marshall had been established in 1865, and its name was changed to Pendleton in 1869.

Pendleton was incorporated in 1880, as railroad fever gripped the area. By 1884, Pendleton was connected by rail to the Midwest, Spokane, and Portland. The 1880 census gave Pendleton a population of 730; by 1910, the year of the first **Pendleton Round-Up**, it was 4,460. The genesis of the **Pendleton Woolen Mills** was in 1893, making use of wool from the extensive sheep ranches in the area. Construction was begun that year on the Eastern Oregon State Hospital, an asylum for the mentally ill; it was completed in 1913. With efforts to de-institutionalize services to psychiatric patients, the facility was converted to the Eastern Oregon Correctional Institution in 1985, and the psychiatric services were continued in an outpatient setting.

Pendleton's role as a transportation hub made it somewhat more ethnically diverse than some other Oregon cities, and it had a population of Chinese and a small African-American community as well, which supported a Union Negro church in 1915. It was also a supply point for sheep and livestock ranchers and wheat farmers. Pendleton's downtown was placed on the National Register of Historic Places in 1986. Stories that Pendleton's Chinese were forced to live underground and out of sight are fictional; they certainly experienced some discrimination, but they lived in daylight. Pendleton's population 11,774 by 1950, and in 2007 was estimated at 17,260.

▶ **Pendleton Round-Up** One of the nation's premier rodeos had its beginning in the aftermath of a Fourth of July celebration, which in 1909 had included bronco riding, foot races, Indian dances and feasts, and other hoopla. Civic leaders came up with the idea of an annual event, scheduled in September to minimize the pressure on ranchers with crops to get in. Established in 1910 as the Northwestern Frontier Exhibition Association, the Round-Up also started off with its "Let 'er buck" slogan and with the participation of Indians from the **Umatilla Reservation** and others in the region. The Round-Up logo associated with the slogan dates from a sketch in 1924 by artist Wallace Smith. Among the early supporters of the Round-Up were Major **Lee Moorhouse**, publisher **C. S. Jackson**, and Harney County rancher **William Hanley**. The Round-Up grounds have been in the same location since 1910. The Pendleton Round-Up and Happy Canyon Hall of

Hazel Walker and Babe Lee are pictured in the trick-riding competition at the Pendleton Round-Up about 1915. Hazel participated in several events at a number of Western rodeos during the 1910s. Walter S. Bowman photograph. University of Washington Libraries, Special Collections, UW27645z.

Fame opened in 1969 to commemorate the rodeo's history.

► **Pendleton Woolen Mills** The Oregon **woolen industry** pioneer Thomas Kay had trained his daughter Fannie in some of the aspects of the business. In 1876, Fannie married a haberdasher named C. P. Bishop; the couple had three sons: Clarence, Roy, and Chauncy. Meanwhile, a wool scouring operation had begun in Pendleton in 1893; in 1895, the operation expanded and began making woolen textiles, and expanded further in 1896 to manufacturing what are known as trade blankets: blankets usually emphasizing strong colors and bold geometric designs favored by many Western American Indian tribes. The name derives from the use of similar blankets in the **fur trade** of the early nineteenth century.

The Pendleton operation failed financially, and in 1909 the Bishop family purchased it and reopened

Employees of the Pendleton Woolen Mills posed beside the factory in 1910 for this photograph by Walter S. Bowman.
Image courtesy of Special Collections and University Archives, University of Oregon Libraries, PH004_0011.

it as the Pendleton Woolen Mills. The company's main blanket trade was located in the Southwest among the Zuni, Hopi, and Navajo nations, but their goods were also popular among Pacific Northwest tribes. By 1912, the company was also producing other fabrics, and in 1924 Pendleton first produced what became the near-legendary Pendleton woolen shirt, using colorful geometric patterns to make an outdoor work shirt that was favored by loggers and mill workers, and eventually by grunge rockers. After World War II, the company entered the business of producing women's clothing, which found a market among new suburbanites and the sporting set. By the 1970s, the company stepped beyond wool for its fashion fabrics, and in the 1980s began to open its own retail stores. The Bishop family still owns the firm.

Pennoyer, Sylvester (1831-1902) Born in New York state, Sylvester Pennoyer graduated from Harvard with a law degree, and came to Oregon in 1855 where he got a job as a teacher. He entered the lumber business in 1862. In 1868-69 he owned and published a Portland daily newspaper, the *Oregon Herald*. Although he was an acknowledged Democrat who had sympathized with the Confederacy, it was not until the mid-1880s that Pennoyer came to the political forefront. It was a time of considerable anti-Chinese agitation along the Pacific Coast, with racial enmity framed as a labor dispute. Pennoyer was the leader of efforts to force the **Chinese in Oregon** to leave the state in 1885-86. In 1886, his prominence in that effort led him to a successful run for governor. Historian Charles H. Carey said that during Pennoyer's eight years in office "he was almost constantly in the public eye by reason of numerous eccentricities."

Among those eccentricities was failing to travel south from Salem to meet President Benjamin Harrison as he entered the state from California, the first sitting president to visit Oregon. He told the president he would be happy to have him call on him at his office in Salem. He was a states' rights Democrat: when President Grover Cleveland named a date for Thanksgiving in 1894, Pennoyer pointedly picked the following Thursday in November for Oregonians to celebrate. And his most prickly act came in 1894 in his response to advice that was telegraphed to him and other governors from the office of President Cleveland on how to handle labor unrest on the nation's railroads. To Secretary of State Q. W. Gresham, Pennoyer wrote, "I will attend to my business; let the President attend to his." Journalism historian George Turnbull relates a story of Pennoyer later being stranded by a storm and seeking shelter. He knocked on a cabin door and identified himself, only to be told from within, "You attend to your business, and I will attend to mine. Go away!" Sylvester Pennoyer also served as mayor of Portland, 1896-98; a street there is named for him.

Peter Britt Music Festival This annual southern Oregon event began when outdoors educator and author Sam McKinney examined the Jacksonville estate of **Peter Britt**, which had recently devolved to the state system of higher education. Thinking it might have possibilities as an outdoor concert venue, in 1963 he persuaded John Trudeau and Gordon Solie of the Portland State College music department to scout the site; all were impressed with the acoustics and the view from the hillside. That same summer, the first chamber orchestra, conducted by Trudeau, was assembled for the first outdoor music festival in the Pacific Northwest. It was a rustic event with a plywood stage, blankets on the lawn and light bulbs in tin cans; the musicians, drawn from around the region and beyond, spent the season in the homes of local hosts. A more formal pavilion was built in 1978, and the festival has matured to become a key part of the economy of **Jacksonville** and southern Oregon.

Trudeau, John. *Touches of Sweet Harmony: Britt Festivals, 1963-1987*. Medford, Oregon: Britt Festivals, 2006.

▶ **Peter Iredale** One of Oregon's pictur-esque sights is the wreck of the British sailing vessel *Peter Iredale*, visible on the beach just south of the mouth of the Columbia River. The *Iredale* was en route to Portland on October 25, 1906 to load a cargo of wheat when a heavy wind drove the ship ashore at dawn. The lifesaving crew at nearby Point Adams helped rescue all hands. Hopes for salvage of the vessel were high, but ultimately the effort proved futile and the hulk became embedded in the sands. The rusted remains, much diminished by scavenging and the elements, are visible at Fort Stevens State Park.

▶ **Petersen Rock Gardens** This tourist attraction near Redmond is the creation of Rasmus Petersen (1883–1952), a Danish immigrant who came to eastern Oregon in 1906. He established a farm and built a Craftsman-style house, and as a

hobby began collecting rocks found on his land, such as obsidian, petrified wood, jasper, malachite, and Oregon agate. Between 1935 and his death in 1952, Petersen constructed a four-acre assemblage of rock

The folk art creations of Rastus Petersen, pictured here about 1950, celebrate his affection for Oregon and his appreciation of American democracy. Mason collection.

The wreck of the British ship *Peter Iredale* has rested on the beach of Clatsop County since 1906. This photograph was probably taken about 1950. Tillamook Head is visible in the distance at the left. Williamson's Marine Photo Shop. Courtesy of Puget Sound Maritime Historical Society, neg. no. 1925-8.

towers, bridges, monuments, and buildings, many somewhat reminiscent of famous American structure. Petersen opened his gardens to the public, and they have remained a tourist attraction.

Pettygrove, Francis W. (1812–1887) Francis Pettygrove was born in Calais, Maine, and went into the retail trade. He came to Oregon in 1843 to do business. He bought land at the future site of Portland from William Overton, and erected a business building there in 1844. The next year he joined with **Asa L. Lovejoy**, owner of an adjacent property, to lay off the first sixteen blocks of a townsite. Lovejoy and Pettygrove used the **Portland Penny** to decide the name of the town, and Pettygrove's choice, after the name of the principal port of his home state, was the winner. Pettygrove sold his share of the townsite in 1847 to Daniel Lownsdale, and moved north to Puget Sound country, where he founded the city of Port Townsend.

PGE Park This Portland athletic stadium was once the site of a tannery on Tanner Creek, and of market gardens operated by Chinese farmers in the 1880s before the **Multnomah Athletic Club** took possession of it in 1893 and developed Multnomah Field there. It soon became a venue for an assortment of public events, lasting into the twenty-first century: presidential visits, college football games, **Portland Rose Festival** events, rock concerts, religious revivals, soccer; a brief fling with a ski jump occurred in the 1950s. In 1926, the athletic club undertook to build a true outdoor arena, designed by architect **A. E. Doyle**. It was not a successful business venture. Dog racing was the major tenant from 1933 until 1955; in 1956, baseball in the form of the Portland **Beavers** became the mainstay. In 1966, the club sold the stadium to the city of Portland, and it became known as Civic Stadium. A major renovation was undertaken in 2001, when the name changed again to honor the money of an electric utility company.

▶ **Philomath** The Benton County town of Philomath is located at the western edge of the Willamette Valley in a region that was settled by farming families in the 1840s. The town initially grew around a school founded in 1867 by the United Brethren Church, Philomath College. The word is Greek, "meaning a lover of learning, an astrologer, or prognosticator," according to geographic names expert Lewis L. McArthur. A post office named Philomath opened in 1868, and the town was incorporated in 1882. The Willamette Valley & Coast Railroad completed its line from Yaquina Bay to Corvallis, passing through Philomath, in 1884. The census of 1900 reported 343 residents in Philomath, and 591 in 1920. In 1915, Philomath had a "large saw mill, ax-handle factory and co-operative creamery," the United Brethren church and one other church, a bank, and a weekly newspaper, the *Benton County Review*.

Philomath College closed in 1927, a victim of changing educational times and the rise of Oregon Agricultural College (now **Oregon State University**) a few miles away in Corvallis. The imposing central hall is now the Benton County Historical Museum. The population of Philomath in 1950 reached 1,289.

The lumber industry was Philomath's chief economic engine after World War II. In 1959 a prominent mill owner, Rex Clemens, and his wife, Ethel, established the Clemens Foundation. The foundation aimed to make college scholarships available to the children of lumber industry workers in the Philomath area, in part a recognition of the inevitable future decline of timber as the city's mainstay. Clemens died in 1985, and his own mill closed at about the same time. In 2006, Peter Richards produced a documentary film, *Clear Cut: The Story of Philomath, Oregon*, about the escalating conflicts in Philomath between the vanishing timber culture and changing educational needs. The city is now adjacent to Corvallis and a bedroom community for its education and high-tech industries. Philomath's population in 1990 was 2,983; the estimate in 2007 was 4,530.

▶ **Phoenix** The city of Phoenix in Jackson County dates from the 1850s; Samuel Colver—whose immense plantation-like house is in the center of town—settled a donation land claim on the site in 1851, and his brother Hiram took an adjacent claim. Samuel laid out a townsite in 1854, and a post office named Phoenix opened in 1857. The name is derived from the Phoenix Insurance Company, although the locality was also at times known as Gasburg, allegedly because of the "loquacity" of a certain woman resident there; the complex interconnection of these two facts may be found in Lewis L. McArthur's *Oregon Geographic Names*. Phoenix prospered in the 1860s as a town with a gristmill in a wheat-growing area. In 1884, it acquired a railroad connection with Portland and Ashland. Phoenix was incorporated as a city in 1910, when it had 250 residents and orchards of apples and pears were replacing the wheat fields; by 1920, that figure was down to 159, reflective of a slump in the orchard industry. Since then,

The house of Samuel Colver in Phoenix, built in the 1850s, as it looked on August 18, 1939. T. J. Edmonds photograph. Federal Writers' Project. Oregon Historical Society, OrHi 36926.

"College Walk" at Philomath College in Philomath, with a venerable oak, photographed about 1915. The former college building became the Benton County Historical Museum in 1980. Steven Dotterrer collection.

Phoenix has milled lumber and shipped fruit. The population reached 746 in 1950 and 2,309 in 1980. Since then, as the **Pacific Highway** corridor between Ashland and Medford has become urbanized, Phoenix has become a bedroom community for the two larger cities. It population in 2007 was estimated at 4,845.

PI (Pacific International Livestock Exposition) *see* Kenton neighborhood, Portland

Pillars of Hercules *see* Rooster Rock

Pilot Butte An extinct cinder cone with rises almost 500 feet above the landscape, Pilot Butte received its name because its distinct shape was a landmark to early travelers. It is located at the eastern edge of **Bend** in Deschutes County. The butte is a park, acquired by the city in 1927, and with a scenic overlook and roadway that was developed during the Depression by the **Civilian Conservation Corps**. Pilot Butte was the namesake of another Bend landmark, the Pilot Butte Inn. This rustic lodge was designed by architect John E. Tourtellotte in the Craftsman tradition. It opened in 1917 and became a headquarters for sportsmen and an early center for outdoor recreation in Central Oregon. The inn was placed on the National Register of Historic Places in 1973; it was almost immediately demolished. The loss helped raise awareness of historic preservation issues statewide.

Pilot Rock The Umatilla County town of Pilot Rock is named for a nearby bluff, and a rural post office with that name opened in 1868. A townsite was platted in 1876, but growth waited until the arrival of a railroad branch line from Pendleton in 1907. Pilot Rock was incorporated in 1911, and the 1920 census reported a population of 347. The surrounding countryside in the early twentieth century was devoted to farming, fruit and poultry raising,

and livestock, and Pilot Rock was equipped with stockyards for shipping cattle, and with warehouses for grain, especially barley, and wool. After World War II, lumber mills boosted the activity, drawing timber from the Blue Mountains to the south. Pilot Rock had a population of 847 in 1950, and 1,612 in 1970; the estimated population in 2007 was 1,560.

pine Four major varieties of pine trees are relatively common or exist in commercial quantities in Oregon: lodgepole pine; ponderosa pine; western white pine; and sugar pine. The lodgepole pine, sometimes called the Sierra lodgepole, *Pinus contorta* var. *murrayana*, grows from twenty to eighty feet in height and is found in the Cascade Range; it is a tall and narrow tree with thin and scaly bark. It is well adapted to forest fires, for the cones can remain on the tree for many years, with the seeds released on exposure to fire; falling to the ground, they begin creating a new forest.

Ponderosa or western yellow pine, *Pinus ponderosa*, was described by Scots naturalist **David Douglas**, who considered its wood to be heavy, or ponderous. This is the most commercially valuable of the pine species in Oregon, found throughout the Blue Mountains of northeastern Oregon, on the east slope of the Cascade Range in the north, and through much of Klamath, Lake, and Deschutes Counties in southern Oregon; a subspecies is found on the western side of the southern Cascades and in the Siskiyou Mountains of Josephine, Jackson, Douglas, and Lane Counties. The ponderosa grows primarily in single-species stands that form extensive forests, but it is also found mixed with other forest conifers; it ranges in height from about 60 to 130 feet or more and has a rough, heavily ridged bark. Ponderosa pine is used to manufacture window frames and panel doors, and the lumber is used for light framing and interior sheathing.

Western white pine, sometimes called mountain white pine or Idaho white pine, *Pinus monticola*, is found in areas of the Blue Mountains and in the

Cascade and Siskiyou Mountains, usually mixed with other conifers but sometimes in concentrated stands. It usually reaches a height of about 100 feet, but can get much higher; one near Medford is 239 feet in height. It is an excellent tree for lumber and for specialty uses such as making matches because the wood is usually free of knots or twisted grain.

Sugar pine, *Pinus lambertiana*, is found in much of the same areas of the Cascade and Siskiyou Mountains as western white pine. It is quite large, usually ranging from 100 to 160 feet in height, with exceedingly large and long cones, which can be as much as twenty-one inches in length, with large, sweet seeds. Like white pine, sugar pine is easily worked and produces framing lumber, cabinetry woods, and door and window frames.

pioneer A pioneer, in Oregon terms, was a Euro-American settler who came to what is today Oregon in the years before statehood, that is, before February 14, 1859. While many of those came over the **Oregon Trail**, the term was also applied to those who came by sea around Cape Horn, or by land routes as fur trappers; even retired French-Canadian trappers with Indian wives could honorably call themselves pioneers. The pioneers formed the Oregon Pioneer Society in 1873 to celebrate themselves; twenty-five years later, the **Oregon Historical Society** was created by later emigrants who also paid fealty to the pioneers. The Oregon Pioneer Society inevitably died out, expiring in the 1950s; the Sons and Daughters of Oregon Pioneers, however, valiantly carry the pioneer torch forward.

Pioneer Courthouse This Portland building, a National Historic Landmark, was completed in 1875 as a federal courthouse, designed by the architect for the U.S. Treasury, Alfred B. Mullett. It also initially housed customs and internal revenue offices and a post office. At the time of its construction, Portlanders felt it was far from the scene of commerce; by 1900, it was in the heart of the new retail and office district. An addition was authorized in 1902. The court and post office operations moved out in 1933, but the post office branch reopened in 1937. In the 1930s, and again in the 1950s and 1960s, efforts were made to demolish the building for a parking lot or office building. In 1969, it was renamed Pioneer Courthouse, and after renovations were completed in 1973, the U.S. Court of Appeals moved into the building. Changes impelled by security issues caused another rebuilding in the early 2000s, which again ousted the post office but retained public access to the glass-enclosed cupola that tops the building.

▶ **Pioneer Courthouse Square** The square block that has held Pioneer Courthouse Square in Portland since 1984 has a distinguished past. It was the site of Central School, Portland's first public school, in 1858. The school was demolished to make room in 1883 for a grand edifice, the Portland Hotel, sponsored by the **Northern Pacific Railroad**; the railroad's finances collapsed, and the hotel was not completed until 1890. But from its opening until it closed its doors in 1951, it was the grande dame hotel of the city; an iron gateway from the hotel has been incorporated in the square. In 1951, the hotel was demolished in order to construct a two-level parking garage of bald ugliness, intended to shore up sales at the **Meier & Frank** department store. Plans by Meier & Frank in the late 1960s to develop even more parking on the site clashed with citizen efforts to consider it the site for a public square. The city acquired the property in the 1970s; the design for the square was by a team headed by Willard K. Martin and including writer **Terence O'Donnell**. Much of the money was raised by "selling" pavement bricks on which the purchaser could have a name or phrase etched; this was one of the first major civic uses of this financing method. Since its opening in 1984, Pioneer Courthouse Square has been the "downtown living room for the people of Portland," in the words of Willard Martin.

This photograph of the courtyard of the Portland Hotel was taken by Minor White during his Portland sojourn in the late 1930s. Designed by the New York firm of McKim, Mead, and White, the Portland Hotel stood on the future site of Pioneer Courthouse Square. The wrought iron gate was preserved when the hotel was demolished, and it was re-erected at its former location. Works Progress Administration, 390322-1. Oregon Historical Society, OrHi 9338.

Pittock, Henry Lewis (1836–1919) and **Georgiana Burton Pittock** (1845?–1918) Henry Pittock was born in England and educated in Pennsylvania. He had had some experience in the printing trade when he came to Portland in 1853; he soon had a job at the weekly *Oregonian* newspaper. By 1860, owner Thomas J. Dryer turned the newspaper over to him to settle his wages. In 1860, Pittock married Georgiana Burton, a recent emigrant from Iowa; the next year, as publisher of the *Oregonian*, he inaugurated a daily edition. A businessman, Henry put the editorship of the paper in the capable hands of **Harvey W. Scott** in 1865. Pittock also invested in the Clackamas Paper Manufacturing Company in 1867, which produced newsprint for the *Oregonian* and for the daily *Telegram*, which he founded in 1877 as an evening newspaper.

Georgiana was a woman with many civic interests, including the Portland Women's Union and other organizations supportive of women and children in need. She was instrumental in the 1889 founding of the Portland Rose Society. Late in their lives, the Pittocks had Edward T. Foulkes design for them a magnificent French Renaissance revival house on a high point of the **Tualatin Mountains** above Northwest Portland. The house was completed in 1914. The house remained in family ownership and use until 1958, when it was put up for sale. It did not sell, and severe damage in the **Columbus Day storm** of 1962 precipitated a proposal to demolish it. The landmark Pittock Mansion was purchased by the city of Portland in 1964, and has since been restored as a house museum—and a stunning scenic viewpoint. The Pittock name was also carried by a sternwheel steamboat, the *Georgie Burton* (1906–47), and by a propeller craft that was a regular passenger vessel on the Portland-Astoria run, the *Georgiana* (1914–39)—she was the last regular passenger vessel on the Columbia River. Henry also invested in the Pittock Building in downtown Portland, long the regional headquarters of the **Union Pacific Railroad** but remodeled in the 1990s to appeal to high-tech startup firms.

Pixie Kitchen Pixie Pot Pies opened in Oceanlake (now **Lincoln City**) in 1948. Renamed Pixie Kitchen in 1953, it quickly became famed for its distorting mirrors that could make you see yourself as fat as you walked in and slim when you left. Although it touted its "heavenly food," it was the kitschy décor that was memorable. A spinoff was Pixieland in nearby **Otis**. The Pixie Kitchen declined in the 1980s and died in the early 1990s.

plums *see* **prunes**

plywood industry *see* **wood products industry**

▶ **politics and government** Native American political structures in the Oregon Country were based on personal and family associations and connections. Among Euro-Americans in the early nineteenth century, the fur-trading companies, in particular the **Hudson's Bay Company**, carried the weight of representing law, order, and a quasi-national connection. By the 1840s, with British and American claims of sovereignty pending, the **Wolf Meetings** led to the formation of a local **provisional government**, headed by provisional governor **George Abernethy**. With the establishment of the Oregon Territory in 1848, American politics and governmental authority were soon in place. **Joseph Lane** was appointed the first territorial governor by President Polk. The years leading up to statehood in 1859 were marked nationally by issues that led to the **Civil War**, including the extension of **slavery** and states' rights. Oregon politics showed the same strains, with newspapers such as the *Statesman* of **Asahel Bush** fanning the flames. In the later years of the nineteenth century, as national politics solidified into the Democratic and Republican Parties, Oregon exhibited Republican tendencies by electing leaders such as Senator **John H. Mitchell** and Representative **Binger Hermann**; a notable exception

For decades, many of the men who were influential in Oregon politics and government stayed at and frequented the Willamette Hotel in Salem when the legislature was in session. It was opened in 1870 as the Chemeketa House, and spent its later years as the Marion Hotel. The photograph was taken about 1895. After many remodelings, it burned in a spectacular fire in 1971. Thomas J. Cronise photograph. Oregon Historical Society, OrHi 0218G041.

was **Sylvester Pennoyer**, elected governor on the Democratic People's Party ticket in 1886.

The twentieth century ushered in a progressive wave, exemplified in Oregon by **William S. U'Ren** in the state legislature and **Oswald West**, a Democrat, in the governor's office. In 1930, Oregon elected a governor who ran as an Independent, **Julius L. Meier,** and followed in 1934 with a maverick Democrat, **Charles H. Martin**. Oregon had a number of senators and representatives with national reputations, including **Charles McNary, Wayne Morse,** and **Richard** and **Maurine Neuberger** in the Senate, and **Nan Wood Honeyman** and **Edith Green** in the House of Representatives. In the last half of the century, two notable governors pursued political agendas that emphasized conservation: Republican **Tom McCall**, elected in 1966, and Democrat **Robert Straub**, elected in 1974. *See also* **Baker, Edward Dickinson; Baker, George L.; Meek, Joseph L.; Nesmith, James W.; Oregon System.**

Polk County The **provisional government** created Polk County from the **Yam Hill District** in 1845, naming it after President James K. Polk; its original boundaries included all of southwest Oregon to the California border. Subsequent redrawing has reduced its area considerably; it now consists of 745 square miles. The county seat is **Dallas**; the first courthouse was built in 1851 when the community was known (perhaps) as Cynthiana; that courthouse was dismantled in the 1850s when the town moved, and a second seat of government was erected. The second building burned in 1898, and was replaced in 1900. The 1900 courthouse still stands in the midst of the town square, and it would be a most handsome edifice but for the 1966 addition to the building. The area that now comprises Polk County is the homeland of the Yamhill and Luckiamute bands of the **Kalapuyan Indians.**

Polk County was perhaps the focal point of interest for those American **pioneer** emigrants of the early 1840s. The soil is highly productive, and the area was quickly settled by farmers who grew wheat and other grains and raised cattle and sheep. River steamboats served the landing at **Independence** beginning in the 1850s, and the county had railroad service by 1880. The 1890s saw the introduction of hops and prunes as major crops. By 1900, Polk County had a population of 10,075, and in 1915 it was noted that "some of the most celebrated dairy farms, fine stock farms, prune orchards, hop yards, and berry and vegetable gardens in the entire state are in the Willamette section of Polk County." It also supported commercial pear and apple orchards, "principally on the hillside slopes." The county was also then one of the leading producers of Angora goats. Lumber mills operated in most Polk County towns, and extensive logging of the Coast Range Mountains began in the 1910s, turning **Falls City** into a lumber town; **Monmouth** has a long history as an educational center. Polk County's population reached 19,989 in 1940; since World War II, population growth in large part reflects residential growth for commuters who work in Salem. The estimated population in 2007 was 67,505.

ponderosa pine *see* **pine**

▶ **Portland** The city of Portland can trace its beginnings to William Overton and **Asa L. Lovejoy**, who jointly claimed in 1843 the land on the west side of the Willamette River where Portland started. Overton soon left, replaced by **Francis W. Pettygrove**, and it was the tossing of the **Portland Penny** that named the townsite. The adjacent land claim of Capt. **John Couch** and his experience as a sea captain helped establish Portland as the effective head of navigation on the Willamette River by 1850: this point was as close as sailing ships could get to the populous and productive lands of the Willamette Valley. Portland had a post office by 1849 and was incorporated in 1851, when its population was likely a bit less than 1,000.

The city made strides in the 1850s: it gained a

newspaper, the quickly influential *Oregonian*, in 1851, saw the beginnings of its most famous department store, **Meier & Frank**, in 1857, and built a road to connect the port with the wheat fields of the **Tualatin Plains**. The population in the 1860 census was 2,874 people—the largest community in the new state of Oregon. During the 1860s, Portland became the headquarters of the **Oregon Steam Navigation Company**, which made its owners rich and made Portland a thriving port. The 1870s brought the beginnings of railroad construction linking the city with the Willamette and Umpqua Valleys; in the 1880s, those links were completed across the continent and via the **Oregon & California Railroad** south to California. The growing international trade in wheat boosted the city as well, as Northwest wheat funneled through the port to cities in Asia and Europe. By 1890, Portland had a population of 46,385; across the Willamette River on the east side were the separate cities of **Albina** (population 5,129) and East Portland (population 10,532), and new **streetcars** connected the three across new bridges. In 1890, the three cities merged into one; the 1900 census reported a population of 90,426 people.

In the early 1900s, Portland planned to celebrate its achievements, which it did with a world's fair, the 1905 **Lewis and Clark Centennial Exposition**. The fair's success presaged a decade of continued economic growth and prosperity, and the first **Portland Rose Festival** took place in 1907. The 1910s brought the growth of residential suburbs on the east side of the river, the development of the **Columbia River Highway** and the beginnings of the **Pacific Highway** as Oregon entered the automobile

One of the state's most elegant bridges crosses the Willamette River at Portland to the Saint Johns neighborhood. The photograph was taken shortly after the bridge opened in 1931. The engineer and designer was David B. Steinman.
Oregon Historical Society, OrHi 4785-a.

age. The municipal airport was opened in 1927 on Swan Island, three new bridges were built across the Willamette in the 1920s, and the Saint Johns bridge opened in 1931. Portland's mayor from 1917 to 1933 was genial theater manager **George L. Baker**. The depression of the 1930s was a difficult time, with homeless people camped in **Sullivan's Gulch**, but it also brought the construction of **Bonneville Dam** and **Timberline Lodge**. Bonneville's electric power was needed during **World War II**, when Portland acquired tens of thousands of new residents including many **blacks**. After the war, the wartime housing project of **Vanport** vanished in a 1948 flood; in 1950, the city elected its first woman mayor, **Dorothy McCullough Lee**. Portland's population in the 1950 census was 373,628.

The last streetcar ran in 1950; buses replaced them, running on the new one-way street system in downtown Portland. The next year, the venerable Portland Hotel, opened in 1890, was demolished to build a parking lot. The declaration of part of **South Portland** as "blighted" in 1957 set in motion the city's first experience with **urban renewal**; it was not until the 1968 opening of the **Keller Auditorium** that tangible, perhaps positive, results were seen from that action. The 1960s opened with the opening of the **Lloyd Center** shopping mall; downtown retail business declined. The **Minnesota Freeway** (1964) and the Marquam Bridge (1969) were elements in a huge network of freeway construction that continued into the 1970s—until the **Mount Hood Freeway** was quashed in 1975, setting off a chain of events that led to the opening of the **MAX** light-rail line in 1986. Portland's population reached 379,967 in 1970; the figure in 1980 was 366,383.

During the 1980s, Portland worked to enhance its downtown retail center in the face of track construction for the MAX line. The 1982 Portland Building, a post-modern be-ribboned office box by designer Michael Graves, made headlines but was not nearly as popular as the 1985 statue **Portlandia** that was erected over the entrance. Annexations and

the urban growth boundary, which was first adopted in 1979, helped propel population growth in Portland; the 1990 census showed 438,802 residents. By 2000, the figure was 529,121; the estimated population in 2007 was 568,380.

Lansing, Jewel Beck. *Portland: People, Politics, and Power, 1851–2001*. Corvallis: Oregon State University Press, 2003.

Portland Art Museum (PAM) The oldest art museum in the state and the region is the Portland Art Museum, established in 1888 and incorporated in 1892 by a group of the city's business men—among them **C. E. S. Wood** and **William S. Ladd**—as the Portland Art Association. The museum's first acquisition was a carefully chosen collection of plaster casts of Greek and Roman antiquities, a seemingly odd purchase but one that fit the organization's aims of bringing great art to a remote locality. Their new home was in rooms at the public library, but by 1905, they had their own building. Anna Belle Crocker was hired as curator in 1909, and served until 1936. The year 1909 also saw the beginning of the Museum Art School; the name changed in 1980 to Pacific Northwest College of Art, which continued to be part of the museum until separating in 1994. The college moved to a new campus in the Pearl District in 1998.

The museum made a great leap forward when funds were raised to construct a new building on the Park Blocks. Designed by **Pietro Belluschi** as a sleek, modern box of brick and travertine, it opened in 1932. The 1956 exhibit of the works from the private collection of Walter Chrysler was curated by the Portland Art Museum and toured the nation, one of the first of the art world's "blockbuster" museum shows. The museum building was added to in 1936 and 1970. In 1994, the museum purchased the adjacent Masonic Temple building, and in 2005 opened it as additional exhibition and research space after an extensive and controversial remodeling.

Portland Civic Theatre (PCT) The Civic grew out of a group called the Art Theatre Players, established in 1925 by three women: Susan Farrell, Florence Bristol, and Delta Spencer. Their first production was *Henrietta the Eighth*, with a cast that included **James Beard**. Under the direction of Mildred Allen Butler, the community theater group changed their name in 1929 to Portland Civic Theatre. Performances were staged in rented quarters until money was raised to build a theater on SW Yamhill Street near the downtown core, which opened in 1942. PCT also established an acting school in 1934, and a Junior Civic Theatre after their new theater opened. While the 1950s and 1960s were very productive, PCT faced severe financial problems by 1971. A succession of innovations was tried, including the introduction of a summer repertory program with paid cast and staging the opening performance—of *Sunday in the Park with George*—at the new Portland Center for the Performing Arts in 1984. But the organization, once one of the largest and strongest community theaters in the country, still struggled, and finally closed in 1990. The theater building was demolished in 1993 and replaced by a parking structure.

Portland Development Commission *see* **Keller, Ira; urban renewal**

Portland Hotel *see* **Pioneer Courthouse Square; Whidden, William Marcy**

Portlandia Installed over the entrance to the city-owned Portland Building, designed in the postmodern style by Michael Graves, is the statue Portlandia, by sculptor Raymond Kaskey. Portlandia is based on the figure of a woman in flowing classical Greek robes who appears on the city seal. She is thirty-six feet tall, and, as one observer noted, if she "was magically to stand up, she would be over fifty feet tall." She is the second-largest hammered copper statue in America; the largest is the Statue of Liberty, and since *she* stands, literally, over 150 feet in height (and on a pedestal of equal height), Portlandia seems to shrink from notice for sheer size. However, she is handsome and exceedingly graceful, and swoops over the street in a welcoming pose, so her size is immaterial. The statue arrived in Portland by barge in 1985 and was trucked to its installation amid much civic festivity.

Portland Institute for Contemporary Art (PICA) Commonly known as PICA, the institute was established in 1995 by artist and art curator Kristy Edmunds to provide a venue for contemporary art programs, a task which it has accomplished very swiftly.

Portland Junior Symphony *see* **Portland Youth Philharmonic**

Portland Penny When **Asa L. Lovejoy** and **Francis W. Pettygrove** platted the future city of Portland in 1844, each proposed a name for the future metropolis. Lovejoy proposed the name of his Massachusetts home town, Boston; Pettygrove opted for the capital and major seaport of his home state of Maine, Portland. The very penny that was used is in the collections of the Oregon Historical Society, a gift of the Pettygrove family.

> Lovejoy, Asa L. Lovejoy's Pioneer Narrative, 1842–1848. Ed. Henry E. Reed. *Oregon Historical Quarterly* 31, no. 3 (September 1930).

Portland Rose see *City of Portland*

▶ **Portland Rose Festival** The genesis of this annual Portland event developed from the 1905 **Lewis and Clark Centennial Exposition**. As the exposition came to a close, mayor **Harry Lane** proposed a Festival of Roses to perpetuate the national recognition that came to the city for hosting that world's fair. But even before Lane's proposal was voiced, roses held an esteemed place in Portland.

The region's climate is highly favorable to rose propagation, and in 1888 **Georgiana Pittock** sponsored a rose show; the next year, attorney Frederick V. Holman and others founded the Portland Rose Society, which continued to hold annual rose shows. In 1902, Holman looked forward to the 1905 exposition and called on Portlanders to plant roses in the gardens and along city streets—and in particular, he encouraged the planting of the Mme. Caroline Testout rose, a pink and aromatic bloom that comes in bush and rambler varieties. The Rose Society held a fiesta in conjunction with its 1904 show, and it included a parade of decorated horse-drawn wagons and carriages (and four automobiles), held on June 10. Holman's idea took root, so to speak.

The first annual fiesta and parade took place in 1907. From 1908 until 1914, the event was presided over by Rex Oreganus, a well-known citizen who was disguised with a beard until the king was unveiled at the festival ball. In 1914, a queen, also chosen from the social elite, ruled the event. Since 1931, the "court" has been made up of young women who are seniors in Portland high schools; one of them is chosen queen. From about 1911 into the 1920s, many of the parade floats were built on the beds of scrapped electric streetcars: propelled by electricity from overhead wires, the floats were also brilliantly lit for an evening spectacle. The route of streetcar lines dictated the parade route. Over the years, the Grand Floral Parade has been the major event of the festival, requiring the use of real flowers in float decorations; it spawned secondary parades such as the evening Merrykhana and Starlight parades, and a junior parade. Visits by United States and foreign

This 1922 photograph shows a float for the Portland Rose Festival evening parade, depicting "Human rosebuds, Oregon's crowning glory." The float is studded with light bulbs, and is built on the frame of a former streetcar. Running on streetcar tracks, the float picked up electricity from an overhead wire through the trolley pole visible at the far right. Mason collection.

naval vessels, and a carnival, have long been a part of the festivities, while others, such as milk carton racing and musical events, have come and gone and come again. In the 1970s, the festival began adding a long list of sporting events, and then an air show. Some roses still play a part in the festival, but Mme. Caroline Testout is difficult to find.

Portland State University After the end of World War II, with returning veterans seeking schools where they could make use of their educational benefits under the GI Bill, the Vanport Extension Center was created in 1946 in **Vanport**. Displaced by the 1948 Vanport flood, the center came to downtown Portland in 1952, occupying the former Lincoln High School. In 1955, the name was changed to Portland State College as it grew into a four-year, degree-granting institution, a move championed in the legislature by **Monroe Sweetland**. Located in the state's largest city, the college experienced tremendous growth, despite being restricted in its offerings in order not to "compete" with established programs at **Oregon State University** and the **University of Oregon**. Master's level programs were added beginning in 1961 and doctoral programs in 1968, and in 1969 the state System of Higher Education designated it as Portland State University. The school has developed along the South Park Blocks in both new and remodeled buildings, creating an urban campus; the motto of the school in recent years has been *Doctrina urbi serviat*, or "Let knowledge serve the city." Portland State University was the largest university in the state system by 2007, with 18,012 undergraduate students and 6,272 graduate students. The school's sports teams are called the Vikings.

Dodds, Gordon B. *The College that Would Not Die: The First Fifty Years of Portland State University, 1946–1996*. Portland, Oregon: Oregon Historical Society Press, 2000.

Portland Symphony *see* Oregon Symphony

Portland Youth Philharmonic Mary V. Dodge was a violin teacher and the director of the Irvington School Orchestra, which became the nucleus of the Portland Youth Philharmonic. In 1924, Dodge and others established the Portland Junior Symphony Association, and they engaged a Russian émigré musician, Jacques Gershkovitch, as conductor. Gershkovitch held the post for twenty-nine years, during which time the group—the first youth orchestra in the nation—became a well-known prototype for similar groups. Gershkovitch was followed by another remarkable musician, conductor and composer Jacob Avshalomov, who directed the orchestra from 1954 until 1994. During his tenure, the Junior Symphony became the Youth Philharmonic, and the group made a half-dozen tours of Europe and Asia.

▶ **Port Orford** The Curry County city of Port Orford dates from the 1850s, when Capt. William Tichenor settled there, hoping to make of it a supply port for the southern Oregon gold fields. As a port, Port Orford has not been a signal success. The name derives from that given to what is now Cape Blanco, which the English Capt. George Vancouver designated Cape Orford, after his friend George, Earl of Orford. In turn, Port Orford has provided a name for the **Port Orford-cedar**. The post office at Port Orford opened in 1855. By 1915, it reportedly had a population of about 200 and its harbor was accessible "nine months of the year." Dairying, lumbering and livestock raising were the nearby industries; "famous Port Orford white cedar" was used to make shingles. A beach of agates north of town gave rise to an annual Agate Carnival each August. Port Orford was not incorporated until 1935, after the **Oregon Coast Highway** gave it a reliable land route to other places; it was the first incorporated municipality in Curry County. The population in 1940 was 755. Port Orford's mayor, Gilbert Gable, was one of the fomenters of the 1941 movement advocating the creation of a new **State of Jefferson** to band together the "forgotten" western sections of southern Oregon and northern California. Portland Orford's population reached 1,037 in 1970, and was an estimated 1,240 in 2007.

Port Orford-cedar This tree is a member of the cypress family, *Chamaecyparis lawsoniana*, also called Lawson cypress and Oregon cedar. Growing only in a narrow band of coastal southern Oregon and northern California, Port Orford-cedar is a tall (from 70 to 200 feet) evergreen whose dense, aromatic wood is used for furniture making and sculpture, and is much favored in Japan for constructing temples, shrines, and woodenware. It is also used for arrow shafts and guitars. In the late nineteenth and early twentieth centuries, Port Orford-cedar was used in **shipbuilding** in the Coos Bay region, where

Asa Simpson and others built both sailing ships and steam lumber schooners from the wood. Several varieties of the tree have also become prime ornamentals in the Pacific Northwest. In the 1950s, a root rot appeared that, along with logging, has threatened the existence of the trees in their native range.

Portsmouth neighborhood, Portland Land in the vicinity of N. Lombard Street and Portsmouth Avenue was platted as a residential subdivision in 1883, but land sales did not materialize until the arrival in 1889 of suburban railroad that connected the area to the **Albina neighborhood**. This became an electric streetcar line in the 1890s, bringing Portsmouth in easy reach of downtown Portland as well as the **Saint Johns neighborhood** to the west. The community briefly—in 1891—had its own post office.

The Battle Rock Cottages has no vacancy, but there appears to be room at the Shoreline Motel and seats at Katie's Kafe in downtown Port Orford, shown in the early 1950s. Clarence I. Christian photograph. Mason collection.

possum *see* **opossum**

potatoes A major food crop, potatoes were common in farm and market gardens from 1825, when they are noted as being planted in gardens at **Fort Vancouver.** They were in the Pacific Northwest even before that time: the Spanish are known to have planted potatoes at their brief settlement at Neah Bay, Washington, in 1791–92, and the Makah Indians continued to grow them. Potatoes are grown for the wholesale market in several areas of Oregon where irrigation waters are available: in **Klamath, Umatilla,** and **Morrow Counties,** in the **Redmond** area, and in the **Treasure Valley** of eastern Oregon. Many of these are turned into frozen potato products, especially French fries.

Powder River The Powder River begins in the Blue Mountains of Baker County and flows east and north some 110 miles to join the Snake River just above Brownlee Dam. The name dates to the fur trade of the 1820s, but the reason for its use remains obscure. The tributaries in the Blue Mountains were the site of gold discoveries in the 1870s, and **Sumpter** on the Powder was a major goldmining town. From 1913 to 1953, the gravels of the Powder River valley downstream from Sumpter were mined by dredge, resulting in miles of piles of gravel. The Baker Valley north of Baker City is irrigated by water from the Powder.

Powers A logging center for more than half a century, Powers is located on the South Fork Coquille River in Coos County. The townsite was named in 1914, honoring A. H. Powers, the general manager of the Smith-Powers Logging Company, and a post office of the same name was established the next year. The railroad connecting the Coos Bay region with Eugene and the wider world opened in 1916, and Powers was at the far southern end of that extension. The logs that came through Powers on their way to mills on **Coos Bay** were converted to lumber that could now be shipped by sea or rail to far-off markets, and the logging continued at a fast pace until 1970. The town was dominated by the lumber company, but it was incorporated as a city in 1945; the 1950 census reported a population of 895, and the estimate for 1957 was 1,300—when it was at the height of its powers, so to speak. Logging declined in the followings decades, and the population fell to 819 in 1980, and to an estimated 730 in 2007.

Powers, Alfred J. (1888–1984) Born in Arkansas, Alfred Powers came west and graduated from the University of Oregon in 1910; his BA thesis was, "Citizens of Pleasant Valley: A Story." Powers made a mark on Oregon as a historian and a writer, and most especially as a writer on the history of Oregon literature. He also served as the dean of extension services for the state system of higher education in the 1930s, and as an editor for the Portland publishing firm Metropolitan Press and its imprint, Binfords & Mort. His monumental *History of Oregon Literature* was published in Metropolitan Press in 1935; among his others works are *A Century of Coos and Curry: History of Southwest Oregon*, with Emil R. Peterson (1952), and *A Long Way to Frisco, a Folk Adventure Novel of California and Oregon in 1852*, which was selected in 2005 by the Oregon Cultural Heritage Commission as one of their "100 Oregon books." Oregon poet Walt Curtis quotes an interview of Powers in about 1983 with Penny Avila where she asks him if Oregon has "a special climate, elixir, that causes people to be creative with words?" His reply was, "I've never been able to analyze it. Whether it's a mixture of sunshine and gloom, whether it's the gorgeousness of our herbage—the riotous show of nature which really is a product of the rain—some kind of germ exists here in Oregon that leads to the creative kind of thing."

Prairie City On the John Day River in Grant County, Prairie City was preceded by a gold-mining camp called Dixie located about three miles north on Dixie Creek, where a strike was made in 1862. The post office of Prairie City opened in 1870 to serve miners and ranchers in the area, and a town developed; it was incorporated in 1891. The census of 1900 gave Prairie City a population of 213. In 1910, the narrow gauge **Sumpter Valley Railway** came to town, and by 1915, it was reported to be a major shipping point for cattle, sheep, and wool. "Heavy freighting into the interior is done by 4- and 6-horse teams," and Prairie City boasted a creamery to serve the local dairy farmers, a planing mill, a sawmill, and a flour mill. Transportation needs changed; the railway pulled out in 1933. The city's population went from 643 in 1920 to 438 in 1930, but rebounded to 867 by 1970. Prairie City is still a service center for nearby ranches and still has a sawmill. The estimated population in 2007 was 1,100.

▶**P Ranch** The headquarters of the eastern Oregon cattle empire of **John William "Pete"**

French was the P Ranch, located about a mile east of the community of **Frenchglen** in Harney County. The ranch was established in 1872, and from it French supervised the immense French and Glenn holdings until his death in 1897. The property has gone through many hands and handlings since; the main ranch house burned in 1947, and the remains— a chimney, fences, outbuildings—are now on the Malheur National Wildlife Refuge.

Oster, Clarence A. The P Ranch House Fire: An Eyewitness Account. *Oregon Historical Quarterly* 106, no. 2 (2005): 284–293.

Prefontaine, Steve "Pre" (1951–1975) Raised in Coos Bay, Steve Prefontaine attended Marshfield High School, where he made a splash as a runner. A charismatic and enthusiastic young man, Prefontaine enrolled at the University of Oregon where he trained with the noted track coach **Bill Bowerman**. He quickly became a star athlete, winning the NCAA

The P Ranch near Frenchglen in the 1930s, surrounded by a stand of cottonwoods. Author's collection.

5,000-meter race four times. He hit the cover of *Sports Illustrated* in 1970 and won a spot on the 1972 U.S. Olympic team, though he missed getting a medal. By the spring of 1975, Pre held the NCAA record in every running event from 2,000 to 10,000 meters. He died in a single-car auto accident at the height of his career; the Prefontaine Classic at the University of Oregon and an annual run in his hometown of Coos Bay remember him.

Prescott This small Columbia County community was named for the owners of a local sawmill and was given a post office in 1905. The post office closed in 1946. The town incorporated in 1947, and in 2007 had a population of about sixty. It is located adjacent to the now-defunct **Trojan** nuclear power plant.

Prineville The county seat of Crook County, Prineville had its beginnings in a rural post office named Prine; established in 1870, it was named for Barney Prine, the first merchant in the area. "His stock consisted of a barrel of first-rate whisky in the front room of his establishment and some blacksmithing equipment in the back room. The prevailing opinion around Prineville is to the effect that most of the business was done in the front room," said historian Lewis L. McArthur. The post office became Prineville in 1872, and one Monroe Hodges filed a plat for city lots and streets in 1877. Prineville was incorporated in 1880, and became the seat of the new Crook County in 1882. Cattle ranching was the chief enterprise in the area in the 1870s and 1880s, and Prineville was a supply point as well as the seat of government. Sheep ranching increased in the 1890s, leading to turf battles between cattle and sheep raisers. Prineville's population in the 1890 census was 460. Railroad construction to Central Oregon raised hopes in Prineville in the early 1900s, but the terrain dictated a Deschutes River route for the **Oregon Trunk Railway** that left Prineville nearly twenty miles from the track when the line opened in 1911. Undaunted, the citizenry succeeded in 1918 in building the City of Prineville Railway, one of the few municipally owned lines in the nation. The city's population in 1920 was 1,144. Logging on national forest lands nearby grew during the 1940s and after World War II, and a number of mills were built in Prineville; the population grew to 3,233 in 1950 and 5,276 in 1980. In 1952, the **Les Schwab** tire-store chain opened its first operations in Prineville and the city remained the headquarters of the company until 2007. Lumber operations fell precipitously in the 1980s, but the city has continued to grow as a center for retirees and outdoor recreation enthusiasts. Its 2007 population was estimated at 11,245.

prohibition Liquor was long a contentious issue in Oregon. In the 1820s, the **Hudson's Bay Company (HBC)** refused to sell or distribute liquor, although a bit was available to some trappers in the field and to executives at **Fort Vancouver**. Those opposed to liquor included many loquacious Christian missionaries, particularly the Methodists; **Jason Lee** and his followers founded the Oregon Temperance Society in 1836. Early settler **Ewing Young** established a still in the 1830s, running afoul of HBC, and his neighbors, in the process. The **provisional government** in 1843 acted to forbid the "introduction, manufacture and sale of ardent spirits," and in the next year destroyed a few distilleries; however, by 1845, the provisional legislature chose to regulate rather than ban alcohol.

The first temperance convention was held in Salem in 1852; many groups, conferences, and movements followed. The IOGT—Independent Order of Good Templars—came in 1865, the WCTU—Women's Christian Temperance Union—in 1880. In the 1870s, praying women were known to enter saloons en masse, bent on changing minds and habits. By the 1890s, prohibition was, in the popular mind, often allied with efforts to give women the vote: many feared that if women voted, prohibition was virtually inevitable. Oregon suffragist **Abigail Scott**

Duniway sought to separate the issues; she herself favored moderation over prohibition.

In 1904, the state passed a local option act; beginning in 1905 with Hood River, a number of individual cities and counties decided to prohibit liquor sales and consumption; nearly a third of the counties subsequently voted to go dry. Then, in 1914, a statewide ban was enacted; it became effective January 1, 1916. Oregon's dry years lasted until federal repeal in 1933. The impact in Oregon included the closure of most **beer and brewing** establishments; the **Blitz-Weinhard Brewing Company** did survive the hiatus with other beverages. In terms of **wine and wine making**, the industry was very small before prohibition, although it was often made at home or by small operations; Italian families in Portland, for example, often pooled resources to buy grapes by the boxcar to make wine at home. The place with the longest reign of prohibition was the city of **Monmouth**, where alcohol was banned from the mid-nineteenth century until 2002.

Caswell, John E. The Prohibition Movement in Oregon, Part I, 1836–1904. *Oregon Historical Quarterly* 39, no. 4 (1938): 251–261.

Caswell, John E. The Prohibition Movement in Oregon, Part II, 1904–1915. *Oregon Historical Quarterly* 40, no. 1 (1939): 64–82.

pronghorn antelope The pronghorn is an antelope-like creature that was once widely distributed throughout eastern and southern Oregon, and indeed throughout the North American West. The herds were greatly diminished by hunters early in the twentieth century, but have since rebounded in southeastern Oregon, particularly on the Sheldon–Hart Mountain National Antelope Refuge, established in 1936.

provisional government The term refers to a period in early Oregon history before the resolution of territorial issues between the United States and Great Britain, and after the influx of a few thousand Euro-American trappers, traders, missionaries, and settlers. The provisional government was established by a group of the more permanent occupants of the territory; it was precipitated by the death of **Ewing Young** and the need to settle his estate, and by concerns about wolves and other predators. The government grew out of a series of what were later called the **Wolf Meetings**, held at **Champoeg** between February 7, 1841, and May 2, 1843. At the last meeting, a group of nine men was named to create a provisional government. **George Abernethy** was selected as the first governor, in 1845; he was re-elected in 1847, although by that time the region's status had been clarified on the international stage with the 1846 Oregon Treaty that placed present-day Oregon under the control of the United States.

▶ **prunes** Fruit trees of the genus *Prunus* produce plums, familiar to most of us as fresh, canned, or frozen fruit. Oregon grows some plums, but once grew a great deal more of them, primarily those known as Italian plums, which were dried to produce prunes. Prunes were widely popular from the nineteenth century well into the 1960s as a natural laxative, and were especially common at the break-

The Willamette Valley Prune Association of Salem issued this booklet of "choice recipes" in 1909. Author's collection.

fast table; they are also delicious. In the 1880s and 1890s, as historian Stephen Dow Beckham wrote, Oregon farmers "went wild for prunes. Thousands of acres of hillside lands were opened and groomed as orchards." The same thing happened in California, and a glut soon developed, but Italian plum orchards—and the wooden dryer structures that turned them into prunes—were common in Polk and Marion Counties and throughout the Willamette Valley until after World War II. Prunes are produced dried and sold in packages or in bulk, and are also dried and then canned in syrup.

public markets Public markets are places, publicly or privately operated, where farmers can rent stalls for the direct sale of farm produce to the public, and which are usually supplemented by stalls leased for longer terms by dealers in other food and agricultural products, such as fish and butcher shops, imported fruit dealers, grocers, bakers, and florists. Market squares for such purposes were often reserved in American city plans from the eighteenth century onward. By the time West Coast cities were being planned, such squares were no longer common. Portland's plan of 1853 did set aside two blocks for this purpose, but their use was sporadic. The first public market in Oregon appears to have been in the New Market Theatre building, erected on First Street near Ankeny in Portland in 1873; it had market stalls on the ground floor, and offices and a theater on the floors above.

Other markets operated on the two public market blocks sporadically from 1890 into the early 1900s. Public markets nationwide enjoyed a resurgence of interest in the early 1900s, partly as a result of Progressive-era political goals in the areas of public health and consumer protection. In the West, the creation and almost instant success of the Pike Place Public Market, founded in Seattle in 1907, led to a spate of similar efforts. In Oregon, Medford began a city-sponsored public market in 1913; it lasted until 1930. Portland opened the Yamhill or Carroll Market in 1914, on Yamhill Street between Fifth and Second; it was named for *Portland Telegram* newspaper editor John F. Carroll, who promoted it. In 1915, the Pomona Grange began a public market in Eugene, which survived until 1959. Smaller public markets operated in Portland neighborhoods and in Astoria; in some cases, such as that of **Fred Meyer**, public market merchants went on to more ambitious endeavors.

The principal Portland public market was targeted for change with the construction of a new Morrison bridge, which required heavy traffic on Yamhill Street, then crowded with farmer's stalls. Over much merchant and farmer opposition, a huge new public market building was erected on the waterfront, opening on December 14, 1933. It was briefly popular, but the market failed and closed by 1942; remnants of the Carroll Market survived on Yamhill Street into the 1980s. *See also* **farmers' markets**; **Saturday Market**.

Eigo, George. *A Market for the City: The History of Portland's Public Markets*. Portland, Oregon: Oregon Historical Society, 2002.

Pudding River The Pudding River rises in the Cascade Range foothills of Marion and Clackamas Counties and flows north to join the Molalla River near Canby. Its course marks the eastern edge of Howell Prairie, and it drains—or once did—**Lake Labish**. The river is frequently of a thick brown color and a mud-like consistency, but these qualities did not give rise to its name. That, it seems, derives from a blood pudding that was created by the Indian wives of two French-Canadian trappers, perhaps Joseph **Gervais** and Etienne Lucier, after a successful elk hunt along the river's banks. The stream was known as Rivière au Boudin as early as 1814, and as Pudding River by 1841.

puma *see* **cougar**

Puter, Stephen A. Douglas (b. 1857) Mr. Puter was a crook; specifically, he was instrumental in the carrying out of some of the immense frauds of the late nineteenth and early twentieth century that bilked the federal government—and thus the public purse and trust—through illegal and specious claims on federal lands. The chief beneficiaries were large timber companies and some politicians, including the redoubtable Senator **John Hipple Mitchell** and **Binger Hermann**. Puter pointed fingers very pointedly in his revealing and confessional book, *Looters of the Public Domain* (1906). *See also* **Oregon and California Revested Lands**.

Quigley, Edward Burns "Ed" (1895–1984) Born in North Dakota, Ed Quigley grew up in Spokane, served in World War I, and went to Chicago after the war, where, off and on, he attended the Art Institute of Chicago and did advertising art. The Depression sent him back to the Pacific Northwest, where he kept a studio in Portland and lived in a log cabin near Sandy. During the Depression, commercials provided little income; Quigley expanded his artistic interests to horses, the rangelands, and, in another direction, the circus. He participated in the **Works Progress Administration** (WPA), painting historical murals at Irvington School in Portland in 1936. By the late 1930s, Quigley became involved with the Yakama Indians, and he began spending his summers as a **buckaroo**. Horses, Indians, the Oregon desert landscape, became major subjects of his art, which by the 1950s had a collector audience. There were circus paintings, too, and small wooden circus sculptures. Quigley was inducted into the National Cowboy Hall of Fame in 1984.

Gohs, Carl. *Ed Quigley, Western Artist*. Portland, Oregon: Geneva Hale Quigley, 1971.

railroads The first railroads in the Oregon Country were built in the 1850s and 1860s to portage goods and passengers around obstacles to navigation: **Willamette Falls** at Oregon City on the Willamette River, and the **Cascades** and **Celilo Falls** on the Columbia River. The prospect of a land grant set off the construction of two railroads in 1869–70, both intending to connect Portland with California. The **Oregon & California Railroad** finally finished the project in 1887; by that date, Oregon was already connected with the upper Midwest by the **Northern** **Pacific Railroad** and with Omaha and points east by an arm of the **Union Pacific Railroad**. A network of narrow-gauge railroads was built in the Willamette Valley in the late 1870s and 1880s; these were swept into the growing system of the **Southern Pacific Company** in 1890, along with the Oregon & California Railroad and the Corvallis & Eastern with its line to **Yaquina Bay** and up the **Santiam River**. The Southern Pacific built lines to Coos Bay and to Klamath Falls in the 1910s and 1920s to complete its Oregon system. In the early

1900s, the Portland-headquartered **Spokane, Portland & Seattle Railway** took over lines to Astoria and Seaside, and assumed the operation of the **Oregon Electric Railway** in the Willamette Valley, and the **Oregon Trunk Railway** to Central Oregon. These lines came into the control of **Burlington Northern Santa Fe Railway**, which, with the Union Pacific, in 2007 controlled all the major rail lines of the state. Since the 1980s, smaller operators have taken over some branch lines, and a number of branch railroads were abandoned.

Passenger train service was operated by individual railroad companies until the formation of Amtrak in 1971. Amtrak instituted the *Coast Starlight* to California, and maintained the **Empire Builder** to Chicago via Minneapolis; it operated service between Seattle and Chicago via Portland and Salt Lake City from 1977 to 1997. In conjunction with the state, Amtrak increased passenger train service from Eugene to Portland and Seattle. *See also* **interurban railways; streetcars**.

Schwantes, Carlos A. *Railroad Signatures Across the Pacific Northwest.* Seattle: University of Washington Press, 1993.

Rainier Like the nearby town of Saint Helens, Rainier is named for a mountain that is visible from the townsite—though both mountains are in Washington state. Situated on the Columbia River in Columbia County, Rainier was founded in 1851; a post office was established in 1852. It was a small lumber and fishing town for many decades. Rainier was incorporated in 1885, and gained railroad connections in 1898; the 1890 census reported 298 inhabitants. Lumber mills boosted the population to 1,359 by 1910. The extension of the **Columbia River Highway** downriver in the 1920s helped the town's economy somewhat, as did the development of the large, planned industrial city of Longview, just across the river in Washington state, at the same time. The ferry crossing was replaced in 1926 by a spindly highway bridge, later named for Lewis and Clark.

Somnolence descended. Rainier's population was 1,285 in 1950, 1,655 in 1980, and an estimated 1,775 in 2007. The town no longer has any lumber mills.

Rajneesh, Bhagwan Shree (1931–1990) An Indian spiritual leader who also went by the names Acharya Rajneesh and, in late life, Osho, the Bhagwan was born Rajneesh Chandra Mohan Jain. He studied and taught philosophy in India in the 1950s and 1960s; in 1968 he created a sensation among Hindu leaders by recommending a more open acceptance of sex. By 1971, he had adopted the spiritual honorific Bhagwan, accepted the first of many disciples or sannyasin, and begun to promote a spiritual life that was not ascetic; in the 1980s it became, in fact, quite materialistic.

The Bhagwan came to the United States in 1981 for medical care; after a brief period in New Jersey, his followers purchased for him the Big Muddy Ranch in Wasco County. Over the next three years, the Rajneeshi swiftly built a city on the ranch, calling it **Rajneeshpuram**. The Bhagwan lived in "a modest home with an indoor swimming pool." He had an affinity for Rolls-Royce automobiles, and his followers—the majority were relatively young and well-to-do professionals—purchased two cars a month for him. He took ceremonial tours of the commune in his Rolls automobiles, showered by flowers tossed by his red-clothed adherents.

The city of Rajneeshpuram had some legal problems, and some of the Bhagwan's staff—most especially his secretary and manager Ma Anand Sheela—engaged in some highly questionable conduct. Indeed, it came to accusations of conspiracy to murder public officials, wiretapping, illegal firearms use, violation of land-use laws, fraudulent voting, and finally in 1984 an instance of mass food poisoning that sickened 751 people in The Dalles: it was perhaps the first instance of mass bioterrorism in the United States. The Bhagwan's advisors fled in 1985, and although he was not directly implicated in any crimes, he was arrested on immigration charges as he was attempting to leave the country. He eventually returned to India in 1986; he took the name Osho, and died in 1990. A few Rajneeshi still live in Oregon.

Rajneeshpuram The former city of Rajneeshpuram was an intentional religious community located on the Big Muddy Ranch in Wasco County. The ranch, some 64,000 acres in size, was purchased in 1981 by followers of the **Bhagwan Shree Rajneesh** for $5.75 million; they proceeded to build a city there, despite the fact that doing so violated state land-use laws and county zoning law. In a short time, Rajneeshpuram grew to a city of about 5,000 people, equipped with a water system, an airstrip, fire and police departments, a shopping mall, restaurants, and armed security guards. In an effort to meet some of the legal objections, the community was incorporated as a city in 1982; however, the next year, the state attorney general filed a lawsuit to invalidate the incorporation on the basis that the city government was in fact an arm of a religious organization, which violated the state's constitution. In a counter move, followers of the Bhagwan in effect took over the government of the nearby existing incorporated municipality of **Antelope** and renamed it Rajneesh. The environmental group **Thousand Friends of Oregon** challenged the city on its violations of state land-use law; neighboring ranchers, including **Bill Bowerman**, also protested the development of a city on rural agricultural lands.

The community unraveled in 1985 in a flurry of crime and indictments, and the city was dis-incorporated as its titular head returned to India and his closest advisors were arrested or fled the country. The abandoned city of Rajneeshpuram was eventually sold, and in the early 2000s was reshaped as the Wildhorse Canyon Young Life camp, operated by an organization that "brings in hundreds of high school and middle school kids each week to tell them about Jesus Christ and give them the 'best week of their lives!'" according to their website.

raspberries Grown extensively in the Willamette Valley, commercial crop raspberries come in red and black varieties. Among the red raspberries, *Rubus idaeus*, two varieties, known as Willamette and Meeker, predominate, and most of the crop is converted to frozen berries, puree, or juice concentrate; some are canned or used in fruit filling products or jams and jellies, and some reach the local markets fresh. Oregon produces about 10 percent of the nation's crop of red raspberries.

Black raspberries, *Rubus leucodermis*, are also often called blackcaps. They are native to North America and have a smaller seed than the red raspberry; less tart, they are used extensively in jams and to flavor ice cream, and their blue-black color makes them an effective food-coloring agent as well. Virtually all the commercially grown black raspberries in the nation are grown in Oregon.

Redmond This Deschutes County city owes its inception to irrigation and the **Oregon Trunk Railway**. The post office opened in 1905, the townsite was platted in 1906, and Redmond was incorporated in 1910. The railroad arrived in 1911. In 1915, Redmond was reported to be "in [the] center of [a] large irrigated district" that already boasted an annual potato show and fair. The population reached 585 in 1920. In 1927, a fire destroyed the downtown core, but rebuilding, symbolized by the red-brick New Redmond Hotel, was rapid. Redmond's population in 1950 was 2,956.

The New Redmond Hotel was placed on the National Register of Historic Places in 1980 and in 2008 was undergoing renovation as the old downtown began to reflect some of the prosperity found at the city's edges. Rapid population growth, with an influx of retirees and seasonal second-home owners, has characterized the area since 1970. The population reached 7,165 in 1990, and an estimated 24,805 in 2007.

redwood The coast or California redwood, *Sequoia*

sempervirens, is the world's tallest tree, a majestic conifer that reaches heights from 200 to 325 feet with a diameter of from ten to fifteen feet. Coast redwoods grow in a narrow strip of land adjacent to the ocean and extending inland from five to thirty-five miles, and up to about 3,000 feet in elevation—an area that experiences frequent damp fogs. The strip reaches from southern Curry County south along the California shoreline to the vicinity of Big Sur. Redwoods often grow in dense, pure forests, but they can also be found growing amidst Douglas-fir, Port Orford-cedar, and mixed conifer trees. A remaining stand of coast redwoods is located in the Rogue River-Siskiyou National Forest in the drainage of the Winchuck River.

Redwood Empire *see* **Redwood Highway**

Redwood Highway The term "Redwood Highway" is used to describe U.S. **Highway 101** from San Francisco north to Crescent City and beyond, via Highway 199, to Grants Pass, Oregon. The idea of such a highway was established as early as 1909 in California, but little happened until the 1920s, when the diversion of highway dollars to southern California prompted the establishment of the Redwood Empire Association in 1927 to promote the northern route. The promoters were the six affected California counties, to which was added Josephine County in Oregon. What has once been a pack-train route from the port of Crescent City to the southern Oregon gold fields, built in the 1850s, was expanded into a toll road by 1887 and was then rebuilt into a highway in the late 1920s. The route provided access to the **Oregon Caves** as well; it was officially opened on June 22, 1929.

Reed, John S. (1887–1920) Journalist, radical, socialist John Reed was born into a moderately wealthy Portland family. He attended Portland Academy and went east to Harvard, where he wrote for the *Harvard Lampoon* and graduated in 1910. He went into journalism, where his leftist political views found voice in periodicals such as *The Masses*. His instincts were to go to the action, and he covered the events of the Mexican revolution in 1914, spending time with Pancho Villa and his cohorts. His reporting resulted in a successful book, *Insurgent Mexico*. In 1915, while back in Portland to visit family, Reed met another writer, **Louise Bryant**, and they began what became a legendary romance. Reed was a noted correspondent during World War I in various European outposts. In 1917, he married Bryant, and they both went to Russia to write about the socialist revolution that was sweeping that land. In 1919, Reed published his firsthand account of the birth of a communist nation, *Ten Days That Shook the World*.

Returning to the United States, Reed carried forward his political beliefs with action as he organized the Communist Labor Party and edited the *Voice of Labor*. In the Red Scare period following the Russian revolution, Reed's political activism forced him to leave the United States. After much tribulation, he again reached Russia, where Bryant joined him and where he was immensely popular. But his life was cut short by typhus; he died October 19, 1920. He was buried, with other heroes of the revolution, beside the Kremlin wall in Moscow.

Reed maintained little connection with Oregon after his school days, and was not fond of Portland; on his last visit in 1915, he found the city to be "awful beyond words." Reed's communism has caused his name to be linked, quite erroneously, to **Reed College**, which has long been associated with leftist politics and, in the 1950s, stood accused of being a hotbed of communism. The college was founded with money acquired through the most rigorous application of capitalism by **Simeon G. Reed**. The story of John Reed and Louise Bryant was captured in the 1981 movie *Reds*, with Warren Beatty as Reed.

Gelb, Barbara. *So Short a Time: A Biography of John Reed and Louise Bryant*. New York: Norton, 1973.

Rosenstone, Robert A. *Romantic Revolutionary: A Biography of John Reed*. New York: Knopf, 1975.

Reed, Simeon Gannett (1830–1895) Born in Massachusetts, Simeon Reed came west to Oregon as a young man, a year after marrying Amanda Wood in 1850. In 1855, he got a job clerking for Portland merchant **Williams S. Ladd**, a position which led to a partnership with Ladd and then, in 1860, to a larger venture. Reed joined with investors Jacob Kamm, a steamboat operator, **John C. Ainsworth**, **Robert R. Thompson**, and others to form the **Oregon Steam Navigation Company (OSN)**. Guided by Ainsworth, OSN made money, and OSN made Simeon Reed wealthy before the company was sold in 1880. Although Reed's venture at iron making at **Lake Oswego** in the 1880s was a failure, he remained a rich man. Reed owned several farms, some in conjunction with Ladd, where he raised blooded horses and cattle, in California, in the Willamette Valley, and at Reedville in Washington County. Simeon and Amanda Reed moved to Pasadena, California, in 1892, where Simeon died in 1895; Amanda remained there, dying in 1904.

Reed College At the death of **Simeon G. Reed** in 1895, his estate devolved to his widow, Amanda, and with it came a suggestion she use some of the money to contribute to "the beauty of the city [of Portland] and to the intelligence, prosperity, and happiness of the inhabitants." Amanda took this to heart, consulted a good deal with the Rev. **Thomas Lamb Eliot**, and established a board of trustees. At her death in 1904, the trustees, guided by Eliot, proceeded to lay the plans for Reed College, which was to be a private, distinctly secular, liberal arts college offering education of high quality. The college was founded in 1908 and held its first classes in 1911. The future campus was acquired in 1910 from the Ladd Estate Company—a portion of the Crystal Springs Farm once owned by Reed's early partner **William S. Ladd**. With a splendid endowment for its time, the college hired noted architect **A. E. Doyle** to design a grand collegiate quadrangle of brick classroom and dormitory buildings, and construction began in 1912. The first president of the college was William Trufant Foster (1879–1950), a young educator who proposed an ideal university that included a ban on fraternities and sororities, a downplaying of intercollegiate athletics, and a strong (but unsuccessful) push for simplified spelling. His tenure (1910–19) set a distinct tone of intellectual rigor and educational innovation that the school has since strived to maintain. The school is noted for its production of Rhodes scholars and future graduate students, its conference teaching methods, and its bohemian scholars, most of whom come from outside the state. *See also* **Reed, John S.**

Reedsport The mouth of the Umpqua River in Douglas County was early on found to be suitable—if barely—for navigation purposes, and it was put to use in the 1850s through the ports of **Gardiner** and, upriver, **Scottsburg**. The construction of a railroad from Eugene to Coos Bay in the early 1900s created the town of Reedsport, on the marshy southern shore of the river. The Reedsport post office was established in 1912, as construction workers built the railroad and the lengthy bridge across the Umpqua estuary. The work was completed in 1916; Reedsport was incorporated as a municipality in 1919, and the 1920 census reported 850 residents in the new city.

Reedsport benefited from the completion of the **Oregon Coast Highway** in the 1930s, but has relied more on lumbering, fishing, and manufacturing than on tourism for its economic base. The city reached a population of 2,288 by 1950, and 4,984 in 1980; since then, the decline in timber harvesting has considerably reduced the city's economy and population; the estimate in 2007 was 4,305.

rheas *see* **emus**

Richland A small ranching community in Baker County, Richland grew around its post office, which was established in 1897. In 1915, the area was described as a center for raising hay, grain, livestock, and fruit, and the town boasted a high school, two churches, fraternal lodges, a bank, and a weekly newspaper, the *Eagle Valley News*. Richland was incorporated in 1917, and the 1920 census credited it with 244 inhabitants. Things have quieted down a bit since that time; the population was 220 in 1950, 181 in 1980, and an estimated 150 in 2007.

Riddle Riddles post office (the *s* was dropped in 1910) was opened along the new Oregon & California Railroad in Douglas County in 1882. Although deposits of nickel were identified in the 1880s on Nickel Mountain, the town remained a small distribution center for logging and gold-mining operations nearby. Riddle was incorporated in 1893; the 1900 census reported a population of 131. By 1915, it was reported that the "goat and sheep industry is growing in importance and conditions are very good for dairying." In 1954, commercial mining and processing of nickel began at Riddle, and has continued—with periodic spikes and lapses—into the twenty-first century. Riddle's population in 1950 was 634; in 1980, 1,265; and in 2007, an estimated 1,040.

Rivergrove This odd bit of political geography in Clackamas County is a purely residential enclave. It was incorporated as a separate city in 1971 to forestall annexation by another municipality; the name derives from the Tualatin River on its south, and the older community of Lake Grove to the north. The population was estimated at 350 in 2007.

river transportation Oregon's rivers and lakes were transportation arteries for Natives using dugout canoes. Early fur trappers plied them with canoes and bateaux, and sail-driven scows and rafts navigated the Columbia in the 1840s. From 1850 until the 1920s, sternwheel steamboats plied the Columbia and Willamette Rivers, as well as many other lesser-known waters, including Klamath and Goose Lakes, the Coquille and Millicoma Rivers, the John Day and Snake Rivers, and several Willamette River tributaries, especially the Tualatin and Yamhill Rivers. Logs also found their way to sawmills by river, with sternwheel and gas- and diesel-powered tugs guiding them. The Willamette Locks and Oregon City eliminated portages at Willamette Falls in 1873; on the Columbia River, it was not until 1896 that locks bypassed the **Cascades**, and 1915 that the Celilo Canal opened to provide through navigation on the Columbia River. Local river traffic, however, declined after the introduction of railroads in the 1880s, and again with improved highways in the 1920s. Passenger traffic ceased in the 1930s on the Columbia River, log movements nearly ceased by the 1970s, and the remaining river traffic is in barges: wheat and hay, petroleum products, and sand and gravel. *See also* ***Bailey Gatzert***; **Canemah**; **Cascade Locks**; *Lot Whitcomb*; **mosquito fleet**; *Oneonta*; **Oregon Steam Navigation Company**; *T. J. Potter*; and names of individual rivers and towns.

"Road of a thousand wonders" This phrase was used as an advertising slogan by the **Southern Pacific Company** for its Shasta Route, the railroad line connecting the San Francisco area with Portland, which opened in 1887. The slogan was promoted during the 1910s and 1920s. *See also* **Aumsville**.

roads *see* **highways and roads**

▶**Rockaway Beach** The resort town of Rockaway Beach in Tillamook County arose with the completion of a railroad linking Tillamook with Portland in 1911. The post office of Rockaway opened that year, and by 1920, numerous cottages and boarding houses lined the railroad tracks. In 1941, Rockaway hot dog stand owners George and Versa Boyington contrived to make a hot-dog-on-a-stick

The main street of the seaside resort of Rockaway Beach about 1920. The railroad station is at the upper left, with a strip of plantings and a welcoming rock garden sign between the tracks and the street. Mason collection.

with a built-in bun of cornmeal, and invented the Pronto Pup, generically known as a corndog. It is only coincidental that the city of Rockaway was incorporated the next year, 1942. Postwar highway travel kept Rockaway busy as a summer resort; in 1987, the town decided that adding the word "beach" to their name would be an improvement: thus, Rockaway Beach. Rockaway had a population of 1,027 in 1950; 970 in 1990; and an estimated 1,360 in 2007.

Rockwell, Cleveland Slater (1837–1907) Born in Youngstown, Ohio, Cleveland Rockwell was trained as an engineer, graduating from New York University in 1856. He was highly regarded for his mapping skills during a long career (1857–92) with the U.S. Coast and Geodetic Survey. Rockwell was appointed chief of the USCGS for the Pacific Northwest, headquartered in San Francisco, in 1867; he was transferred to Portland in 1878 and remained there until his death. **George Davidson** was a colleague in the USCGS.

Rockwell was also a painter, one of the best in Oregon in the nineteenth century, turning out luminous watercolor paintings of regional scenes along the Columbia River, of fly-fishing, of coastal scenes from Sitka to South America. He worked also in oil, and sketched prolifically in pencil, often with watercolor or wash. Rockwell's scenes are romantic and composed, undistorted by lurid color or re-arranged landmarks, and often include men and women and manmade structures; the attention to detail reflects his detailed work drafting coastal charts. His works were exhibited in San Francisco and Portland during his lifetime, and he was active in the Portland Art Club and the Oregon Artists Association. Several exhibits in the late twentieth century bolstered his visibility, and prices for his work have skyrocketed in recent decades. He was also the great uncle of artist Rockwell Kent (1882–1971).

Stenzel, Franz. *Cleveland Rockwell: Scientist and Artist, 1837–1907.* Portland, Oregon: Oregon Historical Society, 1972.

rodeos *see* **Molalla; Pendleton Round-Up; Saint Paul**

Rogue Indians *see* **Athapaskan Indians; Takelma Indians**

Rogue River (body of water) The Rogue River rises in the Cascade Range and flows south and west through Jackson, Josephine, and Curry Counties to enter the Pacific Ocean at Gold Beach. The major tributaries include Bear Creek, the **Applegate River**, and the **Illinois River**. It is about 200 miles long, much of it in remote canyons of the Coast Range Mountains. The Rogue is famous for its whitewater rapids and for its steelhead trout and salmon fishing, and for the **mail boat** trips from **Gold Beach**. The remote sections of the river in the Coast Range were long the haunts of isolated gold miners and subsistence farmers, with an occasional tourist bent on fishing; author **Zane Grey** had a cabin on the river in the 1910s and 1920s. *See also* **Bear Creek Valley**.

> Atwood, Kay. *Illahe: The Story of Settlement in the Rogue River Canyon.* Corvallis: Oregon State University Press, 2002.
> Grey, Zane. *Rogue River Feud.* New York: Harper, 1929–1930.

Rogue River (town) The Jackson County town of Rogue River had its beginnings with a crossing of the river known as Evans Ferry, along the route of the **California-Oregon Trail**. The ferry was established during the gold rush days of the 1850s; there was a post office nearby from 1855 to 1859 with the name Gold River. In 1876, a rural post office was opened with the name Woodville, probably named for the first postmaster, John Woods. The Oregon & California Railroad came through in 1884, and in 1912 Woodville changed its name to Rogue River and became an incorporated municipality. The census of 1920 credited it with 211 residents. That count increased to 590 by 1950, 1,308 in 1980, and an estimated 2,085 by 2007. Rogue River has been primarily a lumbering town; by the 1990s, it was increasingly a suburb of Grants Pass and a retirement community. Since 1953, Rogue River has been the site of the annual Rooster Crow festival, for reasons that remain obscure.

Rogue River Wars This lengthy series of raids, attacks, and battles occurred in southern Oregon between 1851 and 1856, with a brief respite ca. 1854–55. The combatants were Euro-American gold miners, settlers, and volunteer soldiers on one hand, and **Takelma Indians** and **Athapaskan Indians**—Galice, Applegate, Chasta Costa, Chetco, Upper Coquille, Upper Umpqua, and others—on the other hand. The proximate causes were the rapid influx of whites into southwestern Oregon and their disturbing activities, as hydraulic gold mining destroyed fisheries, and farmers and miners removed game habitat. The **Donation Land Act** permitted settlers to claim land and establish farms, despite the fact that Indian title to the land had not been acquired. Miners also brought with them to Oregon the sensibilities that ruled the California gold fields: Indians should be exterminated; and many were. Indian agent **Joel Palmer** negotiated treaties and the creation of three reservations in an effort to settle some of the unrest. However, in 1855 an incident near the **Table Rock** reservation set off a final string of violence that culminated with the Battle of Big Bend on the Rogue River in June 1856. The toll of the war included several hundred Indians and about fifty miners and settlers. Palmer decided that, in good measure to save their immediate lives, the Indians must be removed. Beginning in January 1857, the Indians were forcibly taken to the **Coast Reservation**, relocating an estimated 4,000 people to situations where they were unable to make a living. A poignant reminder of the move is the name of the mighty Rogue River which was applied, in faint tribute, to a rippling creek that is tributary to the South Yamhill River, on the **Grand Ronde Reservation**.

Beckham, Stephen Dow. *Requiem for a People: The Rogue Indians and the Frontiersmen.* Corvallis: Oregon State University Press, 1996.

Romani in Oregon *see* **Gypsies in Oregon**

Roosevelt Military Highway *see* **Oregon Coast Highway**

Rooster Rock This basalt column in the Columbia River Gorge of eastern Multnomah County is a prominent landmark. As Lewis L. McArthur coyly phrased it, "The modern name is of phallic significance originating from rhyming slang." It was long the site of a salmon cannery. It was developed as a state park after World War II, and since the 1960s has had a well-known nude beach. Not far from Rooster Rock are two shorter, similar pillars that were often depicted on postcards. These were known as The Needles (the railroad track once threaded between them) or the Pillars of Hercules. The Needles still stand today beside **Interstate 84**, but few travelers notice them.

Roseburg Along the route of the **California-Oregon Trail**, Roseburg is the county seat of Douglas County. A small community arose around the joining of Deer Creek and the Umpqua River during the 1850s. Aaron Rose from New York via Michigan settled on a donation land claim there in 1851 and opened a stable, tavern, and store and butcher shop. When Douglas County was created in 1852, Winchester was the first seat of county government, but an 1854 election designated Deer Creek as the county seat. Rose gave the land for the new courthouse. The town of Roseburgh was platted in 1857, and a post office was opened (the post office spelling changed to Roseburg in 1894). Roseburg was incorporated in 1868 as a city. The **Oregon & California Railroad** arrived from Portland in 1873, and Roseburg remained the southern terminus until construc-

tion resumed a decade later; the California connection took place in 1887.

Roseburg prospered in the 1870s as a transfer point from train to stagecoach; in 1880, the census reported 822 residents in the city. The Umpqua Valley was a fertile agricultural area that developed with fruit orchards and poultry and dairy farms. In the early 1900s, there was even some grape growing and wine making; lumber mills added to the economy, and by 1910, Roseburg's population was 4,738; it reached 8,390 in 1950.

In the early morning of August 7, 1959, a downtown building caught fire; the fire caused an explosives-laden truck to explode in a blast that demolished buildings in an eight-block radius. Fourteen people died and 125 were injured; the downtown retail core was demolished. The course of the rebuilding was affected by the construction of **Interstate 5** in the 1960s and the consequent rise of suburban retail development north of the downtown, especially near Garden Valley. Roseburg's population rose to 16,644 by 1980; the estimate in 2007 was 21,255.

Rosenberg, Harry and David *see* **Harry and David**

roses *see* **Portland Rose Festival**

Row River This small tributary of the Coast Fork Willamette River rises in eastern Lane County in the **Bohemia mining district** and flows westward to Cottage Grove. The Oregon writer **Opal Whiteley** was raised along the Row River. The Buster Keaton epic comedy silent film *The General* was filmed along the river in 1926. The name, said historian Lewis L. McArthur, is the result of "a dispute between George Clark and Joseph Southwell over a stock trespass. The two men were brothers-in-law as well as neighbors, but the disagreement ran so deep that Clark lost his life as a result."

Rufus On the Columbia River and on the Union Pacific Railroad, which was built down the river in 1884, Rufus was a rural post office that opened in 1886. Rufus C. Wallis was the postmaster and the namesake. In 1965, the community decided to incorporate; the 1970 census reported a population of 317; the estimated population in 2005 was 270.

Russians in Oregon A significant group of immigrants from Russia came to Oregon in the waning days of the Soviet Union and since its collapse. These were Christian Pentecostals who were allowed to leave Russia, and beginning in 1988 thousands of Russians and Ukranians have arrived in Oregon, first making connections with the earlier **Old Believer** Russian immigrants in the Woodburn area. Russian emigrant communities have arisen in Salem and Marion County and in southeast Portland. *See also* **Glendale**.

S

Sacajawea (1780s-ca. 1812); also spelled Sacagawea. A member of the Lemhi band of Shoshone Indians, Sacajawea was apparently captured from her tribe in east central Idaho in 1800 by Hidatsa Indians and taken to the upper Missouri, where she came to marry a French-Canadian fur trapper, Toussaint Charbonneau, in 1804. That year, the **Lewis and Clark Expedition** hired Charbonneau to act as an interpreter, and Sacajawea and the couple's infant son, **Jean Baptiste Charbonneau**, remained with the group until it returned to the upper Missouri River in 1806. Sacajawea had no official place as part of an army corps, but the journals indicate she was often helpful, as she was familiar with several languages and was able to identify edible and medicinal plants. Her presence, especially with her child, was also important in signifying that the party was of peaceful intent. At one point, when the party took an informal vote on a course of action in settling for the winter on the lower Columbia River, Sacajawea is noted as having a voice—said by some to be a first instance of a woman "voting" in the Pacific Northwest. Sacajawea and her husband traveled to Saint Louis in 1809 to leave their son with William Clark, but her fate thereafter is not known; it is likely that she died about 1812 at Fort Manuel in what is today South Dakota. Sacajawea's life was romanticized by many writers, most notably by **Eva Emery Dye**, a suffragist and the author of several historical novels.

Saddle Mountain A visual landmark from the mouth of the Columbia River, Saddle Mountain in Clatsop County reaches an elevation of 3,283 feet. It is part of the **Coast Range Mountains.** The mountain is composed of fragments of basalt fused together, the result of lava flows striking seawater some fifteen million years ago. Saddle Mountain's distinctive two-peak summit was a landmark for early mariners seeking the entrance to the Columbia River.

Sahaptin Indians These people, who ethnologists have described as Western Columbia River Sahaptins, have been commonly referred to as Tenino Indians or Warm Springs Indians. The ethnologists' term is focused on the Sahaptian languages, whose speakers also include the Yakama Indians and the **Nez Perce Indians**. The Sahaptin Indians who lived along the western stretches of the Columbia River, roughly between The Dalles and Arlington, lived in villages located primarily along the north shore of the river and on some islands. They also made extensive treks to the south, especially along the Deschutes and John Day Rivers and their tributaries, in summer and autumn, to harvest and preserve such foods as bitterroot, camas, a variety of berries, lamprey, and trout. The immense salmon fisheries at Fivemile Rapids and **Celilo Falls**, and the trading centers associated them, were also within Sahaptin territory. The Sahaptin Indians ranged over much of the landscape that is now included in Wasco, Sherman, Gilliam, Grant, Wheeler, Morrow, and Jefferson Counties.

The 1855 Middle Oregon Treaty established the **Warm Springs Reservation** and established tribal fishing and hunting rights; however, it was 1969 before some of those fishing rights were fully acknowledged. The completion of **The Dalles Dam** in 1957 and the subsequent flooding of Celilo Falls and Fivemile Rapids gave the Sahaptins some monetary compensation. The **Confederated Tribes of Warm Springs** includes the Sahaptins (Warm Springs Indians), the Kikshts (**Wasco Indians**), and the **Northern Paiute Indians**. Descendants of many Sahaptin Indians are enrolled as tribal members of the Yakama Nation or the **Confederated Tribes of the Umatilla Indian Reservation**.

> Aguilar, George, Sr. *When the River Ran Wild!: Indian Traditions on the Mid-Columbia and the Warm Springs Reservation*. Portland, Oregon: Oregon Historical Society Press; Seattle: University of Washington Press, 2005.

Saint Helens The city of Saint Helens is the county seat of Columbia County; the name reflects the fact that Mount Saint Helens in Washington state is prominently visible from the bluff. Saint Helens is an old settlement, a hoped-for seaport and railroad terminal rival to Portland that was founded in the late 1840s by Capt. H. M. Knighton, who first called it Plymouth. A post office by that name was opened in 1850, but was changed the same year to Saint Helen (the post office did not see fit to add the final *s* until 1913). The Northern Pacific Railroad reached Saint Helens by 1884 and the city was incorporated in 1889. The 1890 census credits it with a population of about 220; it reached 742 by 1910. Though its seaport aspirations had come to naught, Saint Helens did prosper in the late nineteenth century as a center for lumbering and for wooden shipbuilding. By 1915, creosoting lumber, quarrying rock, fishing for salmon, and general farming and dairying were the chief occupations after lumbering and shipbuilding. Saint Helens had a population of 3,994 by 1930, and 6,212 in 1970, when it was growing as a residential suburb of Portland. Its estimated population in 2007 was 12,075.

Saint Johns neighborhood, Portland This Portland neighborhood originally was a thoroughly separate community, which evolved from a settlement made in 1846 by James John (1809–1886), an Ohioan who came to the Oregon Country in 1842. John built a store and house, and in 1852 platted a townsite with the name Saint Johns. The reason for John's sainthood is not known. He also operated a ferry across the Willamette. A post office with the name Saint Johns opened in 1873. In 1890, the Willamette Bridge Railway Company constructed a steam-powered suburban rail line from the **Albina neighborhood** via a zigzag route to Saint Johns, which soon offered connections into downtown Portland. The line was gradually converted to electric power, and by 1903, electric **streetcars** connected Portland with Saint Johns—which was incorporated as a city on February 19, 1903. The Saint Johns post office was discontinued in 1912, and in 1915, Saint Johns approved its annexation into the city of Portland. At the time of its annexation, Saint Johns had a population estimated at 4,872 and had a number of industries: lumber mills, boat building, a woolen mill, iron works, a flour mill, lumber planing mill, a stone works, and factories making baskets, wood veneer (plywood), and excelsior (shredded wood for packaging). There were three banks and a weekly newspaper.

The neighborhood is also the location of a school named for James John (who left his modest estate for public education), and of the Saint Johns suspension bridge, a stunning piece of engineering with serious Art Deco touches that was completed in 1931. Beneath the bridge, in the shadow of the Gothic-arched concrete piers supporting the bridge approach, is Cathedral Park, established in 1980 and so named as a result of a photograph taken in 1968 by Al Monner for the *Oregon Journal*, with a caption that noted the cathedral-like arches of the bridge.

Saint Paul This small Marion County farming community on Mission Creek was founded in the 1830s when retired French-Canadian *voyageurs* of the Hudson's Bay Company settled on **French Prairie** and farmed. In response to entreaties for Roman Catholic priests, Fr. **François Norbert Blanchet** and his associate Fr. Modeste Demers arrived in Saint Paul in 1839 and held the first mass in the Oregon Country. For a brief time in the 1840s, Saint Paul was the headquarters for Roman Catholic mission efforts in the region, with a school and a convent. A brick church was built in 1846; remodeled and enlarged, it is still the focal point of the community. A post office opened in 1874, and for a brief time (1880–90), the ill-fated narrow gauge Oregonian Railway served Saint Paul. City government was established in 1901; in the 1910 census, 103 people lived in Saint Paul. By 1915, nearby farms were producing "grains, hay, clover, alfalfa, hops, fruits, berries, potatoes, corn and vegetables; dairying, hogs, sheep, goats and poultry." Agricultural products were shipped from Saint Paul landing on the Willamette River, about a mile west of the townsite, until the 1920s, when local roads took over most of the traffic.

In the midst of the Depression, Saint Paul sought some excitement, and a rodeo was proposed to provide it. The first of the now-annual Saint Paul July 4 rodeos was held in 1936 in the city park. French Prairie is not exactly cowboy country, but the event has become a Willamette Valley tradition, bolstered by several other small-city rodeos in the area, such as the **Molalla** Buckaroo. Saint Paul's population was about 410 in 2007.

▶ **Salem** The county seat of Marion County and the capital city of Oregon, Salem is situated on the Willamette River at the south end of **French Prairie** and **Lake Labish**; Howell Prairie lies to the east. The open landscape, fertile soil, and the presence of Mill Creek for waterpower made it the site of the relocation of the Methodist Mission of **Jason Lee** in 1840. The Methodists established the Oregon Institute, the predecessor of **Willamette University**, in 1842. While the mission itself faded in the 1840s, the community grew. Territorial status for Oregon brought a post office to Salem in 1849, and the townsite was platted in 1850–51; the name comes from the city in Massachusetts. The territorial capital moved from Oregon City to Salem in 1851, and after a brief fling in Corvallis in 1855, Salem has remained the capital city and the center of state **politics and government**. The city was incorporated in 1857.

The first railroad arrived in 1870, and the first stage of a permanent state capitol building was erected in 1876; its surmounting dome was not completed until 1893. Salem's population in 1880 was 2,538; only Portland, East Portland, and Astoria were larger cities in that year. By 1910, there were 14,094 residents. Agriculture contributed much to the city's economy; by 1915, Salem was the "hop center of the Willamette Valley and the state" and noted also for its **cherries** and prunes, grapes, berries, and other fruit and vegetables. There were fruit and vegetable canneries, lumber mills, a brewery, and a **flax** factory. By the 1950s, Salem was the largest food-canning center in the nation; the census of 1950 gave it a population of 43,140.

The state capitol burned in a spectacular fire in

1935, and was replaced by the present Art Deco building with its gold leaf-plated statue atop the barrel rotunda, "Oregon Pioneer." In 1949, West Salem in Polk County was merged with Salem; it had been a separate city, founded in the late 1880s and incorporated in 1913. Since World War II, state government has increased its presence in Salem with extensive office building additions. Waterfront timber-related industries have disappeared, and Salem has paid some attention to its history with the preservation of the Deepwood estate, the Jason Lee house, the Thomas Kay woolen mill, and the **Asahel Bush** house. Salem's link to **A. C. Gilbert** is marked by a children's museum, and the downtown core district, including the Elsinore Theatre designed by

Ellis F. Lawrence, and the Ladd & Bush bank, which has been listed on the National Register of Historic Places. Salem's population was 68,725 in 1970 and 136,924 in 2000; the estimate in 2007 was 151,895.

Salishan Situated on the dunes and hills south of the mouth of the **Siletz River**, Salishan is a resort and housing development in Lincoln County. It was a project of industrialist John D. Gray, who envisioned it as the state's first high-quality coastal destination hotel and resort. The Salishan landscape was designed by **Barbara Feeley**, while architect John Storrs contributed modern structures that echoed the cedar longhouses of the Salmon River

The Salem waterfront looked like this in the early 1920s. This view shows the sawmill of the Charles K. Spaulding Logging Company; visible in the background is the Center Street Bridge. The mill closed in 1955. Oregon Historical Society, OrHi 92884.

and Siletz **Tillamook Indians** who had inhabited the area. The Tillamook spoke a Salish dialect, giving rise to the name of the resort. Development began in 1962 and the first installment of Salishan opened in 1965.

► **salmon** Four species of salmon live in Oregon waters; but *see also* **steelhead trout**.

The Chinook salmon, *Oncorhynchus tshawytscha*, is the largest, best known, and most celebrated of the salmon. It is also known by the names king salmon, royal Chinook salmon, spring salmon, tyee salmon. Chinook spawn in freshwater gravel beds, swimming upstream from the Pacific in the spring to reach the spawning grounds where they originally hatched. Chinooks once ranged up the entire Columbia River system, reaching above Willamette Falls, up the Deschutes and John Day Rivers, up the Snake and its tributaries, into Idaho and British Columbia. Chinook also spawn in the Klamath River. The Chinook was the primary target of commercial **fishing** for canning purposes from the 1870s, but its rapid decline in the Columbia River caused processors to use other salmon varieties to meet the demand. Chinook can reach thirty pounds or more in weight.

Chum salmon (*Oncorhynchus keta*) is found along the Pacific Coast, south to the Sacramento River. They are a small salmon, weighing about eight pounds, and they head upriver to spawn in the autumn. They have been described as "an inferior food fish," although the particulars of their inferiority appear to be indefinite.

Coho salmon (*Oncorhynchus kisutch*) is sometimes called silver salmon, and was also once common along the Pacific Coast; populations in Oregon and northern California are quite low, however. Silvers run about seven to eleven pounds, and are considered good game fish, as they are found in many coastal rivers and are also caught at sea.

Sockeye or red salmon (*Oncorhynchus nerka*) return from the sea to spawn and rear in lakes; there were only two main runs of sockeye in Oregon: up the Columbia and Deschutes Rivers to Suttle Lake, and up the Columbia, Snake, Grande Ronde, and Wallowa Rivers to **Wallowa Lake**. Both runs have been extinguished by dams. The landlocked, non-migrating variant of the sockeye is the kokanee, which is found in both Suttle and Wallowa Lakes. *See also* **Celilo Falls**; **fishing, commercial**; **fishwheels**.

Sandy The Clackamas County city of Sandy is near the Sandy River. A post office named Sandy opened in 1873 in a country store. It was incorporated in 1911, and in 1915 it was described as the "terminus of three scenic stage lines," with "an unobstructed view of Mt. Hood" in a "picturesque scenic environment." Sandy then had a creamery, lumber mill, and sawmill. The 1920 census gave it a population of 242; by 1940, it was 473. Postwar suburbanization boosted the count to 1,544 by 1970; by 2007, the estimated population was 7,595.

Sandy River The Sandy River rises on the slopes of Mount Hood in Clackamas River, gathers waters from the Salmon River, **Bull Run River**, and the

The Tenino brand of canned salmon was named for the Tenino band of Sahaptin Indians, who lived in the vicinity of The Dalles. The Seufert Brothers Packing Company was a major user of fishwheels to harvest salmon. Author's collection.

Zigzag River, and flows west and north to join the Columbia River at Troutdale. It is about fifty miles in length. The journals of the Lewis and Clark Expedition called the stream Quicksand River, a term that was in use through the 1840s. The historical use of the river to float logs resulted in the determination of it as a navigable stream by the Oregon State Land Board in 2002, which triggered a state claim of ownership of the streambed and banks of the lower thirty-seven and a half miles of the river—a claim which is a boon to those boating, fishing, and otherwise using the river, but a sore spot with adjacent landowners. In 2007, Marmot Dam on the Sandy River, built in 1912 as part of the **Bull Run** hydroelectric project, was decommissioned and demolished, making the Sandy once again a free-flowing river in its entirety. For many years, the Sandy River was a popular place to fish for **smelt**, with entire families dipping and scooping up the small fish.

Santiam Indians *see* **Kalapuyan Indians**

Santiam Pass One of the historic and most tortuous passes over the Cascade Range is Santiam Pass, elevation 4,817 feet, passing between Three Fingered Jack and Mount Washington. From **Sisters** on the east side of the mountains, the route reaches Santiam Pass west of Suttle Lake. On the west side of the mountains, one route continues north and west down the North Fork Santiam River canyon and Salem; another route goes directly west over Tombstone Pass to the South Santiam River; a third route goes to the southwest down the McKenzie River. The Tombstone Pass route was that of the Santiam Wagon Road, a toll road established in 1865 that operated until 1914; the historic transcontinental auto race of the 1905 **Lewis and Clark Centennial Exposition** came over this route, the most difficult portion of their entire trip. The North Fork Santiam route was to be that of Col. T. E. Hogg's transcontinental railroad connection from

Yaquina Bay to the Snake River; the railroad got up the canyon to **Idanha**, but no farther. Hogg Rock near the summit of the pass remembers his grandiose vision.

Santiam River The North, Middle, and South Santiam Rivers head in the Cascade Range of Linn County and flow west to join the Willamette River north of Albany. Flood control and hydroelectric dams such as **Detroit Dam** on the North Santiam and Foster and Green Peter Dams on the South and Middle Santiam were built in the 1950s and 1960s. The South Santiam River canyon was the main route from the Willamette Valley over **Santiam Pass** to Central Oregon. The headwaters of the Middle Santiam reach a former gold-mining district especially along Quartzville Creek.

sasquatch Tales of large, hairy, foul-smelling, humanoid creatures lurking in the woods have merged into "sasquatch," a word popularized in the 1920s. The term was used by **lumberjack** Albert Ostman in 1924 to describe four creatures that he encountered—or was kidnapped by—in the wilderness near Powell River, British Columbia; it is reputed to be of Salish language derivation. A wave of sasquatch sightings in the Pacific Northwest was precipitated by a film taken in the coastal woods of northern California by Ray Wallace in August 1958, which depicted a hairy apparition with large feet. The film was revealed to be a hoax after Wallace's death in 2002. "Bigfoot" is another term for the sasquatch. Despite exhaustive efforts, no tangible proof of the existence of the sasquatch has yet been put forward. While there have been a number of reputed sightings in Oregon, the legend has a firmer hold in British Columbia, northern Idaho, and Washington state.

Saturday Market Two prominent Saturday Markets are held in Oregon. The first was established in Eugene in 1970 as a seasonal venue for craftspeople and artists. In 1974, the Portland Saturday Market began operation, growing to become a nearly year-around event on both Saturdays and Sundays. Both markets feature artisan creations and prepared foods, but not fresh vegetables or foodstuffs, such as would be found at a **public market** or **farmers' market**.

Sauve, Laurent *see* **Sauvie Island**

Sauvie Island A large, fertile, low-lying land bounded by the Columbia River, Multnomah Channel, and the Willamette River, Sauvie Island was the homeland of the Multnomahs, a **Chinook Indian** tribe that thrived on the **wapato**, **camas**, salmon, and sturgeon that abounded there. One of the first, and most ill-fated, early American settlements occurred there in 1834–36 at Fort William, established by **Nathaniel J. Wyeth**. The island is named for Laurent Sauve (d. 1858), a French-Canadian *engagé* of the Hudson's Bay Company who worked on a dairy that supplied the post at Fort Vancouver. Sauvie Island is in both Multnomah and Columbia Counties; it is drained by the Gilbert River and a network of sloughs and ditches. Much of the land is a wildlife refuge, while the remainder is extensively farmed with berries, nursery stock, corn, peaches, cabbage, and garden truck crops. The island landmark is the Greek Revival–style James F. and Julia Bybee house, built in 1856, in Howell Territorial Park; **Thomas Jefferson Howell** also once lived here.

Scappoose With a name of Indian derivation but unknown etymology, Scappoose is a once-rural town in Columbia County that is rapidly becoming a suburb of Portland. The community is located along the edge of the Columbia River floodplain west of Sauvie Island. A post office named Columbia was established in the vicinity in 1868; the name was changed to Scappoose two years later. Railroad service from Portland began in 1883, and fifteen years later, a rail connection to Astoria opened. The devel-opment of the Columbia River Highway in the 1920s helped stimulate the local economy, and the town was incorporated in 1921; the 1930 census recorded a population of 248. The Steinfeld family, which had begun producing pickles in Portland in 1922, acquired a farm in Scappoose in 1934 and did some canning there during World War II. After the war, Steinfeld's grew to become the most notable industry in town, producing pickles and sauerkraut from cucumbers and cabbage grown in the area. The plant closed about 2000 and was demolished in 2006, after the family sold the business to a national firm. In 2007, the population of Scappoose was estimated to be 6,090.

Schwab, Les (1917–2007) Born in Bend and raised in a Central Oregon logging camp, Les Schwab graduated from high school, married his sweetheart Dorothy Harlan, and went to work for the Bend *Bulletin* newspaper; he served in the Army Air Corps in World War II. In 1952, Schwab began the business that made him a household Oregon name: selling tires. Schwab built a small empire on such down-home qualities as sharing his profits with his employees, promoting employees who performed well, promising and delivering quality care with a guarantee, and, once a year, offering a free beef promotion to his customers. The chain had 410 stores in the West by 2007; the headquarters, which were in Prineville during Schwab's lifetime, moved to Bend in 2008.

Scio Located on Thomas Creek in Linn County, Scio was the site of a water-powered flour mill. The fertile land nearby had been extensively settled in the 1840s and 1850s; the mill provided the nucleus of a community. Named for a town in Ohio (in turn named for the Mediterranean island of Chios or Scio), the post office was established in 1860, with city government following soon after in 1866. When the ill-considered Oregonian Railway built down the east side of the Willamette Valley in 1880, it missed the small mill and farming town by a mile. Beginning about 1890 and continuing for some two decades, town merchants built and operated a very unofficial railroad to nearby West Scio. Scio was incorporated in 1890, when its population was 253. In 1915, farming, dairying, fruit growing, hop growing, lumbering, and stock raising were the principal activities, and Scio had a sawmill, planing mill, and a milk condensary. In the late twentieth century, Scio became noted for the concentration of rural **covered bridges** in the vicinity. From his arrival in 1998 until his death by dog in 2006, Scio was the home of Big Red, a community-supported rooster that patrolled the streets. Scio's population in 2007 was estimated to be 760. The West Scio railroad station was moved to Scio in 1985 to become the town museum.

Scotch broom The invasive plant known as Scotch broom, *Cytisus scoparius*, was brought in to help control blowing sand dunes in areas such as **Clatsop Plains**. For some years, it worked, and it was considered an attractive plant. The *Daily Astorian* reported in the spring of 1932 that more than a thousand Clatsop County citizens assembled at Camp Clatsop on the Plains for the annual Scotch broom festival. "Despite gloomy weather forecasts the sun broke through the clouds for most of the festival and hundreds of persons held picnic luncheons on the golden Scotch broom-covered hillsides." It has since escaped its coastal bounds and is widespread on the west slope of the Cascade Range, often dominating **clearcuts** after the trees are gone.

▶ **Scott, Harvey Whitfield** (1838–1910) For four decades, Harvey Scott and his opinions dominated the editorial pages of the Portland *Oregonian*, during the time when it was the leading news journal in the Pacific Northwest. Harvey Whitfield Scott was born in Illinois, and came west with his family on the Oregon Trail in 1852; his mother and a younger brother died en route. Scott studied at

and was the first graduate, in 1863, of **Pacific University** in Forest Grove. He moved to Portland, where he worked as a librarian, studied law, and was admitted to the state bar in 1865. The same year, he was hired by *Oregonian* publisher **Henry L. Pittock** to edit the paper.

In his editorial writings, Scott promoted the need for a sound monetary system, tirelessly championed regional commerce, and frequently philosophized about the value of religion and spiritual journeys. Scott was opposed to women's suffrage, a viewpoint that long angered his sister, the formidable suffragist and journalist **Abigail Scott Duniway**. Yet it is clear that Harvey Scott had great respect for women's abilities; another sister, Catherine (Scott) Coburn, worked closely with him as associate editor of the *Oregonian* from 1888 until his death in 1910; she died in 1913. (She had also worked with sister Abigail at *The New Northwest*.)

Harvey Scott's Portland business connections were cemented by investments in banking and real estate and by civic involvements. He was a staunch

Uncharacteristically sprawled on a sand dune near Seaside, Harvey W. Scott, editor of the Portland *Oregonian*, examines the latest edition with a critical eye. The photograph was taken in 1905. It might be deduced that it was difficult for Scott to relax. Oregon Historical Society, CN 002756.

supporter of the public library and an avid amateur historian, a "pioneer" who had arrived in Oregon during its territorial days. He was a founding member and the first board president of the **Oregon Historical Society**, and a promoter of the **Lewis and Clark Centennial Exposition** of 1905. Scott's wife, Margaret, left a bequest at her death in 1925 to finance a statue of Harvey W. Scott. It was finally completed by the sculptor Gutzon Borglum in 1933, and stands atop **Mount Tabor**, a volcanic butte in southeast Portland. A similar butte nearby is named Mount Scott, occasioned by his purchase and development of property there in 1889–90; it was sold in 1909 to become Lincoln Memorial Cemetery.

Nash, Lee M. Scott of the *Oregonian*: Literary Frontiersman. *Pacific Historical Review* 45, no. 3 (August 1976), 357–378.

Scott, Levi C. (1797–1890) Levi Scott was born in Illinois and came to Polk County, Oregon in 1844. With **Jesse Applegate** he worked to improve the **Southern Emigrant Road**, sometimes called the Applegate or Scott-Applegate Trail, in 1846. In 1848, he settled on a donation land claim in Douglas County, where a mountain and a valley carry his name. In 1850, he founded the town of **Scottsburg** on the Umpqua River; and from 1852 to 1854 he served in the territorial legislature. He participated briefly in the drafting of Oregon's future state constitution in 1857, and then settled down for a bit. He was visiting his son John Scott in Malheur County when he died in 1890, at the age of ninety-three.

Scott-Applegate Trail *see* Scott, Levi; Southern Emigrant Road

Scottsburg The community of Scottsburg is on the Umpqua River in Douglas County, and was founded by and named for **Levi Scott** in 1850. It is sited at the effective head of navigation on the Umpqua, and for a brief period in the early 1850s it was a trading post of great importance to the gold-mining enterprises of southern Oregon. Supplies from San Francisco came by sea to the Umpqua, and were transferred by pack train to the mining areas near **Jacksonville** and in the Illinois River valley. Southern Oregon's first newspaper, the *Umpqua Gazette*, was published here in 1854; in 1855, the plant was moved to Jacksonville to issue the *Table Rock Sentinel*. By this time, Crescent City, California, was developing as a supply point for the southern Oregon mines. Scottsburg was nearly wiped away by **floods** in 1861, and its commercial decline was immediate. It continued into the early twentieth century to be an interchange point for stagecoach travel from the interior valleys destined for the coast; at Scottsburg, river steamers continued down the Umpqua to **Gardiner** and Winchester Bay, where other stages continued south along the beach. The general store of Cyrus W. Hedden, established about 1851, was continued by his son John N. Hedden, in 1941. The Hedden store advertised itself as "the oldest store in the state."

Scotts Mills The Marion County farming community of Scotts Mills grew up around a flour mill on Butte Creek built in the 1860s by Robert H. and Thomas Scott. Thomas Scott was the first postmaster when the Scotts Mills post office opened in 1887. The community was incorporated as a municipality in 1916, and the 1920 census counted 208 residents. The population has wavered slightly thereafter; oddly the 1970 census also reported a population of 208. The estimate in 2007 was an even 300.

Sea Lion Caves This private family-owned enterprise, located north of Florence, encompasses a large natural cave that is home to a group of some 200 Stellar **sea lions**. The cave is more than 200 feet below the level of the **Oregon Coast Highway**, and was first opened to the public in 1932 via a tortuous trail with wooden stairs; an elevator was installed in 1961. The sea lion colony is resident the year around.

sea lions The Stellar or northern sea lion, *Eumetopias jubatus*, was widely distributed along the North Pacific Coast from California into Alaska and Siberia. Sea lions eat a very wide variety of fish, and for that reason have often been targeted for destruction; Oregon once had a bounty on them. They are a protected species, however, since 1972. While the pelt of the sea lion has never been much in demand, the animals themselves are edible and were a traditional food source for Indians along the coast and in the lower Columbia River. Stellar sea lions breed at the **Sea Lion Caves**.

The California sea lion, *Zalophus californianus*, is much more common along the Oregon coast; the range is from British Columbia to Baja California. The populations have increased rapidly in recent decades and the animals are often found sprawling on docks and about piers in great numbers at ports such as Newport and Florence. They too have been accused of eating fish in excessive quantities.

sea otters The sea otter, *Enhydra lutris*, was the first animal whose pelt drew Euro-American traders to the North Pacific Coast. They were once common from the Sea of Japan along the coastline south into Mexico. A market for the furs developed in China in the late 1700s; Russian, British, and American trades competed for them, hunting them themselves and trading with Natives for pelts. The trade peaked in the early 1800s; the **fur trade** changed with changing fashions, and the sea otter had been hunted to near-extinction by 1840. Currently the species is recovering.

Seaside This seaside resort town in Clatsop County is located at the mouth of the Necanicum River just north of **Tillamook Head**. Members of the **Lewis and Clark Expedition** camped at the future location of Seaside in 1806, where they boiled sea water to obtain salt for their eastward trek. In the 1860s, the area was a rustic retreat for some wealthy Portlanders, who came by steamboat down

the Columbia River, and then by wagon reached the seashore, where a few summer boarding houses—one was called Summer House—were built. Transportation impresario **Ben Holladay** built Seaside House in 1871. A post office named Summer House was created in 1871, with the name changed in 1873 to Seaside House; in 1882, it became simply Seaside.

A locally financed railroad, the Astoria & South Coast, connected the resort town with Astoria, beginning in 1890–91; in 1898, the **Spokane, Portland & Seattle Railway** began service between Seaside and Portland. The Grimes Hotel, the Moore Hotel, and dozens of boarding houses and modest bungalows hosted the summer population. There was a summer Saturday afternoon train from Portland for "daddies"—most executives worked a half-day on Saturday; another special left Seaside early Monday morning, taking the family breadwinner back to town for another week of work while wife and children remained at the beach. The city of Seaside was incorporated in 1899; the 1900 census gave it a population of 191; by 1910, the count was 1,270.

In the 1920s, Seaside developed a shoreline walkway, The Prom (from promenade); a natatorium marked the intersection of The Prom and Broadway, the main street from the railroad station. Broadway itself was lined with souvenir shops, carnival rides such as bumper cars, ice cream stands, and other adjuncts of summer life. The privately owned Seaside Aquarium opened on The Prom in 1937. Automobile travel was boosted by the completion of the **Oregon Coast Highway** in the 1930s, and the **Sunset Highway** direct to Portland in 1947. Passenger train service expired in 1952.

For a few years in the 1960s, aimless groups of (alleged) college students made the town the scene of weekend Labor Day riots in September. The population in 1970 reached 4,402 as more retirees chose to live on the Oregon Coast; small hotels such as the Moore were replaced by large chain hotels and motels and the honky-tonk aspect of Broadway faded, replaced by boutiques and ethnic restaurants; some

T-shirt shops and arcades remained, however. A re-routing of Highway 101 to the east of the city center provided the impetus for the construction of Seaside Factory Outlets in the 1980s. Seaside's population in 2007 was estimated at 6,400.

second-growth timber When a stand of **old-growth timber** is cut—logged, or harvested—and the land re-grows as forest, the standing trees are known as second-growth timber.

seed industry Particularly since the end of World War II, Oregon has developed a large seed industry, a specialized crop that requires purity of stock and freedom from weeds and other unwanted plants. Major seed crops include ryegrass, orchard-grass, sugarbeet, fescue, and clover; in 2006, Oregon produced more than three-quarters of the nation's crop for these seeds. The chief production is in the Willamette Valley counties of Lane, Linn, Benton, and Marion.

Sellwood district, Portland The Rev. John Sellwood, an Episcopal minister, bought the land from **Henderson Luelling** in 1866, and in 1882 sold it to the Sellwood Real Estate Company, which platted a townsite in 1883 and began to sell lots. A post office also opened in 1883, and the community was incorporated in 1887. In 1892, the East Side Railway, an electric **interurban railway**, opened from Portland as far as Sellwood to serve the race track at City View Park (now the site of Sellwood Park) and reached Oregon City in 1893. The community was annexed into the city of Portland in the same year, although the post office continued to operate until 1901. A business community developed in the vicinity of Spokane Street at the Milwaukie Road (SE Milwaukie Avenue) and at SE 13th Avenue, the route of the interurban railway; Spokane Street led to the Sellwood Ferry across the Willamette River. The Sellwood Bridge replaced the ferry in 1925. In the 1980s, Sellwood emerged as a shopping district for antiques.

► **Seneca** Located high (elevation 4,675 feet) (and cold: Seneca recorded the state's lowest temperature in 1933, at -54°) in the Blue Mountains of Grant County, Seneca began as a rural post office, established in 1895. The name was bestowed by the first postmaster, Minnie Southworth; her brother in

The brand new company town of Seneca is depicted as it appeared in July 1931. The timber is located miles to the northeast in the Blue Mountains. R. W. Heck photograph. Oregon Historical Society, CN 019579.

law was Seneca Smith, a prominent judge in Portland. Seneca's destiny changed in 1929 with the arrival of the Oregon & Northwestern Railroad and the beginning of large-scale ponderosa pine log shipments from Seneca and the surrounding national forest lands to the huge new mill at **Hines**, some fifty miles to the south. The Hines company also established a planing mill and railroad shops in Seneca, which became essentially a **company town**. Logging operations declined in the 1970s, and the railroad and lumber mills ceased operations in 1984. As company control waned, the town was incorporated in 1970. The 1980 census recorded a population of 285; the estimated population in 2007 was 270.

▶ **Shady Cove** Located on the Rogue River in Jackson County, on the highway from Medford to Crater Lake, Shady Cove was a rural post office that opened in 1939. It developed as a small service community, and incorporated as a municipality in 1972; the 1980 census reported a population of 1,097. In

a misguided attempt to establish a distinctive civic persona in the 1970s, Shady Cove decided to go for a "Western" look: false front stores and hitching posts. The concept has since been abandoned. The estimated population of Shady Cove in 2007 was 2,820.

shanghai tunnels *see* **crimping**

Shaniko the town of Shaniko in Wasco County developed from a community called Cross Hollows, where a post office opened in 1879 with August Scherneckau (1837–1923) as the postmaster. Scherneckau had come to the area in 1874 and purchased land to farm, and had also built a store and hotel. He sold his properties to Gus Schmidt in 1888, a year after the Cross Hollows post office closed. The arrival of the Columbia Southern Railway in 1900 revived the community, and a new post office named Shaniko was established, based on a phonetic spelling of Scherneckau's name. Shaniko was the end of the line, and it was in a booming sheep-raising coun-

The market in Shady Cove is busy on a late summer morning in the 1960s. A sign boasts that this is "The Store that has Everything," which includes livestock and poultry feeds, Holsum bread, Lucky Lager beer, and the office of Houston's Trailer Court; Thrifty Green Stamps are awarded to customers. Mason collection.

try; it soon became one of the largest wool-shipping points in the nation as well as a major cattle-shipping point. The town was incorporated in 1901; its population in 1910 was 495. But decline rapidly set in with the opening of the parallel **Oregon Trunk Railway** in 1911 several miles to the west, and Shaniko's population fell to fifty-five by 1940; the railroad left in 1943. Since then, Shaniko has prospered very sedately as a picturesque **ghost town**. Its estimated population in 2007 was twenty-five.

Shark *see* **Cannon Beach; shipwrecks**

Shasta Indians The Shasta people inhabited the upper reaches of the Klamath River in northern California and in the Siskiyou Mountains and the **Bear Creek Valley** and Cascade Mountain foothills of southern Oregon, perhaps overlapping with the **Takelma Indians**. The region was traversed by the **California-Oregon Trail** and was heavily impacted by an influx of gold seekers by 1851—clashes with

white trappers, explorers, and especially miners were sudden and severe. The Shasta were involved in the **Rogue River Wars** of the 1850s, and some of the survivors were forced onto the **Coast Reservation**.

▶ **sheep raising** Sheep came to the Oregon Country as early as the 1820s for the **Hudson's Bay Company**, and others came from Hawai'i in the 1830s and from California in the 1840s. They were raised in the Willamette Valley for their wool and meat, but the **woolen industry** did not begin to take shape until the 1860s after the importation of several wool-producing varieties such as Australian and American merinos, Hampshire Downs, and Southdowns. Sheep also did well on the **dry side** of the Cascades, and were raised in northeastern and Central Oregon and in Lake County. By the early 1900s, **Shaniko** in Wasco County was said to be the largest single shipping point for wool in the nation. The **Irish** became associated with sheep raising in Morrow and Lake Counties, while the **Basques** were

A crew of men is pictured at work shearing sheep on the ranch of Arthur Minor near Heppner in the early 1900s. Sheep raising was a major industry in **Morrow County**. Benjamin A. Gifford photograph. Oregon Historical Society, Gi 1614.

often sheepherders when the industry grew into Malheur and Harney Counties after 1900. Sheep grazing on federal lands from the 1870s through the 1890s often came in conflict with the **cattle industry**, leading to the "Sheepshooters War," which left as many as 10,000 sheep dead—and a few men as well. The creation of grazing allotments on federal lands reduced the conflicts after 1902. The woolen industry declined but survived; lamb for meat has become a specialty product, especially in the Willamette Valley.

"She flies with her own wings" The state legislature adopted this phrase as the state motto in 1987, replacing the former motto, "The Union," which had been proclaimed in 1957. "The Union" appears on the state seal, which dates from 1857 (statehood came in 1859) and reflects contemporary anxiety about the issues that soon led to the **Civil War**. The seal for the Territory of Oregon, which had been adopted in 1854, included the Latin phrase *Alis volat propiis*. Those words had been crafted for the purpose by Judge Jesse Quinn Thornton (1810–1888) to commemorate the actions of the founders of Oregon's **provisional government** in 1843, forming a government "dependent only upon the inherent political authority of its own people." The 1987 adoption of the territorial motto—now phrased in English—reflected a renewed appreciation for that view. "She flies with her own wings" was also the masthead slogan of the politically independent *Oregon Journal* newspaper, published by **Sam Jackson**.

Sheridan Founded as an agricultural community in the 1860s, Sheridan was named for a Civil War hero, **Philip Henry Sheridan**. Then a mere lieutenant, Sheridan was briefly stationed at nearby **Forts Hoskins** and **Yamhill** in the 1850s. The area along the South Yamhill River was settled by farming families beginning in the 1840s, among them A. B. and Mary Ann Faulconer. Mr. Faulconer platted a small townsite about 1865, and Sheridan post office

was established in 1866. Wheat was the principal local crop, and a steam flour mill was built in 1876. Sheridan became the terminus in 1878 of the narrow-gauge Dayton, Sheridan & Grand Ronde Railroad, connecting it to river navigation at Dayton, which permitted local wheat to be sent to Portland for export. The town was incorporated in 1880, and the census recorded 196 residents that year. The surrounding countryside in the early twentieth century grew wheat, hops, prunes, walnuts, pears, cherries, honey, poultry, and livestock. Sheridan has usually had a sawmill or two. Its population in 1950 was 1,922; the estimate in 2007 was 5,865.

Sheridan, Philip Henry (1831–1888) The famous—or infamous—Phil Sheridan was stationed in the Oregon country from 1855 to 1861, including a stint at Fort Yamhill on the Grand Ronde Reservation Agency in 1856-61, very near the present town of **Sheridan**. Born in New York state, Sheridan attended West Point and graduated in 1853. He was assigned to a post in Texas, and then came to California and Oregon in 1855 working with a topographical survey team. Sheridan was involved in the Yakima and **Rogue River Wars** in 1855-56; in 1857, he helped to complete the construction of **Fort Hoskins** and worked on a road connecting it to the Indian agency at **Siletz**. Lt. Sheridan was in command at **Fort Yamhill** when he was ordered east in the fall of 1861. Sheridan distinguished himself in battle during the Civil War; it was he who stopped Robert E. Lee's escape at Appomattox Court House on April 9, 1865; Lee surrendered the next day. Sheridan later served the army in the Rocky Mountain West and was instrumental in protecting Yellowstone National Park, then administered by the army. Gen. Sheridan was commanding general of the U.S. Army from 1883 until his death.

Sherman County Created in 1889 from a corner of Wasco County, Sherman County is named for Civil War hero Gen. William T. Sherman, who had visited Oregon in 1880 with President Rutherford B. Hayes. The area was adjusted in 1891 when the southern boundary line moved eighteen miles south; the county has 831 square miles. In 1890, it had a reported population of 1,792. The town of Wasco was designated the county seat, but **Moro** contested the placement and after several electoral battles, Moro won the war. An interim courthouse was built in 1892, and in 1899 the current courthouse on a hill above the town of Moro was completed. The Columbia Southern Railway built a line from Biggs to Moro in 1899, and continued it to **Shaniko** in 1900. The county is part of the homeland of the **Sahaptin Indians**.

The economy of Sherman County has always relied on agriculture. Cattle and sheep raising have been carried on in the southern section, but wheat has been the mainstay, supplemented by barley. A 1915 booklet noted that "the open wheat country begins at the canyon rims. There are no mountains or forests in the county—just steep, narrow canyon walls and open, rolling country." Sherman County's population reached 4,242 in 1910, and declined to 2,271 by 1950; the estimated figure for 2007 is 1,855. A larger percentage of Sherman County's acreage is under cultivation than any other Oregon county.

Sherwood The city of Sherwood in Washington County was founded because of the construction of the Portland and Willamette Valley Railway (P&WV). Landowners James C. and Mary Ellen Smock gave a right of way to the P&WV in 1885, and the line was built the next year. The Smocks platted a townsite in 1889, when rail service finally began (the company had financial troubles, repeatedly). The Sherwood post office was established in 1891, the name apparently bestowed by resident Robert Alexander, who was from Sherwood, Michigan. The town was incorporated in 1893, and the 1900 census reported 111 residents. By the 1910s Sherwood was reported to be located in a farming and lumbering district, with dairying and fruit growing the major

activities. Sherwood had three sawmills and a plant for drying, canning, and packing fruit. The station shipped quantities of onions, hops, potatoes, apples, and grains. The rural qualities continued until well after World War II. Sherwood's population was 382 in 1930, 575 in 1950. The figure climbed to 3,093 in 1990; after that came explosive suburban residential and retail growth, giving the city a population of an estimated 16,365 in 2007. The town's 1947 Robin Hood Theatre, rescued several times from abandonment and decay, has been demolished.

shipbuilding Perhaps the best-known instance of shipbuilding in Oregon was one of the first, when in 1855 settlers on Tillamook Bay launched the two-masted schooner *Morning Star of Tillamook* to provide a connection with the outside world. Beginning in 1850, a number of craft were built in Oregon for **river transportation**, and small work and pleasure boats were built in ports such as Portland and Astoria, but building ships for ocean travel was another matter. The Coos Bay shipyard of **Asa Simpson** began building wooden sailing vessels in 1859, especially designed to carry the area's coal and lumber to California ports, and continued until 1903. During World War I, the federal Emergency Fleet Corporation contracted with shipyards in Coos Bay, Tillamook, Astoria, and Portland to produced steel wooden-hull vessels, but the market disappeared with the war's end. A similar push in World War II saw the erection of three large facilities in Portland and Vancouver, Washington, operated by **Henry J. Kaiser**; in Coos Bay, the firm of Kruse and Banks, established in 1905, turned out mine-sweepers during the war. Ship repair and small shipbuilding has continued in the Portland area and several other ports.

► **shipwrecks** The Oregon shores are littered with shipwrecks. The mouth of the Columbia has been so dangerous that the term "**Graveyard of the Pacific**" has been applied to it. Two of the wrecks left prominent remains on the beach. The picturesque and rusting ruins of the British sailing vessel *Peter Iredale* (beached in 1906) rest near the mouth of the Columbia River, while the ominous wreckage of the cargo ship *New Carissa*, which went aground in 1999, littered the shores of Coos Bay until 2008. A California disaster that had a notable impact on Oregon was the sinking of the passenger steamship *Brother Jonathan* off Crescent City in 1865.

A Navy sloop that carried the **Wilkes Exploring Expedition**, the USS *Peacock*, wrecked on a sand spit near the north entrance to the Columbia River on July 18, 1841. The instrument of the vessel's destruction received the name Peacock Spit. Fifteen years later in 1856, the bark *Desdemona* also grounded on shoals near Astoria; her remains were visible for years on what were known as the Desdemona Sands. Another Navy vessel came to its end near the Columbia's mouth in 1846, the schooner USS *Shark*. Part of the *Shark*'s wreckage, encumbered with three cannons, floated south and gave rise to the name **Cannon Beach**. The survivors of the mishap (all on board survived) came ashore at present-day Astoria and carved their names on a rock, now known as Shark Rock. Nearly twenty years later, when the *Industry* sank, Shark Rock received another inscription, "The bark Industry was lost March 16, 1865; lives lost 17, saved 7".

In a short period early in the twentieth century, Oregon endured a series of maritime accidents, be-

One of the more bizarre shipwrecks occurred on October 1, 1913, when the *Glenesslin*, bound for Portland for a cargo of wheat, ran aground at 2:30 in the afternoon of a fine fall day. All twenty-one crewmen were saved, but the ship, built in 1885, was a total loss. In the waning days of sailing ships, good crews were hard to find (which sometimes led to crimping); the *Glenesslin* had a young, inexperienced, and apparently inebriated crew. University of Washington Libraries, Special Collections, UW22300.

ginning with the stranding of the *Peter Iredale* in 1906. A fire engulfed the steam schooner *J. Marhoffer* off Yaquina Head in 1910. The ship's boiler came to rest in what became known as Boiler Bay, just north of Depoe Bay. In a bizarre incident that may have been an insurance scam, the three-masted British square-rigger *Glenesslin* ran headlong into Neahkahnie Mountain in broad daylight 1913 while she was en route to Portland to load wheat. There were no fatalities. In 1914, the passenger and cargo vessel *Francis H. Leggett*, en route from Grays Harbor, Washington, to San Francisco, foundered off Tillamook Bay on the northern Oregon coast. Only two of the sixty-seven persons aboard survived. In 1915, the coastwise cargo and passenger steamer *Santa Clara* went aground at Coos Bay; while ninety-three people were saved, twelve lost their lives.

Riverboats were also subject to disaster. The sidewheeler *Gazelle* was built at **Canemah** in 1854, and she exploded there on April 18 of the same year. The unexplained boiler explosion killed twenty-eight persons, including the pilot of the *Wallamet*, which was moored next to the *Gazelle*. Among the victims of the blast was Crawford Dobbins, a business partner of Colburn Barrell, who was an investor in the *Gazelle*. Dobbins and another blast victim were buried in what became Lone Fir Cemetery in Portland, which was then owned by Colburn Barrell.

Short Sand Beach This small and magical beach is in Tillamook County, where Short Sand Creek and Necarney Creek spill into Smuggler Cove, south of Cape Falcon. The beach is indeed short, hemmed in by cliffs, and the cove provides a meager shelter to fishing and pleasure boats in stormy weather, but it did not shelter the boats of smugglers, despite the name. The area was reached only by trail until the completion of this section of the **Oregon Coast Highway** in 1940. The state park at Short Sand Beach is named for **Oswald West**, in commemoration of his efforts to protect the Oregon seacoast from development.

Siletz This Lincoln County community dates from the mid-1850s, with the establishment of the **Coast Reservation** in 1855 and the Siletz Agency the following year. The Coast Reservation included members of many tribes and bands from western Oregon, especially from the southern coast; its lands shrank in 1865 and 1875 as most of its territory was opened to white settlement; allotment agreements reduced the lands as well until, as Stephen Dow Beckham wrote, "the cessions of remaining tribal properties left later generations of Indians almost landless." Siletz town acquired a post office in 1890, and in 1910, Congress permitted the platting and sale of town lots at Siletz. The community persisted through the federal termination of the **Confederated Tribes of Siletz** in 1955, and their restoration in 1977. Siletz is the headquarters of the reconstituted **Siletz Reservation**, and is located on the Siletz River. The town was incorporated as a municipality in 1946. The 1950 census reported a population of 570; this increased to 596 in 1970 and to an estimated 1,165 in 2007.

Siletz Indians *see* **Tillamook Indians**

Siletz Reservation The remnants of the **Coast Reservation** became the Siletz Reservation after 1875. The **Confederated Tribes of Siletz** own and manage the Siletz Reservation, which is comprised of 3,666 acres in Lincoln County, in a number of parcels including property in the town of **Siletz** and timberlands in the watershed of the **Siletz River**.

Siletz River The Siletz River rises in the Coast Range Mountains of Polk County and flows north and west (its course is exceedingly convoluted) about seventy miles through Lincoln County to Kernville, where it enters the Pacific Ocean just north of **Salishan**. It was long a major fishery for **lamprey**, a staple food of the Tillamook Indians as well as others along the Coast and in the Willamette Valley.

Silicon Forest The term "Silicon Forest" is a parallel construction derived from Silicon Valley, the center of California's high-tech, computer-related research and industrial center south of San Francisco. The Silicon Forest is a mental construct that is centered on such Oregon-based firms as **Tektronix**, Electro Scientific Industries (ESI), and Floating Point Systems, and a host of companies based in California, Japan, and elsewhere, such as Hewitt Packard, Intel, and Sun Microsystems. The Silicon Forest can be said to have grown outward from the Tektronix campus that opened in 1951 near Barnes Road and the Sunset Highway north of Beaverton. It has become dispersed, with physical nodes on the **Tualatin Plains** and along the **Sunset Corridor**, in the **Gresham** area, and in Clark County, Washington; some consider **Corvallis** to be part of the forest as well.

> Dodds, Gordon B., and Craig E. Wollner. *The Silicon Forest: High Tech in the Portland Area, 1845–1986.* Portland, Oregon: Oregon Historical Society, 1990.

Silver Creek Falls Silver Creek drains the timberlands between the Silverton Hills on the east and the Waldo Hills on the west, in southern Marion County. In one concentrated area shortly before their confluence, the North and South Forks of Silver Creek and two tributaries plunge over a series of ten waterfalls, ranging in height from 27 feet to 177 feet. The area was logged in the late nineteenth century, and some of the land was then farmed; the falls were a merely local attraction until Silverton photographer **June Drake** began advocating, through his own photographs, for a park to preserve and promote the falls. The efforts finally succeeded in the mid-1930s when the state began acquiring property and a **Civilian Conservation Corps** (CCC) camp was established at the falls. The CCC workers constructed a network of trails linking the waterfalls, as well as picnic facilities and the rustic South Falls Lodge; their work earned the park facilities a place on the National Register of Historic Places. Silver Creek Falls State Park is Oregon's largest state park, with more than 9,000 acres.

Silver Lake This small Lake County community grew from a rural post office in the Silver Lake valley, established in 1875 to serve a few ranches and farms. The post office closed briefly from 1880 to 1882, but in the 1880s it became the nucleus of a real town. On Christmas Eve in 1894, a large community dance was held on the second floor of the Christman Brothers store building. An oil lamp was jostled and fell to the floor; in the ensuing conflagration, forty-seven people died, many of them children. A plea for medical help was carried to Lakeview, some hundred freezing miles away; by heroic efforts Dr. **Bernard Daly** returned to aid the survivors. Silver Lake revived, and in the early 1900s was a bustling small supply town where dry land farmers were settling public lands. It has led a quiet existence since as an agricultural community.

Silverton The farming town of Silverton is located about fifteen miles east of Salem on the banks of Silver Creek. The creek supplied the power for a sawmill in the 1850s, and later a gristmill. A railroad arrived in 1880, and Silverton was incorporated in 1885; the 1890 census reported a population of 551. In the early 1890s, Silverton was the site of Liberal University, a most unusual, non-Christian school. Silverton was the hometown of cartoonist **Homer Davenport**, who wrote a charming account of his boyhood there. By 1915, Silverton had two weekly newspapers, two banks, a lumber mill, and Fischer's flour and cereal mill; the area nearby grew fruit and hops and raised dairy cows. Lumber mills drove the town's economy in the 1920s, but in the 1930s attention turned to the scenic attractions of the graceful **Silver Creek Falls** to the southeast. Silver Falls State Park was established largely through the efforts of Silverton photographer **June Drake**. Silverton was the hometown of **Bobbie the**

Wonder Dog, who in 1923 is said to have trekked his way 2,551 miles back to Oregon from Indiana. Silverton is also the site of the Oregon Garden, begun in 1999 to showcase the state's nursery business as well as to be a "destination" tourist attraction. Oregon's only Frank Lloyd Wright-designed building, a "usonian" house, was moved to the Oregon Garden in 2002. Silverton's population was 3,146 in 1950, and an estimated 9,205 in 2007.

> Davenport, Homer. *The Country Boy; the Story of His Own Early Life.* New York: G. W. Dillingham Company, 1910.

Simpson, Asa Meade (1826–1915) Asa Simpson was born in the shipbuilding center of Brunswick, Maine, and learned the shipbuilding trade at his father's shipyard. He followed the gold rush trail to San Francisco in 1850, where he was very successful in building vessels. He came to **Coos Bay** in 1855 and there combined **shipbuilding** with lumbering, shipping the products to California. His first Oregon vessel, the brig *Arago*, was launched in 1859. In time, he had lumber and shipping operations along the Pacific Coast. The most famous ship from the Simpson yard in North Bend was the *Western Shore*, built by John Kruse and described as the only true clipper ship ever built on the West Coast. She was launched in 1874 and in 1876 set a record sailing time of 101 days from Portland to Liverpool with a cargo of wheat; alas, the *Western Shore* was wrecked north of San Francisco in 1878. The lumber-carrying *Marconi* was the last ship from the Simpson shipyard, launched in 1902. Asa Simpson kept his residence in San Francisco, but his son Louis B. Simpson, himself a lumber baron, lived in Coos Bay. When the *Marconi* ran aground trying to leave Coos Bay in 1909, lumber that was salvaged from the wreck was used in the building of Louis Simpson's estate, Shore Acres, on the rugged headlands near **Cape Arago**. While that building and a later house burned, the gardens and grounds of Shore Acres remain as a spectacular state park.

> Beckham, Stephen Dow. Asa Mead Simpson, Lumberman and Shipbuilder. *Oregon Historical Quarterly* 68 (1967), 259–273.

Simpson, Samuel Lysander "Sam" (1846–1899) Sam Simpson is remembered today as the author of the quintessential Oregon poem of the Victorian era, "Beautiful Willamette," written at Albany in 1870. Sam was the son of a successful businessman and was sent to Willamette University; he got a taste of journalism when his father, Ben Simpson, briefly owned the Salem *Oregon Statesman*. For four months in 1866, Sam was an editor. He married the legendarily beautiful Julia Humphrey in 1868; they divorced seven years later. Simpson was early on inflicted with a taste for drink, a legendary vice of journalism. After dabbling in the law, Simpson spent the remainder of his relatively short life working for a variety of newspapers in Oregon and Washington, writing poetry and short stories. The final section of his most noted poem is a suitable remembrance of his life:

> On the roaring waste of ocean
> Shall thy scattered waves be tossed,
> 'Mid the surge's rhythmic thunder
> Shall thy silver tongues be lost.
> O! thy glimmering rush of gladness
> Mocks this turbid life of mine!
> Racing to the wild Forever
> Down the sloping paths of Time.
> Onward ever,
> Lovely river,
> Softly calling to the sea;
> Time, that scars us,
> Maims and mars us,
> Leaves no track or trace on thee.

Siskiyou Mountains A range of the Klamath Mountains in southwestern Oregon and northern California, the Siskiyou Mountains take up where the **Coast Range** ends, and arch to the east to nearly meet the Cascade Range. They are wedged between the Klamath River on the south and the Rogue River on the north, and include the headwaters of the Illinois, Applegate, and Chetco Rivers. **Mount Ashland** is the highest peak, but several others exceed 7,000 feet in elevation, and the pass over the range south of Ashland is the winter terror of **Interstate 5**. Much of the range is in national forests, some of it in designated wilderness; the **Oregon Caves** are on the northern edge of the range. The Klamath and Siskiyou Mountains are geological "islands" where a number of plants and animals have developed as unique varieties.

> Wallace, David Rains. *The Klamath Knot: Explorations of Myth and Evolution.* Berkeley: University of California Press, 2003.

Siskiyou Trail see **California-Oregon Trail**

Sisters Taking its name from the magnificent view of the **Three Sisters** in the Cascade Range, Sisters in Deschutes County had its beginnings in a short-lived army post, Camp Polk, which was established nearby in 1865. The area was on the route of the wagon road between Central Oregon and the Willamette Valley that snaked over **Santiam Pass**. Camp Polk post office served rural ranchers from 1875 until 1888, when it was moved a few miles to the present site of the town, and the name was changed to Sisters. A townsite was platted in 1901 and a small town developed; a few sawmills were established in the area, and the Santiam Pass highway was opened in the 1920s. By the mid-twentieth century, the large Bend lumber company, Brooks-Scanlon, had logged most of the privately held pinelands near Sisters. Sisters was incorporated in 1946. In the 1970s, the development of residential properties at **Black Butte** by a Brooks-Scanlon subsidiary bolstered retail trade in the city of Sisters. However, it also brought a mandate from Black Butte that a movie-set version of a Wild West town would be

rather nice, and Sisters retailers complied; the faux frontier look is now part of city building codes. Sisters had a population of 723 in 1950, which fell to 516 by 1970; as the resort trade and the appeal of Central Oregon living appreciated, so did the census, to 959 in 2000 and an estimated 1,825 in 2007.

Sitka spruce see **spruce**

Siuslaw Indians The Siuslaw Indians include two Siuslawan groups: the Siuslaw, who lived at villages around the estuary of the Siuslaw River and along the coast to the north; and the Lower Umpqua, concentrated around Winchester Bay and the mouths of the Smith and Umpqua Rivers. The Siuslaw culture was similar to that of other coastal tribes, with a diet that relied on salmon, lamprey, smelt and other fish, shellfish, seals, sea lions, elk and deer, plus roots, wapato, and berries. Cedar-plank longhouses held entire family groups. Cedar canoes were used for river and bay travel, and for ocean fishing. A treaty with the Siuslaws was made in 1855 but never ratified; despite their non-involvement in the **Rogue River Wars**, many Siuslaw were taken to the **Coast Reservation** in 1860, although those near the Siuslaw River were not affected. As anthropologist Henry B. Zenk noted, "Lacking either ratified treaty or reservation affiliation, the Siuslawans . . . endured an especially difficult and litigious relationship with the federal government." In 1917, a tribal government of Coos, Lower Umpqua, and Siuslaw Indians was established; it was federally recognized in 1984.

Siuslaw River Rising in the Coast Range of western Lane County, the Siuslaw River flows westerly to **Mapleton**, near the head of tidewater and navigation, and then proceeds abut twenty-five miles down a narrow valley to Florence, where it enters the Pacific Ocean. The total length is about 110 miles. The river was once a major artery for logs going to sawmills at Mapleton, Acme, and Florence.

Skidmore Fountain Located at the intersection of SW First Avenue and Ankeny Street in Portland, the Skidmore Fountain was dedicated in 1888 in memory of druggist Stephen G. Skidmore, whose bequest inspired and partly funded the fountain. It was designed by New York sculptor Olin Warner, who had been selected by **C. E. S. Wood**. Wood was instrumental in seeing the work completed and he wrote the uplifting lines carved in the stone base, "Good citizens are the riches of a city." It is said that brewer Henry Weinhard offered to send beer through the fountain at its opening, but the offer was perhaps not terribly serious.

Skidmore/Old Town Historic District, Portland Covering all or part of twenty-four blocks surrounding the core of early Portland, this district was placed on the National Register of Historic Places in 1975. It features a range of mid-nineteenth-century to early twentieth-century commercial buildings in a variety of architectural styles, including Italianate revival and Richardsonian Romanesque, but is especially notable for its Victorian-era masonry and cast-iron façade buildings. The city's first **public market** was held in the New Market Theatre, which was built in 1872 with a cast-iron façade; the theater was above the market hall. The **Skidmore Fountain** is another landmark of the district, as are the 1857 Hallock and McMillen building (the oldest) and the 1859 Delschneider building, both small structures built for warehousing and sales at a time when the city's riverfront port was across the street.

skid road Early logging operations often involved skidding felled logs along a pole road to a stream or landing on their way to the sawmill. The logs were pulled along by oxen or horses, and a boy ran beside to grease the logs so they would skid better. The skid road worked until railroads and trucks replaced the oxen and horses. Such a road is said to have extended from the top of First Hill down to Henry Yesler's steam sawmill in Seattle in the 1850s; after its useful life expired, it remained a road, then a cable car line, finally a city street, named Yesler Way. And by the 1890s, Yesler Way was the "dead line" of Seattle: north of Yesler was the respectable city; south of Yesler was where the city's saloons, bawdy theaters, and houses of prostitution were permitted. And that was also where cheap hotels and rooming houses were available for transient loggers and lumbermen, fishermen, and harvest hands. The term "skid road" was used to apply not only to Yesler Way, but also to the district that was defined by it. Skid road was often corrupted to skid row, and it spread to other cities beyond Seattle. Portland's skid road district—north of West Burnside Street near the waterfront—was known as the North End in the early 1900s; it also included by the 1920s Nihonmachi or Japantown, and New Chinatown; by the 1930s, many people called West Burnside Street, Skid Road. *See also* **New Chinatown/Japantown Historic District, Portland**

skid row *see* **skid road.**

skiing The sport of skiing is relatively new, and its popularity in the West is often tied to a few key resort developments, such as Sun Valley in Idaho (1936) and **Timberline Lodge** (1938). The Bend Skyliners mountaineering club, formed in 1928, also promoted skiing, and Skyliner Bill Healy joined with other investors in 1957 to promote a ski area on Bachelor Butte, which they renamed **Mount Bachelor**. Ski areas were developed on Mount Hood beginning in 1928 with two locations, the Skibowl and Multorpor (derived from Multnomah-Oregon-Portland); a rope tow opened in 1938 and a chairlift in 1946. The ski resort on **Mount Ashland** dates from 1963. Other skiing areas have risen in the Blue Mountains and even at Warner Canyon in Lake County.

Skinner Butte Usually called Skinner's Butte, this is a prominent landmark in Eugene, Lane County. The butte is named for Eugene Skinner (1809–1864), who is also the city's namesake. With an elevation of 682 feet, it rises about 250 feet above the city. The public park dates from 1914, and has been the site of decades of squabbles about a religious symbol, a wooden cross that was erected by private individuals on the butte in the 1930s. The cross (and its replacements as it deteriorated) stood there until 1964, when a new cross, "a fifty-one foot concrete Latin cross with neon inset tubing" was privately erected on the summit. From then until 1997, litigation was in play; the eventual outcome removed the cross to the grounds of a local bible college and replaced it with a flagpole. No similar controversy has dogged the large letters *O* and *E* on the slopes of the butte, which have long represented the University of Oregon and Eugene (now South Eugene) High School, respectively.

Skipanon River The short coastal river in Clatsop County has been saddled with a variety of spellings over the years, including Skipanarwin (the form used in the journals of the **Lewis and Clark Expedition** in 1805) and Skeppernawin and Skippenon, and has often been called a creek; it most resembles a slough. It heads in Cullaby Lake and flows placidly north to empty into Youngs Bay at **Warrenton**.

skunk cabbage A perennial native plant, *Lysichiton americanum*, that grows profusely in damp fields, swamps, and marshy creek beds along the Pacific Coast from northern California north into Alaska, skunk cabbage has large, shiny green leaves. It also has a large bright yellow bract that embraces a spike covered with hundreds of bright yellow flowers, which appears in early spring. The plant, especially the flowers, emits a pungent, skunky odor, highly unpleasant to many but agreeable to some. Northwest Coast Indians used skunk cabbage leaves to line baskets; it could also be eaten, but it was a food of last resort, steamed or roasted.

Skyline Trail *see* **Pacific Crest Trail**

Slabtown neighborhood, Portland The amorphous neighborhood of Slabtown is in the vicinity of NW Sixteenth Avenue and Pettygrove Street, an area that at the turn of the twentieth century consisted of hundreds of small workers' cottages and dozens of street corner grocers, laced with streetcar lines and close to industrial jobs near the waterfront: factories, sawmills, and wood products manufacturers. The cottages were heated with wood, and people cooked with wood, and stacks of slabs of waste wood—the trimmings, bark, knots—lined the streets of Slabtown. Wood was the common fuel of Portland, but in other more spacious neighborhoods it was stacked to the side or in back of the house. The name, once a slight, has lingered as a reminder that where now are vast parking lots shadowed by freeway piers, there once were homes.

slavery The state of Oregon was admitted to the Union on the eve of the **Civil War**, and the slavery issue impacted the politics that led to statehood. A number of the Indians in the Oregon Country owned slaves, but the practice rapidly decreased in the face of population declines from disease and the influx of white emigrants, which dramatically altered traditional lifestyles. Some of the early Oregon settlers of the 1840s came from slave-holding states. Daniel Waldo and his family, emigrants of 1843, brought his slaves with him, including a child fathered by Daniel. They settled in the area known as the Waldo Hills east of Salem. Daniel Waldo was a member of the 1844 provisional legislature, and he voted for a "lash law" that year which required that **blacks in Oregon**—slave or free—be lashed twice a year "until he or she shall quit the territory." The lashing provision was quickly modified to forced labor, but the intent was clear despite the fact that only one black man was actually forced to leave the territory. Efforts to create a slave state on the Pacific Coast failed, but when Oregon did enter the Union in 1859, its constitution not only forbade slavery but also excluded blacks from the state. This provision was not enforced, but still affected the status of blacks, many of whom moved to British Columbia in 1859.

► **smelt** Also known as eulachon, olichan, ooligan, candlefish, and hooligan, smelt are small, silvery, oily fish that travel upriver from the Pacific Ocean in huge swarms to spawn, like salmon, in rivers. Coastal Indians used them for food and oil, and they were a popular food with whites as well. Smelt runs were unpredictable and did not occur every year, so when they were noticed, a call went forth: people rushed out with dipnets, buckets, and coffee cans to scoop up the fish. Smelt need not be cleaned to eat (the fish have been swimming without eating for days); they were commonly fried in large quantities.

In the 1940s, restaurants such as Henry Thiele's in Portland featured huge platters of fried fish when "the smelt are running." Runs were usually especially heavy on two Columbia River tributaries, the Cowlitz River in Washington, and the **Sandy River**. The runs began to decline in the 1950s, and by the 1990s, they were sporadic events. The reasons for the decline are still under study.

Smith, Jedediah Strong (1799–1831) Hunter, trapper, explorer, Jedediah Smith, like his contemporary **John Day**, left his name strewn over the landscape of the American West. Born in New York state, Smith traveled overland to California and Oregon in the 1820s in the pursuit of furs; his adventures left a **Smith River** in both states. His other wanderings ranged from the Tetons and South Pass of Wyoming to the Santa Fe Trail. He was leading a party on that trail when he disappeared in 1831.

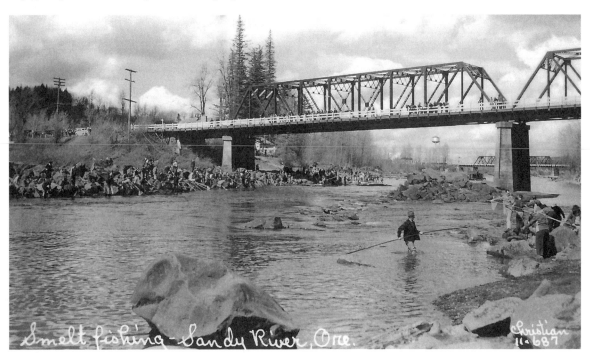

Hordes of eager fishing folk crowd the shores of the Sandy River at Troutdale to catch smelt. The photograph was taken about 1940. Clarence I. Christian photograph. Steven Dotterrer collection.

Smith, Margery Hoffman (1888–1981) Margery Hoffman was the daughter of noted Portland artist and art patron **Julia Hoffman**. She was educated at Bryn Mawr College and took art lessons at the Arts Students League in New York City and the Museum Art School in Portland. The Oregon Society of Artists was founded in 1926, and she was a founding member. Smith was a painter known for floral and still life works, but she achieved fame as an interior designer, especially for her work at **Timberline Lodge** and at the state park that was developed at **Silver Creek Falls**. Smith also donated a collection of Asian art to the **Portland Art Museum** that became the nucleus of their holdings, as well as endowment funds for Asian art. She spent her later years in San Francisco, where she died.

Smith River This river is a tributary of the Umpqua River, draining part of the Coast Range Mountains north of Reedsport in Douglas County. About seventy miles in length, Smith River is one of many geographical features in the American West named for **Jedediah Strong Smith**. Smith was trapping furs with a group of men, heading north from California in the summer of 1828. They pitched a camp near the mouth of the Smith River; while Smith and two companions were away from the camp, Indians attacked it and the fifteen men there were killed; one escaped. Smith and his compatriots made it to **Fort Vancouver** and eventually returned to Saint Louis. Another river in Del Norte County, California, is also named for Smith; a tributary, North Fork Smith River, heads in Curry County, Oregon.

Snake River The major tributary of the Columbia River is the Snake, a tortuous stream of some 1,040 miles in length that has its source in Yellowstone National Park, and meets the Columbia near Pasco, Washington. Along the way, it crosses Idaho and forms the border between Idaho and Oregon; part of that section is known as **Hells Canyon**. In the canyon area, three large hydroelectric-generating dams—Brownlee, Oxbow, and Hells Canyon, built between 1958 and 1967—have stilled the waters and wiped away the sites of such once-flourishing mining camps as **Copperfield**. Farther downstream, between Lewiston, Idaho, and the confluence with the Columbia, four other dams block the stream: Lower Granite, Little Goose, Lower Monumental and Ice Harbor. These dams, all constructed between 1962 and 1975, were built primarily to improve navigation to Lewiston, but they also provide irrigation water and hydroelectric power.

The Snake's major Oregon tributaries are the **Owyhee**, **Malheur**, **Powder**, and **Grande Ronde Rivers**. These rivers, like the Snake itself, are no longer accessible to migrating salmon. **Sturgeon** were also once abundant in the Snake.

▶**Sodaville** The small mineral spring that gave rise to the town of Sodaville was known to settlers in this part of Linn County in the 1840s. Located in the Cascade foothills southeast of Lebanon, Sodaville was platted into lots by Thomas Summerville in 1871, with a block containing the spring set aside for "perpetual public use." A post office was also established in 1871, and the town was incorporated in 1880; the census of that year gave it a population of fifty-six. Its heyday as a small resort town lasted through the 1890s, although the state appropriated monies to maintain the public spring at least until 1921. The post office closed in 1933 and little remains of the townsite, but city government continues to function in the town, which had a population in 2007 of about 290.

Southern Emigrant Road The term "Southern Emigrant Road" was used during the 1840s and 1850s to refer to a variant routing of **Oregon Trail** that crossed present-day Nevada and part of California via the California Trail before veering northwesterly to meet the **California-Oregon Trail** near Ashland. The route was blazed in 1846 by **Jesse and Lindsay Applegate**, **Levi Scott**, and others who were recent immigrants to Oregon. Both Applegates had lost a son to drowning in the Columbia River during the last leg of their journey, a tragedy that prompted them to attempt to forge another, and safer, route. The party intercepted a group of westbound emigrants at Fort Hall, Idaho, and persuaded about 100 wagons to follow them. The first part of the route was already a primitive road, but the cutoff across the Black Rock Desert of Nevada, past Goose Lake and across the Cascade Range was untracked and not ready for wagons: it was a near-disastrous endeavor. The bedraggled emigrants did not reach Oregon until late fall, and a relief party from the Willamette Valley met the emigrants in the Umpqua Valley in November to offer food and assistance. The episode left a bitter taste in many pioneer mouths. The route was gradually improved, but relatively few emigrants chose to use it.

The Southern Emigrant Road, or South Road, or Southern Route, became publicized as the Applegate Trail only after Walter Meacham of the Oregon Council of the American Pioneer Trails Association published a booklet by that title in 1947. Meacham spearheaded efforts to mark and recognize the trail. The descendants of some of those who took the route have attempted to amend the name to Scott-Applegate Trail (to give some recognition to Levi Scott) or to revert to the more contemporary terminology.

Southern Oregon University (SOU) The Methodist church founded Ashland Academy in Ashland in 1869, renaming it Ashland College in 1872. In 1879, it turned its concentration to preparing teachers, and became Ashland College and Normal School. The state of Oregon designated Ashland a state normal school in 1882, but it provided no public funds and the school closed in 1890. Re-organization created the Southern Oregon Normal School—

This modest building, pictured in June 1930, was the springhouse erected by the state of Oregon over the "famous mineral springs" at Sodaville. A full city block was set aside for the springhouse and grounds. *Oregon Journal* photograph. Oregon Historical Society, CN 015007.

with both state and Methodist funding—in 1899, but this too was short-lived; the school lost state dollars and closed in 1909. Finally, Southern Oregon Normal, a new state institution, opened in 1926. It was renamed Southern Oregon College of Education in 1939 as it moved beyond training teachers, and became simply Southern Oregon College in 1956, then Southern Oregon State College in 1975. In 1995, in recognition of added graduate level programs, the school became Southern Oregon University (SOU). The name changes reflect the uncertainty of support and direction that the school has often experienced. By the early 2000s, financial constraints and declining enrollment caused program cuts and further self-examination.

▶ **Southern Pacific Company (SP)** Once a formidable corporation with tentacles throughout the American West, the Southern Pacific railroad had its beginnings in 1865. SP built the western segment of the first transcontinental line, completed to San Francisco Bay in 1869, and by 1883 had another continent-spanning line from Los Angeles. In the 1880s the SP secured its control of numerous allied lines, and in 1887 it leased the **Oregon & California Railroad**, which by the end of the year completed the first and only (until 1927) line connecting San Francisco and Oregon. By the mid-1890s, SP controlled virtually all of the extensive branch railroad lines in the Willamette Valley and a branch to **Yaquina Bay**. In the next three decades, the company extended its reach with new routes to Tillamook, Coos Bay, and Klamath Falls, and in 1927 completed a new California main line via Willamette Pass, called the Natron Cut-off. Between 1914 and 1917, the SP electrified its lines from Portland to Lake Oswego, Forest Grove, McMinnville, and Corvallis to meet the new competition of the **Oregon Electric Railway**'s interurban lines in the Willamette Valley. The electric lines were discontinued in 1929, often replaced by SP-owned **bus transportation**. A great percentage of Oregon's ag-

ricultural, timber and passenger traffic was held by the SP in a near-monopoly until the 1950s. The SP ran several premier passenger trains between Oregon and California, including the overnight *Shasta Limited* and its 1937 replacement, the *Cascade*, and a dawn-to-midnight streamliner introduced in 1949, the *Shasta Daylight*. The Southern Pacific became engaged in truck and bus transportation in the 1920s, and its freight and passenger business lost

The "Million-dollar train with the million-dollar view, " the *Shasta Daylight* train of the Southern Pacific Company connected Portland with San Francisco via Willamette Pass and Odell Lake (pictured here). This 1949 brochure described features aboard the train, such as the Timberline Tavern Car, with décor that was inspired by Timberline Lodge. Author's collection.

ground in the 1960s. Amtrak replaced the *Cascade* in 1971 with the **Coast Starlight**. The company was in deep financial trouble by the 1980s and was purchased and absorbed by the **Union Pacific Railroad** in 1996.

South Portland neighborhood, Portland

South Portland is partly a neighborhood, and partly a vanished neighborhood. In the early twentieth century, the term referred to an area south of SW Jefferson Street and east of the base of the West Hills. It was a district of houses, rooming houses, and small shops, built in the 1880s and 1890s as streetcar lines extended the reach of the city; by the 1910s, it was increasingly an area populated by immigrants, notably **Jews** and **Italians**. Synagogues and Saint Michael's Catholic Church were landmarks, as was the then-new Civic Auditorium (later **Keller Auditorium**). Much of South Portland was demolished as part of an **urban renewal** project in the 1960s; for some years an isolated relic has been the Victorian house whose basement housed the works for making Mrs. Neusihin's kosher dill pickles (still in production, but now somewhere else).

Olsen, Polina. *The Immigrants' Children: Jewish and Italian Memories of Old South Portland*. Portland, Oregon: Smart Talk Publications, 2006.

Spanish-American War, 1898

One of the first units to be sent to the Philippine Islands after the onset of the Spanish-American War was the Second Oregon Volunteer Infantry, mustered into service between May 7 and May 15, 1898. Consisting of fifty officers and 970 enlisted men, the Second Oregon was sent off to tropical conditions with little preparation—they were issued a uniform with a heavy flannel shirt worn beneath a heavy flannel jacket, for example. During their service, the Second Oregon lost fifteen men in action, and thirty-eight to disease. They were mustered out on August 7,

1899. The battleship USS *Oregon* was one of the war's heroes.

Bunnett, Sara, ed. *Manila Envelopes: Oregon Volunteer Lt. George F. Tefler's Spanish-American War Letters*. Portland, Oregon: Oregon Historical Society, 1987.

▶ **Spokane, Portland & Seattle Railway (SP&S)** Headquartered in Portland, the SP&S Railway sloganeered that it was "The Northwest's own railway." Not quite. Despite its name (which reflected early ambitions), the railroad reached only from Spokane to Portland, with an extension to Astoria and Seaside. It was wholly owned by two larger Midwest-centered railroad companies. In 1905, James J. Hill announced that his **Great Northern Railroad** and the **Northern Pacific Railway** would build the line. The "North Bank Road" was opened in 1908, giving both companies direct access from Saint Paul and points east down the north bank of the Columbia River to Vancouver and Portland. The SP&S also took over the operations of the **Oregon Electric Railway** and the **Oregon Trunk Railway**. The principal eastbound traffic was finished lumber; the main westbound traffic was wheat and other grains. For a brief time in 1915–16, the SP&S operated fast trains between Portland and Flavel, near Astoria, to connect with two equally fast steamships to San Francisco, named the *Great Northern* and the *Northern Pacific*. The SP&S carried the Portland sections of two major Chicago-Pacific Northwest passenger trains, the *Empire Builder* of the Great Northern and the Northern Pacific's *North Coast Limited*. The SP&S was merged with its owners and other lines in the Burlington Northern Railroad in 1970, and thence into the **Burlington Northern Santa Fe Railroad** in 1996.

Grande, Walter R. *The Northwest's Own Railway: Spokane, Portland & Seattle Railway and its Subsidiaries*. 2 vols. Portland, Oregon: Grande Press, 1992–97.

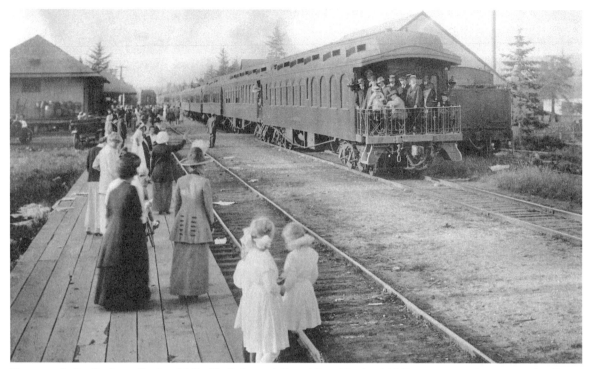

The scene is the Spokane, Portland & Seattle Railway station at Seaside about 1910, as a group of women and well-dressed children wave farewell to a number of men gathered on the back platform of the train. This may be the summer Sunday evening train, or the special early Monday train, when family men headed back to the city of Portland for work, leaving their families to spend another week at the seashore. Author's collection.

spotted owl The northern spotted owl, *Strix occidentalis caurina*, inhabits old-growth forests along the Pacific Coast. It was classed in 1990 as a threatened species under the federal Endangered Species Act and is also on the state list of threatened species. The spotted owl reaches maturity after two years, breeds slowly, feeds at night on squirrels, woodrats and small mammals, and requires a habitat that includes snags and cavities. The owl became a cause célèbre in the 1990s when its protection was cited as one reason for reducing timber harvests on federal lands and for disrupting timber sales on private lands; there were other reasons, too, including overharvesting and overproduction, but the owl (and its defenders) took a great deal of heat in the 1990s for the closure of many mills and logging operations in the Pacific Northwest.

Spray The Wheeler county town of Spray began as a rural post office in 1900, in a region devoted largely to stock raising. In 1915, lumbering and the raising of poultry and fruit were also carried on in the vicinity; the population was estimated at 148. Spray was incorporated in 1958. The 1970 census credited it with 161 residents; the estimate in 2007 was 160.

➤ **Springfield** The Lane County city of Springfield is located on the plain between the McKenzie and Willamette Rivers in an area that was settled by emigrant farm families in the 1840s and 1850s. A sawmill and flour mill were operating in the 1850s, and a townsite was platted in 1856; a post office named Springfield opened in 1868. The town was incorporated in 1885, and the 1890 census credited it with a population of 371. In 1891, the South-

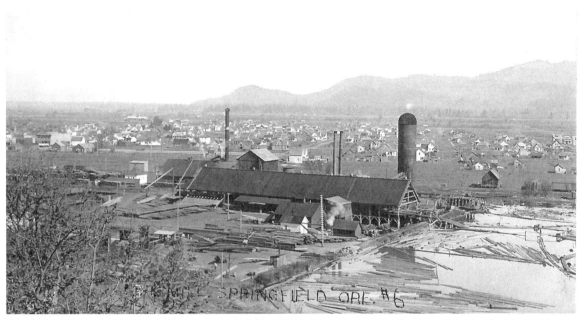

The Booth-Kelly sawmill was a major employer in Springfield in the early twentieth century. This view looking north from Springfield Butte shows the mill about 1915. In 1901, Booth-Kelly bought an existing mill and its millrace, which brought water from the Willamette River to the site. They built a new mill and a log pond to store logs for the mill; that mill burned in 1911. The plant was sold to Georgia-Pacific in 1958, and most of it was closed in 1964. Mason collection.

ern Pacific Company extended its line from Coburg into Springfield and then eastward up the Middle Fork Willamette River to Natron. That same year the city could boast of lumber mills, three hotels, three churches, and a saloon. A streetcar line connected Springfield with Eugene in 1910, when the population reached 1,838. More lumber mills were constructed, including the large Booth-Kelly mill; the population in 1940 was 3,805. In 1949, the **Weyerhaeuser Company** built a huge lumber and plywood operation in Springfield, and the census count reached 10,807 in 1950, 26,874 in 1970. The timber industry began shrinking by the 1980s, and the Weyerhaeuser mills closed in the 1990s. Springfield's economy was closely tied to that of Eugene, of which it became a virtual suburb. Author **Ken Kesey** lived much of his life in nearby Pleasant Hill; his brother, Chuck, and wife, Sue, started the Springfield Creamery in 1960, which used a recipe of their bookkeeper Nancy Hamren to produce acidopholus-cultured yo-

gurt. Nancy's Yogurt was an early and successful product of the natural foods movement. The Dorris Ranch Park in Springfield is the site of one of the state's first commercial **filbert** orchards, and the park still harvests the nuts for sale.

► **spruce** The Sitka spruce, *Picea sitchensis*, sometimes called coast or tideland spruce, is the world's tallest spruce, reaching a height of 160 feet and a diameter of three to five feet or greater. An evergreen with thin gray bark and sharp needles, the Sitka spruce grows in the Pacific Coast fog belt from Alaska to northern California, both in pure stands and in mixed stands with western hemlock. It was little used for lumber until the early 1900s, when the strength and light weight of old-growth spruce proved to be useful in building airplanes. During World War I, the U.S. Army Signal Corps Spruce Division began a crash program to fell and mill Sitka spruce to make warplanes. The war ended

Sitka spruce trees are outlined in the smoke from a campfire on the Oregon Coast, probably near Yachats in the early 1900s. E. A. and C. L. Marshall family collection. Oregon Historical Society, Lot 311-818.

before major production began, but mills built for the Corps, such as those at **Toledo**, began to use the timber. Spruce is used for structural lumber, as wood pulp for paper, and in specialty products such as wooden berry boxes, boats, and piano sounding boards.

Spruce Goose *see* **McMinnville**

Stadium Freeway *see* **Interstate 405**

▶ **Stafford, William** (1914–1993) Poet William Stafford was born and educated in Kansas. He was in graduate school there in 1941 when he was drafted for military service. Stafford became a conscientious objector and was assigned to forest service camps during World War II. He graduated from the University of Kansas in 1947 and the next year joined the English faculty at **Lewis and Clark College** in Portland. Stafford did not begin to write

poetry until the 1960s; his first major collection, *Traveling through the Dark,* came out in 1962, and won the National Book Award the next year. The title poem, like many of his poems, reflects his own

The poet William Stafford pictured browsing in the stacks of the library at Lewis and Clark College. Oregon Historical Society, CN 014269.

experiences, his connections with the natural world, his sense of peaceful coexistence, and his appreciation of particular places, qualities which have made many readers consider him a poet of the place, Oregon. Stafford was a prolific writer, and published fifty-seven volumes of poetry. He was named poet laureate of Oregon in 1975; though he retired from teaching in 1980, he continued to travel and give poetry readings.

staging and freighting transportation

The business of transporting people and freight for hire, on land, emerged as a major enterprise in the 1850s, when packers using mules and horses brought supplies from **Gardiner** and **Scottsburg** and Crescent City, California to the southern Oregon gold mines. Many of the packers were Californians, often **Mexicans** with much experience in the business. As roads improved, packing turned into freighting using wagons to hold the goods rather than saddle packs. During the 1860s gold rushes in eastern Oregon, freight wagons and stagecoaches met the boats of the **Oregon Steam Navigation Company** from Portland at Umatilla Landing. The first through stagecoach service from Portland to California was established in 1860; it took six days to reach Sacramento. As railroad mileage grew from the early 1880s into the 1910s, stages and freight services typically connected railroad stations with mining camps, mill towns, and remote settlements; often the stage services were offered in conjunction with mail contracts, which also went by train whenever feasible. Auto stages and auto freight lines began appearing about 1905, and by the 1910s were especially common in the arid areas of southeastern Oregon. **Bus transportation** supplanted stagecoaches by the 1920s.

▶ **Stanfield** Located along the Umatilla River in Umatilla County, the locality of Stanfield was once on the route of the **Oregon Trail** and later on roads leading from the steamboat landing at Umatilla. When the Union Pacific Railroad built through the area in 1882, it established a station for this agricultural area, called Fosters. Foster post office opened in 1883, and was closed in 1890. Irrigation

Newly shorn sheep fill the feedlot at this ranch near Stanfield, photographed about 1915. Mason collection.

efforts in the early 1900s inspired a second development effort. Robert N. Stanfield (1877–1945) had landholdings in the area for his **sheep** raising and wool shipping business, and he and others subdivided some of the land and platted a townsite. Stanfield was later a state representative, and served in the U.S. Senate from 1921 to 1927. The Stanfield post office opened in 1909; the town was incorporated in 1910, in which year the census recorded 318 residents. That was a high point for several decades; the population was 241 in 1940, but irrigation developments brought new life, and it rose to 845 in 1950. Stanfield's population was 1,568 in 1980, and an estimated 2,155 in 2007.

State of Jefferson The concept of another state along the Pacific Coast has had several incarnations since the 1850s. On the eve of World War II, a band of regional boosters of southern Oregon and northern California who felt the states' politicians were ignoring their needs proposed a new state. In 1941, a group that included mayor Gilbert Gable of **Port Orford** and others in Siskiyou, Modoc, and Del Norte Counties in California, and **Jackson**, **Josephine**, **Klamath**, and **Curry Counties** in Oregon cited the ostensible need to develop the area's mineral resources in the face of impending wartime as a justification. The group came up with a state seal consisting of "xx" in a circle, symbolizing the alleged "double crossing" antics of lawmakers in the two states. In November 1941, a roadblock was set up on **Highway 99** and motorists were handed a leaflet about Jefferson, the future forty-ninth state of the union. But the events of December 7, 1941, shoved aside what historian Cain Allen described as a "half-serious secessionist movement." The idea has persisted as a half-serious concept, both for its novelty value as a tourist lure and as a political tool. The Jefferson Public Radio system serving southern Oregon and northern California from Ashland has made good use of the idea since its inauguration as KSOR in 1969.

Stayton The Marion County city of Stayton developed around several enterprises of Drury Stayton, who by 1870 had built a water-powered sawmill and a flouring mill at the site; he platted the townsite in 1872, and a post office opened the same year. A small wool carding plant operated there in 1880, and a narrow-gauge railroad reached West Stayton, three miles from the town, in the same year. Stayton was incorporated in 1891, and the 1900 census showed it had a population of 324. The establishment of a woolen manufacturing plant in 1905 helped boost the count for the 1910 census to 703. In the 1910s, Stayton had other water-powered mills including a cabinet factory, a sash and door factory and an excelsior mill. Excelsior was a type of fine wood shavings used for upholstery padding and packing material. In 1915, Stayton reportedly had a Lavender Club, "organized by the women to grow lavender for commercial purposes."

Agriculture, an important activity in the area since the 1850s, became more significant in the 1920s with the establishment of a processing cooperative, the Stayton Canning Company. Snap **beans** became a local specialty, honored at an annual Bean Festival. A private irrigation project also developed in the area west of Stayton in the 1920s, an unusual endeavor for the time and place. Stayton's population reached 1,040 in 1940 and 3,170 by 1970. The woolen mill, commonly called the Paris Mill, continued to produce woolen cloth and blankets, with interruptions, until about 1990. In the last decades of the twentieth century, Stayton's economy was based on frozen, canned, and processed food and timber products. Increasingly, the town is a residential suburb of Salem and Albany. Its population in 2007 was estimated at 7,765.

steamboats *see* **river transportation**

steamships *see* **ocean transportation**

Steel, William Gladstone (1854–1934) William Steel was born in Ohio and finished high school in Portland. His younger years were filled with a variety of jobs: he was an apprentice pattern maker, a newspaperman, the publisher of the Albany *Herald*, and in the early 1880s, a letter carrier and mail supervisor in Portland. In the late 1880s, Steel was an investor with two brothers in a suburban development in the **Fulton neighborhood** of Portland. It was 1885 when Steel and a friend took an arduous trip to **Crater Lake**. The lake was still little known; **Peter Britt** of Jacksonville had taken photographs there in 1874 that first publicized the remarkable caldera and its deep blue waters. Steel and his friend went there to meet with the noted geologist Joseph LeConte, who was studying Pacific Coast volcanoes. The lake was a revelation to Steel. After the visit, he wrote, "An overmastering conviction came to me that this wonderful spot must be saved, wild and beautiful, just as it was, for all future generations, and that it was up to me to do something. I then and there had the impression that in some way, I didn't know how, the lake ought to become a National Park."

Crater Lake National Park became Steel's cause. A first step in 1886 withdrew some of the property from homestead entry, and the federal Cascade Forest Reserve of 1893 brought additional protection. Steel brought members of the mountain-climbing club the **Mazamas** (he was one of its founders) to the lake in 1896, where to great publicity they named the mountain in which the lake was cradled: Mount Mazama. The lake was designated a national park, the nation's seventh, in 1902. Steel hoped he would be the first superintendent, but that did not happen; still, he did receive that appointment in 1913, serving until 1916. Although Steel was awed and fascinated by the lake, he also promoted a number of ideas that run counter to ideals of preserving its natural attributes: he pushed the road entirely around the rim of the lake, and advocated one to reach the lake shore; he suggested an elevator from the lodge to the lake; he planted (successfully, alas)

fish in a fishless lake. But he saw the marvels, too. Steel Cliff on Mount Hood is named for him, as is Steel Bay in Crater Lake.

Weiselberg, Erik. He All but Made the Mountains: William Gladstone Steel, Mountain Climbing, and the Establishment of Crater Lake National Park. *Oregon Historical Quarterly* 103, no. 1 (Spring 2002): 50–75.

steelhead trout *Oncorhynchus mykiss*, steelhead trout, are usually called simply steelhead. They are the ocean-going version of the rainbow trout, which remain in fresh water throughout their lives. Steelhead migrate to the Pacific and return to spawn, but unlike **salmon**, they do this individually rather than in schools. The steelhead return primarily in spring and fall, and although most die after spawning, some return to the sea one or two times; salmon inevitably die after spawning. The steelhead can weigh from about four to twenty pounds; although runs in the Columbia River system and several coastal rivers are troubled, fishermen pursue them in the Rogue and Umpqua Rivers.

Steens Mountain Located in Harney County, Steens Mountain is one of many fault-block escarpments—**Abert Rim** is another prominent example—in southeastern Oregon, an area of basin-and-range geology that also describes much of Nevada and Utah. On the west side, the Steens appears to be a slanted tableland, etched with deep ravines such as the Big Indian, Little Blitzen, and Kiger Gorges, which feed waters into the **Donner und Blitzen River**. From its highest point at 9,733 feet, the Steens plunges down on its eastern face to the Alvord Desert at an elevation of about 4,200 feet—nearly a sheer-mile drop. The mountain is named for Maj. Enoch Steen, who in 1860 was in the vicinity on a mission to pursue troublesome Indians. The western slope of the Steens was part of the rangelands of **Pete French** in the 1880s, and the Bureau of Land Management (BLM) has managed much of the mountain as cattle rangeland. The so-called Kiger mustangs are feral horses that have long ranged and bred in the Kiger Gorge and vicinity, and though they are exasperating to both conservationists and ranchers for the damage they do to the land, they have become a feature of the area. The herd is periodically culled and the horses sold by the BLM. Some mining of uranium was done on the mountain in the 1950s. Federal land on the mountain was placed into a management and protection area in 2000 to minimize mining and grazing damage, and some private lands were acquired to add to the protected area.

sternwheel steamboats *see* **river transportation**

Stevens, James (1892–1971) James Stevens only occasionally resided in Oregon, but his authorship of the Paul Bunyan legends from the 1920s into the 1940s made him something of an Oregon-related personality—and this despite the fact that Paul Bunyan is primarily a character of Upper Midwest logging, not that of the Pacific Northwest. Stevens was born in Iowa and lived in many places; in the eighth grade, he was expelled for chewing tobacco, but he was an insatiable reader and library user. He fought in World War I, and on coming back worked in the woods and the sawmills in Oregon, and traipsed through the Midwest and the West. He researched logging history; he took residence in Detroit, Portland, Seattle. *Paul Bunyan* came out in 1925. In 1927, he collaborated with **H. L. Davis** on a small booklet that scandalized the small Pacific Northwest literary community: *Status Rerum: A Manifesto upon the Present Condition of Northwestern Literature, containing Several Near-libelous Utterances, upon Persons in the Public Eye.* He wrote about logging and lumbering and about conservation; his colleague was **Stewart Holbrook**. In the 1940s, he became public relations director for the Western Lumberman's Association and helped promote the "Keep Washington Green" program. In all, Stevens wrote nine books including *Homer in the Sagebrush* (1928) and *Big Jim Turner* (1948), and more than 250 short stories and magazine articles.

Storrs, John *see* **Fealy, Barbara**

Straub, Robert W. (1920–2002) Robert Straub was born in San Francisco and attended Dartmouth College, where he obtained a bachelor's degree as well as an MBA. After serving in the army during World War II, Straub and his wife, Pat, moved to Eugene, Oregon, in 1946, where he became a builder and developer. Straub was elected to the Lane County board of commissioners in 1954, from which he stepped to a state senate seat in 1959. There he voiced his concerns about increasing water and air pollution and advocated for better management of the state's natural resources. A Democrat, he joined with Republican governor **Tom McCall** and other progressives to preserve Oregon's beaches for public use and to create the Willamette River Greenway. Straub was elected state treasurer in 1964, serving two terms before running for governor in 1974 and defeating Victor Atiyeh for the post. As governor, Straub worked to strengthen land-use laws initiated under McCall, to improve education, and to reorganize and improve the management of state agencies and services. His conservation impulses were tested and proven during his tenure as state treasurer, when he vocally opposed highway department plans to route the **Oregon Coast Highway** across a sand spit at the mouth of the **Nestucca River**, damaging the estuary as well as blocking public use of the beaches. The highway stayed inland; the sands are now a state park, named for Straub.

Clucas, Richard A. The Political Legacy of Robert W. Straub. *Oregon Historical Quarterly* 104, no. 4 (Winter 2003): 462–477.

strawberries Three species of wild strawberry grow in Oregon. *Fragaria virginiana* and *F. vesca,* western and wood strawberries, are widely distributed in the state, but the best-known—the most luscious and elusive—Oregon strawberry is *F. chiloensis*, the beach or dune or coast strawberry. This plant is found only along the seashore, usually on dunes or headlands.

Strawberries are a major commercial crop in Oregon. In the 1880s, they were being grown for market in the Portland and Hood River areas; the Willamette Valley was a major producer by the 1910s. Although strawberries can be preserved by drying and in jams and jellies, canning was not a suitable preservation process, and it was not until food-freezing techniques were mastered that frozen strawberries and concentrates became a way of moving Oregon strawberries beyond a local market. The variety known as the Marshall was grown on the Pacific Coast from the 1920s, large, firm and exceedingly tasty, but also not too productive and prone to disease. Still, they were widely planted in Oregon into the 1960s even as other varieties such as Totems were developed and replaced them. In the mid-twentieth century, Oregon grew as much as a hundred million pounds of strawberries annually, but California held and increased its lead. In the 1980s and 1990s, strawberry production declined, battered by California production and the loss of fields to suburban growth. By 2006, Oregon produced only 1 percent of the nation's strawberry crop—but it was the state's twenty-ninth most valuable crop, and Oregon was the nation's third largest producer. The Marshall variety has virtually vanished, despite the efforts of food cultists to find surviving specimens and revive production.

streetcars Streetcars are a form of transit operating in public streets, using steel rails and powered, usually, by electricity from an overhead wire. Some streetcars were hauled by horses or by small steam locomotives. Streetcars operated in a number of Oregon towns and cities: Astoria (1892–1922; beginning with horses in 1888); Forest Grove (ca. 1906); Albany (1889–1918—horse, steam, electric); Salem (1889–1927, beginning with horses); Eugene-Springfield (1907–27); West Linn (1893–1930); Baker City (horse-drawn, ca. 1890–1904); Medford (ca. 1915); and Klamath Falls (horse-drawn, ca. 1907–11).

In Portland, a vast network developed, beginning with a horse-drawn line on First Avenue in 1872, financed by **Ben Holladay**. Many of Portland's neighborhoods such as **Sellwood** and **Montavilla** developed as streetcar suburbs, allowing commuting workers to have country houses and city jobs. Portland also had cable-operated streetcars of the San Francisco type from 1890 to 1904. The Portland system was consolidated into a single network by 1907, by the Portland Railway, Light & Power Company (they also supplied electricity, and eventually became Portland General Electric Company, then PacifiCorp). By 1918, the company operated 273 miles of streetcar lines with more than 600 streetcars. Bus lines began operating in the 1920s, and in the 1930s electric buses replaced some lines. Buses replaced the last Portland streetcar after February 28, 1950. In 1991, replicas of 1905-era streetcars began operating as a tourist attraction on the new **MAX** line. Streetcar service returned to Portland on July 20, 2001. *See also* **interurban railways**.

Stumptown Whitefish, Montana, is called Stumptown. There is a community of Stumptown, Virginia. There was a Stumptown in Ohio, and a mining camp in Colorado. The Stumptown Brewery is in the former redwood logging town of Guerneville, California. In the late twentieth century, the legend arose that **Portland** had been known, almost from its inception in the 1840s, as Stumptown. With regard to the numerous early townsites that were laid out in the vicinity of Portland, in his *Early Portland: Stump-Town Triumphant* (1970) Eugene Snyder noted that the supporters of rival towns "claimed Portland had more stumps than people and gave it the derisive nickname 'Little Stumptown.'" And he quotes a "visitor in 1847" as saying, "The trees are cut down where the streets have been surveyed, but the stumps are left." The use of the Stumptown moniker has spread since the publication of Snyder's book. It is worth noting that virtually all the towns in western Oregon once were stumptowns.

sturgeon The white sturgeon, *Acipenser transmontanus*, is the largest North American freshwater fish. These sturgeon in their natural state spawn and live in fresh water, but also migrate to the Pacific during maturity and can live in brackish water as well; they may transition from fresh to salt water a number of times in their long lives (they can live a century or more). Sturgeon are bottom feeders; they can reach up to fifteen feet in length and may weigh more than 1,500 pounds. In Oregon, they were common in the Columbia River system, including the Snake River. The construction of a succession of dams on the Columbia River has effectively landlocked most of the sturgeon, which cannot use fish ladders; only the lower reaches of the Willamette and Columbia hold sea-going sturgeon. The sturgeon was a valued food fish, and some are still taken commercially on the lower Columbia and by tribal fishers above Bonneville Dam.

Sublimity Suitably sited, Sublimity is a rural town in Marion County. The first postmaster, James M. Denny, bestowed the name in 1852: "for the sublime scenery in the hills around the town," said geographic names historian Lewis L. McArthur. The town grew slowly as a trading center for farm families; a railroad arrived at Aumsville, four miles away, in 1880. Not until 1903 was Sublimity incorporated, and the 1910 census recorded 138 residents there. In 1915, farmers nearby were reported to engage in "dairying, farming and fruit raising; grains, fruits, vegetables, wheat, oats, rye, barley, hops, flax and potatoes," and a local creamery served the dairy farmers. In 1970, the population was 634; since that time, Sublimity has become a bedroom community for commuters who work in Salem, a dozen miles

NO 3, 1500 POUND STURGEON CAUGHT IN SNAKE RIVER, NEAR ONTARIO. ORE. ©W

This sturgeon was caught in the Snake River near Ontario about 1910, and was estimated to weigh 1,500 pounds. Wesley Andrews photograph. Author's collection.

away. The population in 1990 was 1,491, and it was estimated at 2,255 in 2007.

sucker *see* **Klamath Indians; Klamath Lake**

Sucker Lake *see* **Lake Oswego**

sugar pine *see* **pine**

Sullivan's Gulch Though the official terminology is Sullivan Gulch, Sullivan's Gulch is what Portlanders call the winding defile that extends east from the Willamette River near Lloyd Boulevard. The gulch was once a watercourse, but over the years it has become a congested transportation corridor occupied by **Union Pacific Railroad** tracks (1884), the **Banfield Freeway** (1955), and the **MAX** light-rail line (1986). The western end of the gulch was the site of a Hooverville in the 1930s, a shanty-town of itinerant workers made homeless by the Depression.

Summerville The rural town of Summerville in Union County is located in the Grande Ronde River valley, an area whose agricultural potential was noted in the 1840s by emigrants on the Oregon Trail. Among the first American settlers, in the 1860s, was William Patten, who became postmaster at the new post office that opened in 1865. It was named for his friend and former Willamette Valley neighbor, Alexander J. Sommerville; somehow, the spelling changed slightly. The town was incorporated in 1885, and the 1890 census recorded 280 residents; it has never since been so large. A railroad reached Imbler, three miles away, in 1890, permanently damaging its aspirations to become a more important place. Still, Summerville hung on, and its residents continued to engage in farming, fruit growing, and poultry raising. A 1915 report noted that Summerville had a "factory for the extraction of fiber from pine needles"; this was apparently not a profitable product. In 2007, about 120 people lived in Summerville.

Sumpter In the early 1860s, while Civil War raged in the East and the South, Baker County was gold rush country. A party of prospecting miners from South Carolina found **gold** on Cracker Creek, and stayed to work their find; they named the settlement Fort Sumter. Sumter post office opened in 1874, but the gold fields soon played out, and it closed in 1878.

The post office was re-established in 1883, this time with an inexplicable *p* added to the name. Gold mining was revived with the arrival of the **Sumpter Valley Railway** from Baker City in 1896, and placer mining gave way to hard-rock mining, which involved tunneling, drilling, and operating ore crushers. Substantial brick buildings went up in downtown Sumpter, and the railroad also helped to develop a lumber industry, with logs from the Blue Mountains headed to Baker City for milling. Sumpter was incorporated as a municipality in 1901, when it was near the height of its second gold rush period: in 1902, Sumpter had two daily newspapers and a weekly paper as well. The 1910 census showed a population of 643 residents; by 1915, Sumpter boasted four churches, a weekly newspaper (both dailies had died), and a bank, but it was shrinking.

Another method of extracting gold, the dredge, appeared in 1913. The dredges dug through the already worked gravels of the **Powder River** valley downstream from Sumpter, a process that went on for forty years. The last dredge stopped in 1953, and it sits there yet, stranded in a pond of its own making on the edge of town.

A fire gutted downtown Sumpter in 1917, the same year the *Blue Mountain American* ceased its weekly publication. The railroad was abandoned in 1947. The population in 1950 was 146 persons; the estimate in 2007 was 170 residents. Sumpter is a **ghost town**, with a fine municipal museum and a suitably bleak abandoned gold dredge.

▶ **Sumpter Valley Railway** Several Utah industrialists, among them David Eccles, formed the Oregon Lumber Company in Baker City in 1889. The next year, the group began construction on the Sumpter Valley (SV), a narrow-gauge railroad built east toward the Blue Mountains to supply logs for their new sawmill. They got as far as McEwen, some twenty-two miles, by 1891; not until 1896 did the rails reach **Sumpter**, ten miles beyond McEwen. The line gradually extended into the mountains, to Whitney, Austin, Bates, and finally, in 1910, **Prairie City**, eighty miles from Baker City. From the mountain towns, Oregon Lumber and other logging outfits ran many miles of logging railroads into the woods.

The Sumpter Valley Railway twisted its way east from Baker City, and crossed the Powder River on this wooden truss bridge—which was painted, and from the paint took the name Red Bridge. The photograph was taken in the early 1890s by Martin M. Hazeltine. Oregon Historical Society, OrHi 3832.

The rise of auto and truck transport, as well as the national Depression, caused the railroad to abandon the westernmost twenty miles of track in 1933, and to discontinue regular passenger trains in 1937. But the war and heavy log traffic kept the company going until 1947. By then, the Sumpter Valley was a legendary railroad anachronism, since most narrow gauge lines had long before been converted to the national standard gauge, or had been abandoned. The nostalgic esteem in which the SV was held led to efforts to re-create it, beginning in 1970. Sumpter Valley Railroad Restoration has succeeded in relaying several miles of track and acquiring locomotives and other equipment that once operated on the line.

Shaw, Frederic J. *Oil Lamps and Iron Ponies, a Chronicle of the Narrow Gauges*. San Francisco: Bay Books, 1949.

Sunnyside neighborhood, Portland
see **Belmont neighborhood, Portland**

Sunset Corridor The term refers to a section of the **Sunset Highway** west of Portland, extending a mile or two on both sides, that since the 1970s has become an area of high employment by those involved in the electronics industry and its spinoffs—the Corridor may be considered to be a major artery through the heart of the **Silicon Forest**.

Sunset Highway Highway travel between the northern Oregon Coast and the Willamette Valley was difficult—in the 1920s, a road trip to Seaside, for example, required about six hours of travel, via the **Columbia River Highway** to Astoria. A shorter route through the Coast Range was proposed, and construction began in the 1930s on the Wolf Creek Highway. The new stretch of roadway extended from Forest Grove to Necanicum Junction east of Seaside, the junction with the **Oregon Coast Highway**. World War II interrupted construction, which was completed in 1949. In 1946, the project was renamed

Sunset Highway in honor of the U.S. Army 41st Infantry Division, known as the Sunset Division. The Sunset Highway name is generally used to refer to the segment of U.S. **Highway 26** between Portland and Seaside.

► **Sutherlin** The area around Sutherlin in Douglas County attracted emigrant settlers in the 1850s; Fendel Sutherlin came to the valley of Calapooya Creek in 1851 and spent half a century there. Sutherlin had an extensive fruit orchard and practiced irrigation. The area was long known as Camas Swale, for the colorful expanses of **camas** found, then and now, in the valley. The Oregon & California Railroad came through the valley in 1872, but the town itself—located only three miles from old and established **Oakland**—did not develop until early in the twentieth century. Two industries pushed Sutherlin's development: fruit growing, and the rais-

ing of **turkeys** and other poultry. Sutherlin post office opened in 1909, and the town was incorporated in 1911. By 1915, promotional literature described Sutherlin as being the center of a "large agricultural section adapted to fruit and other profitable industries" and a "large turkey and other poultry raising and marketing section." Sutherlin's population in the 1920 census was 515, and it was sited along the new **Pacific Highway**.

Sutherlin's course was steady through World War II. In 1947, **Weyerhaeuser Corporation** began construction of a large sawmill in Springfield, and the company built a thirty-mile logging railroad up Calapooya Creek from Sutherlin to supply logs for that mill. Boosted also by local mill employment, Sutherlin's population reached 2,230 in 1950 and 3,070 in 1970. Subsequently, timber employment has fallen precipitately, but the town's population continued to rise, reaching an estimated 7,610 in 2007.

This structure, Oregon Woods Camp, was built near Sutherlin by Loring A. Wood and is pictured about 1932, the date at the center doorway. The slogan at the top reads, "When dreams come true." The sign at the left indicates that this is the "Largest log entrance of nature in the world, taken from a dream." It was built of "3,200 logs from 464 trees," and was illuminated with colored lights. Its fate is not known. Author's collection.

Swan Island *see* **aviation; dahlia**

Swedes in Oregon The major migration of Swedes to the United States in the late nineteenth century was to the Midwest, but by the early 1900s, second-generation Swedes and new immigrants often came to the Pacific Northwest, attracted by opportunities in logging and fishing, and in farming on the logged-over lands known as stump farms. The largest group came to Portland, but Swedish communities were formed in Astoria (along with **Finns**, **Danes**, Norwegians, and Icelanders), the Coos Bay region, Medford, Bend, and Klamath Falls. The Swedish-language *Oregon Posten* was published in Portland from 1908 to 1936. In 1930, approximately 11,000 Swedish immigrants lived in Oregon, along with more than 15,000 second-generation Swedish Americans.

Sweet Home Once a rural retreat—hence the name—Sweet Home is in Linn County along the South Santiam River. Emigrant farmers settled in the area as early as 1851, and in the mid-1860s, it was reached by the Santiam Wagon Road, a toll route that connected with Central Oregon over **Santiam Pass** until about 1920; this was developed after World War II into the Santiam Highway. The rural Sweet Home post office opened in 1874; the community that grew around it was incorporated as a municipality in 1893. The 1910 census showed Sweet Home with a population of 202; twenty years later, it was 189. A 1915 promotional booklet described Sweet Home as a region of "farming, lumbering, mining, dairying and poultry raising"—the mining being a bit of gold, found several miles to the east up Quartzville Creek.

In 1931, Sweet Home became a railroad and sawmill center. Huge stands of privately owned timberland—much of it the remains of land grants to the Willamette Valley and Cascade Mountain Wagon Road Company in the 1860s—had yet to be tapped, and Sweet Home became the nexus of the tapping. The **Oregon Electric Railway** extended a line from Lebanon to Sweet Home and then up the South Santiam River to Foster, and up the Calapooya River to a log-loading point called Dollar—named for the Robert Dollar Lumber Company. Sweet Home's population jumped to 1,090 in 1940, and to 3,603 in 1950 as local mills geared up. Population reached 6,921 in the 1980 census, but decreases in timber harvesting slowed down the town's growth in the 1980s. The population by 2007 was estimated at 8,995.

Sweetland, Monroe Mark, Jr. (1910–2006) This popular and populist politician was born in Salem and raised in Oregon and Michigan, and educated in the East. Monroe Sweetland was living in New York state in 1934, and there he ran as a socialist for the state senate. Roosevelt's New Deal captivated him, however, and although he was proud to acknowledge his socialist tendencies, he cast himself as a progressive Democrat for the rest of his life. Returning to Oregon, Sweetland was the publisher of several small-town newspapers, such as the Molalla *Pioneer* and the Milwaukie *Review*; for a time he published the *Oregon Democrat*. Sweetland was a tireless advocate for education at all levels, and a state leader in the resurgence of the Democratic party in Oregon after World War II. He was elected to the state senate in 1952, ultimately serving ten years in the legislature. Moving to California for a time to work with the National Education Association, Sweetland also distinguished himself in working for educational opportunities for Japanese-Americans and Latinos, and was a prime mover in the passage in 1968 of the federal Bilingual Education Act. He returned to his home in Milwaukie in the 1990s and continued to be active politically and in promoting education, especially the development of **Portland State University**, which he had helped to found and nurture.

T

> **Table Rock** Jackson County is the location of the best-known Table Rock in the state (there is another in Clackamas County, and a Table Mountain in Lincoln County). Two Table Rocks are located there: Upper and Lower. The flat-topped rocks are basalt, with steep cliffs that rise about 800 feet above the **Bear Creek Valley**. Lower Table Rock is a notable landmark along Interstate 5. In the 1850s, it gave rise to the name Table Rock City for **Jacksonville**, and the first newspaper in that gold rush town was the *Table Rock Sentinel* (1855). Treaties with the **Takelma Indians** in 1853 and 1854 led to the brief establishment of the Table Rock Reservation; one of the last episodes in the **Rogue River Wars** was the 1855 attack by whites on Indians near the reservation, which set off a string of incidents which led to the forcible relocation of most Indians from southwestern Oregon in 1856.

Taft *see* **Lincoln City**

Takelma Indians The Takelma people once occupied a homeland that took in parts of present-day Josephine, Douglas, and Jackson Counties. The area provided a variety of foods, including the acorn, which was a staple; other major foods included camas, berries, seeds, salmon, deer, and elk. Shelter was in the form of winter lodges, partly below ground level and made of pine boards for walls and roof; and summer shelters built of brush. The Takelma were

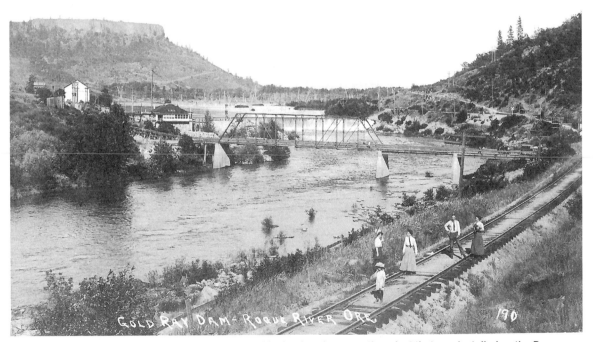

Lower Table Rock is at the left, looms over a dam and hydroelectric generating plant that was installed on the Rogue River near Gold Hill. Built by brothers Col. Frank Ray and Dr. C. R. Ray and completed in 1904, the wooden dam was later replaced with a concrete structure and produced electricity until 1972. The photograph was taken about 1905; behind the dam can be seen a forest of white trees, dead from the dam's backwaters. Steven Dotterrer collection.

located along the **California-Oregon Trail** and hence had encounters with white trappers and explorers as early as the 1820s. Incursions of **Shasta Indians** into the **Bear Creek Valley** combined with the gold-mining excitement of the 1850s to involve the Takelma in the **Rogue River Wars**. The **Table Rock** treaties led to a brief reservation for the Takelma, but ultimately led to their forced relocation in 1856. A few Takelma remained in southwest Oregon through the nineteenth century.

Talent Located in Jackson County, the town of Talent was the creation of the Oregon & California Railroad, which built through the Bear Creek Valley in 1883. The Talent post office, opened in 1883, was named for local resident A. P. Talent, who also platted the townsite. Emigrant farmers settled the area beginning in the 1850s, and the area was known as Wagner Creek or Eden precinct before the railroad came. Talent was incorporated in 1910. The area was primarily devoted to orchards and agricultural use through the 1960s; the population in 1950 was 739. Suburban growth in the area between Ashland and Medford transformed Talent into a bedroom community by the 1980s; the population grew from 1,389 in 1970 to an estimated 6,525 by 2007.

Tamástslikt *see* **Confederated Tribes of the Umatilla Indian Reservation**

Tangent This small farming community in Linn County was founded about 1872 with the construction of the Oregon & California Railroad south from Portland. The name is taken from the term for a perfectly straight section of the railroad track—which extends for nearly twenty miles. The post office opened in 1872, and the town of Tangent was incorporated in 1893; in 1915, Tangent's railroad station was a shipping point for "grain, hops, livestock, fruit and wool," and dairying and poultry raising were carried out in the vicinity. Since the 1970s, Tangent has been noted for the production of grass seed, a product that is shipped internationally. Tangent had a population in 1980 of 478; the estimate in 2007 was 970.

Tektronix The roots of Oregon's **Silicon Forest** are often traced back to the creation of Tektronix, which evolved from the development of "the world's first triggered oscilloscope" in 1946. An oscilloscope is a tool, a type of test equipment used in electronics that provides a graphic view of signal voltages. **C. Howard Vollum** and Melvin J. "Jack" Murdock made this technological breakthrough; they followed up on the development by incorporating Tektronix that same year. Its first headquarters were in southeast Portland at SE Fifty-ninth Avenue and Foster Road. The next year the firm had a dozen employees; it began construction of a manufacturing plant in what became the **Sunset Corridor** of Washington County in 1950, and boasted some 250 employees by 1951. The company headquarters moved there in 1956.

The construction of the major Tektronix campus, on the site of a former private airport, began in 1957; the first public stock shares were issued in 1963. By the mid-1970s, Tektronix was the state's largest single employer, with nearly 10,000 workers on its payroll. It was *the* major electronics manufacturer in the state; its employment peaked in 1981 at more than 24,000 employees worldwide. Tektronix was also an incubator for a number of spinoff and ancillary enterprises, such as Floating Point Systems and Mentor Graphics. The company experienced financial and entrepreneurial troubles in the 1980s and 1990s and underwent major retrenchments, but has survived and continues to stand among the Silicon Forest trees.

Tenino Indians *see* **Sahaptin Indians**

theater Alice Henson Ernst describes the production of several plays by crewmembers of the British sloop *Modiste* while moored at **Fort Vancouver** in

1846 as the first such doings in the Oregon Country. Traveling troupes became fairly common in the nineteenth century, traveling by ship from San Francisco to Portland and Puget Sound ports, and even gold rush camps in the 1850s found halls for visiting thespians. The first temple to theater was the New Market Theatre of 1872 in Portland, which still stands, though there have been no performances there for more than a century. Portland in particular hosted many traveling presentations, and did develop some repertory groups, such as that which brought **George L. Baker** to fame and to election as mayor. The **chautauqua** movement of the 1890s through the 1920s had some theatrical aspects; one was that, after its demise, the space could be used for real theater, which is what **Angus L. Bowmer** did in Ashland in the 1930s; the outcome was the **Oregon Shakespeare Festival**. The **Portland Civic Theatre** was a city institution, one that had **James Beard** among its early players.

Ernst, Alice Henson. *Trouping in the Oregon Country: A History of Frontier Theatre.* Portland, Oregon: Oregon Historical Society, 1961.

The Dalles The city of The Dalles is the county seat of Wasco County. The name is from the Canadian French and refers to the narrow-channeled rapids in the vicinity of **Celilo Falls**. The present town site was an early settlement for Protestant missionaries who were intent on reaching the various Indian populations that congregated in the vicinity of Celilo Falls. One of these was a branch of the Methodist missionary efforts of **Jason Lee**, called Wascopam mission, that was established in 1838 by the Rev. Daniel Lee, nephew of Jason Lee, and the Rev. H. K. W. Perkins. A contorted basaltic knob known as Pulpit Rock that was used for outdoor preaching in the 1830s and 1840s remains today to mark that episode; sitting in the middle of 12th Street, it is the site of a religious service each Easter. When emigrants on the **Oregon Trail** in the 1840s and 1850s reached The Dalles, they had to

choose whether to float their goods and themselves down the Columbia, or pay the toll and take the **Barlow Road** around Mount Hood. The Dalles grew as a mercantile point. The **Cayuse War** and the establishment of **Fort Dalles** in 1850 helped solidify the town. A post office opened in 1851, and The Dalles was incorporated (as Dalles City) in 1857; the 1860 census gave it a population of 805. During the early 1860s, gold rushes to Montana, Idaho, and eastern Oregon, The Dalles was a portage point in the **Oregon Steam Navigation Company**'s transportation system, and this made the city the site for a proposed U.S. mint in 1864. However, the gold rush wound down and the mint was never completed; since 2005 the building has housed a winery.

The railroad line that supplanted the steamboats came through in 1882, and The Dalles became a trade center for an agricultural district that grew wheat, sheep, and livestock, and was a major fish-processing center with the Seufert Brothers cannery. By the 1910s The Dalles was becoming a hub for growing and processing cherries, apples, pears, and a variety of other fruits and vegetables; it also had a wool-scouring plant, flour mill, box factories and planing mills, an ice plant, a creamery, and a fruit cannery. The population of The Dalles was 2,232 in 1880, and 4,880 in 1910; by 1950, it reached 7,676. The construction of **The Dalles Dam** in the 1950s brought in the **aluminum industry**, which played a major economic role in the city for several decades. In 1984, The Dalles was the scene of one of the nation's first bioterrorism attacks. Adherents of the **Bhagwan Shree Rajneesh** sickened 751 persons by food poisoning at several The Dalles restaurants. The population of The Dalles in 2007 was estimated at 13,045.

The Dalles-California Highway
see **Highway 97**

The Dalles Dam The U.S. Army Corps of Engineers completed construction of The Dalles Dam on the mid-course of the Columbia River in 1957. It produces hydroelectric power. The dam inundated many traditional Native American salmon fishing sites, including the spectacular waterfalls and ancient fishery at **Celilo Falls**. The locks at the dam replaced the canal that had provided transit around the falls since 1915.

The Gorge *see* **Gorge, The**

The Needles *see* **Rooster Rock**

Thompson, David *see* **Columbia River**

Thompson, Robert R. (1820–1908) Robert Thompson was one of the Triumvirate: the three principals of the **Oregon Steam Navigation Company (OSN)**, which also included **John C. Ainsworth** and **Simeon G. Reed**. Thompson came west to Oregon Territory in 1846, sought for and found gold in California in 1848–49, and eventually settled near The Dalles with his wife, Harriet. In 1853, he helped bring a large flock of sheep to Oregon. By the late 1850s he was operating boats on the upper Columbia, and became allied with OSN in 1860, to his ensuing immense good fortune. The OSN steamboat *R. R. Thompson* commemorated his investments, which extended into Portland business interests and real estate. He also owned extensive farmlands in Yamhill County near Carlton. Thompson died in San Francisco.

Thousand Friends of Oregon Founded in 1975 by Henry Richmond and **Tom McCall** to give a voice to citizens concerned with land-use planning in Oregon, the Thousand Friends of Oregon aimed to use the tools provided in the 1973 Senate Bill 100 to preserve and protect the state's quality of life. Senate Bill 100 mandated that counties and cities prepare and use a comprehensive plan that examined the limits and potentials of future development and took into account such factors as the future need for open space, utilities, historic preservation, and schools. The Thousand Friends spent its first years making sure that cities and counties—a number of which were exceedingly reluctant—complied with the law.

Three Sisters These three high volcanic peaks in the Cascade Range have been called the Three Sisters since at least the mid-1850s; the peaks were individually named Faith, Hope, and Charity in the 1840s by members of the **Jason Lee** Methodist mission at Salem. The North Sister (Faith) has an elevation of 10,085 feet; the Middle Sister (Hope) is 10,047 feet; and the South Sister (Charity) reaches 10,358 feet. The three peaks have some fifteen glaciers. The town of **Sisters** derives its name from the peaks. The small Deschutes County community of Brothers derives its name from the circumstance that one can view the Three Sisters looming behind three nearby hills.

Thurston, Samuel Royal (1816–1851) Samuel Thurston, born and raised in Maine, was an emigrant to Iowa, then an emigrant to Oregon. He was the first delegate to the U.S. Congress from the Oregon Territory and worked to pass the seminal **Donation Land Act** in 1850. Thurston graduated from Bowdoin College in 1843, studied law, got married, and moved to Iowa. In 1847, he and his family moved to Oregon where he settled in Hillsboro and practiced law. The next year he was elected to the legislature of the **provisional government** from the **Twality District**. In 1849, Thurston was selected to represent the new Oregon Territory in the U.S. Congress. There he helped forward the Donation Land Act, which legitimized many years of land claims by American citizens and set the stage for thousands more. Thurston also allied himself with **Jason Lee** and others of the Methodist colony to deny land claims by **John McLoughlin**, a sad episode in the territory's turbulent beginnings. Thurston was also the voice for a segment of the emigrant populace that opposed the presence of free African-Americans in the Oregon Territory. In an 1850 address to the Oregon territorial legislature, Thurston asserted that the presence in Oregon of blacks could lead to intermarriage with Indians. This might lead to "long bloody wars, . . . the fruits of the comingling of the races." Thurston also helped to block the Senate ratification of the Tansy Point Treaty with the Clatsop and Nehalem Indians, a small move that has led to more than a century and a half of still-unresolved legal maneuvers.

Thurston died at sea off Acapulco, Mexico, in 1851 while en route back to Oregon from Washington, DC He was buried in Acapulco, but the territorial legislature had his body moved, and he was reburied in Salem in 1853. Thurston County, Washington, the site of the capital city of Olympia, is named for him. The prominent Thurston Road in the Eugene area is named for his son, George H. Thurston, who was born in Iowa in 1846 and became a surveyor and a rancher in the Springfield area and in eastern Oregon.

Tigard The Washington County city of Tigard is located in an area that was settled in the 1850s by farming families, including that of Wilson M. Tigard, who arrived in 1852. A community developed, and a post office named Tigardville opened in the Tigard general store in 1886. A number of German immigrants came to the area in the 1890s, and in 1908, the **Oregon Electric Railway** opened its line between Portland and Salem through the town, making it a commuter suburb. The same year, the post office changed the name from Tigardville to Tigard. By the 1910s, the area was still known for growing garden truck for Portland markets, and for fruit, walnuts, prunes, dairy cattle, livestock, and poultry. There was a sawmill, and the town had a new Germania Hall. By the 1930s, Tigard was on major highways from Portland to the Oregon Coast and Corvallis, and more residents were commuters who took the bus or drove to city jobs.

Tigard was incorporated in 1961 as suburban growth began to accelerate. The city's population in the 1970 census was 6,499; ten years later it had grown to 14,799. The completion of the **Interstate 5** freeway and the connecting freeway to Beaverton gave the city a boost as a residential area for workers in the **Silicon Forest**. Commuter train service connecting Tigard with Beaverton and Wilsonville began in 2008. The city's estimated population in 2007 was 46,715.

Tillamook The community of Tillamook developed slowly. The settlement on the muddy banks of Hoquarten Slough was granted a post office in 1866, some thirteen years after the creation of Tillamook County, and it was 1873 before the town was designated the county seat. By the 1890s, Tillamook was a small center of government in the heart of a small county with a developing dairy industry, making cheese and butter for export. The town was incorporated in 1891, and the 1900 census credited it with 894 inhabitants. Development was swift in the next two decades as the arrival of a railroad connection from Portland in 1911 triggered a vast expansion of logging and lumber milling operations in Tillamook. The population reached 1,964 by 1920, and 3,685 by 1950. The great **Tillamook Burn** for a time accelerated timber harvesting, but mills suffered in the 1940s. During World War II, Tillamook was the site of a naval air station for blimps, used for aerial reconnaissance along the Oregon Coast. One of the two immense wooden hangars for the blimps has survived and houses the Tillamook Air Museum; it is among the world's largest wooden structures. The Tillamook County Creamery Cooperative that operates the Tillamook **cheese** business is headquartered in Tillamook and has proven to be an economic underpinning for the city. The lumber business declined again in the 1980s but the maturation of timber in the former Tillamook Burn lands caused some increased harvesting in the 2000s. Tillamook's estimated population in 2007 was 4,690.

▶ **Tillamook Burn** The term "Tillamook Burn" refers not to just one fire, but to a series of **forest fires** that collectively shocked the state, its timber industry, and the practices of forest management. The first fire began on August 14, 1933 at a logging camp in the Coast Range on the headwaters of Gales Creek when a dragging cable caused a spark. The spark became a raging inferno that lasted until early September and consumed some 240,000 acres of old-growth timber; the smoke darkened the skies in the Willamette Valley and debris rained on ships at sea. A second forest fire in the same region in 1939 burned another 190,000 acres, and in 1945 a third fire consumed 180,000 acres. The fires had a devastating effect on an industry already suffering from the effects of the Depression. Since 1948, much of the burned-over land has been incorporated into the Tillamook State Forest, which was systematically re-forested using some seventy-two million seedlings, with the help of state funds and of many civic-minded organizations. In the early 2000s, as the replanted forest lands reached "maturity," questions arose as to whether the forest had been revived only to be cut for timber, or whether other goals regarding wildlife and land and water conservation needed to be more strongly considered.

Wells, Gail. *The Tillamook: A Created Forest Comes of Age.* 2nd ed. Corvallis: Oregon State University Press, 2004.

Tillamook cheese *see* **cheese**

Tillamook County An exceedingly small number of white settlers, and an undetermined number of Tillamook Indians, lived in the country that was designated Tillamook County by the territorial legislature in 1853. Even by the time of the 1870 census, a mere 408 inhabitants were recorded in the county.

A forest fire rages through standing timber and logged-over lands along the route of the Wolf Creek Highway, later known as the Sunset Highway, about 1940. A series of forest fires burned in this region between 1933 and 1945.
Mason collection.

The land was drawn from Polk, Clatsop, and Yamhill Counties; a number of boundary changes between 1855 and 1893—the last being the creation of Lincoln County—resulted in an area of 1,125 square miles. The Nehalem and Nestucca bands of the **Tillamook Indians** inhabited the coastal areas south of Tillamook Head. Treaties with the Tillamook went un-ratified by the U.S. Senate, and although their populace had been severely reduced by disease, especially in the 1830s, many Tillamook continued to live along the shores of Tillamook Bay.

The American settlers of the 1850s were scattered in subsistence farms along the bay as well, and in the valleys of the five streams draining into it: the Tillamook River, Wilson River, **Trask River**, Kilchis River, and Miami River. Until the 1910s, the easiest—or, rather, the least arduous—way to travel from the Tillamook country to the Willamette Valley was by ship up the coast and then via the Columbia River. Early county government met in houses or schools; not until an election in 1873 did the residents denote the town of Tillamook as the county seat. The first courthouse was rented quarters in a general store. A county building was built in 1889, but it burned in 1903; a brick replacement was completed in 1905. A third courthouse was finished in 1933, and the 1905 building became the Tillamook Pioneer Museum.

Agriculture, logging and lumbering, and tourism have long been the bases of Tillamook County's economy. Dairying developed in the late nineteenth century in the well-watered valley around Tillamook Bay and in the lower valleys of the **Nehalem River** and the **Nestucca River**. While milk did not travel well, it could be made into butter and **cheese**, which did. A 1915 promotional booklet noted that Tillamook County's "celebrated dairy and cheese industry" was carried out on only about fifty square miles, but there were twenty-seven cheese-making factories. Regarding the rest of the county, the booklet noted that aside from a "few bare mountain slopes and summits and a few marshes," it was "covered with magnificent timber." Sixty years later, all the magnificent timber was gone, sent to mills at Tillamook, **Garibaldi**, and **Wheeler**. The re-growth from the **Tillamook Burn** forest fires of the 1930s and 1940s began to once again supply mills in the early twenty-first century. Tourism in Tillamook County first blossomed with the completion of a railroad to Portland in 1911, and seaside or bayside resorts blossomed at **Manzanita**, **Rockaway Beach**, and ill-fated **Bayocean**; further development occurred after the **Oregon Coast Highway** was opened in 1940. Fly fishermen were lured to the Nehalem and Nestucca Rivers from the 1910s; beginning in the 1930s, surf fishers went to **Cape Kiwanda**, near Pacific City.

Tillamook County's population in 1900 was 3,477; it reached 8,810 by the 1920 census, and 18,606 in 1950. The estimated population in 2007 was 25,845. The county long promoted itself as the "Land of cheese, trees, and ocean breeze."

► **Tillamook Head** This promontory juts into the Pacific Ocean in Clatsop County, a few miles south of Seaside. Its steep, forested slopes rise about 1,200 feet. In 1806, members of the **Lewis and Clark Expedition** followed a well-worn Indian trail over Tillamook Head to see a whale that had washed ashore at Cannon Beach. In the late nineteenth century, a toll wagon road was built from Seaside around Tillamook Head to the east, avoiding the perilous bluffs.

Tillamook Indians The Tillamook Indians lived in villages along the Oregon Coast from **Tillamook Head** south to Siletz Bay and the headwaters of the Siletz River. Speakers of a Salishan language, the Tillamook spoke at least four dialects, the Nehalem, Nestucca, Salmon River, and Siletz. The villages were located around the region's prominent bays and river mouths, giving easy access to such food sources as salmon and shellfish, lamprey, sea lions, seals, and whales. The Tillamook also harvested salmon-

An aerial view of Seaside about 1940 shows Tillamook Head in the background. Boyer photograph. Author's collection.

berry sprouts, camas, wild strawberries, salalberries, and huckleberries. Beaver, muskrat, and beaver added to the menu. As with most coast tribes, housing took the form of cedar-plank lodges, sometimes partially dug into the ground; as many as four families might live in a single lodge. The interior included sleeping platforms along the sides and central fires, with hanging mats to provide privacy. The Tillamook were, like most Oregon tribes, decimated by malaria and other introduced diseases, especially in the 1830s, and only a few hundred survived into the 1840s. The Tillamook signed a treaty in 1851 ceding their land, but it was never ratified; consequently, although a few Tillamook went to the Siletz or Grand Ronde Reservations, many remained in their homeland. There was a Tillamook village near **Garibaldi** through the 1890s. Congress and the courts settled Indian land claims between 1897 and 1945, and Tillamook received disbursements from the Indian Claims Commission in 1958 and 1962.

Tillamook Rock Tillamook Rock, off the shore of **Tillamook Head** in Clatsop County, housed one of the state's most formidable **lighthouses**, known as "Terrible Tilly." The light was extinguished in 1957, and the structure stood abandoned until 1980. Since then, it has been used as a columbarium.

timber industry *see* **logging and lumbering; wood products industry**

▶ **Timberline Lodge** The lodge was designed and built as a public works project that would serve enthusiasts of a new and growing sport, **skiing**. It is located on the south side of **Mount Hood** above the town of **Government Camp**. Timberline Lodge was built between 1936 and 1938 by the Works Progress Administration using local artisans and local materials and is sited on National Forest lands. President Franklin D. Roosevelt dedicated the lodge on September 28, 1937. Constructed of stone and wood,

Mount Hood and Timberline Lodge, photographed shortly after construction was completed in 1938. Sawyer's photograph. Author's collection.

the lodge abounds in artwork with a regional theme, such as rooms that are named for local flora, with textiles woven to match. **Margery Hoffman Smith** supervised the artwork. Timberline was a difficult inn to operate, with heavy snowfall and maintenance problems; it was closed for a time in the 1950s. The lodge underwent significant refurbishing in the 1980s, and a new day lodge for skiers removed some of the maintenance strain. Timberline Lodge was designated a National Historic Landmark in 1978.

T. J. Potter The *Potter* was a sidewheel passenger steamboat built in North Portland in 1888. She was named for Thomas J. Potter (1840–ca. 1887), the recently deceased first vice president and general manager of the Union Pacific Railroad in Omaha. The *Potter* was built by the Oregon Railway & Navigation Company (OR&N) to serve the Portland-Astoria run as well as Ilwaco, Washington (acoss the Columbia River from Astoria), where connection was made

with the OR&N-owned narrow-gauge railroad that ran up the Long Beach peninsula. The chief patronage came from the affluent Portland families who summered at Seaview, Long Beach and Ocean Park. The *T. J. Potter* was an elegant craft, and she worked the route with other noted vessels such as the *Telephone* and the *Olympian*, lasting into the 1910s. She was retired by 1916 and converted to quarters for shipbuilding crews at Astoria during World War I; finally, she was beached, stripped of her metal fittings, and burned, in 1925. Her remains are still on the shore of Youngs Bay in Astoria.

Toledo The site of Toledo in Lincoln County was claimed in 1866 by John and Joseph Graham and William Mackey under the Homestead Act. First known as Graham's Landing, it became Toledo when a post office was established in 1870; the Grahams had once lived in Toledo, Ohio. The Willamette Valley & Coast Railroad connected Toledo with Corvallis in 1884, and Toledo was designated the county seat of the new **Lincoln County** in 1893. The community was incorporated in 1905. Toledo was a small sawmill town until World War I, when the U.S. Army Signal Corps built a huge mill to produce spruce lumber for airplane construction, and extensive railroad lines to bring in the timber. The war ended before the mill began production, but it was sold to a private operator, and the C. D. Johnson—later **Georgia-Pacific** (GP)—mill became the city's economic mainstay. Toledo's population in 1910 was 541; by 1930, it was 1,656. While the county seat was moved to Newport in 1954, GP built a new pulp and paper mill in 1957, and mill operations have continued to support the city. The estimated population in 2007 was 3,585.

Tongue Point Jutting out into the Columbia River at the east end of Astoria, the peninsula known as Tongue Point was so named by Lt. William Broughton, of Capt. **George Vancouver**'s expedition in 1792. A Navy base was established there in 1939, and after World War II, surplus naval vessels were stored in Cathlamet Bay adjacent to the base. After the Navy left in 1961, a Job Corps center took over the facilities in 1964. Tongue Point is connected to the mainland by Tongue Neck.

Tonquin The ship *Tonquin* was sent from New York City to **Fort Astoria** in 1810, arriving at the Columbia River on April 12, 1811, to supply the fort and the overland members of the **Pacific Fur Company**. From the Columbia, the *Tonquin* sailed north to trade with Indians along the coast of Vancouver Island. At Clayoquot Sound, an altercation with the Natives culminated in an explosion that destroyed the ship and killed sixty-one members of the crew and Indians. The loss helped to sink the Pacific Fur Company venture.

Trailblazers Portland's professional basketball team played its first games in 1970 in Memorial Coliseum. Lanky center Bill Walton joined the team from UCLA in 1974 and helped the team reach the National Basketball Association (NBA) finals in 1977. The regional enthusiasm for the team, known as Blazermania, developed in that season, which culminated in the team's NBA championship. The Trailblazers moved to the new Rose Garden Arena in 1995.

Trask River Rising in the Coast Range of eastern Tillamook County and western Washington County, the North Fork and South Fork Trask River flow west to join about twelve miles east of Tillamook Bay. Just before entering the bay, the Trask is joined by the Tillamook River. The river is named for Elbridge Trask, who came to the area in 1848. His life was the basis of three historical novels by **Don Berry**, the first of which was titled *Trask* (1960).

► **Treasure Valley** The term is used to describe the valley of the Snake River where it is joined by a number of major tributaries, including the Boise, Payette, and Weiser Rivers of Idaho, and the Malheur and Owyhee Rivers of Oregon. In Oregon, Treasure Valley includes the cities of Ontario, Nyssa, and Vale, and the considerable irrigated agricultural land in their vicinity. The Owyhee River Project of

Irrigation water destined for the Treasure Valley area is carried through huge pipes from the Owyhee River at Owyhee Dam, shown in the 1930s. Wesley Andrews photograph. Steven Dotterer collection.

1927–32 brought water to Treasure Valley and transformed its agriculture. The area is a heavy producer of potatoes and onions.

tree farms The tree farm is a concept developed by the **Weyerhaeuser Corporation** to counter the perception that the decimation of old-growth timber by logging would soon mean the end of the industry and the end of private forest lands. The first Weyerhaeuser tree farm was dedicated in 1941 near Grays Harbor, Washington. In 1951, *Time* magazine reported about a **Coos Bay** property: "On this tract, as on the other 1,979,568 acres of Weyerhaeuser tree farms, timber will be treated as a crop just like corn, cotton and cucumbers, [to] be harvested over an 80-year cycle." Tree farms are not without controversy: there are concerns over pesticide use, the problems of monoculture crops, the adverse impact on wildlife, and the difficulty of corporations to continuously look eighty years into their future. Weyerhaeuser could not always do it, and had closed most of their Coos Bay operations by 2003. *See also* **Christmas trees.**

► **Trojan** The Trojan nuclear power plant, the only such facility built in the state of Oregon, was demolished on May 21, 2006. It had been built by the Portland General Electric Company along the Columbia River in Columbia County between 1970 and 1975, and was put into operation in 1976. It was a contentious project, exacerbated by the discovery of construction errors and structural problems in 1978, and in 1980 state voters approved a ban on future nuclear plants. The plant closed in 1992 after a radioactive leak was disclosed. The mothballed plant and its immense, 499-foot-tall cooling tower stood abandoned for more than a decade.

Troutdale A a post office named Sandy operated from 1854 until 1868 at the far eastern edge of Multnomah County on the Sandy River. A new post office named Troutdale opened there in 1880, named

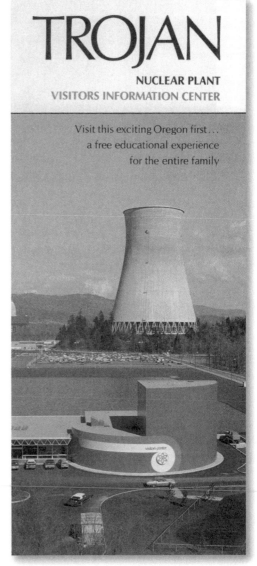

This promotional brochure dates from the 1976 opening of the Trojan nuclear electric power plant, where one will "discover why the atom is essential to the economic and ecological well-being of America." Author's collection.

by Capt. John Harlow (he had a fishpond which he stocked with trout). The Harlow house is now a museum of the Troutdale Historical Society. The **Union Pacific Railroad** built through Troutdale in the early 1880s, and the community was incorporated in 1907, the same year that it was connected to Portland by an electric **interurban railway**. Troutdale was an area of "farming, lumbering, dairying, gardening, poultry raising, [and raising] small fruits" in the 1910s. The town was the gateway to the **Columbia River Highway** from its opening in 1916. Troutdale's population in 1910 was 309; by 1950, it reached 514. The completion of **Interstate 84** put the town off the main thoroughfare, but increased the suburbanization of the area. The 1970 population of 1,771 preceded the building of an outlet shopping mall in the 1980s; by 1990, vegetable fields were receding in the face of a population of 7,852; the estimated population in 2007 was 15,430.

Tualatin The town of Tualatin along the Tualatin River in Washington County arose from a post office that was established in 1869; the original spelling was Tualitin, one of many variants of the word. The community was sometimes called Bridgeport during the 1880s. Tualatin became a suburb in the 1910s as two railroads offered frequent electric train service to Portland, and the town was incorporated in 1913. The area was still agricultural, with numerous dairies and farms that grew onions, potatoes, apples and hogs. Tualatin had a sawmill and a brick and tile factory in the 1910s, and a **golf** links; the river itself was described as "a beautiful stream for boating, fishing and picnicking," and the town as one "of beautiful suburban homes." Tualatin's population in 1920 was 234; by 1950, it was 248, and in 1970, 750. The Tualatin Crawfish Festival had its start in 1951. Growth since that time has been explosive: 7,483 in 1980, and an estimated 26,025 in 2007.

Tualatin County *see* **Twality District; Washington County**

Tualatin District *see* **Twality District**

Tualatin Indians *see* **Kalapuyan Indians**

Tualatin Mountains The Tualatin Mountains are more familiarly known to Oregonians as the West Hills or the Southwest Hills of Portland. They are a branch of the northern **Coast Range Mountains**, separating the Willamette River from the **Tualatin Plains** to the west. The highest point is **Council Crest** at 1,074 feet. Much of the northern section of the West Hills is included in **Forest Park**, a forested city park with many trails but no roads. Several major access points reach from the Tualatin Plains into Portland: Canyon Road, down the defile of Tanner Creek, was developed in the 1850s as a plank road to bring wheat to Portland for shipment. In the 1960s, as the **Sunset Highway** was widened to accommodate western suburban growth, the roadway virtually demolished the canyon. Another route via West Burnside and Barnes Road also dates from the mid-nineteenth century. A route via Macleay Creek and Cornell Road was improved by the **Civilian Conservation Corps** in the late 1930s. Farther north are routes over Cornelius Pass and the Logie Trail, the latter being part of the historic land route from **Fort Vancouver** into the Willamette Valley and onto the **California-Oregon Trail**.

Tualatin Plains The fertile, open plains of northern Washington County were the homeland of the Tualatin or Atfalati band of the **Kalapuyan Indians**. The openness was the result of the Tualatin practice of burning the prairies each fall to improve forage and to better harvest tarweed seeds. The catastrophic decline in the local Indian population in the early nineteenth century, especially from malaria in the 1830s, made this land both attractive and available. By the 1840s, the Tualatin Plains were being settled by emigrants, such as **Joseph L. Meek**, regardless of the still unsettled legal position of their settlement. The heavy production of the wheat fields of the Tualatin Plains and the glowing messages about the area sent to American friends and relatives were the enticements that drew emigrants over the **Oregon Trail** in the 1840s and 1850s.

Tualatin River Rising in the Coast Range Mountains of Washington County, the Tualatin River flows first north, then eastward past Hillsboro and Tualatin to a confluence with the Willamette River near West Linn. Its twisting course extends a bit over eighty miles. Despite the presence of rapids near the mouth of the river, steamboats navigated the Tualatin in the 1860s, going as far as Hillsboro and nearly to Forest Grove.

Tupper Rock *see* **Grandmother Rock**

turkeys Poultry raising has been a popular enterprise in Oregon since the 1840s. In the twentieth century, as poultry raising became an industry that shipped processed, refrigerated birds to market, several communities became centers of turkey culture. Most prominent was **Oakland**, where Ward Cockeram developed a meaty turkey and which in 1929 sponsored the first Northwest Turkey Show. The development of the broad-breasted bronze turkey is Oakland's claim to fame. The Stoller Vineyards at Dayton are the site of one of the once-largest turkey production facilities in the state, and turkeys were raised there until 1993. Nearby McMinnville has an annual Turkey Rama which began in 1938 when the area was a heavy turkey producer; the festival continues despite the disappearance of turkey farms. Once Oregon grew 30 percent of the West Coast supply of turkeys, some three million birds a year. Only a few local producers remained in 2007.

▶ **Turner** Farmers settled the area where Turner is located in the 1850s, and the Oregon & California Railroad built through it in 1870. The railroad intended to erect a station there, but the building materials were accidentally deposited some six miles south. The station was constructed there and named Marion; a second shipment arrived at the intended point, and that station was named Turner for long-time residents Henry L. and Julia Ann Turner. The post office opened in 1871; the community was incorporated in 1905, and the 1910 census enumerated 191 residents. Turner was described in 1915 as the center of an agricultural region producing fruit, livestock, dairy products, wheat, oats, potatoes, and prunes. The Turner family in 1878 donated six acres along mill creek to the Christian Church, which held their Oregon annual meeting there in the 1880s. In 1891, the church completed a remarkable wooden tabernacle; the façade was anchored at each end by a square tower topped by a globe. One of the towers was downed in the **Columbus Day storm** of 1962, but the building was refurbished in the 1990s and is still in use. Turner's estimated population in 2007 was 1,690.

Twality District This was the name of one of the four districts (counties) established in 1843 by Oregon's **provisional government**. Variant spellings are found, including Tuality and Tualatin. It included the northwest corner of present-day Oregon and a western slice of what is now Washington state and the province of British Columbia. *See also* **Washington County**.

The Turner Tabernacle of the Disciples of Christ is shown as it appeared in the early 1900s. Mason collection.

Twenty Miracle Miles This was an advertising slogan used during the 1950s and 1960s to promote highway travel to the Oregon Coast communities between Otis and the Siletz River, including most especially those that now comprise **Lincoln City**. Despite the fact that the splendid shoreline is relatively intact, the area has become known since the 1980s as the Twenty Miserable Miles. Increased highway traffic, a proliferation of roadside retail developments, a flashy casino, and a discount shopping mall characterize the strip.

Tygh Valley Indians *see* **Sahaptin Indians**

UFOs *see* **unidentified flying objects**

Ukiah The range country town of Ukiah in Umatilla County began as a rural post office opened in 1890; it was named for Ukiah, California. In 1915, it was described as being the center of an "extensive cattle range" and as having a creamery—so there were dairy cattle to be found, too. The town was not incorporated until 1969; in 1970, it had a population of 249; the estimated figure for 2007 was 260.

Umatilla The town of Umatilla in Umatilla County dates from the mid-nineteenth century when it was a river landing. The Umatilla post office, established in 1851, marked an official beginning. The development of steam navigation on the Columbia River coincided with gold rushes in eastern Oregon and Idaho, and Umatilla townsite was platted in 1863 and incorporated as Umatilla Landing in 1864. It was a major transfer point for the **Oregon Steam Navigation Company** until the arrival of the railroads in the mid-1880s shifted the focus of transportation. Umatilla's population in 1910 was only 198, and in 1940, 370 residents were recorded. The opening of the Umatilla Army Depot in 1941 provided a new economic support; it began to store chemical weapons in 1962 and in the 1990s sent away all other weapons. Destruction of the chemical weapons began in the 2000s. Umatilla's population was 679 in 1970. **McNary Dam** and increased irrigated agriculture in the area have helped boost the number of residents to an estimated 6,440 in 2007.

Umatilla County Created from a portion of Wasco County in 1862, Umatilla County subsequently shrank as Grant, Morrow, Union, and Wallowa Counties were cut from it between 1864 and 1887. The county has 3,231 square miles, and the county seat—after some deliberation—is **Pendleton**. A courthouse was built in **Umatilla** (then known as Umatilla Landing) in 1866; the first courthouse in Pendleton, a two-story wooden structure, went up in 1869. A substantial three-story brick courthouse replaced that in 1889, but was replaced by the current structure in 1956. Umatilla County (then rather larger in area) had a population in 1870 of 2,916. The land now incorporated in the county includes part of the homeland of the **Umatilla** and **Cayuse Indians**, and the **Umatilla Reservation** is encompassed by the county.

The gold rushes of the early 1860s in eastern Oregon and Idaho brought a swift influx of prospectors and miners, freighters and ranchers through the steamboat landing at Umatilla. The arrival of railroad connections in the early 1880s brought a boom in wheat farming. The county's population in 1890 was 13,381; it was 25,946 in 1920. By the 1910s, Umatilla County was described as "the banner wheat county of Oregon," but the western half also had thousands of acres newly under irrigation, producing potatoes, alfalfa, and melons. The section near **Milton-Freewater** became a center for growing peas in the 1950s, and the county has also long been a producer of fruit, grains, cattle, and sheep. The timber of the Blue Mountains has also supplied mills in Pendleton, Pilot Rock, and other towns. The **Pendleton Round-Up** has marked the county's ranching legacy and Indian heritage annually since 1910. Umatilla County had a population of 41,703 in 1950, and 58,861 in 1980; the estimate for 2007 was 72,245.

Umatilla Indians The Umatilla people's homeland extended on both sides of the Columbia River from near the mouth of the John Day River upstream to the confluence of the Walla Walla River. Their diet and daily lives resembled those of the neighboring **Cayuse Indians** and the Walla Walla Indians. Fish were a staple: salmon, sturgeon, **lamprey**, and others; elk and deer were hunted, and camas, bitterroot, and berries gathered. Houses were mat lodges sited in winter villages near the Columbia, and mat shelters during summer and autumn harvest and hunting rounds. The Umatilla encountered white trappers and explorers in the 1810s and 1820s, and with the Walla Walla and the Cayuse, they signed a treaty in 1855 that created the **Umatilla Reservation** for all three tribes, reserving off-reservation fishing rights. The Umatilla are since 1949 one of the three **Confederated Tribes of the Umatilla Indian Reservation**.

Umatilla Reservation The 1855 treaty between the United States and the Walla Walla, **Cayuse** and **Umatilla Indians** established the Umatilla Reservation of 512,000 acres for the three tribes. The size dwindled almost immediately to 245,699 acres in 1859. From that, the townsite of **Pendleton** was ceded in 1882, and in 1888 the reservation was further reduced to 157,982 acres. The allotment of

lands to individual tribal members reduced the common holdings, and inholdings of non-Indian-owned land proliferated in the first half of the twentieth century, resulting in a reservation that is a checkerboard of Indian and non-Indian land. A tribal council was formed in 1949 (its successor is the **Confederated Tribes of the Umatilla Indian Reservation**), and the council opposed the dissolution of the reservation under the 1954 Termination Act; the reservation continues, managed now by the tribes.

Umatilla River The Umatilla River heads in two forks in the Blue Mountains of Umatilla County, flowing north and then west across the Umatilla Reservation, through Pendleton and then northward to join the Columbia River just below McNary Dam. The total length is about eighty-five miles. The Umatilla once had significant runs of salmon and lamprey; however, the withdrawal of water for **irrigation** projects near Hermiston in the early 1900s was so heavy that by the 1920s, the Umatilla no longer ran the year around. By 1926, no Chinook or coho salmon remained in the river. Beginning in the 1980s, the **Confederated Tribes of the Umatilla Indian Reservation** began efforts to re-hydrate the river and restore fish runs. It required years of negotiations with farmers, the Bonneville Power Administration, environmental groups, and the state to craft a means of replacing the Umatilla River irrigation water with Columbia River water from behind McNary Dam. The first salmon returned to the Umatilla in 1994.

Umpqua County A county named Umpqua was created by the territorial legislature in 1851 in southern Oregon, influenced by the recent gold discoveries and a rapid influx of miners. On January 7, 1852, Douglas County was created from the eastern part of Umpqua County; the northern section was lost to Lane County in 1853; in 1862, the remainder of Umpqua County was folded into Douglas County.

No formal county seat was established nor court-house built; Elkton, Green Valley, and Yoncalla all saw meetings of the Umpqua County court. This is Oregon's only "vanished" county.

Umpqua Indians *see* Athapaskan Indians; Siuslaw Indians

Umpqua River Flowing from a legendary "hundred valleys," the Umpqua River drainage includes the southern side of the **Calapooya Mountains**, the west slope of the Cascade Range in Douglas County, and some of the eastern slope of the Coast Range. Its course of about 111 miles takes it north through the Umpqua Valley around **Roseburg** and then northwesterly in a twisted course to Elkton. It then flows westward, cutting through the Coast Range, to Winchester Bay, where it meets the **Smith River** before entering the Pacific Ocean. The Umpqua is navigable to **Scottsburg**, and from the late 1800s into the 1910s, river steamboats connected Scottsburg with **Gardiner** and other towns. In 1870, one Nicholas Haun tried to demonstrate the navigability of the Umpqua all the way to Roseburg—if it could be done, funds might be found to improve the waterway. Haun built the sternwheel steamer *Swan* and launched her at Gardiner on January 20; it took eleven days of steaming and struggling and pulling to reach Roseburg. Folklorist and historian Randall Mills reported that "It is not exactly truthful to say that she navigated the Umpqua; part of the way she walked, and a fair share of the way she was hauled bodily along." There was an appropriation to improve the channel, which was spent, but no one ever took another boat upriver; the *Swan* managed to get back downstream and spent the rest of her days on the "navigable" portion.

unidentified flying objects (UFOs) The famous first instance of sighting "flying saucers" was that of pilot Kenneth Arnold, who reported seeing nine unidentified shiny, speeding objects near Mount Rainier in Washington state, on June 24, 1947. Another famous sighting occurred in Oregon on May 11, 1950, when Paul A. Trent and his wife, Evelyn, observed a saucer-shaped object in the sky from their farm near McMinnville. Mr. Trent took two photographs of the strange craft, which were displayed in a local bank; the *Telephone Register* newspaper published them with a story on June 9, 1950. The photographs also appeared in *Life* magazine on June 26, 1950. The authenticity and interpretation of the images has been debated inconclusively ever since. The event precipitated the establishment of an annual UFO festival in McMinnville in 2000.

Union The community of Union was formed about 1862, and named with the same patriotic impulses that created **Union County** in 1864. The place is at the southern edge of the valley of the **Grande Ronde River** along the route of the **Oregon Trail**. A post office was established in 1863, and in 1874, the county seat was moved from La Grande to Union. Union was incorporated in 1878, and the 1880 census reported a population of 416. The **Union Pacific Railroad** built through the valley in 1884, but passed about two miles west of Union; in 1890, a private company built a connecting railroad, which remained in service until the last sawmill in town closed in 1989. The county seat moved again in 1905, back to La Grande, and in the early 1900s, Union was a supply center for an agricultural area that engaged in dairying, fruit raising, and general farming. The Eastern Oregon Agricultural Experiment Station and farm opened near Union in 1901. The population climbed to 1,483 by 1910, sank somewhat in the next two decades, and in 1950 was 1,307. **Highway 30** went through Union, but **Interstate 84** bypassed the town by several miles, and the city has promoted its history and heritage to attract visitors. The commercial district with structures from the 1870s was placed on the National Register of Historic Places in 1997; the Union Hotel, built to serve highway travelers in the 1920s, offers rooms and meals.

Union County The **gold-mining** rushes of the early 1860s in eastern Oregon induced the state legislature to form Baker County in 1862, and then to carve Union County out of Baker County in 1864. The name reflects support for the Union side in the **Civil War** that was then raging. Border adjustments occurred between 1875 and 1913; since then the county's area has remained stable at 2,038 square miles. The county seat was at **La Grande** from 1864 to 1874, then was moved to **Union**, and in 1905 was wrenched back to La Grande. Court was usually held in rented quarters, but Union built a new brick structure when it got the county seat honor in 1874. When it returned to La Grande in 1905, county government was quartered in a building that had been erected in 1904 as the La Grande city hall. That building was razed in 1996 and county offices were then relocated to other buildings.

Historically the Cayuse Indians and the Nez Perce Indians occupied the area now in Union County. The Grande Ronde River Valley attracted farmers in the 1860s and 1870s, and the arrival of the transcontinental railroad in the 1880s made the area even more attractive. By the 1910s, the valley was described as a "checkerboard" of farms. Fruit orchards were joined by wheat fields, and cattle and sheep raising were carried on. Logging in the Blue Mountains brought lumber mills to La Grande and Union; the Mount Emily Logging Company of La Grande built miles of railroads to bring out logs from the 1920s into the 1950s. Union County's population reached 12,094 in 1890, and 16,191 by 1910; it remained rather stable for several decades, reaching 19,377 in 1970. The estimated population in 2007 was 25,250.

Union Pacific Railroad (UP) The Union Pacific was a partner in the first transcontinental railroad that connected the Midwest with San Francisco Bay in 1869. In the late 1870s and early 1880s, UP began building a branch to the Pacific Northwest. The two major subsidiaries formed to complete this project were the Oregon Short Line Railroad (OSL), which built west from Wyoming to **Huntington** on the Snake River, and the Oregon Railway & Navigation Company (OR&N), which built east from Portland. **Henry Villard**, who was attempting to complete the Northern Pacific Railway to the Pacific Coast, organized the OR&N in 1879. In the process, Villard purchased the **Oregon Steam Navigation Company** and its portage railroads, which gave him a right-of-way for the OR&N tracks along the south shore of the Columbia River from Portland upstream to Wallula, Washington, connecting there to the Northern Pacific in 1883. The OR&N continued east from Umatilla over the Blue Mountains to Huntington, making another transcontinental route from Portland in 1884. Villard had to step aside at the end of 1883, and the OR&N came into the Union Pacific network. In addition to its main line across northern Oregon, the UP built a number of branches south from the Columbia River onto the great wheat-growing plateau to the south between 1888 and 1911, and also built branches that reached Joseph (1908), Bend (1911), and Burns (1924). UP also had lines to Spokane from Umatilla and in 1910 opened a line from Portland to Seattle. The Union Pacific also maintained some steamboats such as the *T. J. Potter* on the Columbia River route to Astoria, and operated steamships connecting Portland with San Francisco. Famous passenger trains of the UP included the streamlined *City of Portland* and the *Portland Rose*. In 1996, UP purchased the **Southern Pacific Company**, making it the dominant railroad in Oregon.

Unity The rural post office of Unity in Baker County opened in 1891. In 1915, Unity was described as an "agricultural community near Burnt River, 30 miles southwest of Lockhart," the nearest railroad station on the Sumpter Valley Railway. Unity decided to incorporate as a city in 1972; the 1980 census recorded 115 residents, while the estimate in 2007 was also 115.

▶ **University of Oregon** The University of Oregon had its beginnings in 1872 when its establishment in Eugene was authorized by the legislature. In 1873, J. H. D. Henderson donated land for a campus on a slight rise on the east side of the town, and construction was started on the first building. This brick temple of learning was designed by William W. Piper in the French Second Empire style with a mansard roof, and was not completed until 1876, when the first classes began. Financial woes brought a substantial donation to the school from railroad magnate **Henry Villard** in 1881, and led to a second building in a more elaborate rendition of the same architectural style. This was designed by Warren H. Williams and completed in

1886; it was named Villard Hall. The first building was named Deady Hall in 1893 for **Matthew Deady**, who was president of the university's board of regents from 1873 to 1893. The first football game was held in 1894. **Prince Lucien Campbell** served as the school's president from 1902 until 1925. In 1926, the university graduated its first PhD and completed its indoor athletic arena, McArthur Court.

Autzen Stadium opened in 1967, inaugurating decades of sports events. Track coach **Bill Bowerman** and track student Phil Knight developed their first running shoes in 1970, leading to the formation of the Nike sports empire, and **Steve Prefontaine**'s track accomplishments enhanced the school's athletic luster. The renovated and renamed Knight Library was dedicated in 1994; the renovated Autzen Stadium was completed in 2003. By 2007, the university had an enrollment of about 16,475 undergraduate students and 3,900 graduate students,

Built in the 1920s, the College Side Inn in the Westgate Building was a social gathering point of the University of Oregon. It was designed by university architecture professor W. R. B. Wilcox and was located on the edge of the campus at 13th Avenue and Kincaid Street. Despite intense opposition, the building was demolished in 1961 to make way for a new bookstore. The photograph was taken in the late 1940s. Dot Dotson photograph. Steven Dotterrer collection.

making it the second-largest state institution of higher learning. The school mascot is a duck, and **Ducks** are the name of its athletic teams.

University of Portland The campus of the University of Portland on Waud's Bluff overlooking the Willamette River was established in 1891 as Portland University by the Methodist Church. In those heady times, a real estate venture was used to help finance the school: the University Park subdivision was laid out in residential lots, with streets named for American colleges, assorted educators and authors, and prominent Methodists, and sales income would help the new university. Unfortunately, a nationwide depression was on the horizon when classes opened in West Hall in 1891, and both real estate and the new school failed to take off. The Catholic Church acquired the campus; the Congregation of the Holy Cross established Columbia University there in 1901. The school opened with fifty-two students, all male, and eight professors. The school was renamed University of Portland in 1935. By the early 2000s, the university had a co-educational student population of about 3,200 and a faculty of 280.

► **Unthank, DeNorval** (1899–1977) DeNorval Unthank was born in Pennsylvania and raised in Kansas City by an aunt and uncle. He graduated from the University of Michigan and received his medical degree from Howard University in 1926. He came to Portland to open a medical practice at a time when very few **blacks** lived in Oregon, and the reception given to him and his family was not welcoming. His perseverance in remaining and in confronting and overcoming racial barriers in the city brought him respect; in 1958, he was named Doctor of the Year by the Oregon Medical Society. He had a strong voice during racial unrest in the **Albina neighborhood** in 1967; the city named a park in North Portland for him in 1969. Dr. Unthank was a co-founder of the Urban League in Portland, president of the local chapter of the National Association

for the Advancement of Colored People, and the first African-American to become a member of the Portland City Club.

One of the five children of DeNorval and Thelma Unthank was son DeNorval (1929–2001), who also attended Howard University and graduated in architecture from the University of Oregon in 1952. He went on to a distinguished career as an architect. Among the projects associated with him are designs for Central Oregon Community College in Bend, Lane Community College in Eugene, the Lane County Courthouse, and Albina Community Bank in Portland. He also encouraged historic preservation, such as the restoration of the Smeed Hotel and the Fifth Street Public Market in Eugene. Like his father, he was active in the Portland Urban League and did design work for them. He was also noted for his residential projects.

Upper Klamath Lake *see* **Klamath Lake**

Dr. DeNorval Unthank is pictured speaking during the period of racial strife in the Albina neighborhood, Portland, in 1967. Oregon Historical Society, OrHi 103651.

uranium *see* Lakeview; Steens Mountain

urban renewal In the late 1940s and early 1950s, new federal legislation was enacted that encouraged American cities to stave off or reverse "urban blight": the proliferation of deteriorating housing and infrastructure in central cities, often accompanied by suburban and exurban growth and development. The laws permitted the use of the power of eminent domain and allowed cities to sell property to developers, with the cities eventually benefiting not only from the improved infrastructure but also from enhanced tax revenues. In the 1950s and early 1960s, urban renewal took hold; it almost always involved clearing the "blighted" land and rebuilding from the bare ground. This was the practice in Portland, where two major ventures were undertaken by the Portland Development Commission under the leadership of **Ira Keller**: the South Auditorium Renewal Project in the **South Portland neighborhood**, and another project in the **Albina neighborhood**. Both were fraught with controversy and neither was successful. The programs evolved to include preservation and rehabilitation in addition to level clearance as a means of reusing properties, shifting the emphasis from housing to include other kinds of property, and including greater citizen input and smaller project scale. Urban renewal projects were also carried out in Eugene, Salem, Coos Bay, and other smaller cities. Since the 1970s, the urban renewal process has continued in Portland, and has expanded to other political jurisdictions such as counties, making particular use of tax-incremental financing to pay for the work: the future increase in property tax revenues guarantees the paying of the bonds that finance the original work.

U'Ren, William S. (1859–1949) Born in Wisconsin and raised in the Midwest, William U'Ren studied at a business college and read law in Colorado; he practiced law there until he moved to Oregon City in 1889, where he also entered into Republican party politics. U'Ren was a supporter of populist and direct democracy, and as a candidate of the People's party he won a seat in the state legislature beginning in 1897. Through some legal wrangling, U'Ren and others produced a constitutional amendment— the first since the constitution's adoption in 1857— that brought the political processes called the initiative and the referendum to the public; the amendment was ratified in a public vote in 1902. The initiative permitted the public to initiate legislation, rather than requiring it to go through legislative processes; the referendum allowed a public approval or rejection of laws that had been enacted through the legislative process.

The initiative and referendum proved to be the first of a series of changes to the political process in the next few years. They included the direct primary (1904), the direct (rather than legislative) election of U.S. senators (1906), the ability to recall elected public officials (1908), the presidential preference primary (1910), and woman's suffrage (1912). As a group, these reforms were sometimes referred to as the **Oregon System**, although of course they were being tried and implemented in many states during what is known as the Progressive era. Some of the reforms have proven to have flaws that enable interest groups to abuse their populist intent; an example is paying for signatures on initiative petitions. U'Ren was a vocal leader, along with other players such as **Oswald West** and **Abigail Scott Duniway**, in the Progressive movement.

V

Vale Situated on the Malheur River at the western edge of the **Treasure Valley**, Vale had its beginnings as a ranching community, where a post office was established in 1883. Vale became the county seat of Malheur County after its creation in 1887, and it was incorporated in 1889. The 1890 census shows it with a population of 131. By the 1910s, Vale had a railroad connection to Ontario and was a center of agricultural endeavors: "Farming, stock raising, fruit growing. Chief crops grain, corn, potatoes, alfalfa, hay and alfalfa seed. Ships wool, honey, cattle, horses, hogs, sheep and alfalfa seed. Center of sheep and wool industry." The population was 992 in 1910, 1,083 in 1940. Increased irrigation from the Owyhee Project boosted agricultural production in the Treasure Valley, and Vale continued a slow growth, reaching a population of 1,558 in 1980 and an estimated 2,040 in 2007.

Valsetz The now-vanished logging and mill town of Valsetz was located in western Polk County. It was built in 1919 by the Cobbs and Mitchell Lumber Company to process a large tract of timber in the Coast Range. The Valley & Siletz Railroad was constructed to connect Valsetz with **Independence**; the railroad's name was elided to form the name of the **company town** that housed the loggers and lumbermen and their families. Valsetz achieved national notice when Dorothy Anne Hobson, aged nine, began writing and producing the *Valsetz Star* in 1937; her quips on life in the Oregon woods reached the approving eyes of the likes of Eleanor Roosevelt (although Dorothy was an ardent young Republican). The *Star* was published until 1941; the town of Valsetz was sold to Boise Cascade Corporation, which closed the last operations in the area in 1984 and razed the town and mill.

Vancouver, George (1758–1798) British navy captain George Vancouver commanded the ship *Discovery* on its voyage of exploration in the North Pacific Ocean. The *Discovery* and its accompanying tender ship, the *Chatham*, set sail from England in April 1791; sailing via South Africa and Australia, the two ships made landfall on the North American continent on April 17, 1792. On the 29th, Vancouver's party encountered the American Capt. **Robert Gray**, who a few weeks later crossed the Columbia River bar. Vancouver's party spent the summer in the vicinity of Vancouver Island and Puget Sound, and in the fall proceeded south, where they paused to reconnoiter the mouth of the **Columbia River** that Gray had already entered. The *Discovery* did not make it over the bar, but the *Chatham*, under the command of Lt. William Broughton (1762–1821), did, and Broughton then took small boats farther upriver. They saw, and named **Mount Hood**, for a British naval figure, on October 29, and on October 30 the party went at least as far as the Sandy River, east of Troutdale. Broughton returned to the *Chatham*, and then with the *Discovery* sailed to the Golden Gate and then to a wintering in Hawai'i. The expedition returned to England in the autumn of 1795. Vancouver's voyage bestowed many place names in North America, especially in the Puget Sound area, but also Mount Hood and a promontory that Broughton labeled Point Vancouver. **John McLoughlin** applied the name to **Fort Vancouver** in 1825. In 1926, the bluff above the Sandy River at Troutdale was named Broughton Bluff for the commander of the *Chatham*. An island in the Columbia was named Chatham Island and a stretch of the river was designated Broughton Reach, both in 1975 on the occasion of the opening of an exhibit about another noted British naval captain and explorer, Capt. **James Cook**, at the Oregon Historical Society.

Fisher, Robin. *Vancouver's Voyage: Charting the Northwest Coast, 1791–1795.* Seattle: University of Washington Press, 1992.

▶ **Vanport** In the brash and hectic years of World War II, the Portland metropolitan area became the site of several vast shipbuilding enterprises. They were located both in Portland and in Vancouver, Washington, across the Columbia River. **Henry J. Kaiser** brought thousands of workers to Portland to work in his shipyards, many of them from the Midwest and the South, and many of them African-American. Portland had no housing to spare, and the real-estate industry did not support public housing nor did it wish to supply housing to **blacks** except in the prescribed **Albina neighborhood**. To house these working families, Kaiser created the planned community of Vanport, located on low-lying land on the south shore of the Columbia River. Officially known as Vanport City, the project was constructed in short order, beginning in September 1942. At its height in 1944, nearly 40,000 people lived there, 6,000 of them African-Americans—it was the state's second-largest city. Built to be temporary, it was a complete city, with schools, stores, churches, and nursery facilities for working mothers. With the end of the war, Vanport shrank, but did not disappear; the postwar Vanport Extension Center grew into **Portland State University**. Many black families stayed, unable to find housing elsewhere in the city, and some **Japanese**, returned from wartime incarceration, also moved to Vanport; post-war housing was in short supply. On Memorial Day of 1948, the flooding waters of the Columbia River breached a railroad embankment and inundated the city. While only sixteen people died in the flood, it left some 18,000 persons homeless. Vanport was not rebuilt.

Maben, Manly. *Vanport.* Portland, Oregon: Oregon Historical Society Press, 1987.

Veneta The Lane County community of Veneta had its beginnings in 1912, when it was named for

Awash in a sea of debris, the flooded city of Vanport is a dismal sight. The slow-rising waters enabled most of the residents to escape safely, but the buildings, built for temporary wartime use, were not salvageable. Mason collection.

Veneta Hunter, daughter of the founder. It had a post office by 1914. Veneta was incorporated as a city in 1962; the 1970 census gave it a population of 1,377. It has since become a commuting suburb of Eugene. Its estimated population in 2007 was 4,640. Veneta Hunter Vincent, the town's namesake, died in 2000 at the age of ninety-one. Veneta is the site of the **Oregon Country Fair**.

Vernonia Located on the Nehalem River in Columbia County, Vernonia began as a rural post office serving a farming community in 1878. Vernonia was incorporated in 1891, and the 1900 census reported it had a population of sixty-two; by 1920, the figure reached 142 residents. In 1917, the Eccles family estate purchased 27,000 acres of timberland in the vicinity of Vernonia, and formed the Oregon-American Lumber Company. A branch railroad was extended to the town in 1922, and construction began on a large lumber mill, which opened in 1924. The population jumped to 1,625 in 1930. Logging continued at a good pace into the 1950s, when the timber was gone and the mill was aging; it closed at the end of 1957. In a final burst of glory, some of the mill buildings were burned to the ground for the 1960 filming of *Ring of Fire*, a cop-and-robbers flick with a forest fire twist, starring David Janssen. Vernonia's population in 1970 was 1,643; the estimate in 2007 was 2,365.

Kamholz, Edward J., Jim Blain, and Gregory Kamholz. *The Oregon-American Lumber Company: Ain't No More*. Stanford, California: Stanford University Press, 2003.

Victor, Frances Fuller (1826-1902) Born in New York state to a peripatetic family, Frances Fuller received an education in Ohio and, like her sister Metta Victoria Fuller (1831-1885), she began writing poetry and fiction rather early; her first novel appeared in 1848. The two sisters produced a collection published in Boston in 1851, *Poems of Sentiment and Imagination*. After a stint of editing

in Detroit and a brief fling at marriage and writing in Omaha, Frances Fuller went to New York City, where she and sister Metta worked for the Beadle Company, which issued dime novels and popular magazines. She also married her sister's husband's brother, Orville Victor. In 1863, she went to San Francisco, and came to Oregon in 1865; she spent much of the remainder of her life in Oregon and San Francisco. And she wrote: *The River of the West*, based on the life of mountain man **Joseph L. Meek** (1869); *All Over Oregon and Washington* (1872), a descriptive travelogue; and then a series of writings for Hubert H. Bancroft's History Company of San Fransisco, including all or parts of Bancroft's monumental *History of California* (1884–90; 7 volumes), History of Oregon (1886–88; 2 volumes), and *History of Washington, Idaho and Montana* (1890). She capped her career with the *Early Indian Wars of Oregon* (1894). She was never wealthy; she had many friends in literary and historical circles, but she also made enemies when her histories were judgmental or insufficiently patronizing to those discussed.

Martin, Jim. *A Bit of a Blue: The Life and Work of Frances Fuller Victor*. Salem, Oregon: Deep Well Publishing Co., 1992.

Vietnam War, 1961—75 Oregon had a reputation for being a hotbed of opposition to the Vietnam War, a reputation that was due in part to the strength of antiwar demonstrations in Portland, but also to the vocal opposition of two successive Oregon senators. The first voice was that of Democratic Senator **Wayne Morse**, "the Conscience of the Senate," who was one of only two senators to vote against the Gulf of Tonkin Resolution that legitimized American intervention in Vietnam. However, Morse's defeat at the polls in 1968 was partly due to his views on the war. Republican Senator Mark Hatfield, who took office in 1967, was also a strong voice against the war, and in that instance, his views likely helped his campaign.

Villard, Henry (1835–1900) Born in Germany, Henry Villard came to the United States in 1853. He studied law, but began working as a reporter in the late 1850s; during the Civil War, he wrote for the *New York Herald* as well as the *New York Tribune*. Villard married the daughter of famed abolitionist William Lloyd Garrison in 1866. On a trip to Germany in 1870, Villard agreed to act as the agent for a group of Germans who held bonds of American railroads, which brought him into the arena of high finance. He was involved in the reorganization of the **Oregon & California Railroad** in the mid-1870s, and in 1879 purchased the **Oregon Steam Navigation Company**. He also formed the Oregon Railway & Navigation Company and, in 1881, took control of the **Northern Pacific Railroad**, which completed a transcontinental link to Portland in 1883. Villard made generous contributions to the **University of Oregon** in those flush times, and Villard Hall there is named for him. Villard spent a great deal of effort in attracting settlers to Oregon and the Pacific Northwest in the early 1880s, including emigrants from Germany. His financial edifice crumbled at the end of 1884 and he left the western scene, although he served as head of the Northern Pacific's board of directors from 1888 to 1893. Villard formed the Edison General Electric Company in 1889 and was president until 1893 when it became General Electric. University of Oregon geology professor E. T. Hodge named Villard Glacier on Mount Hood for Henry Villard.

vine maple *see* **maple**

virgin timber *see* **old-growth timber**

Vista House *see* **Crown Point**

viticulture *see* **wine and wine making**

Vollum, Charles Howard (1913–1986) and **Jean Vollum** (1927?–2007) Born in Portland and a graduate of Reed College with a degree in physics, Howard Vollum was a tinkerer with radios and electronic devices; his 1936 thesis title was "A stable beat frequency oscillator equipped with a direct reading frequency meter." He served in the Army Signal Corps during World War II, and resumed tinkering with oscilloscopes in 1946. In 1947, he and Jack Murdock founded **Tektronix**, beginning the electronics industry in Oregon. He married a schoolteacher, Jean Kettenback, whom he met while ice skating, in 1950. Tektronix was a financial success, and Howard and Jean began putting energies into philanthropy. Howard contributed to the 1965 founding of the Oregon Graduate Institute (now part of **Oregon Health and Science University [OHSU]**) and also supported Reed College and the Vollum Institute at OHSU. Howard and Jean were benefactors of the **Oregon College of Art and Craft**, and of the Mount Angel Abbey Library, designed by Finnish architect Alvar Aalto. After Howard's death, Jean supported the emerging "green" movement with such projects as Ecotrust, which is headquartered in the Jean Vollum Natural Capital Center, a renovated historic warehouse building.

Waldport After the dissolution of the **Coast Reservation**, white settlement took place around Alsea Bay, and Waldport post office was created in the 1880s to serve those Lincoln County settlers near the **Alsea River**. Isolated from coastal traffic by an inadequate port, and with only a rudimentary road to the interior, Waldport did not prosper. It did incorporate as a municipality in 1911, and its 1920 population was recorded as 121. A few years earlier, it was reported that Waldport shipped lumber and livestock and some wool and fruits, and there were two small salmon canneries, a creamery, and a saw- and planing mill—and an oar factory. Coastal travel improved immensely in the early 1930s with the completion of the **Oregon Coast Highway** and a bridge to replace the ferry service over Alsea Bay. Waldport became a tourist stopover, and the population climbed to 689 by 1950. In the 1970s, Waldport was the location of a cult headed by Marshall Herff Applewhite, which recruited followers to undertake a rendezvous with a spacecraft to take them to a higher plane; the cult came to attention again in 1997 as a group called Heaven's Gate; Applewhite and thirty-eight others committed suicide in San Diego, again aiming for a higher plane.

Walla Walla Indians *see* **Umatilla Indians**

Wallowa The small trading town of Wallowa was a rural post office in 1873, when whites began settling in the Wallowa Valley. The town was incorporated in 1899, and had a population of 243 in the 1900 census. A railroad line from La Grande arrived in 1908, which provided an outlet to market lumber, and by the 1910s Wallowa was a lumbering center with three planing mills, a sawmill, and a box factory. Dairying and livestock raising went on nearby, and a creamery took care of the dairy products; there was also a flour mill. Wallowa's population reached 1,055 by 1950, but has since declined; it was 847 in 1980, and an estimated 945 in 2007.

► **Wallowa County** Created in 1887 from the eastern portion of Umatilla County, Wallowa County

The post office at Promise, Wallowa County, as photographed in 1937. The community was located on a remote ridge south of the Grande Ronde River, in an area that W. Mann, who settled there about 1891, called Promised Land and Land of Promise. The post office operated from 1896 to 1944. Author's collection.

is at the most northeasterly corner of the state. Boundary adjustments with Union County were made in 1890, 1900, and 1915, resulting in the current area of 3,153 square miles. The county includes the homeland of the Wallowa band of the **Nez Perce Indians**; the elder **Joseph** is buried at the foot of Wallowa Lake near the town named for him. Joseph was the initial county seat, but an 1888 election placed it in Enterprise. A courthouse was finally constructed in 1909 and continues to house county offices. Wallowa County's population in 1900 was 5,538; it increased to 9,778 in 1920, fell to 7,264 by 1950, and to 6,911 by 1990. The estimated population in 2007 was 7,130.

Wallowa County's economy was long based on cattle ranching, with an admixture of gold mining, farming, and lumbering. The scenic appeal of Wallowa Lake and the rugged Wallowa Mountains led to the construction of the Wallowa Lake Lodge in the 1920s, along with other resorts. The town of Joseph developed as a small center for art bronze casting in the 1990s and tourism and recreation emerged as small industries. Wallowa County joined with Union County in 2002 to purchase the railroad connecting Joseph with La Grande, continuing to offer freight service while adding excursion trains to the remote and roadless **Grande Ronde River** Canyon.

▶ **Wallowa Lake** Sited at the base of the forbidding and jagged peaks of the Wallowa Mountains, Wallowa Lake was formed when a retreating glacier left moraines that blocked in the scoured valley. The lake became a popular rustic retreat in the 1910s, with boats and a small amusement park. An aerial tramway was built from the south end of the lake in 1970, climbing to the top of Mount Howard, at an elevation of 8,150 feet.

Wallowa Mountains Sometimes considered to be an extension of the Blue Mountains, the Wallowa

A postcard view of the north end of Wallowa Lake, with the town of Joseph at the far end, about 1940. Author's collection.

Mountains range about forty miles between the Minam River and the Imnaha River south of Joseph. Most of the range is national forest land, and much of it is within the Eagle Cap Wilderness Area. Its highest point is Sacajawea Peak (9,838 feet), the tallest mountain in Oregon outside the Cascade Range and the sixth tallest peak in the state.

► **walnuts** In the first decades of the twentieth century, walnuts, like **filberts** and **prunes**, were a popular new crop in Oregon orchards. Those known as English walnuts (*Juglans regia*; and also known as Persian, Circassian, European, Madeira, French, and Italian walnuts) were widely planted in the Willamette Valley, and also were grown in the Umpqua and Rogue River valleys. California is the major United States producer, but Oregon was long the second-ranking state in walnut production into the 1960s. By 2006, California produced 99 percent

Written by C. J. Lewis, chief of the division of horticulture at the Oregon Agricultural College (now Oregon State University) and published by the Southern Pacific Company, "Walnut Culture in Western and Southern Oregon" was issued in 1916. It was distributed throughout the nation to attract farmers to the state and encourage them to plant walnuts. Author's collection.

of the nation's crop; Oregon was still the number two producer.

The black walnut (*Juglans nigra*) is a native American tree, but not native to Oregon, nor is it grown commercially in Oregon. It is often found as an ornamental, however, such as those that were planted at the house of William and Mary Ann Barlow in **Barlow**.

wapato *Sagittaria latifolia* is a member of the arrowhead family. It is an aquatic plant that is widely distributed across North America, and in other localities may be called duck potato or Indian potato for its edible tubers. The common name in the Pacific Northwest is wapato. Wapato grows in ponds, lakes, and swamps, usually in large colonies held together by a network of thin white roots. It is the tubers on the roots that are edible and were sought as a major food source by many Native people. To gather wapato in lakes or ponds, a common approach was to walk and kick one's way through the patch while holding on to a canoe, to dislodge the tubers. Using a fork or stick could also dislodge the tubers, which float to the surface for collection. Wapato were eaten raw or were cooked by roasting, boiling, or steaming; they were also dried and pounded to make a flour. Notable wapato sites include the lakes of **Sauvie Island**, the marshlands of Klamath County, and the seasonal Lake Wapato near Gaston.

wapiti *see* **elk**

Warm Springs Indians *see* **Sahaptin Indians**

Warm Springs Reservation The treaty with the Middle Oregon Tribes, signed in 1855 and ratified by the U.S. Senate in 1859, established the Warm Springs Reservation of about 600,000 acres for the Sahaptin bands known as Tygh, Wayampam, Tenino, and John Day, and the Upper Chinook bands known as The Dalles, Ki-gal-twal-la, and Hood River;

see **Wasco and Wishram Indians**; **Sahaptin Indians**. The reservation also included many **Northern Paiute Indians** in the late 1870s after the **Bannock War**. A survey error in the 1870s was corrected in 1972; the current size of the reservation is 661,360 acres. The Warm Springs Reservation is one of the few reservations that retained its entire original land base and did not undergo the process of assigning allotments, which has resulted in a checkerboard of ownerships at many other reservations. The reservation is the home of the **Confederated Tribes of Warm Springs**, organized in 1937.

> Stowell, Cynthia K. *Faces of a Reservation: a Portrait of the Warm Springs Indian Reservation.* Portland, Oregon: Oregon Historical Society, 1986.

Warrenton The city of Warrenton in Clatsop County dates from the late 1880s with the work of Daniel Knight Warren to dike the saltwater tidal flats at the mouth of the **Skipanon River**. The townsite was platted in 1889 and a post office opened in 1892; a railroad was built through Warrenton connecting Astoria and Seaside in the early 1890s, and Warrenton was the location of the company shops. Warrenton was incorporated in 1899, and by 1910, it could boast a population of 339 residents. In 1915, it was reported that Warrenton had two sawmills and two clam canneries—razor clams were a delicacy dug from the seashore sands—and that cranberry culture and vegetable truck gardening were extensively engaged in. Warrenton's population reached 1,365 by 1940, when sawmills were active. After World War II, charter fishing-boat operations became popular, carrying sports fishermen out on the Columbia and over the bar into the ocean. Warrenton's population was 1,825 in 1970; annexations, including the town of **Hammond** in 1991 and residential and commercial growth at the eastern outskirts boosted the figure to an estimated 4,645 in 2007.

Wasco The town of Wasco takes its name from Wasco County, where it had been since its inception about 1870. However, in 1889 Sherman County was split off from Wasco County, and the town went to the new county. Located in wheat country, Wasco was connected to the Union Pacific Railroad by a branch line in 1897. Wasco was briefly the Sherman County seat, but that distinction went to Moro in 1899, the year the branch line railroad reached farther south to that point. Wasco was incorporated in 1901, when its population was about 300. Wheat-induced prosperity increased the population to 701 in the 1920 census, when Wasco boasted a bank, two flour mills, an opera house, and a weekly newspaper. The count dropped below 400 for the rest of the century and was estimated at 400 in 2007.

► **Wasco County** Named for the Wasco or Wascopam Chinook Indians, Wasco County was created by the territorial legislature in 1854 from portions of Clackamas, Marion, Linn, and Lane Counties. It then extended from the crest of the Cascade Range all the way to the Rocky Mountains, between latitudes 42° and 46°—the California and Washington borders—some 130,000 square miles. A good deal of whittling down has since taken place, reducing the area to 2,396 square miles. The county seat has always been at **The Dalles**, where courthouses were built in 1859, 1884, and 1914. All are still standing; the 1859 structure is used as a community hall, the 1884 building became a funeral chapel, and the 1914 building is still the seat of county government. Wasco County has a long agricultural history, producing wheat and fruit (especially **cherries**). In 1915, Wasco County was described as an ideal place for grape growing and **wine making**; however, the timing was inopportune, as Oregon had just adopted statewide **prohibition**. Grape growing and wine making have made a return to the region since the 1980s. The county also had an **aluminum industry** that came in the 1950s with the completion of **The Dalles Dam**; that industry declined in the 1980s. Lumber and tourism have long added to the economic mix. Wasco County's population in 1900 was 13,481; in 1950, 15,552; in 2007, it was estimated at 24,125.

Wasco and Wishram Indians The Wasco and Wishram people are Chinook-speaking Indians living near the Columbia River east of the Cascade Range. They wintered near the river, as did other Chinook-speaking bands to the west, including the Cascades, Hood River, and White Salmon people. As anthropologists David and Kathrine French note, "There is no simple, unequivocal term referring to the Wasco, Wishram, intermediate, and Cascades populations collectively and exclusively."

These Chinookan people lived on and near the river, which fed them with salmon and provided transportation. In summer, treks were made into higher elevations to procure berries and roots; spring and fall fish runs supplied salmon, and other fish included lamprey, sturgeon, and smelt. The Wasco and Wishram people lived in an area where many other tribes visited for trading and fishing, and they were exposed to white travelers and trappers at an early date.

After treaty negotiations in 1855, most Wishram became associated with the Yakama Reservation in Washington, while most other Gorge Chinookans were assigned to the **Warm Springs Reservation**; some went to the **Grand Ronde Reservation** in the Willamette River Valley, while others continued to live in the Gorge on non-reservation lands.

Washington County The antecedent of Washington County was the **Twality District**, established by the provisional legislature in 1843 as one of the four original counties of the Oregon Country. The western boundary was the Pacific Ocean; to the south, Yamhill County, and to the east, Clackamas County; and, on the north, the line was ostensibly

Orchards and vineyards cover the hillside in this scene in Wasco County by photographer Benjamin A. Gifford, taken in the early 1900s. Oregon Historical Society, Gi 563.

at 54°40', or somewhere north of present-day Prince George, British Columbia. In 1844, the Columbia River became the rather more workable northern boundary, and Clatsop County was carved from its northwest corner. The name was changed in 1849 by the territorial legislature from Twality or Tuality County to Washington County, in honor of George Washington. The creation of Multnomah and Columbia Counties in 1854 resulted in establishing the county boundaries as they have remained; the area is 727 square miles. The county seat is **Hillsboro**, where a wood-frame courthouse was built in 1852. A brick courthouse replaced it in 1873, only to be replaced again in 1928; several additional county buildings have been added since. Washington County's population in 1860 was 2,801; that figure increased to 11,972 in 1890, and to 21,522 in 1910.

Washington County was a prime location for land seekers in the 1840s and 1850s, when the fertile soils of the **Tualatin Plains** were settled by farmers. Agriculture was the prime economic engine from the beginning, as wheat fields blanketed the plains. By the 1910s, more than half of the county's land area was being actively farmed, "including some of the most celebrated nurseries, hop yards, onion beds, gardens, prune orchards, berry patches, and dairy farms of the state." At the same time, the county was served by two electrified **interurban railways** that provided suburban commuter trains connecting the major towns with Portland. Highway development spurred further residential growth; the county's population reached 39,194 by 1940.

Postwar development in the county was encouraged by the location of **Tektronix** in Beaverton in the 1950s, and the construction of the **Sunset Highway**, which replaced the Tualatin Valley Highway as the chief automotive thoroughfare. The building of **Cedar Hills** indicated the future of suburban growth in the county; the 1950 population count was 86,330. By 1980, the figure was 245,860; the estimate in 2007 was 511,075. Despite the tremendous loss of farmland to housing and development, the county was still the third largest producer of agricultural products in terms of monetary value. The high value comes through crops such as grapes for **wine making**, strawberries, nursery stock, pears, and berries.

Waterloo This small Linn County community is on the banks of the South Santiam River, where rapids produced waterpower for sawmills and a gristmill. Also, mineral springs were located nearby which attracted health seekers. Waterloo post office opened in 1875. The prospects for a woolen mill induced the platting of the townsite in 1892, and Waterloo was incorporated in 1893. The woolen mill was opened in 1895 and brought instant prosperity, but prosperity was cut short when the mill burned in 1898. A year later, a visiting journalist said things had been quiet since the fire; "he saw 17 men sitting on a fence watching a man gardening," reported historian Alfred L. Lomax. The 1900 census counted a modest population of fifty-nine residents.

By 1915, an emigration bulletin noted that the area was one of farming, lumbering, and the raising of small fruit, vegetables, and livestock, and that there were "wonderful caves" nearby that attracted visitors; no other information has been found about the mysterious caves. Waterloo has continued to be an incorporated city; its population in 1920 was eighty-two; in 1950, 195; in 1980, 211; and the estimate in 2007 was 210. The post office was closed in 1974.

Watkins, Carleton E. (1829–1916) This San Francisco-based photographer is famed for his landscapes of Yosemite, Mendocino, and other California points in the mid-nineteenth century. Carleton Watkins also made two extended trips to Oregon and produced remarkable views of the Columbia River Gorge. His first trip was in the summer of 1867, when he photographed Portland and **Oregon City** as well as the operations of the **Oregon Steam Navigation Company**, such as the sidewheeler *Oneonta*.

Watkins made several additional trips in the 1880s, again concentrating on the Gorge and, this time, on the operations of the Oregon Railway and Navigation Company. Watkins' views of such iconic places as Multnomah Falls and Cape Horn were widely distributed as large art pieces and as stereopticon slides.

Palmquist, Peter E. *Carleton E. Watkins, Photographer of the American West.* Albuquerque: University of New Mexico Press for the Amon Carter Museum, 1983.

▶ **webfoot** An early nickname for an Oregonian, based on the fact that the **wet side** is mighty damp. It seems to have originated as a derisive term among gold miners in California in the late 1840s. However, by 1862, the term was "suddenly adopted [by Oregonians] as a descriptive badge of honor and even as a term of affection," according to historian Hazel Mills. It has been used as a moniker for students at the **University of Oregon** and their athletic teams, and was briefly the name of the school yearbook; "webfoot" has morphed into "duck" at the University, although the earlier term is still sometimes used.

Mills, Hazel E. The Constant Webfoot. *Western Folklore* 11, no. 3, (1952): 153–164.

Weinhard, Henry *see* **Blitz-Weinhard Brewing Company**

PORTLAND OREGON
FAVORITE PASTIME
OF THE NATIVES..

While a webfoot might be found anywhere in Oregon, the species was exceedingly abundant in Portland. This postcard depiction is from about 1915. Steven Dotterrer collection.

West, Oswald (1873–1960) Oswald West was born in Ontario, Canada. His family moved West in 1877, and West went to school in Salem, Oregon; he worked at a Salem bank until 1899, when he trekked north to seek gold in Alaska, but then returned to a bank job in Astoria. In 1903, West was appointed to the office of State Land Agent, where he worked to recover some of the vast acreage of state school lands that had been effectively stolen by land speculators, a set of schemes detailed by **S. A. D. Puter** in his confessional book, *Looters of the Public Domain.* His reform-minded work led him to be appointed in 1907 to the new Railroad Commission of Oregon. In 1910, West ran for governor on the Democratic ticket—though he ran a nonpartisan, Progressive-influenced campaign—and he won.

Although the legislature was in the hands of the Republicans, West pushed progressive legislation, using the initiative and referendum in some cases. In his one term, West saw the approval of woman's suffrage, statewide liquor **prohibition**, better control of working conditions and compensation, a workman's compensation act, stronger state regulation of railroads, banks and utilities, and reforms in prison operation. His administration oversaw the creation of a state office of forestry and state fish and game commissions. Among his notable achievements was the "saving" of the Oregon coastline from private ownership through the mechanism of declaring, in 1913, that all lands between the mean high and low tides were a public right-of-way: in other words, a public highway. At this early point in the state's development, the effect was to protect most of the beach lands from private ownership (however, later unfortunate repercussions occurred when auto enthusiasts insisted the law permitted auto use on all beaches, regardless of wildlife damage or sunbathers' plaints). His opposition to liquor, vice, and political corruption was exemplified in the **Copperfield** affair, which also highlighted his support of equal rights for women.

West did not seek a second term, and in 1915

moved to Portland to practice law. He continued to use his voice in the political arena for many years, and wrote numerous newspaper and magazine articles on a variety of topics, from horse racing to pioneer life. West's rustic beach cabin, located on a dramatic site in Cannon Beach, was placed on the National Register of Historic Places in 1992. The dramatic **Short Sand Beach** south of Cape Falcon is included in Oswald West State Park.

West Coast Airlines West Coast was one of the nation's first regional airlines, headquartered in Seattle and linking smaller communities in Oregon, Washington, Idaho, western Montana, and Utah with major airports. It began scheduled service in 1947. In Oregon, West Coast initially provided service with DC-3 propeller planes, and later added DC-9 and Fairchild F-27 aircraft as well as smaller Pipers. In Oregon in 1953, West Coast took off from Portland for Albany/Corvallis, Eugene, North Bend/Coos Bay, Medford, Astoria, Pendleton, La Grande, Baker City, and Ontario/Payette. By 1961, La Grande was dropped from the routings, but Klamath Falls, Salem, and Roseburg were added, along with thrice-weekly service to Burns and Lakeview. West Coast Airlines was merged with Pacific Air Lines and Bonanza Air Lines in 1968 to form Hughes Airwest. **Air Oregon** was created in 1981 to continue service to smaller airports. *See also* **aviation**.

western meadowlark *see* **meadowlark**

Western Oregon University This state university in **Monmouth** had its start with a group of Campbellites: members of the Disciples of Christ; later, the Christian church. The group came from Illinois in the mid-1850s with the express purpose of founding a new town and a denominational college. The site was selected in 1854, the first trustees were chosen in 1855, and Monmouth University began in 1856. In the mid-1860s, nearby Bethel College was consolidated with Monmouth and the name was changed to Christian College. Thomas F. Campbell became the second president in 1869 and oversaw construction of the first permanent, brick building; it was later named Campbell Hall. Students in 1872

did not bring intoxicating beverages to the college premises or use it elsewhere, abstained from all things immoral, disorderly, such as gambling, card playing—even for amusement, profanity, did not leave town without permission of the president or faculty, did not attend a ball, visit a saloon or billiard hall or other improper place of amusement, [and] did not visit another student except at the home of that student's parents in Monmouth.

There were 237 students enrolled.

In the 1880s, enrollment fell, and the college began a "normal" department to train teachers. Although the state supplied no funds for a number of years, it did designate Christian College as the Oregon State Normal School; similar peculiar situations prevailed at normal schools in **Drain**, **Weston**, and **Ashland**. In 1889, **Prince Lucien Campbell** became president of the Monmouth school; he left in 1902 to head the University of Oregon. After closing due to lack of funds in 1910, in 1911 the school finally received permanent funding from the state. Teacher training was the focus through the 1920s and into the 1930s, such that in 1939 the school became the Oregon College of Education; still, the legislature considered closing the institution several times. The first four-year degrees were granted in 1943, but the war depleted the student body to 147 students—only three of them men. The school added a master's program in elementary education in 1952. By 1965, enrollment topped 2,000; in 1973, closure was discussed again, and once more in 1980. The name was changed for the fourth time in 1981, to Western Oregon State College; that became Western Oregon University in 1997. Despite continued talk of closing the school, it grew rapidly in the 1980s. It opened the Jensen Arctic Museum in 1985 and a new library in

2000. In 2007, the university had about 4,500 undergraduate students and 400 graduate students.

Westfir The Western Lumber Company established and named a mill at Westfir in Lane County in 1923, the same year the post office opened. Located on the North Fork of the Middle Fork Willamette River in the midst of Willamette National Forest, Westfir was a **company town**, where the timber company operated the housing and businesses. The Southern Pacific Company was constructing its railroad line through Westfir and over Willamette Pass between Eugene and Klamath Falls in the 1920s, and was a major customer of the mill. After some troubled times during the 1930s, the mill was purchased by the Edward Hines Lumber Company in 1945. Hines established a large plywood mill in 1952. With declining timber resources, Hines closed their operation in 1977, and the remaining residents, now property owners, incorporated their town in 1979; the last remnant mill operations ceased in 1985. The population in 2007 was estimated at 335. The **covered bridge** spanning the river, built in 1945 and able to support loaded log trucks, is the longest in Oregon at 180 feet.

West Hills *see* **Tualatin Mountains**

West Linn The city of West Linn had its first incarnation when Robert Moore arrived in Oregon from Peoria, Illinois, in 1840 and claimed land on the west side of the Willamette River below Willamette Falls. He established a townsite called Linn City, named for the same Missouri senator who is honored by **Linn County**. The west side of the falls became the chief portage point between boats above and below the falls, and Linn City was a bustling place in the 1850s. However, the tremendous **floods** of December 1861 virtually erased the town, which was not rebuilt. The Willamette Falls Locks were built through the site in 1873, and other industrial uses have occupied much of the land.

When the Portland General Electric Company began to expand its new hydroelectric power generation at Willamette Falls in the early 1890s, it established the town of Willamette near the mouth of the Tualatin River, and built an electric **interurban railway** to connect Willamette with the power plant near West Linn. The Willamette post office opened in 1895; the interurban line was extended north to the Bolton neighborhood. The city of West Linn was incorporated in 1913, and the West Linn post office opened in 1914; in 1916, the Willamette townsite was incorporated into West Linn, although a separate post office was operated until 1955 and there is still a distinct, historic business district called Willamette. The census of 1920 showed West Linn with a population of 1,628; it reached 2,945 by the time of the 1950 census.

After World War II, the city grew into a substantial residential suburb, a process that grew rapidly after the construction of **Interstate 205** in the 1970s. West Linn's population was 7,091 in 1970, 16,389 in 1990, and an estimated 24,180 in 2007.

Westmoreland neighborhood, Portland The Westmoreland neighborhood was a real estate development of the Ladd Estate Company, derived from the land holdings of pioneer Portland merchant **William S. Ladd**. It was platted in 1909, and was already served by an electric streetcar line on its western edge. At SE Milwaukie Avenue and Bybee Boulevard, a new streetcar line was built east into the **Eastmoreland neighborhood** and Erroll Heights in 1911. The intersection began to develop into a retail shopping area, which was fully realized by 1925, when the Moreland Theatre opened there.

Weston The city of Weston in Umatilla County developed around a post office established in 1869. Weston was incorporated in 1878, and the 1880 census gave it a population of 446. The Union Pacific Railroad built through the town in 1887—and the next year, fire destroyed most of Weston's downtown. Weston-made brick had constructed the rival town of Pendleton in the 1880s, and so in the early 1890s, Weston rebuilt its own retail core with a number of impressive brick stores and fraternal lodges; the downtown district was placed on the National Register of Historic Places in 1982. An academy was started at Weston in 1882, which in 1885 was designated as Eastern Oregon Normal School, a training school for public school teachers. But the state designation brought little in the way of funds, and the school ceased in 1909; it was reincarnated in La Grande in 1929 and grew into **Eastern Oregon University**. In the early 1900s, Weston-area farmers grew wheat, barley, and potatoes. Irrigation brought new crops such as corn and peas, and food processing became a town industry. The Smith family began a canning operation in 1919, which grew into Smith Frozen Foods.

The novelist and journalist Nard Jones (1904–1972) is known as a Washington state writer (*Swift Flows the River* [1940]; *Seattle* [1942]), but his first novel was *Oregon Detour* (1930), set in a small town named Creston that was uncannily like Weston, where he lived from 1919 to 1927. Weston residents adjudged Jones's raw realism as virtual slander, and the book was locally condemned and hidden from view. But for many years, local residents talked of the book and its characters, trying to figure out what neighbor appeared as what character.

Weston had a population of 679 in 1950; the estimate in 2007 was 745.

West Salem *see* **Salem**

West Shore *see* **newspapers and journalism**

west side *see* **wet side**

wet side The west side of the **Cascade Range** is often called the wet side, because it is so much more moist than the east or **dry side** of this range.

Weyerhaeuser Corporation The Weyerhaeuser Timber Company was established in 1900 by Friedrich Weyerhaeuser and some fifteen partners. They purchased 90,000 acres of timbered land in the Pacific Northwest from the Northern Pacific Railway. Weyerhaeuser had the money and the experience to head the enterprise, having spent forty years in the timber industry in the upper Midwest. The company's operations, headquartered in Tacoma, were primarily in Washington state, but it acquired timberlands in Klamath County beginning in 1905 and built large operations at **Klamath Falls** starting in 1929; its lumber mill closed in 1991, and its plywood and particleboard operations were sold in 1996. Weyerhaeuser opened a lumber mill at **Springfield** in 1949, where it produced lumber, pulp, paper, plywood, and particleboard, and also launched operations at **North Bend** and **Coos Bay** in the 1940s. The company purchased Portland-based Willamette Industries in 2002. The company has substantial timberland holdings and other wood-products-related operations in Oregon.

➤ **wheat** One of the very first crops brought to the Oregon Country was wheat, which was planted at **Fort Vancouver** in the 1820s. By the 1830s, wheat was being grown on **French Prairie** and on the **Tualatin Plains**. Homeseeking emigrants often planted wheat within a few weeks of establishing a land claim. By 1846, more than 160,000 bushels of wheat were grown annually, and wheat was accepted as legal tender in a cash-starved society. The California gold rush provided an export market for wheat for a few years, most of which was grown in the Willamette Valley. Andrew Kilgore was one of the first to try growing wheat on the "dry side," planting wheat in Umatilla County in 1863; wheat production rapidly expanded on the Columbia Plateau, contributing to the stream of wheat from eastern Washington state, Montana, and the Dakotas that flowed to Portland after the completion of the **Northern Pacific Railway** in 1883. Wheat made

Portland a major port city, with shipments for Liverpool and other European markets and for Asian ports. In the first decades of the twentieth century, eastern Oregon wheat fields were harvested using massive combine harvesters pulled by teams of up to sixteen horses. Wheat has remained a significant crop in Oregon throughout the twentieth century, and has even returned to the Willamette Valley to some extent.

Small water-powered grist and flour mills were once common in the Willamette Valley and in other wheat-growing areas, producing flour but also processing corn, barley, and other grains for feed. Mills such as those at **Mulino** and other small towns were strictly local (although the Mulino mill sent flour to California during the gold rush times of shortage in the 1850s). By the 1920s, most of the small mills had closed or ground only animal feed, leaving major flour mills only in Portland and one in Astoria. These too have since closed, the last being Centennial Mills in Portland, which closed in 2000. Small

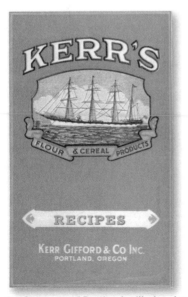

Kerr Gifford & Company of Portland milled and exported flour and other grain products. The ship logo symbolizes their worldwide trade. The recipe booklet, issued in 1921, advertises several types of wheat flours as well as wheat flakes and farina wheat cereal. Author's collection.

specialty mills such as Pendleton Flour still produce flour; the Butte Creek Mill in Eagle Point still grinds flour with water power as it has since the 1870s, and the Boston or Thompson's Mill near Shedd, now a state heritage park, preserves the state's oldest water-powered flour mill.

Wheatland Wheatland in Yamhill County began as a ferry landing, sited in a landscape that was characterized by fields of wheat as early as the 1840s. Daniel Matheny purchased a land claim there in 1844 and began the ferry service. A post office opened in 1867. As river transportation developed in the 1850s and 1860s, warehouses for grain and general merchandise were erected, along with a gristmill and two hotels. But railroad construction in the 1870s and 1880s nipped Wheatland's modest prosperity, and river traffic declined dramatically. The post office closed in 1903, and by 1915, some eighty-five people were reported to live in the vicinity, engaged in "fruit growing, general farming and hop raising." Peaches were planted in the early 1900s and are still grown there a century later. The Wheatland ferry still crosses the Willamette River here. *See also* **ferries**.

► **Wheeler** This Tillamook County town on Nehalem Bay developed around sawmill operations that date from the late nineteenth century. The community of Vosburg preceded Wheeler in the 1900s, and Coleman H. Wheeler built a major mill in 1910. The Wheeler post office opened in 1910, shortly before the completion of the Pacific Railroad & Navigation Company railroad line from Portland. The Wheeler Lumber Company mill was enlarged in 1913, and Wheeler was incorporated in 1914. In 1915, a promotional publication gave the town's population as 150, with "lumbering, salmon fishing, dairying and general farming" being its economic engines. Wheeler then had a sawmill, a salmon cannery, a weekly newspaper (the *Reporter*, founded in 1915), and a bank.

The mill of the Wheeler Lumber Company at Wheeler, capable of producing 150,000 board feet of finished lumber daily. The photograph probably dates from the 1920s. Oregon Historical Society, OrHi 106085.

Wheeler also had Dr. Harvey Earl Rinehart, who had come to Wheeler with his bride Ella in 1913, a new graduate of the University of Oregon Medical School. Dr. Rinehart established the Rinehart Clinic in 1920, which specialized in treating arthritis. By the 1950s his son and daughter-in-law, Drs. Robert E. and Dorothy White Rinehard, had joined the clinic. The establishment of Medicare and other changes in the medical system caused the clinic to change focus and decline later in the century. In the 1990s, it was revived as a nonprofit rural health clinic; the medical director since 1992 was Dr. Harry H. Rinehart, grandson of the founding physician. Wheeler's population in 2007 was estimated at 445.

Wheeler County Created in 1899, Wheeler County was formed from parts of Grant, Gilliam, and Crook Counties. There have been no boundary changes since 1899; the area is 1,713 square miles. Henry Wheeler operated the first stage line through the county, and it is named for him. The town of **Fossil** was named the temporary county seat in 1899, and in 1900 an election was held to determine the permanent seat of government. Fossil won out over the rival towns of **Spray** and the now-vanished Twickenham. An imposing courthouse was erected in Fossil in 1902, and still serves in that capacity. The area now comprising Wheeler County was part of the historical spring and summer gathering areas of the **Sahaptin Indians**, whose annual rounds included gathering a variety of roots.

Wheeler County's population in 1900 was 2,443. The county was described in 1915 as "mountainous, deeply seamed with canyons"; there were then some 450 miles of public roads in the county, ten miles of which were improved with gravel. No railroad came until 1929, when the Condon, Kinzua, and Southern Railroad built south from Condon to the new **company town** of Kinzua, where a lumber mill provided traffic for the railroad. The mill, the county's major employer for years, operated until 1976, when it and the railroad were abandoned. The town was demolished by 1979, although a small golf course occupies part of the townsite. Otherwise, the county's economic base has been primarily agricultural, with livestock raising being a prime occupation. The John Day Fossil Beds National Monument has become a tourist destination. Wheeler County's population in 2007 was estimated at 1,570.

Whidden, William Marcy (1857–1929) Born in Boston, William Whidden graduated in 1877 from the Massachusetts Institute of Technology and then spent four years studying architecture at the famed École des Beaux Arts in Paris. He stepped directly into the New York City offices of McKim, Mead & White, perhaps the most august of the city's architectural firms. At their behest Whidden came to Portland and the Pacific Northwest in 1881–82 to consult on projects for **Henry Villard** and his **Northern Pacific Railroad**. In 1883, he returned to Portland to supervise construction of the Tacoma Hotel and the similar Portland Hotel, but the collapse of Villard's finances stalled the projects; meanwhile, he married Alice McLoughlin Weygant in Portland. After a short term back in Boston, Whidden again came to Portland in 1888 to supervise the construction of the Portland Hotel for a group of local investors. He designed **Cloud Cap Inn** in 1889, the same year that his Boston colleague **Ion Lewis** came for a visit and stayed; they formed the partnership of Whidden & Lewis, which became the leading architectural firm in the city for the next two decades, noted for their commercial and office buildings, and their residences for the well-to-do. Among their notable projects were Portland City Hall (1895), the Forestry Building at the **Lewis and Clark Centennial Exposition**, the Imperial Hotel (1910; later Hotel Lucia), and the Multnomah County Courthouse (1914), and houses for Richard and Bertha Koehler (1905) and Winslow B. Ayer (1905).

Their protégé and successor to the mantle of "society" architects in Portland was **A. E. Doyle**.

> Marlitt, Richard. *Matters of Proportion: The Portland Residential Architecture of Whidden & Lewis*. Portland, Oregon: Oregon Historical Society Press, 1989.

Whitcomb, Lot *see Lot Whitcomb*; **Milwaukie**

► **White, Minor Martin** (1908–1976) Born and raised in Minnesota, Minor White graduated from the University of Minnesota in 1933 with a major in botany and a minor in poetry; he also studied photography. In 1937, he picked up a 35mm camera and went west; he found work as a night clerk at a cheap Portland hotel. White lived at the YMCA and spent

A photograph of Minor White taken by Lawrence Smith, a member of the camera club that White formed at the Portland YMCA. The photograph was snapped in the spring of 1938 along the Clackamas River. White's camera is a Kodak Duo-620 Series II, a medium format folding camera that was introduced to the market in June 1937.
Historic Photo Archive, 0001-A64 (00299).

his available time photographing and teaching, and in 1938 began working with the **Works Progress Administration** as a photographer. He shot an extensive series of photographs of nineteenth-century buildings with cast-iron façades along the Portland waterfront, capturing many shortly before or during their demolition. In 1940, White went to eastern Oregon to teach at the WPA art center at La Grande, returning to Portland in 1941. The **Portland Art Museum** presented his recent work in a one-man show in 1942 and also commissioned him to photograph two of the city's Victorian-era houses.

White served in military intelligence during World War II, and later enjoyed a distinguished career as a photographer and a teacher and historian of photography. He was a co-founder of the magazine *Aperture* in 1952 with Ansel Adams and others, and edited it until 1975. *See also* **Pioneer Courthouse Square**.

> DeWolfe, Fred. *Heritage Lost: Two Grand Portland Houses through the Lens of Minor White.* Portland, Oregon: Oregon Historical Society Press in collaboration with the Portland Art Museum, 1995.

White City After World War II, the site of **Camp White** in Jackson County was converted to industrial purposes under the name White City, although it is not an incorporated city. The industries, including lumber products firms and chemical plants, are served by a railroad line that was built to serve Camp White. There were few residences in the area until the 1970s, but residential population has increased rapidly since then.

Whiteley, Opal (1897–1991) Opal was born in Washington state, and lived briefly as a child in the Oregon logging town of Wendling. The family moved near her grandparents' farm on the **Row River** in Lane County when Opal Whitely was five years of age. A precocious child, she took to writing a diary, and was known for her love of nature and an ethe-

real personality. Opal taught nature classes and became involved in Junior Christian Endeavor, an evangelizing youth group, and in 1918 she self published *The Fairyland Around Us*, a nature book for young people. Opal became an overnight American literary sensation in 1920 when *The Story of Opal: The Journal of an Understanding Heart* was published in *Atlantic Monthly* and then issued as a book. The manuscript was based on her childhood diaries, endowed with a fine and loving look at the natural and human world of Mosby Creek and the Row River, the Walden school and her grandparents' house. It is a fantasy world with a horse named William Shakespeare, fairies and princesses, the Man Who Wears Gray Neckties and is Kind to Mice, and a fir tree named Raymond of Toulouse. First hailed as a masterpiece, *The Story of Opal* was soon attacked as something a child could not have created, as a literary fraud. Opal proclaimed that she was really a French princess, and she left Oregon for France and then India; and then she disappeared. She emerged to public view in 1948 in London, unable to care for herself, surrounded by books. She spent the remainder of her life in an institution. Her books had a revival in the 1990s, and one can visit **Cottage Grove** at the junction of the Row and the Willamette Rivers, and take a tour from there of the rural countryside where Opal lived and learned and taught.

white oak *see* **oak**

white pine *see* **pine**

White Stag In 1906, Max and Leonard Hirsch (affiliated with **Meier & Frank**) bought the Willamette Tent & Awning Company. They took on Harry Weis of Willamette Tent and renamed the company Hirsch-Weis Canvas Productions, makers of sails, tarpaulins, and outdoor wear. In 1929, Max's son Harold S. Hirsch (1909–1990) began a line of outdoor apparel which evolved in the 1930s into White

Stag (in German, Weis is white, Hirsch is deer or stag), which soon found favor among the adherents of a newly developing sport, **skiing**. According to historian Stan Cohen, "a button-front ski suit made in 1941" was much favored by women working in the wartime shipyards and aircraft factories. Harold Hirsch built the White Stag Manufacturing Company into an international sportswear firm and was a supporter of higher education and a civic leader. In 1940, a prominent neon sign based on an outline map of Oregon was erected by locally produced White Satin sugar, overlooking the Burnside Bridge. The sign was modified in 1959 to advertise White Stag Sportswear, with the company's leaping stag at the top of the sign. The sign was altered again in 1997, when the White Stag name was replaced by that of Made in Oregon, but the leaping stag was retained. For some years, the stag has sported a red nose during the Christmas season. The White Stag brand was sold to Wal-Mart in 2003.

Whitman, Marcus (1802–1847) and **Narcissa Whitman** (1808–1847) Marcus Whitman was born in New York state and trained and practiced as a physician; he also became an elder in the Presbyterian church and a volunteer with the American Board of Commissions for Foreign Missions. He sought a missionary position, and traveled to the Oregon Country in 1835 in search of potential mission sites. Through the American Board he met Narcissa Prentiss, also born in New York, who had yearned for missionary work since the age of sixteen. The two married, and in 1836 the Whitmans joined another young missionary couple, the Rev. Henry Spalding and his wife Eliza, and William H. Gray for a westward trek that brought them to the Walla Walla River. Here the Whitmans settled at Waiilatpu, intending to bring Christianity to the **Cayuse Indians**. It was a difficult assignment, made harder by cultural differences and the susceptibility of the Indians to introduced diseases. The American Board, unimpressed with the results of

the effort, decided to close the mission in 1842; Whitman went east to plead for continuation, and made his case. He came back to Waiilatpu with the **Great Migration** of 1843. When an epidemic of measles killed many Cayuse children, while most white children recovered, Dr. Whitman's standing became precarious. A group of Cayuse attacked the mission on November 29, 1847, killed the Whitmans and twelve other whites, burned the buildings, and took hostage fifty-three women and children. The event set off the **Cayuse War** and provided ample material for the creation of several grand legends of early Oregon history, such as that "Whitman saved Oregon" from British dominion. The Whitmans are writ large in the Oregon Country: Whitman College, the Whitman Mission National Historic Site, the major hotel in Walla Walla, a national forest, a Washington county, and a Portland school all commemorate an adventurous and committed couple. Marcus Whitman represents Washington state in the National Statuary Hall.

Drury, Clifford Merrill. *Marcus and Narcissa Whitman, and the Opening of Old Oregon.* Glendale, California: A. H. Clark Company, 1973.

wigwam burner The term "wigwam burner" describes the shape of a particular type of structure used at sawmills and other wood-products plants to burn waste; a more general term is waste burner or refuse burner. Constructed of sheet metal, the cone- or tepee-shaped burners were topped with a screen and usually were from thirty to fifty or more feet tall. There were also straight-sided or silo burners, though common speech often rendered them wigwams as well. From the early 1900s into the 1970s, wigwam burners were a signature feature of the timber industry, used to burn the bark, sawdust, knots, and trimmings. Wigwam burners suffered a quick demise with the implementation of federal and state air pollution regulations and the development of other ways to utilize wood waste, such as the manufacture of toilet tissue, cardboard, and bark mulch. *See also* **Hines; Long Creek**.

Wilkes Exploring Expedition The United States Exploring Expedition was a scientific exploring and surveying venture that was conducted in the Pacific Ocean between 1838 and 1842 under the command of Lt. Charles Wilkes (1788–1877) of the U.S. Navy. The party explored the West Coast of the United States in 1841, including ascending the Columbia River and sending an overland party to California via the **California-Oregon Trail**. One of the expedition's artists, Alfred T. Agate (1812–1846), made drawings depicting Astoria, the longhouses of the **Chinook Indians**, and the wreck of one of the expedition's vessels, the *Peacock*, at the mouth of the Columbia River. No lives were lost, but the ship gave its name to the sandbar on which she foundered, Peacock Spit. The detailed Wilkes maps of the Ore-gon Country proved valuable as negotiations went on between Great Britain and the United States over the sovereignty of the region.

Barkan, Frances B. *The Wilkes Expedition: Puget Sound and the Oregon Country*. Olympia, Washington: Washington State Capital Museum, 1987.

➤ **Willamette Falls** The falls of the Willamette River at Oregon City are about forty feet in height, and in volume of water are the largest in the Pacific Northwest, since the silencing of **Celilo Falls** in 1957. The river is constricted between basalt cliffs, and the horseshoe-shaped falls cascade over a basalt shelf. The falls were a significant Native fishing site where **salmon** and **lamprey** were easily caught as they ascended the falls to spawn. Engineering changes to stabilize the falls for industrial use destroyed much of those runs, although a fish ladder

WILLAMETTE FALLS

Native men are pictured fishing with dip nets at Willamette Falls in an engraving prepared from a sketch done in 1841 by Joseph Drayton, an artist with the Wilkes Exploring Expedition. University of Washington Libraries, Special Collections, NA3995.

was implemented in 1882, and rebuilt in 1971. **John McLoughlin** of the **Hudson's Bay Company** was the first to make industrial use of the waterpower from the falls, building a sawmill and gristmill there in 1829. The **papermaking industry** in Oregon had its beginnings here in 1866. In 1888, the Willamette Falls Electric Company was established to generate hydroelectric power; electricity was transmitted fourteen miles to Portland on June 3, 1889, the first successful long-distance transmission of electrical power in the nation. Willamette Falls effectively blocked navigation from the upper Willamette River, requiring portages for goods and passengers until the opening of the Willamette Falls Locks in 1873. The system has four locks, built of wood and operated, since 1915, by the U.S. Army Corps of Engineers; it is the nation's oldest operating multiple-lift navigation canal. The decline and virtual disappearance of commercial navigation on the Willamette put the continued operation of the locks in jeopardy by 2008, despite use by pleasure craft. The locks were placed on the National Register of Historic Places in 1974.

► **Willamette Meteorite** This is the largest meteorite to have been found in the United States, having been "discovered" in 1902, although it was known to local Indians. Its contentious history has included competing ownership claims (it was removed from private property to adjoining private property), display as a curiosity at the **Lewis and Clark Centennial Exposition** in 1905, having pieces ignominiously chopped from it, and being sold to Mrs. William E. Dodge, who gave it to the American Museum of Natural History—where it has resided since 1906. The meteorite, severely weathered, weighs about fifteen and a half tons; its composition is about 91 percent iron and 8 percent nickel. The **Confederated Tribes of Grand Ronde** have an agreement with the museum permitting annual access to the meteorite for sacred purposes.

Willamette Mission The first site for the Methodist Indian mission established in 1834 by **Jason Lee** was on the Willamette River near the later site of **Wheatland**. The mission moved to Salem in 1840. The original site is now a state park; one of its features is the representation of the original mission buildings in framed outline form, termed "ghost structures." The Wheatland ferry landing is included in the park.

Willamette River A tributary of the Columbia River, the Willamette River is about 185 miles in length, flowing north between the Coast Range and the Cascade Range to its confluence with the Columbia near Portland. The North and Middle Forks of the Willamette rise in the Cascade Range of Lane County, flowing northwesterly to a point near Eugene, where the Coast Fork joins the stream. The Coast Fork rises in the hills of the Calapooya Divide south of Cottage Grove. From Eugene north, the

The Willamette Meteorite is posed in a warehouse prior to its display at the Lewis and Clark Centennial Exposition in 1905. University of Washington Libraries, Special Collections, UW27642z.

river once followed a meandering, often-changing course through the wide valley. From the Cascade Range flow several rapid-flowing tributaries: the McKenzie, Santiam, Calapooia, Clackamas, and Molalla Rivers. Flowing east from the Coast Range are shorter, slower streams such as the Long Tom, Marys, Luckiamute, Yamhill, and Tualatin Rivers.

The valley between Eugene and Oregon City is extremely fertile, the homeland of the **Kalapuyan Indians**. This was the proverbial Eden to those **pioneers** of the 1840s and 1850s who sought a farmstead, and its productivity and healthful climate were the lures that set them on their way over the **Oregon Trail**. The Willamette was navigable by river steamboats during normal water levels as far upstream as Corvallis, and on occasion to Harrisburg, Eugene, and even Springfield. Steamboats began running on the river in 1850, with the launching of the *Lot Whitcomb*. The obstruction at **Willamette Falls** was dealt with by portages until the opening of the Willamette Falls Locks in 1873, about the time that river transportation began to decline due to the construction of paralleling railroads. The Willamette has long been subject to winter and spring **floods**; the construction of dams on several tributaries after World War II reduced their severity. Initially, **ferries**, three of which remain in operation, were used to cross the main channel of the Willamette; beginning in the 1880s, **bridges** were built to span the stream. The decline of commercial river traffic by the 1920s left several once-thriving steamboat-landing communities to fade into oblivion.

Corning, Howard McKinley. *Willamette Landings*. 3rd ed., with a new introduction by Robin Cody. Portland, Oregon: Oregon Historical Society, 2004.

Willamette Stone The Willamette Stone marks the nexus of official government land surveying of the Oregon Country. It was initially a cedar stake, driven by the first surveyor general of Oregon, John B. Preston, on June 4, 1851. The stone marks the Willamette Meridian, the north-south survey line, and the Base Line, the east-west line. The stone was installed July 25, 1888, and is located in a small state park located off SW Skyline Boulevard, about four miles from downtown Portland.

Willamette University By some accounts the oldest higher education institution in the West, Willamette University in Salem can trace its history to an academy established by **Jason Lee** in 1842. It was associated with the Methodist Church. The name Wallamet University was adopted in 1853. Willamette was a co-educational institution from its inception, and it established the first school of medicine in Oregon in 1866 (later merged with the University of Oregon program). The region's first law school was opened in 1883, and Willamette has made the study of law one of its specialties. Willamette had an enrollment of 2,642 students in 2005.

Willamette Valley *see* **Willamette River**

Willamette Valley Project *see* **Detroit Dam; floods; Lowell**

Willamina A rural post office named Willamina was established near Willamina Creek and the South Yamhill River in 1855; it moved around a bit as the postmasters changed, and in 1866 ended up at the site of **Sheridan**; so the name was changed to Sheridan. In 1878, another post office near Willamina Creek was created, again named Willamina; this one persisted. The town was incorporated in 1903, and in 1907, a railroad line was extended from Sheridan to Willamina, primarily to serve the brick and tile works that were established there. Willamina's population in the 1910 census was 376. In 1915, the town was noted as having a factory that made wood handles for tools and that it was located in a countryside where general farming, fruit growing, dairying, and stock raising were carried on. The brick and tile factory was described as one of the most important in the Pacific Northwest, producing high-grade face brick and terra cotta. The brick works retained its importance and was in production until it closed in 1974; it was the last major brick works in the state. Willamina's population grew to 1,082 by 1950 and 1,749 in 1980. The estimated population in 2007 was 1,880.

Williamson River The Williamson River and its tributary, Sprague River, lie in Klamath County, draining the highlands north and east of **Klamath Lake**. The Williamson is about seventy-five miles in length; the two rivers provide more than half of the water flowing into Klamath Lake. The Williamson has been used for irrigation in the ranching areas at the north end of the lake; some of this network is being removed and diked lands returned to natural delta area as bird habitat.

▶ **Wilsonville** Situated on the Willamette River in Clackamas County, Wilsonville was a rural post office established in 1880 near Boones Ferry. Jesse V. Boone, a great grandson of Daniel Boone, established the ferry crossing about 1847; Boones Ferry Road extends from Portland south beyond Woodburn. In 1908, the **Oregon Electric Railroad** opened from Portland to Salem through Wilsonville, with a half-mile-long steel bridge over the Willamette, bringing suburban commuter train service to the town. By 1915, Wilsonville was described by the Oregon Almanac as a small center of "lumbering, logging, general farming, fruit and berry growing, dairying, stock and poultry raising." The trains were discontinued in the early 1930s, and the town languished on a country road. The construction of **Interstate 5** in the 1950s put it back on an artery of commerce; the ferry was discontinued in 1954,

A wagon and a team of horses are shown approaching the west bank of the Willamette River aboard Boone's Ferry. The town of Wilsonville is located up the hill behind the point where the photographer was standing when he took this picture about 1910. Three of the once-numerous ferries that crossed the Willamette are still in service; this one was replaced by a bridge in 1954. Wesley Andrews photograph. Steven Dotterer collection.

replaced by the freeway bridge, now named the Boone Bridge. Wilsonville was incorporated in 1969; its population in the 1970 census was 1,001. That figure jumped to 7,106 in 1990, 13,991 in 2000, and an estimated 17,360 in 2007. A commuter train link to Tigard and Beaverton opened in 2008.

wine and wine making In his *History of Southern Oregon* (1884) A. G. Walling stated, apropos of the valley of the Rogue River, that

> enthusiastic wine-drinkers and virtuosos, have foreseen a time when all the hillsides would be covered with vineyards, and when an over-flowing population, appeased of their own beverage, should be enjoying life in the shade of the vines. Soberly speaking, they have predicted that the laurels of France, Germany, and every foreign wine-producing country, as well as California, would be wrested from them and worn by the lovely vale of the Rogue River, which will then be the most abundant producer of the best of wines.

In the early 1880s, Raphael Morat (1835–1898) and J. N. T. Miller (1826–1900) were among several growers of grapes and producers of wine near **Jacksonville**, as was **Peter Britt**, the town photographer and horticulturist, who produced wine under the label Valley View Vineyard.

Grape growing and wine making took place also in the Willamette and Umpqua Valleys, but markets were very limited. In 1915, as Oregon was on the verge of statewide **prohibition**, it was reported that in Wasco County grape culture had made great progress in the vicinity of The Dalles, where

> the semi-tropical varieties are grown, and in this northern latitude attain a superior flavor similar to that of the same varieties in France, Spain, Northern Italy, and along the Rhine, a flavor far superior to that of California grapes. It is predicted that the low altitude hillsides along and near the Columbia River will some day be covered with vineyards.

In the 1910s and 1920s, **Italian** immigrant families in Portland were said to pool their funds to buy California grapes by the railroad carload to produce homemade wine. During prohibition years, **loganberries** were legendarily favored for the production of homemade wine in Oregon; commercially, a small bit of sacramental wine was produced.

In 1933, with prohibition over, Ron Honeyman and John Wood established the Honeywood Winery in Salem; the company alleges that there is a story behind the name of the winery, but denies that Honeywood is created from the founders' names. Honeywood made fruit cordials, liqueurs, and wines from the likes of loganberries, and is still in business. In 1961, Richard Sommer began planting grape vines at Hillcrest in Douglas County; David Lett of Eyrie Vineyards planted the first pinot noir grapes in 1965; Richard Ponzi began his vineyard in Washington County in 1969. It was only a short time until 1976, when Lett's Oregon pinot noir made industry news for its quality. From these and other viticultural pioneers, Oregon has grown a wine industry—a cottage industry for the most part, for none of the more than three hundred wineries is a mass production facility. Only thirty-five acres were planted in wine grapes in 1970; by 2006, the figure was more than 15,000 acres.

Blosser, Susan Sokol. *At Home in the Vineyard: Cultivating a Winery, an Industry, and a Life.* Berkeley: University of California Press, 2006.

Pintarich, Paul. *The Boys up North: Dick Erath and the Early Oregon Winemakers.* Portland, Oregon: Wyatt Group, 1997.

Winnemucca, Sarah (1844?–1891) Born in northern Nevada into the family of a **Northern Paiute Indian** leader named Winnemucca, or Poito, Sarah Winnemucca spent part of her childhood with the family of William Ormsby, where she learned English and first became a woman of two worlds. Much of her life was spent trying to connect the two. William Ormsby died in 1860 in the Pyramid Lake

War between whites and Paiutes. The establishment of the Malheur Reservation in Oregon in 1873 promised to alleviate some of the conditions, and Sarah Winnemucca taught there and acted as an interpreter. The reservation was dissolved in the early 1880s as the **Bannock War** developed, in which Winnemucca served as an Army interpreter. In the late 1870s, Winnemucca began to lecture in California and Nevada about the plight of the Paiutes; while doing this, she met and married Lewis H. Hopkins, an employee of the Indian Department. They traveled east, with Sarah giving hundreds of lectures; in Boston, the Peabody sisters sponsored her and later helped her to turn her talks into her book, *Life among the Piutes: Their Wrongs and Claims* (1883). Winnemucca returned to Nevada and established a school for Indian children; the passage of the Dawes Act in 1887 that sent Indian children to boarding schools such as that at **Chemawa**, crippled her school, which promoted an Indian lifestyle. She died in Idaho of tuberculosis.

Zanjani, Sally Springmeyer. *Sarah Winnemucca.* Lincoln: University of Nebraska Press, 2001.

Winnemucca-to-the-Sea Highway One of the odder named highways in the state is this route that begins at Winnemucca (population in 2000: 7,174) in northern Nevada, traverses the basin-and-range topography of southeastern Oregon, and crosses the Cascade Range and the Coast Range Mountains to terminate at Crescent City, California (population in 2000: 4,006). Distance: 493 miles, via Denio, Lakeview, Klamath Falls, Medford, and Grants Pass. The route was promoted in the 1950s as a direct route from the Midwest to the Pacific shore.

Winston Winston's beginnings were as a rural post office named Winstons in Douglas County, from 1893 to 1903. As Winston, the post office was re-established in 1948, and the community was incorporated in 1953; its population in 1957 was 2,490.

Located off the I-5 freeway, Winston became the site of a private zoo, Wildlife Safari, in 1972; this has since become a nonprofit educational institution. Its population in 2007 was about 5,780.

Wishram Indians *see* **Wasco and Wishram Indians**

Wobblies *see* **Industrial Workers of the World (IWW)**

► **Wolf Creek** An unincorporated community in northern Josephine County, Wolf Creek was located on the **California-Oregon Trail**. By the early 1850s, Six Bit House (a "bit" is twenty-five cents) catered to travelers in the area, and regular stagecoach service began in 1860. The Wolf Creek Inn was built about 1883, just at the time the railroad came through and dispatched the stagecoach. However, the hotel enterprise continued, and under the name Wolf Creek Tavern it was a popular stop along the **Pacific Highway** for many decades; additional rooms were added in the 1920s. Jack London reputedly finished his manuscript for *Valley of the Moon* at the Wolf Creek Tavern, and Clark Gable was once a guest. By the 1910s, residents of Wolf Creek grew some fruit, farmed, and raised poultry. The construction of **Interstate 5** took Wolf Creek off the main travel path. Beginning in the 1960s, several countercultural communal groups found a congenial location in the Wolf Creek area. The combination of a back-to-the-land impulse and the rise of feminist and queer philosophies brought to Wolf Creek groups such as Magdalene Farm, a "Maoist sissy" commune. It was founded in the 1970s; in 1987, the farm became the property of Nomenus, which created a spiritual retreat for Radical Faeries. The state of Oregon acquired the Wolf Creek Tavern in the 1970s and restored it as an inn and restaurant. Just off the I-5 freeway, the inn is on the National Register of Historic Places.

Zan 783

Built in 1857
Wolf Creek Tavern
Wolf Creek, Oregon

Despite the caption on this postcard view, the inn at Wolf Creek was built about 1883, not 1857. The photograph was taken circa 1940, and shows the addition that was built onto the inn in the 1920s; behind that is the public school. Zan Stark photograph. Steven Dotterrer collection.

Wolf Creek Highway *see* **Sunset Highway**

Wolf Meetings These meetings were held in 1843, ostensibly to resolve the question of how to deal with predatory wolves in the Willamette Valley. The Wolf Meetings turned out to be the culmination of discussions held since 1841 that had dealt with the need for a code of laws, and were prompted by the estate problems after the death of **Ewing Young**. The first Wolf Meeting was held in Salem, and the second at the home of Joseph Gervais on **French Prairie** (where bounties on wolves were established); the third meeting at **Champoeg** in effect led to the formation of the **provisional government** of 1843.

▶ **Wood, Charles Erskine Scott** (1852–1944) C. E. S. Wood was a dashing Army lieutenant who came to hate war, a corporate attorney who delighted in representing anarchists, a poet and an

artist. Born in Pennsylvania, Wood came to Vancouver Barracks after his 1874 graduation from West Point. His participation in the **Nez Perce** War in 1877 led him to meet Chief Joseph and record his surrender speech; **Joseph** became a lifelong friend. Admitted to the Oregon bar in 1884, Wood left the Army and practiced corporate law in Portland, building up a profitable practice that enabled him to engage his many other interests, especially writing and painting. His paean to the Oregon landscape, *The Poet in the Desert*, was published in 1915. Although Wood left Oregon for California after World War I, a most visible legacy is carved into the base of the **Skidmore Fountain**, itself sculpted by his friend Olin Warner: "Good citizens are the riches of a city." Wood himself was one of this city's great treasures. His daughter, **Nan Wood Honeyman**, was Oregon's first woman representative in Congress.

Wood, Charles Erskine Scott. *Wood Works: the*

Life and Writings of Charles Erskine Scott Wood. Ed. Edwin Bingham and Tim Barnes. Corvallis: Oregon State University Press, 1997.

Woodburn Located on French Prairie, this farming supply center was platted by J. A. Settlemier in 1871 with an orientation to the main line of the Oregon & California Railroad, which built south from Portland in 1870. The Woodburn post office opened the same year. In 1880, Woodburn became a railroad junction point with a branch line heading south along the east side of the Willamette Valley. The community was incorporated in 1889 and was

Poet and lawyer, soldier and rake, C. E. S. Wood is pictured here with William Hanley at the dedication of a monument to John S. Devine, early Harney County cattleman. The marker was erected by the Good Roads Club at Devine Canyon north of Burns on July 22, 1928. R. W. Heck photograph. Historic Photo Archive, 9336-AB96.

reported in the 1890 census with a population of 405. The Settlemier nursery and the production of fruit, berries and vegetables anchored the local economy.

By 1915, diversified farming still held sway, including dairy production and poultry raising, and growing onions, hops, and potatoes. The MacLaren School for Boys—later the MacLaren Youth Correctional Facility—has been in Woodburn since 1926, when it was founded as the Oregon State Training School. After the Pacific Highway was rerouted to the east of the downtown in the 1940s, a second business district developed along the new road. Food processing—canning and freezing—continued to grow in importance.

The post–World War II period saw a substantial growth in the population of Mexican immigrants, drawn by work opportunities in nurseries, berry cultivation, and other agricultural pursuits. In the 1960s, Woodburn became the new home of a group of Russian religious refugees, known as **Old Believers**. The opening in 1954 of the I-5 freeway to the west of the town led to the development in the 1960s of the adjacent Woodburn Senior Estates, a housing development and golf course for retirees. The freeway prompted yet another retail cluster, capped by Woodburn Company Stores, a brand-name outlet mall that opened in the 1980s. Woodburn's population in 1950 was 2,395; in 1990, 13,404; in 2007, it was estimated at 22,875.

wood products industry Dimensional lumber for building construction was not the only product of the **logging and lumbering** industry. In the nineteenth century and into the twentieth century, other wood products included ship's masts; **shipbuilding** timbers; timber for railroad ties, bridge trusses, and joists and beams; shingles and shakes; fence posts; poles for telephone, telegraph, and electrical transmission lines; wood for ornamental trim and gutters, doors, and window surrounds; and wood for furniture making. By the mid-twentieth century, driven in part by the disappearance of **old-growth timber**, the industry developed new wood products such as particleboard, laminated wood beams, and plywood. During and after World War II, plywood boomed as a building material; historian Gail Wells noted that "More than seventy plywood plants opened their doors in Oregon between 1940 and 1960, including plants in Astoria, Garibaldi, Tillamook, Gardiner, Reedsport, North Bend, Coos Bay, Coquille, Port Orford, Gold Beach, and Brookings." The downturn in logging and lumbering since the 1980s affected these products as well as lumber. Environmental issues, exemplified by the **spotted owl** but including questions about forest management, **forest fires**, and overharvesting, dampened the industry into the 2000s.

Woodstock neighborhood, Portland This was one of several Portland real estate subdivisions that was platted in the later nineteenth century with names derived from the Waverley novels of Sir Walter Scott (1771–1832), which had a revived popularity at the time. The Woodstock plat was laid out in 1890 on a ridge overlooking the city to the northwest. Located several miles from downtown, Woodstock was linked to it by a new electric streetcar line, which traversed active farmland and damp ravines on its route. A post office named Woodstock opened in 1891 and operated until 1912, by which time the area was within the city limits. The business district also catered to **Reed College** and the **Eastmoreland neighborhood** to the west, both of which developed after 1910.

Wood Village Wood Village in eastern Multnomah County was built in the 1950s to house workers for an aluminum manufacturing plant, which closed in 2001. Wood Village was incorporated in 1951, and a 1957 census reported a population of 815. By 1970, the population was 1,553, in 1990, 2,814. The estimate in 2007 was 3,100.

woolen industry Although Oregon's first woolen mill opened in Salem in 1857, the early history of the woolen industry in large part revolved around Thomas L. Kay (1837–1900). Kay was an English immigrant trained in the industry; he came to Oregon in 1863 and helped to found and run the state's second woolen mill at **Brownsville**. He subsequently worked at mills in Ellendale (near Dallas), Ashland and Salem, finally establishing the Thomas Kay Woolen Mills in Salem in 1889. Kay and his son, Thomas B. Kay, turned out woolen cloth for suits and other clothing, flannel, cashmere, and blankets; the factory operated until 1962. The Kay mill was sold in 1965 and became the Mission Mill Museum. Kay's daughter married C. P. Bishop, whose family developed the **Pendleton Woolen Mills**, which specialized in blankets for the Indian market and in the 1940s branched into sportswear design and manufacture.

> Lomax, Alfred L. *Pioneer Woolen Mills in Oregon; History of Wool and the Woolen Textile Industry in Oregon, 1811–1875*. Portland, Oregon: Binfords & Mort, 1941.
>
> Lomax, Alfred L. *Later Woolen Mills in Oregon: A History of the Woolen Mills which Followed the Pioneer Mills*. Portland, Oregon: Binfords & Mort, 1974.

Works Progress Administration (WPA) Created by President Franklin D. Roosevelt in 1935, the WPA was a federal Depression-era program to provide jobs and training to the unemployed. It became the Work Projects Administration in 1939, and in 1940 shifted to vocational training before it was terminated in 1943. In Oregon, the WPA was instrumental in a large number of highly visible projects, ranging from the construction of **Timberline Lodge** and the state capitol building in **Salem**, to compiling and writing the history and guidebook *Oregon: End of the Trail* (1940). The research for Howard McKinley Corning's *Dictionary of Oregon History* was done by the WPA. WPA artists such as

Ed Quigley painted murals in Oregon schools, post offices, and other public buildings, **Margery Hoffman Smith** supervised crafts workers at Timberline Lodge, and **Minor White** taught and photographed in Portland and La Grande. The Historic American Building Survey documented Oregon's early built environment through photographs and measured drawings.

World War I, 1914—18 The first world war affected Oregon in several ways. **Fort Stevens** was reinforced. Persons of **German** heritage experienced some harassment, and some Portland streets were given less Teutonic names. **Shipbuilding** increased vastly, at Portland and on Coos Bay and in Astoria, where wooden vessels were turned out with amazing speed. The war also brought a demand for spruce lumber; the light weight and strength of spruce made it desirable for airplane construction. The U.S. Army Signal Corps Spruce Divisions were created to get the spruce out as fast as possible. The war ended before the logging railroads and mills were completed to carry on this work, but the construction did not go to waste; the mill at **Toledo**, for example, went into private production immediately.

World War II, 1939—45 The war had numerous impacts on Oregon. Training camps such as **Camp Adair** and **Camp White** (now White City) arose instantly; **Fort Stevens** was fitted for new duties. The power generated by **Bonneville Dam** gave impetus to the establishment of an **aluminum industry** that in turn fed the construction of armaments and ships. Wartime **shipbuilding** was concentrated at Portland and at Vancouver, Washington, and workers immigrated to Oregon from the Midwest and the South, including many **blacks**. Industrialist **Henry J. Kaiser** built housing for war workers, including the city of **Vanport**. Another major impact was in the forced removal under executive order 9066 of all **Japanese** and Japanese-Americans from western Oregon. Most residents from the Willamette Valley, Portland, and the Hood River valley were sent to a camp at Minidoka, Idaho; most Japanese in the Treasure Valley area remained, since they were "inland."

Oregon was also affected by some of the few physical attacks made on the U.S. mainland. A Japanese submarine shelled the beach at Fort Stevens in the summer of 1942, without damage; later that year, the same submarine launched a seaplane that dropped bombs in southern Oregon, again without major effect. Finally, in late 1944, the Japanese launched a bizarre fleet of some 9,000 balloons over the Pacific, designed to trigger forest fires on alighting. The balloons were reported as far inland as the Dakotas, but caused little damage and no forest fires. However, in the spring of 1945 a child found one of the balloons during a family picnic near Bly, Oregon; it exploded, killing six people.

French, Chauncey Del. *Waging War on the Home Front: An Illustrated Memoir of World War II.* Portland: Oregon Cultural Heritage Commission; Corvallis, Oregon: Oregon State University Press, 2004.

Wy'east *see* **Mount Hood**

Wyeth, Nathaniel J. (1802–1856) Nathaniel Wyeth was born in Massachusetts, and he got into the ice business early in his life; he shipped ice from New England to the West Indies in the 1820s, insulated with sawdust. In 1831, Wyeth became intrigued with a plan advocated by Boston teacher Hall Jackson Kelly to send a colonizing force to the disputed **Oregon Country**. Wyeth adapted the plan, with himself in charge, and departed in 1832 with a party of twenty for Oregon, overland; only eight made it to **Fort Vancouver**—others died or deserted, and his supply ship was wrecked en route to Oregon. Wyeth returned East in 1833, and began planning another venture. In 1834, he ambitiously left Saint Louis with a party of some seventy men—Methodist missionary **Jason Lee** among them—intending to trade with the Indians and to export furs and salmon when he arrived in Oregon. Stopping midway near Pocatello, Wyeth founded Fort Hall, which later became a landmark on the **Oregon Trail** (and which Wyeth sold to the **Hudson's Bay Company (HBC)** in 1837). Arriving at Fort Vancouver in the fall, Wyeth established Fort Williams on **Sauvie Island** and tried to execute his trading plan. While he did manage to trade and fish and to ship some goods,

he was unable to compete with the powerful HBC. He returned to the East in 1836 and went back to shipping ice to the Caribbean, but some of his party remained to become early American settlers in the Oregon Country. A historical marker notes the site of Fort Williams; in Hood River County, a park and railroad station are named for him, and a post office named Wyeth operated there from 1903 to 1936.

Yachats The seaside resort of Yachats in Lincoln County is located at the mouth of the Yachats River. The region was the homeland of the Alseas, a group of **Alsean Indians** who remained in the area with the establishment of the Coast Indian Reservation in 1855. The reservation was terminated in 1875, which opened the area to white settlers. A rural post office prosaically named Ocean View operated in the vicinity from 1887 to 1893 and again from 1904 to 1912 north of the river; in 1912 it was moved to a point near the river mouth, and the name was changed to Yachats in 1916. The picturesque Little Log Church was built in 1930. The completion of the **Oregon Coast Highway** in the 1930s ended Yachats' isolation. Yachats was incorporated as a city in 1967, and the 1970 census showed it with a population of 441. The estimated population in 2007 was 765.

▶ **Yamhill** Sited in Yamhill County at the north end of the valley of the North Yamhill River, the town of Yamhill developed around the post office named North Yamhill, which opened in 1851. It was a fruitful farming area where wheat was long the most popular crop; a small town arose in the 1860s. In 1872, the Oregon Central Railroad built down the valley from Portland; the line ran a short distance east of North Yamhill town. By the 1880s, North

Yamhill was the transfer point for mail en route to Tillamook, on the Oregon Coast. Rather than use the uncertain ocean route into Tillamook Bay, the mail went by train to North Yamhill and then over the Coast Range via the Trask Wagon and Toll Road, and unusual arrangement that lasted until the completion of a direct railroad line to Tillamook in 1911. North Yamhill was platted in 1889 and incorporated in 1891; the name was changed to plain Yamhill in 1908. The noted children's author Beverly Cleary spent her early childhood on a Yamhill farm, and the Queen Anne style house where she lived stands at the edge of the town. In the early twentieth century, the Yamhill area was "primarily a grain producing section," but also grew fruit, hops, and vegetables. Lumbering, raising hogs and poultry, and dairy farming were also carried on. The 1900 census gave Yamhill a population of 254; by 1940, it reached 418, and by 1970, 516. Yamhill is located in a region where grape growing and winemaking have been increasing since the 1980s; its estimated population in 2007 was 820.

Yamhill County Formed in 1843 out of the **Yam Hill District**, Yamhill County originally extended from the Willamette River west to the Pacific, and from the Yamhill River south to the California border. Eleven other counties were eventually carved from that body of land, leaving Yamhill County with an area of 709 square miles. The first county seat was at **Lafayette**; the government moved to McMinnville in 1889. Yamhill County's population in 1870 was 5,012, and 18,285 by 1910. The area was part of the homeland of the Yamhill band of the **Kalapuyan Indians**; the 1855 treaties established the **Grand Ronde Reservation** for them, although members of other tribes were soon placed there also.

The population of Yamhill County in 1860 was 3,245; by 1880, it reached 7,945, and in 1910, 18,245. The economy has been rooted in agriculture since the 1840s; by the early 1900s, Yamhill County was noted for raising hops, prunes, filberts, and walnuts; dairying and livestock breeding were also important. A 1915 booklet said that "Gathering hoop poles from the hazelwood bushes, chittim bark and crawfishing are minor industries." Lumber became important in the 1920s in towns such as Carlton and Sheridan. The population increased to 33,484 by 1950; after World War II, suburban pressures transformed towns such as Newberg. The wine industry took a foothold in the early 1980s, and within twenty years transformed the county into the pinot noir center of the state, and grape culture has pushed aside hops and prunes. Still, the county's economy has remained agricultural, and it produces dairy products, nursery stock, wheat, and barley; logging and lumbering have also retained importance. Yamhill County's population reached 65,551 in 1990, and in 2007 was estimated at 93,085.

Yam Hill District The Yam Hill, or Yamhill, District was one of the original districts (counties) established in 1843 by the **provisional government**. It encompassed all the land west of the Willamette River to the Pacific Ocean, and south of the Yamhill River to California. The other districts were the **Champooick District**, the **Clackamas District**, and the **Twality District**.

The farming community of Yamhill, which had been known as North Yamhill until just recently, is pictured in 1911 by Southern Pacific Company photographer George M. Weister. Oregon Historical Society, OrHi 50505.

Yamhill Historic District, Portland A concentration of nineteenth-century commercial buildings in the vicinity of SW Second Avenue and Yamhill Street in Portland was placed on the National Register of Historic Places in 1976. The district includes a number of two- and three-story Italianate-style store and office buildings, including a number with cast-iron façades, built in the 1870s and 1880s.

Yamhill Indians *see* **Kalapuyan Indians**

▶ **Yaquina Bay** It was through the efforts of Col. T. Edgenton Hogg and his magnificently conceived but disastrously executed railroad and steamship enterprise focused on Yaquina Bay that New-

The winsome young woman, holding the shell of a creature not found near Yaquina Bay, is nonetheless urging us to visit that place. This is the cover of a booklet issued in 1903 by the Southern Pacific Company to send Willamette Valley residents to spend the summer at Newport and vicinity, and to travel thence by train. Author's collection.

port became a viable resort, albeit still one that was not all that easily reached. Col. Hogg (ca. 1835–1896) schemed to build a railroad from Yaquina Bay to Corvallis, up the Santiam River, and east across Central Oregon to a connection with the **Union Pacific Railroad** and all points east—with connecting steamships from San Francisco. The railroad to Corvallis was completed by 1885, and tracks went up the Santiam, but the steamships failed, the money ran out, and the terminal of Yaquina City failed to grow. Yaquina was once home to native oysters, similar to the tiny, famed Olympia oysters, and the demand for these in San Francisco was an impetus to close the **Coast Reservation** and open the area to white settlement in the 1870s. The native oyster vanished; the widely cultivated Pacific oyster was introduced in 1918 and has been farmed there since.

Yaquina Indians *see* **Alsean Indians**

Yaquina River The twisty, turning Yaquina River heads in the Coast Range of western Benton and eastern Lincoln Counties and flows west about fifty miles to join **Yaquina Bay** near Toledo, thence into the Pacific at Newport.

Yeon, Jean Baptiste "John" (1865–1928) Born into a French-speaking farm family in Ontario, John Yeon went to Ohio and worked as a lumberjack when he was a teenager. He pressed west, arriving in Portland in 1885, where he worked in the woods and ran a lumber camp before going into the business himself with a $1,200 investment. His Yeon & Pelton Lumber Company became one of the major outfits on the lower Columbia River. He sold the firm in 1906 and went into real estate investment in Portland. Yeon was active in the early "good roads" movement, serving as Multnomah County roadmaster from 1913 to 1917, and was one of the backers of the construction of the **Columbia River Highway**. He built one of downtown Portland's first terra cotta-clad office towers, the Yeon Building, in 1911.

His son **John Yeon** extended some of his father's interests. A scenic corridor of the Columbia River Highway is named for John B. Yeon.

Yeon, John (1910–1994) The son of wealthy lumber magnate **John B. Yeon**, John Yeon was a conservationist, promoter of parks, architect, and art appreciator. At the age of seventeen, he spent his own money to purchase a bit of seacoast north of Cannon Beach, Chapman Point; it is now a notable part of Ecola State Park. He was appointed to the state parks commission at the age of twenty-one, and at twenty-six, he designed a remarkably modern and sophisticated house for lumberman Aubrey Watzek in Portland's West Hills. His only training had been a few odd jobs as draftsman and office boy in architectural offices, but the house is a tour de force in the use of wood both structurally and for interior finishes, and is remarkable for integrating house with landscape. Yeon did other residential designs, using modern and inexpensive wood materials such as plywood. A collector of Asian art, Yeon used Asian touches in his architectural work; he also designed museum galleries, especially those for Asian art. Yeon gave much effort and time and money toward the preservation of the Columbia River Gorge, efforts that in the 1960s included persuading federal officials to modify their design of **Interstate 84** to be just a little more sensitive to the river's natural contours. Yeon purchased a significant tract of land on the Washington side of the river that he carefully preserved and conveyed to a land trust. Landscape architect Wallace Huntington said of Yeon that "he cared about every blade of grass."

yew The Pacific or western yew, *Taxus brevifolia*, is an evergreen tree that grows to a height of about fifty feet, and is often found in the understory of coniferous forests and along stream banks. The wood is notable for its strength, and it is used to make archery bows and in cabinetwork, but it is not a common tree in Oregon. The foliage and seeds are poisonous; however, a derivative has been used in cancer treatments.

Yoncalla The community of Yoncalla is located in Douglas County. The Yoncalla Valley was the homeland of the Yoncalla band of the **Kalapuyan Indians**. White settlers came to the area to farm in the 1840s, among them the Charles and **Jesse Applegate** families. The Yoncalla post office was opened in 1851, and a railroad came through in the 1880s. The city was incorporated in 1901; the population in the 1910 census was 233. Agriculture and logging have been the economic mainstays. Yoncalla was on the **Pacific Highway**, but the construction of **Interstate 5** put it on a side road. The population reached 626 in 1950, and 919 in 1990; the estimate in 2007 was 1,110.

Applegate, Shannon. *Living among Headstones: Life in a Country Cemetery*. New York: Thunder's Mouth Press, 2005.

Yoncalla Indians *see* **Kalapuyan Indians**

Young, Ewing (ca. 1800–1841) Ewing Young achieved more fame through his death than he garnered during his short lifetime. The settlement of his estate became one of the defining events in the political history of the Oregon Country. Born in Tennessee, Young was an American adventurer, a fur trapper and trader who helped open the Santa Fe Trail and who ventured into California in the 1830s. He arrived in the **Oregon Country** in 1834 and settled in at the base of the **Chehalem Mountains** in 1834—the first American to establish residence in the Willamette Valley. There he built a sawmill and gristmill and began to farm. In 1837, he and others formed a company to go to California and bring back cattle, a project that marked the beginning of the livestock trade. Young's farm became a trade center and an information hub. His sudden death in 1841 precipitated a local crisis; a wealthy man, Young left no will, and the process of settling the estate led to the **Wolf Meetings** that, in 1843, formed the Oregon **provisional government**. A school in Newberg is named for Young, as is one of Oregon's heritage trees. The Ewing Young oak was planted on his grave near the site of his cabin on May 6, 1846, by Miranda Bayley and Sidney Smith, and has grown there ever since.

Zigzag River One might mistakenly think that this Clackamas County river was named for its twists and turns. The Zigzag is about ten miles long; it and its tributary Little Zigzag River drain Zigzag Glacier on Mount Hood, and flow into the **Sandy River** near the community of Zigzag. According to geographic names historian Lewis L. McArthur, the name derives from a description in the 1845 diary of **Joel Palmer** of his zigzag descent and crossing of the ravine in which the river flows.

Bibliography and Websites

The sources and resources in this bibliography offer readers other ways to build up a history-based understanding of the state. For most titles, there are a few lines of annotation about the work's subject matter, and its virtues (or vices). All the works are widely available through public and academic libraries, and new or used copies should also be within reach. The bibliography includes fiction—and even a few works of poetry—that speak to Oregon themes and regions. A selection of websites is also included: those listed have given evidence of being historically accurate, easy to use, and likely to persist for some time in some form.

More expansive but un-annotated bibliographies are available online. The Oregon History Project of the Oregon Historical Society at www.ohs.org/education/oregonhistory/index.cfm includes extensive bibliographies for its narrative sections on Oregon, Oregon's geographical regions, and Oregon topics. The Portland Bureau of Planning has a number of extensive bibliographies in its historic resources research guide series: topics include Portland, general Oregon history, Oregon architectural history and historic preservation, and African-American and women's history in Oregon. They are available at www.portlandonline.com/planning/index.cfm?c=eeabd.

Abbott, Carl. *Greater Portland: Urban Life and Landscape in the Pacific Northwest.* Philadelphia: University of Pennsylvania Press, 2001.
A synopsis of recent Portland development by an urbane urban historian.

Allen, Barbara. *Homesteading the High Desert.* Salt Lake City: University of Utah Press, 1987.
A story of early twentieth-century dry-land agriculture related through oral interviews.

Applegate, Shannon, and Terence O'Donnell eds. *Talking on Paper: An Anthology of Oregon Letters and Diaries.* Corvallis: Oregon State University Press, 1994.

Atwood, Kay. *Blossoms and Branches: A Gathering of Rogue Valley Orchard Memories.* Ashland, Oregon: Kay Atwood, 1980.
Based on extensive oral histories.

Atwood, Kay. *Illahe: The Story of Settlement in the Rogue River Canyon.* Ashland, Oregon: Kay Atwood, 1978. Reprint. Corvallis: Oregon State University Press, 2002.

Baehr, Russ. *Oregon's Outback: Tales and Legends from Beyond the Cascades.* Bend, Oregon: Maverick Publications, 1988.
Derived from interviews done in the 1960s with Central Oregon settlers.

Bailey, Barbara Ruth. *Main Street Northeastern Oregon: The Founding and Development of Small Towns.* Portland, Oregon: Oregon Historical Society, 1982.
A geographical and historical investigation.

Bancroft, Hubert Howe. *History of the Northwest Coast.* 2 vols. San Francisco: A. L. Bancroft & Co., 1886.
The Euro-American history of the Oregon Country prior to 1848.

Bancroft, Hubert Howe. *History of Oregon, 1848–1888*. 2 vols. San Francisco: History Co., 1888. Researched and written by Frances Fuller Victor; the quintessential nineteenth-century comprehensive history.

Battaile, Connie Hopkins. *The Oregon Book: Information A to Z*. Newport, Oregon: Saddle Mountain Press, 1998.
A comprehensive alphabetical handbook to all things Oregonian, with an emphasis on contemporary conditions and politics.

Beckham, Stephen Dow, ed. *Many Faces: An Anthology of Oregon Autobiography*. Corvallis: Oregon State University Press, 1993.

Beckham, Stephen Dow. *Requiem for a People: The Rogue Indians and the Frontiersmen*. Norman: University of Oklahoma Press, 1971. Reprint. Corvallis: Oregon State University Press, 1996.
A compelling account of the Rogue River Wars of the 1850s and their consequences.

Berg, Laura Berg, ed. *The First Oregonians*. 2nd ed. Portland, Oregon: Oregon Council for the Humanities, 2007.
A series of essays on Oregon tribes and Oregon Indian culture.

Berry, Don. *Trask: A Novel*. New York: Viking Press, 1960. Reprint. Corvallis: Oregon State University Press, 2004.
A novel set on the Oregon Coast in the 1840s as Native and white cultures meet.

Bingham, Edwin R., and Glen A. Love, eds. *Northwest Perspectives: Essays on the Culture of the Pacific Northwest*. Seattle: University of Washington Press, 1979.

Boag, Peter. *Environment and Experience: Settlement Culture in Nineteenth-Century Oregon*. Berkeley: University of California Press, 1992.
A case study of agricultural development in the Calapooia River valley.

Bosker, Gideon, and Lena Lencek. *Frozen Music: A History of Portland Architecture*. Portland, Oregon: Western Imprints, the Press of the Oregon Historical Society, 1985.
A sweeping populist manifesto on Portland architecture, albeit with some wide steps and pratfalls.

Bowen, William. *The Willamette Valley: Migration and Settlement on the Oregon Frontier*. Seattle: University of Washington Press, 1978.
A detailed, academic study of familial and geographic interconnections among American emigrants to Oregon in the mid-nineteenth century, with many maps.

Brogan, Phil F. *East of the Cascades*. Ed. L. K. Phillips. 4th ed. Portland, Oregon: Binfords & Mort, 1977.
Central Oregon as seen by a journalist and amateur historian.

Clark, Malcolm, Jr. *Eden Seekers: The Settlement of Oregon, 1818–1862*. Boston: Houghton Mifflin, 1981.
Who came to stay, and why.

Clark, Rosalind. *Oregon Style: Architecture from 1840 to the 1950s*. Portland, Oregon: Professional Book Center, 1983.
Oregon history from the perspective of its formal architecture.

Corning, Howard McKinley. *Dictionary of Oregon History*. Portland, Oregon: Binfords & Mort, 1956.
"Compiled from the research files of the former Oregon Writers' Project with much added material." An

alphabetical handbook with numerous errors, it is nevertheless fascinating and useful.

Cressman, Luther. *The Sandal and the Cave.* 2nd ed. Portland, Oregon: Beaver Books, 1964. Reprint. Corvallis: Oregon State University Press, 2005.
The prehistory of Oregon Indians; there have been new discoveries and interpretations, but this was a pioneering study.

Davis, H. L. *Honey in the Horn.* New York: Harper, 1935. Reprint. Moscow: University of Idaho Press, 1992.
A Pulitzer Prize–winning novel of Oregon set at the beginning of the twentieth century; perhaps the fictional embodiment of Oregon-ness.

Dicken, Samuel N. *Pioneer Trails of the Oregon Coast.* 2nd ed. Portland, Oregon: Oregon Historical Society, 1978.
The hazards of sea travel led to a network of trails paralleling the coastline.

Dicken, Samuel N., and Emily F. Dicken. *Two Centuries of Oregon Geography.* 2 vols. Portland, Oregon: Oregon Historical Society, 1979–82.
Geography with a historical perspective.

Dodds, Gordon B. *Oregon: A Bicentennial History.* New York: W. W. Norton, 1977.
A lucid general history.

Dodds, Gordon B. *Varieties of Hope: An Anthology of Oregon Prose.* Corvallis: Oregon State University Press, 1993.

Douthit, Nathan. *A Guide to Oregon South Coast History: Traveling the Jedediah Smith Trail.* Corvallis: Oregon State University Press, 1999.

Douthit, Nathan. *Uncertain Encounters: Indians and Whites at Peace and War in Southern Oregon,* *1820s to 1860s.* Corvallis: Oregon State University Press, 2002.

Due, John Fitzgerald, and Frances Juris Rush. *Roads and Rails South from the Columbia: Transportation and Economic Development in MidColumbia and Central Oregon.* Bend, Oregon: Maverick Publications, 1991.

Edwards, G. Thomas, and Carlos A. Schwantes, eds. *Experiences in a Promised Land: Essays in Pacific Northwest History.* Seattle: University of Washington Press, 1986.

Evans, Elwood. *History of the Pacific Northwest: Oregon and Washington; Embracing an Account of the Original Discoveries on the Pacific Coast of North America.* Portland, Oregon: North Pacific History Company, 1889.
A nineteenth-century "mug book" that features biographies of notable residents of the business class, as well as a general narrative history.

Ferriday, Virginia Guest. *Last of the Handmade Buildings: Glazed Terra Cotta in Downtown Portland.* Portland, Oregon: Mark Publishing, 1984.
The development of Portland's downtown office and retail core in the first quarter of the twentieth century.

Friedman, Ralph. *In Search of Western Oregon.* Caldwell, Idaho: Caxton Printers, 1990.
This is a one-man attempt to update the "wet side" portion of the 1940 WPA guide, *Oregon: End of the Trail.* It is folksy, comprehensive, and detailed.

Gibson, James R. *Farming the Frontier: The Agricultural Opening of the Oregon Country, 1786–1846.* Seattle: University of Washington Press, 1985.

Hanley, Mike, and Ellis Lucia. *Owyhee Trails: The West's Forgotten Corner.* Caldwell, Idaho: Caxton Printers, 1973.
Anecdotal history and geography of the region where the borders of Oregon meet those of Idaho and Nevada.

Hawkins, William J., III. *The Grand Era of Cast-Iron Architecture in Portland.* Portland, Oregon: Binfords & Mort, 1976.
A specialized work, but one with wider Oregon references; provides insight into nineteenth-century commercial life.

Hawkins, William J., III, and William F. Willingham. *Classic Houses of Portland, Oregon, 1850–1950.* Portland, Oregon: Timber Press, 1999.
A special topic that has broader connections, since similar residences and designs are found around the state.

Holbrook, Stewart H. *The Columbia.* New York: Rinehart & Co., 1956.
A compendium of stories, folklore, and history linked together by the Columbia River.

Holbrook, Stewart H. *Far Corner: A Personal View of the Pacific Northwest.* New York: Macmillan Co., 1952.
A grab bag of regional folklore and history that characterized the Oregon Country in mid-century.

Igler, David. *Industrial Cowboys: Miller & Lux and the Transformation of the Far West, 1850–1920.* Berkeley: University of California Press, 2001.
Mostly about California, but Miller & Lux loomed large in southeastern Oregon as well.

Jackman, E. R., and R. A. Long. *The Oregon Desert.* Caldwell, Idaho: Caxton Printers, 1964.
A rancher and an agronomist examine the southeastern Oregon landscape and its history, in fact and folklore.

Johansen, Dorothy O., and Charles M. Gates. *Empire of the Columbia: A History of the Pacific Northwest.* 2nd ed. New York: Harper & Row, 1967.
A sweeping, academic panorama that still reads well.

Jones, Suzi, ed. *Webfoots and Bunchgrassers: Folk Art of the Oregon Country.* Salem, Oregon: Oregon Arts Commission, 1980.

Jones, Suzi, and Jarold Ramsey, eds. *The Stories We Tell: An Anthology of Oregon Folk Literature.* Corvallis: Oregon State University Press, 1994.

Kesey, Ken. *Sometimes a Great Notion: A Novel.* New York: Viking Press, 1964. Reprint. New York: Penguin Books, 1988.
Rain, damp, rust: a novel depicting how coastal logging can take a toll on families and the environment.

King, Bart. *An Architectural Guidebook to Portland.* 2nd. ed. Corvallis: Oregon State University Press, 2007.
A straightforward handbook that is more historical than architectural and is well flavored with anecdote and observation.

LaLande, Jeffrey M. *First Over the Siskiyous: Peter Skene Ogden's 1826–1827 Journey through the Oregon-California Borderlands.* Portland, Oregon: Oregon Historical Society, 1987.
Euro-American explorations in the fur-trapping era of the Hudson's Bay Company.

Langston, Nancy. *Where Land & Water Meet: A Western Landscape Transformed.* Seattle: University of Washington Press, 2003.

The story of water manipulation in the Harney Basin.

Lansing, Jewel. *Portland: People, Politics and Power, 1851-2001*. Corvallis: Oregon State University Press, 2003.
Similar in scope to MacColl's *Merchants, Money and Power*, but with greater emphasis on politics and a slightly softer tone.

Love, Glen A. *The World Begins Here: An Anthology of Oregon Short Fiction*. Corvallis: Oregon State University Press, 1993.

Loy, William G., Stuart Allan, Aileen Buckley, and Jim Meacham. *Atlas of Oregon*. 2nd ed. Eugene: University of Oregon Press, 2001.
A masterful and beautiful assemblage of topical and geographical mapping.

Lucia, Ellis. *The Big Woods: Logging and Lumbering from Bull Teams to Helicopters in the Pacific Northwest*. Garden City, New York: Doubleday & Co., 1975.
A comprehensive but rather-too-glowing account of the timber industry.

Lucia, Ellis ed. *This Land Around Us: A Treasury of Pacific Northwest Writing*. Garden City, New York: Doubleday, 1969.
An idiosyncratic and wide-ranging anthology of both fiction and factual writing.

MacColl, E. Kimbark. *The Growth of a City: Power and Politics in Portland, Oregon, 1915 to 1950*. Portland, Oregon: Georgian Press, 1979.

MacColl, E. Kimbark, and Harry H. Stein. *Merchants, Money, and Power: The Portland Establishment, 1843-1913*. Portland, Oregon: Georgian Press, 1988.
A synthesis that developed from MacColl's two earlier works; a relentless interweaving of the three title elements that depicts the city's political and economic underpinnings.

MacColl, E. Kimbark, and Harry H. Stein. *The Shaping of a City: Business and Politics in Portland, Oregon, 1885 to 1915*. Portland, Oregon: Georgian Press, 1976.

McArthur, Lewis A., and Lewis L. McArthur. *Oregon Geographic Names*. 7th ed. Portland, Oregon: Oregon Historical Society Press, 2003.
The definitive and invaluable guide to place names. It is also wise and witty, and can be read from cover to cover.

McCulloch, Wakter F. *Woods Words: A Comprehensive Dictionary of Loggers Terms*. Portland, Oregon: Oregon Historical Society and the Champoeg Press, 1958.

Meinig, D. W. *The Great Columbia Plain: A Historical Geography, 1805-1910*. Rev. ed. Seattle: University of Washington Press, 1995.
A classic look at the wheat country of eastern Oregon and Washington.

Nash, Tom, and Twilo Scofield. *The Well-Traveled Casket: A Collection of Oregon Folklife*. Salt Lake City: University of Utah Press, 1992. Reprint. Eugene, Oregon: Meadowlark Press, 1999.

Neuberger, Richard. *Our Promised Land*. New York: MacMillan, 1938.
Journalism in a package that extols the Pacific Northwest's natural resources and looks forward to their exploitation—and conservation.

Oliphant, J. Orin. *On the Cattle Ranges of the Oregon Country*. Seattle: University of Washington Press, 1968.
Details the consequences of overgrazing.

Oregon State Immigration Commission. [*1915 Oregon Almanac*]: The State of Oregon: Its Resources and Opportunities; Official Pamphlet Published for the Information of Homeseekers, Settlers and Investors. Salem, Oregon: State Printing Department, 1914.

Peterson, Emil R., and Alfred Powers. *A Century of Coos and Curry: History of Southwest Oregon.* Portland, Oregon: Binfords & Mort, 1952.

Pomeroy, Earl. *The Pacific Slope: A History of California, Oregon, Washington, Idaho, Utah, and Nevada.* Seattle: University of Washington Press, 1965. Reprint. Reno: University of Nevada Press, 2003.
A gracefully written history of the Pacific Coast that portrays western Oregon as essentially urban from a very early date.

Ramsey, Jarold, ed. *Coyote Was Going There: Indian Literature of the Oregon Country.* Seattle: University of Washington Press, 1977.
A selection of myths and other literary pieces from around the state.

Ramsey, Jarold. *New Era: Reflections on the Human and Natural History of Central Oregon.* Corvallis: Oregon State University Press, 2003.

Robbins, William G. *Hard Times in Paradise: Coos Bay, Oregon.* Rev. ed. Seattle: University of Washington Press, 2006.
The rise and fall of the timber economy on the southern Oregon coast.

Robbins, William G. *Landscapes of Conflict: The Oregon Story, 1940–2000.* Seattle: University of Washington Press, 2004.
The continuation of *Landscapes of Promise.*

Robbins, William G. *Landscapes of Promise: The Oregon Story, 1800–1940.* Seattle: University of Washington Press, 1997.
Presents a history of the state in terms of its natural resources and environment.

Ross, Alexander. *Adventures of the First Settlers on the Oregon or Columbia River, 1810–1813.* London: Smith, Elder & Co., 1849. Reprinted, with an introduction by William G. Robbins. Corvallis: Oregon State University Press, 2000.
An account of the establishment of Fort Astoria; "one of the charter literary documents for the Pacific Northwest," avers William Robbins.

Schwantes, Carlos A. *The Pacific Northwest: an Interpretive History.* Rev. ed. Lincoln: University of Nebraska Press, 1996.
An expansive, well-written, well-illustrated overview history.

Simpson, Peter K. *The Community of Cattlemen: A Social History of the Cattle Industry in Southeastern Oregon, 1869–1912.* Moscow: University of Idaho Press, 1987.

Snyder, Eugene F. *Portland Names and Neighborhoods: Their Historic Origins.* Portland, Oregon: Binfords & Mort, 1979.
An alphabetical account of the origin of the names of streets, parks, and schools, with additional information on city development.

St. John, Alan D. *Oregon's Dry Side: Exploring East of the Cascade Crest.* Portland, Oregon: Timber Press, 2007.

Sturtevant, William C., and Warren L. D'Azevedo. *Handbook of North American Indians.* Vol. 11, Great Basin. Washington, DC: Smithsonian Institution, 1986.

Part of the indispensible, anthropologically oriented guides to the prehistory and history of the Indians of Oregon.

Sturtevant, William C., and Robert Fleming Heizer. *Handbook of North American Indians*. Vol. 8, California. Washington, DC: Smithsonian Institution, 1978.

Sturtevant, William C., and Wayne P. Suttles. *Handbook of North American Indians*. Vol. 7, Northwest Coast. Washington, DC: Smithsonian Institution, 1990.

Sturtevant, William C., and Deward E. Walker. *Handbook of North American Indians*. Vol. 12, Great Basin. Washington, DC: Smithsonian Institution, 1998.

Throckmorton, Arthur L. *Oregon Argonauts: Merchant Adventurers on the Western Frontier*. Portland, Oregon: Oregon Historical Society, 1961.
An account of the impact of commerce and business on early Oregon affairs.

Trombold, John, and Peter Donahue, ed. *Reading Portland: The City in Prose*. Portland, Oregon: Oregon Historical Society Press; Seattle: University of Washington Press, 2006.
An anthology that includes history, journalism, and fiction.

Vaughan, Thomas, ed. *High and Mighty: Select Sketches of the Deschutes Country*. Portland, Oregon: Oregon Historical Society, 1981.

Vaughan, Thomas, and Virginia Guest Ferriday, eds. *Space, Style and Structure: Building in Northwest America*. 2 vols. Portland, Oregon: Oregon Historical Society, 1974.
A sweeping review of the region's architectural history by a number of authors.

Victor, Frances Fuller. *All Over Oregon and Washington: Observations on the Country, Its Scenery, Soil, Climate, Resources, and Improvements*. San Francisco: John G. Carmany & Co., 1872.
A description of the region by one of its first and foremost historians.

Walling, Albert G. *A History of Southern Oregon: Comprising Jackson, Josephine, Douglas, Curry, and Coos Counties*. Portland, Oregon: A. G. Walling, 1884.
An early regional narrative celebrating Progress and Civilization.

Wells, Gail. *The Tillamook: A Created Forest Comes of Age*. 2nd ed. Corvallis: Oregon State University Press, 2004.
The Tillamook Burn of the 1930s resulted in a new, managed forest.

Wendt, Ingrid, and Primus St. John, eds. *From Here We Speak: An Anthology of Oregon Poetry*. Corvallis: Oregon State University Press, 1993.

Winther, Oscar Osburn. *The Old Oregon Country: A History of Frontier Trade, Transportation, and Travel*. Stanford, California: Stanford University Press, 1950. Reprint. Lincoln: University of Nebraska Press, 1969.

Writers' Program (U.S.). *Oregon: End of the Trail*. Portland, Oregon: Binfords & Mort, 1940.
The Oregon volume of the Depression-era American Guide Series; a guidebook to a landscape in transition and a compendium of legend, lore, and history.

Zucker, Jeff, Kay Hummel, and Bob Høgfuss. *Oregon Indians: Culture, History and Current Affairs, an Atlas and Introduction*. Portland, Oregon: Oregon Historical Society, 1983.

Oregon Websites

Oregon Blue Book
http://bluebook.state.or.us/
Prepared and updated by the Oregon State Archives from the office of the Oregon Secretary of State, the Oregon Blue Book is concise guide to state and local government and all that it touches, from agriculture to military affairs, education to labor, and including history and culture.

Oregon Encyclopedia Project
http://www.oregonencyclopedia.org/
Launched in 2008, the Oregon Encyclopedia Project is sponsored by Portland State University and the Oregon Historical Society. It aims to have a comprehensive encyclopedia of Oregon history and culture online in 2009, to mark the sesquicentennial of Oregon statehood; a published version may be issued later. This is a major academic undertaking with extensive editorial and advisory boards.

Oregon Historical Society Research Library
http://librarycatalog.ohs.org/WebOPAC/index.asp
The Society's store of research materials includes books, maps, historical photographs, artwork, periodicals, newspapers, letters and diaries, business records, personal papers, and paper ephemera ranging from brochures and pamphlets to menus and timetables. The research library is open to the public; it charges a fee for those who are not members of the Society, so joining is a worthwhile move for those doing extensive research. The library has an online catalog, which includes items from the Society's artifact collections and also includes images, such as historical photographs. The online catalog has limitations but can at least suggest what is available: http://librarycatalog.ohs.org/WebOPAC/index.asp.

Oregon History in the Oregon Blue Book
http://bluebook.state.or.us/cultural/history/history.htm
The concise and flowing narrative is by Steven Dow Beckham.

Oregon History Project at the Oregon Historical Society
http://www.ohs.org/education/oregonhistory/narratives/histories.cfm
The Oregon History Project was developed to provide both students and the general public with a guided set of narratives about Oregon history, coupled with extensive illustrations and primary source materials and a sophisticated search capability. By and large, it succeeds in providing this. Additional narratives are planned; as of 2008, the following were available:
As Long as the World Goes On: The Land and People of Southwestern Oregon, by Kay Atwood and Dennis Gray
Canneries on the Columbia: A New Western History, by Elliott West, Katrine Barber, Chris Friday, Ellen Eisenberg, and Joseph Taylor, III.
Central Oregon: Adaptation & Compromise in an Arid Landscape, by Ward Tonsfeldt and Paul Claeyssens
Commerce, Climate & Community: A History of Portland & Its People, by William Toll
Forests and Green Verdant Lawns: The Oregon Coast, by Gail Wells
High Desert History: Southeastern Oregon, by Jeffrey M. LaLande
Lewis & Clark: From Expedition to Exposition, 1803–1905, by William L. Lang and Carl Abbott
Nature and History in the Klamath Basin, by Stephen Most
Oregon Folklife: Our Living Traditions, by Joanne B. Mulcahy
This Land–Oregon, by William G. Robbins

Wooden Beams and Railroad Ties: The History of Oregon's Built Environment, by Richard H. Engeman

The World Rushed In: Northeastern Oregon, by David Peterson del Mar

Oregon State Archives
http://arcweb.sos.state.or.us/
This is the gateway to research materials created by state (and territorial) government. It includes the Oregon Historical County Records Guide, histories of state agencies and guides to their records, legislative archives, and records of genealogical interest.

Oregon State University Archives
http://osulibrary.oregonstate.edu/archives/
Created initially as the archives of the university itself, the OSU Archives have become a general resource through their holdings of historical photographs, the papers of faculty members, and departmental records, especially in such fields as agriculture, forestry and the sciences.

Portland Historical Timeline
http://www.portlandonline.com/auditor/index.
    cfm?c=27408.
Prepared by the Stanley Parr Archives, City of Portland. The Archives themselves are excellent resources for the study of city government and its services.

Salem Online History from Salem Public Library
http://www.salemhistory.net/
This fact-filled site includes thousands of historical photographs (from around the state, though most are from the Willamette Valley) and a wide variety of illustrated topical essays, handily arranged. Uneven in some areas, it is yet a valuable resource.

University of Oregon Libraries, Special Collections and University Archives
http://libweb.uoregon.edu/speccoll/
This unit of the UO Libraries includes not only the institutional archives, but also a wide-ranging collection of Oregon-related historical materials, ranging from historical photographs and early personal and business papers to literary manuscripts, paper ephemera, and periodicals. The University is also the headquarters of the Oregon Newspaper Project, which has been microfilming the state's newspapers—all of them—for several decades; the next step will be digital access to them. For more information, go to
http://libweb.uoregon.edu/speccoll/image_svcs/onp/
    index.html

University of Washington Libraries, Special Collections
http://www.lib.washington.edu/speciaLcoll/
The UW Libraries have extensive research materials on Pacific Northwest history. In addition to books and periodicals, Special Collections includes extensive holdings of regional maps, photographs, architectural plans and drawings, postcards, posters, and paper ephemera. Some materials—especially historical photographs, but also government documents, menus, and many other items—are available online through the University of Washington Libraries Digital Collections website: http://content.lib.washington.edu/

The Oregon Coast Highway was a route for adventurers in the 1920s.
Frank Patterson photograph. Steven Dotterrer collection.

About the Author

Richard H. Engeman is a historian and archivist with wide research and writing experience in Pacific Northwest history. A graduate of Reed College, he also holds graduate degrees in librarianship from the University of Oregon and in history from the University of Washington. His writing has appeared in *Pacific Northwest Quarterly, Oregon Historical Quarterly, Portland Monthly,* and other publications. He is the author of an award-winning unit of the Oregon Historical Society's online Oregon History Project, *Wooden Beams and Railroad Ties: the History of Oregon's Built Environment.*

Formerly public historian of the Oregon Historical Society, Engeman has also worked at the University of Washington Libraries, the Southern Oregon Historical Society, and the National Maritime Museum at San Francisco. He serves on the Portland Landmarks Commission and is on the board of the Oregon Museums Association and the Oregon Century Farm & Ranch Program. He is the principal of Oregon Rediviva LLC, which does historical research and writing and museum and archives consulting. Author photograph by Laural Engeman.

This covered bridge over Mill Creek was located near Scottsburg, along the lower Umpqua River. Built in 1925, it was demolished in the 1950s. Steven Dotterrer collection.